Upgrading PCs Illustrated

QUE®

Upgrading PCs Illustrated

by Jim Boyce with

Sheldon Dunn, Chris Turkstra, Jason Massarelli, Keith R. Aleshire, and Kevin Kloss

Upgrading PCs Illustrated

Library of Congress Catalog No.: 96-72221

ISBN: 0-7897-0986-4

99 98 97 6 5 4 3 2 1

Interpretation of the printing code: the rightmost double-digit number is the year of the book's printing; the rightmost single-digit number, the number of the book's printing. For example, a printing code of 97-1 shows that the first printing of the book occurred in 1997.

Screen reproductions in this book were created using Collage Plus from Inner Media, Inc., Hollis, NH.

Credits

PRESIDENT
Roland Elgey

PUBLISHER
Joseph B. Wikert

PUBLISHING DIRECTOR
Brad R. Koch

EDITORIAL SERVICES DIRECTOR
Elizabeth Keaffaber

MANAGING EDITOR
Michael Cunningham

DIRECTOR OF MARKETING
Lynn E. Zingraf

ACQUISITIONS MANAGER
Elizabeth South

ACQUISITIONS EDITOR
Angie Wethington

SENIOR PRODUCT DIRECTOR
Lisa D. Wagner

PRODUCT DIRECTOR
Kevin Kloss

PRODUCTION EDITORS
Lisa M. Gebken
Thomas F. Hayes

EDITORS
Kate Givens
Christopher Nelson

STRATEGIC MARKETING MANAGER
Barry Pruett

PRODUCT MARKETING MANAGER
Kris Ankney

ASSISTANT PRODUCT MARKETING MANAGERS
Karen Hagan
Christy M. Miller

TECHNICAL EDITOR
Curtis Knight

MEDIA DEVELOPMENT SPECIALIST
David Garratt

TECHNICAL SUPPORT SPECIALIST
Nadeem Muhammed

ACQUISITIONS COORDINATOR
Tracy C. Williams

SOFTWARE RELATIONS COORDINATOR
Susan Gallagher

EDITORIAL ASSISTANT
Virginia Stoller

BOOK DESIGNER
Ruth Harvey

COVER DESIGNER
Nathan Clement

PRODUCTION TEAM
Dan Julian
Daryl Kessler
Julie Searls
Lisa Stumpf

INDEXER
Tim Tate

Composed in *Galliard* and *Frutiger* by Que Corporation.

About the Authors

Jim Boyce is a contributing editor and monthly columnist for *WINDOWS Magazine*. Jim has authored and co-authored more than 30 books about computer software and hardware. He has been involved with computers since the late 1970s, and has used computers as a user, programmer, and systems manager in a variety of capacities. Jim has a wide range of experience in the DOS, Windows, and UNIX environments.

Sheldon Dunn has been involved in the software development field for the last 15 years. He has worked with Novell, Borland, Microsoft, Broderbund, and MicroPro International, as well as consulted for companies in other fields. He is the author of the Xbase Cross Reference, a programmers' guide to dBASE, FoxPro, and Clipper, and has contributed to a dozen other books on computer software. He can be reached in Sebastopol, Sonoma County, California at **sheldunn@sonic.net**.

Chris Turkstra is the kid who was always disassembling his toys. He has been involved with PC technology since he received his first IBM PC in 1983. Chris is a technical architect who spends much of his time designing and implementing networked systems for clients. You can reach him at **75507.720@compuserve.com** or **turkstra@cris.com**.

Jason Massarelli has been in love with technology ever since he plugged his first Commodore 64 into his 8-inch black-and-white TV. Jason is a technical consultant who specializes in designing and implementing network solutions for clients. Jason also advises large clients on cutting edge and future technology, most of which he is still trying to figure out himself. You can reach Jason at **mazz@suba.com** or **104136,2657** on CompuServe.

Keith R. Aleshire is president and CEO of Strike Twice Corp., a computer consulting and high-tech advertising firm. He has worked for various firms, including Northgate Computer Systems, Digi International, and LaserMaster Corp. Keith has been a senior producer and columnist for the Prodigy service and writes for several computer magazines. He has authored and co-authored nine books. Keith is a Phi Beta Kappa graduate from the University of Minnesota School of Journalism.

Kevin Kloss is a product director for Que Corporation. He has co-authored *Platinum Edition Using Windows 95*, and directed more than a dozen books on Windows NT/95, Visual Basic, and networking. In a previous position, Kevin was a technical consultant for Quality Systems, Inc., where he demonstrated, sold, and implemented customized information management systems. Kevin has a B.S. in chemistry from Eastern Michigan University. He now lives in Carmel, Indiana, with his wife Michelle and two cats Tac and Tara.

Acknowledgments

Many people helped in the creation of this book in one way or another. Jim Boyce offers his thanks to:

Brad Koch and Kevin Kloss for the opportunity to do the project and all the help structuring and organizing the book and photographs.

Elizabeth South and Angie Wethington for their usual outstanding job of putting together the project.

Tom Hayes, Lisa Gebken, and the editors for an outstanding job of editing and fine-tuning the book.

Don Distel, for the great photographs and patience, and of course, for the tea and bagels.

Curtis Knight, for an outstanding job of technical editing. The book is much better because of his thoroughness and testing.

The production department of Macmillan Computer Publishing, for turning text and illustrations into a real book.

John Schmitt, the second-nicest guy on the planet.

A special thanks goes to Mike Taylor, owner of Eagle Micro of Indianapolis. We purchased most of the major components used for the upgrades shown in this book from his local shop. It just goes to show you do not have to mail order to get a good deal. Thanks, Mike.

We'd Like to Hear from You!

As part of our continuing effort to produce books of the highest possible quality, Que would like to hear your comments. To stay competitive, we *really* want you, as a computer book reader and user, to let us know what you like or dislike most about this book or other Que products.

You can mail comments, ideas, or suggestions for improving future editions to the address below, or send us a fax at (317) 581-4663. For the online inclined, Macmillan Computer Publishing has a forum on CompuServe (type **GO QUEBOOKS** at any prompt) through which our staff and authors are available for questions and comments. The address of our Internet site is **http://www.mcp.com** (World Wide Web).

In addition to exploring our forum, please feel free to contact me personally to discuss your opinions of this book: I'm **74201,1064** on CompuServe, and I'm **kkloss@que.mcp.com** on the Internet.

Thanks in advance—your comments will help us to continue publishing the best books available on computer topics in today's market.

Kevin Kloss
Product Development Specialist
Que Corporation
201 W. 103rd Street
Indianapolis, Indiana 46290
USA

Contents at a Glance

VI Maintenance and Disaster Recovery

VII Appendixes

Table of Contents

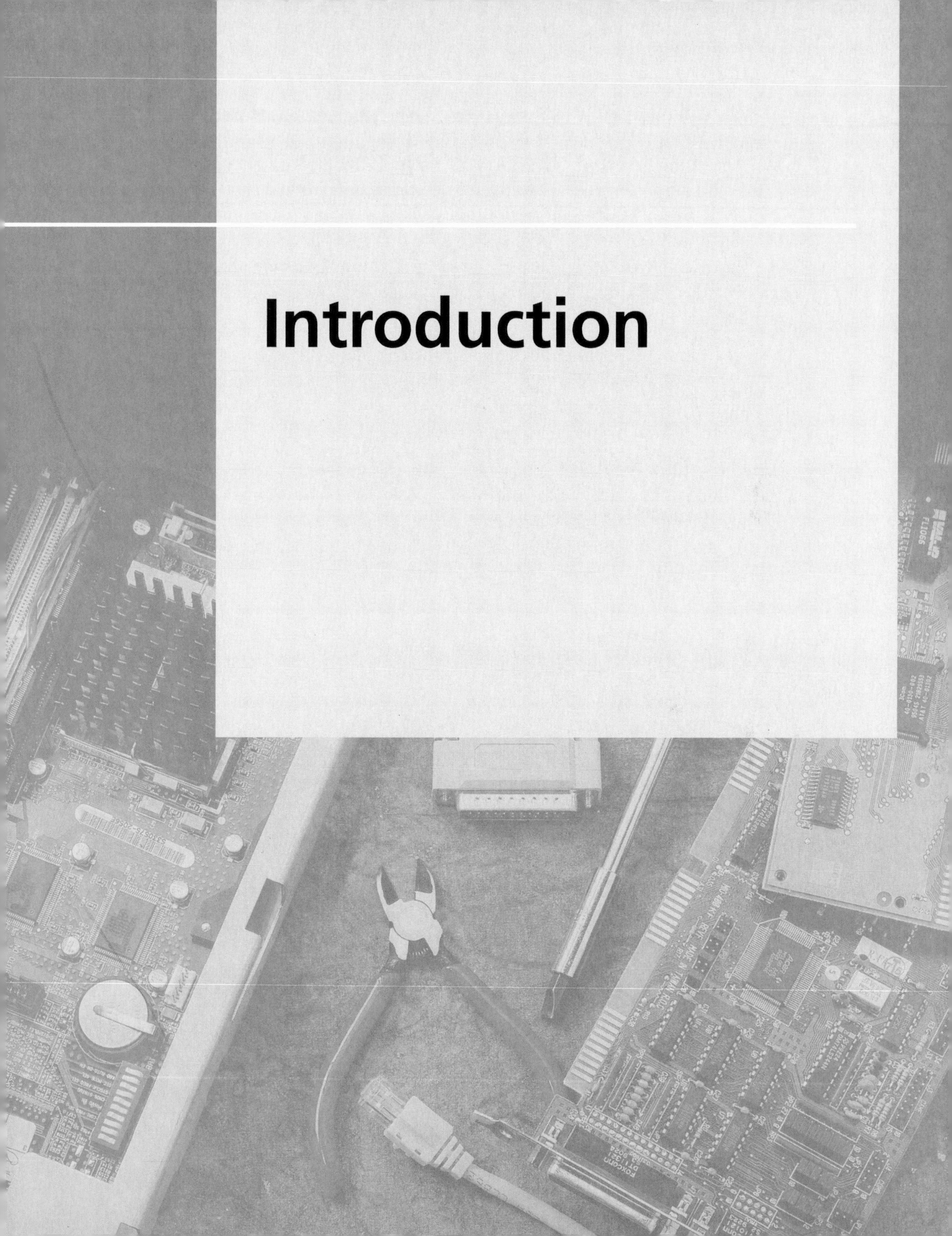

Introduction

In 1969, John Muir first published *How To Keep Your Volkswagen Alive, a Manual of Step By Step Procedures for the Compleat* [sic] *Idiot.* In my mind, John's book remains one of the best how-to books ever written. Why? First, the book is geared not toward mechanics or even the mechanically inclined, but instead toward the average person who simply wants to perform some, if not all, maintenance on his or her Volkswagen. John coined the "Complete Idiot" moniker to describe people who are as intelligent as anyone else, but who simply don't know anything about a particular topic. He intended his book to enable these people to diagnose and fix problems with their beasts of burden.

The second thing going for John's book is the complete, detailed steps he provides to help the reader diagnose and fix problems. It doesn't matter that you have never done anything more than change the oil in the car; you too can rebuild the engine from top to bottom by just following some simple, detailed steps.

Upgrading PCs Illustrated certainly won't help you get back together that rusty VW Beetle hiding in the back forty. But, it can help you save a few dollars performing your own computer upgrades and teach you about your system in the process. All you have to do is follow the step-by-step instructions. I've included plenty of photographs and illustrations to keep you on the right track.

Who This Book Is For

Upgrading PCs Illustrated isn't meant for the techno-wizard who can recite from memory all the IRQ and base address settings for all the gadgets in his computer. Instead, it's designed for the average person who has the desire to rummage inside his computer to upgrade and install new components. You don't need any special training or a lot of mechanical or technical aptitude. All you really need are a few cheap tools and the capability to read and follow simple directions. Even the most major upgrades, such as replacing the computer's motherboard (the main circuit board where the brains of the computer live), are fairly simple tasks that require nothing more than a screwdriver and an hour or so of time. Don't worry that you don't understand how the silly thing works—you don't have to.

The explanations and steps in the book are not geared toward just the uninitiated, however. Even if you have some experience working inside a computer, you can still benefit from the no-nonsense explanations on why and how to perform an upgrade in areas that might be new to you. So whether you're just starting out with computers or are an old pro, *Upgrading PCs Illustrated* is your best source for learning when, why, and how to upgrade your PC. Best of all, I've included lots of pictures to make the procedures crystal-clear.

What About Repairs?

Many people who have no experience repairing electronic devices like computers believe that a repair, either minor or major, involves testing all those tiny electronic components and replacing the ones that are fried, loose, or otherwise discombobulated. In some cases that's true, but by and large, a repair involves throwing out the dead part and replacing it with a new one. If your video card (which creates what you see on the monitor) suddenly dies, a computer repair shop isn't going to repair the card. Instead, the technician simply removes the card and installs a new one.

So, repairing a PC is really not much different from upgrading one. Installing a new video card to replace a malfunctioning one is exactly the same as installing a *better* video card to upgrade the PC's capabilities. So although much of *Upgrading PCs Illustrated* doesn't focus on troubleshooting and repair, you can use the book to help you replace components that aren't working. Plus, later chapters in the book do help you with troubleshooting.

TIP If a part does break down and you have to replace it, you might as well upgrade the component at the same time. Rather than simply replace the part with another of the same type and capability, look for a replacement that enhances the system's capabilities. In most cases, the upgrade costs the same or less than the original part did. For example, four years ago I installed a 2X CD-ROM drive for about $700. Today, 6X CD-ROM drives, which are three times as fast, are selling at around $100.

How This Book Is Structured

Upgrading PCs Illustrated divides system upgrades into distinct parts, with each part covering related types of components.

Part I: Preparation

Part I serves as an introduction, offering tips to help you decide when and how to upgrade your system:

- Chapter 1, "Justifying and Planning an Upgrade," helps you decide when it's time to upgrade your PC. It also helps plan the process to make sure you're not stuck without a crucial item when you're ready to perform the upgrade.
- Chapter 2, "Building a Software Safety Kit," explains how to create a set of startup disks that enable you to recover from disaster should it occur. Don't skip this chapter!
- Chapter 3, "Physical Safety and Tools," offers an important look at the steps you should take to ensure your own safety and protect the PC from harm. You also find a discussion of useful tools in Chapter 3.
- Chapter 4, "Systems Overview," explains PCs in general to give you an understanding of how a PC works. Chapter 4 doesn't give you a detailed technical background in PC operation, but it does help you understand the processes that enable your PC to function and run programs.
- Chapter 5, "Taking Inventory," takes you on a guided tour of your own PC. You open up the case to figure out what you have and where you can go with it. You also start a set of logs that serve as an inventory for your system.
- Chapter 6, "Basic Device Configuration and Installation," explains adapter cards and their functions. Learning how to configure an adapter card and install it covers a fair percentage of all system upgrades.

Part II: Processors, Motherboards, and Memory

Part II provides step-by-step directions to help you upgrade your system's processor, replace the motherboard, and add memory:

- Chapter 7, "Working with the BIOS," explains the PC's Basic Input/Output System (BIOS) and its function. You learn not only how to configure common BIOS settings, but also how to update the BIOS.

- Chapter 8, "Upgrading the CPU and FPU and Cache," explains CPU upgrades, such as replacing a 486 with a Pentium, that make your computer run faster. Additionally, you learn how to add a *Floating Point Unit (FPU)*, also called a *math coprocessor*, to a 486SX system that lacks one.
- Chapter 9, "Replacing the Motherboard," covers one of the most major upgrades. For example, you might decide to replace the motherboard in your old 386 computer with a fast, new Pentium motherboard.
- Chapter 10, "Adding Memory," covers an important upgrade concept for today's PCs. Today's newest operating systems, Windows 95 and Windows NT, require a lot of memory, as do applications. Increasing the amount of memory in the system can have a dramatic impact on performance.

Part III: Mass Storage Devices

Part III explains how to upgrade or add various mass storage devices in your PC. These include the PC's hard disk drive, tape drive, and removable drives (floppy and optical drives):

- Chapter 11, "Hard Disks," explains how hard disk drives work and provides instructions on replacing existing drives, adding new drives, and replacing the host adapter that controls the drive.
- Chapter 12, "Floppy and Other Removable Media Devices," explains how to add removable drive devices such as standard floppy drives and new high-capacity optical and mechanical drives.
- Chapter 13, "Tape Drives," explores different options for adding a tape drive to your system for backup. This chapter also explains how to install and begin using the drive.

Part IV: Multimedia Devices

Part IV examines a topic in which almost everyone is interested: multimedia. This part of the book looks at video and sound options for your PC:

- Chapter 14, "Video," covers standard video cards, as well as those that offer full-motion video. In addition to learning how to configure and install video cards, you also learn how to upgrade the video memory on a video card to increase the number of colors and resolution it can display.

- Chapter 15, "Sound," looks at sound cards and related components such as microphones and speakers. You learn how to configure a sound card, install it, and begin using sound on your system.
- Chapter 16, "CD-ROM and CD-R Drives," explains two closely related types of components: CD-ROM and CD-R drives. CD-ROM drives are read-only devices, and CD-R drives let you create your own CD-ROMs.

Part V: Communications, Internet, and Networking

Part V covers a hot topic—Internet and communications. This part of the book helps you add modems, network cards, and other communications components to your PC so you can access resources outside your PC:

- Chapter 17, "I/O Adapters and System Ports," explains how to add serial (COM) and parallel (LPT) ports to your system.
- Chapter 18, "Modems," explains how modems work and how to install and use them. You find tips on choosing the modem that's right for you, as well as steps for installing the hardware and adding any necessary software to make your modem work.
- Chapter 19, "Network Interface Cards and Software," shows you how to configure and install a network adapter in your computer so you can share resources on a local area network (LAN) with other users. This chapter can be particularly important if you're setting up a small office and need to use the hardware you have most efficiently.
- Chapter 20, "Making Internet Connections," shows you how to connect to the Internet to use the World Wide Web and other Internet resources such as FTP (File Transfer Protocol). You also learn important configuration and troubleshooting tips.
- Chapter 21, "Using Dial-Up Networking," explains how to use the Dial-Up Networking feature in Windows 95 and Windows NT to connect your computer to others over a modem. Dial-Up Networking offers one method for connecting to the Internet. You also can use Dial-Up Networking to enable others to dial into your computer.
- Chapter 22, "Voice and Fax Messaging," explains how to incorporate voice messaging and fax send/receive into your PC.

Part VI: Maintenance and Disaster Recovery

Part VI is the place to turn for general maintenance tips, troubleshooting, and overcoming component and system failures:

- Chapter 23, "General System Cleaning," explains when and how to handle those general cleaning jobs that keep your PC working at peak performance.
- Chapter 24, "Basic Troubleshooting," gives you the background you need to troubleshoot problems with your system. You find the steps to take in order to find and fix specific problems.
- Chapter 25, "The Computer Won't Start," offers steps that help you get the PC back up when all hope seems lost.

Part VII: Appendixes

I've included a couple of resource appendixes to supplement all those mail-order catalogs you've been browsing:

- Appendix A, "Manufacturers Listing," gives you contact information for lots of computer hardware and software manufacturers, including their Internet addresses.
- Appendix B, "Online Resources," lists resources on commercial online services and the Internet that are not vendor-specific. This appendix can help you find files, addresses, and other items you need for your upgrades.
- Appendix C, "Glossary of Common Terms," is a list of common terms used during the upgrading and repairing process.

Conventions Used in This Book

In Windows 3.x, Windows 95, and Windows NT, you can use either the mouse or keyboard to activate commands and choose options. You can press a command's or menu's hot key, use the function keys, or click items with the mouse to make your selections. In this book, command and menu hot keys are underlined as in the following example:

Choose File, Open to display the Open dialog box.

In this book, key combinations are joined by a plus (+) sign. For example, Ctrl+C means to hold down the Ctrl key, press C, and then release both keys. The following example shows a typical command:

> Choose Edit, Copy, or press Ctrl+C.

Occasionally, you might need to press a key, release it, and then press another key. If you need to press Alt, then F, then O, for example, the command would be similar to the following:

> Press Alt,F,O to display the Open dialog box.

Names of dialog boxes and dialog box options are written as they appear on your display. Messages that appear at the command prompt are displayed `in a special font`. New terms are introduced in *italic* type. Text that you type is shown in **boldface**. If you see an instruction to "Enter **some text**," it means to type the text **some text** and then press Enter. If the instruction tells you to "Type **some text**," it means to type the text but not press Enter.

The checklists help you make sure you have everything you need to perform a procedure. Think of it as a pre-flight checklist:

To Replace the Motherboard, You Need:

- ☑ New motherboard on hand, with documentation for switch settings and connectors
- ☑ Motherboard mounting hardware on hand
- ☑ Memory installed on motherboard
- ☑ Phillips screwdriver
- ☑ BIOS settings recorded, including hard drive type

NOTE Notes provide additional information that might help you avoid problems, or offer advice or general information related to the current topic.

TIP Tips provide extra information that supplement the current topic. Often, tips offer shortcuts or alternative methods for accomplishing a task.

CAUTION Cautions warn you if a procedure or description in the topic can lead to unexpected results or even data loss or damage to your system. If you see a caution, proceed carefully.

TROUBLESHOOTING

This paragraph provides guidance on how to find solutions to common problems. The problem you may encounter appears in bold face, and the solution appears in the paragraph(s) following the problem.

What About Sidebars?

Sidebars are sprinkled throughout the book to give you the author's insight into particular topics. The information in a sidebar supplements the material in the chapter.

Internet references, such as the following one, point you to sites on the Internet where you can find additional information about a topic being discussed:

Microsoft's Internet Web Site
http://www.microsoft.com

Where to Go for More Information

Que offers other titles that can help you master the intricacies of your PC and its operating system. For more information about these titles, Que, Macmillan Computer Publishing, and other Macmillan online services, check out the Macmillan USA Information SuperLibrary on the Internet at **www.mcp.com\que**. You'll find a wealth of information, online shopping, and more. Or, check out the **MACMILLAN** forum on CompuServe.

For other online sources of information about Microsoft Windows 95, check the **WIN95** forum on CompuServe or connect to the Microsoft Web site at **www.microsoft.com**. For other online sources of information about Microsoft Windows NT, check the **WINNT** forum on CompuServe or connect to the Microsoft Web site.

PART

I

Preparation

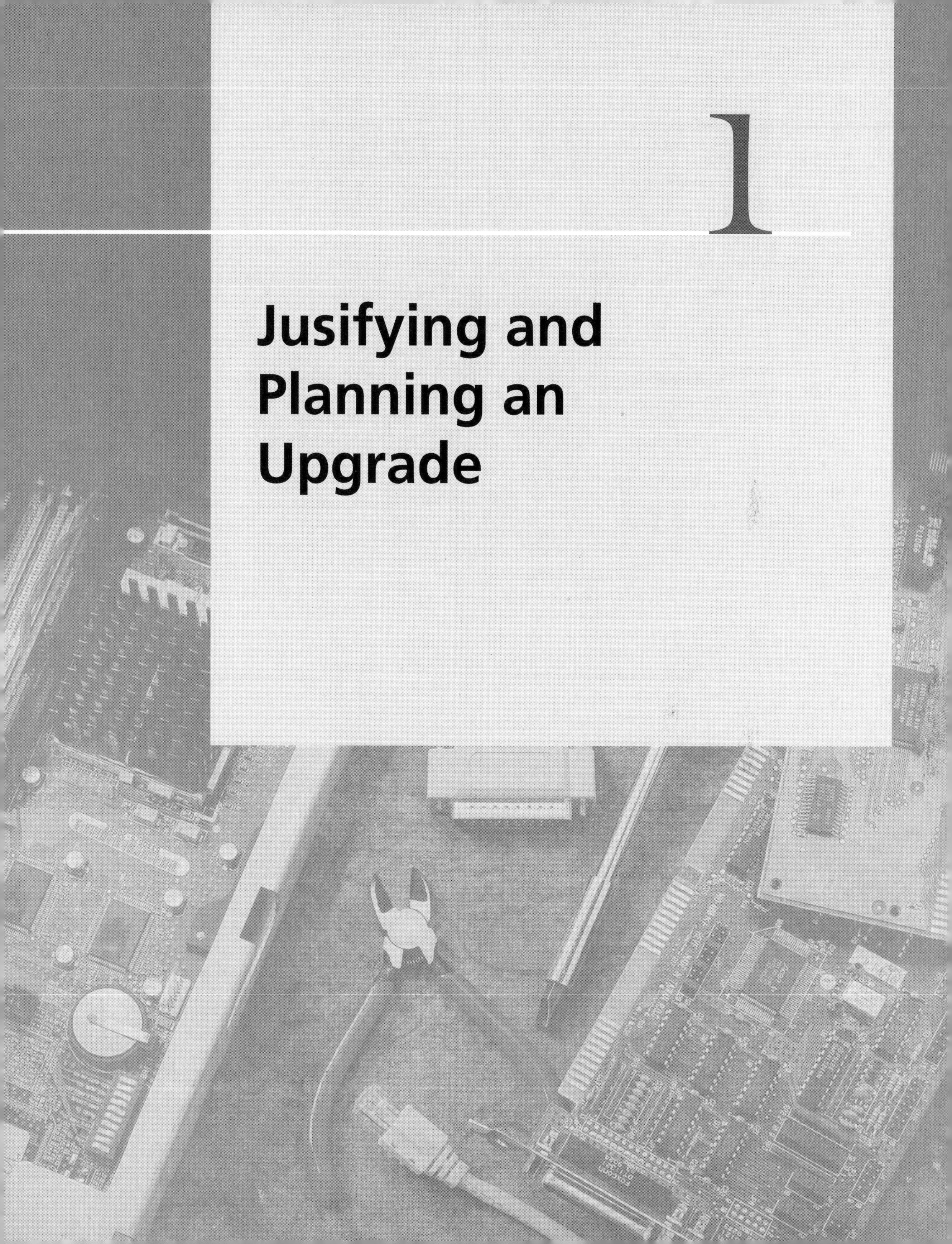

1

Jusifying and Planning an Upgrade

You're probably ready to open up your computer and dive right in on some upgrades. Before you invest a lot of money in hardware, software, and time, you need to pause and take stock of what you have and where you want to go. This brief chapter gives you an overview of upgrade options and helps you decide what changes are right for your system. The topics covered in this chapter include:

- When to upgrade your system and what components to upgrade
- When to buy a new system instead of upgrade
- Where to locate parts and supplies for the upgrade

What and When to Upgrade

Every year when the new automobile models come out, last year's model suddenly becomes obsolete. With computers, obsolescence is even worse. It seems like a faster, better system shows up every six months or so. New processors, new storage devices, and new whiz-bang gadgets are constantly vying for your attention and money.

A few people are well-served by their old PCs and do not want or need to to upgrade their systems. But most of us like to take advantage of the latest games, productivity programs, and new operating systems, so we're obligated to keep our systems as up-to-date as we can. For some, money is no object. For most of us, though, money is very much an object, and we need to make sure we get the best bang for the buck. It is, therefore, important to have a good grasp not only of what you should upgrade, but also when.

There is hardly a component in your PC that can't be upgraded, stepped-up, boosted, or in some way improved. Some of these upgrades are relatively cheap to perform. Others mean a sizable investment—sometimes as much as half (or more) of what a new PC would cost. Most make sense to perform, although some give you more benefit than others.

Although the following sections don't detail every possible reason for upgrading specific items, they do give you a good foundation on which to base your decisions about upgrading your PC. Later chapters delve more deeply into each component and explain the rationale and processes for choosing and installing an upgrade. This chapter serves mainly as an overview, bringing together all of your upgrade possibilities in one place to help you pick and choose where your upgrade dollars will go. Narrow your choices in this chapter, and before going shopping, read the other chapters that apply to your choices to make sure you're on the right track.

The BIOS

BIOS stands for *Basic Input Output System.* The BIOS, essentially, is a set of mini-programs and functions that reside on a Read Only Memory (ROM) chip in your PC (see Figure 1.1). You can think of the BIOS as the PC's low-level nervous system. Its programs enable the CPU and other components in the PC to communicate and function. The BIOS processes all keyboard input, communication through the PC's ports, the characters that appear on the display, and much more. In effect, the BIOS serves as a middleman between your PC's hardware and its software (which includes the operating system such as Windows 95 or Windows NT). The BIOS enables your software to access the PC's hardware. Because the BIOS sits midway between your hardware and software, it often is called *firmware.*

FIG. 1.1
A BIOS contains low-level programs that enable the PC to perform the most basic functions.

Today's PCs use BIOSes from a handful of different BIOS manufacturers. The programs in these BIOSes are different, although the BIOSes themselves all provide the same types of low-level functions. The functions that a BIOS performs are very basic, but that doesn't mean there isn't room for upgrade. Plug and Play and support for new hardware are two reasons to upgrade your PC's BIOS.

Plug and Play (PnP) refers to the computer's capability to automatically set up and use a new hardware component without any intervention by you. In other words, in a PnP system, you can install a new device and let the computer and operating system configure it for you so it doesn't conflict or interfere with any other devices in the computer. So, you might want to upgrade the BIOS in your system to provide PnP support.

NOTE Windows 95 provides PnP support for many devices, even on systems that do not include a PnP BIOS. Adding PnP support to the BIOS provides an additional layer of integration and further simplifies installing new devices.

Another reason to upgrade the BIOS is to ensure that all the latest hardware is supported by your PC. Early BIOSes, for example, didn't support hard disks of more than a certain size. BIOS upgrades enabled PCs to handle the new, higher-capacity disks that came along without requiring special driver software to enable the PC to communicate with the device. These drivers added to the system's complexity and, in some cases, slowed down performance and caused compatibility problems.

A third reason to upgrade the system's BIOS is to obtain bug fixes. Your current BIOS might have a few bugs in its routines that prevent it from working properly with certain devices. Keeping the BIOS current helps avoid those types of problems.

Depending on your current system's BIOS, updating the BIOS can be as easy as running a program. Most of today's BIOS chips are *flash programmable*, which means they can be reprogrammed by running an update program that you acquire from the BIOS manufacturer. With these types of systems, it's a good idea to check every three to six months to find out if a new BIOS update is available, and perform the update.

Other systems require that you remove the BIOS chip and replace it. The cost can be as high as $80 or more, so you don't want to perform this type of upgrade often. But, an upgrade can give you the same benefits as a flash upgrade—namely, an up-to-date BIOS that supports all the latest hardware and system features. See "Overview of the BIOS" in Chapter 7 for more information.

TIP If your system contains a flash BIOS, you should consider updating the BIOS prior to performing any other system upgrade. This ensures that your system will support all the latest hardware and system features. If your system requires a chip replacement to update the BIOS and you haven't replaced the BIOS for a few years, it's a good idea to replace it prior to performing any other upgrades.

Justifying the cost of a BIOS upgrade is easy. Most flash BIOS upgrades are free—just download the latest update from the BIOS manufacturer or from the PC manufacturer's bulletin board system (BBS) or Internet Web site. Also, spending $80 after two or three years to upgrade your system's BIOS (for a chip replacement) is a relatively inexpensive way to ensure bug-free performance and support for a wide range of additional hardware.

The CPU

The *Central Processing Unit (CPU)* is the brains of your PC (see Figure 1.2). Essentially, the CPU is where all the computing takes place, although in today's PCs, special-purpose processors often handle video and certain other functions. Even so, switching your PC's CPU is one of the two upgrades that has the most impact on its performance. (Adding memory is the second.)

FIG. 1.2
The CPU performs the majority of the actual computing that takes place in your PC.

How you upgrade the CPU depends on your system's design and its current CPU. In some systems, you can simply replace the existing CPU with a faster one. You might, for example, replace a 25MHz 486 chip with a 100MHz 486 to get a big jump in performance for a relatively minor cost. Or, you might install an Intel OverDrive chip in your system to take it from a 486 to a Pentium. Upgrade CPU modules also are available that let you upgrade a 286 or 386 system to a 486 or 586 (the functional equivalent of a Pentium-based system).

Most CPU upgrades range from as little as $100 to around $650. When you start considering an upgrade near the high end of that range, you need to take a look at the overall picture and decide if you might be better off simply buying a new system. The section "Upgrade versus New" later in this chapter offers advice on when to opt for a new system rather than an upgrade.

In general, if you want to improve the performance of your PC, you need to upgrade the CPU. In most cases, a CPU upgrade is cost-effective. If yours is a very old system, however, you're probably better off buying a new system. It usually doesn't make sense to try to upgrade a 286 or 386, for example, although it's certainly a good option if you just want more speed and don't have the money to spend on a new system.

Memory

Regardless of what type of system you have, one of the best upgrades you can perform is to add more memory (see Figure 1.3). This is particularly true with the Windows 95 and Windows NT operating systems. Going from 4M to 8M or 12M of RAM in a system can be nearly as effective in improving performance as replacing the CPU or motherboard (though not quite). Adding memory is therefore a very cost-effective way to improve your system's performance.

FIG. 1.3
In today's PCs, memory is contained on modules called SIMMs, which stands for Single Inline Memory Modules.

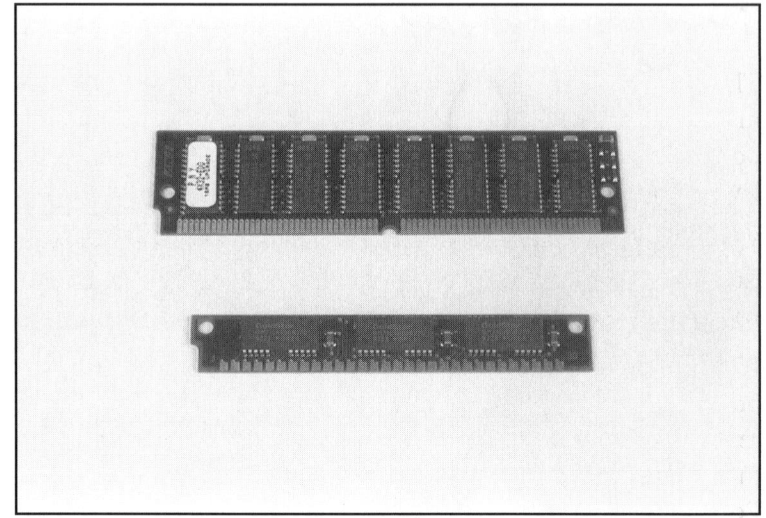

Everyone sees a big boost in performance by raising the amount of RAM in the system to 16M. Beyond that point, however, the average user typically doesn't notice a big jump in performance. The exception is if you're running programs that generate large data files (like a computer-aided-design program such as AutoCAD) or doing a lot of multitasking (running lots of programs at one time).

Memory has dropped in price over the last few years, however, so it isn't nearly as expensive as it used to be to have a lot of RAM in your system. Most new systems contain 16M of RAM, and it's not uncommon for power users to have 32M or more. If you're buying a new system or replacing the motherboard, and you want to be able to accommodate full-motion video and other up-and-coming features, buy as much RAM as you can afford in the 16–32M range. If you're performing an interim upgrade and will be buying a new system in a year or so, 16M will probably work well for you until then.

TIP There are a few issues to consider before rushing out to buy more memory. You need to take stock of your system to determine how many, if any, memory slots are available on the motherboard. You also need to get the correct memory package type (30-pin or 72-pin) and speed to match your PC's requirements. Make sure you read Chapter 10, "Adding Memory," before buying more RAM. For tips on checking what type of memory you have now, read Chapter 5, "Taking Inventory."

The Motherboard

The most major upgrade, short of buying a new system, is replacing the system's motherboard (see Figure 1.4). The *motherboard* is the computer's main circuit board and is where the CPU lives. The PC's memory, BIOS, and other major low-level components also reside on the motherboard.

You might think that replacing your PC's motherboard is a herculean task, but it isn't. All it takes is a few hours, some patience, and a screwdriver. Oh, and, of course, a new motherboard.

If yours is an older system, such as a 286 or 386, it's a good candidate for a motherboard replacement. Most 486 and Pentium-based systems can be upgraded with the replacement of the CPU, so they are less likely candidates for motherboard replacement. Even so, you can make a case for replacing a 486 motherboard with a new Pentium or Pentium Pro motherboard.

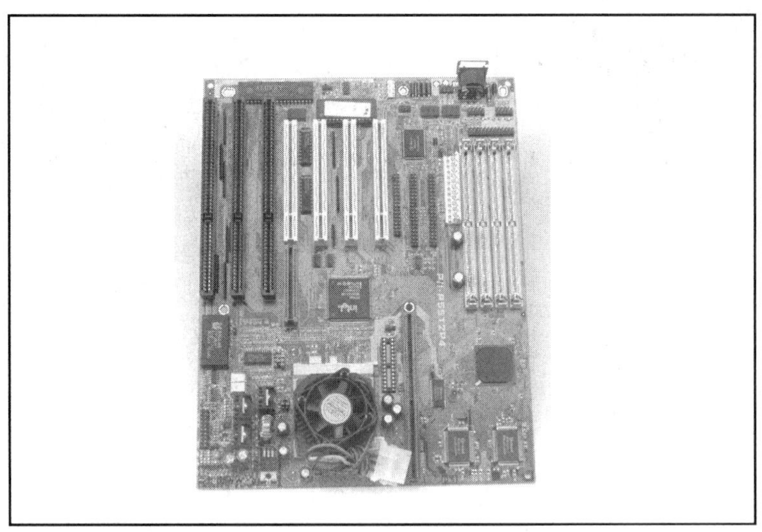

FIG. 1.4
Replacing the motherboard is a major, but relatively easy, upgrade.

Many of the earlier, slower 486 systems, for example, don't accommodate Intel OverDrive CPU upgrades even though they contain an upgrade socket. Intel changed the OverDrive specifications after these systems were built, which means the OverDrive chips don't work in them. In some cases, you can replace the CPU with a faster version, such as replacing a 25MHz 486 with a 50MHz 486. That change doesn't have a very profound impact on the system, so you're better off replacing the motherboard.

Whether you opt for an upgrade or replacement of the motherboard really boils down to a few points:

- *You're strapped for cash.* CPU upgrades are cheaper than a motherboard replacement. If you just can't afford a new motherboard, a CPU replacement is a good interim step.
- *You're intimidated.* A CPU upgrade is easier to accomplish than a motherboard replacement. Read Chapter 9, "Replacing the Motherboard," to see what's involved. If you still feel it's beyond your skills, opt for a CPU upgrade.
- *Memory.* You might not be able to use your existing memory on the new motherboard. Most older motherboards use 30-pin memory modules, and today's motherboards typically use 72-pin modules. Some let you use both, and you can get adapters to make them work. Figure in the possible cost of new memory in your motherboard purchase.

- *You are performing other upgrades.* If you're adding a new hard disk, CD-ROM drive, sound card, and other gadgets, you're probably better off buying a new PC. If the cost of the upgrade is within 30 percent or so of a new PC, spend the extra money and buy new.

TIP One final tip: Buy a PCI motherboard rather than a VESA local bus motherboard. PCI is largely replacing VESA, and you'll enjoy a better choice of upgrades later. For more information about VESA versus PCI, see Chapter 9, "Replacing the Motherboard."

Video

A new, fast video card can have a really dramatic impact on your system's performance. If you're still using a tired VGA video card, a new VESA or PCI local bus video card gives you faster graphics, more colors, and support for neat features like full-screen, full-motion video. Best of all, you can get a reasonably fast, capable video card for less than $150. Figure 1.5 shows a typical video card.

FIG. 1.5
Today's video cards usually contain between 1M and 2M of video RAM, which usually can be expanded further.

TIP The term *local bus* refers to a system in which devices are able to communicate more or less directly with the CPU, bypassing the PC's regular bus. This improves performance for those devices and the overall system. Devices that are available in local bus versions include video cards, network cards, and hard disk host adapters. The two common local bus standards are VESA and PCI, with PCI surpassing VESA in terms of device availability.

If you're replacing the system's motherboard and you currently don't have a local bus video card (VESA or PCI), spend the extra money for a new local bus video card. If your current system contains a VESA local bus video card and the new motherboard uses a PCI local bus, you'll need a new PCI local bus video card.

Buy a TV Instead!

Last year I decided to upgrade my primary system. In addition to replacing its 486 motherboard with a Pentium-166, I added a second, faster CD-ROM drive and loaded it with memory. I also decided to pick one of the fastest video cards available. As usual, the price for the video card dropped right after I bought it because the company came out with a new, faster model. *C'est la vie.*

Thinking that everyone should be able to watch CNN and daytime soaps while they work, I decided to include a TV card in the system. The TV card required that I get an MPEG upgrade for the video card, which I did. By the time I'd purchased the video card, MPEG upgrade, TV card, and paid the tax on it all, I'd spent nearly $1,000. The moral of the story is this: If you really want a TV in your office, buy a TV. It'll be cheaper.

Multimedia: Sound and CD

Probably one of the most common upgrades is adding multimedia capability to your PC. This typically includes adding a CD-ROM drive and sound card to the system. Although you can add one and not the other, it's unlikely you will because today's multimedia titles make extensive use of sound, and nearly all come on CD rather than disk.

You can buy CD-ROM drives and sound cards separately, or you can opt for a multimedia kit. These multimedia kits include a CD-ROM drive, sound card, and, usually, a selection of multimedia titles on CD.

Even if you're not planning to buy any multimedia titles now or in the future, you still might want to add a CD-ROM drive and sound card. While most software has traditionally been distributed on floppy disk, an increasing number of software publishers are distributing their software on CD. This trend makes sense for the publisher: CDs are cheaper to mass-produce than floppy disk sets, and the CD enables the publisher to distribute much larger programs and support materials than would be practical with a floppy. So, if you want to be able to continue to upgrade your software and buy new software, you'll have to have a CD-ROM drive in your system.

With the advent of voice messaging systems for the computer and voice e-mail, the sound card becomes an important productivity tool in addition to an add-on for playing games. So, a multimedia upgrade makes sense for nearly any system that lacks multimedia capability. If you're also considering replacing the motherboard, however, take a close look at buying a new system instead. You might find that when you total all your upgrades, a new system is only a few hundred dollars more.

Unless you can't find the combination of CD-ROM drive and sound card that you want, buying a multimedia kit makes sense. All the components, cables, and drivers you need are included in the kit, along with (usually) a nice selection of software to get you started.

Storage and Backup

The first computer I owned had a 40M disk drive, and I thought that would be plenty. No sooner had that thought escaped to my conscious mind than the disk filled up. Today, my primary system contains its original 340M disk, as well as a 1.2G upgrade. Both are nearly full, even though both contain compressed volumes to increase their capacity. The moral of my story is that you can never have enough disk space.

If the rest of your system is pretty much up-to-speed but lacks free disk space, adding a hard disk is a good idea. You gain more space for the ever-expanding operating system and new applications, more swap space to improve the system's performance, and more breathing room for your documents and other data. Figure 1.6 shows a hard disk and host adapter.

FIG. 1.6
Adding a new hard disk (and host adapter if necessary) gives your PC more room to store programs and data.

TIP The term *swap space* refers to the area of the hard disk that the operating system (such as Windows 95) uses to simulate memory. The operating system moves blocks of memory called *pages* to and from the disk as needed. Here's an analogy to help you understand paging: Think of your PC's total memory requirements as a pile of paper pages. You have a box in which to put those pages, which represents the available memory in your PC. You have more pages than will fit in the box, so you can only have in the box those pages you're using at the time. So, you *swap* pages in the box that you're currently not using for pages that you do need. In your system, the swap space on disk contains the pile of pages the system currently isn't using.

In most cases, you can replace your existing drive, but I generally recommend that you supplement the existing drive rather than replace it. The only reason to ditch a drive altogether is if the system case doesn't have room to accommodate the old drive and the new one.

TIP If your current drive is IDE and you want to add a new SCSI drive for the best possible performance, the two should be able to coexist without any problems. This means you can leave your operating system alone and simply add a new disk to increase capacity. But, to truly optimize performance, you should consider installing the new, faster drive as the boot drive and placing the operating system on it. Chapter 11, "Hard Disks," explores these upgrade options and others.

If you decide you need a new drive, don't think that you necessarily need the largest drive you can get. Unless you intend to add a lot more applications, a 1G drive probably will serve you well for quite a while, particularly when you consider that you can compress the drive to nearly 2G of storage space.

TIP If you do decide to get a new drive and want to compress it to get extra space, leave a large enough uncompressed host drive to contain your operating system and your critical document and data files. Although it isn't common to experience problems with compressed volumes, it can be more difficult to recover data from a trashed compressed volume than from a trashed uncompressed disk. For example, I store all of my documents on an uncompressed drive.

If, on the other hand, you intend to upgrade a lot of your applications, install new applications, or experiment with creating sound, capturing video, or other disk-intensive applications, a 2G drive is probably more appropriate. And if you're a real space-hog, you can always opt for a 4G drive, although you'll pay a premium price for it.

Networking and Communications

Other popular upgrades include adding network capability and adding modems and faxmodems. With an increasing number of people working either part-time or full-time from home, user-installed networks have become more common. Even if you have only two computers in your small office, a network gives you a lot of flexibility in sharing files, disk space, printers, faxmodems, and other resources. With Windows for Workgroups, Windows 95, and Windows NT all including their own built-in network capability, creating your own network is a simple task that only requires the addition of a little bit of hardware and cabling. So, upgrading your PCs to support networking is a good idea, even in a home environment. Figure 1.7 shows a typical network card, cables, and terminators.

With increasing use of the Internet and online services, a fast modem saves you connect time, and also saves you money. If you're currently using a 9600bps (bits per second) modem, you should think about upgrading to a faster one, such as a 28.8Kbps (thousand bits per second) or 33.6Kbps model. If you're currently using a 14.4Kbps modem, you need to take a closer look. Your Internet service provider or online service might not support connection speeds higher than your 14.4Kbps modem accommodates, and, until they do, a faster modem won't do anything to decrease your online time or associated costs. When your service provider or online service does upgrade its modems to accommodate higher connect speeds, spend the money for a 33.6Kbps modem.

FIG. 1.7
This network card uses coaxial cable similar but not identical to the cable used for your TV.

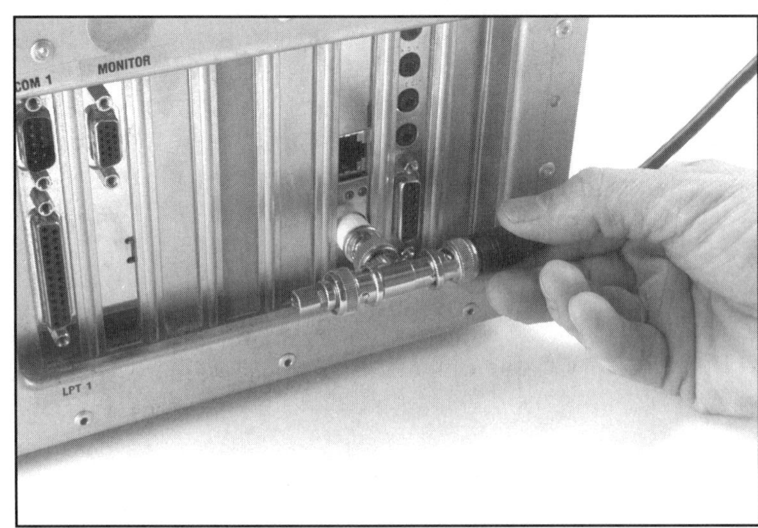

POTS, ISDN, Cable TV, or...?

Modem speeds are starting to reach the upper end of the telephone infrastructure's capability to carry data traffic. In some areas, Integrated Services Digital Network (ISDN) lines are available that provide much higher speeds. Currently, though, ISDN is not widely available and is still relatively expensive. Rural areas, for example, may never have ISDN capability.

If you're interested in Internet access, you should also be aware that a shift is underway from dial-up access to hard-wired access. Within a few years, most areas of the country will have Internet access available through the local cable-TV operator. The Internet traffic will piggyback on your cable-TV cable. Whether the access goes through your Internet-ready TV or your computer will depend on how your cable company designs the systems, but it's likely that you'll be able to connect your cable modem to your PC.

I have a hunch that entertainment (television shows, movies, and so on) will move from being distributed by cable to being distributed by satellite, and each home will have a small satellite dish. All that cable left buried in the ground will then provide the infrastructure for networking (Internet) and video-phone service. Who will own that cable and provide the Internet and telephone service remains to be seen.

All That Other Stuff...

Unless you've thumbed through a computer catalog lately, you might be amazed at the gadgets, doo-dads, and programs you can get for your PC. Although none of the following items are a necessity for most people, you might find a gadget or two that you can't live without.

Digitizing Tablet

This input device consists of a tablet and stylus that you can use in conjunction with a wide range of art programs to draw and paint electronically. If you or your kids are artistically inclined, this is a great add-on. Figure 1.8 shows a typical digitizing tablet.

FIG. 1.8
If you're interested in graphics or art, a digitizing tablet is a great add-on.

Scanner

A *scanner* enables you to convert paper documents to electronic documents. You can, for example, scan photos, letters, and forms into the computer to edit or use within documents you create on the computer. You also can use a scanner to fax paper documents through your faxmodem. Figure 1.9 shows a typical desktop scanner and a hand-held scanner.

FIG. 1.9
Desktop scanners let you scan an entire page in one pass, but hand-held scanners are less expensive.

Multi-Function Printers

These devices include a printer, copier, scanner, and fax in one unit. In addition to cutting down the clutter in your office, bringing all these functions together in one device cuts overall cost, because a multi-function device is cheaper than the individual components it replaces. Figure 1.10 shows a typical multi-function device.

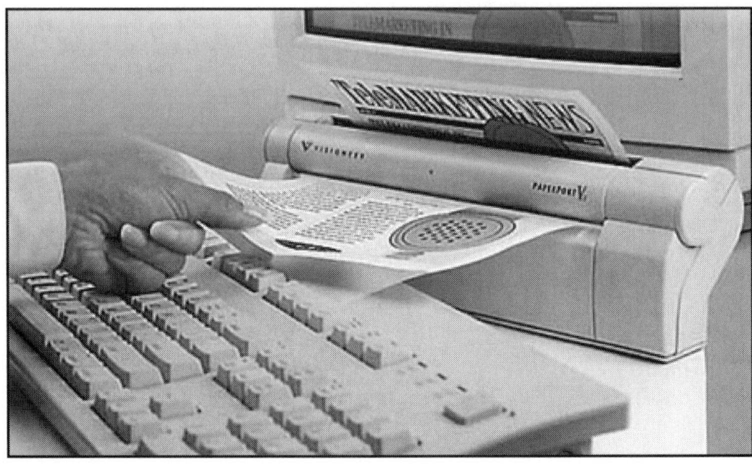

FIG. 1.10
Multi-function devices combine a printer, scanner, fax machine, and copier into one self-contained unit.

Ergonomic Keyboard

This new type of keyboard splits the keys in the middle and angles each set to provide a more ergonomic hand position while typing. Although this type of keyboard might feel a little awkward for a few minutes, you're soon glad you switched. Any carpel tunnel problems you have with your wrists will likely go away (unless you already have severe problems). Figure 1.11 shows a typical ergonomic keyboard.

TIP Before you buy a keyboard, try out a few at your local computer store. Not all keyboards are created equal, and they all have a slightly different feel to them. You might prefer one over another just by the way the keys respond.

FIG. 1.11
An ergonomic keyboard relieves wrist strain and possibly improves your typing speed.

15-inch or 17-inch Monitor

There is nothing special about these except the size. If your system currently includes a 14-inch monitor, you'll enjoy the extra size, which enables you to use a higher screen resolution (assuming your video card supports it) and still be able to read the display. If you can wait a year or so, hold off and buy one of the new flat panel LCD hybrid displays that will hit the market next year. Sure, they'll be more expensive, but they're extremely cool. Figure 1.12 shows a 17-inch monitor.

FIG. 1.12
A 15-inch or 17-inch monitor can give you more available screen space.

Many companies are working on flat panel display units, such as CTX, Dolch, and Sony. The problem has been cost. The manufacturing yield is typically quite poor, which drives the unit cost up.

This has been improving, however, and a search on the Internet can produce several vendors willing to sell you a flat panel display. PixelVision has a broad range of flat-panel monitor products ranging in sizes from 12-inch to 16-inch with resolutions up to 1,280×1,024. U.S. list prices range from $3,000 to $10,000.

You can find PixelVision at the following Web address:

http://www.pixelvision.com/prod.htm

Film and Slide Scanner

These scanners enable you to digitize (scan) positive or negative film and slides into your PC. If you're an avid photographer, this is a great way to bring your photos in to your PC for editing. Figure 1.13 shows a typical film/slide scanner.

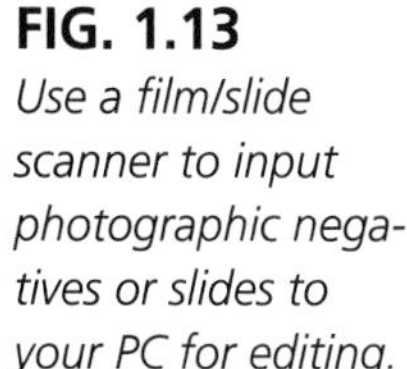

FIG. 1.13
Use a film/slide scanner to input photographic negatives or slides to your PC for editing.

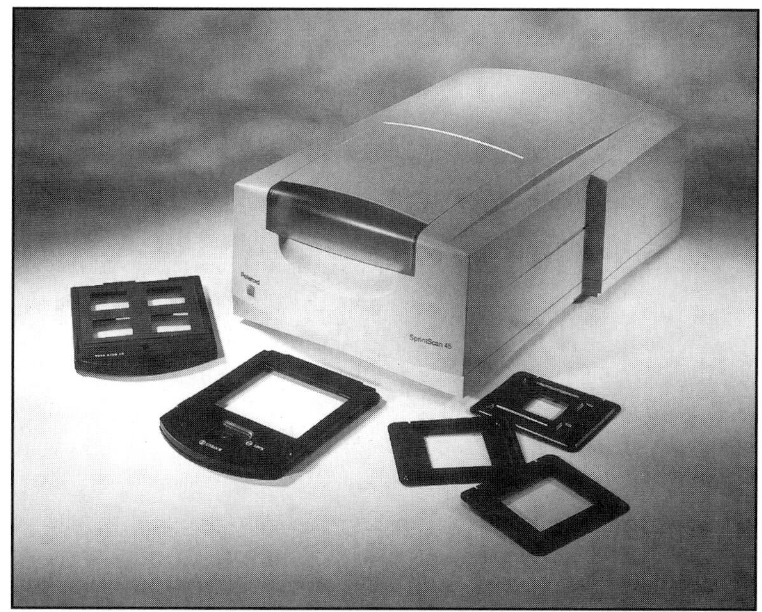

Upgrade versus New

Upgrading is a great means of keeping your PC up-to-date, and is a good option when you're repairing your PC. After all, if you're going to the trouble of opening it to replace a component, you might as well do a little "tune-up" while you're at it, assuming you have the extra money to spend on it.

Upgrading isn't always the best option, however. In some cases, buying a new system makes more sense than trying to upgrade your existing system. In particular, the overall cost should be your overriding concern. If you're replacing the motherboard, RAM, and hard disk and adding a multimedia kit, you're probably going to find that buying a new system is in the same price range. The small amount of money you might save is typically not worth the trouble you're going to go through to perform the upgrade.

To determine if the upgrade makes sense in your situation, price all of the components you want to install, including tax and shipping, if applicable. Add in the cost of Windows 95 if you're currently using Windows 3.1, because a new system will include Windows 95. Compare the cost of the upgrade to the cost of a new, similarly configured system. If you're not upgrading your monitor, don't include the cost of a monitor in the new system. The difference in cost between the two options is your cost savings to perform the work yourself. If the difference is only a few hundred dollars, you might decide that the time and effort involved in the upgrade isn't worth the savings.

NOTE If you've found an old IBM-XT computer at a garage sale and have visions of upgrading it, don't bother. The XT case is shorter than the AT case, and all of today's adapters are designed to fit the AT case. You'll have to replace the case and power supply, and because none of the components in the XT will be of any use to you, there won't be anything of the old system left in the new system. Use the old XT for a doorstop instead.

Locating Parts and Supplies

You can buy the majority of your upgrade components locally. Many discount retailers—such as Wal-Mart, Best Buy, and others—sell memory, multimedia kits, modems, and most other PC components. You'll probably be able to buy any other components, such as motherboards, from a local computer retailer or repair shop.

Another option is to order through one of the many mail-order companies that deal in computer components. The prices from a mail-order company generally fall in the same range as those from a discount retailer when you figure in shipping and handling costs. If yours is a large order, though, you might need to determine how sales tax affects the final cost. If the mail-order company is located in a different state, it might not charge you sales tax, which could save you a few dollars in the end. Check to make sure when you're pricing an upgrade.

WINDOWS Magazine and *PC* Magazine provide a good source of information about mail-order companies that sell computer components. In particular, you'll find literally hundreds of mail-order companies listed in *Computer Shopper*, the mother of all upgrade magazines.

An important point to consider when you are upgrading your system is how you will gather all the driver and other software updates you might need. In many cases, the hardware comes with the necessary drivers, but in some cases, those drivers might not be up-to-date. Most companies host sites on the Internet and make driver updates available at those sites. Many also maintain BBSes from which you can download drivers. And if nothing else, you should be able to call the company and ask for the necessary updates. Before you go through any of these steps, however, check with the company to find out what the latest driver revision is.

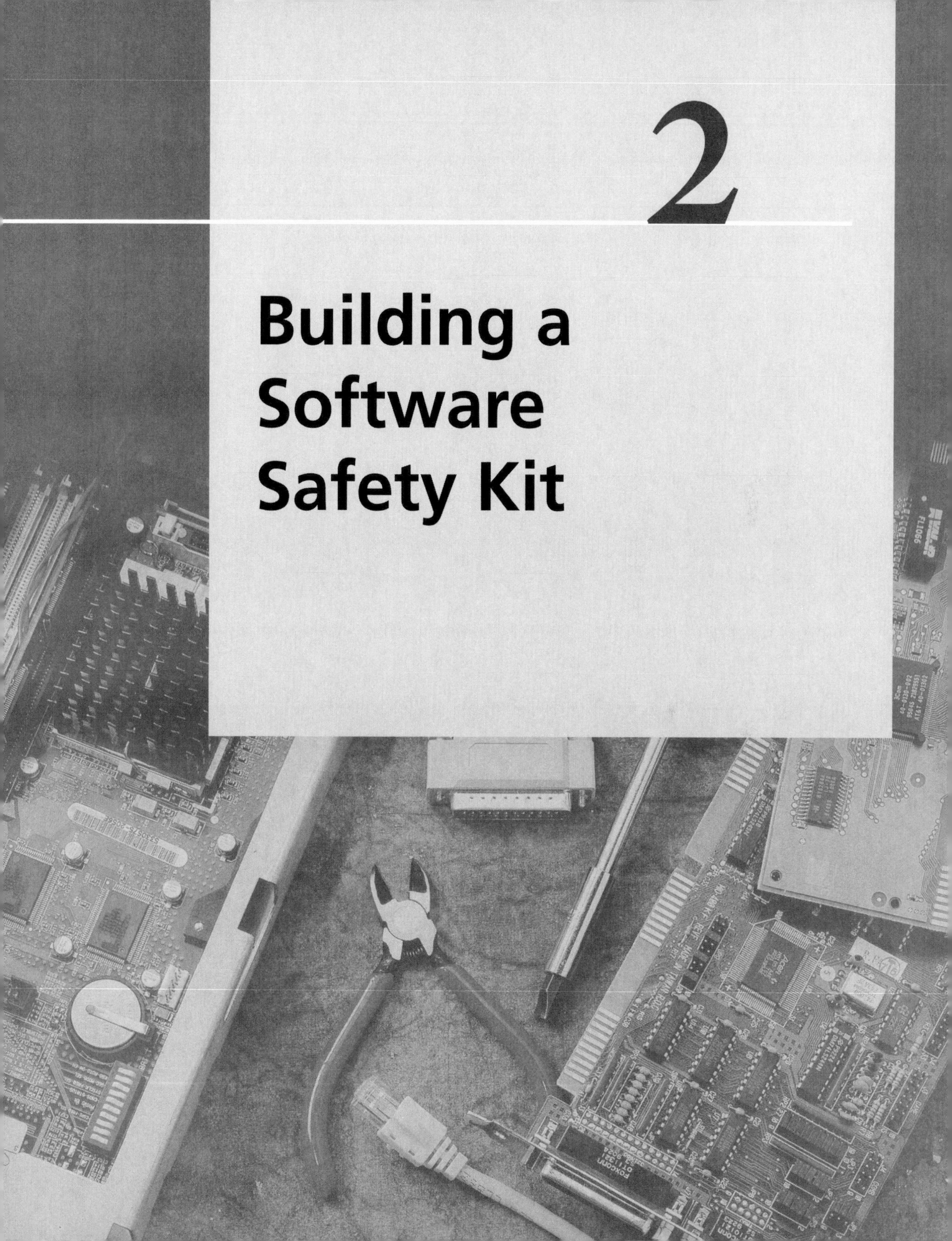

2

Building a Software Safety Kit

The first thing you should do before you even think about opening your PC's case to perform an upgrade or repair is to create a software safety kit. The tools you place in this kit help ensure that if something does go wrong during the installation process, you aren't left with a fancy computer that won't boot. So, before you head down to the store to pick up all your new goodies, or while you're waiting for them to arrive in the mail, read this chapter and follow every step!

Here's a list of what you'll do as a result of this chapter:

- Create a set of boot and recovery disks
- Back up your PC's system files and Registry
- Create a system log that details the contents of your PC
- Back up the PC's BIOS
- Back up your important data files

Although all of these steps are important to safeguard your computer now and in the future, having a recovery or boot disk is one of the most important.

Creating Boot/Recovery Disks

Chapter 4, "Systems Overview," explains how your PC works in a general sense, including how the system boots the operating system. For now, I'll just explain that when you turn on your PC, it runs through a set of simple diagnostic procedures called the POST, which stands for Power On Self Test. In general, the PC checks its memory and a few other items, and, if all is well, begins looking for an operating system such as DOS, Windows 95, or Windows NT.

By default, your PC looks first in drive A for a *bootable floppy disk*, which is one that contains the necessary files to boot the system. That doesn't mean it kicks it into next week. The term *boot* comes from the word *bootstrap*, and simply means that the computer looks for and loads an operating system to control the PC.

NOTE If you're not very familiar with the term *operating system*, you find a description in Chapter 4. For now, just know that the operating system is the collection of software on your computer that enables the PC to run programs, and also enables you to interact with the PC and those programs.

If no disk is found in drive A, the system looks on the hard disk for a bootable operating system. When it finds the necessary files, it begins booting the operating system. When the operating system has been loaded, it takes over control of the PC. To you, this typically means that you see Windows 95 or Windows NT appear on your display.

TIP Many viruses transfer from one computer to another by infecting boot disks. So, your computer is susceptible to being infected by a virus when you boot from a floppy disk. Most of today's PC BIOSes contain a setting that lets you specify the boot seek order, or the order in which the BIOS searches the disks for an operating system (A then C, or C then A). Changing this setting to make the system check drive C first for an operating system can reduce the risk of virus infection, because the system does not attempt to boot from the floppy unless it can't find an operating system on drive C. The only time this happens is when you're having a problem with the hard disk or have installed a new hard disk to replace your old one.

During the upgrade, software you install might need to modify your system files, Registry, or other information on your hard disk. It very rarely happens that something goes so wrong that your PC no longer boots. But it is possible, so the first thing you should do is create a boot disk (also called a *recovery disk*) for your PC. The following sections explain how to do so for DOS/Windows 3.x, Windows 95, and Windows NT.

Creating a Boot Disk for DOS/Windows 3.x

Create Boot/Recovery Disk—DOS/Windows 3.x

- ☑ Your system boots and works properly now.
- ☑ You have two blank high-density disks for drive A.

The first phase of the process requires that you format a disk and transfer the system files to it.

Phase One

1. Boot the system and start Windows.
2. In File Manager, choose Disk, Format Disk to display the Format Disk dialog box (see Figure 2.1).

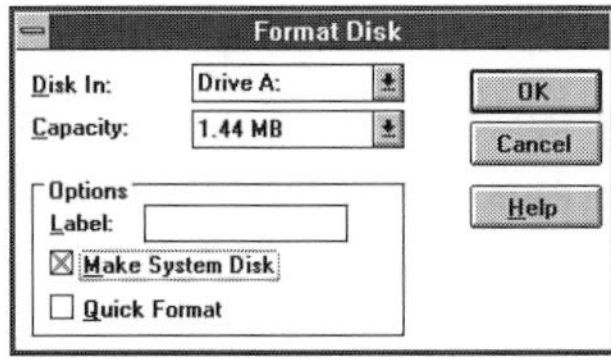

FIG. 2.1
Create a boot disk using the Format Disk dialog box.

3. Select Drive A from the Disk In drop-down list.
4. Choose the appropriate disk capacity from the Capacity drop-down list.
5. Place a check in the Make System Disk check box.
6. Make sure the Quick Format check box is cleared.
7. Choose OK, then Yes to begin formatting the disk.
8. Label this disk **DOS Boot Disk**.
9. Repeat steps 2–7 with the second disk, and label this second disk **DOS Repair Utilities**.

You now have two bootable floppy disks containing a few hidden DOS operating system files and the file COMMAND.COM. You use one as a boot disk and the other (which also is bootable) as a disk to store some useful troubleshooting and repair utilities. You copy those files in the next phase.

Phase Two

1. Using File Manager or the DOS COPY command, copy the files AUTOEXEC.BAT and CONFIG.SYS from the root directory of drive C to the DOS Boot Disk.
2. Copy the file AUTOEXEC.BAT from the hard disk to a file named AUTOEXEC.FLP on the DOS Boot Disk. For example, you can use the DOS command **COPY C:\AUTOEXEC.BAT A:\AUTOEXEC.FLP** to copy and rename the file.
3. Copy the file CONFIG.SYS from the hard disk to a file named CONFIG.FLP on the DOS Boot Disk.

NOTE At this point, you should have identical files named CONFIG.SYS and CONFIG.FLP, and identical files AUTOEXEC.BAT and AUTOEXEC.FLP, on the floppy.

4. Copy the files SYSTEM.INI and WIN.INI from the Windows directory to the DOS Boot Disk.

5. Copy the files HIMEM.SYS, EMM386.EXE, and SMARTDRV.EXE from the DOS (or Windows) directory to the DOS Boot Disk.

NOTE If your system contains these three files in both the DOS and Windows directories, copy the ones with the latest dates to the floppy.

6. Insert the DOS Repair Utilities disk in the floppy drive. Copy the files ATTRIB.EXE, EDIT.COM, FDISK.EXE, FORMAT.COM, and QBASIC.EXE from the DOS directory to the floppy disk.

You now have a bootable system disk that contains the files necessary to boot the system and load basic memory management drivers. The second disk contains useful utility programs.

The CONFIG.SYS and AUTOEXEC.BAT files on the boot floppy load drivers from the hard disk if the statements in these two files include the correct path to the driver files. If the paths are not included, the system tries to load the drivers from the floppy disk at boot time. So, you need to edit CONFIG.SYS and AUTOEXEC. BAT, and change any lines that reference drivers to point to the correct location on the hard disk. That is Phase Three.

Phase Three

1. Open Notepad and load the file CONFIG.SYS from the DOS Boot Disk (see Figure 2.2).

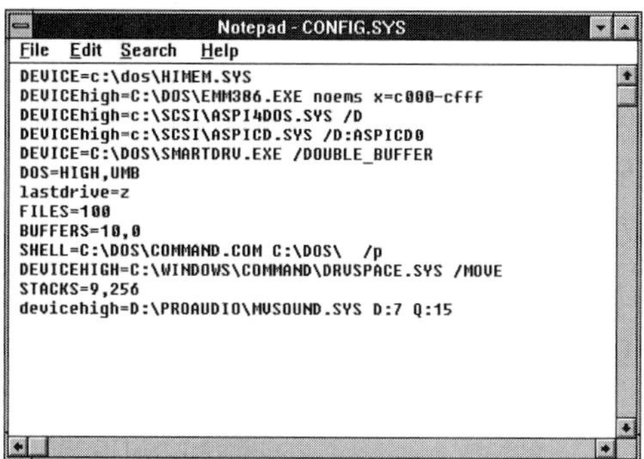

FIG. 2.2 *You can use Notepad to edit text files such as CONFIG.SYS and AUTOEXEC.BAT.*

2. Locate all the lines in CONFIG.SYS that begin with `DEVICE=` or `DEVICEHIGH=`. If no path is specified in front of the driver file name, add the correct path. You have to verify the location of the driver file on the hard disk in order to specify the right location. For example, if the line reads `DEVICE=ASPICD.SYS`, and the file is located in the root directory of the hard disk, change the line to read `DEVICE=C:\ASPICD.SYS`.

TIP If a driver doesn't have a path before it in the CONFIG.SYS file, the driver file is probably located in the root directory of drive C. If you can't find the file, try entering the command **DIR *file.ext* /S**, where *file.ext* is the name of the driver file. This command performs a directory listing of your entire drive C and locates the file.

3. When you finish with the changes to CONFIG.SYS, save the changes on the floppy.
4. Still in Notepad, open AUTOEXEC.BAT from the floppy disk.
5. Search through the file and note any lines that load programs. The programs have a COM or EXE extension, and might be preceded by the `LH` or `LOADHIGH` statement. For each such line, specify the correct path to the file. For example, if a line reads `LOADHIGH MOUSE.COM`, and the MOUSE.COM file is located in the root directory of drive C, change the line to read **LOADHIGH C:\MOUSE.COM**.
6. Save the changes to the floppy.

At this point, booting the system with the floppy disk causes it to load all the same drivers as it would from the hard disk. All you've done is change the AUTOEXEC.BAT and CONFIG.SYS files to make sure DOS knows where those files are located, and loads them from the hard disk instead of trying to load them from the floppy. If your hard disk isn't working, though, DOS still tries to load the drivers from the hard disk. So, you should have a separate set of CONFIG.SYS and AUTOEXEC.BAT files that load the device drivers from the floppy disk.

Remember those two files, AUTOEXEC.FLP and CONFIG.FLP, that you copied to the boot disk back in Phase Two? Those are the files you'll edit to point to drivers on the floppy disk.

Phase Four

1. Open Notepad, then load the file CONFIG.FLP from the DOS Boot Disk.
2. Locate each line that begins with `DEVICE=` or `DEVICEHIGH=`, and copy (using File Manager or the COPY command) the specified driver file from its location on the hard disk to the root directory of the floppy disk.
3. Edit the file, changing all of the lines that begin with `DEVICE=` or `DEVICEHIGH=` to point to the driver file on drive A instead of the hard disk. For example, if the line reads `DEVICE=C:\SCSI\ASPICD.SYS /D:ASPICD0`, change the line to read **DEVICE=A:\ASPICD.SYS /D:ASPICD0** (and make sure you've copied the file to the root directory as indicated in step 2).
4. Save the changes on the floppy.
5. In Notepad, open the file AUTOEXEC.FLP from the floppy.
6. Edit the file, changing all the lines that load device drivers or other programs to reference drive A instead of drive C.
7. Copy from the hard disk to the floppy disk the program files referenced by the lines you identified in step 7.
8. Place the DOS Boot Disk and the DOS Repair Utilities disks in a safe location.

You now have two disks. The DOS Boot Disk contains the files necessary to boot DOS and a copy of the CONFIG.SYS and AUTOEXEC.BAT files. Included on the disk are backup copies of your Windows configuration files, SYSTEM.INI and WIN.INI, although these files aren't used when booting DOS.

This disk also contains a set of AUTOEXEC and CONFIG files (with an FLP extension) that you can rename to AUTOEXEC.BAT and CONFIG.SYS if your hard disk isn't readable. The disk includes the driver files and terminate-and-stay-resident (TSR) programs loaded by CONFIG.SYS and AUTOEXEC.BAT to be used as backups in case your hard disk isn't readable. Normally, however, the AUTOEXEC.FLP, CONFIG.FLP, and driver/TSR files aren't needed unless the hard disk can't be read.

The second disk, DOS Repair Utilities, contains programs you'll find useful for editing system files and recovering your hard disk. These utilities and the use of a boot disk are explained in Chapter 24.

Creating a Boot Disk for Windows 95

Startup Disk—Windows 95

- ☑ Your system boots and works properly now.
- ☑ You have three high-density disks for drive A.
- ☑ You have the Windows 95 CD or distribution disks. This is required only if the Windows 95 distribution cabinet files are not on your system's hard disk. These files have names like Win95_04.cab. If you purchased your system with Windows 95 already installed, the CAB files probably are on the hard disk in a subfolder of the Windows folder (such as \Windows\Options\Cabs).

The process for creating a boot disk for a Windows 95 computer is less complex than for a DOS/Windows 3.x computer. Windows 95 automates much of the process, as you see in Phase One.

Phase One

1. In Windows 95, open the Control Panel and double-click the Add/Remove Programs icon.
2. Click the Startup Disk tab to display the Startup Disk page (see Figure 2.3).

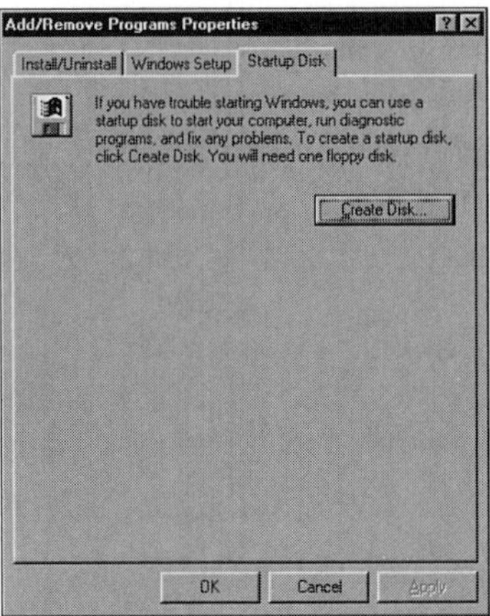

FIG. 2.3
The Startup Disk page's only function is to start the process of creating a startup disk for Windows 95.

3. Click the Create Disk button. Windows 95 starts the process of creating a startup disk and prompts you to insert the Windows 95 CD or disks, if needed.

4. Windows 95 prompts you to insert a blank disk in drive A. Do so and click OK. Windows 95 creates the startup disk for you.
5. Label the disk **Windows 95 Startup Disk**.
6. Place the disk in a safe location.

In addition to creating a disk with which you can boot the system, the previous procedure places a few support programs and support files on the Windows 95 Startup Disk. These include:

- *Attrib.exe*. Enables you to change the attributes (read-only, hidden, archive, system) of files. It's sometimes necessary when troubleshooting a system to change file attributes.
- *Chkdsk.exe*. Performs simple diagnostic checks on a disk.
- *Command.com*. The Windows 95 command interpreter, which provides the command-line interface you see when the system boots from the floppy.
- *Debug.exe*. Lets you test and edit other programs. It is sometimes useful for troubleshooting and system configuration, although you probably won't use it often.
- *Drvspace.bin*. A support file that is used by the DriveSpace compression driver and is only necessary if your system contains a compressed volume.
- *Edit.com*. A simple text editor you can use to edit files such as Config.sys, Autoexec.bat, System.ini, Win.ini, and other text files.
- *Fdisk.exe*. Enables you to view, manage, and create partitions on a hard disk.
- *Format.com*. Enables you to format a disk, including hard disks.
- *Io.sys*. Support file that is part of the Windows 95 operating system.
- *Msdos.sys*. Support file that is used by Windows 95 to store startup information such as whether to display a boot menu.
- *Regedit.exe*. The Registry Editor, which enables you to view and modify the Registry. Windows 95 uses the Registry to contain settings and information about your system and its software.
- *Scandisk.exe*. Enables you to scan a disk for errors and repair those errors.
- *Scandisk.ini*. Initialization file used by Scandisk to store its operating settings.

- *Sys.com.* Lets you copy the system files to a disk, which makes the disk bootable.
- *Uninst.exe.* This program can be used to uninstall (remove) Windows 95 programs.

Phase Two

The second disk, Windows 95 Recovery Disk, contains a backup copy of your system configuration files. Some of the files will duplicate those on the startup disk you created in Phase One, but others will not be duplicates. As with the startup disk, Windows 95 provides a shortcut method to create the disk. The utility you need to create the disk is located on the Windows 95 CD.

NOTE The ERU (Emergency Recovery Utility) is located in the \Other\Misc\Eru folder of the Windows 95 CD. If you have the Windows 95 diskette set instead of the CD, you can download the Windows 95 CD utilities and optional files from the Microsoft Windows 95 Software Library Web site at **http://www.microsoft.com/windows/software/cdextras.htm** in the Other Utilities link. If you can't get ERU, you can use the manual backup method I explain later in this section.

ERU attempts to back up as many of the system configuration files as will fit on the floppy. In most cases, not all of the files fit. Rather than run ERU twice and back up the files on two disks, you should back up the files onto the hard disk, then compress the files onto a floppy. To compress the files, you need a compression utility such as WinZIP or PKWare (PKZIP.EXE and PKUNZIP.EXE), which are readily available on BBS, commercial information services, and the Internet. If you prefer not to get the compression utility, you can simply run ERU as many times as necessary to back up all your configuration files onto as many floppies as necessary. The following procedure assumes, however, that you have a compression utility.

The WinZIP Internet site is at
http://www.winzip.com/winzip/

Create Emergency Recovery Disk

☑ You have already created a Startup disk per Phase One.

☑ You have the Windows 95 CD or have downloaded the Emergency Recovery Utility from the Microsoft Web site.

☑ You have a compression utility such as WinZIP or PKWare.

1. Open the folder \Other\Misc\Eru on the Windows 95 CD, or open the folder in which you installed the ERU program.
2. Start Eru.exe.
3. ERU prompts you to specify the location for the backup file set. Choose the Other Directory option button, then choose Next.

NOTE If you prefer to back up your files onto a floppy, choose the Drive A option button instead. Note that you'll probably have to run the ERU program at least twice with two different floppies to back up all the files. Also, some of the files might not fit on a floppy.

4. In the Directory text box, type the path to the directory in which you want the files backed up (or accept the default of C:\ERD). Then, choose Next.
5. ERU displays a list of files it will back up (see Figure 2.4).

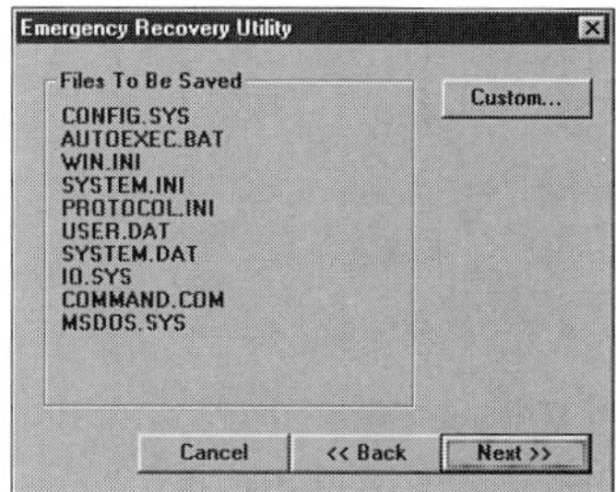

FIG. 2.4
ERU lists the files it will back up by default.

6. Click the Custom button to display a dialog box you can use to specify which files to copy (see Figure 2.5).

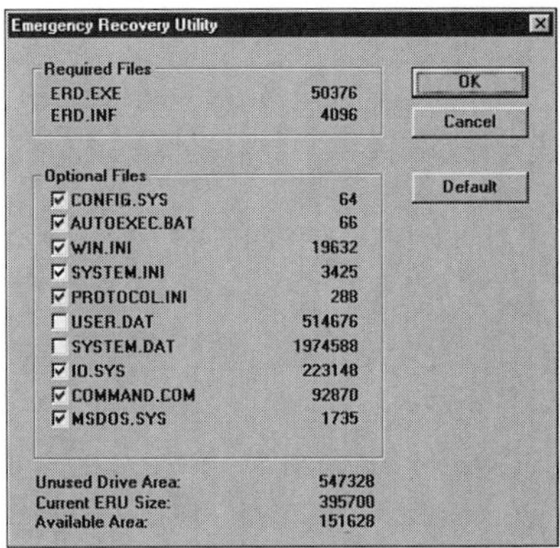

FIG. 2.5
By default, ERU tries to back up all the configuration files if they will fit on the floppy. If not, ERU only backs up those files that will fit.

7. Verify that all of the files are selected, then choose Next. ERU backs up the files to the specified directory.
8. Use your compression utility to compress all of the files in the backup directory to a floppy disk. If the compression utility supports it, create a self-extracting archive so you won't need the compression utility to decompress the archive later.
9. Label the disk **Emergency Recovery Disk** and place it in a safe location.

Registry Backup—Manual Method

You have two options for backing up the Registry manually. You can export the Registry entries from the Registry Editor, or you can simply copy the two Registry files, System.dat and User.dat, to a backup location. The following procedure explains the former.

If you want to back up the Registry files individually, boot the system to a command prompt (not to the Windows 95 GUI), then copy the files System.dat and User.dat from the Windows folder to a floppy disk. If the files don't fit on a disk, compress the files into an archive using WinZIP or a similar compression utility.

1. Choose Start, Run, and enter **regedit** in the Open combo box to start the Registry Editor.
2. In the Registry Editor, choose Registry, Export Registry File.
3. The Registry Editor prompts you for the backup location. Because the entire Registry will be backed up, it's unlikely the file will fit on a disk. So, choose a directory on your hard disk and specify the desired file name, such as **Registry Backup**.

Creating a Recovery Disk for Windows NT

A *Windows NT recovery disk* stores system configuration files that enable you to reconstruct your system and operating environment if problems occur. When you install Windows NT, Setup gives you the option of creating a recovery disk. If you no longer have that disk, or have changed the system's configuration or installed new software since then, you should update the recovery disk. Phase One explains how to create a recovery disk, and Phase Two explains how to update one.

Creating a Recovery Disk for Windows NT

- ☑ Windows NT boots and runs properly.
- ☑ You have a high-density disk for drive A. (Windows NT formats the disk, erasing any data currently on the disk.)
- ☑ For updating a recovery disk only: You have a recovery disk previously created for this workstation.

Phase One

1. For Windows NT 3.5x, choose File, Run, and enter **RDISK.EXE** in the Command Line text box. For Windows NT 4.0, choose Start, Run, and enter **RDISK.EXE** in the Open combo box.
2. In the Repair Disk Utility dialog box, click the Create Repair Disk button. Rdisk prompts you to insert a disk in drive A. Do so, and choose OK.
3. Put the disk in a safe location.

Phase Two

1. For Windows NT 3.5x, choose File, Run, and enter **RDISK.EXE** in the Command Line text box. For Windows NT 4.0, choose Start, Run, and enter **RDISK.EXE** in the Open combo box.
2. In the Repair Disk Utility dialog box, click the Update Repair Info button. Rdisk prompts you to verify that you want to update the repair disk. Insert the disk in drive A and click Yes.
3. Put the disk in a safe location.

Using a Boot Menu—Windows 95

One final step you might want to take on Windows 95 systems is to configure Windows 95 to display a boot menu when you start the system. The boot menu gives you the opportunity to select various startup options, rather than simply booting the Windows 95 GUI. For example, one of the options enables you to boot the system to a command prompt (essentially, a DOS environment). Using the boot menu can be particularly useful when performing upgrades, because you might need to boot the system to a command prompt or boot the system without network support during troubleshooting.

The following procedure helps you configure your system to display a boot menu:

1. Open My Computer, then open drive C.
2. Choose View, Options, and then click the View tab in the Options property sheet.
3. Choose the Show All Files option button, and then choose OK.
4. Locate the file Msdos.sys in the root directory of drive C. Right-click the file and choose Properties. Remove the read-only and hidden atttributes.
5. Load the file Msdos.sys into Notepad or WordPad.
6. In the `[Options]` section of the file, add the following settings:

   [Options]
   BootMenu=1
   BootMenuDelay=10
7. If your system contains a previous version of DOS, as well as Windows 95, and you want to be able to boot to that version of DOS, also add the setting **BootMulti=1** to the [Options] section.
8. Save the file, and then restore its hidden and read-only file attributes.
9. Restart the system.

When you restart the system, you should see a boot menu offering choices that control how Windows 95 starts. The setting `BootDelay=10` causes the menu to remain on the screen for 10 seconds, after which the system chooses the default, option 1 (Normal, which boots the Windows 95 GUI).

Creating a System Log

A *system log* is a detailed list of the components in your computer and their settings, such as the IRQ and base address settings of your adapters (sound card, network card, and so on). The system log also contains a list of the devices in your system, such as your video card, that don't typically have settings associated with them. In addition, the log contains a list of the drivers required by each device.

A system log is particularly useful when you're upgrading the system because it effectively gives you a snapshot of your computer's contents. If you're installing a new network card, for example, you can look in the log for the old card's settings and duplicate them. Checking the log helps you avoid device conflicts (such as two devices trying to use the same IRQ or base address setting).

The system log also is indispensable for troubleshooting problems when they occur. Therefore, it's absolutely imperative that you make a system log and update it from time to time.

Creating a System Log for DOS/Windows 3.x

Although it won't give you as complete a log as you can get in Windows 95, the MSD (Microsoft Diagnostics) utility included with DOS and Windows 3.x gives you a comprehensive log of your system's contents and settings. You can use this log as a starting point to add other information about specific adapters and drivers.

Creating a System Log for DOS/Windows 3.x

☑ You have the MSD.EXE program in either your DOS or Windows directory.

☑ Your printer is connected and functioning.

---

1. Start Windows.
2. Open the Main program group, and double-click the MS-DOS Prompt icon to open a DOS box.
3. At the DOS command prompt, enter **MSD** to start the program.

4. In the MSD program window, choose File, Print Report.
5. In the Report Information dialog box, place a check in the Report All check box.
6. Because the report can be very long, you should print it to a file. Click the File option button and type a file name in the associated text box (or accept the default name of REPORT.MSD).
7. Choose OK to print the report.

Now that the log is stored in a file, you can open it with a word processor (such as Write) and scan it before printing the hardcopy.

Creating a System Log for Windows 95

Windows 95 makes it easy to create a system log. You can use the Device Manager, which you find through the System icon in the Control Panel.

If you haven't already done so, you should install the Generic/Text Only printer driver. This driver enables you to print the system log to a text file, and is useful with other programs when you need to print to a file without embedding printer control codes in the document. To install the Generic/Text Only driver, open My Computer, and then open the Printers folder. Double-click the Add Printer icon to start the Add Printer Wizard. When you are prompted to select a printer, select Generic from the Manufacturer's list. The Text Only printer is the only one listed under that option.

Although you can print the log to a printer, it's a better idea to print it to a file. You then can load it into WordPad or another word processor and scan through it before printing it. You should, however, print a copy of it in case the disk on which the log is stored becomes corrupted or unreadable:

1. Open the Control Panel and double-click the System icon.
2. Click the Device Manager tab to display the Device Manager page (see Figure 2.6).
3. Click the Print button to display the Print dialog box (see Figure 2.7).

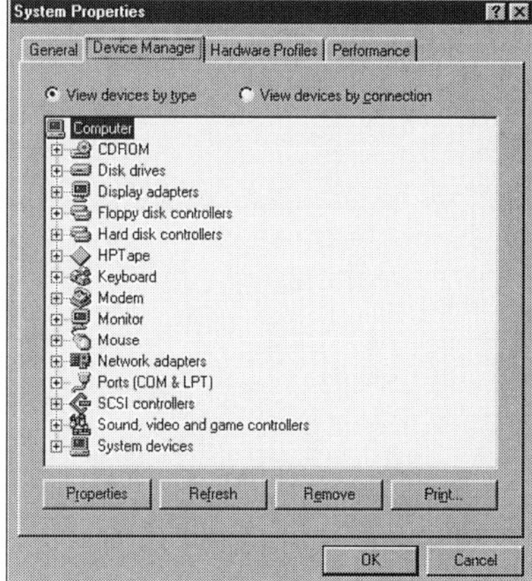

FIG. 2.6
Use the Device Manager page to view information about your system's configuration.

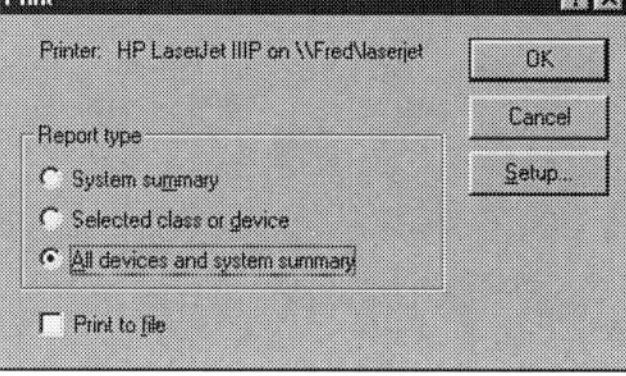

FIG. 2.7
In addition to printing a complete system log, you also can print just a system summary.

4. Choose the All Devices and System Summary option button, and then choose Setup and select the printer you want to use (such as the Generic/ Text Only printer to print to a file).
5. If you're printing to a file, place a check in the Print to File check box.
6. Choose OK to print the report.

Creating a System Log for Windows NT 3.5x

Windows NT 3.5x provides a useful utility called Windows NT Diagnostics that you can use to view information about your system. The utility also prints a system log for you. Unlike the Windows 95 Device Manager, however, the Windows NT Diagnostics can save the report to a plain text file without a special printer driver.

1. Open the Administrative Tools program group.
2. Double-click the Windows NT Diagnostics icon.
3. In the Windows NT Diagnostics window (see Figure 2.8), choose File, Print Report.

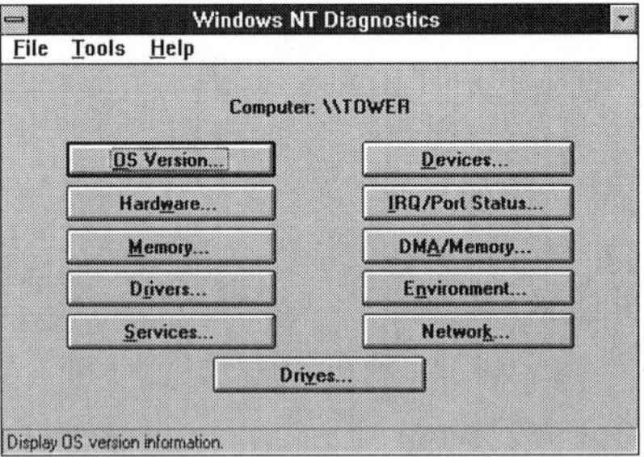

FIG. 2.8
Use the Windows NT Diagnostics utility to view your system's configuration and print a system log.

4. In the Print Report Options dialog box (see Figure 2.9), choose the Report All option button, and then choose OK.

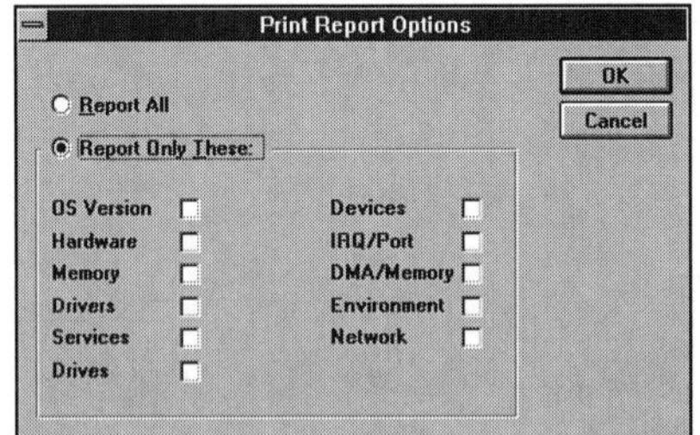

FIG. 2.9
You can print a complete log or a partial one through the options in the Print Report Options dialog box.

5. Specify a file name and choose OK.
6. After reviewing the file (in Write, for example), print a hardcopy of the log.

Creating a System Log for Windows NT 4.0

Like Windows NT 3.51, version 4.0 includes a Windows NT Diagnostics utility you can use to view your system's configuration and print a log.

1. Choose Start, Programs, Administrative Tools (Common), and Windows NT Diagnostics.
2. In the Windows NT Diagnostics property sheet (see Figure 2.10), click the Print button.

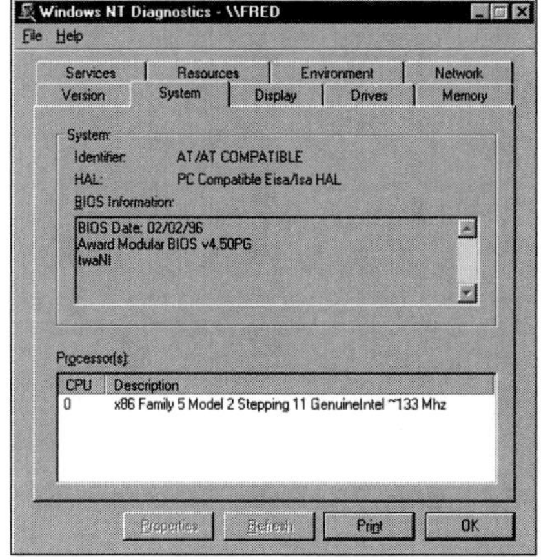

FIG. 2.10
Windows NT Diagnostics provides a multi-tabbed property sheet to organize information about your system's configuration.

3. In the Create Report dialog box, choose the All Tabs, Complete, and File option buttons, and then choose OK.
4. Specify a file name, and then choose Save.

Using Your System Log

You'll find the system log indispensable for helping you track your system's settings. Refer to it any time you're changing settings for a device or installing a new device. Each time you make a change to the system, either print a new log or make notations in the hardcopy to keep the log up-to-date.

Backing Up the BIOS

Equally important (perhaps more important) than creating a system log is creating a backup of your BIOS settings. For example, you might experience a problem that causes your BIOS settings to be lost. Or, you might make a change to the BIOS setup that induces problems, and need to restore the original settings. And, knowing your old BIOS settings is often important when replacing your motherboard—more than likely, your hard disk settings are stored in the BIOS. Your system won't be able to read the hard disk until you enter those settings into the new motherboard's BIOS.

TIP Most of the new Pentium motherboard BIOSes have the capability to sense the type of hard disk installed and adapt to its settings automatically. With these types of systems, you only have to configure the BIOS to auto-sense the disk, and you don't have to enter specific hard disk values for heads, cylinders, and so on. However, you still should make a backup of your BIOS settings.

There are a few utility programs that can back up specific BIOSes, and your system BIOS might have a feature that enables you to store the BIOS settings to a file for later retrieval. But, I'm going to show you a method that, although it might seem like the Neanderthal method, works for everyone and gives you a hardcopy at the same time.

One step that I can't help you with is accessing your BIOS Setup program. On some systems, you access the BIOS Setup program by pressing the Delete (Del) key when the system is first starting. Other systems must be booted to a DOS prompt, and then you press a key combination such as Ctrl+Alt+Esc. Your system manual explains how to access the BIOS Setup program.

If your system automatically boots Windows 95 without displaying a boot menu, you can press Shift+F5 when you see the `Starting Windows 95` message on the monitor. If you prefer to have a boot menu appear that gives you the option of booting to a command prompt, as well as other options, use the procedure given earlier in this chapter to configure your system to use a boot menu.

Recording BIOS Settings

- ☑ A printer is connected to your system and turned on.
- ☑ You know how to access the BIOS Setup program on your system.

1. Restart your system and, before the operating system boots, enter the BIOS Setup program. If your system is running Windows 95 and you need to boot to a command prompt, press Shift+F5 when you see the message, `Starting Windows 95.`
2. In the BIOS Setup program, choose the first configuration option to display its associated settings.
3. Press Shift+Print Screen to print the display.
4. Repeat the same process to print each of the other BIOS Setup program pages, recording all your BIOS settings.

Backing Up Data

Before you begin any major upgrade, particularly those involving hard disks or motherboard replacement, you should back up your data files. It isn't likely that other upgrades will have any negative effect on your files, and your hard disk should be unaffected by a motherboard replacement, but it's still a good idea to back up your files anyway. In fact, you should get in the habit of backing up your files on a regular basis. Then, if something happens to your disk or any of the files on it, you'll have a backup copy.

The method you use to back up your system depends on what backup equipment, if any, your system contains. If your system contains a tape drive or a CD-R (CD-Recordable) drive, perform a full backup, which backs up everything. If you don't have a tape drive or CD-R drive, you have to use floppies, which means you're probably limited to backing up only your document files.

The software you use to back up your files depends on the hardware, so I can't offer guidelines that apply to everyone. But, there is one important point to consider. If you're going to be changing operating systems (Windows 3.x to Windows 95, Windows 95 to Windows NT, and so on), you need to make sure that your backup program will run under the new operating system. Check with the program's publisher to find out if it is compatible as is, or if you can get an updated backup version for the new operating system that will be able to read your old backup sets.

One solution, if you're not going to be backing up your entire system, is to just use WinZIP or another archive utility to compress the files onto disk. These utilities let you create a compressed file that spans multiple disks, so you don't have to worry about running out of space on the disks.

CAUTION You probably think your data is safe from loss. Nothing could go wrong with the upgrade. So you're replacing the motherboard...big deal! You'll just enter the correct BIOS parameters for the hard drive and everything will be fine.

Don't count on it. I've experienced the problem with some systems (though very infrequently) that the system can't read the hard drive, even after entering the appropriate disk settings in the BIOS. Because the data was backed up, I just reformatted the hard disk and continued to march. If you run across this problem and your data isn't backed up, you'll have to reinstall the old motherboard, back up the system, and then perform the upgrade. The moral: Back up first.

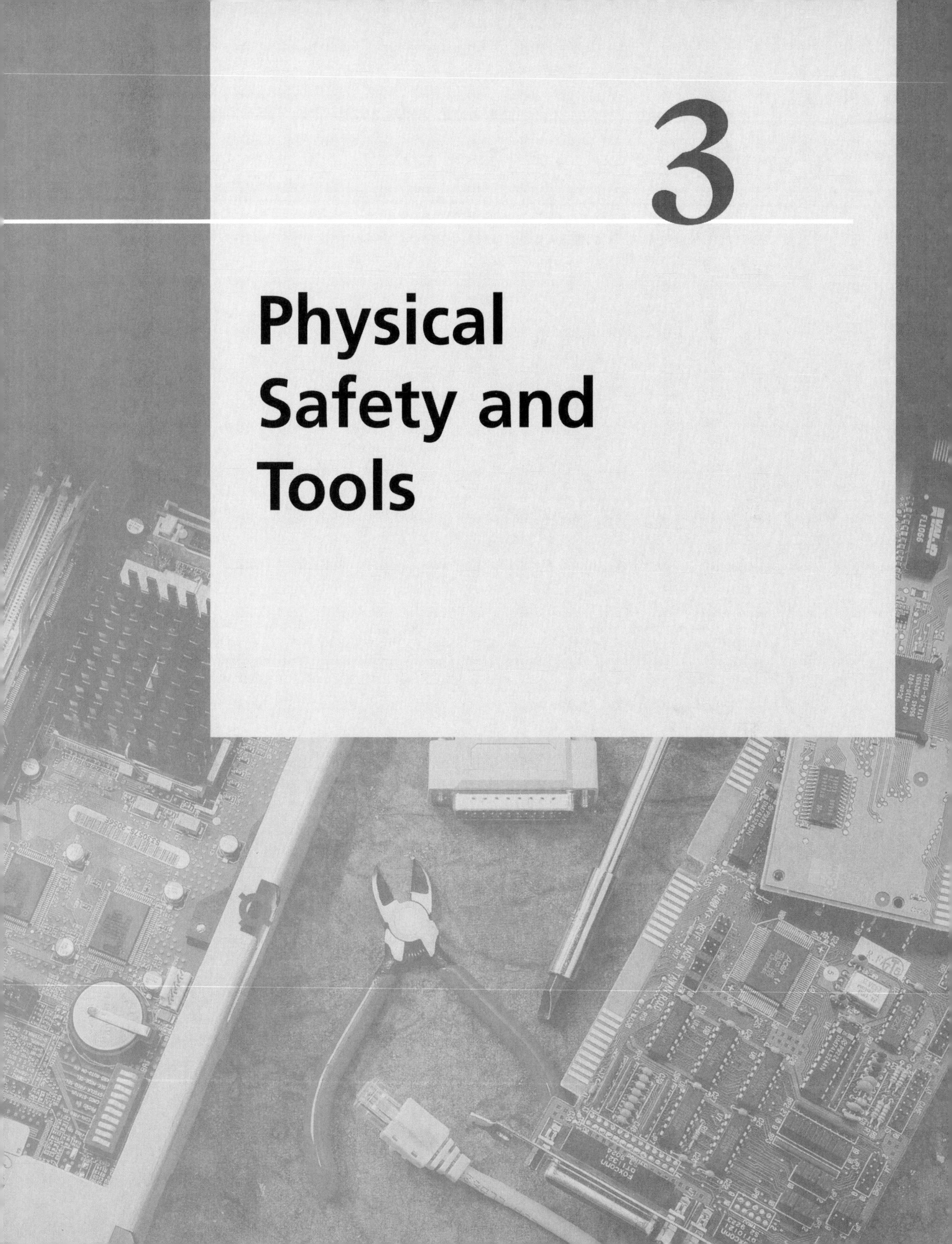

3

Physical Safety and Tools

This is the part of the book where I try to absolve myself of any responsibility for your personal safety. Sure, it's unlikely you'll have any problems or be in any danger working inside your computer, but there are a couple of things you *shouldn't* do if you want to stay safe. I explain these things and other general safety issues in this chapter. You'll also learn what tools you should have on hand to perform upgrades and troubleshooting. The chapter covers these topics:

- General safety—things to do and not do
- Components to leave alone
- How to keep your computer safe from *you*
- What tools are needed for most upgrades

Above all, I want you to be safe when you're working inside your computer. So, let's cover general safety first.

General Safety

Working on any device has its risks. You can get hurt changing the oil on your car if you aren't careful. The same is true with working inside a computer. Sure, you don't have to worry about a jack slipping and the computer falling on you while you're changing the CPU, but there are a few things you should watch out for.

You can get an electrical shock working inside a computer that is plugged in and turned on. Most of the devices in the computer use, at most, 5 to 12 volts at low amperages, so your chances of getting zapped are somewhat remote. But, that doesn't mean it isn't possible to receive a shock, so you should *always* turn off the PC and unplug it before removing the case or doing any work inside it.

There is nothing at all wrong with running the PC for testing and troubleshooting with the cover off. There is no sense putting the cover back on before you're sure everything is working properly. After you're sure the system is working, you can replace the cover. But while the cover is off and the computer is running, keep your hands on the keyboard and the mouse, not on your tools!

> **CAUTION** Unless you have a desire to screw up your computer or have a death wish, never work inside your computer when it is turned on. Never, ever! Even if you don't zap yourself, you could drop a screwdriver on the motherboard and potentially zap something. For your computer's sake, if not your own, stay out of the computer while it's running.

Depending on how your system is set up, you might have a hard time getting to the wall socket where your computer is plugged in. Maybe the plug is behind the desk, for example. You don't have to unplug the computer from the wall socket—just unplug the computer's power cord from the back of the computer. Just don't let the cord fall behind the desk, or you'll be moving furniture after all.

The Power Supply

After you are inside the computer, the only item that poses any significant danger is the *power supply*, which supplies power to the computer and all its internal components. If yours is a desktop case, you'll find the power supply at the right-rear inside the computer inside a shiny metal box (the power cord plugs into the power supply, so you can't miss it). In a tower case, the power supply is located at the top-rear of the tower.

The power supply converts the alternating current (AC) coming from the wall socket into the clean direct current (DC) required by all those gadgets inside the computer case. The major components inside the power supply are some large capacitors that store electricity (there are other components in there, too). The danger to you comes from the fact that those capacitors store their charges even when the system is turned off and unplugged. Figure 3.1 shows the inside of a PC power supply for those of you who are more curious than you should be.

Because those capacitors can still be energized when you open the power supply's housing, there's a strong possibility of getting a nasty shock. Next time you have the PC open, take a look at the power supply. You'll find a note on the power supply that reads something like this:

> Do not remove this power supply cover under any circumstances. There are no serviceable components inside. Serious shock hazards are present inside this power supply case, even with the power switched off.

Sounds pretty serious, doesn't it? The power supply manufacturer doesn't want to be sued because you opened the power supply case and got fried. I don't want to be sued either, so stay out of the power supply!

FIG. 3.1
Inside a PC power supply live a few components that can give you a nasty shock.

TIP Because *Upgrading PCs Illustrated* focuses on upgrades instead of repair, I don't cover power supply replacement, per se. I do, however, cover power supply testing and troubleshooting in Chapter 25, "The Computer Won't Start." If you find that the power supply is bad, replacing it is a simple matter of unscrewing the few screws that hold the power supply to the case, removing the power supply, and installing a new one. If you want a more detailed exploration of the power supply, check out Scott Mueller's book, *Upgrading and Repairing PCs*, from Que.

Yeah, But What About the Fan?

Okay, so there is one part of the power supply that can be replaced. Occasionally, the cooling fan dies, which bodes ill for your computer. Without the fan to keep them cool, the components in the computer can overheat, which can lead to system malfunctions and even damage. In the last 15 years, I've seen two power supply fans die.

Even so, I don't recommend that you try to replace the fan in your computer's power supply if it fails. Pull the power supply and install a new one. There is some slight possibility that whatever caused the fan to fail could have damaged other components in the power supply. Because they don't cost a lot, it's best to just replace the power supply with a new one.

The Monitor

If your monitor goes dead, you might be inclined to open it up to locate the fuse you think must have popped. Well, forget it. Don't even think about it. There's nothing in the monitor that you can service, and, as with a television set or power supply, you can get zapped working inside the monitor. Take it to a reputable service center and have them fix it for you. Or, if it's a 14-inch monitor, consider upgrading to a 15-inch or 17-inch monitor.

Static Electricity and the Computer's Safety

Most of the advice I offer in this chapter is not so much for your safety as it is for the computer's safety. I've already mentioned that it's a bad idea to work inside a running computer. Even if you don't zap yourself, you might drop a screwdriver or other tool on the motherboard and potentially short something out. The result is a new motherboard and the expense that goes with it. In addition, you can't install adapters or other devices while the computer is running. Trying to do so will probably destroy the adapter and possibly the PC.

Many of the microchips inside your PC are susceptible to damage from static electricity. A single discharge can render the chip useless, which in turn can render the PC useless. Because static electricity can and does build up in your body, you need to take a few precautions when handling computer components.

Devices such as motherboards, memory modules, video adapters, and other adapters are shipped in anti-static bags that prevent them from being damaged during packaging and shipping. When you receive a new device, leave it in its anti-static bag until you're ready to install it. There's no need for any undue curiosity—the thing will still be in the bag when you're ready to install it.

In addition, you need to take care when handling adapters, motherboards, hard disks, and other devices that contain microchips. When you open the PC's case, make sure you touch any metal part of the case before touching other components. Touching the case discharges any static in your body. While working inside the computer, you should use an *anti-static wristband.* This gadget fits on your wrist and connects to a ground source (like the metal part of the case) to keep you static-free (see Figure 3.2). These wristbands are described in the following section, also. You can get one from many electronics stores. If you can't find one locally, call JDR Microdevices at 408-494-1400.

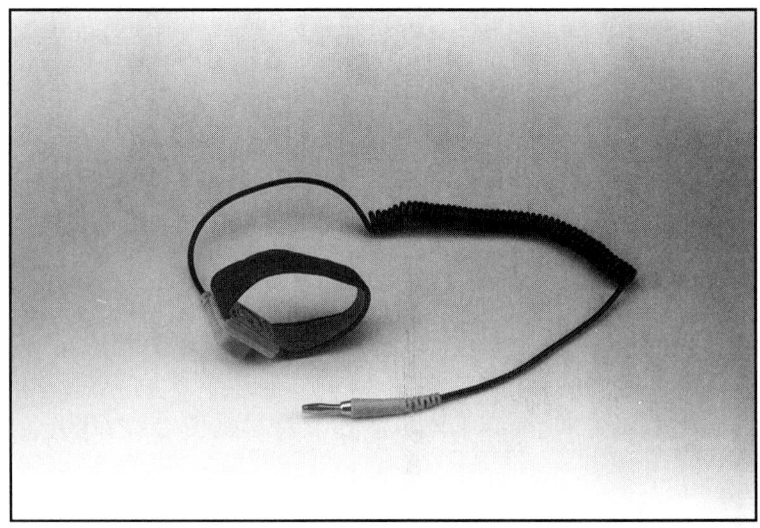

FIG. 3.2
Use an anti-static wristband to help prevent static from building up in your body as you work and possibly damaging components.

You also should avoid touching the edge connectors (see Figure 3.3), components, or backside of a memory module, adapter, motherboard, or other printed circuit card. These connectors conduct electricity, including static charges, that can damage the device. Always handle memory modules by the ends, and, whenever possible, handle a motherboard by its edges, and an adapter card by its edges or mounting bracket. Never touch the components on the boards without first discharging your static.

Many technicians use anti-static mats when working on computer components. These devices are essentially insulating mats with ground wires that you connect to a ground source to dissipate any static that might build up. But, I've also seen many technicians who don't go to this extra trouble. If you're careful about discharging the static from your body before working with components, you shouldn't have any problems.

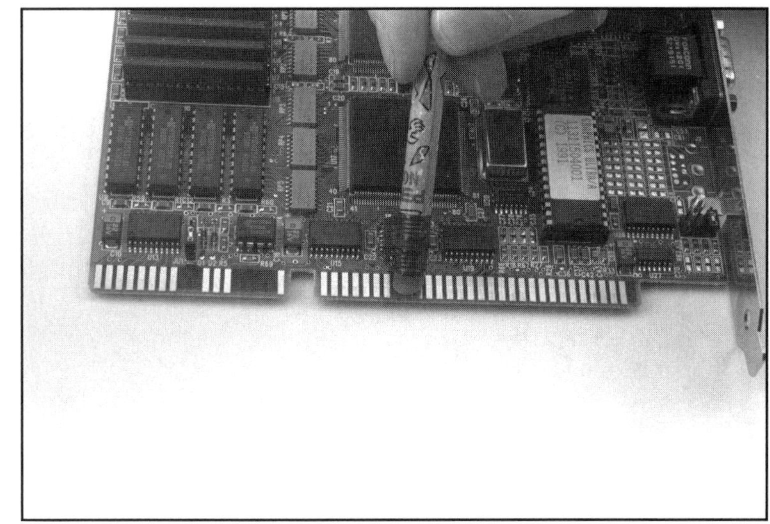

FIG. 3.3
The edge connector on an adapter connects it to the motherboard. Avoid touching them to prevent static discharge to the device.

TIP Do you have carpet in the room where you'll be working on the PC? If so, be extra conscious about discharging the static that definitely builds up in your body. Some people go so far as to take their shoes off to help prevent static buildup. In any case, don't shuffle your feet a lot while you're working in the computer. You'll build up less static that way.

Putting Together a Tool Kit

A small set of tools is all you need to perform nearly any upgrade to your PC. The majority of the time, all you need is a single Phillips head screwdriver. In some cases, a few other tools can come in handy. Table 3.1 lists the items you should consider having on hand or available for your upgrade projects. Figure 3.4 illustrates those tools.

NOTE Each procedure in *Upgrading PCs Illustrated* lists the tools you'll need to accomplish that upgrade or procedure.

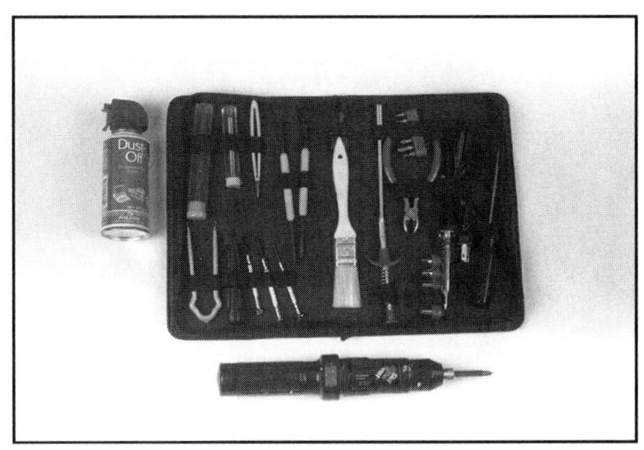

FIG. 3.4
You can accomplish most upgrades with a Phillips screwdriver, but these other tools can come in handy for some jobs

Table 3.1 Your PC Upgrade Toolkit

Tool	Description
Medium Phillips screwdriver	Used for removing the screws that hold the case together, as well as most other screws in the computer.
Small Phillips screwdriver	Good for the screws that hold the adapters in place, as well as screws on the motherboard.
Small flat-bladed screwdriver	Needed to remove and reinstall some of the connectors that attach to the back of the PC. It's also good for removing chips from their sockets.
Cordless screwdriver	A luxury, and great for those case and adapter screws.
Double-ended screwdriver	My favorite tool that has a flat blade on one end and a Phillips on the other. It's great for pointing, poking, and even screwing.
A long Phillips bit	Use in the cordless screwdriver to reach the adapter screws without having to stick the screwdriver in the case.

Tool	Description
A multitester (VOM)	For checking cables and power supply; LCD digital types are more expensive but nicer.
A few paper clips	Use with the multitester when checking cables for continuity.
A nut driver	Use on the case screws instead of a screwdriver.
A stiff-bristled brush	Great for brushing the dust off the power supply, motherboard, and other places it tends to accumulate.
Bent-nosed needlenose pliers	Can be useful for straightening bent pins and grabbing small objects you accidentally drop in hard-to-reach spots.
Can of compressed air	Okay, it's really compressed difluoroethane, but it's like compressed air in a can. Use it to blow the dust and other nasty crud that builds up in your keyboard and on the inside of the PC.

TIP Before you start blowing crud out of your computer, take the thing outside. Otherwise, you'll just be blowing the dust back into your office where it will get sucked back into the computer. If nothing else, take the dirty part down to the local gas station and use the air compressor to blow it out. Chapter 23, "General System Cleaning," has some additional information about cleaning your system.

In reality, one Phillips screwdriver and one small flat-bladed screwdriver are all you need to perform any upgrade. If you have a double-ended screwdriver, you have it all in one tool.

Some of the items listed in Table 3.1 are by no means required. The cordless screwdriver, for example, is simply faster to use than the hand-operated, manual sort, and can speed up the whole process a bit.

The multitester (also called a *voltammeter*) lets you check voltage, continuity (whether the wire in a cable is broken, for example), and amperage. You'll never need it for an upgrade, but it is handy for troubleshooting the power supply, testing cables, and making your own cables. The types of multitesters you find at the average discount retailer or department store cost anywhere from about $10 to $25. So, unless you want to have one on hand for testing batteries, wall sockets, or other electrical things around the house, don't buy one until you really need it.

You can find the can of compressed air at most computer retailers, electronics retailers, and some department stores. You'll find that over time, dust, hair, dead skin cells, and peanut fragments will find their way into your keyboard. Blow that stuff out with the compressed air. It's also good for blowing the dust off of the power supply and other components inside the computer.

TIP Don't shake up the can of compressed gas. Doing so might cause liquid to be ejected from the can, rather than just gas. If you drop the can, let it sit for a few minutes to settle.

Good and Bad Habits

Whenever I work on my old Volkswagen, I always end up with a few left-over washers or screws. I think the engine spontaneously grows new ones to replace the ones I've left out, because it's still running. Here are a few tips to keep you from ending up with spare parts or getting lost in the middle of the operation:

- Keep track of what you remove from the computer, placing small parts in a cup or other container so you won't lose them. In most cases, this only amounts to a few screws, but it's still a good idea.
- Draw diagrams of where things are located, which wires connect to which connector, and so on. Make sure to label your notes with the color code used on the wires.
- Use stick-on labels to identify cables when you disconnect them. Floppy disk labels work great for this.
- If you have an Instamatic camera, take three or four pictures of the inside of your PC before you start an upgrade. In particular, take a shot of where the cables are connected. If you get lost during the upgrade, you can refer to the photos to regain your bearings.

- Don't leave any of the adapter covers off when you replace the cover. The adapter covers are the thin metal things that look like the mounting brackets on the adapters (see Figure 3.5). They cover the holes in the back of the case where an adapter would otherwise be mounted. These covers mount over the holes with a screw, just like the adapters screw into the case. Leaving these covers out reduces the efficiency of the cooling fan and allows a lot of extra dust to get into your system.

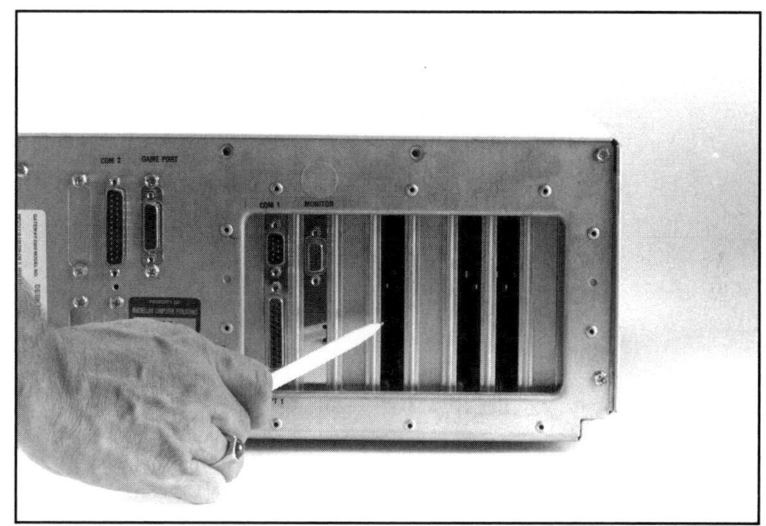

FIG. 3.5
Always cover the adapter holes to keep dust out and allow for proper ventilation and heat dissipation.

- Take notes and mark down any system changes in your system log. Write down in the log the IRQ, address, and other settings you use when installing adapters and similar gadgets. This is one of the best habits you can get into, and you'll thank me for it later. I promise.

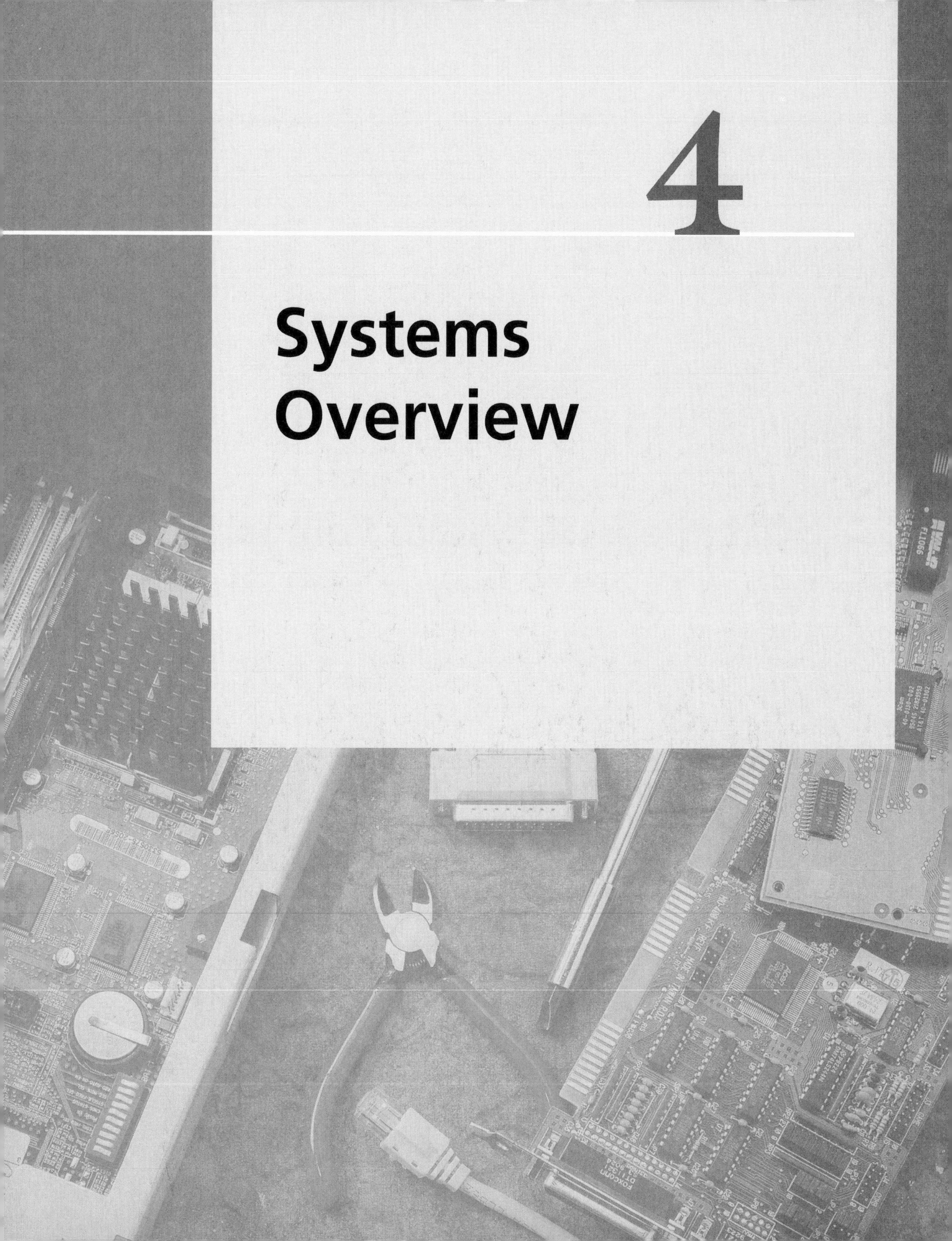

4

Systems Overview

Before you start tearing into your system, you need to have an understanding, at least in general, of what the major components are and how they work together. You also need to understand the *boot process*, which comprises the steps the system goes through to start up and load the operating system (such as DOS, Windows 95, or Windows NT). This chapter gives you an overview of your system and how it works, covering these topics:

- An overview of your system's components
- How the system boots
- The role the operating system plays
- Controlling the boot process
- What the system's startup files do

First, you should understand what the system contains.

Overview of System Components

Your system contains many components that work together to create a working computer. Each of these components is explained in detail in Chapter 5, "Taking Inventory." This chapter provides an overview of the major components to help you understand how the components work together and how the system boots. If after reading the following sections you don't feel you have a very strong grasp of what each component is and does, don't worry. You'll find plenty of background about each component in Chapter 5.

The Motherboard, CPU, and BIOS

Inside your computer's case you'll find the *motherboard*, which is the computer's main circuit board (see Figure 4.1). The motherboard is where the majority of the computer's non-removable components and support circuitry reside. It's a big circuit board measuring roughly 12×13 $^3/_4$ inches (the standard size of an AT-class motherboard), although some motherboards might be slightly different in size.

In a few systems, the motherboard is actually fairly small. In these systems, adapters (such as video cards) don't plug into the motherboard. Instead, a *riser card* plugs into the motherboard and the adapters plug into the riser card. Some manufacturers use this system to enable them to make the case smaller. If your PC uses this type of design, you might not be able to upgrade the motherboard, because an after market motherboard might not fit in the case. Instead, you might have to also buy a new case. Fortunately, cases are not very expensive.

FIG. 4.1
The CPU resides on the motherboard and serves as the brains of the computer.

NOTE An *aftermarket* motherboard is one sold as a replacement motherboard for an existing system. When you buy replacement windshield wiper blades, those are aftermarket blades.

In addition to containing a lot of support circuitry, the motherboard contains the *CPU*, or *Central Processing Unit*. The CPU is the brains of the computer and is where the majority of the computing takes place. It's the mother of all microprocessors in your PC. Your system might contain a 386, 486, 586, or Pentium CPU.

NOTE In the early days of the PC, Intel Corporation was the only manufacturer of CPUs for the PC. Today, other companies also manufacture CPUs, although Intel still makes a majority of the CPUs in use in today's PCs. The numbers 386 and 486 come from the Intel's part numbers for the CPUs, which are 80386 and 80486. Intel originally planned to release a 586 chip, but decided to name it *Pentium* instead so it could copyright the name. Other manufacturers continued with the numbering scheme and name their Pentium-compatible chips the 586 (or something similar). You'll learn more about CPUs in Chapter 8, "Upgrading the CPU and FPU and Cache."

Also on the motherboard are all sorts of other components that support the CPU. One of these components is the *BIOS*, which stands for *Basic Input Output System*. The BIOS is a microchip that stores a small set of programs that enable the PC to perform very basic functions such as accessing the hard disk (see Figure 4.2). The BIOS also contains the code that enables the computer to perform its Power On Self Test (POST), and start up, or *boot*, the operating system.

FIG. 4.2
The BIOS is an important component that enables the PC to perform basic services.

The important concept to understand about the BIOS, at this point, is that it contains program code (called *firmware* because it falls logically between hardware and software) that enables the computer to perform certain functions even without the help of the CPU. It also contains program code that lets the CPU access various other hardware components before any operating system is present.

RAM

RAM stands for *Random Access Memory.* The RAM in your system (see Figure 4.3) serves as short-term memory for the computer, while the hard disk serves as long-term storage. When you're running a program, some or all of the program is loaded into RAM. Also, a document or data file you're working with in the program usually is stored in RAM. When you save the document, the program essentially copies it from RAM to disk.

In addition to your programs and documents, much of the operating system resides in RAM. Some portions of the operating system that aren't required at the moment for the system to operate are stored on disk until they're needed. You learn more about operating systems later in the section "Operating Systems."

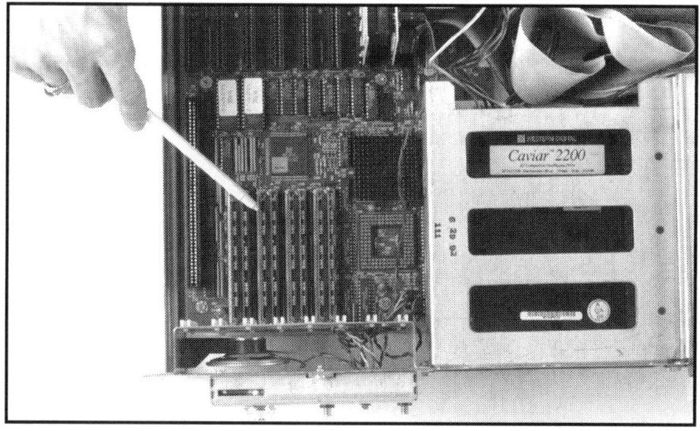

FIG. 4.3
RAM serves as temporary working memory to contain the operating system, programs, and data while the PC is on.

Hard Disk and Floppy Disk Drives

Your system's disks serve as long-term storage. The system contains at least one ***hard disk*** and one ***floppy disk***. The hard disk is located inside the computer's case where you can't see it. Trust me—it's there. Figure 4.4 shows a hard disk mounted inside a PC. The front of the floppy disk drive is accessible in the front of the computer so you can insert floppy disks into it.

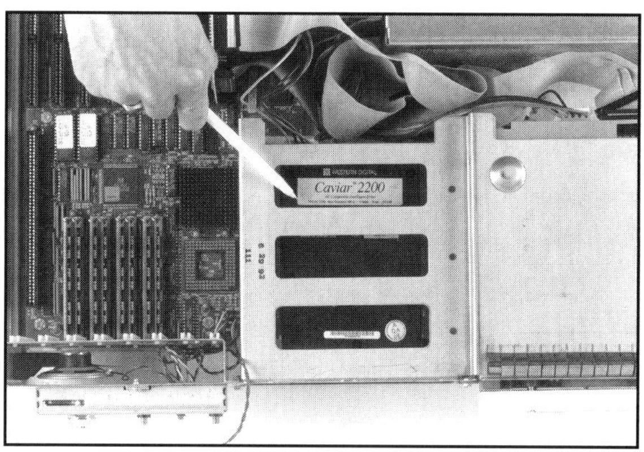

FIG. 4.4
The hard disk mounts inside the computer, usually where you can't see it from the outside.

The hard disk is where the majority of your files reside. The operating system is stored on the hard disk, as is the vast majority of your programs and documents. When you run a program, the operating system reads the program from the hard disk, copying various parts of the program into RAM (enough to run the program). The program then can read more of its program code from the disk as needed. For example, the part of the program that lets you print a document might not be loaded into memory until you actually choose the menu command that starts the printing process. Fortunately, all that stuff happens automatically.

An important point to understand is that when you run a program, the system doesn't move the program from the hard disk to RAM. It just reads it from the disk. It's like reading a book: When you read, you don't lift the words off the paper and stuff them in your head. You just copy them into your brain for temporary use.

NOTE An increasing number of programs are being published on CD instead of (or in addition to) floppy disks. With many of these CD-based programs, you can run the program from the CD. This means that the majority of the program is read from the CD and is never copied to your hard disk. In effect, the CD acts as long-term storage for the program.

In a lot of cases, however, at least a small portion of the program is copied to the hard disk. Usually, this is done to make the program start or run faster. Even with a portion of the program on your hard disk, keeping the majority on the CD is still a great idea. Instead of using hundreds of megabytes of space on the hard disk for the program, the program might only require a few megabytes.

Although you might store some of your documents on floppy disks, you're more likely to use the floppy disk drive only when installing a program or when backing up files. Two common sizes of floppy disks are used: 5 1/4-inch and 3 1/2-inch. The 5 1/4-inch floppies really are floppy—their flexible sleeves let you bend them (but don't do it, because you could ruin the disk and lose its contents). More prevalent today are the 3 1/2-inch disks that use a rigid plastic case to house the disk. The disk itself is still floppy, just like the 5 1/4-inch disks. Disks come in four different formats: 360K and 1.2M for the 5 1/4-inch disks, and 720K and 1.44M for the 3 1/2-inch disks.

Another important use for the floppy disk drive is to enable you to boot the system when the hard disk is unreadable for some reason. Chapter 2, "Building a Software Safety Kit," explains how to create a boot disk.

The important point to understand about the floppy drives is that if the system contains two drives, they are recognized by the system as drive A and drive B. The system is only able to boot from drive A, so you need to use drive A when you make a system disk. In almost every case, drive A is located above drive B in the case.

TIP You might have a system with only one floppy disk drive. If yours contains only a 5 1/4-inch drive, it's probably a fairly old system. If your system has only a 3 1/2-inch drive, or you're going to be replacing the 5 1/4-inch drive with a 3 1/2-inch drive, you might be worried about not being able to read 5 1/4-inch floppies you might have. If so, you can get a combination drive that contains both a 3 1/2-inch drive and 5 1/4-inch drive in one unit. I installed such a drive in one of my systems a few years ago, and as far as I can recall, I've never used the 5 1/4-inch part of the drive.

3 1/2-inch drives are more popular because they have a higher total capacity than 5 1/4-inch drives. Also, the disks are smaller, which means they take up less storage space. Their hard cases also make them less susceptible to damage.

Adapters

Also inside the computer you'll find a few *adapters*. These are circuit cards that plug in to the motherboard's *bus slots*. These adapters mount to the back of the PC's case and typically include connectors that stick out the back of the PC. The computer's video card is an example of an adapter (see Figure 4.5). Network interface cards, hard disk controllers, internal modems, and sound cards all are examples of adapters. Basically, any card that plugs into the motherboard and mounts to the back of the case is an adapter.

FIG. 4.5
Adapters plug into the motherboard's bus slots and mount to the back of the PC's case.

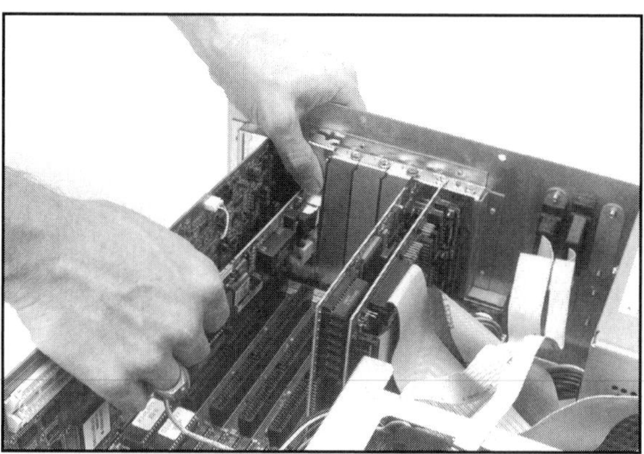

NOTE If yours is a relatively new system, some of the functions that used to be handled by adapters are handled directly on the motherboard. For example, most

continues

continued

recent PC motherboards include the serial and parallel ports, IDE (for hard disks, CD-ROM drives, and tape drives), and mouse connectors right on the motherboard. In these systems, connector brackets are mounted on the back of the case where an adapter would otherwise mount, and connect to the motherboard. This gives you an easily accessible place to plug in various gadgets, such as the mouse. Rather than plug it directly into the motherboard, you plug it into the connector on the back of the PC.

Operating Systems

Without software, hardware is useless. Without software to make it run, hardware is just a collection of electronic components, metal, glass, and so on. You might be able to turn it on, but it won't do anything except hum contentedly.

The program code stored in the system's BIOS gives the system a very small level of functionality. Even so, the code in the BIOS does very little except provide a means for the system to perform some self-diagnostics and access peripherals like hard disks on a very basic level. But in addition, the BIOS also is responsible for getting the operating system booted.

What Is an Operating System?

An *operating system* is a collection of programs and related software that enable a computer to function. By *function*, I mean that the computer recognizes and controls hardware, both at the very low level on the motherboard and at the higher level on peripheral devices such as disk drives, the display, printers, and so on. It also runs programs, takes input, and generates output. These basic functions essentially enable the CPU to interact with all of the components in the computer. The operating system provides this capability typically through device drivers.

What Are Device Drivers?

In generic terms, a *driver* is a program that enables an operating system to communicate with and control a device. Some capabilities for controlling and accessing devices are built into DOS. For example, DOS can read a hard disk without having to load any special drivers in CONFIG.SYS because the program code to read the disk is built into the core operating system that gets loaded through IO.SYS and MSDOS.SYS.

DOS doesn't have the built-in capability to communicate with a CD-ROM drive, and that's a good example of where DOS needs an external driver. If your DOS system contains a CD-ROM drive, you'll find a line in CONFIG.SYS that specifies the driver for the drive. This driver gets loaded and becomes part of the operating system when CONFIG.SYS is read and processed during boot. Other common devices not directly supported by DOS include, among others, sound cards and mice.

Some devices require more than just a driver. A CD-ROM drive, for example, typically requires two drivers. The first enables the system to access the device and communicate with it, and the second (usually MSCDEX.EXE) enables DOS to work with the CD's file system. MSCDEX is loaded by the second configuration file, AUTOEXEC.BAT.

The key concept about drivers is that they enable the operating system to control and use devices for which it doesn't have built-in support. This is true for any operating system.

This portion of the operating system is geared toward the internal workings of the computer rather than to giving you a means to work with the computer. An additional function of most operating systems is to provide a mechanism that lets you, the user, interact with the computer and its components.

The portion of the operating system that lets you interact with the computer is called a *user interface.* In DOS, the user interface is a cryptic command prompt generated by the command interpreter, COMMAND.COM. With Windows 3.x, the *graphical user interface (GUI)* is not actually part of the operating system. Instead, Windows 3.x is a program that provides a graphical interface to your computer and also gives you a consistent means of running other programs.

In Windows 95 and Windows NT, the GUI is an integral part of the operating system. It performs the same function as Windows 3.x in giving you a consistent, easy-to-use interface with which to use your computer.

You don't need a technical understanding of how operating systems do their job. You just need to understand that without an operating system, your computer is a great big doorstop that only a junk dealer could love. With an operating system and slick GUI, your computer is an indispensable tool.

How does the operating system get onto your computer? Either you install it or the manufacturer or vendor installs it. In either case, the operating system resides on the computer's hard disk. When the system is turned on, the operating system boots, as explained in the next section.

The Boot Process

Now that you have a little bit of background about the components in your PC, you're ready to learn how the system *boots*. The term *boot* comes from the word *bootstrap*, which refers to the PC's ability to figuratively pull itself up by its bootstraps and load its own operating system. Understanding the process the system goes through to boot will help you when it comes time to troubleshoot an upgrade. It also helps you understand how and when devices become recognized and accessible by the system.

If you feel like you're reaching information overload when you read the following sections, don't worry; it's enough at this point that you understand the general concepts, if not the specifics. If you're really not interested in any of the technical aspects of the boot process, skip to the section "The Big Picture—Controlling the Boot Process" later in the chapter.

NOTE The boot process involves a lot of steps, many of which would be interesting only to the terminally curious. For example, the first thing that happens in the entire process is the power supply performs a power-on self test, and when the voltages and current levels it is generating are acceptable, it sends a Power Good signal to the motherboard. I've left out these gut-level steps and concentrated in the following sections on the high-level steps in the boot process that you can recognize and/or control yourself.

If you're one of those terminally curious people, check out *Upgrading and Repairing PCs* from Que for a complete description of every step in the boot process.

Low-Level Testing

Initially, the system's ROM code begins executing. This is program code stored in a read-only memory chip on the motherboard. The system tests basic functionality, including scanning memory for video adapter ROM BIOS program code. In other words, the system looks for a video adapter and instructions on how to handle it when it finds it.

The POST

The acronym POST stands for Power On Self Test. The POST is a program routine built into the system's BIOS, which is stored in a chip on the motherboard. The POST, which executes each time you turn on the PC or perform a cold reboot (such as pressing the Reset button), is essentially a mini-program that tests some of the PC's hardware.

For example, the POST tests the PC's RAM to make sure it is working properly. The POST tests the CPU, motherboard support circuitry, and other major components, including the keyboard. If the POST can't find the keyboard, for example, or the keyboard isn't working, the POST displays an error message similar to `Keyboard failure` to let you know there is a problem.

The diagnostic tests that the POST performs are not very thorough, but they can identify major problems. For example, the memory test can locate gross memory failures, but probably won't detect more subtle memory problems. Nevertheless, the POST serves an important function in identifying problems. If an error occurs during the POST, it generates an error message on the monitor. Many errors also generate audible error tones (series of beeps).

Reading the Boot Sector

After the POST completes successfully, code in the BIOS starts looking for a boot sector. A *boot sector* is a sector on a disk that contains a bootstrap program. This *bootstrap program* contains the instructions necessary to locate and load an operating system.

The BIOS code looks first on the disk in drive A for a boot sector. If the floppy disk contains a valid boot sector and bootstrap program, the BIOS loads the bootstrap program and turns over execution to it. If no drive is inserted in drive A, the system looks on the hard disk for the boot sector. If there is a disk in drive A, but it isn't a system disk (and therefore doesn't contain a bootstrap program), the BIOS generates a message informing you that the disk isn't bootable and that you need to replace it with one that is.

NOTE Most recent BIOSes enable you to specify the order in which the BIOS checks for an operating system on drive A and drive C. Most systems default to searching drive A first. However, configuring the BIOS to search drive C first can overcome the potential for infecting your system with a boot virus from a floppy disk.

The Bootstrap Program and Beyond

When the BIOS finds a bootstrap program, the BIOS turns over operation to it. What the bootstrap program does at that point depends on the operating system with which the disk was formatted.

NOTE In the following sections and throughout this book, file names that pertain to DOS systems are all in uppercase, as in CONFIG.SYS. File names for Windows 95 and Windows NT systems are shown with an initial capital letter only because that's the way they appear in Explorer. Also, the terms *directory* and *folder* are used interchangeably.

DOS Systems

The DOS bootstrap program is rather self-centered and doesn't recognize the possibility of other operating systems. It assumes you want to boot DOS, regardless of whether the hard disk might contain other operating systems also. The DOS bootstrap program looks for two hidden system files, IO.SYS and MSDOS.SYS (IBMBIO.COM and IBMDOS.SYS on some systems), that reside on the boot disk. These two files contain the core DOS operating system.

IO.SYS loads first. The code in it then loads MSDOS.SYS, which initializes base device drivers, enabling the system to begin accessing the file system and devices connected to the system.

Next, the system configuration file CONFIG.SYS is processed. The CONFIG.SYS file is a text-only file that contains settings and commands that basically configure the system hardware and the way it runs. For example, most device drivers required by the system, such as a driver to enable the system to read the CD-ROM drive, are specified in CONFIG.SYS. The important point to understand about CONFIG.SYS is that you can change the way the system boots just by editing the file and changing CONFIG.SYS' contents. You learn more about CONFIG.SYS in the section "Startup Files" later in this chapter.

NOTE DOS actually reads CONFIG.SYS multiple times during boot. The `DEVICE`, `INSTALL`, and `SHELL` statements are processed first, then remaining statements are processed. So, the order in which commands other than these three appear in CONFIG.SYS isn't important.

After processing CONFIG.SYS, COMMAND.COM processes the file AUTOEXEC.BAT, which, like CONFIG.SYS, is located in the root directory of the boot disk. While CONFIG.SYS generally controls the system's hardware configuration, AUTOEXEC.BAT more generally controls its software configuration.

AUTOEXEC.BAT can contain settings the system uses to operate. An example is the `PATH` statement, which defines the directory path DOS searches for files that aren't located in the current directory. AUTOEXEC.BAT can also be used to start programs, including loading device drivers. On many systems, the last statement in AUTOEXEC.BAT, `WIN` executes the WIN.COM program that starts Windows 3.x. Whether or not AUTOEXEC.BAT loads Windows, processing AUTOEXEC.BAT is the last step in the boot process for DOS systems.

NOTE If no AUTOEXEC.BAT file exists, COMMAND.COM executes its internal `DATE` and `TIME` commands, then displays a command prompt.

As with CONFIG.SYS, the important point to understand about AUTOEXEC.BAT is that it is a text file whose contents you can edit to control the way the system boots and runs. You learn more about AUTOEXEC.BAT in the section "Understanding Startup Files" later in this chapter.

Windows 95 Systems

On a Windows 95 system, the bootstrap program executes the file Winboot.sys, which is responsible for loading the Windows 95 operating system. Winboot.sys has the capability to display a boot menu at startup. The menu looks like this:

```
1. Normal
2. Logged (\BOOTLOG.TXT)
3. Safe mode
4. Safe mode with network support
5. Step-by-step confirmation
6. Command prompt only
7. Safe mode command prompt only
8. Previous version of MS-DOS
```

NOTE The boot menu only appears automatically if the setting `BootMenu=1` appears in the Msdos.sys file. You can cause the menu to appear by pressing F8 when you see the `Starting Windows 95` message on the display. Option 8, which enables you to boot your previous version of DOS, only appears if the setting `BootMulti=1` is included in the Msdos.sys file. You also can boot DOS by pressing F4 when you see the `Starting Windows 95` message.

How Winboot.sys proceeds depends on whether the boot menu is displayed and what action you select from the boot menu (or whether you press a function key during the boot process to choose a specific boot mode). For a normal boot, Winboot.sys first processes Config.sys, if it exists. If Autoexec.bat exists, Winboot.sys loads Command.com to process Autoexec.bat. Then, Winboot.sys looks for and processes the first part of the Registry, which is contained in the file System.dat.

Because Winboot.sys automatically loads Himem.sys, Ifshlp.sys, and Setver.exe, these commands don't need to be present in Config.sys. In fact, you don't need a Config.sys file at all with Windows 95 unless you need to load drivers that aren't included with Windows 95. You also don't need a Win.ini file, although Windows 95 will create a generic one if one doesn't exist when the system starts.

The last step Winboot.sys performs is to execute Win.com, which loads the graphical portion of Windows 95. If you boot the system to a command prompt and then want to load the GUI, just enter **WIN** at the command prompt.

Windows NT Systems

When you install Windows NT, its Setup program modifies the boot sector of the hard disk to enable it to boot Windows NT. The code in the boot sector runs the NTLDR program, which is stored in the root directory of the boot disk. One of the first things that NTLDR does is read the Boot.ini file, which is located in the root directory of the hard disk. Boot.ini lists, among other things, the operating systems that are present on the computer and their boot locations. NTLDR then displays a boot menu you can use to select which operating system to load.

If your system was formatted with Windows 95 and you then installed Windows NT, for example, you'll see an item in the boot menu for Microsoft Windows; selecting that item boots Windows 95. You'll also see two options for booting Windows NT. The first boots Windows NT with its normal video mode, and the second forces Windows NT to boot using a standard VGA display. This VGA option is useful for reconfiguring your display if the current setting causes a problem.

After you choose one of the Windows NT items from the boot menu, NTLDR runs the program NTDETECT, which also is located in the root directory of the boot disk. NTDETECT checks the system's hardware and places that information in the appropriate keys in the Registry. Then, Windows NT starts loading the device drivers necessary to operate. Finally, it loads the GUI.

The Big Picture—Controlling the Boot Process

Now you have some information about how your system boots. What good is it? Aside from being useful for small talk at really boring parties, you can use the information to control the way your system boots. This is particularly helpful when you're installing new equipment and troubleshooting the system. First, though, you need a little more background about your system's startup files.

TIP The following sections explain the startup and configuration files your system uses. There is a lot of information provided—all certainly useful—but it might be more than you need at the moment. If you're just looking for some quick tips to control how your system boots, skip forward to the sections "Controlling Boot Under DOS," "Controlling Boot Under Windows 95," and "Controlling Boot Under Windows NT."

Understanding Startup Files

Regardless of the operating system your system contains, it uses one or more files to determine how to start the system. The following list describes the files as they relate to specific operating systems:

- *DOS/Windows 3.x.* DOS systems use the files CONFIG.SYS and AUTOEXEC.BAT to control the boot process. Windows uses the files SYSTEM.INI, WIN.INI, and PROGMAN.INI to control its startup.
- *Windows 95.* Windows 95 systems can use the files Config.sys and Autoexec.bat, although these two files are not needed in most cases. Windows 95 uses System.ini and Win.ini files for compatibility with Windows 3.x. Windows 95 also uses the system portion of the Registry, System.dat, to control startup. Finally, items in the Startup folder execute automatically after you log on.
- *Windows NT.* Windows NT systems use the file Boot.ini to control startup options. Like Windows 3.x and Windows 95, Windows NT uses System.ini and Win.ini for compatibility with Windows 3.x. Windows NT also uses the system portion of the Registry to define how it starts. Windows NT 3.x can use the Startup group to automatically start programs. Windows NT 4.0 uses the Startup folder for the same purpose.

CONFIG.SYS—DOS and Windows 95

As mentioned briefly earlier in this chapter, DOS uses a file named CONFIG.SYS to control the system's hardware configuration. CONFIG.SYS is located in the root directory of the boot disk and typically contains statements that load device drivers and perform a handful of other possible tasks. Windows 95 checks for the presence of CONFIG.SYS and processes it if the file exists.

CONFIG.SYS is not required to boot either DOS or Windows 95. Most DOS systems do use a CONFIG.SYS file, however, because almost all DOS systems require device drivers to be loaded through CONFIG.SYS to access hardware and run Windows 3.x. Windows 95 systems need a CONFIG.SYS file only if you need to load a driver not included with Windows 95. An example is a real-mode driver for a sound card not supported directly by Windows 95.

NOTE The CPU can run in different modes, two of which are *real mode* and *protected mode*. Windows 95 runs in protected mode, and so do Windows 95 drivers. If you have a device that doesn't include a Windows 95 driver and isn't supported directly by Windows 95, you can still use the device by loading a real-mode driver through CONFIG.SYS. The only real disadvantage to this is that the CPU has to switch between protected mode and real mode to work with the device, which slows down the system.

CONFIG.SYS is a text file, which means you can view and edit it with any text editor or word processing program such as the DOS EDIT program, Notepad, WordPad, System Editor, and so on. Figure 4.6 shows the System Editor (SYSEDIT.EXE) with CONFIG.SYS displayed.

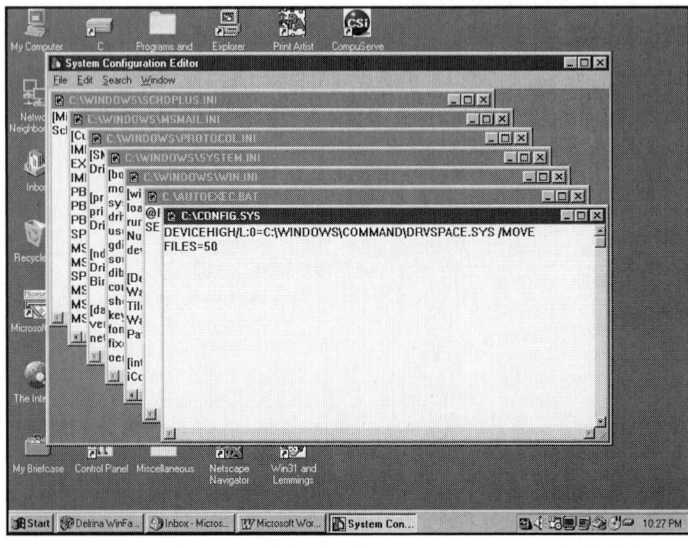

FIG. 4.6
CONFIG.SYS is a text file located in the root directory of the boot disk, and contains settings that primarily configure the system's hardware.

NOTE This chapter doesn't cover DOS configuration commands in detail, because you're probably upgrading to Windows 95 or Windows NT, which doesn't require CONFIG.SYS or AUTOEXEC.BAT statements. Instead, the material is intended to help you understand what your system contains and why, and also to help you troubleshoot problems later. Also, understanding these settings enables you to customize the way your Windows 95 system starts, because Windows 95 can use (but doesn't require) CONFIG.SYS and AUTOEXEC.BAT files.

The following list explains the most common statements (but not all) you'll find in the CONFIG.SYS file:

- `BUFFERS=`*`nnn`*. This statement creates a specified number of disk buffers when the system starts. The disk buffers are used to temporarily hold disk data as it is moving between the disk and CPU, which speeds disk performance. Example: `BUFFERS=10`.
- `DEVICE=` or `DEVICEHIGH=`. These two statements load device drivers. The device driver is specified after the equal sign. An example that would load a mouse driver is `DEVICE=C:\LOGITECH\MOUSE.COM`. The statement can also include optional switches that control how the driver loads and operates. A *switch* is just additional information supplied on the same line, such as `DEVICE=C:\LOGITECH\MOUSE.COM /COM2`. The `DEVICE` statement loads the device driver into memory below 640K, and the `DEVICEHIGH` statement loads the device driver into upper memory, which is between 640K and 1M.
- `DOS=`. This statement specifies that DOS maintain a link to the upper memory area, also known as UMA, (above 640K); load itself into upper memory; or both. For example, typing **DOS=HIGH,UMB** directs DOS to load itself into upper memory and maintain a link to the UMA so it can access drivers that are loaded into the UMA.
- `NUMLOCK=ON¦OFF`. This statement determines the state in which the NumLock key is set when you boot the system. Example: `NUMLOCK=OFF`. Most recent BIOS have an option to set the state of the NumLock key at boot.
- `SHELL=`. This statement specifies the location of the command interpreter, which, in almost all systems running DOS, is COMMAND.COM.
- `FILES=`*`nnn`*. This statement specifies the number of files that can be open at any one time.
- `INSTALL`. This statement installs memory resident programs, which are programs that wait in memory until you need them.

- `LASTDRIVE=`. This statement specifies the maximum number of drives the system recognizes. If CONFIG.SYS doesn't contain this statement, the last available drive letter is one letter higher than the last drive currently available. If you have a hard disk as drive C and a CD-ROM drive as drive D, for example, the last available drive is E.

On Windows 95 systems, Io.sys automatically incorporates a group of settings and commands that are otherwise handled (on a DOS system) by settings in CONFIG.SYS. These include:

- *Himem.sys.* This driver provides extended memory management for the real-mode Windows 95 command-line environment and MS-DOS mode. You can place an entry for Himem.sys in Config.sys to override the default settings provided by Io.sys for Himem.sys.
- *Ifshlp.sys.* This is the Installable File System Helper, which loads device drivers and enables the real-mode environment to perform disk I/O. Only minimal disk I/O services, provided through Io.sys, are available until Ifshlp.sys is loaded.
- *Setver.exe.* Some DOS applications must run under a specific version of DOS. Setver.exe enables you to "fool" applications into thinking they are running on a specific version of DOS by having Setver.exe report a specific DOS version number to the application.
- *Dblspace.bin or Drvspace.bin.* If your system uses DoubleSpace or DriveSpace disk compression (included with MS-DOS 6.*x*), Io.sys loads the appropriate driver.
- `dos=high,umb`. This setting directs the system to load DOS into the UMA and provide memory management of the UMA.
- `files=60`. This setting specifies the number of file handle buffers to be created to handle files opened by standard DOS I/O calls. This setting has no effect on files opened by Windows 95. It's provided primarily for compatibility with older applications.
- `buffers=30`. This setting specifies a number of file buffers created to handle file I/O generated by Io.sys file calls. This setting is not required by Windows 95.

- `stacks=9,256`. This setting specifies the number and size of stack frames. The setting is not required by Windows 95 and is included only for compatibility with older applications.
- `lastdrive=z`. This setting specifies the last drive letter that the system can assign a drive. If Setup finds this setting in Config.sys during installation, Setup moves the setting to the Registry. This setting is provided for compatibility with older applications and isn't required for Windows 95.
- `shell=command.com /p`. This setting specifies the command-line interpreter, the program that provides the Windows 95 command line.
- `fcbs=4`. This setting specifies the file control blocks to be created. The setting is provided for compatibility with older applications and isn't required for Windows 95.

You don't have any way to modify Io.sys to change these default settings, but you can override them by creating a Config.sys file and placing in it corresponding entries with different settings. In the vast majority of cases, though, you shouldn't need to override these settings.

AUTOEXEC.BAT—DOS and Windows 95

Like CONFIG.SYS, AUTOEXEC.BAT is a text file located in the root directory of the boot disk, and is optional. AUTOEXEC.BAT is called a *batch file* because it processes a batch of statements or a batch of programs at one time.

Generally, AUTOEXEC.BAT contains statements that set environment variables and start terminate-and-stay-resident (TSR) programs. The *environment variables* define global settings for the computer, such as the directory path. The *directory path* is the path the operating system searches for files if it can't find them in the current directory. *TSR programs* often are drivers or programs that work in conjunction with drivers.

Because AUTOEXEC.BAT executes automatically at startup, it also can be used to execute other programs automatically at startup. The `CALL` statement lets you initiate another batch file. When that other batch file finishes running, control returns to AUTOEXEC.BAT and it continues processing with the next statement.

One common statement you find at the end of most AUTOEXEC.BAT files on DOS systems that also contain Windows 3.x is the `WIN` statement. This statement actually initiates the program WIN.COM, which loads Windows.

On Windows 95 systems, you don't need an Autoexec.bat file per se, but your system still might contain one. The primary reason to use an Autoexec.bat file under Windows 95 is to specify environment variables and load drivers that aren't included specifically with Windows 95. And, as you can under DOS, you can use Autoexec.bat under Windows 95 to automatically start programs when the system starts. As you learn later in the section "The Startup Group and Startup Folder," there are other methods for automatically starting Windows-based programs when Windows starts.

Systems with DOS and Windows 95

If your system contains both DOS and Windows 95, you actually have two sets of Autoexec.bat and Config.sys files. Windows 95 automatically renames the files according to which operating system you choose. Regardless of which operating system is running, the current, working copies of the files are always named Autoexec.bat and Config.sys.

When Windows 95 is running, the DOS configuration files are renamed to Config.dos and Autoexec.dos. When DOS is running, the Windows 95 configuration files (if any) are named CONFIG.W40 and AUTOEXEC.W40. So, if you boot the system to DOS and want to edit your Windows 95 startup files, make sure you edit CONFIG.W40 and AUTOEXEC.W40. If Windows 95 is running and you want to edit your DOS configuration files, make sure to edit Config.dos and Autoexec.dos.

NOTE You can see from the file names Config.w40 and Autoexec.w40 that Microsoft originally intended to follow the numbering scheme for the Windows 95 revision and call it Windows 4.0. Marketing reasons and a desire to differentiate Windows 95 from Windows 3.x won over logic, however, and the name Windows 95 was born.

SYSTEM.INI—Windows 3.x, Windows 95, and Windows NT

The SYSTEM.INI file is used by all versions of Windows. In Windows 3.x, SYSTEM. INI is one of the primary means through which Windows stores its operating settings. In Windows 95 and Windows NT, the System.ini file is used primarily to provide compatibility with Windows 3.x programs. On these two operating systems, most settings are stored in the Registry instead.

SYSTEM.INI is a text file and is located in the Windows directory. Like CONFIG.SYS, SYSTEM.INI primarily controls hardware settings. The file is divided into sections, each section labeled with a header in brackets and settings for that section immediately following:

```
[386Enh]
device=mxvgrab.386
DEVICE=DVA.386
keyboard=*vkd
mouse=*vmouse
```

In this example, the `[386Enh]` label identifies the section, and the four settings following it all load Windows device drivers. Unlike CONFIG.SYS and AUTOEXEC.BAT, drivers specified in SYSTEM.INI do not load until Windows loads. Also, drivers that have an extension, such as mxvgrab.386, are located on disk in the Windows or Windows System directory (unless the driver callout includes a path). Drivers that are preceded by an asterisk are contained internally within Windows itself.

Generally, you won't need to edit SYSTEM.INI yourself, because settings are added to it automatically by Windows or by an application's Setup program. Occasionally, however, you might need to edit SYSTEM.INI yourself to remove a conflicting driver, add a driver manually, or make other minor changes. You can use the System Editor or any text editor to edit SYSTEM.INI.

> **CAUTION** If you use a word processing program to edit your system's configuration files, make sure you save the files in text-only format. If you save the files using the word processor's native file format (like a DOC file), the system won't be able to read the files.

WIN.INI—Windows 3.x, Windows 95, and Windows NT

All versions of Windows use a WIN.INI file to store various settings, most of which define operating parameters or software settings for Windows. Like SYSTEM.INI, the WIN.INI file is a text file located in the Windows directory. The structure of the WIN.INI file is similar to SYSTEM.INI, with multiple sections labeled by headers in brackets:

```
[windows]
load=C:\WINDOWS\CDIDLL.EXE
run=
NullPort=None
device=HP LaserJet IIIP,HPPCL5MS,\\Fred\laserjet
```

This example includes a variety of settings, including one (the first) that loads a program at startup. As with SYSTEM.INI, Windows modifies WIN.INI automatically. Applications also often use WIN.INI to store their own settings.

You will probably not have to modify WIN.INI yourself very often, but occasionally you might need to make minor changes to it to change the way Windows or other programs run. You can use the System Editor or any text editor to edit WIN.INI.

TIP If one or more programs starts automatically when you start Windows, and you can't find a reference to those programs in the Startup group or folder, check the `load=` and `run=` lines in WIN.INI. These two settings can be used to start programs automatically when Windows starts.

PROGMAN.INI—Windows 3.x and Windows NT 3.x

Program Manager uses the PROGMAN.INI file to store its operating settings. PROGMAN.INI is similar in structure to WIN.INI and SYSTEM.INI, with different sections labeled by headers in brackets:

```
[Groups]
Group1=C:\WINDOWS\MAIN.GRP
Group2=C:\WINDOWS\PROGRAMS.GRP
Group3=C:\WINDOWS\ACCESSOR.GRP
Group4=C:\WINDOWS\STARTUP.GRP

[Settings]
Order= 6 7 9 1 8 10 13 3 14 12 4 2 11 5
Window=65 49 699 537 1
```

The `Group`*n* settings specify the file name of Program Manager's group files (the files in which your program groups are stored). The `[Settings]` section contains settings that define the way Program Manager looks.

Program Manager modifies PROGMAN.INI as necessary to store its settings, but you can modify it manually, also. If you move a program group file, for example, you can simply change the `Group`*n* setting that references it to point to the correct location.

TIP You can include a `[Restrictions]` section in PROGMAN.INI that applies various levels of restrictions to Program Manager. You can use these restrictions to control users' ability to create and delete groups and program items and perform other actions. These restrictions aren't covered in this book because they don't really apply to upgrading PCs. For more information about the `[Restrictions]` section, check out *Maximizing Windows* from New Riders Publishing, or search the Microsoft Knowledge Base on Microsoft's Web site.

Microsoft's Knowledge Base Web site is located at
http://www.microsoft.com/kb

Msdos.sys—Windows 95

Windows 95 uses the Msdos.sys file to store settings that control the way the operating system boots. Msdos.sys is located in the root folder of the boot disk. It is a hidden, system, read-only file. You can, however, change the file's attributes so you can edit it and control the way Windows 95 starts. I explain how in just a bit.

Msdos.sys contains two sections: `[Options]` and `[Paths]`. The `[Paths]` section includes settings that specify paths to various Windows 95 files:

- `WinDir=`*`path`*. This setting specifies the path you specified for installation during setup. It points to your Windows 95 directory.
- `WinBootDir=`*`path`*. This setting, by default, points to the same path you specified during setup to contain Windows 95, and points to the files needed to boot Windows 95.
- `HostWinBootDrv=`*`path`*. This setting specifies the location of the root directory of the boot disk.

The `[Options]` section is the one you're most likely to need or want to modify. It can contain a variety of settings that determine how Windows 95 boots. Here are the settings you can use in the `[Options]` section:

- `BootMenuDelay=`*`n`*. This setting specifies the number of seconds the system pauses to display the message `Starting Windows 95` before it begins to boot the operating system.
- `BootFailSafe=1` or `0`. Using a value of 0 prevents Windows 95 from booting in safe mode. Using a value of 1 doesn't cause Windows 95 to boot in safe

mode, but instead only makes safe mode available during boot. You can press F6 or F8 during boot to select safe mode. Safe mode boots the system with a minimal set of drivers for troubleshooting purposes.

- `BootGUI=1` or `0`. The default value of 1 causes Windows 95 to boot the GUI. Setting this value to 0 causes Windows 95 to boot to a command prompt, after which you can type **WIN** to start the GUI and remaining portions of the Windows 95 operating system. You can duplicate the effect of `BootGUI=0` by creating an empty file named **Win.bat** in the root directory of the boot disk (because Win.bat takes precedence over Win.com).
- `BootKeys=1` or `0`. Setting this value to 1 enables the F4, F5, F6, and F8 keys during boot. Setting this value to 0 disables the boot keys.
- `BootMenu=1` or `0`. A value of 1 causes the boot menu (described earlier in this chapter) to appear at boot time. Or, you can simply press F8 during boot to display the boot menu. A value of 0 causes the system to automatically boot Windows 95 without displaying a boot menu.
- `BootMenuDefault=#`. This setting specifies the menu item that Windows 95 boots by default. The default is 1 when the system boots normally, and 4 when the system boots in safe mode.
- `BootMenuDelay=#`. This setting specifies the number of seconds that Windows 95 displays the boot menu before choosing the default option.
- `BootMulti=1` or `0`. A value of 1 enables you to boot your system's previous version of DOS if it exists on the disk. You also can press F4 during boot to boot the previous version of DOS. A setting of 0 disables the capability to boot the previous version of DOS.
- `BootWarn=1` or `0`. A value of 1 causes Windows 95 to display a warning when it is booting the system in safe mode. A value of 0 disables the warning.
- `BootWin=1` or `0`. The default value, 1, causes the Windows 95 operating system to be booted. A value of 0 causes your previous version of DOS to boot, even if you select the Normal option from the boot menu. If you set `BootWin=0` and `BootMenu=1`, also set `Logo=0` to avoid showing the Windows 95 boot logo, which prevents you from seeing the DOS prompt.
- `DblSpace=1` or `0`. This setting controls whether or not Windows 95 loads Dblspace.bin, which is required for compressed volumes created using DoubleSpace. A value of 0 disables loading of Dblspace.bin.

- `DoubleBuffer=1` or `0`. Specify a value of 1 to have Windows 95 use double-buffering for any SCSI host adapters in the system. *Double-buffering* is required by many SCSI adapters to ensure error-free I/O. Setup adds this setting automatically if it determines that the SCSI adapter requires it.
- `DrvSpace=1` or `0`. A value of 1 (the default) enables Windows 95 to load the Drvspace.bin driver for DriveSpace compressed volumes. A value of 0 prevents the driver from being loaded.
- `LoadTop=1` or `0`. A setting of 1 causes Windows 95 to load Command.com and/or Drvspace.bin in the UMA. A value of 0 causes them to be loaded below 640K.
- `Logo=1` or `0`. A value of 1 (the default) causes Windows 95 to display a logo while the system is booting. Set this value to 0 if you don't want to see the logo.
- `Network=1` or `0`. A value of 1 (the default) enables Windows 95 to load real-mode network drivers for safe mode. A value of 0 prevents these network drivers from being loaded.

Some of these settings are not very useful for the average person, but some can be very useful. In particular, all of the settings that begin with `Boot` offer an easy way for you to control the way your system boots in normal operation as well as when troubleshooting the system.

Before you start fiddling with Msdos.sys, you should make a backup copy on disk. If you screw up the file so badly that you can't get it back to normal, you can restore the backup copy.

To edit Msdos.sys, you first need to change its attributes. If you're working from the command prompt, use this command:

```
C:\>ATTRIB -S -H -R MSDOS.SYS
```

If you're working from within Windows 95, double-click My Computer, then double-click the boot disk's icon (probably drive C). If you don't see Msdos.sys in the folder, choose View, Options. Click the View tab, then choose the Show All Files option button and click OK. This lets you view the hidden files on the disk, of which Msdos.sys is one.

To change the attributes of Msdos.sys within Windows 95, right-click the file's icon and choose Properties. In the Attributes area of the property sheet, clear the Read-Only and Hidden check boxes.

Next, open Notepad or WordPad and load the Msdos.sys file into it. Make the changes you want, then save the file and close the text editor. Restore the read-only and hidden file attributes and restart the system to test your changes.

Boot.ini—Windows NT

Windows NT uses the Boot.ini file to control the Windows NT boot process. Boot.ini is a read-only, hidden system file in the root directory of the boot disk. Like many other Windows-related configuration files, Boot.ini includes sections labeled by headers in brackets, with settings for that section following underneath. Here's an example of a Boot.ini file:

```
[Boot Loader]
Timeout=15
Default=C:\
[Operating Systems]
C:\="Microsoft Windows 95"
multi(0)disk(0)rdisk(0)partition(1)\WINNT="Windows NT Workstation Version
➥ 4.00"
multi(0)disk(0)rdisk(0)partition(1)\WINNT="Windows NT Workstation Version
➥4.00 [VGA mode]" /basevideo /sos
multi(0)disk(0)rdisk(0)partition(1)\WINNT351="Windows NT Server Version
➥3.51"
multi(0)disk(0)rdisk(0)partition(1)\WINNT351="Windows NT Server Version
➥3.51 [VGA mode]" /basevideo /sos
```

In this sample, the system actually contains four operating systems, although only three are apparent from the Boot.ini file: Windows NT Workstation version 4.00, Windows NT Server version 3.51, and Windows 95. This particular system also contains MS-DOS, which can be booted by selecting the Microsoft Windows 95 option from the NTLDR boot menu, then choosing Option 8 from the Windows 95 boot menu.

The `[Boot Loader]` section contains two settings that help define the boot process:

- `Timeout=`*`n`*. This setting specifies the amount of time the boot menu is displayed before the system boots based on the default menu selection.

- `Default=aaa`. This setting specifies the default boot option. In this sample, the system automatically boots Windows 95 if no action is taken to choose a different option. If Windows NT Workstation 4.00 were the default, the setting would read

  ```
  multi(0)disk(0)rdisk(0)partition(1)\WINNT
  ```

The `[Operating Systems]` section defines the operating systems that are available from the boot menu. Note that each of the Windows NT installations includes an option to boot the system in VGA mode. The switches at the end of each VGA mode entry in the file, `/basevideo/sos`, cause Windows NT to boot in VGA mode, which enables you to boot the system when a problem occurs with the currently installed video driver.

You can edit Boot.ini manually, but it's easier to edit it from within Windows NT. To do so, open the Control Panel and double-click the System icon. On Windows NT 4.0 systems, click the Startup/Shutdown tab. Use the System Startup group of controls to specify the default operating system and boot delay (which correspond to the Default and Timeout settings, respectively). Figure 4.7 shows the System property sheet.

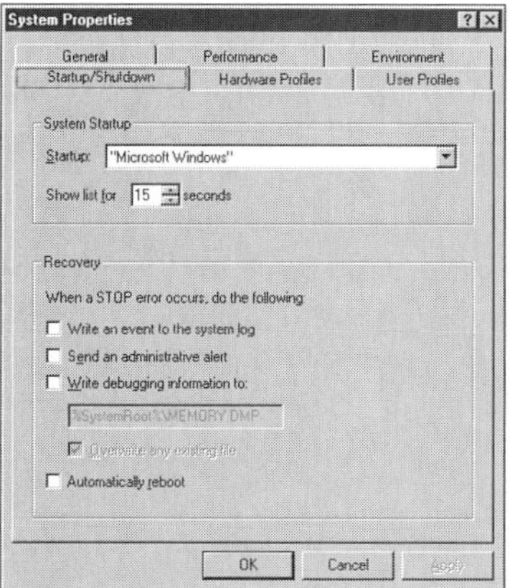

FIG. 4.7
You can control system startup in Windows NT 4.0 through the Startup/Shutdown tab of the System property sheet.

On Windows NT 3.5x systems, use the two controls in the Operating Systems group in the System dialog box (see Figure 4.8) to control the default operating system and the boot delay.

FIG. 4.8
On Windows NT 3.5x systems, use the System dialog box to control the boot process.

The Registry—Windows 95 and Windows NT

Windows NT and Windows 95 both use a *Registry* to store settings and other information that defines the way the system boots and runs. Microsoft likes to tout the Registry as a replacement for all those INI files and other configuration files required under Windows 3.x. Don't believe a word of it. Even on a system that has never contained anything other than Windows NT or Windows 95, you find plenty of INI files, many created by the operating system itself.

On Windows NT systems, the Registry comprises the six files located in the *Ntroot*\System32\Config directory. You don't deal with the files individually, so their names are not important here.

On Windows 95 systems, the Registry comprises two files: System.dat and User.dat. The System.dat file incorporates global and system-specific settings, and User.dat incorporates user-related settings such as for desktop configuration.

It isn't terribly important that you understand where the Registry is stored. What's more important is that you understand how to modify settings in the Registry. You can make most changes through the Control Panel. When you change the wallpaper pattern through the Desktop icon in Control Panel, for example, you indirectly change a setting in the Registry. Whenever possible, you should modify the Registry only indirectly by using the Control Panel.

If you do need to edit the Registry, you can do so with the Registry Editor, which is included with Windows NT and Windows 95. Figure 4.9 shows the Windows 95

Registry Editor. To start the Registry Editor in Windows 95 and Windows NT 4.0, choose Start, Run, and enter **REGEDIT** in the Run dialog box. Under Windows NT 3.5x, choose File, Run in Program Manager and enter **REGEDT32** in the Run dialog box.

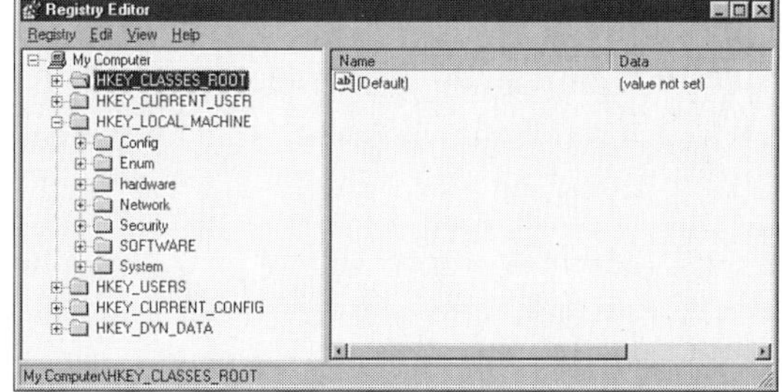

FIG. 4.9
You can modify the Registry directly using the Registry Editor.

I won't go into a lot of detail on the Registry or Registry Editor because you seldom need to use it. It's covered simply to let you know what the Registry is and how you can edit the Registry if you're instructed to do so by an installation manual.

The Startup Group and Startup Folder

Under Windows 3.x and Windows NT 3.x, the *Startup group* enables you to start programs automatically as soon as Windows starts. The Startup group is no different from any other program group. Windows and Windows NT simply look for a group by that name and execute any programs in it during startup.

Windows 95 and Windows NT 4.0 systems use something very similar—a *Startup folder*. The Startup folder is like every other folder (directory) on your system, except that it is named Startup. These operating systems look for the Startup folder in the \Windows\Start Menu\Programs folder by default.

In short, you can place any executable object (program, shortcut, and so on) in the Startup group or folder and it executes automatically as soon as Windows starts. Here's the important part: To bypass the Startup folder or group, hold down the Shift key while Windows is starting, and keep holding it down until you see the desktop appear. Why would you want to bypass Startup? An application in the group or folder might be causing problems and locking up your system. After bypassing Startup, you can open the group/folder and remove the offending item.

TIP In all versions of Windows, Windows 95, and Windows NT, the `run=` and `load=` lines in WIN.INI also can start programs automatically at startup. If your Startup group/folder is empty, but programs are still starting anyway, have a peek at WIN.INI.

Editing Startup Files

Except for the Registry, you can edit all of the configuration files with a text editor. In the case of some, like Msdos.sys and Boot.ini, you must first change the attributes of the file so it isn't read-only or hidden.

For DOS systems, the `EDIT` command works great for editing files. EDIT.COM is located in your DOS directory, and also requires the file QBASIC.EXE be on your system in the DOS directory. At a command prompt, just type **EDIT *filename***, where *filename* is the name of the configuration file you want to edit. An example is **EDIT C:\CONFIG.SYS**.

In all versions of Windows, Windows 95, and Windows NT, you can use Notepad to edit configuration files. Or, use the System Editor, a special text editor designed specifically for editing the system configuration files (previously shown in Figure 4.6).

System Editor (SysEdit) displays each of the configuration files in a separate window, which makes it easy to edit multiple files at one time. To start System Editor under Program Manager, choose File, Run, and enter **SYSEDIT** in the Run dialog box. To start System Editor under Explorer, choose Start, Run, and enter **SYSEDIT** in the Run dialog box.

Controlling Boot Under DOS

The previous sections that discussed CONFIG.SYS and AUTOEXEC.BAT explained that you can control, to some degree, the boot process on DOS systems by modifying these two files. You also can control the boot process with some function keys.

When the message `Starting MS-DOS` appears on the display, you can use these function keys to control how the system boots:

- *F5.* Pressing F5 when the `Starting MS-DOS` message appears causes DOS to bypass the CONFIG.SYS and AUTOEXEC.BAT files altogether.

- *F8.* Pressing F8 when the `Starting MS-DOS` message appears causes DOS to single-step through the CONFIG.SYS and AUTOEXEC.BAT files, letting you verify whether you want to execute each line. This lets you bypass only certain lines in the files.

MS-DOS 6.x also lets you create a multi-configuration setup in CONFIG.SYS, which effectively lets you create different configurations and select a configuration at boot time. This can be particularly useful if you want to use a certain device only part of the time. When you don't want to use it, you can boot the system and choose a configuration that doesn't include the driver for the device. This leaves the system with more memory, because the memory isn't taken up by the driver.

Another common use for a multi-configuration setup is to run DOS games that conflict with Windows. You can create a configuration just for that game, and boot the system to an appropriate DOS environment to run it. When you're finished with the game, you can reboot the system with the configuration you use to run Windows.

Creating a multiple configuration CONFIG.SYS file isn't difficult, but it does take a little explanation. Rather than cover it here, I'll point you to your DOS manual for an explanation of how to do it.

Controlling Boot Under Windows 95

Like DOS, Windows 95 supports the use of function keys during boot to control boot options. Before the `Starting Windows 95` message disappears from the display, you can press one of the following function keys to control the boot process:

- *F4.* This function key causes the system to boot your previous version of DOS if one exists on the system. It is equivalent to choosing Option 8 from the boot menu.
- *F5.* This function key causes Windows 95 to start in safe mode.
- *F6.* This function key causes Windows 95 to boot in safe mode with network support, if possible.
- *F8.* This function key causes Windows 95 to display a boot menu, and is equivalent to adding the setting `BootMenu=1` to the Msdos.sys file.

TIP You can press any of these function keys at any time after the PC finishes the POST—you don't have to wait until you see `Starting Windows 95`.

You read earlier in this chapter about the Windows 95 boot menu. When you press F8 (or add the setting **BootMenu=1** to the Msdos.sys file), you'll see the following boot menu appear when Windows 95 starts to boot:

- *Normal.* This option starts the full Windows operating system and GUI.
- *Logged (\BOOTLOG.TXT).* This option boots the full Windows 95 operating system and GUI, and also creates a boot log called Bootlog.txt in the root directory of the boot disk. The log is useful for troubleshooting startup problems.
- *Safe Mode.* This option excludes the majority of drivers and boots a minimal Windows 95 operating system. Only the drivers needed for basic services such as disk access are loaded. This mode uses a standard VGA display driver, which can help overcome startup problems caused by an incompatible or improperly configured display driver. Use safe mode when you suspect that a driver is causing a startup problem.
- *Safe Mode with Network Support.* This option starts Windows 95 in safe mode but loads the network drivers (which are not loaded with plain safe mode).
- *Step-by-Step Confirmation.* This option is similar to the single-step boot option MS-DOS offers, and single-steps through the Config.sys and Autoexec.bat files.
- *Command Prompt Only.* This option boots the Windows 95 command line, but does not boot the GUI or full set of drivers. If the system uses a 32-bit Windows 95 CD-ROM driver to access your CD-ROM drive, for example, you cannot use the CD-ROM drive from the command prompt. This is because the driver doesn't load until the full operating system and GUI load. Booting to the command line enables you to boot a minimal operating system quickly to perform file maintenance and troubleshooting. Essentially, you're booting to DOS when you boot to a command prompt, and you can run DOS programs and commands.
- *Safe Mode Command Prompt Only.* This option boots a minimal operating system similar to the Safe mode option, except the system boots to a command prompt rather than to a GUI. Only critical drivers load, and a standard VGA driver is used to overcome potential display problems.

TIP If your system still contains a copy of DOS, and the setting `BootMulti=1` is present in the Msdos.sys file, the boot menu will contain an Option 8 that enables you to boot the system to the previous version of DOS.

Controlling Boot Under Windows NT

As explained earlier in the section "Boot.ini—Windows NT," the settings in the Boot.ini file control the way Windows NT boots. Boot.ini defines the operating systems installed on the computer, which operating system boots by default, and the amount of time the boot menu is displayed before Windows NT boots using the default option. As explained earlier, you should use the System icon in the Control Panel to control the way Windows NT boots.

5

Taking Inventory

You've probably read the previous chapters and you're chomping at the bit to get busy. Before you whip out the screwdriver and dig into the system, however, you need to take inventory so you know what is in your system. This helps you decide what you can upgrade and how you can do it. Plus, taking inventory helps you learn about your computer. With that in mind, this is what you experience through this chapter:

- Open and take a tour through your PC
- Learn about the motherboard, its sockets, and connectors
- Learn about the PC's memory and disk drives
- Learn about adapters and which ones you have in your PC
- Reassemble the PC
- Learn about external devices connected to the PC
- Plan your next upgrade

Whether you're installing, upgrading, or just rummaging around in the PC to take inventory, you need to know how to open the PC's case. So, that first step is explained in the following section.

Opening and Touring Your System

Some upgrades, like attaching a new external modem, don't require that you open the PC. Most upgrades, however, do require that you open the case. It isn't difficult to do, though.

What Type of Case Do You Have?

PC cases come in three general configurations: desktop, tower, and mini-tower. Figure 5.1 shows a desktop case. A desktop case generally sits horizontally on your desk with the monitor on top of it.

Desktop cases come in two general sizes: compact and standard. The compact cases are shorter and often smaller in width and depth than a standard case. Figure 5.2 shows a compact case and a standard desktop case.

FIG. 5.1
A desktop case typically sits on a desk with the monitor resting on top of the computer.

FIG. 5.2
Some manufacturers design their own compact cases to conserve desktop space.

These compact cases use a proprietary motherboard design that includes a riser card. The *riser card* installs in a slot in the motherboard, and then the adapters (video, modem, and so on) install horizontally in the riser card. These types of systems have two major disadvantages at upgrade time:

- You have to buy a replacement board directly from the manufacturer.
- You can't add as many adapters to the system as you can a standard case.

Figure 5.3 shows a compact case with the riser card installed, and Figure 5.4 shows a close-up of the riser card.

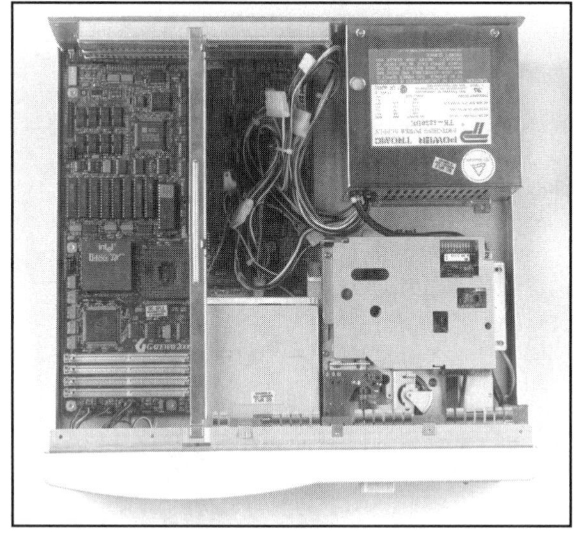

FIG. 5.3
Compact desktop systems use a riser card to connect the system's adapters to the motherboard, which limits your upgrade options.

FIG. 5.4
Video, modem, and other adapters install in the riser card.

If you find that your system uses a riser card and you're interested in replacing the motherboard, you can contact the manufacturer to find out whether an upgrade motherboard is available that fits your system. You'll probably find, though, that it makes more sense to buy a new standard size case and motherboard (or an ATX motherboard and case). A new case gives you more expansion slots and probably more drive bays (where the disk drives and similar peripherals install). You might spend an extra $100 or so on the case (perhaps less), but that additional expense should be offset by the lower cost of a standard motherboard.

NOTE You can find more information about the ATX case and motherboard in Chapter 9, "Replacing the Motherboard."

If you have a desktop case and want to move it from the desk to the floor for more room, you can. You can get a special case floor stand from most computer retailers to rest the desktop case on its side on the floor (see Figure 5.5).

FIG. 5.5
You can use a special stand to mount a desktop vertically on the floor.

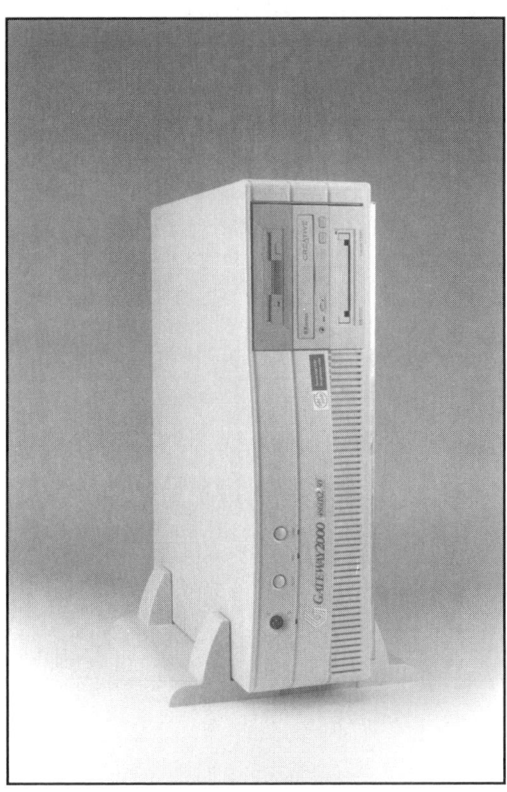

NOTE If you decide to move your case from horizontal to vertical (or vice versa), keep in mind that you might have to reformat the hard disk to do so. The hard disk can have problems reading and writing to the disk if it is used in a position that is different from the one in which it was formatted.

If you decide to mount your desktop case upright on the floor or use a tower case resting on the floor, you might need to get some cable extenders (see Figure 5.6), because the computer is farther away from the monitor, keyboard, mouse, and other external peripherals. You should be able to find these extension cables at any computer retailer or mail-order house.

A tower case is designed to sit on the floor or upright on the desk beside the monitor. A mini-tower case is just shorter than a tower case and usually sits upright on the desk beside the monitor, although you certainly can stand a mini-tower on the floor. Figure 5.7 shows a mini-tower case.

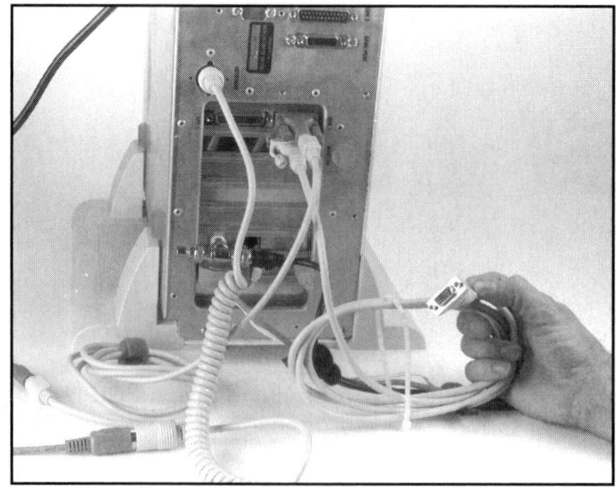

FIG. 5.6
You can get cable extenders for the keyboard, monitor, mouse, and joystick.

FIG. 5.7
A mini-tower case sits vertically on the desk or on the floor.

Of these three types of cases, the tower offers the most room for additional drives because it has the most bays. A *bay* is a slot in which a device like a hard disk, floppy disk, CD-ROM/CD-R, or tape drive installs (see Figure 5.8). Desktop cases typically have five bays, mini-tower cases have seven bays, and tower cases have 10 bays (the actual number sometimes varies).

FIG. 5.8
A bay is a slot in which a device such as a hard disk, CD-ROM, or tape drive installs.

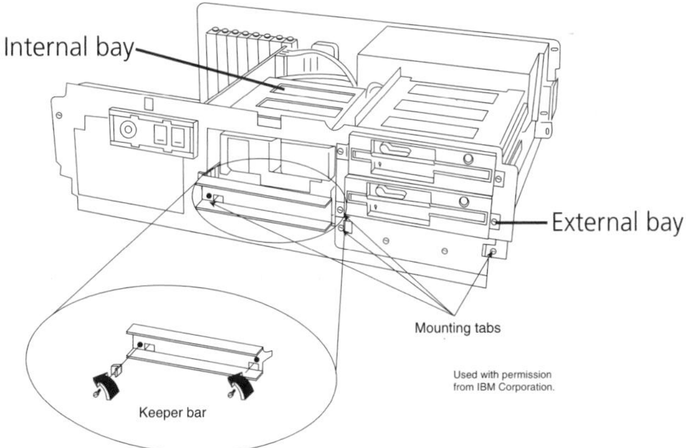

Some of the bays in your PC are external bays and others are internal bays. *External bays* open to the outside of the case. Floppy disk drives, CD-ROM drives, CD-R drives, optical drives, removable hard drives, and tape drives all mount in external bays because you need to be able to access the front of the drive to insert the media (disk, tape, CD, and so on).

Internal bays don't open to the outside of the case but instead are tucked inside the case. Hard drives mount in internal bays because you don't need to be able to see or touch the hard disk in order to use it. Many tower cases have internal bays at the very top of the case above the power supply (see Figure 5.9), as well as below the floppy and CD-ROM drive bays.

FIG. 5.9
Tower cases have drive bays tucked in just about every nook and cranny. Here's one over the power supply.

NOTE Early systems such as the IBM XT and AT often mounted the hard drives in external bays. These drives had face plates with drive activity lights that covered the drive. Being able to see the activity light was about the only reason the drives needed to be mounted in an external bay. Today, the cases have a drive activity light that connects to either the motherboard or to the hard disk adapter.

If you find that you don't have any more drive bays available for an upgrade, after you tour your PC in this chapter you might consider buying a new, larger case. Or, you might be able to remove a device or put it in its own external case. Check out the section "Planning the Upgrade" later in this chapter for more information about these options.

Pick the Position that Works For You

Unless you're ready to reformat the hard disk, you shouldn't just yank your desktop case off your desk and stand it on its side on the floor even if you have the floor stand. The way the hard disk's heads fly over the surface of the disk makes them susceptible to misalignment if the drive is formatted horizontally and then placed on its side. If you're willing to reformat the hard disk, it's not a problem.

Most CD-ROM drives are designed to work in either the horizontal or vertical position. If your CD-ROM drive requires the use of a CD cartridge, you're in good shape in either position. Most CD-ROM drives that use trays in which you place the CD also work in either position. These drives use small tabs or spring-loaded gadgets to hold the CD in place.

Personally, I prefer tower and mini-tower cases on the floor over desktop cases because I have lots of other junk taking up space on the desktop. The extra drive bays also give me more room to expand in the future. Plus, moving the computer to the floor lets me get it and its gene-altering electromagnetic radiation a little farther away from my body. Maybe it will never cause any genetic mutation, but I need all the help I can get.

Most motherboards, particularly aftermarket ones (those you buy as replacements), are a standard size and have mounting holes in the same locations so they will fit a standard case. Desktop, mini-tower, and tower cases all have the same motherboard mounting configuration, so a replacement motherboard should fit in any one of these cases. This standard motherboard configuration is called an *AT-style motherboard* because they follow the same general layout as the IBM AT. Figure 5.10 shows the general configuration of a standard AT-style case and motherboard.

FIG. 5.10
Standard AT-style cases and motherboards are currently the most common type, although a new version called ATX also is available.

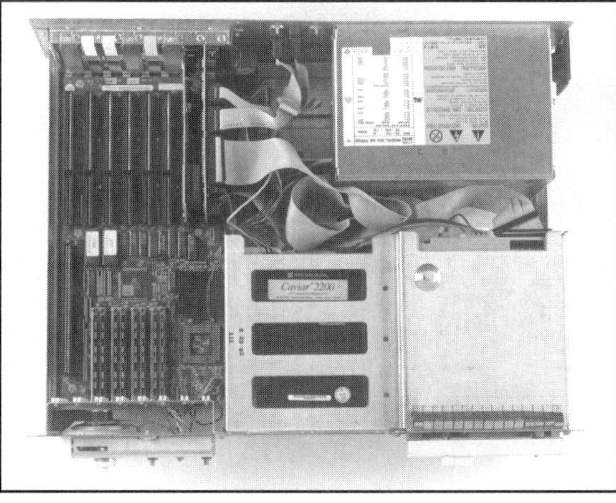

NOTE Chapter 9, "Replacing the Motherboard," covers motherboard shapes and types in detail. Before you buy a new motherboard or case, make sure you read the following section, as well as Chapter 9.

ATX Cases—The Latest Thing

The newest type of case is called the *ATX case*. The ATX case uses a different internal configuration than the standard AT-style case, with the power supply mounted in a different location. The motherboard for an ATX case is different in configuration from an AT-style motherboard. The ATX motherboard is turned 90 degrees from the orientation of an AT-style motherboard. This puts the long edge of the motherboard along the back of the case and the adapter bus slots perpendicular to the long side rather than the short side. Figure 5.11 shows an ATX-style motherboard and case.

FIG. 5.11
The ATX form factor is different from the AT form factor, but your adapters will still work with the new style.

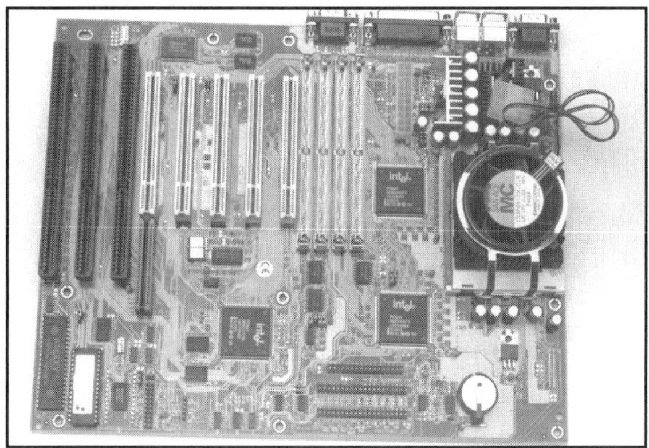

Why switch from a tried-and-true design to the new ATX design? Intel, the primary manufacturer of CPUs for PCs, designed the ATX specification and proposes that system manufacturers use the ATX layout for their systems. The ATX design moves the CPU away from the bus slots and adapters for better cooling. It also eliminates the problem of full-length adapters interfering with the CPU or CPU fan.

NOTE Chapter 9, "Replacing the Motherboard," covers the ATX design in more detail. Before you buy a motherboard, read Chapter 9 to be sure you're getting the right type of board and case.

Opening the PC's Case

Generally, opening the PC's case requires only that you remove a few screws from the back of the case and then slide off the cover. Some of the newer cases don't use screws at all. Instead, these cases have a pop-up front panel—just pull the thing off. After you pull off the front panel, you simply slide the case cover forward an inch or so, then lift it off. The following procedure covers both types of cases.

To Open the PC's Case, You Need:

- ☑ Phillips screwdriver or nut driver for case screws
- ☑ Small flat-bladed screwdriver for cable connections
- ☑ Computer is turned off!

---

1. Verify that the computer is turned off.
2. Unplug the computer from the wall socket, or unplug the PC's power cord from the back of the computer.
3. Disconnect the monitor cable from the back of the PC. This cable runs from the monitor to the video card at the back of the PC. You'll probably have to use the small flat screwdriver.
4. Unplug the monitor and place it out of the way, preferably on the floor so you don't knock it off the desk while working on the PC.
5. Look at the back of the PC. If it has screws in the four corners, unscrew these screws. Desktop cases usually have a screw at each corner and one in the middle on top (see Figure 5.12). Tower and mini-tower cases have two or three screws on each side of the back of the case. Put the screws in a cup, your pocket, or some other place where you won't lose them.

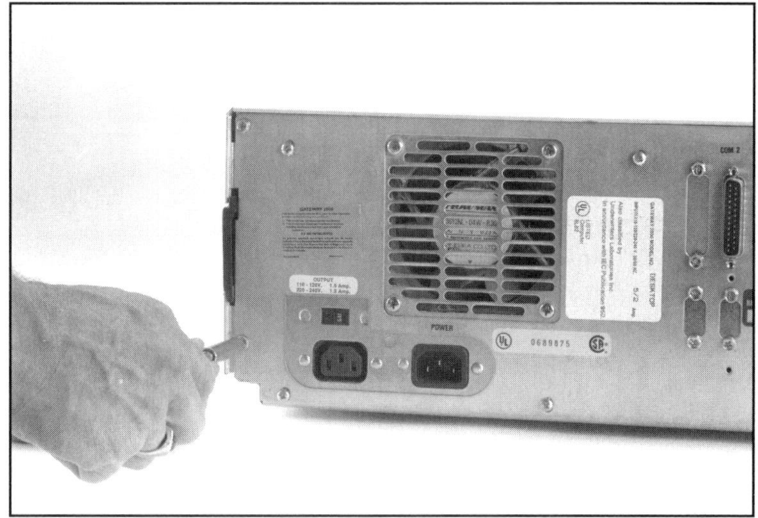

FIG. 5.12
Unless the front panel pops off, your case should have five or six screws holding on the cover.

NOTE If there are only four screws near each other in the back of the case, your PC uses a pop-off front panel and the cover just slides off. The four screws you see in the back hold the power supply to the case (see Figure 5.13). Don't unscrew them. See step 6 for how to proceed.

FIG. 5.13
The power supply attaches to the case with four screws. Don't loosen these screws.

6. If your PC doesn't have screws in the back, feel under the front of the case. You should feel a handhold that lets you grab and pull off the front panel (see Figure 5.14). Gently pull off the front panel.

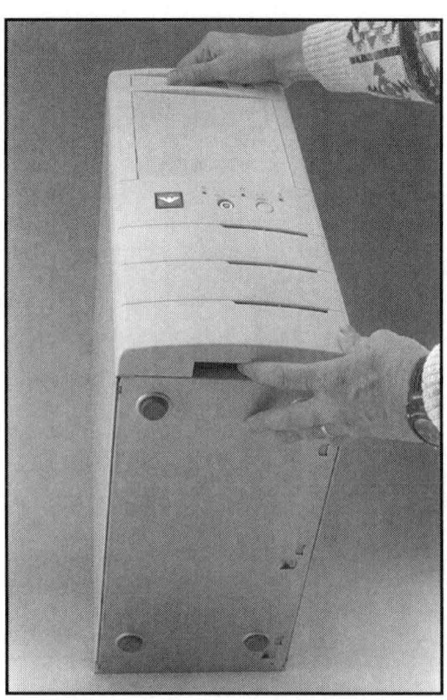

FIG. 5.14
Cases that have a pop-off front panel include a hand-hold at the bottom of the case you use to grasp the front panel to pull it off.

7. Slide the case cover forward and lift it off. Some cases require that you pull the cover all the way forward before removing it (see Figure 5.15), but others require that you pull it forward only an inch or so, then lift it up and off (see Figure 5.16).

FIG. 5.15
Desktop cases typically require that you slide the cover all the way to the front before lifting it off.

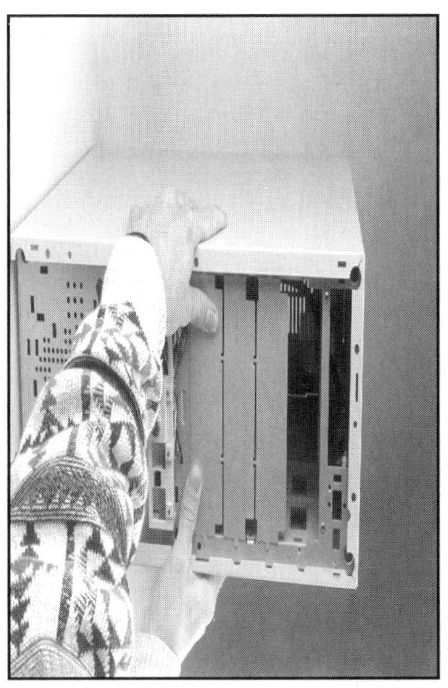

FIG. 5.16
Tower cases typically require that you slide the cover forward an inch or so and then lift it off.

8. Set the cover aside where you won't trip over it or knock it over.

With the cover off, you can see the arrangement of the components in the computer. Figure 5.17 shows a typical AT-style PC with its components labeled.

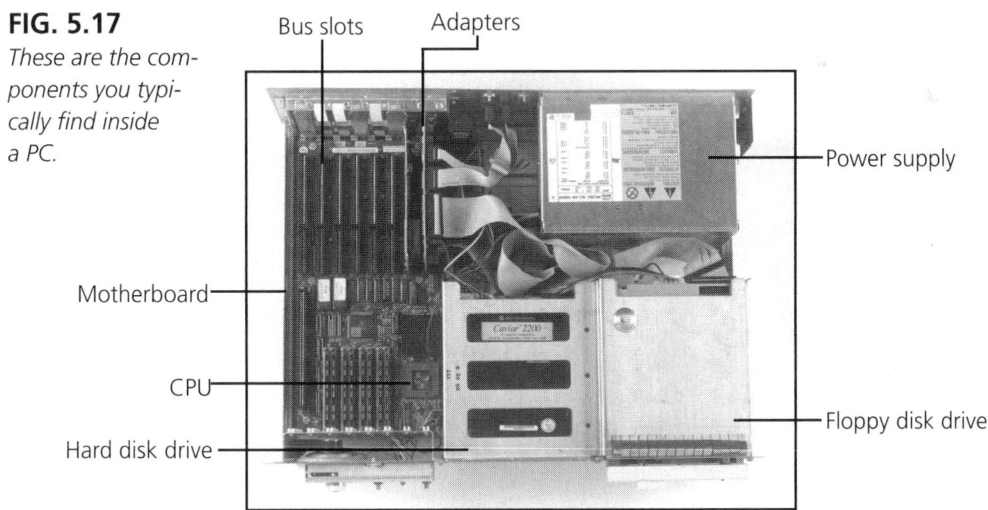

FIG. 5.17
These are the components you typically find inside a PC.

Now that your system is open, you're ready to take a tour through its guts.

The Motherboard: Slots, Sockets, and Connectors

Even if you're not replacing your motherboard, it's a good idea for you to know what is on the motherboard and where each major item is located. Figure 5.17 shows the major components in your system, and Figure 5.18 focuses on the motherboard to illustrate what it contains and help you identify its sockets, connectors, and other items.

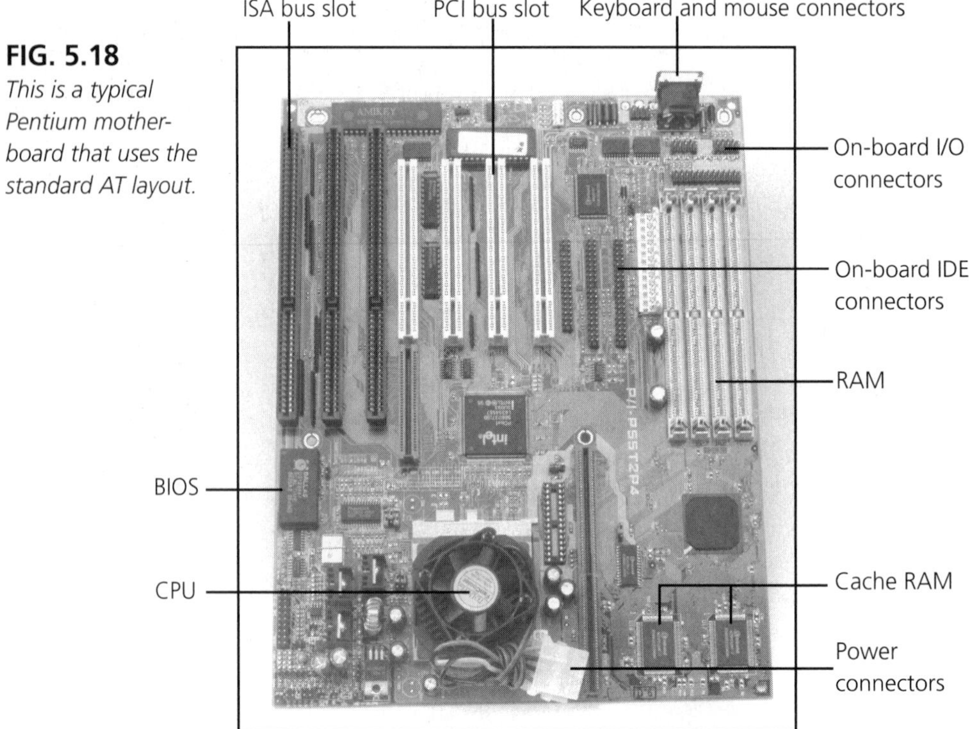

FIG. 5.18
This is a typical Pentium motherboard that uses the standard AT layout.

As you go through the following sections, taking a tour of your PC, you should consider writing down what you find. In other words, take a written inventory of your system so that when you close the system back up again, you have a clear picture of what it contains and what can be upgraded.

Bus Slots

The *bus slots* are the connectors on the motherboard in which the system adapters install. These adapters typically include the video card, hard disk controller, internal modem, sound card, and so forth. The appearance of the slots depends on the type of *bus* the system uses. The bus is basically the type of connections the system uses to connect the adapters to the computer. You find these types of buses in today's PCs:

- *ISA Bus.* This standard bus originated with the IBM AT Personal Computer. It offers the lowest performance of the three bus types discussed here. ISA stands for *Industry Standard Architecture.*
- *VESA Local Bus, or VL bus.* The VESA local bus provides for high-speed connections between adapters and the CPU, bypassing the normal communications channels used by ISA adapters. Local bus adapters offer much better performance than ISA bus adapters because of this.
- *PCI Local Bus.* The PCI bus also offers improved performance over the ISA bus. PCI came after VESA but has rapidly become more popular and is included on most Pentium and Pentium Pro motherboards.

TIP You can tell a PCI adapter from an ISA adapter by two characteristics. First, the edge connector is smaller on a PCI adapter than it is on an ISA adapter, and the contacts on the PCI adapter are smaller and closer together. Second, you can tell the difference by the side of the adapter on which the components are mounted. Hold an ISA adapter with the mounting bracket in your right hand and the components will be on the side of the adapter facing you. Hold a PCI adapter the same way, and the components will be on the back side of the adapter.

Nearly all 386 systems use the ISA bus. A single bus slot consists of two separate sockets butted end-to-end. An 8-bit adapter uses only the larger of the two sockets, and a 16-bit adapter uses both sockets. (You learn more about adapters in the section "Internal Adapters" later in this chapter.) Figure 5.19 shows a 486 motherboard with ISA slots.

Most 486 motherboards and some early Pentium motherboards use a VL bus. The VL bus slots incorporate a standard ISA bus slot along with an additional slot. You can install a regular ISA adapter in the ISA portion of the slot (the two end-to-end connectors), or install a VL bus adapter that takes up all three connectors.

FIG. 5.19
ISA slots consist of two connectors butted end-to-end for each connector.

Most Pentium and Pentium Pro motherboards use a combination ISA/PCI bus, containing three or four ISA slots and three or four PCI bus slots. As you can see in Figure 5.20, the PCI bus slots are smaller than the ISA slots.

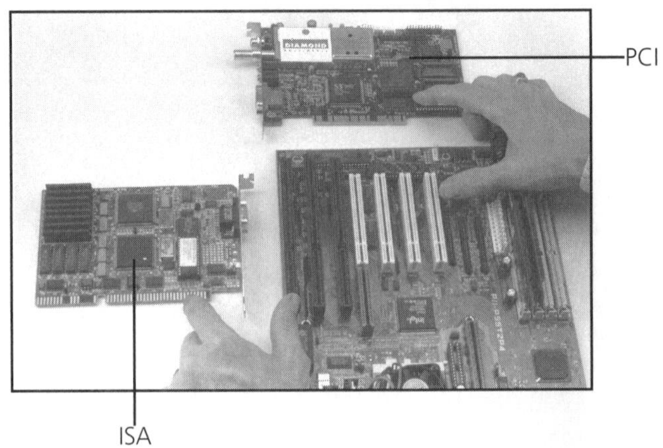

FIG. 5.20
PCI bus slots are smaller than the ISA slots. PCI adapters also have their components mounted on the opposite side from an ISA adapter.

NOTE You can install an ISA adapter in an ISA or VL bus slot. A VL bus adapter can install only in a VL bus slot, and a PCI adapter can install only in a PCI slot. You can't install an ISA adapter in a PCI slot.

If yours is a 386 or 486 motherboard, it might also contain a special, proprietary memory expansion slot. These slots expand the amount of memory a system can hold beyond what the motherboard's SIMM sockets can take. A special adapter containing memory chips or SIMMs installs in this special slot. Figure 5.21 shows a memory expansion slot. Note that it's an extension of the standard ISA slot—you could install an ISA adapter in the slot or install a memory card in the slot (which would use all of the connectors).

FIG. 5.21
Proprietary memory expansion slots are common on 386 and 486 motherboards.

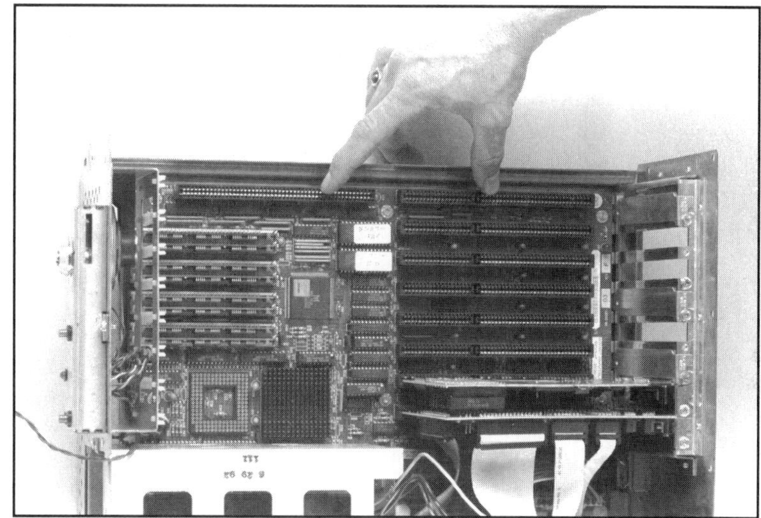

The important points for you to understand about your system's bus at this point are how the bus affects your upgrade options and in which slots you can install adapters.

If you have a system with a local bus and won't be upgrading the motherboard, any new adapters you buy should be local bus devices, assuming you have a local bus slot available for them. If the system contains an ISA adapter that is installed in a VL bus slot, and you have an open ISA slot, move the adapter to the ISA slot to make the VL bus slot available.

If you're going to replace the motherboard, you'll probably end up with a PCI bus system since most new motherboards incorporate a PCI bus. An advantage to choosing a system with a PCI bus rather than a VL bus is that PCI devices are now more commonly available than VL bus devices. So, you have a wider range of hardware from which to choose.

TIP You might think that having only three or four slots of each type on a motherboard limits your capability to add adapters to the system. Actually, three or four should be plenty because most new motherboards provide on-board IDE and

continues

continued

I/O connections, eliminating the need for hard disk adapters or I/O adapters. The slots that would otherwise be used by these adapters are available for other devices such as internal modems, sound cards, and so on.

CPU

The CPU is the brain of the computer. *CPU* stands for *Central Processing Unit*, and this is where the majority of the computing takes place in the computer. Figure 5.22 shows a CPU with a heat sink installed on it. The *heat sink* helps dissipate heat away from the CPU. Figure 5.23 shows a CPU without a heat sink. Instead of a heat sink, your CPU might include a CPU fan, which is a small fan mounted on the top of the CPU to help keep it cool.

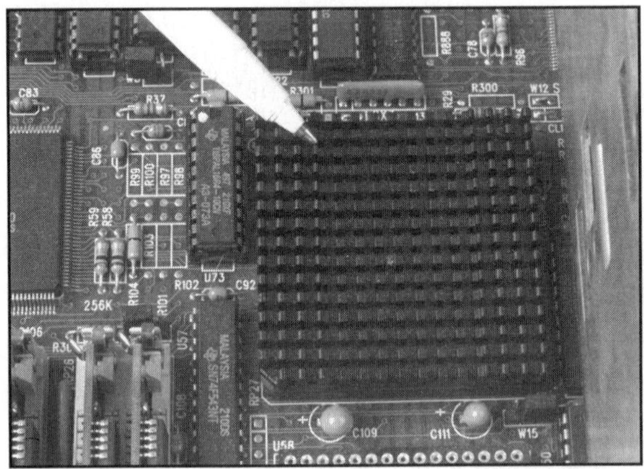

FIG. 5.22
This CPU has a heat sink mounted on its top to help dissipate heat away from the chip.

You probably already know what type of CPU your system contains. But, maybe you've just purchased a used system or just aren't sure about the CPU type. You can tell what type of CPU your system contains by the message that appears when the system first starts to boot. Most BIOS startup routines display a list of equipment just before the operating system starts to boot. This list typically includes the processor type, hard disks installed, and other general hardware information.

With the system open, you should be able to tell what type of CPU your system contains by reading the information that's printed on the top of the chip. You'll probably see a combination of numbers and letters that include the numbers `386`, `486`, or `586`, or the words `Pentium` or `Pentium Pro`. The 386 and 486 designations indicate that your system contains a processor compatible with the Intel 80386 or 80486 CPU, respectively (or most likely, contains an actual Intel processor).

FIG. 5.23
This CPU does not include a heat sink.

A Pentium designation indicates your system contains an Intel Pentium processor. The Pentium chip is one step up the evolutionary chain from the 486 processor, and the Pentium Pro is one step above the Pentium. A designation of 586 indicates that the chip is a non-Intel chip compatible with (or offering essentially the same performance as) a Pentium processor. If the CPU has a heat sink mounted on its top, you can find the processor designation on the bottom side of the chip (see Figure 5.24).

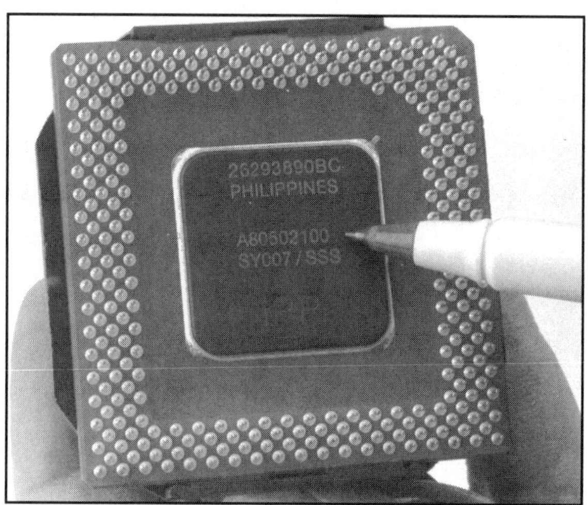

FIG. 5.24
You should find the chip's designation on the bottom, as well as the top.

After you locate the chip designator, look in the same spot for an indication of the chip's speed, which is expressed in *megahertz*. Basically, the speed of the chip defines the number of commands it can perform per second. The faster the speed, the faster the CPU and the faster your PC's performance with that CPU type. In other words, a 166MHz Pentium performs faster than a 100MHz Pentium. But, a 100MHz 486 might not perform faster than a 90MHz Pentium.

To determine the system's speed (if you don't already know it), look in the same spot you found the CPU's type designation (see Figure 5.25). Look for 25, 33, 50, 60, 66, 90, 100, 120, 133, 150, 166, or 200. This number indicates the chip's speed.

FIG. 5.25
You'll find the CPU's speed designation in the same place as its type designation.

RAM

RAM stands for *Random Access Memory*. RAM serves as short-term storage. Generally, the system's RAM is located on SIMMs (*Single Inline Memory Modules*) that install in sockets on the motherboard. Figure 5.26 shows two types of SIMMs. One uses a 30-pin configuration and the other uses a 72-pin configuration.

A third type of slot accommodates DIMMs, or *Dual Inline Memory Modules*. DIMMs use a 168-pin configuration. DIMMs effectively pack twice as much memory in one package compared to SIMMs, although DIMMs are slightly longer than SIMMs.

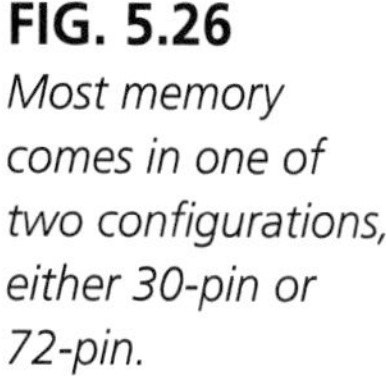

FIG. 5.26
Most memory comes in one of two configurations, either 30-pin or 72-pin.

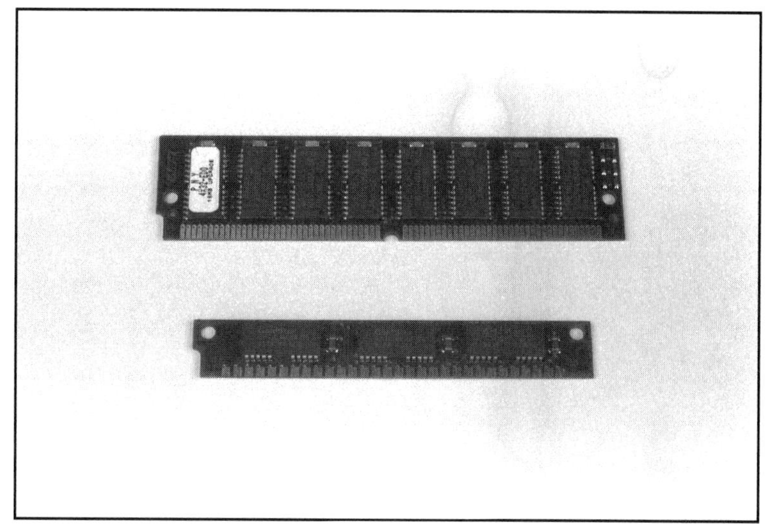

Some higher end systems use DIMMs exclusively, others use SIMMs exclusively, and still others provide a mix of SIMM and DIMM sockets.

DIMMs typically are more expensive than SIMMs, but they offer better performance because they contain onboard buffers and the DIMM sockets are designed to offer better reliability.

One other type of memory you might have in your system is EDO memory. EDO stands for *Extended Data Out*. Without launching into a detailed technical explanation, I'll just say that the internal design of EDO memory makes it more efficient so it offers faster performance over non-EDO memory. If your system is designed for EDO memory, you must use EDO memory in it. If the system is designed for non-EDO memory, you can't use EDO memory in it.

EDO memory uses a 72-pin SIMM configuration, so it's difficult to tell EDO memory from non-EDO memory. All that is different is the type of chips used on the SIMM. To find out if your system contains EDO memory, you need to look closely at the SIMMs themselves. In all likelihood, the SIMM has EDO printed somewhere on it. You might have to remove one of the SIMMs to tell. See Chapter 10, "Adding Memory," for instructions on removing and installing RAM.

Another consideration about RAM is its speed. The RAM speed is measured in nanoseconds, with a smaller number indicating faster performance. Most systems today use memory speeds between 60ns and 100ns. For now, take a look at one of your computer's SIMMs and try to locate a speed indicator on one of the memory chips. Probably, it reads either 60 or 70, indicating 60ns or 70ns.

The important point to understand about your system's memory at this stage is that your motherboard's RAM slots are designed to take a specific type of memory configuration. Some have only 30-pin sockets, some have only 72-pin sockets, some have a mix of 30- and 72-pin sockets, and yet others include DIMM sockets.

If you're thinking of adding more memory to your system, you need to know what types of sockets the motherboard contains, which ones are full and which are empty, and what combinations of memory you can use. In some cases, this means removing some of the existing RAM and replacing it with higher capacity RAM. At this point, make a note of what types of RAM sockets your system contains, which ones are filled, and what is in them. Also, start hunting for your motherboard manual, because it will tell you what combinations you can use.

If you're replacing the motherboard, you're probably hoping to use the same memory in your new board. That might not be practical or even possible because the existing memory might not fit the configuration supported by the new motherboard. Before you buy the new motherboard, read Chapter 10, "Adding Memory," to determine whether you can use your existing memory.

NOTE You can get a gadget called a *memory adapter* that lets you install 30-pin SIMMs in a 72-pin socket and vice-versa. The type of memory adapter you use depends on your system's configuration and the location of the CPU and RAM sockets. In other words, you need a memory adapter that fits your situation. Memory adapters are covered in more detail in Chapter 10, "Adding Memory."

Cache RAM

The *cache RAM* on the motherboard serves as a temporary storage space for data moving to and from the CPU. The cache speeds up performance because the CPU can access often-used data from the cache much more rapidly than from RAM. If the data already resides in the cache, the system doesn't have to retrieve the data from RAM.

486, Pentium, and Pentium Pro CPUs contain a cache, called an *internal cache*, that is built directly into the CPU. Most systems also include an *external cache* that consists of memory chips mounted on the motherboard. Figure 5.27 shows an external cache.

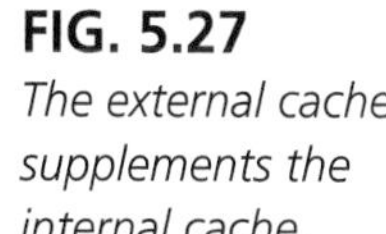

FIG. 5.27
The external cache supplements the internal cache.

In general, more cache is better than less cache, but you're probably not going to see any major improvement by increasing the external cache size on your system, even if your motherboard supports adding more cache. So, I don't even cover the process for adding cache RAM in the book.

NOTE The systems that benefit the most from a larger cache are servers. This book is geared toward the average user, another reason that increasing cache RAM isn't covered.

BIOS

Figure 5.28 shows the BIOS chips on a motherboard. The BIOS contains program code that performs very basic, low-level functions that enable the PC to boot and the CPU to access various components in the system. BIOS chips are manufactured by a handful of companies, including Phoenix, AMI, and Award.

The primary reason to upgrade the BIOS is to add new capabilities not supported by your current BIOS. For example, many old BIOS don't support disk drives greater than 512M. In some cases, you have to upgrade the BIOS because the current BIOS contains bugs or outdated code that prevent it from working properly with certain devices.

How you update the BIOS depends on your system. Many older BIOS must be physically replaced with a new BIOS, meaning you remove the existing BIOS chip and install a new one. Newer BIOS chips are *flash programmable*, meaning you upgrade the BIOS by running a program that changes the BIOS's internal program code—you don't have to replace these BIOS.

FIG. 5.28
Some BIOS are upgradable through software, but others must be physically replaced.

For now, you should make note of which BIOS the system contains and its version number. You don't actually have to open the system and look at the BIOS to do so. Instead, watch the initial startup screen that appears when you first turn on the computer. You see the BIOS manufacturer's name and the BIOS version displayed on the monitor. In Chapter 7, "Working with the BIOS," you learn more about the BIOS and how to update it.

I/O Connections

Your PC contains one or more serial ports (COM1, COM2, and so on) and one or more parallel ports (LPT1, LPT2, ...). Serial ports are most commonly used to connect mice, trackballs, and external modems to the system. In the case of internal modems, the modem is *configured* as a specific COM port (such as COM2). If there is an existing COM port in the system that is configured the same as the internal modem, that COM port has to be disabled to allow the modem to function as that port.

If yours is a 386 or older 486, it probably uses an I/O adapter to provide serial and parallel ports. The card itself probably has one serial and one parallel port sticking out the back of the PC. If your PC includes a second serial port, it probably connects to the I/O card by a thin ribbon cable. The same is true for a second parallel port. Also, the I/O functions might be incorporated on your hard disk host adapter, which means just about every cable inside your computer is connected to that one card.

Newer PCs have the port circuitry built onto the motherboard, with pins on the motherboard to which you connect the serial and parallel ports (see Figure 5.29). These motherboards are shipped with brackets that mount the actual serial and parallel connectors to the back of the PC, and ribbon cables connect these to the motherboard connections.

FIG. 5.29
Newer motherboards have the I/O circuitry built right onto the motherboard, so you don't need a separate I/O adapter.

At this point, you should take a survey of your I/O ports to see how many of each you have. If you plan to replace the motherboard, your new one will no doubt contain two serial ports and one parallel port. You should think about whether you need more than those ports, and if so, you need to locate the manual for your current I/O card so you know how to configure its settings so they don't conflict with the onboard ports.

Disk Adapter or Connections

Your system should contain at least one floppy disk drive and one hard disk drive. The floppy disk drive(s) is installed in the external drive bay(s), and the hard drive(s) in the internal drive bay(s). Figure 5.30 shows a hard disk drive being installed in a system.

If you're planning to expand your available disk space, take a look in the system to determine how many empty drive bays there are. If you don't have any empty drive bays, you either have to replace the existing drive or install an external drive. For now, just make note of the available bays so you can begin planning for the upgrade.

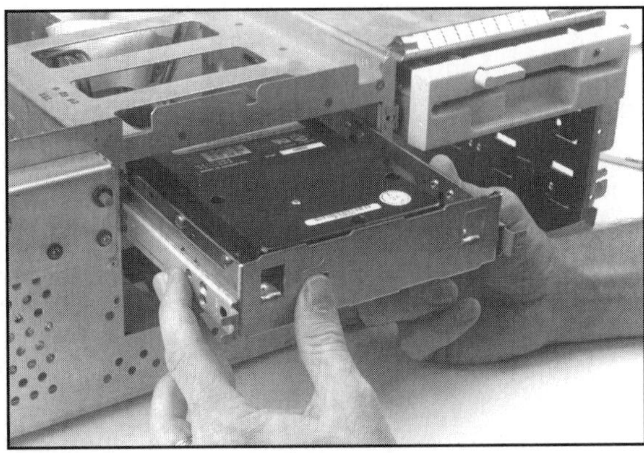

FIG. 5.30
Hard disk drives are usually installed in internal drive bays.

Miscellaneous Connectors

Notice that there are at least four or more sets of wires running from the front panel of the case to the motherboard. These connect the reset switch, turbo LED, and other front panel devices to the motherboard. The system also probably has a speaker wire connected to the motherboard from the PC's speaker, as well as a hard disk drive activity light.

In general, these connections are only a factor if you're going to be replacing the motherboard. If so, at some point before you disconnect the wires you should make a note of their locations and how they're connected. If you have an instamatic camera, take a few close-up shots of the connections. Otherwise, draw a diagram. I remind you about these connections again in the motherboard chapter.

NOTE The motherboard also has other connections, including keyboard, power supply, and sometimes, mouse connections. These aren't really relevant at this point, but you find mention of them in other chapters where they are relevant.

Internal Adapters

Your system contains one or more *adapters*, which also are called *cards*. These adapters provide specific functions not provided by the motherboard. Video cards, internal modems, hard disk adapters, and sound cards are examples of adapters. Figure 5.31 shows a typical adapter.

FIG. 5.31
Adapters provide functions not performed by the motherboard.

At this point, take an inventory of the adapters in your system so you know what you have. Also, take an inventory of the empty bus slots so you know how many additional devices you can install.

Reassembling Your System

After you have finished poking and prodding inside the PC and have a nice inventory list, you're ready to reassemble the system. Generally, its just the reverse of the disassembly process.

To Reassemble the PC, You Need:

- ☑ A complete inventory of your system
- ☑ The PC is turned off!
- ☑ Phillips screwdriver or nut driver for the case screws
- ☑ Small flat-bladed screwdriver for cable connections

---

1. Make sure all the internal cables are tucked back inside the PC so they won't interfere with the cover.
2. Slide the cover on the PC, making sure to engage the tabs at the bottom of the cover (if any) with the edges of the case.
3. Carefully slide the cover back into position, making sure not to pinch any cables. You might have to pay special attention to the floppy drive(s) and CD-ROM drive (if there is one) to get the opening in the case past the drive(s).

4. After the cover is repositioned fully on the case, install the retaining screws.
5. If you disconnected the monitor, reconnect it.
6. Plug in the system and turn it on to make sure everything still works.

External Devices

You no doubt have a keyboard and a mouse connected to your PC. Most people also have at least one other external device connected to the PC—a printer. You might have other devices such as a scanner or external modem connected to the PC.

Now that you've completed the internal inventory, take an inventory of the external devices connected to the PC. Just note the device, manufacturer, and model number.

Planning the Upgrade

With a good inventory, you're ready to start planning any upgrades. There are many issues to consider, but most of those issues are specific to the individual items you're upgrading. For example, if you want to increase the system's available disk space, you need to decide whether to add a drive or replace the existing one, whether to use an internal or external drive, which disk should be the boot disk, and so on. Rather than cover these types of issues here, I've left them for the chapters in which each specific upgrade is addressed.

At this point, you should decide *which* upgrades you want to perform. By far, one of the most cost-effective upgrades you can make is to add more memory to the system. This is particularly true if you're running Windows, Windows 95, or Windows NT, but not much of a factor for DOS-only systems.

NOTE Adding memory to a DOS system can have a positive impact, but generally only if you're running very memory-intensive programs that can make use of extended memory.

Other upgrades really depend on your situation and how you use the system. If you have a 14.4Kbps modem and do a lot of online communication, an investment in a 28.8Kbps or faster modem is a good idea. If you're low on disk space, adding another hard disk makes sense.

Regardless of what upgrades you decide to do, you should take a little time to plan them. This includes more than just finding the component you want at a reasonable cost. Here are some things you should consider when planning an upgrade:

- *Will I have all the parts I need?* When you buy a new component, make sure you have all the parts you need to install it. When you buy a new motherboard, for example, it probably won't come with any mounting hardware. But, you should be able to use the hardware from the old motherboard. If you buy a disk drive, you might need a set of mounting rails. Before performing an upgrade, read through the chapter that covers it to make sure you have everything you need.
- *Is this device supported by my operating system?* When you buy a new device, find out if it is supported by your operating system. With DOS/Windows 3.x, the device probably comes with a device driver disk that contains the software you need to make it work on your system. Windows 95 and Windows NT users can check the Hardware Compatibility List (HCL), which comes with the operating system, to determine whether the driver is included or needs to be supplied with the device. You also find the HCLs at the Microsoft Web site by searching the Knowledge Base.

You can find the Microsoft Knowledge Base at http://www.microsoft.com/kb

TIP Here's a way to check whether Windows 95 directly supports a device: Open the Control Panel (choose Start, Settings, Control Panel) and double-click the Add New Hardware icon. Click Next; then choose the No option button and click Next. In the Hardware Types list, choose the type of device you're going to be installing and choose Next. Windows 95 displays a list of manufacturers and devices. Scroll through the list to find the manufacturer and see if the device is listed. If the device is fairly new, but it isn't listed in the Models list, you can be fairly sure it includes a Windows 95 driver disk. When you're finished browsing the list, choose Cancel.

- *Will my system support the new device?* Most devices work in any system. But if you're adding a disk drive, for example, you need to make sure the BIOS supports drives of the size you are buying. Make a call to the BIOS manufacturer to make sure the new device you're buying is supported by your BIOS.

- *Can I afford the potential downtime?* Think about how long it will take you to perform the upgrade and whether you can afford to not have the use of your system for that time. Double the amount of time you figure for the upgrade just in case it doesn't work and you have to undo it.
- *Would it be more cost effective or less work to buy new?* If you're going to be performing a major upgrade, take a look at the overall cost and how much you think your time is worth. You might decide it makes more sense to buy a new computer with all the latest gizmos and gadgets.
- *Do I feel competent to perform the upgrade?* If you read through the chapter that covers the upgrade you're considering and still don't feel confident to do it, check with a local PC retailer to see if they can perform the upgrade for you.

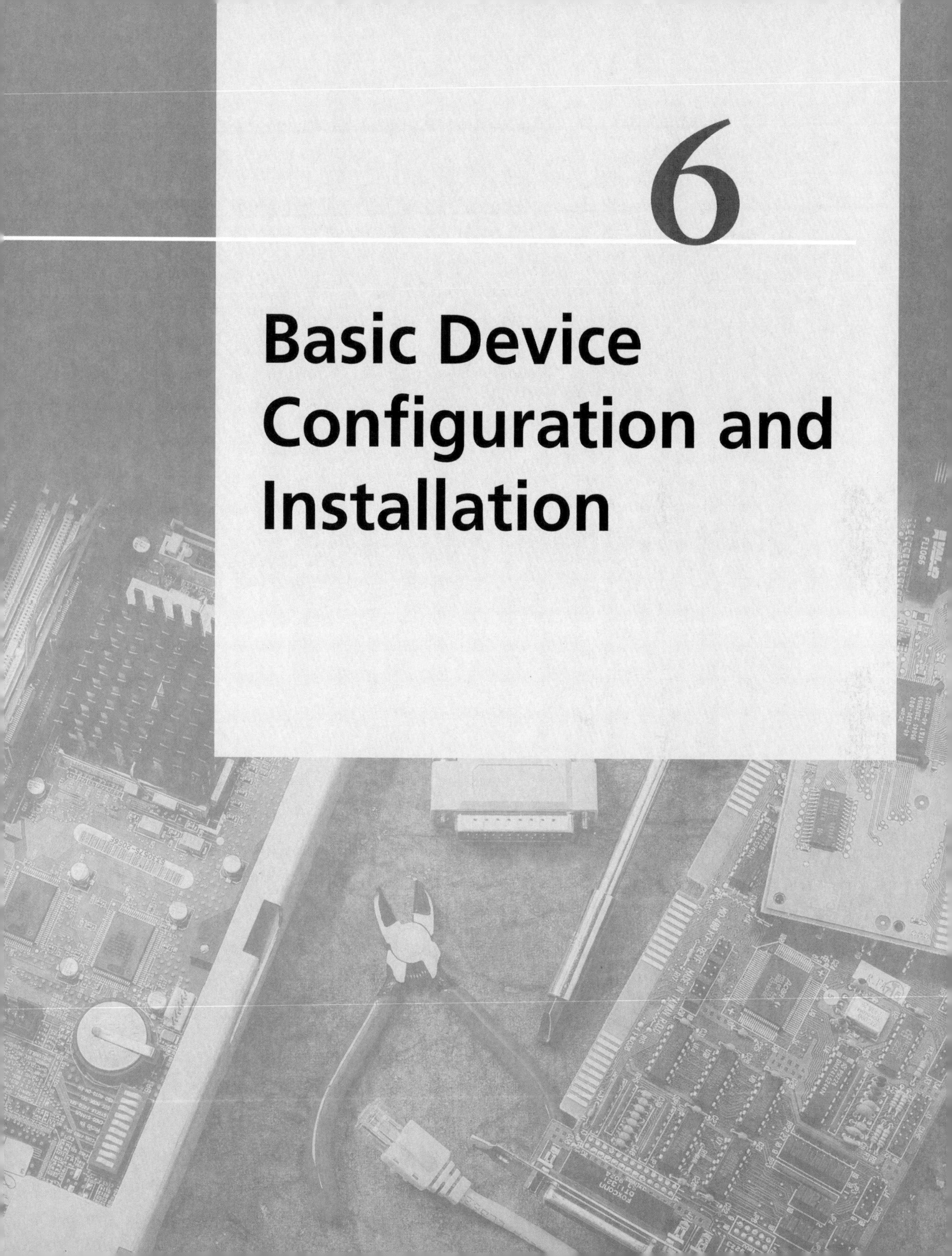

6

Basic Device Configuration and Installation

In the bad old days when computers weren't quite as "intelligent" as they are today, just about every upgrade that involved an adapter card also involved setting switches and performing other feats of magic on the adapter. Today's PCs eliminate a lot of the configuration hassle by supporting Plug and Play, which enables the computer to configure the device for you automatically. But even in a Plug-and-Play compatible PC, you will probably run across situations in which you need to know how to configure an adapter.

This chapter explains adapter configuration in detail, covering the following topics:

- Understanding IRQ, DMA, and memory addressing
- Understanding Plug and Play
- Configuring adapter switches and jumpers
- Installing and removing adapters and connecting cables

Understanding Adapters

Most PCs contain at least one *adapter*—sometimes called a *card* (from *printed circuit card*). Figure 6.1 shows a typical adapter.

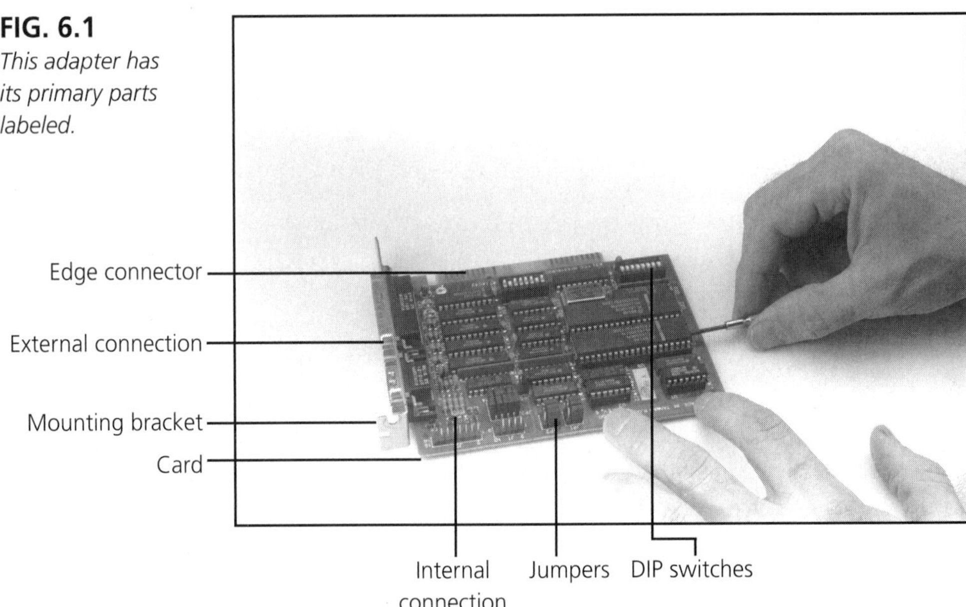

FIG. 6.1
This adapter has its primary parts labeled.

The adapters install in the PC's bus slots, which were explained in Chapter 5. Adapters perform functions not performed by the motherboard itself, and examples include video cards, sound cards, internal modems, network interface cards, TV cards, and disk host adapters.

More and more features are being built into today's motherboards. In fact, for a while, many motherboards even included video circuitry so the PC didn't need a separate video card. Today, the IDE disk host adapter and communications ports (COM and LPT) are included on most motherboards, although video typically is not. Some high-end motherboards also include a network interface right on the motherboard. Even so, you'll probably have at least one or two adapters in your system.

All adapters, regardless of what they do, have some traits in common. The following list identifies these parts (refer to Figure 6.1):

- *Card*. The adapter card itself is just a printed circuit card on which various electronic components are mounted.
- *Mounting bracket*. The mounting bracket attaches the adapter to the back of the PC's case. At the bottom of the bracket is a tab that slides down behind the edge of the motherboard. At the top is a notch through which a screw goes to fasten the card to the case. This secures the card in its slot and prevents it from moving when you connect cables to it.
- *DIP switches*. DIP stands for *Dual Inline Package*, and DIP switches are just a collection of very small switches. You use these switches to configure the card's settings. You'll find a close-up photo of a DIP switch later in this chapter in the section "Configuring Adapters."
- *Jumpers*. These are small plastic plugs that you install on rows of pins on the card. They connect two pins together, enabling electricity to *jump* between the two, and thus the name jumpers. You'll find more information about jumpers in the section "Configuring Adapters" later in this chapter.
- *Edge connector*. The edge connector is the part of the card that inserts into the PC's bus slot. The edge connector contains *contacts*, which are metallic strips that connect the circuitry on the card to the PC's bus. The configuration of the edge connector has to match the type of slot in which the card is inserted. An ISA card, for example, can't go in a PCI slot, or vice versa, because the edge connector isn't designed for that type of slot.

- *Internal connection.* Many adapters include one or more connections on the card to which you connect cables. A sound card, for example, almost always includes connections on the card for a CD-ROM drive and various audio connections.
- *External connection.* Many adapters (but not all) include external connectors that mount to the card's bracket and therefore are visible and accessible from the back of the PC. You connect external devices (like the monitor, for example) to these connectors.

TIP You can tell a card's type (ISA, EISA, VL, PCI) by two traits: the location of the card's components and the size and shape of its edge connector. Hold the card with the bracket in your right hand with the top of the card facing away from you. If the components are on your side, it's an ISA, EISA, or VL bus card. If the components are on the opposite side, it's a PCI bus card.

You also can tell the card's bus type from the shape and size of the edge connector. If the connector is only a few inches long and contains very thin contacts, you have a PCI card. An 8-bit ISA card's connector is about 3 inches long, and the contacts are about 0.1 inch wide. A 16-bit ISA card's connector consists of two separate connectors—a short one on the left and a longer one on the right.

Cards that communicate with the PC using 8 data bits at a time are called *8-bit cards.* Cards that use 16 bits are called *16-bit cards.* Cards that use 32 bits are called—you guessed it—*32-bit cards.* In general, the more data bits the card can transfer at a time, the faster the card. Some cards, though, don't need to transfer more than 8 bits at a time, so an 8-bit design is fine for them.

An 8-bit ISA card has only one section to its edge connector, and a 16-bit ISA card has two sections. The 8-bit card uses only one of the two end-to-end connectors on the bus slot, and the 16-bit card uses both connectors in the slot. The VL and PCI cards fit only in their specific slots.

Understanding Configuration Steps

Later in this chapter you'll learn about some of the physical components on adapters, including DIP switches and jumpers. First, though, you should learn about some of the things you might need to configure on an adapter before you install it.

Understanding IRQ

Some adapters require an *IRQ assignment.* IRQ stands for *Interrupt ReQuest line.* When an adapter needs to signal the CPU that it needs attention, it does so using its assigned IRQ. Today's PCs use 16 IRQ lines, although some of those 16 are used only by the system and can't be assigned to an adapter. Table 6.1 lists IRQ numbers and the most common device assignments.

Table 6.1 Common IRQ Assignments

IRQ	Device
NMI	Nonmaskable interrupt, reports parity errors
0	System timer
1	Keyboard
2	EGA/VGA and cascade interrupt for second IRQ controller
3	COM2 or COM4
4	COM1 or COM3
5	LPT2 (printer port 2), or sound card
6	Floppy disk, or hard disk/floppy disk controller
7	LPT1 (printer port 1)
8	Real-time clock
9	Software redirected to IRQ2
10	Available
11	Available
12	Available (PS2 mouse)
13	Math coprocessor
14	Hard disk controller
15	Available, or hard disk controller

There are two main points to understand about IRQ assignment:

- Not every device needs an IRQ line assigned to it.
- Unless your system allows *IRQ sharing*, each device that requires an IRQ must have a unique IRQ setting. This means that you need to keep track of the IRQ assignments in your system and when you install a new device, make sure it doesn't conflict with another device's IRQ setting.

TIP MicroChannel Architecture (MCA) and EISA (Enhanced Industry Standard Architecture) bus systems do support IRQ sharing, which enables multiple devices to use the same IRQ line. ISA systems, however, don't support IRQ sharing per se.

When you're installing in your system an adapter that requires an IRQ, you need to check your system log to determine which IRQs are available. Chapter 2, "Building a Software Safety Kit," explains how to create a system log. Also study Table 6.1 to help guide you in your selection. Keep in mind that some of the IRQs are assigned at the system level and can't be changed. IRQ0 and IRQ1, for example, are never available to you. Generally, the most commonly available IRQs are 3, 4, 5, 7, 10, 11, 12, and 15.

NOTE Because of the way the ISA bus is designed, 8-bit cards can use only IRQ settings up to IRQ9. 16-bit cards can use any available IRQ setting, including those above IRQ9. Keep that in mind when configuring an adapter.

Most often, an adapter's IRQ is set by either a DIP switch or a jumper on the card. Some adapters are *software configurable*, which means they come with a setup program that lets you set the IRQ and other settings for the card. Under Windows 95 and Windows NT, software configurable adapters typically can be configured by the operating system when you install the device.

Check the section "Configuring Adapters" later in this chapter for instructions on using DIP switches and jumpers to configure a card.

Understanding DMA

Many devices need to access memory, and they do so through the CPU. The device makes a request to the CPU, and the CPU processes the request, reading or writing to memory as requested. All this memory access can tie up the CPU when it could be doing something else, slowing down the system overall and also slowing down the device's performance. So, many devices that perform memory access a lot support *DMA*, which stands for *Direct Memory Access.* DMA provides a direct, high-speed link between a device and memory, bypassing the CPU.

Devices such as SCSI host adapters and sound cards, to name a few, often require a DMA channel assignment. As with IRQ settings, devices require a unique DMA channel assignment. If you have conflicting IRQ or DMA assignments, strange and unpleasant things are going to happen. For example, your sound card will develop a really bad stutter, or your hard disk will go nuts. So, it's important to come up with unique settings.

AT-class systems support 8 DMA channels, 0 through 7. Table 6.2 lists common DMA channel assignments. As with IRQ settings, DMA channels are limited to either 8-bit or 16-bit availability. Table 6.2 also lists the 8-bit/16-bit availability for DMA channels.

Table 6.2 16-Bit DMA Channel Default Assignments

DMA	Function	Bus Slot	Card Transfer	Type
0	Available	Yes	16-bit	8-bit
1	Sound/Available	Yes	8/16-bit	8-bit
2	Floppy Controller	Yes	8/16-bit	8-bit
3	Available	Yes	8/16-bit	8-bit
4	DMA Cascade	No	N/A	N/A
5	Sound/Available	Yes	16-bit	16-bit
6	Available	Yes	16-bit	16-bit
7	Available	Yes	16-bit	16-bit

As you can see from Table 6.2, some DMA channels are available only for 16-bit adapters. Also, 8-bit transfers are slower than 16-bit transfers because only half as much data is transferred at a time. So, if you're installing a 16-bit card, you should use a DMA assignment of 5, 6, or 7, if available, to get the best possible performance from the adapter.

Also, you should know that even though a device supports DMA transfers, it might not require it. DMA simply enables the device to perform better. So, if you run out of DMA channels, you might be able to disable DMA on a non-critical device from which you don't need optimum performance, making its DMA channel available for another device.

Another point to understand is that one device can use two DMA channels. Many sound cards, for example, use DMA 1 for sound Blaster compatibility mode and DMA 5 for their native mode.

As when assigning an IRQ line, you need to check your system log and manuals to make sure you select a DMA channel that doesn't conflict with another device already in the system. You usually set a device's DMA channel through a DIP switch or jumper on the card, or through a configuration program included with the card. You'll find more information on each method later in the section "Configuring Adapters."

Understanding Base Addressing

In addition to IRQ and DMA settings, many devices require an *I/O base address.* Your PC contains a range of memory addresses that are set aside for input and output, or communication between the device and the CPU. For example, COM1 is usually assigned to the hexadecimal memory address range 3F8 through 3FF. This memory address range serves as the "window" through which the CPU communicates with the COM port. As far as the CPU is concerned, the address range 3F8 through 3FF *is* the COM port.

NOTE Memory addressing, including hex addresses, is explained in Chapter 10, "Adding Memory." For now, just understand that a memory address, in whatever form, identifies a specific location in memory. A *memory range* is a sequential range of addresses, or *block* of memory.

When you configure a device, keep in mind that it might require a base address setting. If it does, you'll have to pick out an address that doesn't conflict with anything else in the system. Adapters are, by convention, only supposed to use base addresses in the range 100 through 3FF. The device's manual and its default setting will be your best bet for determining what base address to use. Usually, the device's designers will have selected a default base address setting that fits the "industry standard" for that type of device.

Even if you choose to use the device's default address, you still should check your system log to make sure the address isn't already in use by another device. If it is, you'll have to use one of the device's alternate addresses. As with IRQ and DMA, base addresses usually are set with a DIP switch, jumper, or configuration program. Check the device's manual to determine how to set its base address.

Understanding RAM and ROM Addressing

In addition to a base address, some devices require a RAM address range, or a range of RAM memory addresses that it can use to store its own data. A good example is a network card—many of them use a RAM buffer to temporarily hold data moving between the card and the network. The address range needs to be unique so that no other device tries to use addresses in the range for its own data.

When you install a device, check its manual to see if the device needs a RAM address range. If it does, you need to check your system log and the other devices in the system to make sure you pick a unique range. Often, these devices use RAM blocks in the Upper Memory Area (UMA), which is the range of memory addresses in the computer between 640K and 1023K.

The adapter manual will indicate which ranges you can use for the device, and you'll probably see suggested addresses such as D0000–D3FFF, D4000–D7FFF, and so on. You learn about memory addressing in Chapter 10, "Adding Memory." For now, just understand that the specified range identifies a specific block of memory. All you need to do is choose a range that isn't being used by any other device, and configure the adapter accordingly. You'll configure the RAM address range just like you do IRQ, DMA, and base address settings: with a DIP switch, jumper, or configuration program.

Another issue you might have to consider with some devices, particularly SCSI host adapters, is the address range the adapter uses for its ROM BIOS. Some devices include their own BIOS that supplement the system BIOS and enable the device to function in the system. The program code is actually contained on the adapter in its BIOS, but the BIOS is mapped to a range of memory addresses in the PC. *Mapping* the BIOS to a range in memory enables the CPU to jump to the appropriate address and execute the BIOS code when necessary.

For example, a SCSI host adapter might use the address range CA000–CBFFF for its BIOS. To help avoid conflicts, the adapter will also support two or three other address ranges. If something else in the system is already using the default address range, you can configure the adapter to use an alternate range. As with other settings, you accomplish this with DIP switches, jumpers, or a configuration program that comes with the card.

TIP If you're running DOS and using EMM386.EXE to manage the UMA, you'll find an entry in CONFIG.SYS that loads EMM386.EXE. You should add an Exclude switch to the EMM386 line to exclude from use the range of memory you've assigned to the device. The following example excludes the range CA00H–CBFFF (note that only the first four values of each address are used):

```
DEVICE=C:\DOS\EMM386.EXE X=CA00-CBFF
```

Refer to Chapter 2, "Building a Software Safety Kit," for more information on editing CONFIG.SYS and other system startup files.

Understanding Plug and Play

Now that you understand some of the potential conflicts when configuring a device, and before you get into actually configuring adapters, you need to learn about systems in which it isn't necessary to configure devices. Many new systems and devices support *Plug and Play*, which enables the computer to automatically configure cards so they don't conflict with one another. Plug and Play has been available in the MCA and EISA buses since their inception, but hasn't been available in the most common bus type, ISA. Plug and Play is often abbreviated as *PnP*.

To work properly, true Plug and Play requires three different components:

- *PnP BIOS*. The BIOS has to support PnP calls that enable it to detect and configure PnP-compatible hardware at startup.
- *PnP Hardware*. The adapters in the system need to support PnP to enable them to be configured automatically by the system. You still can use standard, non-PnP adapters in the system, but they won't be auto-configurable.
- *PnP Operating System*. The operating system needs to recognize and support PnP for complete implementation. The operating system needs to be able to detect conflicts and step you through the process of resolving the conflict. Currently, Windows 95 supports PnP, but Windows NT does not. Future versions of Windows NT will support PnP.

In its ideal implementation, PnP enables you to install a new device, then turn on the computer and let the system configure the device without requiring you to provide any configuration information. The BIOS scans all the devices, assigns settings as necessary, then boots the operating system. You don't have to worry about fiddling with switches, jumpers, or configuration programs—you just plug it in and start playing.

Not all devices support PnP, so you might have a mix of devices in your system. This means that even though some of the devices will auto-configure, you might have to configure some of them yourself. Whether or not your system supports PnP, the next section helps you set up those devices that require manual configuration.

Configuring Adapters

As you read earlier, configuring an adapter often requires choosing and assigning IRQ, DMA, and base address settings for the device. Generally, this means setting DIP switches or jumpers on the board, or using a configuration program that comes with the device. To determine which method your card requires and to locate the switches or jumpers you need to work with, check the manual that came with the device. It provides you with specific information on how to configure the card's settings. The following sections provide some general explanation on how to work with switches and jumpers.

Setting DIP Switches

DIP just refers to the construction of the package that contains the switches. And that's all DIP switches are—a group of really small switches (see Figure 6.2).

Each switch in a DIP has two positions, on or off. If you look closely at the DIP, you'll probably find either a 0 and 1 or the words `on` and `off` printed on the top to indicate which position is on and which is off. If you see a 0 and a 1, the 0 indicates off and the 1 indicates on. Sometimes the words `open` and `closed` are used to indicate off and on, respectively. (When you turn on a switch, you're *closing the circuit.*) For some settings you just have to set one switch in the DIP, and other settings require a combination of switch settings in the DIP.

FIG. 6.2
DIP switches are just tiny switches mounted together in a block.

Sometimes the switches rock from one position to another, but usually the switch slides. The switches are really small, so you'll often have to use something other than your finger to change the switch setting. For example, use a ball-point pen or something similar to push the switch into the necessary position. The manual that comes with the device will include a table or list of switch settings required to configure specific settings or options.

CAUTION Make sure the device is turned off before you change its DIP switch settings.

One other point about DIPs: each DIP on a card will be labeled (on the card) with a designation such as `DSW1`, `SW1`, `DSW2`, `SW2`, and so on. This simply differentiates one DIP from another on the card. So, if the card contains more than one DIP, you need to make sure you're setting the right one. The manual will tell you to set—for example, switch 3 on SW1. This means to set switch number 3 on the DIP labeled `SW1`.

Using Jumpers

Jumpers are small plugs that fit on a couple of pin contacts on the card (see Figure 6.3). All you're doing when you install a jumper is making contact between two pins, closing the connection between them. So, jumper settings are usually referred to as being either *open* or *closed*. When the jumper is installed on the pins, the connection is closed. When no jumper is installed on a set of pins, the connection is open. In a way, jumpers are a little like switches because they let you make a connection (close the switch) or open the connection (open the switch).

Usually, the pins that accept jumpers come in one of two configurations: two pins per row or three pins per row. With a 2-pin configuration, you either install a jumper on a set of pins or not—the connection is either open or closed. With a 3-pin configuration, you can choose between three different possible settings: no jumper, installing a jumper on pins 1 and 2, or installing a jumper on pins 2 and 3. Figure 6.3 illustrates these different configurations.

FIG. 6.3
Jumpers are tiny plugs that connect together two pin contacts.

If a jumper is located by itself, it's usually fairly easy to remove or install the jumper with your fingers. When the jumper is next to another, however, you might need to use tweezers or needle-nose pliers to gently remove or install the jumper (see Figure 6.4). Small, curved needle-nose pliers are particularly helpful for this.

FIG. 6.4
Sometimes you'll have to use tweezers or needle-nose pliers to install or remove a jumper.

As with DIPs, you'll find the necessary jumper configurations for different settings in the adapter's manual.

You'll find jumpers not only on adapters, but also on other devices. Hard disk drives and CD-ROM drives, for example, often use jumpers to set the drive ID and other settings. Regardless of the device, it should come with enough jumpers to configure all the necessary settings. Make sure you save any jumpers you don't use so you'll have some available if you need them later, on the same or a different device. If you don't have any spares, check with your local computer retailer or service shop. They'll probably give you some if you ask nicely.

TIP I usually throw my spare jumpers in one of my desk drawers. If you prefer, you can leave the jumpers on the card, even if they aren't doing anything. Just install the jumper only on one pin, rather than two. That way, it will remain on the board in case you need it later, but won't be connecting together any pins.

Some Final Tips

Before you tear into the system, here are a few general tips that apply to all types of adapters:

- *Static discharge.* Always make sure you touch a metal part of the computer chassis or use a static wristband to discharge your static before handling an adapter. Handle the board by the edges to lessen the chance of touching components and discharging static into them. Never touch the edge connector, for the same reason.
- *Dirty pins.* Although it isn't a major problem, the contacts on a card's edge connector can get dirty or oxidized, preventing the pins from making good contact. You can buy special wet-wipes that are formulated specifically for cleaning edge connectors, but I have a much cheaper (and much more readily available) option—a clean pencil eraser. Set the card on the table or work surface and use the eraser from a pencil to "erase" the connectors, removing any crud from them (see Figure 6.5). Remember to erase both sides of the connector if both sides have contacts. Make sure you clean the contacts with the board away from the PC, because you don't want eraser crumbs floating around inside the computer. Dust off any crumbs from the card with compressed air or a brush.

FIG. 6.5
You can use a pencil eraser to clean edge connector pins.

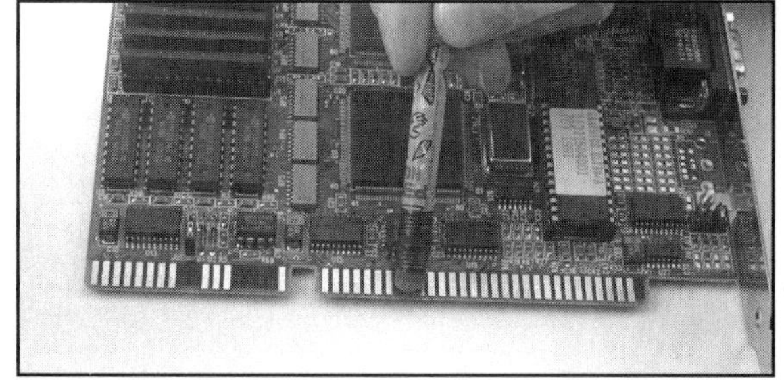

- *Socketed components.* Most of the components on a typical adapter will be soldered to the card. But, some of the chips might be installed in sockets. It doesn't happen often, but chips can work their way loose from a socket. If you're having problems with a card that contains socketed chips, remove the card and place it on a secure surface. Discharge your body static, then press gently but firmly on the chip to seat it fully into the socket (see Figure 6.6). Don't touch the pins of the chips if you can avoid it.

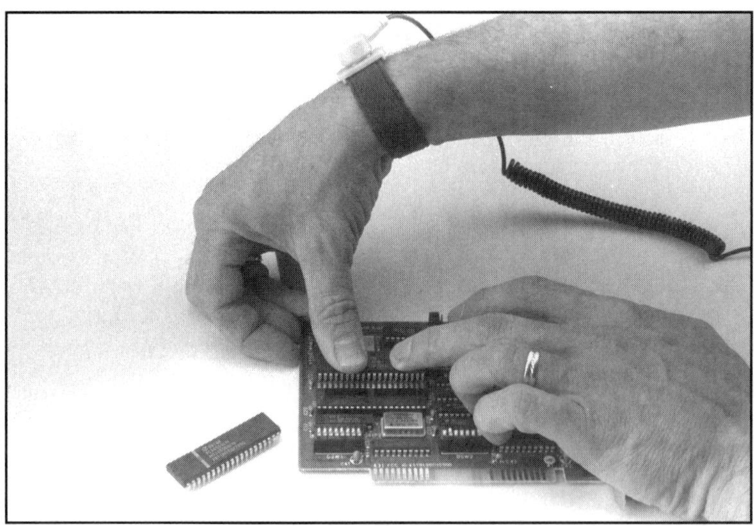

FIG. 6.6
Push gently but firmly on a socketed chip to seat it in its socket.

- *Cover those holes!* Make sure you don't leave any bracket holes uncovered in the back of the computer (see Figure 6.7). Leaving the bracket holes uncovered cuts down the cooling efficiency of the power supply fan, which makes the PC run hotter than it should. Also, the open holes are magnets for dust.

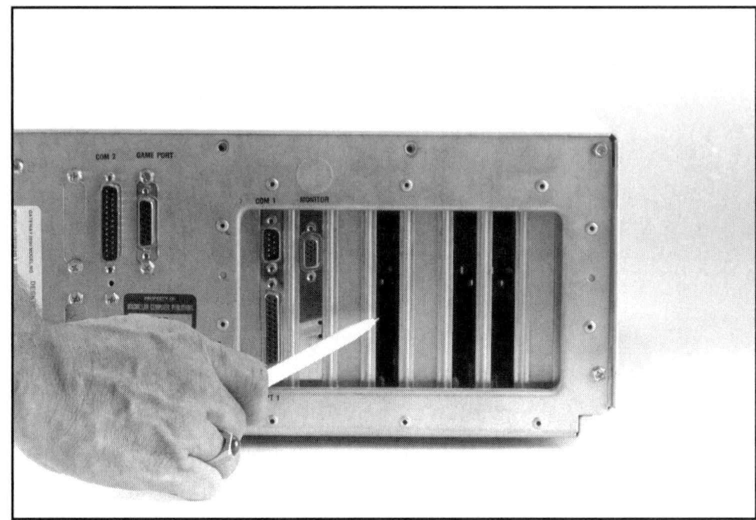

FIG. 6.7
Open bracket holes are a magnet for dust and decrease cooling efficiency.

Removing and Installing Adapters

Removing and installing adapters are among the most common upgrade tasks, and also the easiest to perform. If you're removing an adapter to replace it with a new one, this procedure is explained first.

Removing Adapters

Before you tear into the system, here are a few cautions about adapters. First, *always* make sure the system is turned off before you try to remove or install an adapter. Before touching the adapter, make sure you touch a metal part of the computer to discharge any static in your body that might damage the adapter by damaging some of the components on it. When you're removing the adapter, try not to touch the components on it any more than you have to. You probably won't hurt anything if you do, but better safe than sorry.

To Move an Adapter, You Need:

- ☑ Phillips screwdriver to remove bracket screw
- ☑ Small flat screwdriver to remove cable screws (if any) from back of adapter
- ☑ Computer is *turned off!*

---

1. Shut down the computer and make sure it is turned off.
2. Open the PC.
3. If the adapter you're removing has any cables attached to it at the back of the PC, disconnect these cables. You might need to use the small flat-bladed screwdriver for this. Note where the cables go if you're not familiar with them, and label them if necessary.
4. If the adapter has any cables attached to it inside the PC, first make sure you know where the cables go (label them if necessary). Gently disconnect the cables from the adapter and move them out of the way.
5. Unscrew the adapter's bracket from the PC's chassis and set aside the screw where it won't get lost. I suggest your pocket as an adequate storage facility.

6. Put the screwdriver down and grab the adapter at both ends of its top (see Figure 6.8). Pull straight up to remove the adapter from its socket. You might need to gently tilt it from back to front rather than straight vertically to get it out of the socket (pull up first on the bracket end).

FIG. 6.8
Pull up on the bracket end first to tilt the adapter out of its socket.

NOTE If the adapter is stuck in the slot so tightly that you can't get it out no matter how hard you try, here's a solution: Very carefully stick the blade of a flat screwdriver between the bracket and the computer case (where the screw came out) and twist the screwdriver to lift the bracket end of the adapter out of the socket. Once you get it started, it should come out without any further problems.

Installing Adapters

As when removing adapters, it's vitally important that the PC be turned off; otherwise, you run the risk of destroying not only the adapter, but the PC as well.

To Install an Adapter, You Need:

- ☑ Phillips screwdriver to install bracket screw
- ☑ Small flat screwdriver to install cable screws (if any) on back of adapter

☑ The computer is *turned off!*

☑ Adapter is properly configured for IRQ, DMA, base address, RAM address, and any other required settings (consult the adapter's manual).

☑ All the cables needed to hook up the adapter, both internally and externally, as required (consult the adapter's manual).

---

1. Check the adapter's manual to determine how to configure the adapter's settings. If the PC and the adapter both support PnP, you should not have to perform any manual configuration.
2. Shut down the computer and turn it off.
3. Open the PC.
4. Pick the slot in which you want to install the device, making sure it's the right type of slot (ISA for an ISA card, PCI for a PCI card, and so on.)
5. If the slot currently has a bracket slot cover in place, remove the screw and the cover. Keep the cover because you might need it later.
6. Carefully align the adapter's edge connector with the bus slot. I usually line up the end farthest from the bracket first.
7. When the edge connector is properly aligned, gently push straight down to seat the adapter into the socket (see Figure 6.9).

FIG. 6.9
Push straight down, gently but firmly, to seat the adapter in its socket.

8. When the adapter is firmly seated, install the retaining screw to hold the bracket firmly to the PC's chassis.
9. Connect any internal or external cables. If the external cables have retaining screws, screw them into their connectors.

NOTE If the adapter is a full-length adapter (rare these days), you'll need to make sure it slides into one of the adapter guides mounted to the inside front of the PC (see Figure 6.10). Make sure you get the card in the correct guide slot, or the card will be bent and stressed (not a good thing).

FIG. 6.10
Card guides mounted to the inside front of the PC are for full-length cards only.

Connecting Cables

Connecting cables to an adapter is fairly straightforward, but there are a couple of things you need to know. First, one of the most common types of cable used inside the PC is the *ribbon cable*. A ribbon cable looks something like a ribbon (usually gray) with individual insulated wires side-by-side inside the ribbon. Figure 6.11 shows a ribbon cable.

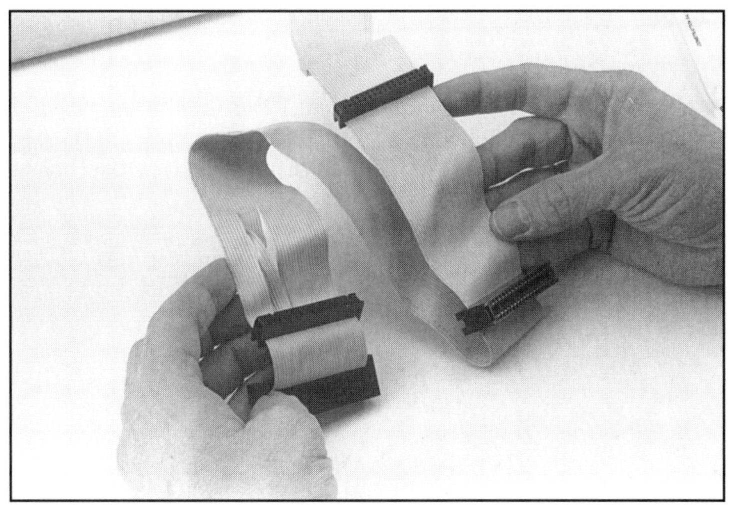

FIG. 6.11
Ribbon cables are usually gray and have multiple wires in them.

Another feature you'll see on a ribbon cable is a colored stripe (usually red) running along one edge of the cable. This stripe indicates pin 1. If you look at a connector for a ribbon cable, you'll see it consists of (usually) two rows of contact pins. If you look closely at the connector, you'll see that one of the pins is labeled as pin 1 (see Figure 6.12). So, when you connect the ribbon cable, make sure you connect it so the colored stripe is on the same side of the connector as pin 1.

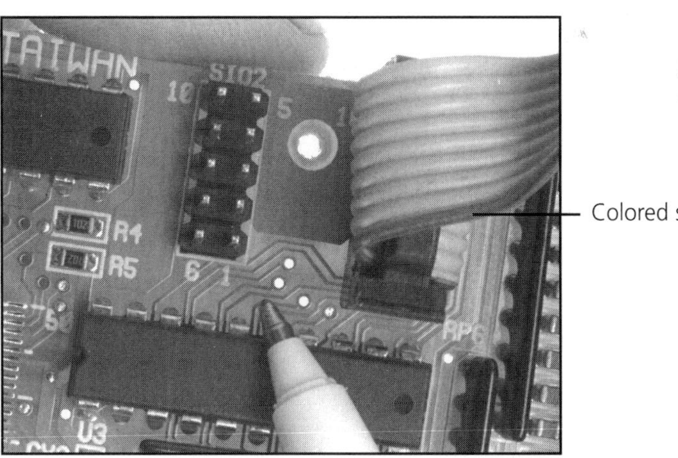

FIG. 6.12
You should find pin 1 labeled on most connections by a number printed on the card.

Sometimes the connectors on one or both ends of the ribbon cable are keyed so they can only install one way in a keyed socket. In a lot of cases though, the pins are not inside any kind of keyed slot, so you have to make sure to pay attention to the location of the colored stripe and pin 1. When you're connecting a ribbon cable, make sure you have the pins lined up with the connector, then gently but firmly push the connector onto the pins.

External connectors are almost always keyed in some way so they can only be connected in one way. Usually, external cables have some kind of retaining screw to hold them securely to the adapter.

PART II

Processors, Motherboards, and Memory

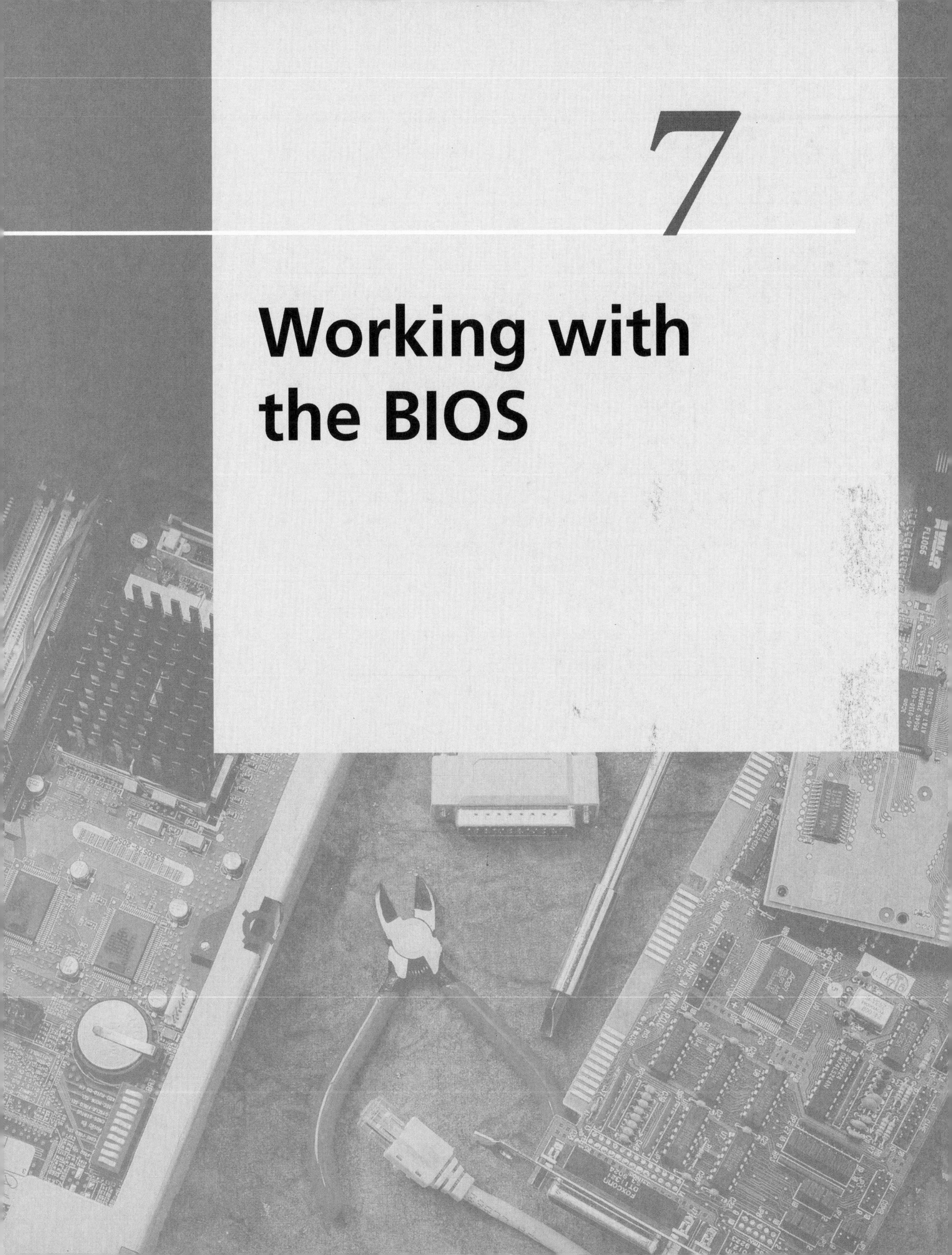

7

Working with the BIOS

Your system BIOS (Basic Input/Output System) has an impact on just about every part of your system because it provides the underlying interface between the CPU and the other components. If yours is an older system, there are some advantages to upgrading the BIOS. If yours is a relatively new system, the BIOS probably is fairly current. Even so, the BIOS manufacturer might have released an update to the BIOS to incorporate new features or fix a possible bug. So, keeping your BIOS up-to-date is important regardless of how old your system is.

This chapter takes a close look at the BIOS, explaining what it is and how you can configure and update your system's BIOS. The chapter covers these topics:

- An overview of the BIOS and what it does
- Replacing a BIOS
- Upgrading a BIOS through software
- Configuring Phoenix, Award, and AMI BIOS settings
- Where to find BIOS upgrades and information

First, you should understand exactly what it is the BIOS is doing in your system.

Overview of the BIOS

The BIOS resides in one or more chips on the computer's motherboard. The BIOS is an *EEPROM (Electrically Erasable Programmable Read-Only Memory)* chip to which the BIOS manufacturer has written program code. This program code, called *firmware* because it represents a blend of hardware and software, enables the computer to perform many basic functions:

- *POST.* The Power On Self Test (POST) tests the computer's hardware. When you see those numbers zipping by on the display during boot, it's the POST performing a memory test. The BIOS POST uses various *beep codes*, or patterns of beeps, to identify specific problems. These beep codes are different from one BIOS to another.
- *Boot the operating system.* The BIOS contains a program called the *bootstrap loader* which is responsible for searching for and starting the operating system boot program. The operating system boot program then takes over control of the computer and boots the operating system.

- *Provide low-level hardware access.* After the operating system is running, program code in the BIOS provides many low-level hardware access functions. These functions enable the CPU to access the hard disk, video controller, and other peripherals.

The BIOS chip on your PC's motherboard is designed specifically for that motherboard's *chip set.* The chip set is a group of one or more special-purpose chips that provide much of the support circuitry for the motherboard. Not every motherboard uses the same chip set, so not every BIOS can be the same. This means that two BIOSes from the same manufacturer are not necessarily the same. Just because two BIOSes are manufactured by AMI, for example, doesn't mean they contain the same code or will work in the same computer.

The link between the chip set and the BIOS also means that you can't just shuffle down to your local discount electronics store and pick up a new BIOS. The BIOS upgrade has to be specifically designed for the chip set used on the motherboard.

But why upgrade the BIOS at all? Your computer has been working just fine, so why tinker with it? Here are a few reasons to upgrade your BIOS:

- *Support for Plug and Play.* Plug and Play (PnP) enables a computer to automatically configure the adapters it contains. Upgrading from a non-PnP BIOS to one that supports PnP enables you to take advantage of automatic configuration. Support for PnP can greatly simplify device configuration during upgrades, but requires adapters that support PnP. Many of the latest and greatest gadgets do support PnP configurations.
- *Support for new hardware.* One of the primary reasons for upgrading the BIOS is to enable your computer to support new hardware that wasn't around when the computer was first built. This includes support for high-capacity floppy disks, improved hard disk support and higher capacity, support for SuperVGA displays, support for additional serial (COM) and parallel (LPT) ports, Universal Serial Bus (USB), and more. Some hardware just won't work if you don't have a BIOS that is recent enough to accommodate it.

- *New BIOS Features.* Most BIOSes include features not related to hardware that make an upgrade desirable. These features include, among others, built-in virus protection and password protection for your system and its BIOS settings.
- *Overcome a BIOS bug.* It isn't very common, but occasionally you'll run into a bug in the BIOS code or a compatibility problem that prevents certain hardware from working properly or at all. The BIOS manufacturers fix the bug in the code and make the updated BIOS code available.

It's a good idea to keep your BIOS relatively current because you'll have fewer compatibility problems and be able to just plug in those new gadgets without worrying about whether they'll be supported by your computer's BIOS. That doesn't mean you should upgrade the BIOS every month, but every six months, at the least, wouldn't be a bad idea.

I'm not suggesting that you physically replace the BIOS every six months. I'm working from the assumption that your current BIOS will be *flash upgradable*, which means you only have to run a program to upgrade the BIOS, not physically replace the BIOS chip. If your system is a 486, you probably will have to replace the BIOS chip to upgrade. In that case, you might upgrade the BIOS now and not upgrade again unless you specifically need some function in the future that the previous upgrade didn't provide.

NOTE Unfortunately, if your current BIOS isn't flash-upgradable, you can't just replace it with one that is. This is due mainly to the fact that the flash programmable BIOS chips use a different pin configuration from the non-flash chips. In other words, the sockets for the chips are different. If your system uses a non-flashable BIOS now, it always will, although you can upgrade the BIOS by a physical replacement.

So, how do you determine what BIOS you have, how current it is, and how to go about upgrading it? Read on.

Collecting Information About Your BIOS and Motherboard

You have to know where you are before you can know where to go. With your BIOS, that means you first need to know what type of BIOS you have and its version number. This one is easy: When you turn on the computer, watch the display closely. During the startup process, the BIOS manufacturer and version number will be displayed, if only for a few seconds. When you first see the BIOS information, press Shift+Pause to pause the display. After you jot down all the necessary information, you can press the spacebar to continue the boot process.

In addition to the BIOS manufacturer and version number, check the initial boot screen for other information about the BIOS. For example, at the bottom of the display you'll probably find additional information about the BIOS, including its date and other information. If nothing else, just write down everything you see and let the people you buy the upgrade from sort out what they need.

The next piece of information you need is the manufacturer of the computer's motherboard. In general, the BIOS upgrade company you talk to should be able to tell what kind of motherboard you have just from the information in the startup screen. If not, you can get the information from your system manuals, which should include a motherboard manual.

If you're buying a BIOS upgrade from the manufacturer of your PC, you'll probably only have to tell them what model you have. If you purchased a Gateway or Dell computer, for example, all you'll have to do is give them your customer number and they should be able to tell you exactly what system you have and what you need to do to upgrade the BIOS. In any case, be armed with the BIOS information from the PC's initial boot screen when you make the call. But, the manufacturer isn't the only source for a new BIOS, as you'll read next.

Finding a BIOS Upgrade

Once you have the information about your current BIOS and motherboard, you're ready to locate a BIOS upgrade. It's important to understand that you're not locked into a specific BIOS manufacturer just because your system's current BIOS is made by that manufacturer. Your system might contain an Award BIOS, for example, but you could switch to an MR BIOS if you choose.

Why switch? You might find that the upgrade BIOS you get from a different company offers additional performance or features not found in the latest BIOS from the company that manufactured your current BIOS. The important point is that you understand that regardless of who you get the BIOS from, it has to be tailored to your computer's motherboard.

You'll find that most BIOS manufacturers don't offer upgrades to end users. Instead, they license their BIOS code to others and let them manufacture and sell upgrades. In particular, Micro Firmware Inc. and Microid Research (Unicore Software) are good bets for locating a BIOS upgrade. This list can help you locate information about your BIOS as well as upgrades:

- *Award*. You'll find a considerable amount of information about Award BIOS and its settings on the Award Web site at **http://www.award.com**. Award doesn't typically provide BIOS upgrades, but instead points you to Unicore Software (see below) for BIOS upgrades.
- *Phoenix*. Phoenix offers some BIOS information on its Web site at **http://www.ptltd.com** but not as much as you'll find at some of the other BIOS manufacturers' sites. Phoenix doesn't provide end-user upgrades, but instead points you to Micro Firmware (see below).
- *American Megatrends Inc. (AMI)*. American Megatrends offers a lot of information on its Web site at **http://www.megatrends.com** about BIOS upgrades. You find a lot of configuration tips and other information. AMI doesn't do end-user BIOS upgrades, but instead points you to Unicore Software (see below).
- *Micro Firmware Inc*. This independent company licenses and markets BIOS upgrades primarily for Phoenix BIOS. If you have a system with a Phoenix BIOS that is old, Micro Firmware can fix you up even if the motherboard is no longer manufactured. You can find Micro Firmware at **http://www.firmware.com**. The phone numbers are 800-767-5465 or 405-321-8333. The fax number is 405-573-5535.
- *TTi Technologies*. This independent company provides upgrades for AMI BIOS. The company also sells Microid Research's MR BIOS. You can reach TTi Technologies at 800-541-1943, or check out its Web site at **http://www.ttitech.com**. You'll find plenty of upgrade information and technical support information about AMI BIOS.
- *Unicore Software (Microid Research)*. Unicore Software is the parent company of Microid Research. Unicore provides a variety of BIOS upgrades, and Microid Research markets MR BIOS, a BIOS upgrade to fit a variety of systems. The phone numbers for Unicore Software are 800-800-BIOS (2467) and 508-686-6468. The fax number is 508-683-1630. You'll find their Web sites at **http://www.unicore.com** and **http://www.mrbios.com**.

It certainly doesn't hurt to shop around a little bit when you're looking for a BIOS upgrade. First, check with the vendor who sold you the computer and see what the price is for an upgrade (and what version you'll get). Then, call up a third-party vendor such as Micro Firmware or Unicore Software and get a price/feature comparison.

What About CMOS Settings?

The BIOS works in conjunction with another chip to store information about your system. When you run the BIOS Setup program, the settings for disk types, memory, and other settings are stored not in the BIOS chip itself, but rather in a non-volatile RAM *(NVRAM)* device on the motherboard. The NVRAM device incorporates the system clock, which enables the system to keep track of the date and time.

You'll often hear these settings referred to as being "stored in CMOS." *CMOS* stands for *Complementary Metal Oxide Semiconductor*, and refers to the type of material used to construct the NVRAM chip. It has nothing to do at all with its function (except that CMOS chips can store and maintain data on very small amounts of current, and are therefore very efficient storage devices). *CMOS settings* are just your system's configuration settings, which you set using the BIOS Setup program, that are stored in NVRAM on the motherboard.

The system settings are maintained by a battery backup that takes many different forms. In many older designs, this battery backup consisted of a battery pack of AA batteries. Some systems used a small sealed battery pack that plugged onto the motherboard. Others use a battery that is either soldered right onto the motherboard or is a replaceable disk battery similar to the ones used in cameras, watches, and other gadgets (only bigger). Other systems use a *capacitor*, which is an electronic device that stores an electrical charge and functions something like a battery. In still other systems, the battery is built right into the NVRAM chip that contains the system clock and stores the system settings.

When the system is on, the battery (or capacitor) is constantly being recharged. When the system is off, the battery backup keeps the configuration information stored in NVRAM. If you disconnect the battery source or the battery goes bad, the settings remain in NVRAM only for a short period of time (typically less than an hour). Then, they're gone and you have to reset everything.

NOTE If you turn on your system one day and it can't access the hard disk, the battery backup might have gone belly up and the system settings have been lost. The fix might be as simple as replacing the battery and restoring the settings.

So, why is all this important? Other than helping you understand where all those settings you provide in the BIOS Setup program are stored, it also will help you overcome a potential problem: losing your BIOS password. Some BIOSes include a feature that lets you specify a system password or a BIOS password. The system password lets you protect the system at boot time—if you don't enter the right password, the system won't even boot. The BIOS password protects the BIOS Setup program—if you don't specify the right password, you can't get into the BIOS Setup program to make any changes.

If you do lose your password, you can discharge the CMOS settings by essentially disconnecting the battery and leaving it disconnected for a few hours. In the case of a system with a built-in battery, you'll have to actually discharge the battery (or capacitor). This can be accomplished by shorting across a couple of jumpers on the motherboard, but typically requires that you use a resistor to prevent frying anything. Therefore, I'm not going to tell you how to do it, as it's different for each system. If you run across this problem, call the technical support department for the PC manufacturer and ask for help. They can steer you toward the right solution.

Physical BIOS Upgrades

If your system doesn't include a flash-programmable BIOS and you want to upgrade the BIOS, you'll have to replace it with a new one. Replacing a chip on the motherboard isn't as difficult as you might think. In fact, it's just as easy as any other upgrade. I'll give you a brief overview before you get into the actual upgrade procedure.

The BIOS is comprised of one to four chips on the motherboard. Consult your system's motherboard manual to locate the BIOS chip(s). Usually, they're located just forward of the adapter bus slots (see Figure 7.1). If all else fails, discharge your static and carefully open the BIOS upgrade package, being careful not to touch the pins on the chips if at all possible (to reduce the risk of static zap). Then compare the new chips with the ones on the motherboard to find ones like it.

FIG. 7.1
The BIOS chips are usually located near the adapter bus slots.

After you locate the BIOS chips, you need to orient yourself a little as to how they are installed. Take a look at the chips and locate the notch on the top of the chip. This notch identifies the location of pin 1 on the chip, which is just to the left of the notch (viewing the chip with the notch facing up). The pins are then numbered sequentially counterclockwise around the chip. The notch corresponds to an identifier on the board to help you install the chip in the slot in its correct orientation.

Figure 7.2 shows the orientation notch on top of a chip, although the chip shown is a 16550 UART chip from an I/O card, not a BIOS chip. If you look closely at the socket and the board, you'll see a notch in the socket, as well as in the outline painted on the board. Match the notches, and you'll have the chip inserted in the right orientation.

FIG. 7.2
This UART chip has a notch at one end that indicates the position of pin 1 and the chip's orientation in its socket.

> **CAUTION** Make sure you install the chip in the right orientation in its socket. If you don't, you'll fry the chip as soon as you turn on the PC, and you'll be paying for another BIOS upgrade.

In addition to noting the correct chip orientation, you also need to keep track of where each chip goes (if your system uses more than one chip in the BIOS set). The motherboard or your motherboard manual might have an indication that one is "high" and the other "low," or one is "odd" and one "even." If you install the BIOS chips in the wrong BIOS chip sockets, you won't hurt the chips, but the system won't start up. If that happens, swap the chips in their sockets and try again.

When you've identified the correct chips and how they should be oriented, you're ready to remove the old ones and install the new ones (make sure you back up your old BIOS settings first, though). Often, a BIOS upgrade will come with a chip extractor, which is a special tool for removing the old chips. If you didn't get a chip extractor, don't worry. You can make do with a small, flat-blade screwdriver or one of the bracket covers from the back of the case. Figure 7.3 shows a socketed UART chip being removed from its socket. You can use the same technique to remove a BIOS chip.

FIG. 7.3
You can remove a chip from its socket by very carefully prying up each end with a small, flat-bladed screwdriver.

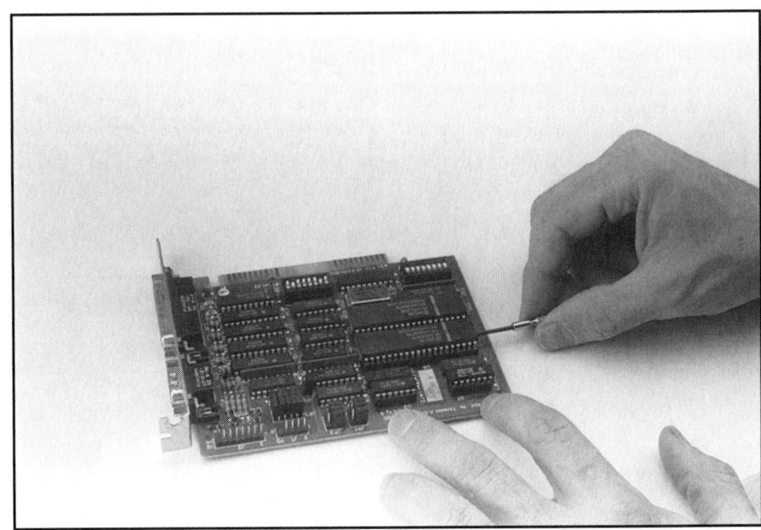

CAUTION Whenever you're working on the motherboard or an adapter, be careful not to scratch the surface of the board. Doing so could damage the *conductor traces,* which are those zillions of lines on the board that look like little wires (and basically, that's what they are).

To get the chip out, first discharge your static, and then insert the tip of the screwdriver under the end of the chip between the chip and the socket. Very gently and slowly pry the end of the chip out of the socket a little way, and then work on the other end of the chip. Move the chip just a little at a time to avoid bending the pins too much.

NOTE You'll find that the short end of a bracket cover (the part that screws to the case) makes a good chip puller. You can put the end of the bracket under the chip and pry *gently* like you would with a screwdriver. Just use care to avoid messing up the socket and chip pins.

When you have the chips out, set them aside where they won't get squashed, mangled, or otherwise abused. After you install the new BIOS chip, you can put the old one in the package that the new ones came in. You might want to save them to make into tie tacks, earrings, electronic cockroaches, or something equally weird.

Before you install the new BIOS chips, you need to make sure the pins are straight. Before picking up the chips, discharge your static. Then look at the chips from an end view. More than likely, the pins will be bowed out slightly from the chip (see Figure 7.4). Holding the ends of the chip, push the pins against a table top or other flat surface until the pins are perpendicular to the chip. Flip the chip over and do the same for the other side.

NOTE The pins don't have to be exactly perpendicular. If the pins aren't bowed out very far, you can simply line up one row of pins in the socket, and then push against the chip slightly as you lower it, lining up the opposite row. Figure 7.5 shows this technique using the UART on an I/O card.

FIG. 7.4
Push the pins against a flat surface until they are perpendicular to the chip body.

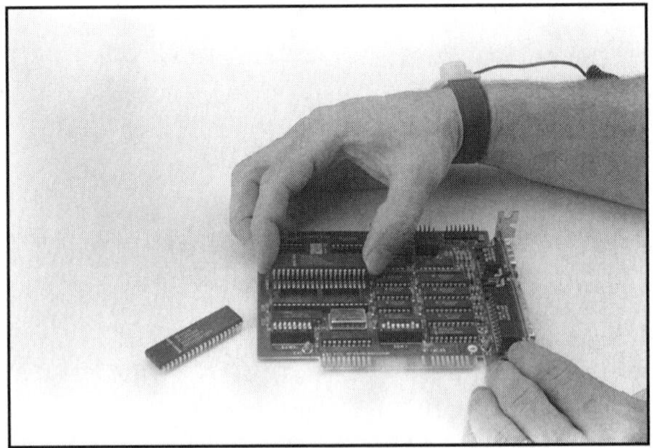

FIG. 7.5
Line up one side of the chip; then jockey the other set of pins into position.

After you have the pins lined up correctly on both sides, take one more look to make sure all of the pins are lined up and none are bent out or underneath the chip. Then, apply gentle but firm pressure using your thumbs or fingers to push the chip firmly into its socket. Figure 7.6 illustrates this, again using a socketed UART chip for the example.

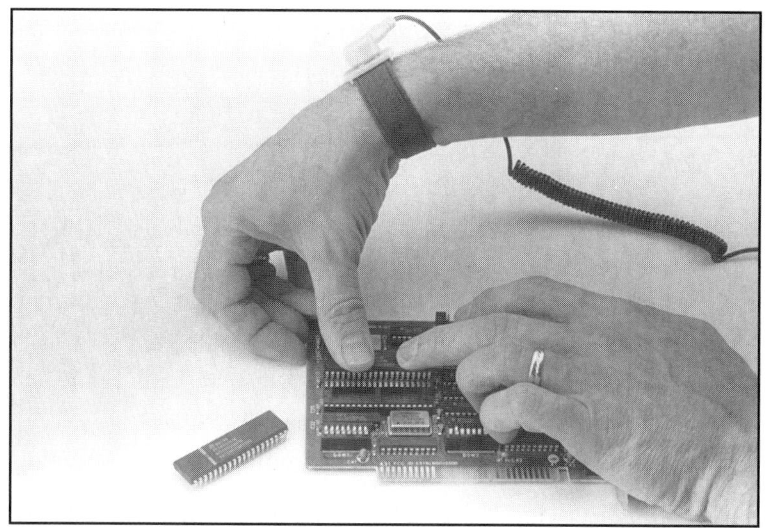

FIG. 7.6
When you're sure all the pins are lined up correctly, push down on the chip gently but firmly to seat it in its socket.

After the chips are in place, double-check your work to make sure you have the chips in the right slots and that they are oriented properly in their slots. When everything looks right, you're ready to turn on the system and set the BIOS settings according to the PC's hardware configuration.

To Replace the BIOS, You Need:

- ☑ The correct BIOS upgrade chips
- ☑ To find the old BIOS chips on the motherboard
- ☑ Chip extractor or small, flat-bladed screwdriver to remove chips
- ☑ A Phillips screwdriver
- ☑ Anti-static wristband or adequate static protection

Now that you have some background, here are the specific steps for replacing the BIOS:

1. Make sure you have backed up your BIOS settings and have a hard copy ready of your hard disk's BIOS settings. See Chapter 2, "Building a Software Safety Kit," if you're not sure how to do that.
2. Shut down and turn off the system.

3. Remove the PC's cover and set it aside.
4. Discharge your static and slip on an anti-static wristband if you have one.
5. Locate the BIOS chips on the motherboard. Use your motherboard manual if you need help locating them. The chips probably are located near the left edge of the board forward of the bus slots.
6. If there are any adapter cards in the way of the BIOS chips, remove them and set them aside. This will require disconnecting the external cables, if any, from the cards, but you might be able to leave any internal cables connected to the cards and just push the cards out of the way.
7. Using either the chip extractor or a small, flat-bladed screwdriver, gently and carefully remove the BIOS chip. (Replace one at a time.)
8. Make sure the pins on the replacement chip are straight, then install the chip, taking care to align the notch on the chip with the notch on the socket.
9. Verify that all the pins are aligned properly; then push the chip into its socket.
10. Repeat steps 6–8 for other BIOS chips if your system uses more than one.
11. Check your work to make sure the chips are installed correctly, especially the orientation of the chips in their sockets.
12. Reinstall any adapters you removed in step 6.
13. Check your work to make sure all the cables are reconnected.
14. Replace the cover, and turn on the system.
15. If the BIOS is installed properly, the system begins to boot. Enter whatever key sequence is required by your BIOS to enter the BIOS Setup program (check your BIOS upgrade manual for the keystrokes needed).
16. Enter the hard disk settings and any other basic system configuration information, leaving the more complex settings alone. For now, you just want to verify that the system can still read the hard disk and boot properly.
17. Save the BIOS Setup configuration settings and let the system reboot.

Flash BIOS Upgrades

If yours is a fairly new PC, it probably contains a flash programmable BIOS. As you read earlier in this chapter, a flash programmable BIOS is a type of EEPROM that can be programmed right in the computer using a special program called a *BIOS loader*. When you program a BIOS this way (sometimes called *flashing the BIOS*), you're actually accomplishing the same thing you do when you physically replace a BIOS—you install new BIOS program code. The only difference is that with a physical upgrade, you have to replace the chip with one containing new BIOS code. With a flash programmable chip, you just replace the old code with new code, but the chip stays the same.

NOTE Before you upgrade the BIOS, make a hard copy of your primary settings, including the hard disk settings.

Even with a flash programmable BIOS, you still need to make sure you get the right version of the BIOS update software designed specifically for your motherboard and chipset. Also, you need to use the correct *loader program* for your particular BIOS. This loader, which is what actually performs the update of the BIOS chip's contents, will come with the updated BIOS software.

Where you get the BIOS update will depend on what type of BIOS you use. Generally, PC vendors make BIOS updates available from their BBS or Web sites. In many cases, the BIOS updates are free, particularly if your system is very new. In some cases, the vendor might charge you something for the update, particularly if the vendor has to send you a disk containing the update.

The actual method and commands you use to upgrade the BIOS will vary according to the BIOS and loader used, but will follow some general guidelines. First, nearly all systems that contain flash programmable BIOS require that a switch or jumper be set on the motherboard to enable the BIOS to be reprogrammed. Without this safeguard, any program that knew how could reprogram the BIOS. Think of a virus programmed to trash your BIOS, and you can see why the safeguard is so widely used. Unless that switch or jumper is set, *nothing* can reprogram the BIOS.

You'll have to check your motherboard and system manual to determine which switch or jumper to set to enable the BIOS to be reprogrammed. Set the switch or jumper, reprogram the BIOS, and then set the switch or jumper back to its safeguard position.

The process you use to actually reprogram the BIOS depends on the BIOS and the loader program. Typically, all you have to do is boot the system to a command prompt and run the upgrade program that you downloaded or which came on a disk from the BIOS company. But, this might pose a bit of a problem for you if you're running Windows 95 or Windows NT. It isn't a major obstacle, but might require a little extra work on your part. Regardless of what operating system your PC is running, you should boot the system without any drivers to ensure that there are no programs in memory that might try to write to the disk or perform some other action while the BIOS is being reprogrammed.

If your system is running DOS 6.x, press the F5 function key when you see the message `Starting MS-DOS` to bypass the CONFIG.SYS and AUTOEXEC.BAT files. If the DOS version is earlier than 6.x, just rename your CONFIG.SYS and AUTOEXEC.BAT files to CONFIG.BAK and AUTOEXEC.BAK. Then, reboot the system. After you perform the BIOS upgrade, rename the files to their original names and reboot the system again.

TIP You might want to use CONFIG.*aaa* and AUTOEXEC.*aaa*, where *aaa* is replaced by your initials. This might help you remember which files are your backup copies.

If you're using Windows 95, you can boot the system to a command prompt by pressing Shift+F5 when you see the `Starting Windows 95` message on the display.

With Windows NT, however, you don't have the option of booting to a command prompt. So, you need to create a bootable system diskette that will allow you to boot the system to a command prompt. This means you need a system running DOS or Windows 95 on which to create the boot disk. If you don't have such a system, find a coworker or friend who has one and ask him or her to make a system disk for you. If all else fails, tell the folks at your local computer store about your problem, and ask if they will make a system disk for you.

General BIOS Configuration Information

The remaining sections of this chapter cover the top four BIOSes used in today's PCs, from Award, Phoenix, AMI, and Microid Research. This section provides some generic information about disk drive configuration and BIOS configuration that apply to all BIOS types.

General Disk Configuration

There are a couple of points you should understand about hard disk configuration before starting to work with your BIOS Setup program. First, you'll find that systems typically support two IDE controllers, each of which is referred to as an *IDE chain*. Each chain can contain up to two hard disks.

With IDE drives, a method called *translation* is needed to convert physical disk locations into logical addressable units. Older IDE drives were limited to less than 504M. Many drives these days are larger than that, and the BIOS typically provides support for an extended translation method to accommodate the larger capacity. You'll generally see translation support referred to as LBA (Logical Block Addressing), ECHS (Extended Cylinder Head Sector), or Large. When you see a drive or translation type of Normal, it typically refers to standard CHS (Cylinder Head Sector) translation, which is the old style with less than 504M.

CAUTION The method the BIOS uses to translate cylinder, head, and sector information is very critical to its capability to read data correctly from the disk. Unless you're sure of the settings, you should use the Auto option to enable the BIOS to choose the right setting automatically. If you choose Auto but the system still can't read the drive, and you know the correct type, choose it in the BIOS Setup. You can get the correct type setting from the hard disk manual or from the drive manufacturer's technical support staff.

I won't go into detail about the differences between the translation methods, because you really don't need to understand them. You just need to be aware that if your disk is larger than 504M, the BIOS needs to be configured for the appropriate extended translation mode.

Also, the new enhanced IDE (EIDE) drives support faster data transfer modes than standard IDE drives. These modes are called *Programmed I/O (PIO) modes.* Table 7.1 lists the PIO modes and their values.

Table 7.1 PIO Modes and Values

PIO Mode	Cycle Time (ns)	Transfer Rate (M/s)	Spec
0	600	3.3	ATA
1	383	5.2	ATA
2	240	8.3	ATA
3	180	11.1	ATA-2
4	120	16.6	ATA-2

If your drive supports PIO, using the highest supported mode gives you the best performance. Using too high a mode, however, results in lost and corrupted data. Use the fastest mode your drive manual indicates it will support, but no higher.

TIP It's very important that you make a hard copy of your system's hard disk parameters before you replace the BIOS, fiddle with its settings, replace the motherboard, or install a new hard disk. If nothing else, write down the disk settings.

General BIOS Configuration

Because a BIOS is tailored specifically to the chipset used on the motherboard, many of the BIOS settings pertain only to a specific chipset. These settings are already optimized by the manufacturer for the system. So, you should avoid fooling with the chipset BIOS settings unless you're working under the guidance of the computer manufacturer's technical support staff.

Rather than cover all of the BIOS settings for each BIOS type, which would be difficult considering the number of possible chipsets involved, the following sections cover the generic settings that are common to most versions of the BIOS. The sections also explain how to enter the Setup program for a particular BIOS, and what special features you should look at in the BIOS to optimize your system's performance.

Configuring an Award BIOS

You enter the Award BIOS Setup program by pressing Delete as soon as you turn on the computer, or by pressing Delete or Ctrl+Alt+Esc when you see a message similar to the following:

```
TO ENTER SETUP BEFORE BOOT PRESS CTRL-ALT-ESC OR DEL KEY
```

Once the Setup program has started, you can use the function keys, cursor arrow keys, Page Up/Page Down keys, and +/– keys to move through the program and choose options.

TIP The Award BIOS provides an override feature that lets you override the stored BIOS settings with system defaults. Using the system defaults enables you to restore the original default settings in the event you make a BIOS setting change that causes problems or causes the system to hang. To invoke the override settings, press the Insert key as soon as the system begins to boot.

Generic BIOS Settings

The specific menu items in the Award BIOS Setup program vary from one motherboard type to another because they are tailored to the motherboard, but most Award BIOSes share a generic set of Setup sections. These include the following:

- *Standard CMOS Setup.* This page includes common system settings such as date and time, hard disk type, floppy disk type, and other basic hardware configuration settings.

- *BIOS Features Setup.* This page contains BIOS-specific features such as type of virus warning, system boot sequence (A:C or C:A), Quick POST, and other general settings.
- *Password Setting.* This page lets you specify a password for the system or for the BIOS Setup program itself.
- *Chipset Features Setup.* This page enables you to set chipset-specific BIOS features. You should only change these if you fully understand the ramifications of the change or at the direction of a technical expert.
- *Power Management Setup.* This entry only appears if your system supports Power Management, Green PC, standards. Its settings control power management features of your system.
- *PCI Configuration Setup.* This entry only appears if your system contains a PCI bus. It enables you to control various aspects of the PCI bus, including how interrupts are assigned to the PCI slots.
- *Load BIOS Defaults.* These settings have been configured by the system manufacturer, and should provide optimum performance for your system. Use this option if you think some of the current BIOS settings are causing problems with the system.
- *Load Setup Defaults.* These settings apply to the chipset-specific features of the BIOS. Load these defaults if you think system performance is being negatively affected by some of the current chipset settings.
- *IDE HDD Auto Detection.* This option enables the BIOS to automatically detect and configure the settings for your IDE hard disk.
- *HDD Low-Level Format.* This option provides a low-level hard disk format utility if your system supports it.
- *Save & Exit Setup.* This item lets you save setting changes to CMOS and exit setup.
- *Exit Without Save.* This item lets you abandon all setting (not save them) changes and exit setup.

Many of the generic settings are self-obvious. For example, I don't need to tell you what the date and time settings are for. However, some of the settings might be a little confusing to you, particularly if you're fairly new to the internals of a computer. The following sections explain some of these settings.

Advanced Award BIOS Settings

The following list explains some of the advanced BIOS settings you might want to modify (not all settings are included):

- *Virus Warning.* If you enable this setting, the BIOS monitors the boot sector and partition table for any attempted modification. If a program tries to modify either, the system halts and displays a message prompting you to accept whether or not the program can alter the boot sector or partition table. Because many disk diagnostic programs attempt to write to the boot sector or partition table, you should disable this BIOS setting before running the disk diagnostic software.
- *Quick Power On Self Test.* Enable this setting to speed up the boot process. When this setting is enabled, the BIOS shortens and skips some hardware tests.
- *Boot Up System Speed.* The default setting—high—places the CPU at its fastest speed. Generally, the only reason to use the slow speed is to run an old DOS program that won't run at the higher speed.
- *IDE HDD Block Mode.* If enabled, the BIOS can read to and write from the hard disk using block mode, which transfers data in blocks, rather than in bytes. This means that more data can be transferred in one read/write operation, speeding up performance. Enable this setting only if your disk supports block transfers.
- *Memory Parity Check.* When the system boots, the BIOS tests the system's memory for *parity errors,* which effectively tests the consistency of the memory. If this setting is enabled and a parity error is encountered, the system halts. Otherwise, the system continues to boot, giving you the choice of using the system even with questionable memory (possibly beneficial for troubleshooting).
- *Security Option.* Use this setting to determine whether or not the system or the BIOS Setup program will be protected by passwords. Bear in mind, though, that if you forget the password, you won't be able to boot the system or access the Setup program. Your only recourse is to discharge the CMOS to clear out the settings. If you choose the System option, the password is required at boot and also when you enter the Setup program.

Choosing the Setup option requires the password only when you enter Setup. Choose the Password Setting option from the main menu to specify the password. To disable the password, just press Enter at the Enter Password prompt without typing a password.

- *System BIOS Shadow.* If this setting is enabled, the system BIOS code is copied to RAM for faster execution, speeding up the system.
- *Video BIOS Shadow.* If this setting is enabled, the video BIOS code is copied to RAM, speeding up video performance.
- *annnn-annnn Shadow.* The memory ranges included under this setting (such as in the form C8000-CFFFF) let you specify whether or not the ROM BIOS ranges specified will be copied into RAM for faster performance. If you have a SCSI host adapter at the address range C8000-CFFFF, for example, enabling shadowing for that range could increase disk performance.

In addition to these settings, your BIOS supports a wide range of chipset-specific settings. In general, you should use the default values because they have been optimized for your system by the manufacturer.

Configuring a Phoenix BIOS

When you boot a system containing a Phoenix BIOS, you should see a message indicating that you can press F2 to enter the BIOS Setup program:

```
Press <F2> to enter Setup
```

After the Setup program is running, you can use the cursor keys, plus and minus keys, and other keys as indicated at the bottom of the Setup screen to select menu items and options.

The Phoenix Setup program includes the following main menu items:

- *Main.* This item contains general system information such as the date and time, hard disk type, floppy disk type(s), and other common hardware settings.
- *Advanced.* This item enables you to set advanced chipset-specific settings.
- *Security.* You can use this item to set User and Supervisor passwords, as well as backup and virus protection settings.

- *Power.* You can use this item to set power management features.
- *Exit.* Use this option to exit the Setup program.

The following list describes some of the settings you might want to modify to optimize the way your system runs:

- *Plug and Play OS.* You can set this to Auto, Yes, or No. If you set it to Yes, the operating system will configure PnP devices. If set to No, the BIOS configures PnP devices. Auto selects Yes if the OS is PnP-aware. Until Windows NT supports PnP, this only pertains to Windows 95 (which does support PnP). If you're having problems with Windows 95 correctly setting up devices, choose No and let the BIOS configure them.
- *Autotype Fixed Disk.* This option enables the BIOS to automatically detect and configure the hard disk settings, which allows the BIOS to correctly identify the disk type in most cases. If the BIOS can't properly detect your disk's type, choose the correct type from the Type setting, or choose User to specify your own settings. You'll find a discussion of disk settings in Chapter 11, "Hard Disks."
- *Multi-Sector Transfers.* This setting specifies the number of sectors to be transferred in one block. The Standard selection is one sector per block. If Block PIO is enabled, the MAX *n* option specifies the maximum possible block size, but the maximum size doesn't necessarily mean the fastest transfer speed.
- *LBA Mode Control.* This setting enables/disables Logical Block Addressing, which provides support for disks larger than 504M. The default is Disabled. If your disk requires LBA addressing, you should enable this setting.
- *32-Bit I/O.* This setting enables/disables 32-bit communications between the CPU and IDE adapter. A 32-bit transfer speeds performance but requires a PCI or VL bus.
- *Transfer Mode.* This setting specifies the mode used to transfer data between the disk and memory. The available options depend on the disk subsystem's capabilities. If the disk supports a PIO or DMA transfer method, choosing one of these options gives the best performance.
- *Cache System BIOS.* Enable this setting to cache the area of RAM in which the system BIOS has been shadowed (copied). Caching can improve system performance.

- *Cache Video BIOS.* Enable this setting to cache the area of RAM in which the video BIOS has been shadowed. This can improve video performance.
- *Cache annn-annn.* Indicates whether or not to cache the specified range of memory. Use these settings to cache secondary BIOS, such as from a SCSI disk adapter, to improve performance.
- *System Shadow.* Enable this setting to copy the system BIOS from ROM into RAM to make the system perform better.
- *Video Shadow.* Enable this setting to copy the video BIOS from ROM into RAM for better video performance.
- *Shadow Option ROMs.* Enable shadowing of individual ranges with these settings if you have secondary BIOS in the system, such as for a SCSI hard disk adapter. Shadowing the ROM can make the device perform better.
- *Boot Sequence.* Use this setting to specify the order in which the BIOS searches for a boot device. You can choose A: then C:, C: then A:, or C: only. Choosing C: only prevents the system from trying to boot from a floppy and can help avoid boot sector virus infections, which occur when booting from a virus-infected disk.
- *Setup Prompt.* When this setting is enabled, the message `Press <F2> for Setup` appears during boot. Disable this setting if you don't want this message to appear (making it potentially more difficult for someone to access your BIOS Setup program in your absence).
- *Floppy Seek.* Disable this setting if you don't want the BIOS to attempt to detect the floppy drives at boot. This doesn't affect the drives' abilities to function and speeds the boot process.
- *Summary Screen.* Disable this setting if you don't want the hardware summary screen to appear during boot. Disabling it speeds up the boot process slightly.
- *Supervisor Password.* Use this option to specify a password to be entered in order to access the BIOS Setup program. When you enter the supervisor password, you have unrestricted access to all Setup menus.
- *Set User Password.* Use this option to specify a user password for accessing the BIOS Setup program. When you enter the user password, you have limited access to the Setup program (to change date, time, and so on).
- *Password On Boot.* If enabled, the system prompts for a password at boot. You also must set the Supervisor password and enter that password at boot time to boot the system.

- *Diskette Access.* You can set this to Supervisor or User. Setting it to Supervisor prevents a user from accessing the floppy drives, a good way to prevent introduction of viruses and unwanted software, and prevent theft of data or programs.
- *Fixed Disk Boot Sector.* Set this to Write Protected if you want the system to warn you when the boot sector is about to be modified (a possible indication of a virus attack).
- *System Backup Reminder* and *Virus Check Reminder.* You can set these to Disabled, Daily, Weekly, or Monthly. If not disabled, these settings cause the system to display a reminder to back up the system and run virus software.

Configuring an AMI BIOS

American Megatrends Inc. not only develops and licenses its own BIOS, it also develops and sells a line of motherboards. AMI provides BIOS upgrades for its own motherboards, but does not provide end-user upgrades for other motherboards that use AMI BIOS. Instead, AMI points you to TTi Technologies and Microid Research for a BIOS upgrade.

When you boot a system containing an AMI BIOS, you should see the following message:

```
Hit <Del> to run Setup
```

Just press the Delete key to enter the Setup program.

Generic BIOS Settings

More than likely, your system's BIOS supports a selection of hard disk configuration settings for each drive in the system. You'll probably see the following terms in the BIOS Setup screen relating to disk drives:

- *Pri Master.* The master drive on the primary chain. The system supports two IDE chains, each of which can support two devices.
- *Pri Slave.* The slave drive on the primary chain. Note that *slave* simply refers to the secondary drive and doesn't indicate that the drive is in any way physically or logically slaved to the master.

- *Sec Master.* The master drive on the secondary IDE chain.
- *Sec Slave.* The slave drive on the secondary chain.

The following list will help you decipher the options in the drive parameters:

- *LBA/Large Mode.* LBA stands for *Logical Block Addressing*, and this mode enables support for IDE hard disks with capacities larger than 504M. LBA mode was introduced for IDE with the ATA-2 specification but has always been used for SCSI disks. Large Mode refers to Extended CHS (Cylinder Head Sector) translation, and provides the same support for high capacity drives as LBA. Large mode is for disks with more than 1,024 cylinders but which do not support LBA. See the caution immediately following this list.
- *Block Mode.* Block mode enables the disk to read larger amounts of data at one time (called a *block*) rather than individual bytes. This setting should be on for drives that support block mode and off for those that do not.
- *32-Bit Mode.* This setting enables 32-bit access to the drive through the BIOS, which speeds performance. Most IDE drives do support 32-bit access; however, the system also must contain a PCI or VL bus.
- *PIO Mode.* There are various levels of PIO that support different cycle times and transfer rates (refer to Table 7.1). Choosing Auto enables the BIOS to automatically detect and configure the correct mode.

CAUTION If your system is working fine and can read the disk, don't switch from one disk mode to another. Doing so could prevent the system from being able to read the disk.

The following settings are generally available on the Advanced Setup page:

- *Quick Boot.* This option, if enabled, causes the POST to execute more quickly because it bypasses some of the tests.
- *Boot Up Sequence.* This setting specifies the order in which the BIOS will search for a boot device. The default is C:, A:, CDROM, which means it looks on drive C for the operating system first, then drive A, then the CD-ROM drive.

- *Boot Up CPU Speed.* Use this setting to specify whether the CPU starts up in high or low speed. The only reason to use low speed is to run a DOS program that won't run at fast speed.
- *Floppy Drive Seek.* This setting determines whether or not the BIOS performs a seek test on the floppy disk drive(s) at boot. Disable it to speed up boot time (has no effect on the disks' abilities).
- *Password Check.* This setting determines whether a password is required at boot to run the BIOS Setup program. Choosing Always causes a password to be requested each time the system is turned on. Choosing Setup causes the password to be requested only for running Setup.

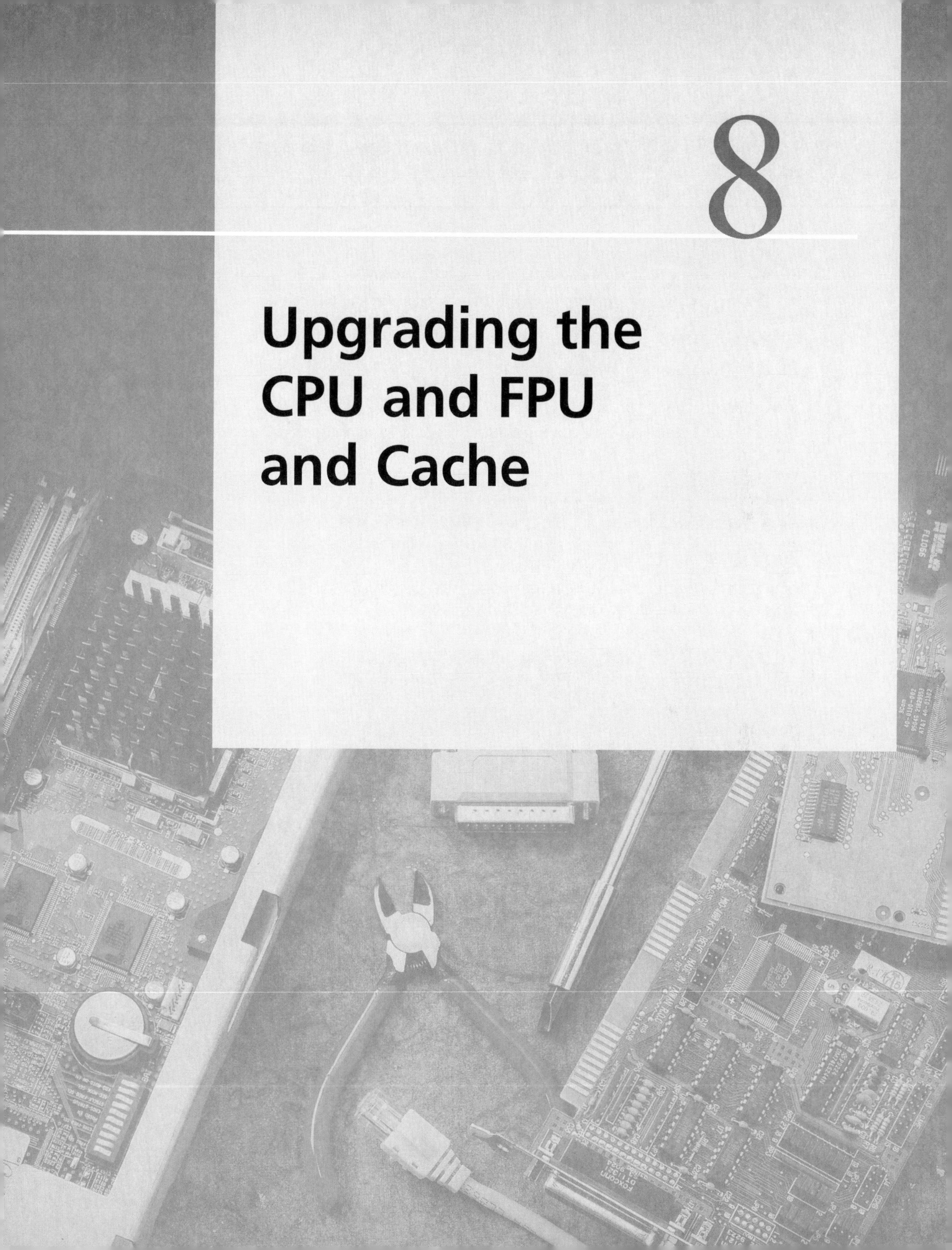

8

Upgrading the CPU and FPU and Cache

One of the best, most cost-effective upgrades you can perform short of replacing the PC's motherboard is to replace the CPU. In some cases with just a few hundred dollars, you can make a tremendous impact on your PC's speed and capabilities.

This chapter covers CPU upgrades, and also takes a look at the *Floating Point Unit (FPU)*, also called a *math coprocessor*. The chapter covers these topics:

- Overview of CPU and FPU upgrade options
- Replacing the CPU
- Installing an Intel OverDrive processor
- Installing a processor upgrade module

You should first have some background about the CPU and FPU to learn what they do. This will give you a better understanding of what your upgrade options are.

CPU and FPU Overview

CPU stands for *Central Processing Unit*. The CPU is the brains of the computer and is where the majority of the actual computing takes place. Figure 8.1 shows a typical CPU—an Intel 80486-DX33 (a 33MHz 486 chip).

FIG. 8.1
This Intel 486-33 CPU is shown installed on a motherboard.

In the early days of the IBM-compatible PC, all PC CPUs were manufactured by Intel Corporation. The first IBM PC used an Intel 8088 CPU. Six CPU generations later features the Intel Pentium Pro (see Figure 8.2), which can think circles around the old 8088 chip. Table 8.1 lists some interesting information about the Intel CPU line.

FIG. 8.2
The Pentium Pro processor is considerably larger than the Pentium processor.

Table 8.1 Intel CPU Specifications

CPU	Maximum Addressable Memory	Internal FPU	Internal Register Size	Data Bus Width
8088	1M	No	16-bit	8-bit
8086	1M	No	16-bit	16-bit
286	16M	No	16-bit	16-bit
386SX	16M	No	32-bit	16-bit
386SL	16M	No	32-bit	16-bit
386DX	4G	No	32-bit	32-bit
486SX	4G	No	32-bit	32-bit
486SX2	4G	No	32-bit	32-bit
487SX	4G	Yes	32-bit	32-bit
486SL	4G	Optional	32-bit	32-bit
486DX	4G	Yes	32-bit	32-bit
486DX2	4G	Yes	32-bit	32-bit
486DX4	4G	Yes	32-bit	32-bit
Pentium OD	4G	Yes	32-bit	32-bit
Pentium	4G	Yes	32-bit	64-bit
Pentium Pro	64G	Yes	32-bit	64-bit

NOTE The part numbers of the Intel chips are actually different from those shown in Table 8.1. The 286, for example, is actually the 80286. The 386 is the 80386, and so on. Intel originally planned to name the Pentium the *586*, but decided on the name *Pentium* so it could copyright the name.

The Maximum Addressable Memory column indicates the maximum amount of memory the CPU can address. As you can see, the 8088 and 8086, which were functionally identical except for the width of the data bus, were limited to just 1M of memory. The Pentium Pro, by contrast, can address 64G of memory—65,535 times as much memory as the 8088/8086. The capability to address more memory means the computer can use memory more efficiently and work with larger operating systems, more programs, and bigger data files without having to use memory voodoo (like expanded memory) to accommodate it all. (For a more in-depth explanation of memory, see Chapter 10, "Adding Memory.")

NOTE If you know much about DOS, you know that it is limited to 1M, even when running on a new processor. This is because DOS was written for the 8088 processor, which also had a limit of 1M. Newer operating systems like Windows 95 and Windows NT aren't limited by this 1M barrier.

The Internal FPU column indicates whether or not the CPU contains an internal FPU. The FPU speeds up math operations and improves the performance of programs that can take advantage of the FPU. Some programs require an FPU, but most do not. Many programs that do support the FPU don't require it, but simply take advantage of it if it's present. Unfortunately, Windows doesn't take advantage of the FPU to improve its own performance. With today's fast processors, though, it really doesn't need to.

NOTE The early 486SX CPUs actually do have an FPU, but Intel disabled it and marketed the chip as a lower-cost alternative to the 486DX.

The Internal Register Size column essentially indicates how much information the CPU can process at one time. The higher the number of bits, the more information it can handle. The Data Bus Width column indicates the number of bits of data the CPU can transfer at one time. The more bits it can transfer at a time, the faster and more efficiently the system will operate.

NOTE There are a lot of other specifications for the chips that aren't included in Table 8.1 simply because it is information you really don't need to know. For example, the 8088 contains 29,000 transistors and the Pentium Pro contains

5,500,000 transistors—quite a difference and a big indicator of why the Pentium Pro is so much more powerful than the 8088. It might be interesting party conversation, but not useful upgrade information.

Other companies have come along in recent years to challenge Intel's dominance in the IBM-compatible PC CPU market. Cyrix, AMD, and Texas Instruments all manufacture Intel-compatible CPUs, and it's possible that your system contains one of these chips. These chips provide roughly the same performance as their Intel counterparts.

A Little About Processor Modes

CPUs run in different *operating modes*. These include *Real mode*, *Protected mode*, and *Virtual Real mode*. Real mode emulates the mode in which the 8088, or original IBM PC, ran. When a 486 chip runs in Real mode, it's just like a really fast 8088 chip.

Protected mode provides more advanced memory management, including access to much more memory than the 1M limit of Real mode. Protected mode also opened the door to *multitasking*, or the computer's capability to run more than one task at a time.

Virtual Real mode, usually referred to as just *Virtual mode*, offers the capability to run multiple Real mode sessions under Protected mode. This means that the processor can create "virtual 8088 computers" and run a different DOS program in each one. Virtual mode is the mechanism by which Windows can multitask DOS programs.

The 286 supports Real and Protected modes, but isn't able to switch from Protected mode to Real mode without resetting the computer. It can, however switch from Real mode to Protected mode without a reset. The 386 and later processors support all three modes and can switch among them without a hardware reset.

What About Speed?

Each CPU has a specific *clock speed*. The clock speed indicates the number of cycles per second at which the CPU operates internally. The speed of a CPU is measured in *megahertz (MHz)*, or millions of cycles per second (one hertz equals one cycle per second).

One *cycle* is the smallest amount of time the processor can use. The old 8088 systems take about 12 cycles to execute one instruction. The Pentium takes on average just one cycle to execute an instruction. So, the clock speed on the chip isn't an absolute rating of its performance. A 100MHz 8088 chip would still take 12 cycles per instruction compared to a 100MHz Pentium and its one cycle per instruction. Roughly, this means the Pentium would run about 12 times faster than the 8088 at the same clock speed (not absolutely true, but close enough for us).

Within the same CPU type, however, clock speed *is* significant, with higher clock speeds meaning faster performance. A 200MHz Pentium system will definitely outperform a 100MHz Pentium system by a wide margin. The overall performance of the system is called its *throughput*, and takes into account how much the system can get done in a given amount of time, not just how fast the clock runs. The more efficient the system's design, the greater its throughput. So, two 200MHz systems from different manufacturers will perform somewhat differently in terms of overall throughput.

What's in Your System?

Before you start thinking about a CPU upgrade, you need to determine exactly what you have. The surest way is to remove the PC's cover and have a look at the chip. In some cases, though, you won't be able to see the chip itself because it will have a *heat sink* (see Figure 8.3) or a fan (see Figure 8.4) mounted to its top. The heat sink and the fan both serve to draw away the heat that the chip generates. The heat sink consists of cooling fans not much different in theory from the fans on a radiator. The cooling fan is actually a small *muffin fan*, complete with a spinning fan blade, that draws heat away from the CPU. Some fans are mounted permanently to the CPU with a heat-transferring adhesive, while others clip or screw on.

FIG. 8.3
A heat sink adds surface area to the top of the chip to help draw heat away from the chip.

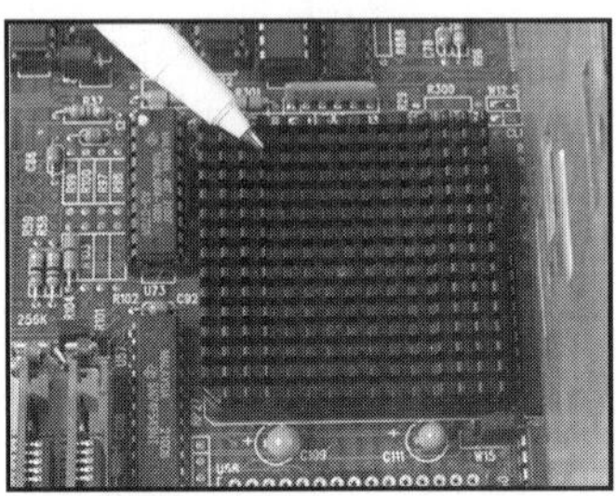

NOTE In many cases, you'll find that the CPU has both a heat sink and a CPU fan for the best possible cooling.

Depending on your BIOS, you'll probably be able to find the information about your CPU on one of the system's initial boot screens. Most systems display information about the system's hardware just before beginning to load the operating system. This information typically includes not only the CPU type and speed, but also the hard disk type, amount of memory, and other information. Be ready to press Shift+Pause when this information screen appears, because it will zip by very quickly otherwise. Press the spacebar to continue the boot process after you've noted the CPU type and speed.

FIG. 8.4
A fan mounts to the top of the CPU and draws heat away from it.

If you do decide to open the PC to check out the CPU, you'll find the CPU type and speed printed on top of the chip (assuming it isn't obstructed by a heat sink or fan) as shown in Figure 8.5. In some cases, you'll also find the chip information printed on the bottom of the chip (see Figure 8.6). If you're taking the chip out anyway, this is a good way to determine the chip type.

If you're having trouble locating the CPU, just look for the largest chip on the motherboard. It will be the CPU. In most motherboard designs, the CPU is located forward (toward the front of the PC) of the bus slots where the adapters install. In an ATX design in which the motherboard sits in the case with the long side parallel to the back of the PC, the CPU is located near the right edge of the motherboard near the power supply cooling fan (see Figure 8.7).

NOTE When you see references to *orientation* in this book, keep in mind that the orientation changes from a desktop case to a tower or mini-tower case. Unless you read otherwise, assume that references to orientation are about desktop cases. If you place a tower case on its right side so you're looking down at the motherboard, the orientation will be the same as for a desktop case.

FIG. 8.5
You'll find the CPU type and speed printed on top of the chip.

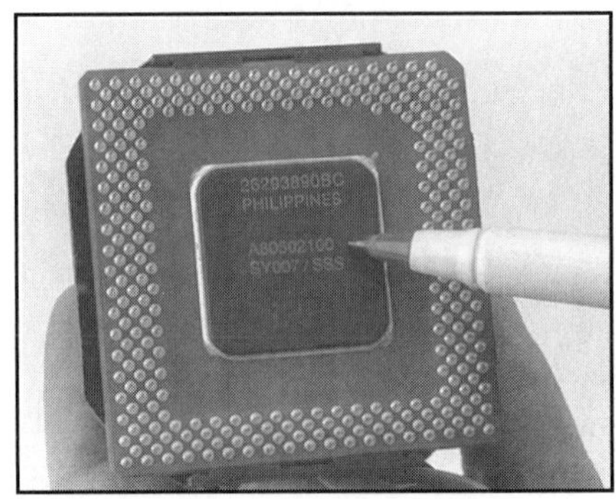

FIG. 8.6
The chip type and speed is often printed on the bottom of the chip.

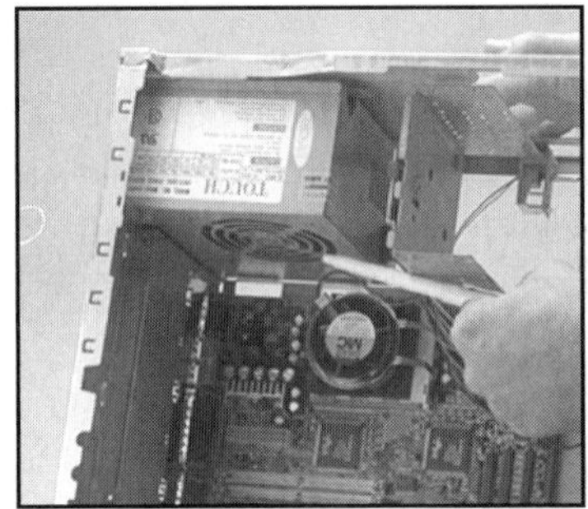

FIG. 8.7
In an ATX configuration system, the CPU is mounted near the power supply for better cooling.

Make sure to note the CPU manufacturer (Intel or other), CPU type (386, 486, and so on), and CPU speed. The speed is expressed in multiples of 25 or 33, with a higher number meaning a faster clock rate. Today's top CPU speed for PCs is 200MHz, although faster chips will be available as soon as new manufacturing techniques are used.

Another thing to take note of when you inventory your PC's CPU is the type of socket in which the chip is installed. There are two primary types: LIF and ZIF. In both cases, the CPU has pins that stick out of the bottom and are inserted into holes in the sockets.

LIF Sockets

LIF stands for *Low Insertion Force*, which means (theoretically) that it doesn't take much force to insert or remove the CPU. Figure 8.8 shows a LIF socket. You insert a CPU in a LIF socket by simply aligning the pins and pushing the CPU down into the socket for a snug fit.

FIG. 8.8
Friction (a tight fit) holds the CPU in place in a LIF socket.

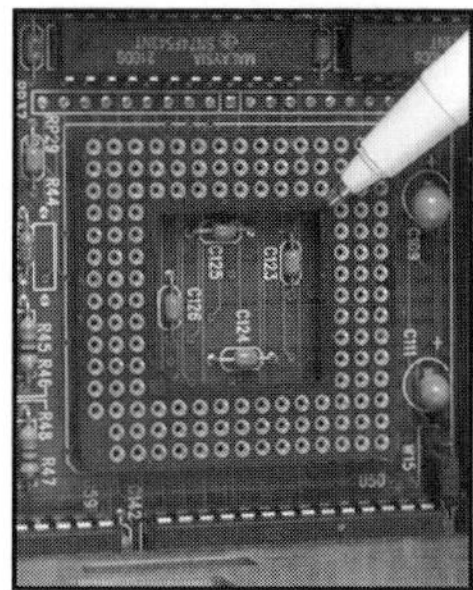

You need a special tool to remove a CPU from a LIF socket, although a flat object like a small screwdriver or a blank case bracket will work if you're very, very careful (more on that later). The correct tool for the job is just a piece of thin metal bent at one end that slips between the socket and the chip. You pry the CPU out with the tool by prying gently on alternate edges of the chip until it comes free of the socket. Typically, upgrade processors come with this tool so you can remove the old CPU. If you don't have one, you can probably borrow one from a local computer retailer/ repair center.

ZIF Sockets

ZIF stands for *Zero Insertion Force*, and that's just how much force you need to install and remove the CPU—zero. The ZIF socket has a small locking lever at one side that closes to lock the CPU in place. You just place the CPU in the socket and push down the locking lever. When you need to remove the CPU, you just pull up the lever and lift out the CPU. Figure 8.9 shows a ZIF socket with the lever being lowered to lock the CPU into place.

NOTE The processors on some older motherboards are soldered in place. You can't desolder these and solder a new one in place. Okay, technically you can, but you'll probably burn up the CPU and components on the board. There are upgrade modules available that accommodate these types of systems, but *Upgrading PCs Illustrated* doesn't cover them because such systems are so old that it's typically best to replace them altogether or replace the motherboard.

FIG. 8.9
A ZIF socket requires no force at all to insert or remove the CPU because a special locking mechanism holds the CPU in place.

OverDrive Sockets and Processors

A third type of CPU socket you'll find on many 486 motherboards is the *OverDrive socket*, which was designed to accommodate the Intel OverDrive upgrade processors. Intel conceived the OverDrive line of processors as a way for users to easily upgrade their systems without having to replace the motherboard.

There actually are multiple types of OverDrive sockets, each of which is designed for a particular type of CPU. If you open your PC and find that there is a large, empty socket on the motherboard roughly the size (or larger) of the system's CPU, that's the OverDrive socket.

Originally, Intel intended the OverDrive chip to be installed in the OverDrive socket and the old CPU removed or disabled. However, Intel later redesigned the OverDrive processors to be pin-compatible with the original CPU and installed in place of the CPU, rather than in the OverDrive socket. If you buy an OverDrive processor today, you'll be removing the old CPU and replacing it with the OverDrive. This means you can upgrade the system with an OverDrive chip even if the system doesn't contain an OverDrive socket.

The only situation in which you need to use the OverDrive socket is if your CPU is soldered in place, as it was on some 486 systems. The original CPU will remain in place but be disabled.

Some systems require an *interposer* be installed between the OverDrive CPU and the socket. The interposer eliminates a problem in the lack of support on some motherboards for the Pentium OverDrive's write-back cache, which can manifest itself as a nonfunctioning floppy drive, among other ways. The interposer simply disables the write-back cache. Figure 8.10 shows an OverDrive processor and interposer. Note that the interposer is really just a special socket adapter for the OverDrive chip.

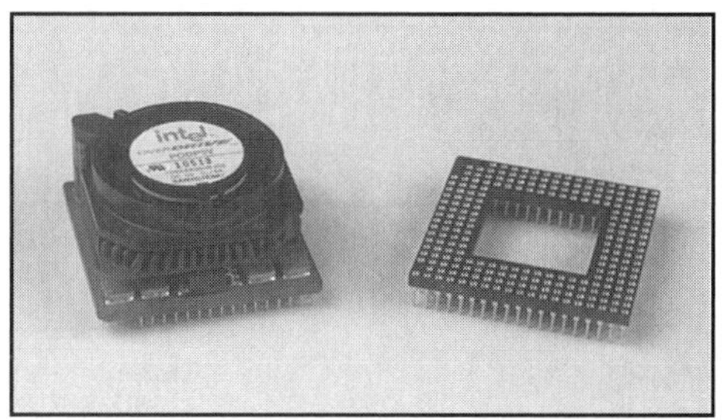

FIG. 8.10
Some systems require that an interposer be installed between the OverDrive processor and the socket.

Before buying a CPU upgrade, check with your system manufacturer's technical support staff to determine if your system requires an interposer.

Choosing a CPU/FPU Upgrade

The CPU upgrade you choose depends on your system motherboard's design and its current CPU. The following sections explore the options you have for upgrading specific processors.

Upgrades for 286 and 386 Systems

You can buy upgrade modules that will bring a 286 or 386 system up to the performance of a relatively fast 486 system. The best thing about these upgrades is their price—upgrades range from $100 to about $150. Because a motherboard replacement will probably cost from $250 to $350 excluding memory to bring the system up to a 100MHz Pentium, the processor upgrade is a good alternative if you don't have the bucks for a more complete upgrade.

Make-It 286 to 486, from Improve It Technologies, is one option for upgrading your old 286 system (see Figure 8.11). At about $150, it's a good investment if the rest of your system is up to speed (enough disk space, acceptable video, and so on).

For upgrading 386 systems, another product to check out is Evergreen REV to 486, from Evergreen Technologies (see Figure 8.12). Upgrade prices range from $100 to $200, depending on your current processor. You'll end up with a 66MHz or 75MHz 486 system. Improve It Technologies also offers a 386 upgrade called Make-It 486 that sells for about $100. As with a 286 upgrade, you should also check out the price of a motherboard replacement to see which one makes more sense for you. You might decide that the extra $150 or so is worth having a Pentium motherboard.

FIG. 8.11
Make-It 286 to 486 upgrades a 386SX system to a 486 system.

FIG. 8.12
The Evergreen REV to 486 upgrades a 386 system to a 486 system.

NOTE When you're pricing a motherboard replacement, keep in mind that you might need to buy new memory for the motherboard rather than use the existing memory in your old system. Include the cost of 16M of new RAM for the motherboard in the price comparison.

For the most part, upgrading a 286 this way makes sense if you intend to continue using DOS on the system. If you want to also upgrade to Windows 95, I'd replace the motherboard instead or just buy a new system. You'll get better performance and be happier with the system overall. Just bear in mind that you might also have to add another hard disk, replace the video card (for better performance), and make other changes to the system if you decide to upgrade to Windows 95.

Upgrades for 486 Systems

A lot of upgrade options exist for 486 systems. Evergreen Technologies offers the Evergreen 586 that upgrades a 486 system to the equivalent of a 75MHz Pentium. Prices range from $130 to $160 depending on your current processor type. Gainbery offers a similar product called CPU MAXimizer GB586 that ranges in cost from $120 to $150. Improve It Technologies markets the Make-It 586/100 that sells for about $170. These are all great upgrade options for 486 systems, because unlike the Pentium OverDrive upgrade from Intel, they will work in all 486 systems.

Another upgrade option for 486 systems is a 486DX4, which brings your system from its current 486 processor to a 100MHz 486 (see Figure 8.13). The 486DX4 replaces the existing processor so you don't need an OverDrive socket. This is a good option for early 486 systems that contain a nonfunctional OverDrive socket (which was designed prior to the OverDrive chip and won't work with it). The 486DX4 upgrade is a way to double, triple, or quadruple the clock speed of your system. It's a quick upgrade, requiring only a replacement of the CPU. And at $100, it's a good investment. If you have the little extra to invest, however, I'd go with one of the upgrade options from Evergreen, Gainbery, or Improve It Technologies.

FIG. 8.13
The 486DX4 replaces the existing 486 CPU to bring the system speed up to 100MHz.

Many 486 systems will accommodate a Pentium OverDrive processor upgrade. Table 8.2 lists the Intel Pentium OverDrive processor upgrades for 486 systems.

Table 8.2 Intel Pentium OverDrive Upgrades for 486 Systems

Current 486 CPU	CPU Speed	OverDrive Upgrade
486SX/DX	33MHz	83MHz Pentium
486DX2	66MHz	83MHz Pentium
486SX/DX	25MHz	63MHz Pentium
486SX2/DX	250MHz	63MHz Pentium

Prices for an Intel OverDrive upgrade from a 486 CPU to a Pentium range from about $160 to around $200. You won't get the same performance as you would from a motherboard upgrade, but the price is considerably less and you'll still see a marked improvement in performance. If you're looking for an inexpensive, easy upgrade, this is the way to go.

Before you buy an OverDrive processor upgrade, check with your system manufacturer's technical support staff to find out which upgrade will work for your particular system. If yours is an early 486, the OverDrive socket might not work for the OverDrive chip. In such a case, you can switch to a 486DX4 or choose a processor upgrade from Evergreen, Gainbery, or Improve It Technologies (described previously in this section).

TIP A good way to tell if the Intel Pentium OverDrive CPU upgrade will work in your existing 486 CPU socket is to look at the socket with the 486 CPU installed. If you can see an extra row of pin holes in the socket around the 486 CPU, the socket will accommodate the Pentium OverDrive processor. If there are no spare holes, you're out of luck—if the motherboard doesn't have a functioning OverDrive socket, your only upgrade option is the 486DX4. But, you can't count on that option forever. Intel began phasing out the 486DX4 in late 1996.

Windows 95 CD-ROM Extras

For technical information, installation tips, and pricing information, check out Intel Corporation's Web site:

http://www.intel.com

If you need help determining which processor upgrade your system can use, and you don't have access to Intel's Internet site, first find out which CPU your system contains. Then, contact Intel's PC Enhancement Operations sales information department at 800-538-3373 or 503-696-8080 to find out which processor upgrade your system can use.

Upgrades for Pentium Systems

Early Pentium systems ran at 60 or 66MHz. Today's fastest Pentium runs at 200MHz, although faster chips are on the way. The 60 and 66MHz versions are 5-volt chips, and everything from 75MHz and up are 3.3-volt chips. The Intel Pentium OverDrive processor upgrade (see Figure 8.14) lets you speed up your system with a new, faster processor. Table 8.3 lists the Intel Pentium OverDrive options.

FIG. 8.14
The Intel Pentium OverDrive processor lets you upgrade Pentium systems to faster Pentium processors.

Table 8.3 Intel Pentium OverDrive Upgrades for Pentium Systems

Current CPU	CPU Speed	OverDrive Upgrade
Pentium	60MHz	120MHz Pentium
Pentium	66MHz	133MHz Pentium
Pentium	75MHz	125MHz Pentium
Pentium	90MHz	150MHz Pentium
Pentium	100MHz	166MHz Pentium

Prices for the Pentium OverDrive upgrade range from around $280 to about $480. All simply replace the existing CPUs, so you'll have the old Pentium chip to make into a big tie tack or very small lawn ornament.

Depending on the design of your motherboard, you also might be able to replace the existing Pentium CPU with a faster CPU. For example, the motherboard in the system I have now supports a Pentium processor from 75MHz to 200MHz. One system currently has a 133MHz CPU and the other a 166MHz CPU. If I wanted to, I could replace both with 200MHz CPUs. Check your system's motherboard manual to see if it supports higher CPU speeds. If so, you can bump up the speed of the system by replacing the CPU.

NOTE Typically, you must set jumpers on the motherboard to specify the speed of the CPU. If you replace the CPU, you'll need to set these jumpers accordingly. Check the motherboard manual to learn what changes you need to make on the motherboard to accommodate the new CPU. You'll probably have to set jumpers for the CPU speed and system clock speed.

Although it isn't supported by any of the motherboard manufacturers or Intel, you can bump up the speed on some systems without doing anything to the CPU. Instead, you continue to use the same CPU but increase the clock rate. This makes the CPU run faster than it is certified to go (which is why no one supports this method).

In some cases, bumping up the speed this way just locks up the system. In others, the system will run for a few hours, but things will begin to go wrong and the system will eventually crash. In some systems, though, everything will continue to work without problems.

What About FPU Upgrades?

You read earlier that FPU stands for Floating Point Unit. The FPU performs math operations more quickly than can be accomplished in software, which speeds up programs that do a lot of floating-point math. The 386DX, 486DX, Pentium, and Pentium Pro processors contain a built-in FPU. In other words, the FPU is an integral part of the CPU.

The 386SX and 486SX processors, however, don't have a built-in FPU. 386SX systems include a separate FPU socket, usually located near the CPU socket, for a 387 chip (the FPU). Most 486 systems also contain an FPU socket to accommodate a Weitek FPU (manufactured by Weitek, not by Intel). Or, you can replace the 486SX with a 487SX, which is a 486DX chip with internal FPU that replaces the 486SX.

Unfortunately, the 387 and 487 chips were discontinued by Intel, and it would be a long shot for you to find one. A better use of your money would be to upgrade the processor to one that includes an internal FPU.

Orienting the CPU Properly (Finding Pin 1)

It's very important that you install the CPU in the socket in its correct orientation. Take a look at a CPU and you'll find that it is chamfered at a 45-degree angle on one corner as shown in Figure 8.15. This indicates the location of pin 1 on the CPU. If you take a look at the top of the CPU, you'll find a dot painted on top in that same corner to indicate the location of pin 1 from the top (see Figure 8.16). If you take a look at Figure 8.2 again, you'll see the corner chamfer and dot on both the Pentium Pro and Pentium CPUs.

FIG. 8.15
The corner of the CPU that is chamfered at a 45-degree angle is where pin 1 is located.

FIG. 8.16
A dot on top of the CPU in the same corner as the chamfer indicates pin 1.

TIP If you look at the back of the CPU, you'll probably find two other well-hidden indicators of pin 1's location. One of the pins will have a square solder pad around it rather than a round one. In that same corner you'll probably also find a solder line pointing to the pin. The easiest way to determine the correct orientation, though, is to look for the chamfered corner.

Next, you need to determine on the CPU socket where pin 1 is located so you can install the CPU properly. In every case, there will be something different about that corner from the other three. For example, it will have some pin holes plugged, a square tab sticking out in the inside corner (toward the center of the socket), or a pin hole at the inside corner where the other three have none. Better still, look at the motherboard to see if there is an outline painted around the socket. Look for a chamfered corner in the painted outline.

CAUTION It's very important that you install the CPU in the socket in the correct orientation. If you install the chip incorrectly and power up the system, you could fry the chip.

Replacing the CPU

With just a few exceptions, you'll be replacing the CPU with an upgrade processor, rather than installing the new CPU in a separate OverDrive socket. In general, the process is the same regardless of the system. You remove the old CPU, install the new CPU, and change any jumper settings as required on the motherboard. The actual process does differ a little depending on whether you need to install a CPU fan and whether the system uses an LIF or a ZIF socket. The first step, though, is to install the CPU fan.

Installing a CPU Fan

Although not technically required on a 486DX4, it's a good idea to install a CPU fan on top of the CPU to dissipate the extra heat that the CPU will generate. Pentium and Pentium OverDrive processors require a fan (OverDrive processors have them built right onto the CPU). There are two basic types of fans:

- Those that glue to the top of the processor
- Those that clip on

Avoid the kind that glue on (unless it comes that way already installed on the processor), and instead choose one that clips onto the CPU.

You'll also find two different levels of fans:

- Cheaper ones less than $10
- Others from $20–$30

The more expensive ones typically use ball-bearing motors and should last longer than the cheaper ones.

If the CPU in your system already has a fan, you might be able to use it on the new CPU if the new CPU is the same size as the old one. Just unclip the fan and install it on the new one. Otherwise, buy a new fan to fit the processor.

Some fans come in two parts that sandwich the CPU. You set the CPU in the bottom part of the fan housing, then clip on the fan. Regardless of what type of fan you choose, it should be obvious by looking at the fan how it installs. And, the fan should come with a diagram to show its installation.

Removing the CPU from Its Socket

You've already read a little about LIF and ZIF sockets. If your system uses an LIF socket, it's a little more difficult to remove the CPU, but certainly not impossible. The processor upgrade you buy will probably come with a CPU extraction tool. It has one end that looks like a comb, with small rounded teeth. This end slips between the CPU and the socket, and you gently pry up one edge at a time. Just pry a little at a time, moving from one edge to another, until the CPU lifts out of the socket.

If you don't have a CPU extraction tool, a small, flat-bladed screwdriver or a spare bracket hole cover will work as a substitute. Just slide the gadget between the socket and CPU and carefully pry the CPU out, working on one edge after another until the CPU lifts out. Just take care that you don't damage the socket.

Replacing the Processor in an LIF Socket

Before Replacing the CPU in an LIF Socket, You Need:

- ☑ New processor and removal tool (usually comes with the processor, but a small, flat-bladed screwdriver or spare bracket cover will work)
- ☑ Anti-static protection
- ☑ CPU fan for the new CPU

To replace the CPU in an LIF socket, follow these steps:

1. Shut down, turn off, and unplug the PC.
2. Open the PC's cover.
3. Locate the existing CPU.
4. Carefully examine the CPU before you remove it, and locate pin 1.
5. Discharge your static and remove the existing CPU with the removal tool. If you're using a screwdriver or bracket to remove the CPU, be *very, very* careful not to chip the CPU or damage the socket. Work it out a small amount at a time.
6. Mount the CPU fan to the new CPU.
7. Check the pins on the CPU and gently, carefully straighten any that are bent (see Figure 8.17). Don't break any!

FIG. 8.17
Carefully straighten any bent pins, but be careful not to break any.

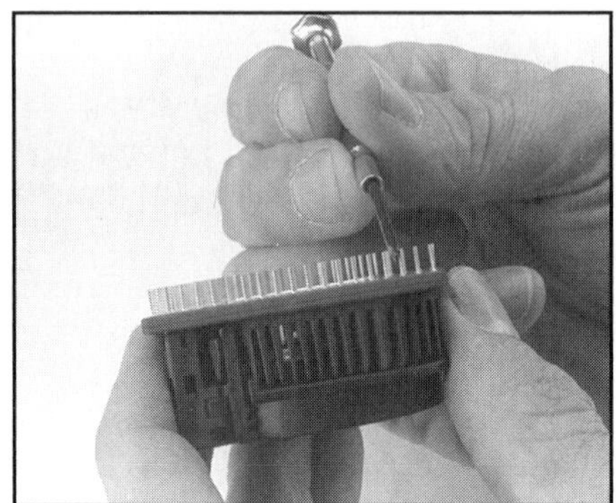

8. Line up pin 1 on the chip with pin 1 on the socket and carefully place the CPU in the socket, making sure all the pins are lined up with the holes.
9. Start at the center, then work on each corner, pushing the CPU into the socket. When you can't see the pins anymore, it's in all the way.
10. Verify that you have the CPU oriented properly in the socket.
11. If you're using a CPU fan, connect it (see Figure 8.18). If your system doesn't have an available power supply connection, get a power supply splitter cable (shown later in Figure 8.21) from your local computer store.

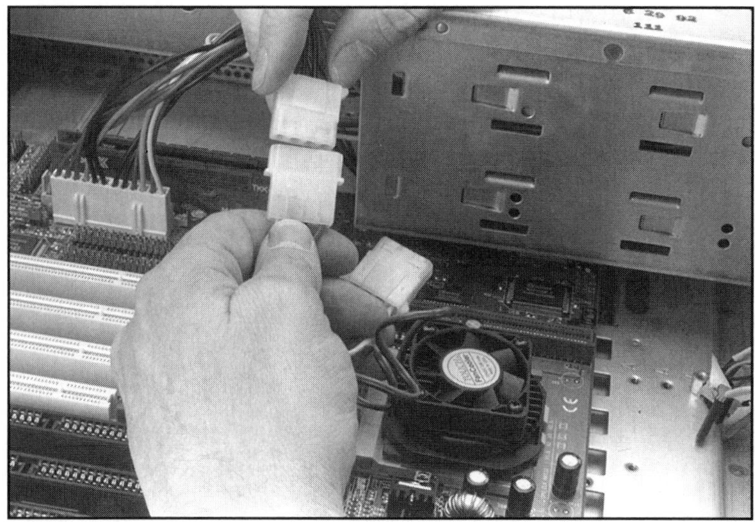

FIG. 8.18
Connect the CPU fan to the power supply.

NOTE OverDrive processors include built-in fans that get their power from the CPU connection. They don't have a separate power supply connection.

12. Reassemble the system and power it up to test it.

Replacing the CPU in a ZIF Socket

Before Replacing the CPU in a ZIF Socket, Check that You Have:

- ☑ New processor
- ☑ Anti-static protection
- ☑ CPU fan for new processor

To replace the CPU in a ZIF socket:

1. Shut down, turn off, and unplug the PC.
2. Open the PC's cover.
3. Locate the existing CPU.
4. Carefully examine the CPU before you remove it, and locate pin 1.
5. Discharge your static, then lift up the retaining lever on the ZIF socket. If the CPU fan is clipped to the socket, release the clip. Then lift the CPU out of its socket.
6. Mount the CPU fan to the new CPU.
7. Check the pins on the CPU and gently, carefully straighten any that are bent (refer to Figure 8.17). Don't break any!
8. Line up pin 1 on the chip with pin 1 on the socket and carefully place the CPU in the socket, making sure all the pins are lined up with the holes. It should just drop into the socket without any pressure (see Figure 8.19). If it doesn't, you probably have a bent pin.

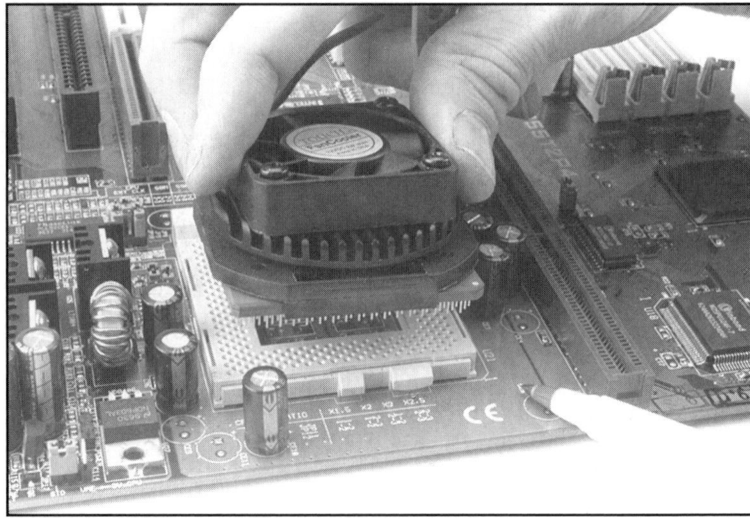

FIG. 8.19
The CPU should just drop into place in the ZIF socket without any pressure.

9. Push down the locking lever to lock the CPU into position (see Figure 8.20).

FIG. 8.20
The lever attached to the ZIF socket locks the CPU into place.

10. Verify that you have the CPU oriented properly in the socket.
11. Connect the CPU fan to a power supply connector. If you don't have any available power supply connectors, get a power supply splitter cable from your local computer store (see Figure 8.21).

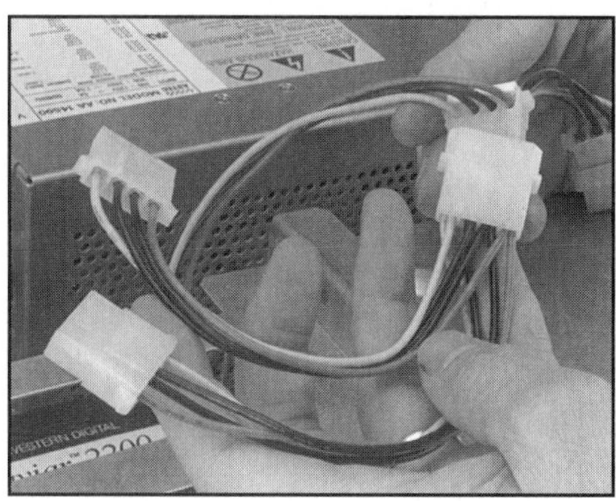

FIG. 8.21
Use a power supply splitter cable to connect the fan if you don't have an available power supply connection.

12. Reassemble the system and power it up to test it.

Installing an OverDrive Chip

Before Installing an OverDrive Processor Upgrade, You Need:

- ☑ OverDrive Processor upgrade
- ☑ Anti-static protection
- ☑ Interposer, if required by your system

To install an OverDrive chip:

1. Shut down, turn off, and unplug the PC.
2. Open the PC's cover.
3. Locate the existing CPU.
4. Carefully examine the CPU before you remove it, and locate pin 1.
5. Discharge your static, then lift up the retaining lever on the ZIF socket. If the CPU fan is clipped to the socket, release the clip. Then lift the CPU out of its socket (see Figure 8.22).

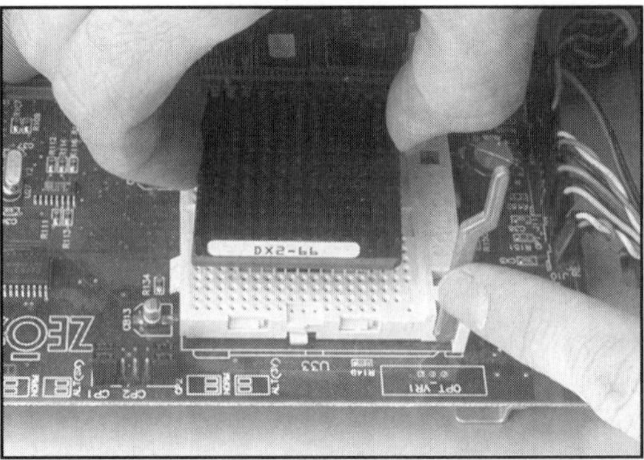

FIG. 8.22
Remove the existing CPU from its socket.

6. Check the pins on the CPU and gently, carefully straighten any that are bent (refer to Figure 8.17). Don't break any!
7. If your system requires an interposer, carefully line up the OverDrive processor on the interposer, making sure to align pin 1 on the CPU with pin 1 on the interposer (see Figure 8.23).

FIG. 8.23
Carefully align the OverDrive on the interposer, making sure to orient the chip correctly, matching pin 1 on the CPU to pin 1 on the interposer.

8. When you're sure the OverDrive is aligned properly with the interposer and all the pins will engage properly, push the OverDrive into the interposer until it is fully seated.
9. Line up pin 1 on the chip with pin 1 on the socket and carefully place the CPU in the socket, making sure all the pins are lined up with the holes. It should just drop into the socket without any pressure (see Figure 8.24). If it doesn't, you probably have a bent pin.

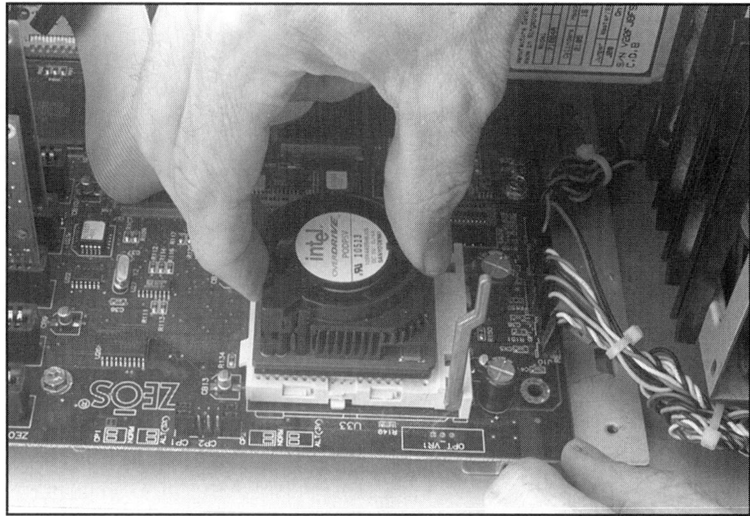

FIG. 8.24
The CPU should just drop into place in the ZIF socket without any pressure.

10. Push down the locking lever to lock the CPU into position (refer to Figure 8.20).
11. Verify that you have the CPU oriented properly in the socket.
12. Reassemble the system and power it up to test it.

Installing a CPU Upgrade Module

Generally, you'll use either the procedure "Replacing the CPU in a ZIF Socket" or "Replacing the Processor in an LIF Socket," given previously, to install a CPU upgrade module from a manufacturer such as Evergreen, Gainbery, or Improve It Technologies. The only real difference is that the CPU might include an interposer that performs voltage regulation for the new chip. If that's the case, the upgrade will include the interposer and instructions on how to install it (if it isn't already installed).

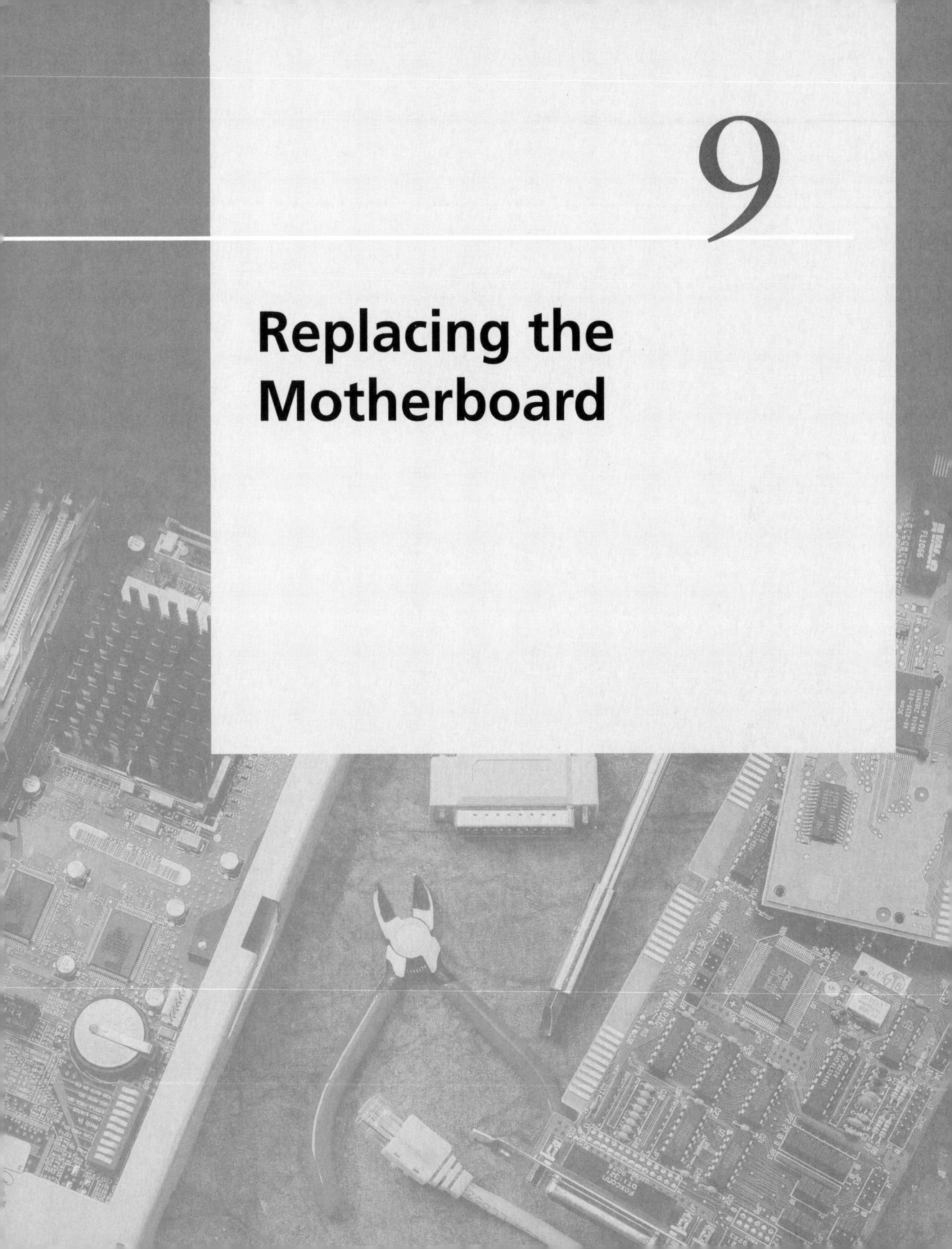

9

Replacing the Motherboard

By far the most radical upgrade you can perform is to replace the system's motherboard. You might think that this task is way beyond your capabilities. Think again. It's a job anyone can do in an hour or so with a screwdriver, some patience, and some guidance. You'll end up with a system that will run circles around your old one. And believe it or not, a motherboard upgrade doesn't have to be expensive.

This chapter takes a look at motherboard replacements, covering the following topics:

- Overview of what the motherboard is and does
- Choosing the best motherboard for your situation
- Getting the new motherboard ready for installation
- Replacing the motherboard
- Reassembling the system

First, you should have some background on what the motherboard is and does.

Motherboard and Case Overview

The main system board in the computer is generally called the *motherboard*. Yes, it's the mother of all computer boards—it's by far the biggest circuit card in the computer. The motherboard is where many of the major components live in the PC, including the CPU, RAM (memory), and in today's PCs, most of the I/O circuitry. Figure 9.1 shows a typical AT-style Pentium motherboard with some of its major components labeled.

The motherboard in Figure 9.1 is shown in the same orientation in which you'd see it mounted in the computer if you were standing in front of the PC. As you can see from the callouts in the figure, the Pentium CPU is located near the front of the computer. The bus slots are located near the rear of the computer. The system's adapters—such as for video, sound, networking, and so on—install in these bus slots. The adapters are screwed to the back of the chassis to hold them in place. The RAM sockets, where the memory is located, are situated at the right edge of this motherboard.

FIG. 9.1
This is a typical AT-style Pentium motherboard with some of its major parts labeled.

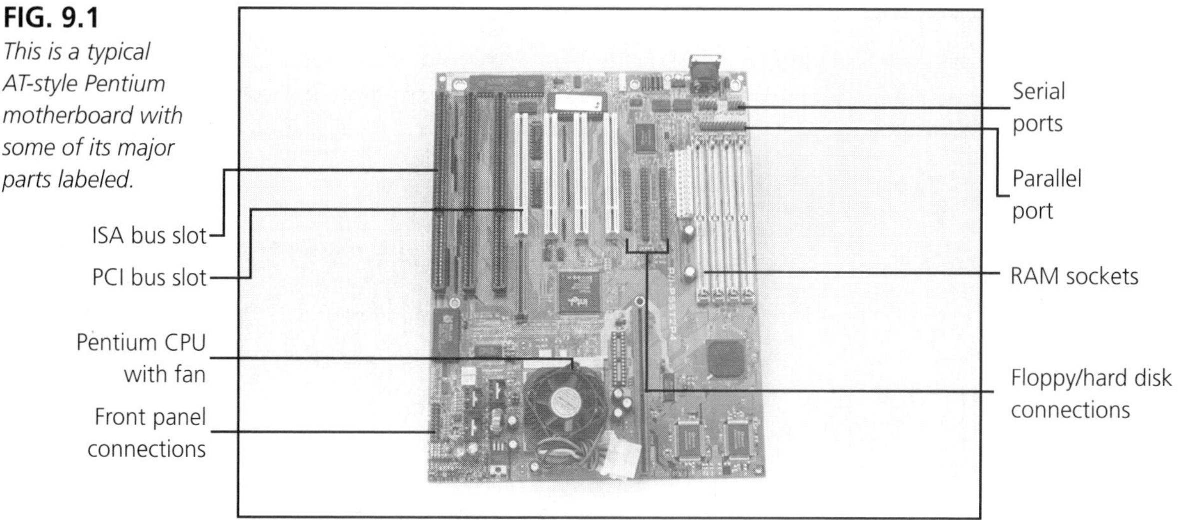

This motherboard, like most new motherboards, has the I/O circuitry built right onto the motherboard. As you can see in Figure 9.1, the motherboard includes connectors for two serial ports, a parallel port, floppy drive, and two IDE chains (for IDE devices such as hard disks and CD-ROM drives). Located just to the left of the keyboard connector, but not pointed out in the photo, is a PS/2 mouse connection on the motherboard. These connectors will have ribbon cables connected to them that attach to ports on the back of the computer, the floppy drive(s), and hard drives/CD-ROM drives.

NOTE It's important to note that not all motherboards are laid out like the one in Figure 9.1, which is an AT-style motherboard. In other words, it uses the same general layout and orientation as the motherboard used in the original IBM AT computer. The long edge of the motherboard runs front to back in the PC, and the bus slots are parallel to the long side.

Figure 9.2 shows the same Pentium motherboard beside an older 486 motherboard. Note that the CPU has been removed from the 486 motherboard—it used to sit in the large socket nearest the bus slots. It will soon be replaced with an OverDrive processor.

As you can see in the photo, the two boards are different sizes. The 486 motherboard uses a standard AT size, and the Pentium motherboard on the right uses a *baby AT* size. This means it uses the same mounting hole pattern, but the actual board is a little smaller.

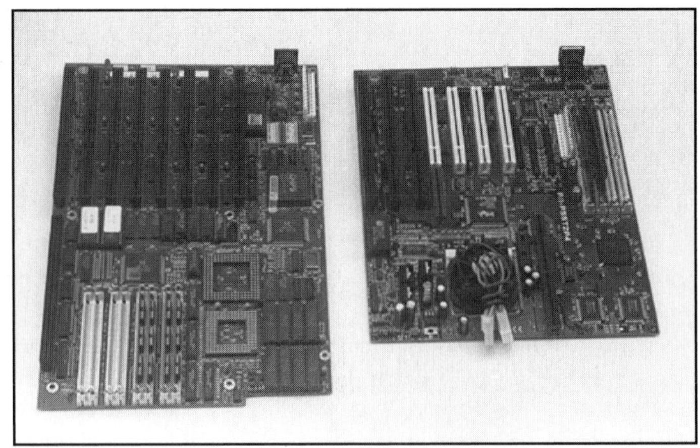

FIG. 9.2
On the left is a 486 motherboard, and on the right a Pentium motherboard.

The size of the board has nothing to do with the CPU it uses. The main reason the Pentium motherboard is smaller is that it is newer. More functions are incorporated into fewer components these days, so the components take less space on the newer board. So, it can be smaller than the older 486 motherboard.

You can also see that the general layout of the boards is a little different. On the 486 motherboard, the RAM sockets are located near the front of the motherboard, but on the Pentium motherboard are located at the right rear. The bus slots are still in the same spot on both boards, although the 486 motherboard contains only ISA slots and one proprietary RAM slot (on the far left). The Pentium motherboard contains three ISA slots and four PCI slots. The location of the slots in relation to the left edge of the board and one another is the same on both boards, however. This is because both boards have to fit in a standard AT-style chassis.

Intel, the primary manufacturer of PC CPUs, has proposed a new motherboard layout called the *ATX form factor.* Figure 9.3 shows an ATX-style motherboard with some of its major parts labeled. The board is oriented in the figure just as you would see it mounted in the computer if you were standing at the front of the PC.

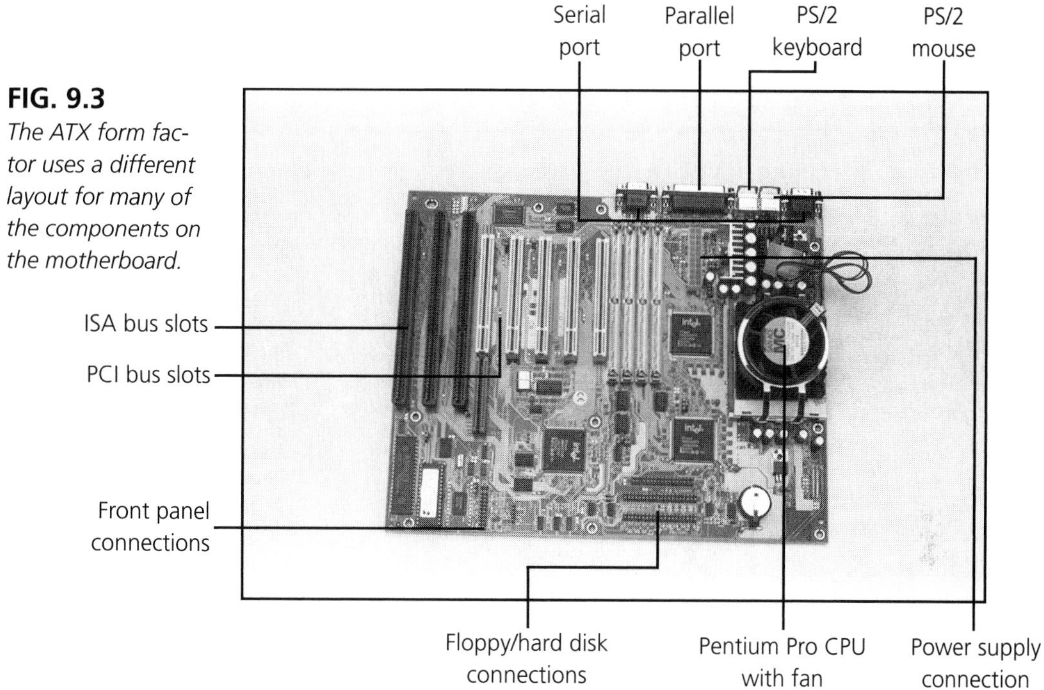

FIG. 9.3
The ATX form factor uses a different layout for many of the components on the motherboard.

As you can see in the figure, the bus slots are parallel to the short side of the motherboard. Instead of the long side of the motherboard running front to back in the PC, the short side runs front to back. The bus slots are located in the same general location, and the adapters still install in these slots and mount to the back of the computer's chassis.

You'll also notice one other difference from the AT-style motherboard: the serial, parallel, keyboard, and mouse connectors are built right onto the motherboard and stick out the back of the chassis when the motherboard is installed. With an AT-style motherboard, you have ribbon cables connected to the motherboard and running to the appropriate bracket connectors on the back of the chassis. This simplifies installation, because you don't have to connect any cables inside the computer.

One of the main reasons for the ATX design is to move the CPU closer to the power supply fan for better cooling, which means the CPU will last longer and suffer fewer faults. The next section explores this and case layout.

About Chasses and Cases

In case you haven't already guessed, *chassis* refers to the metal skeleton of your computer. Figure 9.4 shows a typical AT-style mini-tower chassis. As you can see from the photograph, the power supply is located a few inches below the top of the chassis, leaving enough room above it for a hard drive to be mounted. The plate on which the motherboard mounts hinges down and pulls out for easy installation of the motherboard.

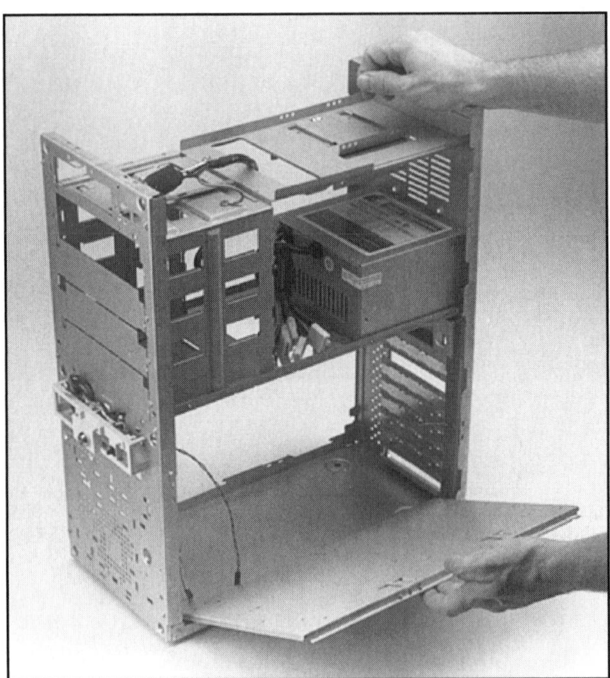

FIG. 9.4
This is a typical AT-style mini-tower chassis.

NOTE The chassis and its cover are generally called a *case*. Throughout this book, you'll see "case" used interchangeably with "chassis."

Figure 9.5 shows an ATX-style mini-tower case. As you can see in the photograph, the power supply is mounted at the very top of the chassis. When the motherboard is installed in the chassis, the CPU is located right underneath the power supply fan, which helps keep the CPU cooler (see Figure 9.6).

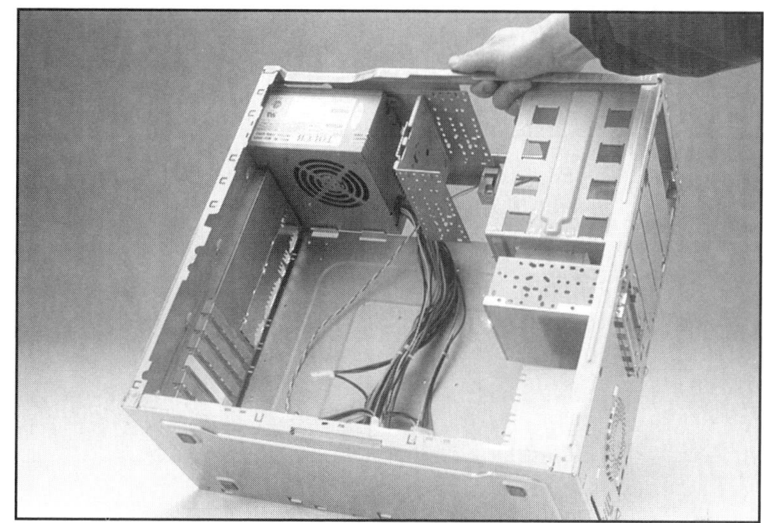

FIG. 9.5
A typical ATX-style mini-tower chassis.

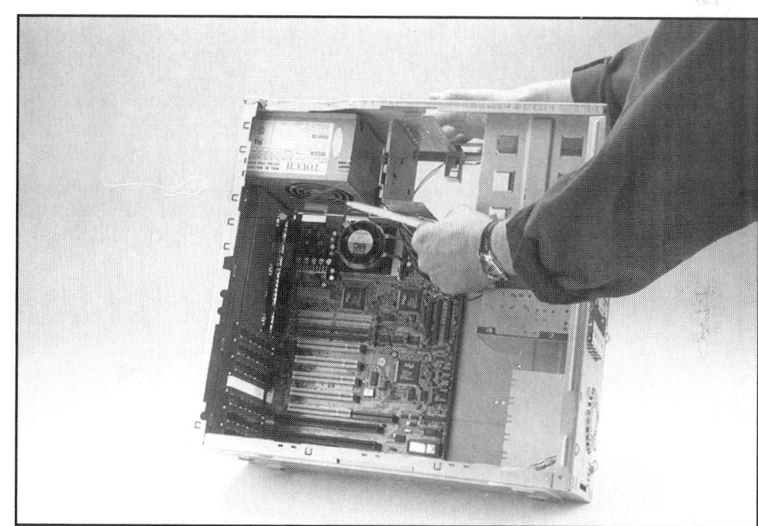

FIG. 9.6
The CPU is located right by the power supply cooling fan in an ATX case.

Like the AT case shown in Figure 9.4, the plate where the motherboard mounts comes off to make it easier to install the motherboard (see Figure 9.7).

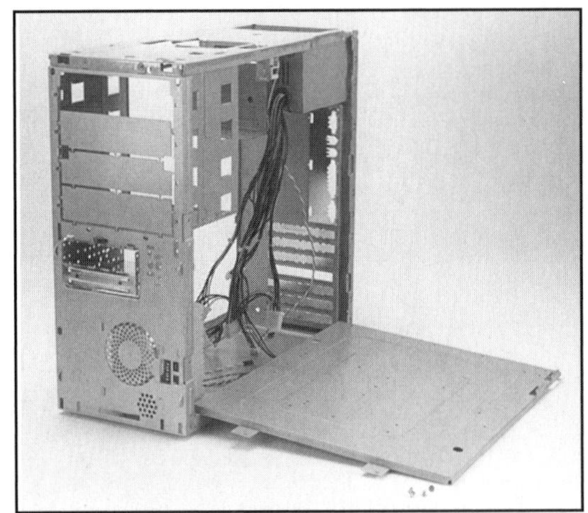

FIG. 9.7
The motherboard mounting plate comes off for easy installation of the board.

An AT case uses special I/O bracket adapters and mounting holes in the back of the chassis for I/O connections (serial and parallel ports). The ATX motherboard has these I/O connectors built right onto the board. These connectors stick out the back of the ATX chassis (see Figure 9.8). This eliminates the need to connect ribbon cables from the motherboard (see Figure 9.9) to the I/O connectors on the back of the chassis as you must on an AT-style system.

FIG. 9.8
The I/O connectors stick out the back of the ATX chassis.

One commonality between new AT and ATX motherboards is the on-board IDE and floppy drive circuitry and connections (see Figure 9.10). The controller circuitry for these drives is built onto the motherboard. Instead of using a separate IDE host adapter and floppy controller, you just connect the drives directly to the motherboard.

FIG. 9.9
Most new AT style motherboards have connectors on the motherboard for the serial and parallel ports.

FIG. 9.10
Most new motherboards include built-in IDE and floppy drive support.

Another thing that is common to all motherboards—old and new—is the front panel connections (see Figure 9.11). Wires connect from these connections on the motherboard to various switches and *LEDs (Light Emitting Diodes)* on the front of the case, and to the PC's speaker. Connections typically include the reset switch, keyboard lock, speaker, turbo switch, and turbo LED.

FIG. 9.11
All motherboards include connections to switches and lights on the case.

You'll read more about these connections later in the section "Mapping the Current Board."

Choosing a Motherboard

Now that you know a little about motherboards and cases, how do you choose a good motherboard? There really aren't a lot of issues to consider, but there are a few.

What Case Style?

First, you need to decide what form factor (motherboard layout) you need—either AT or ATX. If your system uses an AT-style case, you'll need an AT-style motherboard. Or, you can choose to buy an ATX motherboard, but you'll also need to buy a new ATX case and swap all the stuff from the old case to the new one. If your current system uses an ATX-style case, you'll need an ATX motherboard.

NOTE If I were building my own computer today, I'd opt for a fast Pentium Pro and ATX case. The Pentium Pro offers the best performance, and the ATX design provides for excellent cooling and considerable flexibility for adding new devices and creating a custom system.

Which Processor?

Next, you need to decide which processor you want on the board. I don't recommend anything less than a Pentium, and you might be hard-pressed to find a 486 motherboard these days, anyway. If you're going through the trouble of replacing the motherboard, you might as well spend the extra few dollars and get a good Pentium or Pentium Pro motherboard. Which processor you get depends on the amount of money you're willing to spend. The Pentium Pro offers better performance than the Pentium, but is naturally more expensive.

TIP The Pentium Pro is optimized for 32-bit operating systems such as Windows NT. When running 16-bit code, however, the Pentium Pro can actually perform at the same rate or more poorly than a Pentium CPU. Windows 95 for the most part consists of 32-bit code, but still contains some 16-bit code. Windows 3.x is, with a few exceptions, mostly 16-bit code. So, you'll get the best performance from a Pentium Pro system if you're running Windows NT or any other full 32-bit operating system.

When you buy the motherboard, make sure you get it with the CPU. Some vendors advertise their boards without the CPU, which makes the price look *really* good. Include the cost of the CPU in your price comparison if the boards you're looking at don't have the CPU already installed. Also, make sure to match the CPU you buy to the motherboard's capability. If the board is only recommended for a CPU up to 133MHz, for example, don't install a 200MHz CPU on it.

What Bus Type?

Unless you have a lot of VL-bus adapters to reuse, forget VL-bus and choose a board with a PCI bus. In the long run, you'll enjoy better performance and have more choices for adapters. Even if you do have a couple of VL-bus adapters, you might consider selling them to a friend and buying new PCI versions to replace them.

The number of bus slots on the motherboard is a consideration, but not a big one because most of them will have roughly a mix of half and half. Before you buy the motherboard, take an inventory of the adapters you'll be using. Include video and sound as a minimum. If the motherboard you're going to buy has onboard IDE and your current system contains one or more IDE hard drives, you won't need a slot for an IDE host adapter. If you're using SCSI devices, though, you will need a slot for the SCSI host adapter.

Also, take into consideration an internal modem if you have one or will be buying one. Personally, I prefer external modems because they don't tie up a bus slot, and I can reset them easily by just turning them off, then on again. The downside is that external modems are more expensive, and require an external power supply.

The new motherboard will very likely include two onboard 16550 UART serial ports and one parallel port. If you're going to need additional ports, reserve a slot for an I/O adapter.

Finally, after you've identified all the gadgets you're going to install in the bus slots, count which are ISA and which are PCI. Then, choose a motherboard that has enough of each type of slot to accommodate your needs.

TIP I recommend PCI for video and SCSI host adapters for the best performance. Check out Chapter 11, "Hard Disks," to decide if you want or need an ultra-wide SCSI host adapter and disk drive for best performance. Check out Chapter 14, "Video," to decide which type of video card you should have.

Which Chipset?

You should give a little consideration to which chipset the motherboard uses. The most commonly used chipsets in today's motherboards are manufactured by Intel, Chips and Technologies (C&T), and Opti. You'll also run across chipsets from SiS, IDC, Toshiba, Texas Instruments, and UMC, among others. The longer the chipset manufacturer has been around, the less likely it will be that you'll have any compatibility problems or chipset bugs.

Which Manufacturer?

Consider who makes the motherboard. Intel, Micronics, AMI, Mylex, and ASUS all make good motherboards, but they're not the only ones who do. Some motherboards are manufactured in the U.S., while others are manufactured in the Pacific Rim. Whichever motherboard you choose, make sure the vendor will provide support and service after the sale. It won't matter who manufactured the board if it fails after the first month and you can't get it replaced under warranty. I would be satisfied with a system using any of the aforementioned motherboards, but would probably buy an Intel board if I were performing the upgrade on my own system.

Read the Manual?

I've found one sure way to tell if a motherboard was not manufactured in the U.S.—read the motherboard manual. It's obvious that many companies don't spend a lot of money or time on translating the manuals. Here's an example: "For the purpose of power saving, there are two jumpers, J4 and J5, to make sure the power saving function doing well. The J4 is a switch to force the system get into green mode immediately." It's tough enough to understand most technical manuals when they are translated properly, but even more so when they are not.

The manual isn't always a sure sign that the motherboard was manufactured outside the U.S. ASUS Computer GmbH, which is located in Germany, has excellent manuals that are not only well-written but properly translated. And perhaps most importantly is the fact that the manual has nothing to do with how well the motherboard performs.

Can You Use Your Existing Memory?

Another point to consider when shopping for a motherboard is whether or not you'll be able to use the memory from your current motherboard. If your current memory is in the form of 30-pin SIMMs and your new motherboard will take only 72-pin SIMMs, you'll have to either buy new memory or use a SIMM adapter. The SIMM adapter will allow you to install the 30-pin SIMMs in a 72-pin socket.

NOTE Some motherboard designs accommodate both 30-pin and 72-pin SIMMs.

Even if you choose to use a SIMM adapter and your existing memory, you still might want to buy some new RAM to increase the total capacity of the system. When you buy the motherboard, talk to the salesperson about your existing RAM and whether or not you'll need a SIMM adapter.

TIP Consider 16M of RAM to be the minimum you'll want in the system. If you can afford it, shoot for more, say from 24M to 32M. This will accommodate all those memory-hogging programs you're sure to run, as well as all those operating system components. Keep in mind that if you can't afford the extra RAM now, you can always add it in the future. Check out Chapter 10, "Adding Memory," for more information about your system's RAM.

Don't Forget Mounting Hardware!

One final thing to consider when buying the motherboard is mounting hardware. If you're replacing an existing motherboard, you should be able to use all the existing standoffs, which are the metal and nylon mounting gadgets that hold the motherboard in place. If you buy a new case, the case should come with a bag full of mounting hardware.

Mapping the Current Board

Before you start tearing the motherboard out of your computer, you need to take the time to map out its connections and mounting points. This will help you ensure that you connect everything properly to the new motherboard.

First, you need to take note of the connections from the old motherboard to the front panel (case). These connections go to the speaker, keyboard lock, turbo switch, turbo LED, and reset switch (occasionally there are others). Some cases label the connection right on the end of the connector that attaches to the motherboard. Others have no indication and all you have to go by is the color coding on the wires.

You'll generally find all the case connections along the front edge of the motherboard, nearest the front of the case (see Figure 9.12). They might be at the left edge, near the center, or at the right edge. In any case, you can't miss them—just look for five or six wires running from the front of the case to the motherboard.

FIG. 9.12
You'll find a set of wires running from the front of the case to the motherboard.

Before you disconnect any of these wires, you need to note where they go. Take a look at one of the connectors to see if it has a label that indicates what it is for (KLCK for keyboard lock, TSW for turbo switch, and so on). If all of the connectors are labeled, you're in good shape. If not, make a label from a piece of masking tape or floppy disk label (or some other label) and tape it to each connection (see Figure 9.13). You should be able to determine each connection by a description painted on the motherboard for each connection. If all else fails, consult your motherboard manual. It will tell you which connections go where. Do them one at a time, and label each one right after you remove it so you don't forget where it went. Also, pay attention to the color coding of the wire and jot down the colors and how they are connected on the board. You might need that information later when you hook up the new motherboard.

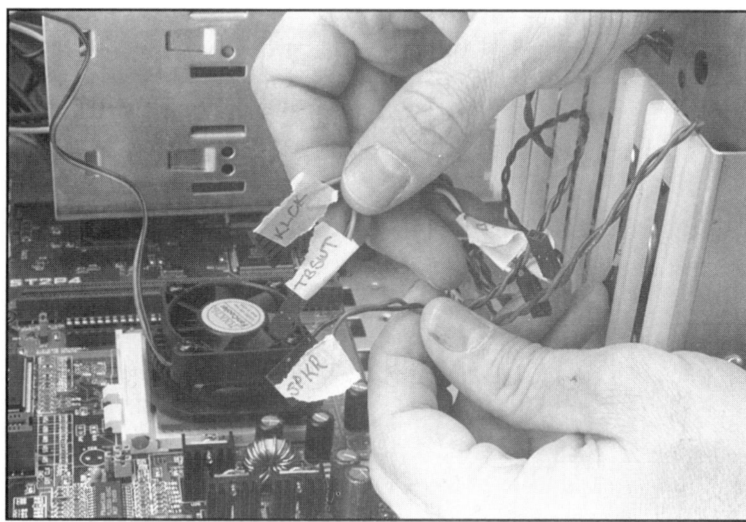

FIG. 9.13
It's important to label all the motherboard connections before you remove them.

TIP If you have an instamatic camera, take a close-up photograph of the connections. You can use the photograph as a reference to remember where all the connections went.

In addition to taking note of where all the front panel connections go, also take note of any other connections to the motherboard such as onboard I/O, IDE, and other connections. If you're not sure what a cable is for, look at the motherboard near the connection. You should find some type of reference painted on the board to tell you what the connection is for. If nothing else, track the cable to its destination (hard disk, floppy disk, and so on) and put an appropriate label on the cable.

When all the connections are identified, take note of where the mounting screws for the board are located. Some of the mounting holes have nylon (plastic) retainers instead of screws.

Setting Up the New Board

When you buy a new motherboard, you'll typically get the board, a set of I/O cables with brackets, a manual for the board, and possibly a driver disk (see Figure 9.14). The board comes in an anti-static bag to protect its delicate electronic parts from being zapped to death. Leave the board in the bag until you're ready to start checking out and configuring the new board. And before you do take the board out of its bag, make sure to discharge your static.

FIG. 9.14
This is a typical motherboard replacement kit.

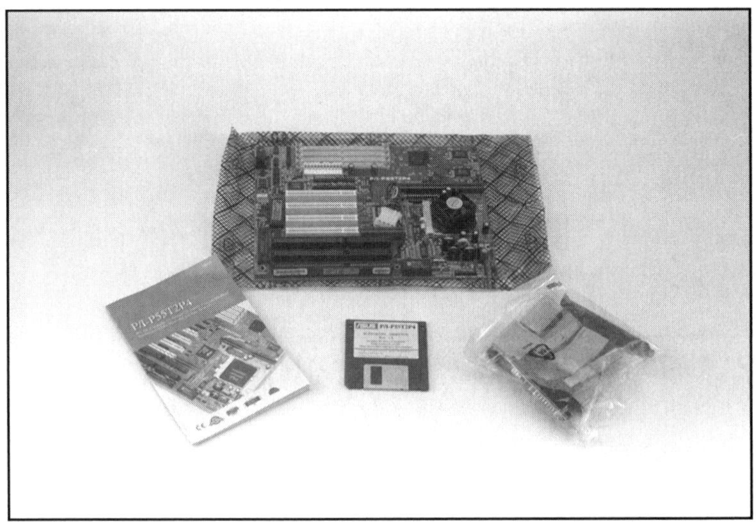

If you bought the motherboard with the CPU installed, there is probably little, if any, configuration you need to do to the board. Although many older motherboards required that you configure jumpers on the motherboard to specify the amount of RAM installed, today's motherboards automatically detect the amount of RAM, so you don't have to mess around with configuration jumpers. Configuration steps that you might have to take are covered in the following sections.

NOTE The motherboard manual has step-by-step instructions on how to configure the board for installation. In many cases, all you have to do is install the RAM and then mount the board in the case. The following sections should help you configure nearly any board, but you should also refer to the motherboard manual to make sure you haven't missed any steps that are specific to that board. Even if you think the motherboard is properly configured, you should take the time to go through the manual to check the settings anyway. If nothing else, it's a good way to become familiar with the board and its layout.

Install the CPU

If the CPU was already installed on the motherboard when you received it, you should be in good shape. If not, you need to install the CPU. Installing a CPU is explained in Chapter 8, "Upgrading the CPU and FPU and Cache." Check the new motherboard's manual to determine which jumpers you need to set in order to configure the CPU speed and clock speed. You should find a table in the manual that lists the different CPU speeds and the corresponding bus speed you need to choose for each one.

Install Memory

After you've installed the CPU, you should install the RAM on the motherboard. You could wait until the board is installed in the case, but it's much easier to do when the motherboard is out of the case. Installing memory is explained in detail in Chapter 10, "Adding Memory." Make sure you check the motherboard manual to determine which banks need which type of SIMM. You'll find a table in the manual that explains how the motherboard's memory sockets can and should be populated with RAM.

NOTE The ATX design offers an advantage for memory placement, making the memory more accessible and easier to install with the motherboard in the case.

Set Switches and Jumpers

You probably won't have to set any switches or jumpers unless you had to install the CPU or are adding more cache RAM. But, you should go through the motherboard manual to determine if there are any jumpers or switches that you do need to set. For example, if you are using a multi-I/O card instead of the motherboard's onboard I/O, you need to disable the onboard I/O so it won't conflict with the card. Typically, you disable the onboard I/O through a jumper on the motherboard. The manual tells you where the jumper is located and how to install or remove the jumper(s) accordingly.

Other Possible Configuration Tasks

About the only other task you might have to perform is installing more cache RAM, which serves as a temporary storage for data moving to and from the CPU. Most motherboards contain 256K of cache RAM, although some motherboards—particularly those intended to be used as network servers—contain 512K of cache RAM.

In general, bumping a workstation's cache from 256K to 512K isn't going to have much of a noticeable impact on your computer's performance. So, I don't recommend that you go through the expense and hassle of doing it. If you're building a dedicated network server, then the extra cache will probably improve performance enough to be worthwhile. Because this book isn't really geared toward the type of user who would be building a dedicated network server, I don't cover cache RAM expansion in the book. If you do decide you want to bump up the motherboard's cache RAM, check the motherboard manual—it tells you how to do it.

Removing the Old Board

Removing the old motherboard is fairly easy, and you should have it out within just a few minutes. If you're reusing your existing memory on the new motherboard, you should remove the old motherboard, remove the memory from it, and install the memory on the new motherboard while the new board is still out of the case.

Before Removing the Motherboard, You Need:

- ☑ Anti-static protection
- ☑ Phillips screwdriver

1. Shut down and turn off the computer, then unplug it.
2. Remove the computer's cover and discharge your static.
3. Note and label each of the internal connections to the adapters.
4. Remove the adapters from their bus slots.

NOTE It isn't absolutely necessary to disconnect ribbon cables or other internal cables from the adapters. Leaving them connected will save you the hassle of reconnecting them later. But, the ribbon cables might get in the way while you're installing the new motherboard, or they might not be long enough to let you move the adapters out of the way. Use your judgment here.

5. Disconnect the power supply connections from the motherboard. They are labeled P4 and P5 or P8 and P9 (see Figure 9.15).

FIG. 9.15
The power supply connectors are located fairly close to the power supply itself.

6. Locate and label all of the wires from the case (front panel) to the motherboard (shown previously in Figures 9.12 and 9.13).

7. Disconnect the case connections.
8. Remove the screws that hold the motherboard in place (see Figures 9.16 and 9.17). There will probably be anywhere from four to seven screws.

FIG. 9.16
Remove the screws holding the motherboard in place.

FIG. 9.17
You should find about four to seven screws.

9. Carefully slide the motherboard to the left and up to remove it from the case (see Figure 9.18).

FIG. 9.18
You'll have to slide the motherboard to the left a little to disengage the standoffs from the chassis.

TIP If you have a mini-tower or tower case with a removable mounting plate for the motherboard, you might as well remove the plate from the chassis, then remove the motherboard from it. Having the plate out will also simplify installing the new motherboard.

10. If you are reusing the RAM, remove the RAM from the motherboard and set it aside for installation on the new motherboard.

NOTE After you remove the new motherboard from its anti-static bag, put the old motherboard in the bag for safekeeping. You might want to sell or trade the motherboard, and wouldn't want it to get damaged in the meantime.

Installing the New Board

Installing the new motherboard is pretty much the reverse of the previous removal procedure, but there are a few extra steps you need to perform.

Before Installing a Motherboard, You Need:

- ☑ Anti-static protection
- ☑ Phillips screwdriver
- ☑ Needle-nose pliers (maybe)
- ☑ Pliers or nut driver (maybe)
- ☑ Utility knife or wire cutters (maybe)
- ☑ New motherboard, properly configured, with memory and CPU installed
- ☑ Mounting hardware (use hardware from old motherboard and case)

1. Verify that the new motherboard is properly configured and has the CPU and RAM installed.
2. Discharge your static, and test-fit the motherboard to see which holes need nylon standoffs and which take a mounting screw.
3. Remove the standoffs from the old motherboard (see Figure 9.19), then install them in the appropriate holes in the new motherboard. Note that some motherboards will come in the box with the standoffs already installed.

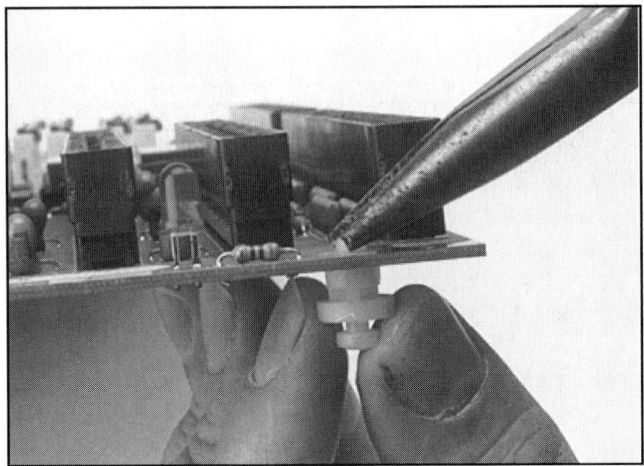

FIG. 9.19
You might need to use pliers to remove the standoffs from the old motherboard.

4. Make sure that the standoffs are installed in the correct location in the case (see Figures 9.20, 9.21, and 9.22).

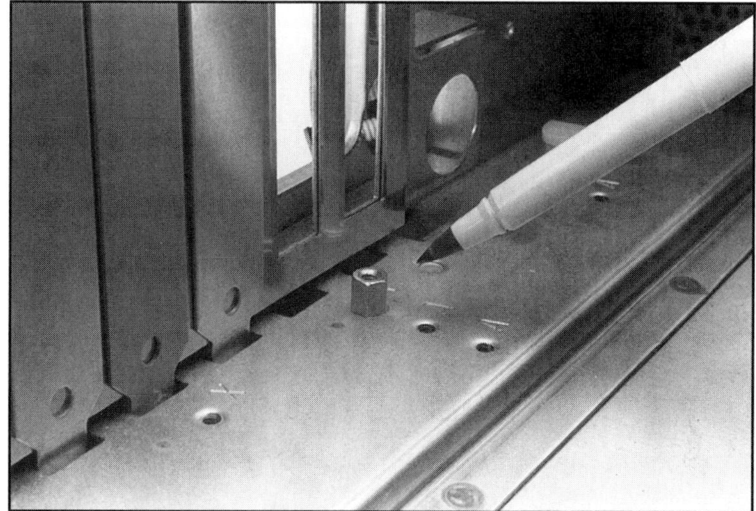

FIG. 9.20
Install standoffs in the chassis if they aren't already present in the correct locations.

FIG. 9.21
This type of standoff simply slides into the chassis, and the motherboard slides into it.

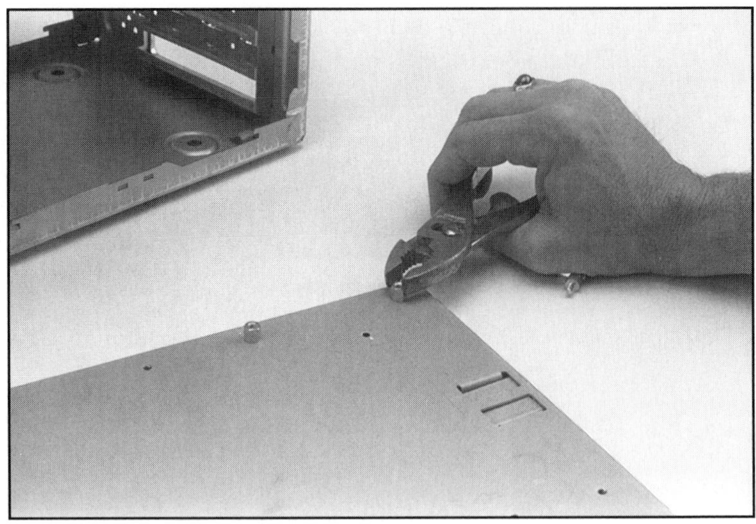

FIG. 9.22
If you're working with a new case, the standoffs probably won't be installed, so you'll have to install them.

5. Test-fit the motherboard on the mounting plate. You might find that the standoffs on the right side interfere with components on the top of the motherboard. If so, trim the standoff as shown in Figure 9.23. Set the motherboard aside when you're sure all the standoffs are in the correct spot.

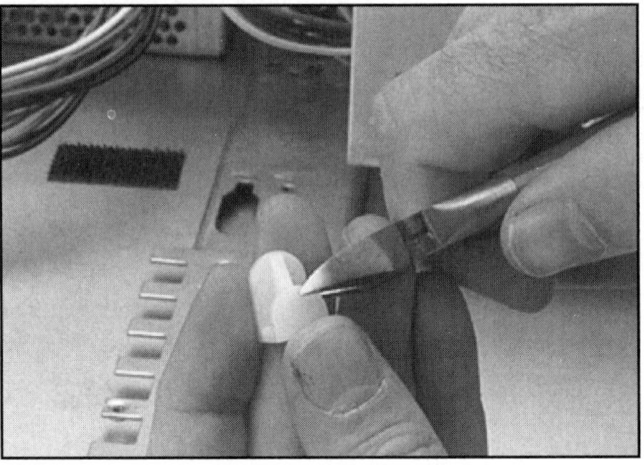

FIG. 9.23
Trim the standoffs if they interfere with any of the components on top of the motherboard.

6. If the computer contains a battery backup for the CMOS and the new motherboard contains its own battery backup (it more than likely does), remove the old battery pack (see Figure 9.24).

FIG. 9.24
If the new motherboard has its own onboard battery backup for the CMOS, you can remove the old battery pack.

7. If the new motherboard has a metal spring plate around the keyboard connector, remove the existing one, if there is one, from the chassis (see Figure 9.25).

FIG. 9.25
Remove the spring plate from the keyboard connector hole if the new motherboard has one.

NOTE In the next step, you install the motherboard in the case. You might want to jump ahead to the section "Attaching Cables" to learn how to connect the serial port and parallel port cables to the motherboard. Connecting them now before you install the motherboard might be a little easier than trying to connect them later. If you decide to connect them now, just set the brackets on top of the motherboard until you get it in place.

8. Slide the motherboard into position in the case, as shown in Figure 9.26. Or, if you have the mounting plate out of the case, attach the motherboard to the mounting plate.

FIG. 9.26
Slide the motherboard into position on the standoffs.

9. Attach the motherboard in place with screws in the appropriate places (see Figure 9.27).
10. If you have the mounting plate out of the chassis, reinstall it (see Figure 9.28).

FIG. 9.27
Screw the motherboard in place.

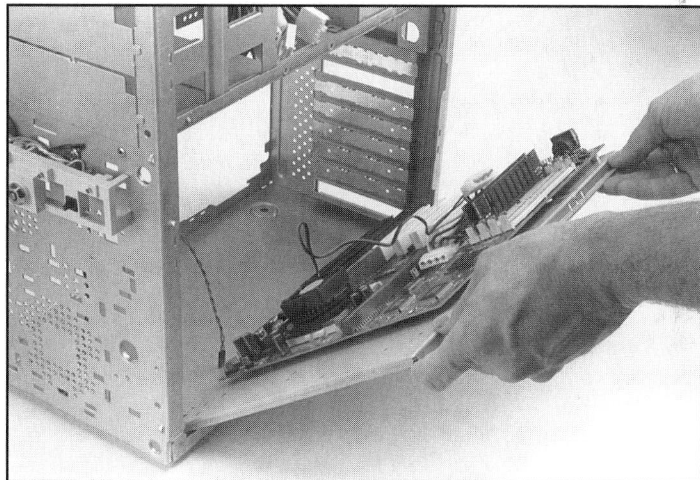

FIG. 9.28
Reinstall the mounting plate in the chassis and secure with clips or screws.

Attaching Cables

Now that the motherboard is installed in the case, you can start connecting that rat's nest of cables.

Before Attaching Cables, Check That:

- ☑ The computer is still unplugged!
- ☑ New motherboard is installed in case
- ☑ Anti-static protection
- ☑ You have the motherboard manual

1. Make sure the computer is still unplugged.
2. Discharge your static.
3. Connect the power supply cables, which will probably be labeled P4 and P5 or P8 and P9 (see Figure 9.29). The connectors are keyed, but make sure the black wires are together in the center of the connectors and the red and orange wires are on opposite ends. Check the motherboard manual if you're not sure which way to connect the wires. In the case of an ATX motherboard, you only have one connector, and it is keyed for proper insertion (see Figure 9.30).

FIG. 9.29
Connect the power supply cables to the motherboard.

FIG. 9.30
The ATX motherboard has a single power connector.

4. Connect the serial port cables to the motherboard, making sure to orient the colored stripe on the cable on pin 1 of the connector (see Figure 9.31).

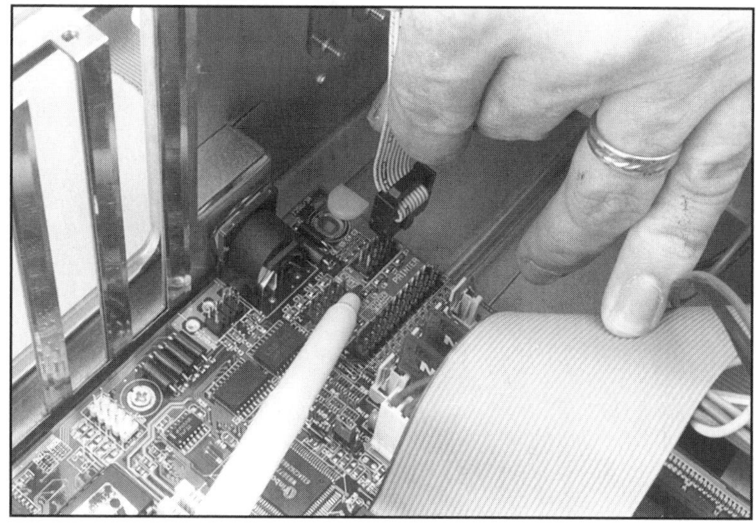

FIG. 9.31
Connect the serial port cables, making sure to connect the side with the colored stripe on pin 1.

5. Connect the parallel port cable (see Figure 9.32) to the motherboard, correctly orienting the cable on the connector (see Figure 9.33).

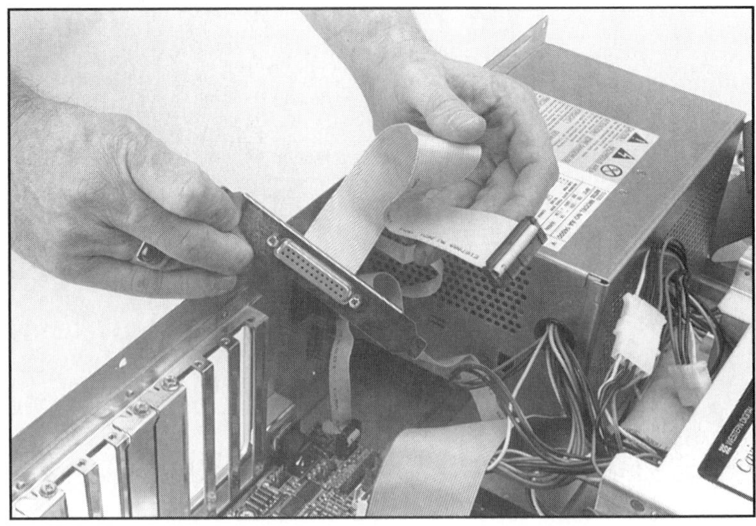

FIG. 9.32
Install the parallel port cable.

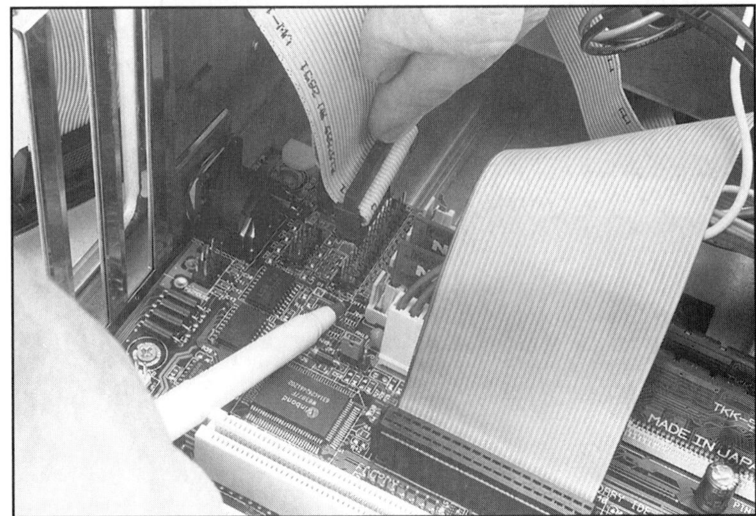

FIG. 9.33
Make sure to line up the stripe on the cable with pin 1 on the connector.

6. Install the I/O brackets in slots in the back of the chassis (see Figure 9.34), or remove the connector from the bracket and install the connector in the appropriate hole in the case (see Figure 9.35).

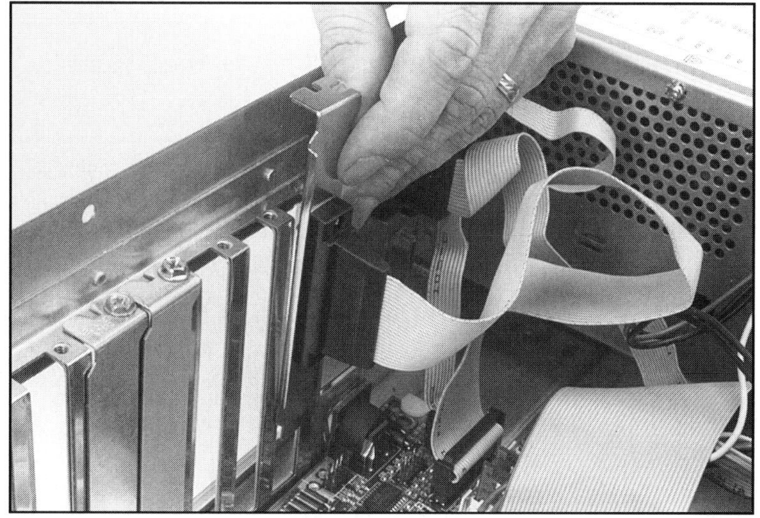

FIG. 9.34
You can install the I/O bracket in one of the slots in the back of the chassis...

FIG. 9.35
...or install the connector in a mounting hole in the back of the chassis.

7. If you're using the onboard IDE controller, connect the IDE cable to the motherboard (see Figure 9.36). If you only have one or two IDE devices, connect the cable to IDE1 (chain 1). If you have more than two devices, connect the cable for the primary boot drive to chain 1. Make sure you connect the side of the cable with the stripe to pin 1 on the motherboard.

FIG. 9.36
Connect the IDE cable(s) to the IDE connectors on the motherboard.

8. If you're using the onboard floppy drive controller, connect the floppy drive cable to the floppy controller connection on the motherboard. Make sure to orient the stripe on pin 1.
9. Check the wires from the front panel to see if they will reach the connectors on the motherboard. If not, you should be able to remove the metal bracket on the front of the chassis where the keylock will expose some extra wire (see Figure 9.37). Pull some more wire through the chassis if you need it.
10. Using your labels, the notations on the motherboard, and the motherboard manual as a guide, attach the front panel connections to the motherboard (see Figure 9.38). Check the manual for the polarity of the connections if necessary. Typically, black is ground (–) and red is hot (+), but you'll also find other colors used like yellow, blue, orange, and white. Usually, orange means hot (+).
11. Connect the hard disk drive activity LED to the connector for that purpose on the motherboard. Check the motherboard manual for its location. Or, if you're using a disk drive host adapter instead of the onboard IDE controller, connect the LED wire to the correct pins on the adapter.
12. Check all your connections one more time to make sure they're right.

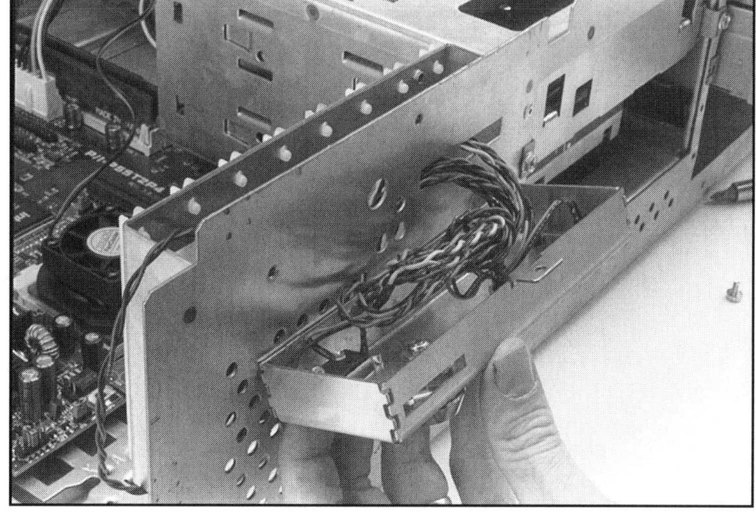

FIG. 9.37 *You'll find more wire hiding under the bracket that holds the keylock and LEDs.*

FIG. 9.38 *Attach all the front panel connections to the motherboard.*

Adapters, Cables, and Reassembly

You're almost home free on this upgrade. All you have left is to reinstall the adapters, connect the cables to the back of the computer, and reassemble the case.

If you don't have any new adapters, I suggest you simply install all the old adapters (unless you're no longer using some), connect the cables, and turn on the system for a smoke test. If it doesn't smoke, you did something right (yes, that is a joke). If you have some new adapters, I recommend you install them one at a time, testing after each one.

You might need to install more than one to get started. For example, you definitely need the video adapter, and if you're not using the onboard IDE controller, you'll also need the hard disk host adapter. After you attach the cables to those adapters, turn on the system to see if it will boot. If it does, shut it off and install the sound card, network card, and so on, testing the system after each one. By installing and testing the cards this way, you'll quickly identify any potential resource conflicts (IRQ, DMA, and so on).

> **CAUTION** Never, ever work inside the PC while it is turned on! Although it's okay to run the system with the cover off while you're testing the adapters, make sure you shut off the computer before getting anywhere near the inside of the PC.

After all the adapters are installed, the cables connected, and everything is working, reinstall the cover.

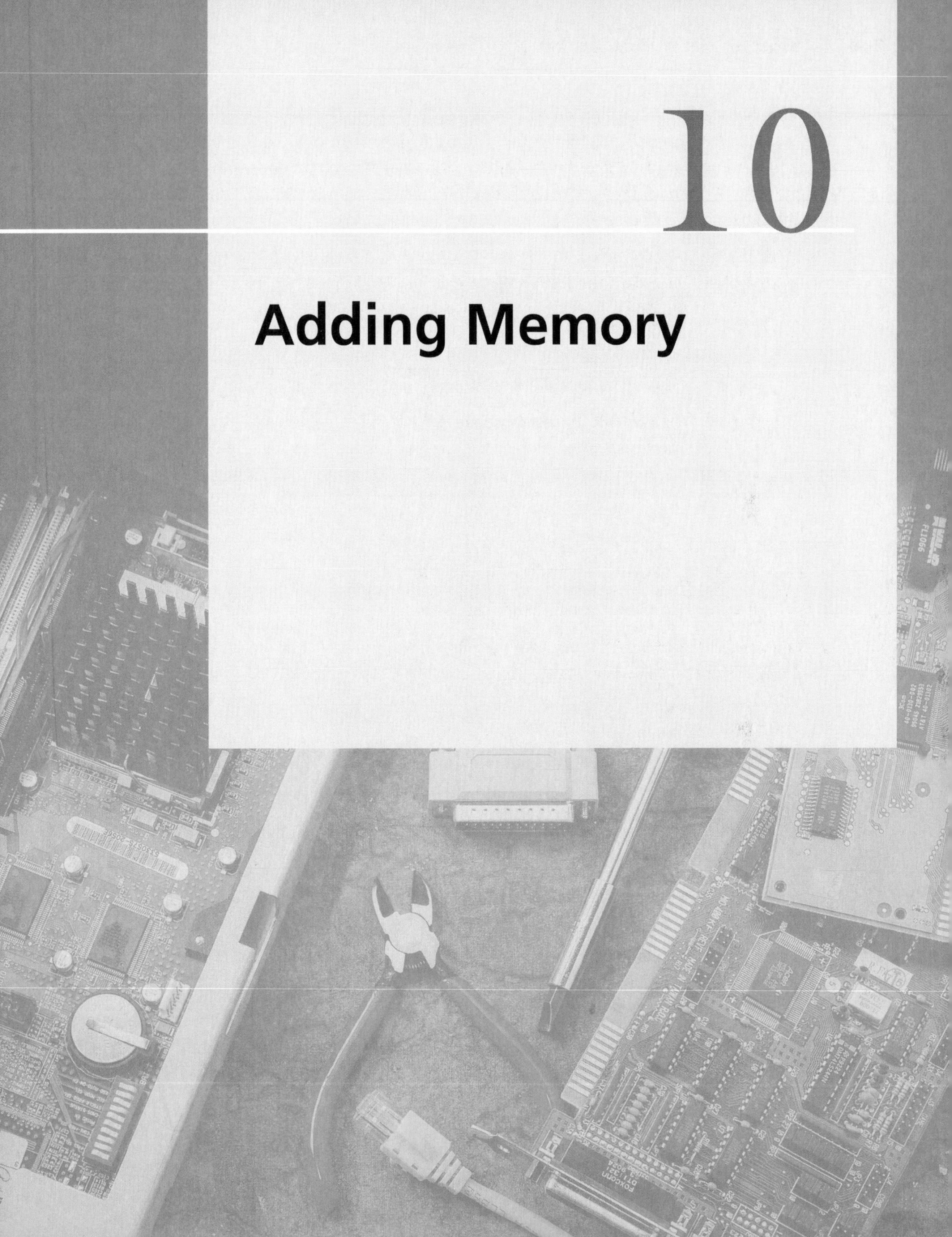

10

Adding Memory

If you're happy with your current motherboard and CPU, but you're looking for a way to speed up the system, maybe you need more memory. Adding more memory to your computer is a good way improve its performance without spending a lot of money. By increasing the amount of RAM in the system, you make more memory available for the operating system, for programs, for cache, and for data.

This chapter takes a look at memory and how adding more can improve the system's performance, covering the following topics:

- Why adding memory can improve the system's performance
- How memory is organized on the motherboard
- How to understand memory addressing
- Choosing the right memory for your system
- Installing memory
- Using a SIMM adapter so you can reuse your old memory

Why Add Memory?

The first question you probably have is, "Why add memory in the first place?"

The memory in your PC acts as a working and temporary storage area for the operating system and the programs you run. Your programs are stored on disk, but those programs are copied into memory to run. So, every program you run needs at least some memory.

Your documents also need to be stored somewhere while you're working on them. Like programs, the documents are copied into memory while you're using them. When you save and close a document, it is copied back to the disk and then removed from memory.

Do programs and documents really use that much memory? You bet they do. The operating system I use most of the time is Windows 95. I typically run three programs all the time: WinFax Pro, Windows Messaging, and Microsoft Word. These three programs alone consume an average of 22M of memory! When I total up all the little utility programs that are running behind the scenes (can't do without that CD player), and throw in the memory used by Windows 95 itself, the grand total comes to more than 40M (see Figure 10.1).

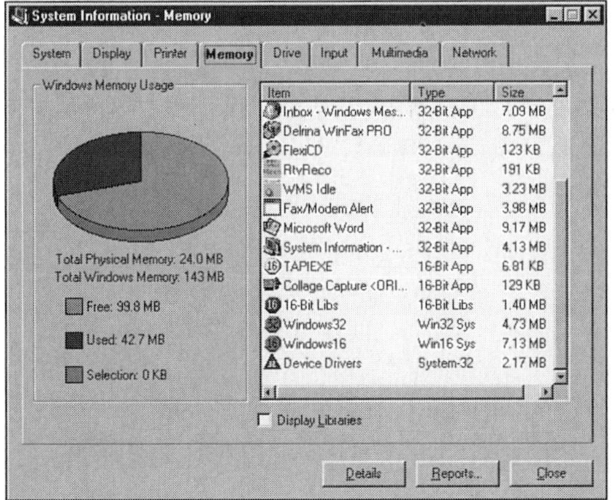

FIG. 10.1
Norton Utilities shows this system using more than 40M of RAM.

But wait a minute! This particular computer contains 24M of RAM. If the programs are using 40M, where is it putting the overflow? It's putting it into virtual memory.

The RAM in your system is *physical memory*—microchips that store data. *Virtual memory*, as its name implies, doesn't really exist. Instead, hard disk space is used to simulate memory, and this is called virtual memory. Here's how it works: the operating system manages the memory in your system as *pages* of memory. As long as there is plenty of physical memory, it doesn't have to use much, if any, virtual memory. If the programs and operating system are only using 8M (fat chance), and the computer contains 16M of RAM, you're in good shape—the computer has plenty of RAM to accommodate everything.

But more than likely, the operating system, programs, and documents are using more memory than your computer contains. So, the operating system sets up a special file called a *swap file* or *paging file* on the hard disk. It then copies some of the memory pages—the ones that aren't being used at the moment—from physical memory to the hard disk for temporary storage. It then has more room in physical memory for more pages. When it needs a page that it has copied to the paging file, it swaps a page from memory to disk and copies the page on the disk back into memory.

Here's an analogy that might help this make sense: Let's say you have a 300-page report you have to read and edit in hardcopy. You have a stack of 300 pages on the desk, and your little, overworked hands can only hold 20 pages at a time. So, when you're through with some of those 20 pages, you set them on the desk and pick up some more. If you need to go back to page 3 again, you set down page 45 and pick up page 3. You always have about 20 pages in your hands (in memory), with the extra pages that you need but aren't using at the moment on the desk (on the disk).

So how does adding more physical memory help the situation? Memory, which is all solid state (no moving parts except electrons), operates much faster than a disk, which consists of spinning data platters and moving heads. Each time the operating system needs to copy a page of memory from the disk, it has to determine which page it needs, locate it on the disk, tell the heads to move to the right spot, wait for the platter to spin the data under the head, and so on. So, any time you can cut down the amount of data going to and from the disk, the better the system will perform. If you have plenty of RAM, you reduce the amount of disk paging the operating system has to do. That speeds up performance.

How Much Is Enough?

With today's memory-crazed operating systems and bloated programs, the average person who uses a couple of programs at a time would need as much as 60M or more of RAM to accommodate everything. Memory is a lot cheaper than it used to be, but it's still too expensive for most people to have that much RAM in their computers. Someday in the not-too-distant future, computers will probably have at least 128M or more built right onto the motherboard (maybe right inside the CPU). It's just a matter of finding new technologies to create higher-capacity memory modules at lower cost.

But you're worried about your computer *today*, and you're stuck with today's memory modules. In just about every case, you should consider 8 to 12M to be the minimum amount of memory you'll need for Windows 3.x, and 16M to be the minimum for running Windows 95 or Windows NT. You can run with less, but the system will be slow.

If you like to run more than a few programs at one time, you're using a memory-hungry program like a CAD (Computer Aided Design) program, or simply want the best possible performance, consider 24M or even 32M. If you're independently wealthy, load the sucker up with as much memory as it will hold!

Overview of Memory and Addressing

There are quite a few things you need to understand about computer memory to be able to pick out the right memory for your system and install it correctly. First, you need to understand the different ways in which memory is packaged for installation in the computer.

Memory Packaging

Although older systems use individual memory chips, most of today's computers use memory modules called *SIMMs*, which stands for *Single Inline Memory Module.* Figure 10.2 shows two types of SIMMs—a 30-pin SIMM and a 72-pin SIMM. A SIMM is just a small printed circuit card with memory chips mounted to it with a few other components necessary for the RAM chips' proper function and well-being. As the names imply, the 30-pin SIMM has 30 pins that connect it to the motherboard socket, and the 72-pin SIMM uses 72 pins.

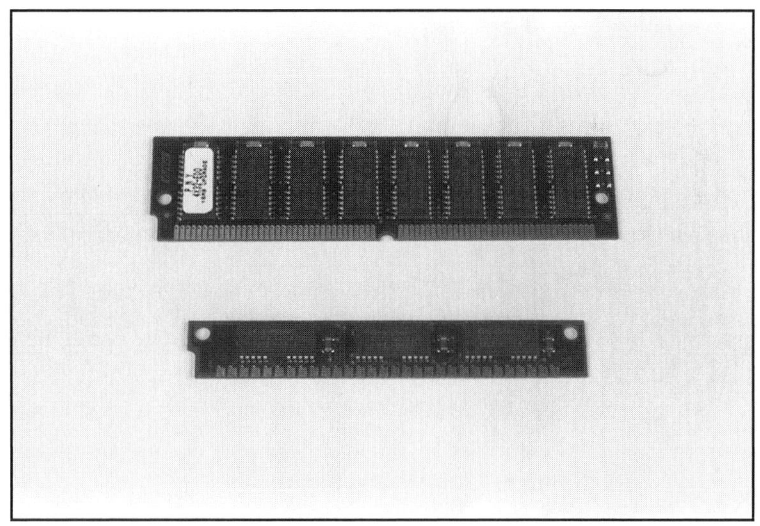

FIG. 10.2
The two most common memory formats these days are the 30-pin SIMM and 72-pin SIMM.

TIP The memory chips on the SIMMs are commonly called *DRAM chips* or *dynamic RAM chips*. In older computers, the DRAM chips were installed in individual sockets on the motherboard. Although individual DRAM chips are used on some of today's motherboards for cache RAM, the main memory is almost always installed as SIMMs or DIMMs.

Most older motherboards use 30-pin SIMMs, and most newer motherboards use 72-pin SIMMs. Typically, 30-pin SIMMs are more expensive than 72-pin SIMMs of the same capacity. 30-pin SIMMs also are limited in capacity to about 4M. You can get 72-pin SIMMs of up to 64M, which makes it a lot easier to get the most memory possible in the computer using 72-pin SIMMs.

Another type of memory package you'll find used in some newer computers is the *DIMM*, which stands for *Dual Inline Memory Module*. DIMMs use a 168-pin configuration that offers better performance over SIMMs. But, the motherboard and chipset have to be designed to accommodate DIMMs. Also, DIMMs are not as common as SIMMs and therefore are more expensive than SIMMs. If your motherboard supports a combination of DIMMs and SIMMs as some do, use DIMMs for the best performance, but expect to pay more for them.

Speed

Memory is rated to operate at a specific speed, which is measured in *nanoseconds* (*ns*), or billionths of a second. Most of today's PCs use memory with a rated speed of 60 to 70ns. The smaller the number, the faster (and more expensive) the memory. So, when you're buying more memory for your PC, you need to match the speed of the new memory with what the system requires (and the speed of the existing memory).

TIP You can use different speed RAM in different banks, but there is no reason to do so unless you already have the different speed RAM. Putting faster RAM in a system designed for slower RAM just means you're spending more for the RAM and not getting the extra speed advantage from it. Using slower RAM in a system designed for faster RAM reduces performance.

Parity and Configuration

The word *parity* refers to a method used in computers to check for errors. In most older computers, the memory design uses parity to check for memory errors. Typically, eight chips made up 1 unit of memory, such as 1M. A ninth chip was used to handle parity checking. So, each 1M SIMM had nine chips on it.

In recent years, memory became so reliable that some manufacturers dropped the parity requirement for their systems. So, a *non-parity SIMM* is used that doesn't contain a parity chip. You can install a parity SIMM in a computer that doesn't require parity and it will work fine. But, a non-parity SIMM won't work in a computer that requires parity.

What does that mean to you, other than the fact that you have to make sure to get the right type? It means you need to be able to read a RAM chip description and know whether or not it supports parity. Table 10.1 shows typical RAM designations and capacities you might see in a vendor's memory configuration table.

Table 10.1 Memory Configuration and Capacity

Organization	Size
1M×32	4M
1M×36	4M
2M×32	8M
2M×36	8M
4M×32	16M
4M×36	16M
8M×32	32M
8M×36	32M

As you can see in Table 10.1, the designation will include 32 or 36. Remember that the original memory organization was eight chips with a ninth chip for parity? Well, 4×8=32, and 4×9=36. So, a value of 32 indicates a non-parity SIMM (no logical ninth chip), and a 36 indicates a parity SIMM. If you multiply the first value in the description (1M, 2M, and so on) by 4, you'll get the capacity of the SIMM. For an 8M×36 SIMM, for example, you'd come up with 32M because 8×4=32.

Lastly, when you locate the configuration you need and the capacity, look for a speed indication of either 60ns or 70ns, depending on the requirements of your system.

EDO

Many new systems employ a type of memory called *Extended Data Output*, or *EDO RAM* as it is commonly called. EDO RAM provides about 15 percent better performance overall than non-EDO chips of the same speed because of its internal design. EDO RAM is also a little more expensive.

To take advantage of EDO RAM, however, your system's chipset must support it. You can use EDO RAM in a non-EDO system, but you won't get the advantage of the extra speed. You'll just end up paying more for the memory. So, when you're shopping for more memory, buy EDO RAM if your system supports it, and buy non-EDO RAM if it does not.

Sockets and Banks

Whether your motherboard uses SIMMs or DIMMs, they'll install in sockets in the motherboard. Typically, the sockets are white, and have lots of metal contacts that connect the SIMM circuitry to the motherboard (see Figure 10.3).

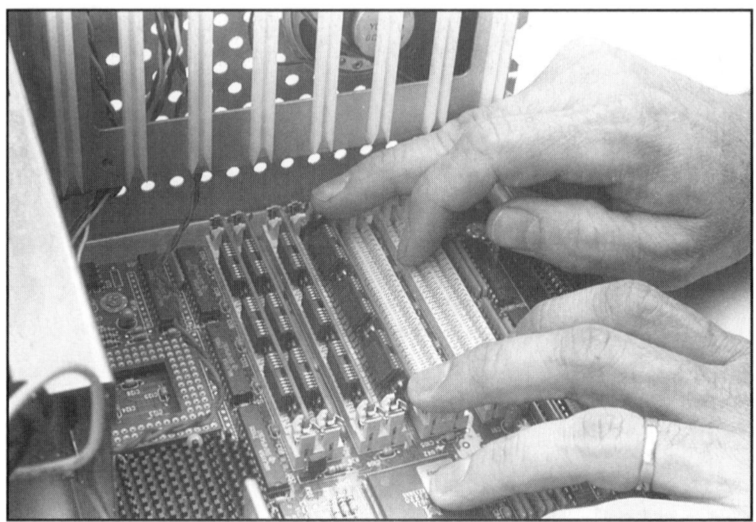

FIG. 10.3
SIMMs and DIMMs install in sockets on the motherboard.

If you take a close look at the memory sockets, you'll probably find that the sockets are grouped together in *banks*. The location of the memory banks varies from one motherboard to the next, but they're always together. The number of memory banks depends on the motherboard design. Some have two and others have three or four. The banks are numbered sequentially starting with 0. If your motherboard has two banks, for example, they are bank 0 and bank 1. Your motherboard manual probably will have a diagram that shows all the major components on the motherboard and identifies the memory banks by number.

Why are the number of banks and their ID numbers important? You have to fill up the banks in a certain way, depending on the design of your motherboard. Your motherboard manual contains a table that explains how to fill up the banks.

Also, you have to install matching SIMMs in a bank—two 4M SIMMs, two 8M SIMMs, and so on. You can't install a 4M SIMM and a 16M SIMM in one bank. Also, bank 0 always has to be filled first. What does this all mean? It means you need to check the manual to determine how the banks can be filled before you decide what memory to buy. You'll read more about this in the section "Choosing the Right Memory for Your System" later in this chapter.

Proprietary RAM

Some system manufacturers use a proprietary design for their memory modules rather than a standard configuration. You can't just buy run-of-the-mill SIMMs and have them work in the system. Instead, you have to buy memory modules made specifically for your brand and type of computer. This is more likely with large, name-brand manufacturers.

Your system manual will tell you if your system uses a proprietary memory module. If you're not sure, let the salesperson know what kind of computer you have when you buy the RAM. The salesperson should be able to steer you to the right kind. Keep in mind that although the memory design might be proprietary, you might not have to buy it from the manufacturer. Many hardware vendors carry brand-specific memory modules as well as standard configuration modules.

Proprietary RAM Cards

Many 386 and 486 motherboards supported a proprietary RAM slot that used one ISA slot and a second connector in line with it. Figure 10.4 shows a proprietary RAM slot on a 486 computer.

FIG. 10.4
A proprietary RAM slot is one way to add more RAM to your system.

The proprietary RAM slot accommodates a special memory adapter card made specifically for the system by the manufacturer. These adapter cards were intended to give you a way to boost the total memory capacity of the system beyond what could be accommodated by the SIMM sockets. Why were they necessary? In the days when these motherboards were designed, SIMM capacity was limited. The only way to load up the system with more than say, 32M, was to add a secondary RAM card.

The drawback to these RAM cards is their proprietary nature: You had to buy it from the system's manufacturer, which typically meant they were expensive, sometimes hard to get, and usually no longer carried by the manufacturer by the time you decided you needed one.

With today's high-capacity SIMMs, you can easily load up a system with 256M of RAM. That should be enough RAM for you, no matter how many hands of solitaire you want to play at one time! So, avoid proprietary RAM cards unless your system already contains one.

NOTE Many 486 and older systems were not designed to handle 256M of memory. Check your system manual to find out how much memory the motherboard will accommodate.

Choosing the Right Memory for Your System

Now that you know a little about RAM, you're ready to go shopping. First, you need to determine if your system uses proprietary RAM modules or standard modules.

Next, you need to check out what you already have.

Checking What You Have Now

The first thing you should do is determine what your system contains now for RAM. You can get the total capacity from the boot screen when the POST checks your system's memory. A value of 8096 would indicate a total of 8M of RAM; 16,192 would be 16M; and so on (1,024K per 1M).

If you're running Windows 95 or Windows NT 4.0, you can use the Control Panel to find the total memory installed in the computer. Here are the steps to follow:

1. Open the Control Panel and double-click the System icon.
2. In the General page of the System Properties sheet (Memory page under Windows NT), you'll find the amount of installed RAM listed under Computer along with the processor type. Figure 10.5 shows the General page of the System Properties sheet on a Windows 95 computer. Figure 10.6 shows the Memory page on a Windows NT computer.

TIP You can display the System Properties sheet by right-clicking the My Computer icon and choosing Properties from the context menu.

After you know how much memory your system contains, you need to open up the system to find out how the memory is configured. Rather than give you a procedure to follow, I'll just explain the process.

Shut down and turn off the computer, then open the system and look for the memory sockets. Count how many sockets there are in total. If you have eight sockets, each one contains a SIMM, and your system reports that it has 8M of RAM, the answer is easy: you have eight 1M SIMMs.

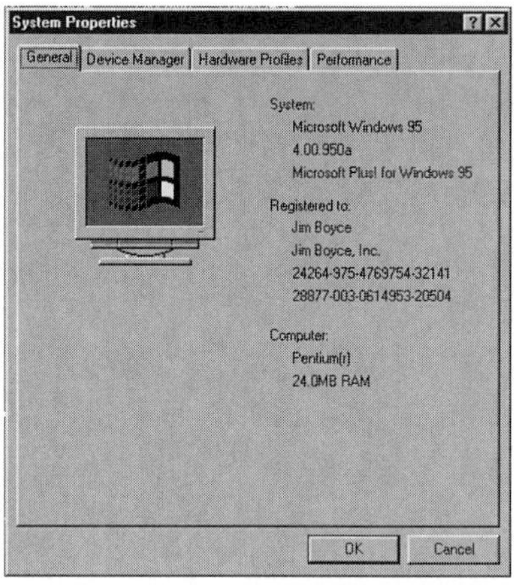

FIG. 10.5
Click the System icon in the Control Panel to determine the amount of RAM in the system.

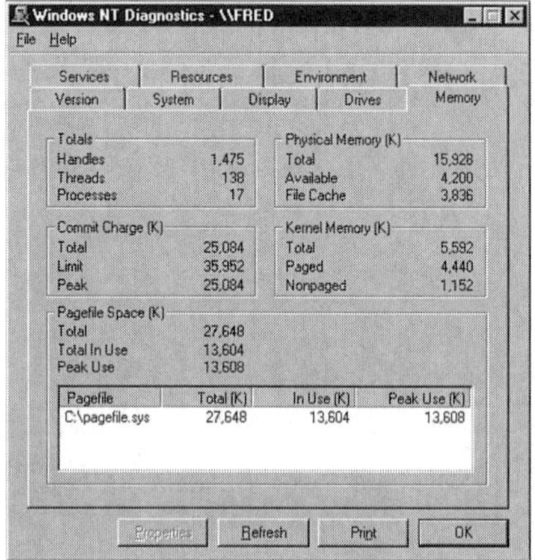

FIG. 10.6
Use the Memory page in Windows NT to check the amount of RAM in the system.

The answer might not be that easy, however. If only one bank (comprising two sockets) is filled, divide the total number of RAM by 2 to determine the capacity of each SIMM. If the system reports 8M of RAM, you have two 4M SIMMs. If the system reports 16M of RAM, you have two 8M SIMMs. I'm sure you get the idea.

But what if you have more than two banks and the total is not a multiple of 8? For example, you might have two banks full (four sockets) and a reported total of 20M. In such a case, you can bet that you have two 8M SIMMs in one bank and two 2M SIMMs in the other:

$$2\times8+2\times2=20$$

The math won't work out any other way to give you a combination of SIMMs that total 20M.

In some cases, the capacity in each bank might not be obvious. In such a case, you'll have to read the descriptions on the SIMMs. Many times, the memory capacity and memory configuration will be printed on one side of the SIMM. Unfortunately, this means you sometimes have to remove the SIMM in order to read it.

CAUTION Before you remove any SIMMs, make sure you discharge your static to avoid damaging the chips on the SIMM.

If the SIMM doesn't have its capacity or configuration listed on it, you'll have to ferret out the information from the part numbers on the chips. Look for a part number that begins with 1, 2, 4, 8, or 16, which generally indicates the capacity (2 for 2M, 4 for 4M, and so on). You'll probably have to remove the SIMM to read the part numbers on the chips. Again, make sure you discharge your static before handling the SIMMs.

TIP If you can't tell the SIMMs' capacities by looking at them, find a computer store in your area that has a SIMM tester. Take the SIMMs to the store and have them tested (it might cost $1 or so per SIMM). The testing process determines the SIMM capacity.

Finally, make a note of which banks are full (*populated*) and which are not. You'll need this information to decide how you can add memory to the system. The next section explains why.

Can You Use All the Existing Memory?

If all of the sockets on the motherboard are populated, you're going to have to remove some SIMMs to add higher-capacity ones. For example, let's say the motherboard has eight sockets and each one contains a 1M SIMM, for a total of 8M. They are configured in two banks of four sockets each. You could remove four SIMMs from bank 0 and replace them with 4M SIMMs, giving you a total of 20M.

So, when you're determining how much memory you can add to your computer and what capacity SIMMs you need, bear in mind that you might have to replace some SIMMs, not just install more SIMMs. Or, you could use a SIMM adapter.

Using SIMM Adapters

What if you can't reuse all the existing memory in the slots as they are? Or, what if you are replacing the motherboard that uses 30-pin SIMMs with a new one that uses 72-pin SIMMs? What if you have some 72-pin SIMMs you like to use on a motherboard that only accepts 30-pin SIMMs? Fortunately, you do have an option: Use a SIMM adapter. Figure 10.7 shows a typical SIMM adapter.

FIG. 10.7
This SIMM adapter adapts 30-pin SIMMs to a 72-pin socket.

A SIMM adapter lets you use more than one SIMM per slot, which can overcome all of these problems:

- *Multiple SIMMs per socket.* You can use a SIMM adapter to install multiple SIMMs in one motherboard memory socket. This is a great solution if you're trying to reuse all the existing memory in your system when you add new memory. You might use two SIMM adapters to install eight 1M SIMMs in two sockets, for example, then fill the other sockets with new, higher capacity SIMMs.
- *30-pin SIMMs in a 72-pin socket.* In this case, the sockets on the adapter are 30-pin sockets. The adapter itself fits into a 72-pin socket. This is a good solution when you're moving your old memory to a new system that uses only 72-pin SIMMs.

- *72-pin SIMMs in a 30-pin socket.* The sockets on the adapter accommodate 72-pin SIMMs, and the adapter itself fits into a 30-pin socket. This is a good solution when you want to use new 72-pin memory in an older system that has only 30-pin sockets.

When you use SIMM adapters, keep in mind that you still have to satisfy the capacity requirements of the bank. This means that the total memory installed in each motherboard socket must match in a bank. For example, if you install a single 8M SIMM in one socket of the bank, the SIMM adapter in the other socket must contain a total of 8Ms worth of SIMMs. Also, keep in mind that you must populate both sockets in the bank. You can't use a SIMM adapter in one socket and leave the other empty. Finally, understand that in some systems, each bank consists of a single slot.

TIP You can use SIMM adapters in two sockets in a bank. But, they'll have to be *opposite-hand adapters*, meaning the SIMMs must mount to opposite sides of the adapters, facing away from one another. This way, the SIMMs on one adapter won't interfere with the SIMMs on the other adapter.

Getting the Right Adapters

Don't just rush out and buy some adapters. You need to take the time to make sure you get the adapters that will fit your situation and the layout of the motherboard and sockets. The following checklist will help you pick out the right ones.

When Choosing SIMM Adapters, You Need to:

- ☑ Map out where you want to use adapters and where you can use individual SIMMs.
- ☑ Check the overall height of the adapter. Make sure that it won't interfere with something above it (like an adapter card installed in a bus slot or the power supply) when you install it in the intended slot. The solution might be to get an adapter that faces the SIMMs in the opposite direction, get a shorter adapter, or move the adapter to a different socket.
- ☑ Make sure the SIMM adapter won't interfere with the next socket in the bank. If you're using two SIMM adapters, you'll have to get opposing adapters (left hand and right hand) that face the SIMMs in opposite directions from one another. Also, you might need to get a taller adapter so the bottom SIMM on the adapter clears the SIMM in the next socket.

- ☑ Check the capacity of the adapter. Some adapters will accommodate only certain capacity SIMMs.
- ☑ Get adapters with the correct pin configuration for the SIMMs and for the motherboard socket (30-pin versus 72-pin). This depends on how you are using the adapter.
- ☑ Some SIMM adapters cause a performance drop, making the RAM run at a slightly slower speed. Look for adapters that compensate for this potential performance drop.

Getting the Right Stuff

Here's one final checklist to help you choose the right memory for your system.

When Getting the Right Memory for Your System, You Need to:

- ☑ Check the total amount of existing RAM in your system and the number of empty banks, if any.
- ☑ Determine how much total memory you want to have.
- ☑ Map out the banks, deciding what combinations of SIMMs and adapters (if any) you'll need in each bank. Remember that SIMMs in a bank must match one another in capacity. Use the motherboard manual to make sure you populate the banks properly.
- ☑ If you're using SIMM adapters, use the previous checklist to make sure you get the right ones.
- ☑ Note the pin configuration (30-pin or 72-pin) you need for each SIMM or SIMM adapter.
- ☑ Note whether you need parity or non-parity SIMMs.
- ☑ Note whether or not your motherboard supports EDO RAM.
- ☑ Note the correct speed of RAM required for your system.

Adding and Replacing Memory Modules

Now that you have plenty of background on SIMMs, DIMMs, and memory in general, you're ready to start removing and installing memory. The following procedures assume that your motherboard uses SIMMs, but the procedure also will work for DIMMs.

Removing SIMMs

Like any upgrade task, removing SIMMs isn't difficult. But, you do need to be careful to make sure you don't damage the SIMM or the socket. The following procedure explains these cautions.

To Remove SIMMs, You Need:

- ☑ Phillips screwdriver to open and close the case
- ☑ Anti-static protection
- ☑ Anti-static bag to hold removed SIMMs if not reusing

1. Shut down, turn off, and unplug the PC.
2. Open the system.
3. Discharge your static, then locate the SIMMs to be removed.

NOTE Because the SIMMs tilt out of their sockets, you'll have to remove them in a specific order. Otherwise, you won't be able to tilt a SIMM because the one behind it is in the way. (Think falling dominoes, and you'll understand.) Look for the little retaining clips that hold the SIMM in place (see Figure 10.8). You'll be tilting the SIMMs away from these clips. In some cases, you'll have to remove a SIMM you intend to leave in the PC simply because it is in the way of the ones you need to remove.

4. On each side of the SIMM to be removed is a small metal or plastic spring clip (see Figure 10.8). Pull back the clip on each side and tilt the SIMM in the socket past the clips.

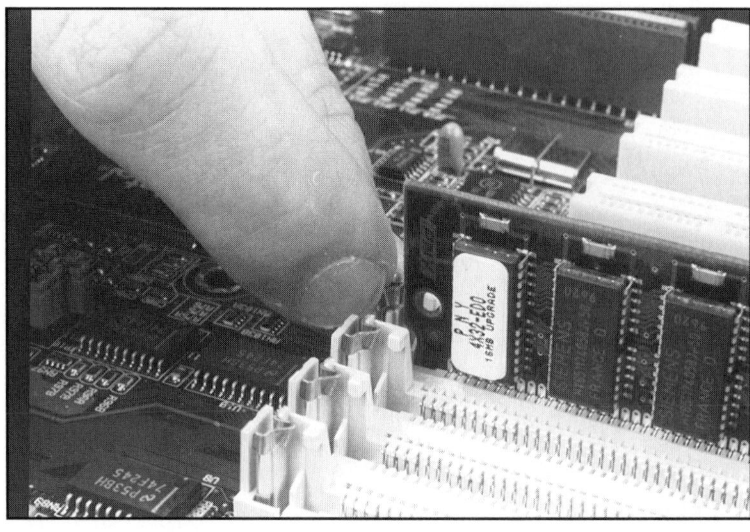

FIG. 10.8
The memory socket has a spring clip that holds the memory module in place.

5. Once clear of the clips, tilt the SIMM at about a 45-degree angle away from the clips (see Figure 10.9).

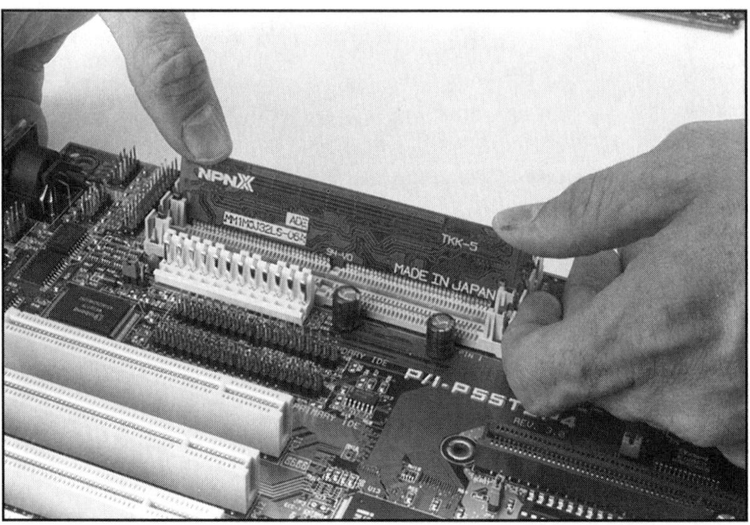

FIG. 10.9
After releasing the clips, you have to tilt the SIMM out of the socket.

NOTE I assume you're going to be putting a new SIMM in these sockets. As you're removing the SIMM, check its two bottom corners for a little notch (shown later in Figure 10.10). Make a mental note at which end of the socket the notch is located. You'll also have to orient the new SIMM according to its notch.

6. Carefully lift the SIMM free of the socket and set it aside.

Installing SIMMs

Installing a SIMM is pretty much the reverse of removal. You just need to make sure you install the SIMM in the proper orientation. Fortunately, the SIMM is keyed so it will only install in the correct orientation.

Before Installing Memory Modules, You Need:

- Phillips screwdriver to open and close the case
- Checklist, "Getting the Right Memory for Your System"
- Anti-static protection

---

1. Shut down, turn off, and unplug the PC.
2. Open the system.
3. Discharge your static, then locate the new sockets in which you want to install SIMMs. Use the checklist in the earlier section, and the motherboard manual as a guide.
4. Note that the SIMM is notched on one corner (see Figure. 10.10). The socket is keyed so the SIMM will only install in the socket in the correct orientation.
5. Carefully place the SIMM in the socket at an angle—about 30–45 degrees—making sure it is oriented properly by the notch and key (see Figure 10.11). The SIMM won't go down all the way if it isn't oriented properly.
6. Push the SIMM down all the way into the socket, then tilt it up towards the retaining clips (see Figure 10.12).
7. Make sure the hole at each end of the SIMM fits over its tab (shown in Figure 10.12), and make sure the retaining clip is holding the SIMM in place.

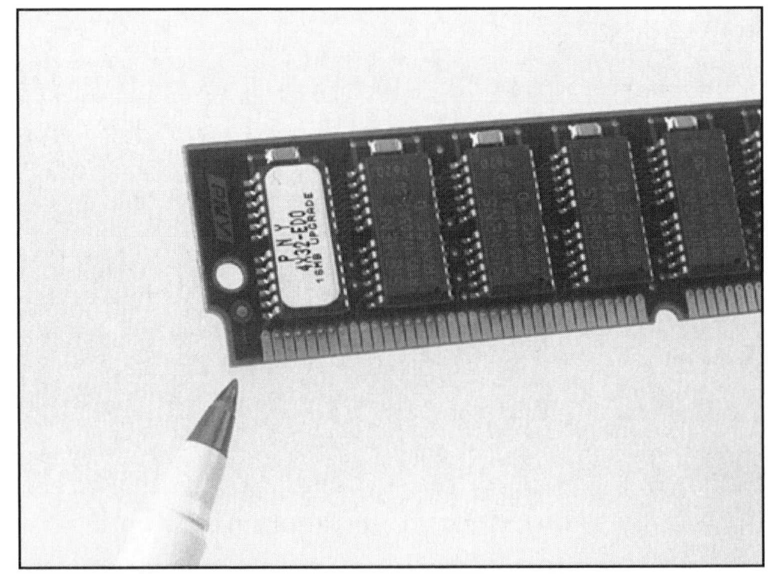

FIG. 10.10
The SIMM is notched to go around a key in the socket, which prevents you from installing it backwards.

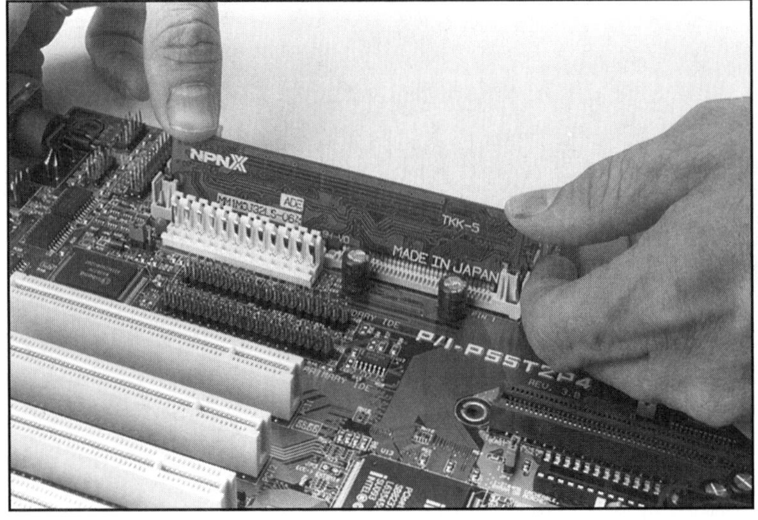

FIG. 10.11
Set the SIMM in the socket at an angle, making sure the notch and key are oriented properly.

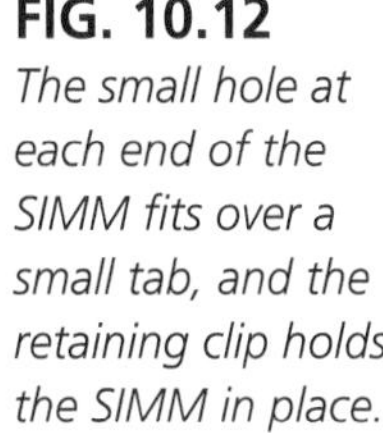

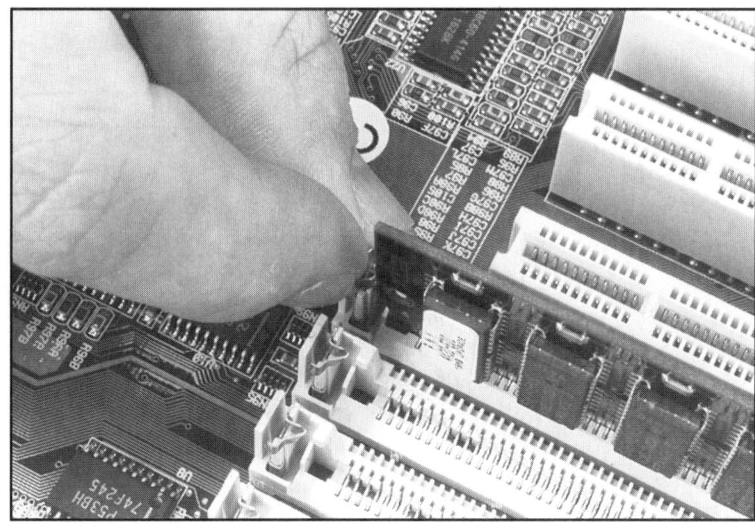

FIG. 10.12
The small hole at each end of the SIMM fits over a small tab, and the retaining clip holds the SIMM in place.

Installing a SIMM Adapter

The hard part of installing a SIMM adapter is choosing the right one to begin with. The easy part is installing it.

To Install a SIMM Adapter, You Need:

- Phillips screwdriver to open and close the case
- Anti-static protection
- Correct SIMM adapter to fit your system and sockets
- SIMMs to go on the adapter

---

1. Shut down, turn off, and unplug the computer.
2. Open the case.
3. Discharge your static.
4. Put the SIMM adapter on a work surface, then mount the SIMMs on the adapter (see Figure 10.13). Use the previous procedure for installing SIMMs as a guide.

FIG. 10.13
Use the procedure "Installing a SIMM Adapter" as a guide to install SIMMs on a SIMM adapter.

5. Place the SIMM adapter in its intended socket, making sure to align the notch in the corner of the adapter with the key in the socket (see Figure 10.14).

FIG. 10.14
Like a SIMM, the SIMM adapter is inserted into the socket at an angle.

6. Push the adapter down all the way into the socket, then tilt it up toward the retaining clips.
7. Make sure the holes in the adapter line up with the tab on the socket and that the retaining clips engage to hold the adapter in place.
8. Reassemble the system for testing.

Configuring the Motherboard

Most new motherboards automatically detect the amount of RAM installed. You don't have to configure anything on the motherboard to specify how much memory is installed. In some cases, particularly with older motherboards, you have to set one or more jumpers or DIP switches to let the motherboard know how much memory is installed. Each one is different, so you'll have to rely on your motherboard's manual to tell you whether or not you have to configure anything on the motherboard. If there is no mention in the manual of jumper or switch configuration for memory capacity, the motherboard detects it automatically.

Changing the BIOS Memory Setting

After you install the memory and configure the motherboard jumpers/switches accordingly (if required), the next step is to configure the BIOS for the amount of RAM installed. If this setting is wrong, it won't prevent the motherboard from using all of the installed memory, but it will cause an error message when the system boots.

The setting for the amount of memory installed is almost always on the first page of the BIOS setup program. Check your system manual and Chapter 7, "Working with the BIOS," to learn how to enter the BIOS Setup program and specify the amount of memory installed in the computer.

After you reset the CMOS setting and save the changes, the system reboots. As it is booting, you should see a larger number in the memory test as the POST tests the new amount of RAM.

Troubleshooting

Usually, your memory upgrades work without a hitch as long as you do your homework and get the right equipment to suit your computer. If you receive an error message during boot (other than something like `Memory type mismatch`, which indicates a different value in CMOS from what is installed), or the POST doesn't report the correct amount of RAM, try these solutions:

- Make sure the SIMMs are all seated properly in their sockets and that the retaining clips are holding the SIMMs in place.

- Make sure you've added memory in the correct banks and in the correct capacities. Remember that the sockets in each bank must match in total capacity.
- Make sure each bank is full. You can't fill up only one socket in a bank of, say, two sockets.
- Check the motherboard manual to see if you need to set jumpers or switches on the motherboard for the new memory.

If you receive a parity error during boot, you probably have installed non-parity RAM in a system that supports parity. More than likely, your BIOS provides a setting that lets you disable the use of memory parity checking. The actual setting and its location within the BIOS Setup pages varies from one BIOS to the next. Look for a setting that references *system parity* or *memory parity* and set it to off or disabled. Save the changes to CMOS and reboot to see if the error goes away.

If everything is installed correctly and you're still getting errors, you either have one or more bad SIMMs (or a bad SIMM adapter), or one or more memory sockets on the motherboard is bad. Take the SIMMs to a local computer repair shop and have them tested. If you find a bad one, replace it. If they all are good, the problem must be with the motherboard. Call the manufacturer's technical support line for help in getting it fixed.

Mass Storage Devices

11

Hard Disks

The PC hard disk is one of the "big three" components you can upgrade, relatively painlessly, to gain a noticeable improvement in your system's performance, just behind memory upgrades. You might be thinking, "What about the CPU?" The fact is that even a relatively slow CPU such as an i386/33 (by today's standards) spends most of its processor time waiting for input, whether from you or the I/O subsystem (the hard disk). Therefore, replacing an older, slower hard disk with a faster, newer one will not only get you more storage space, but will also boost your perceived overall system performance. Your Excel spreadsheets won't recalculate any faster, but they sure will load faster.

In this chapter, you will:

- Determine some of the more important things to look for when shopping for a new hard disk
- Understand the differences between major hard disk types
- Choose the proper hard disk for an upgrade
- Prepare a new hard disk for installation
- Install a new hard disk

Hard Disk Overview

NOTE Many people use the term *hard disk* and *hard drive* interchangeably, as I do. However, the more accurate term is *hard drive* because the hard disk or *platter* is merely a component of the hard drive.

The technology that comprises a modern hard drive (HD) is so amazing that it's a wonder that they work at all. An analogy has been floating around for years that helps put things in perspective, because the speeds, distances, and sizes relevant to a typical hard drive don't mean much to the average user. As with most magnetic recording devices, a typical HD has a read/write head and recording media or disk sometimes referred to as a *platter*. So the analogy goes like this: Imagine that a read/write head as big as a 747 is cruising at around mach 1 just a few feet above the ground (the platter)! Now you can see why the case is hermetically sealed. Even something as small as a smoke particle is large enough to get wedged between the head and the platter and scorch the surface.

Let's get started with a brief overview of the main hard disk drive components as shown in Figure 11.1.

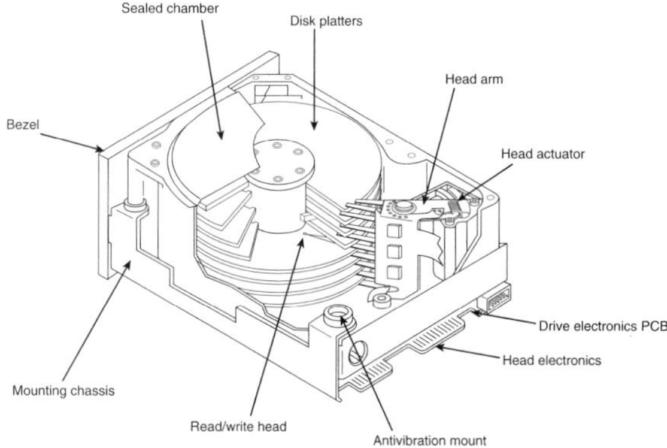

FIG. 11.1
The main hard disk drive components.

Platters

A *platter* is little more than a disk of aluminum, glass, or ceramic. By comparison, a floppy disk simply uses a disk of thin plastic. Platters are then coated on both sides with a layer of magnetic material (the actual media), and coated with a protective layer. Finished and polished platters are then stacked and coupled to the *spindle motor*; some drives may only use one platter. Before the platter stack is fixed to the frame, the read/write heads are fitted in between each disk. There is usually one head per platter side, so a drive with two platters should have three or four heads. During drive operation, the spindle motor spins the platter stack at 3,600 to 7,200 RPM (rotations per minute) for AV (Audio Video) drives.

Read/Write Heads

Read/Write heads (or *R/W heads*) form the interface between a drive's electronic circuitry and magnetic media on the platters. During writing, a head translates electronic signals into magnetic flux patterns that magnetize points on the media where those transitions take place. A read operation works roughly in reverse. Flux patterns along the disk induce electrical signals in the head which are amplified, filtered, and translated into corresponding logic signals. It is up to the drive's electronics to determine whether a head is reading or writing. Early drive heads were big and bulky, which limited the number of tracks that a platter could hold. Today, thin-film heads are extremely small and light, allowing faster high-capacity drives.

The most recent advances in hard drive R/W heads use *magneto-resistive* (*MR*) *technology*. MR heads are two or three times more sensitive than thin-film heads. This technology has historically been expensive, but has dropped quit a bit in price. I recently bought an IBM UltraSCSI 2G HD for $449, which works out to only 22 cents per 1M!

When assembled, the heads themselves are attached to long metal arms that are moved by the head actuator motor. Read/write preamp ICs are typically mounted on a small PC board that is attached to the head/actuator assembly. The entire subassembly is sealed in the platter compartment, and should be considered inaccessible unless opened in a clean room environment.

Head Actuators

Hard drives swing the heads along a slight arc to achieve radial travel from edge to spindle. Many hard drives use *voice coil motors* (also called *rotary coil motors* or *servos*) to control head movement. Cylinders are selected by incrementing the servo signal and maintaining the signal at the desired level. Voice coil motors are very small and light assemblies that are well suited to fast access times and small HD assemblies.

The greatest challenge to head movement is to keep the heads centered on the desired track. Otherwise, aerodynamic disturbances, thermal effects in the platters, and variations in voice coil driver signals can cause head positioning error. Head position must be constantly checked and adjusted in real-time to ensure that desired tracks are followed exactly. The process of track following is called *servoing the heads.* Information is required to compare the head's expected position to its actual position; any resulting difference can then be corrected by adjusting the voice coil signal. Servo information is located on the platters.

Spindle Motor

One of the major factors that contribute to hard disk performance is the speed at which the media passes under the R/W heads—by spinning the platter(s) at a high rate of speed (at least 3,600 RPM). The spindle motor is responsible for spinning the platter(s). A spindle motor is typically a brushless, low-profile DC motor (similar in principle to the spindle motors used in floppy disk drives).

An *index sensor* provides a feedback pulse signal that detects the spindle as it rotates. The drive's control electronics use the index signal to regulate spindle speed as precisely as possible. Today's drives typically use magnetic sensors that detect iron tabs on the spindle shaft, or optical sensors that monitor holes or tabs rotating along the spindle. The spindle motor and index sensor are also sealed in the platter compartment.

Older hard drives used a rubber or cork pad to slow the spindle to a stop after drive power was removed, but newer drives use a technique called *dynamic braking*. When power is applied to a spindle motor, a magnetic field is developed in the motor coils. When power is removed, the magnetic energy stored in the coils is released as a reverse voltage pulse. Dynamic braking channels the energy of that reverse voltage to stop the drive faster and more reliably than physical braking.

Choosing a Disk Type

There are many parts to a hard disk that a real "gear head" might argue are important in selecting a new drive. Most people really only use one criterion when considering which HD to choose: cost. You can get into a lot of trouble if that is your sole consideration, and I speak from experience. Here are the basic things to consider when comparing, in order of importance:

- *Interface type, such as IDE (Integrated Drive Electronics).* The interface type goes without saying. You wouldn't buy a SCSI (Small Computer System Interface) HD if all you have is an IDE controller, unless you want to add the benefits of a fast SCSI drive without eliminating the existing IDE drive.

  Also, make sure to match the controller with the drive. An Ultra Fast SCSI drive will not be "Ultra Fast" if you only use a SCSI 2 controller. The same can be said for an EIDE (Enhanced Integrated Drive Electronics) HD and an IDE controller.
- *Maximum formatted storage capacity.* HD manufacture's and vendors usually quote you the maximum storage capacity, which is always more than the formatted capacity due to many factors including file system (FAT16, FAT32, NTFS), cluster size or allocation unit, type of files being stored, and so on.
- *Transfer rate.* The transfer rate is the rate at which the drive *and* controller can send data to the system. The greater the value, the better. UltraFast Wide SCSI subsystems hold the current record at 40M/sec.

- *Rotational speed (RPM).* Rotational speed and transfer rates are closely related. The faster the RPM, the more data passes under the read/write head in a set period of time, allowing for higher total transfer. Faster is not always better, however. The faster the RPM, the more chance you have to drop some data. Not a problem for digital video, as in AV drives, but not so good for your spreadsheet.
- *Average seek time (also known as access time).* The access time is the amount of time that lapses between a request for information and its delivery. The lower the value, the better. Most modern HDs have an access time of 10ms or less.
- *Cost per megabyte.* This is a good way to compare two drives of different storage capacity. For example, the IBM 2G drive I mentioned earlier cost $449 (449/2,000M), which translates to about 22 cents per 1M. A 1G drive costing $299 ran me 30 cents per 1M; therefore, I'm getting a better deal with the larger drive even though it might cost me more.
- *Onboard cache (or just cache).* Onboard cache acts as a buffer for data being transferred to and from the HD. The larger, the better.

NOTE For a more comprehensive and technical understanding of the factors influencing hard drive capacity, get a copy of Que's *Upgrading and Repairing PCs, Sixth Edition*. Make sure to read Chapter 14, "Hard Disk Drives."

SCSI versus EIDE

When people ask me, "Which is better: SCSI or EIDE?" I say, "It depends." The real answer for you is: Make your choice based on a combination of the current state of your system and your future needs. In general, SCSI is the better way to go if you are going to have more than one physical disk, and if that disk will be running a modern operating system like Windows 95 or, better yet, Windows NT.

Why? SCSI controllers have enough on-board "intelligence" to multitask; neither IDE nor EIDE (Enhanced Integrated Drive Electronics) do. When the CPU makes a request of a SCSI subsystem, the CPU is then free to process other tasks while it waits for the previously requested data. The time it takes to find and return the data is an eternity to the CPU, which is used to dealing with RAM on a nanosecond basis. Even 9ms is 1,000 times slower than cache RAM access. In contrast, a request made of an EIDE or IDE subsystem holds the CPU hostage until the data is returned, which is time spent *not* working on your other requests.

Also, when using two or more drives, SCSI drives work independently of each other or in parallel. EIDE/IDE work serially, so a request made for data on two separate physical drives can take twice as long to return as the same request made of a similar SCSI system. SCSI controllers support seven devices; EIDE only four. SCSI is also the current king of transfer rates at 40M/sec for Ultra Fast Wide SCSI 3 subsystems.

With that in mind, there are still times when EIDE is the way to go:

- If your system already supports EIDE devices. Then you will not need to upgrade the controller, but you could add a new EIDE disk (up to four are supported). This is your cheapest way out, and you can still use the original HD.
- If your current system uses an older IDE controller and disk. You could upgrade to an EIDE controller and add an EIDE disk. EIDE components are more readily available and are usually cheaper than the SCSI equivalent.
- If your system will have only one physical disk. Single-disk EIDE systems usually edge out a single disk SCSI system in performance comparisons, because the IDE system has 100 percent of the processor's attention.
- If you are buying a new motherboard. Most new motherboards come with on-board EIDE controllers built right in, as shown in Figure 11.2. Again, it's cheaper.

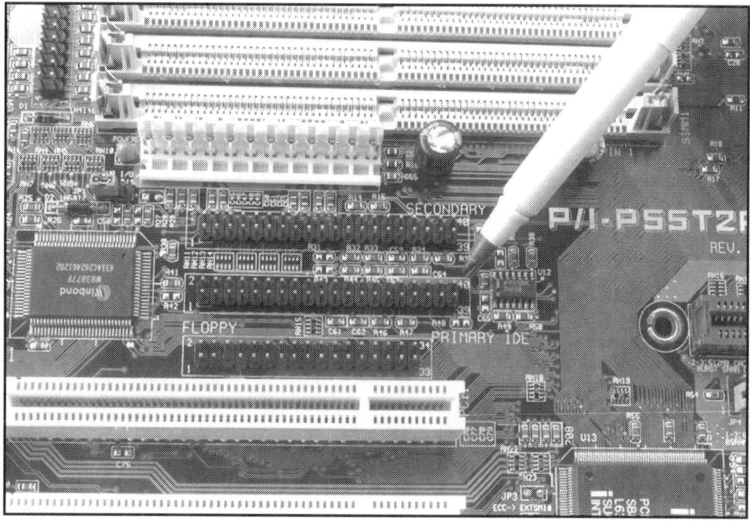

FIG. 11.2
On-board primary and secondary EIDE controllers.

- If (for some unknown reason) your primary operating system will be DOS. DOS is not a multitasking OS, and will not be able to take full advantage of the SCSI performance benefits.

NOTE Older IDE hard disks are fully compatible with EIDE controllers. They use the same 40-pin signal interface cable.

Adding a SCSI Drive to an IDE System

If you would like to free yourself from the bindings that IDE imposes on you, but can't bear the idea of pitching a perfectly functional IDE drive, consider adding a SCSI drive as your upgrade instead of another IDE/EIDE drive. This will allow you to take advantage of the greater performance/expandability that SCSI has to offer, while retaining your current investment. And if you ever decide to invest in a new SCSI-based system, you can take the SCSI drives with you while retaining a completely functional IDE system.

TIP In an IDE/SCSI system, the IDE drive must be the boot drive. Very few computer systems have the ability to allow the SCSI drive as the boot drive with an IDE drive installed.

Planning the Installation

Once you have decided on the type of drive to buy (and you've picked out a controller, if necessary), it's time to plan your actual installation process. Drive upgrades are usually straightforward, but proper planning is the key to avoiding problems later on.

Data Backups

Before you attempt to perform any type of HD upgrade, you should perform a full system backup of your current hard disk(s). If you are replacing a disk outright, a backup is vital for restoring your work to the new disk. If you are adding a second drive, a backup is not quite so critical, but will still protect you in the event you might accidentally lose data on your original disk.

Backups can take many forms: you can use floppy disks, Syquest cartridges, Iomega Zip or Jazz cartridges, or any type of tape drive. Most of these drives come bundled with some form of backup software, so once the "backup drive" is connected, you should be able to start the backup software and proceed almost automatically.

TIP Skip to Chapter 12 or 13 to install a backup device first, if you do not have one already installed. It's better than trying to back up 300M of data on 209 floppies.

Power Considerations

Power is the first issue to consider. A typical hard disk requires about 10 watts of power for proper operation. This may not sound like much, but you must be sure that your power supply is able to provide that much power. Otherwise, your supply may become overloaded. Overloaded supplies often cause unpredictable PC operation, or prevent the PC from booting at all. In extreme cases, a severely overloaded power supply can even break down. Here are some rules to help avoid power problems:

- If you're just replacing an existing hard drive with a new one, power should not be a problem.
- If your system has not been upgraded before, it can usually support an extra drive without any problem.
- If your system has been significantly upgraded already, pay attention to the system's operation after you add a new drive. If the system behaves erratically, you may need a higher voltage power supply.

You also need to have a 4-pin power connector available for the new drive. If you're just replacing an existing hard disk outright, you can just reuse the power connector on the replacement drive. When adding a new drive, be sure that there is an extra power connector available from the power supply.

If you don't have a power connector available, you can purchase a *Y-connector* that splits an existing connector into two separate connectors, as shown in Figure 11.3. You simply remove a power connector from a drive, install the Y-connector, plug one arm of the Y-connector back into the original drive, and you've got a spare connector for that new drive.

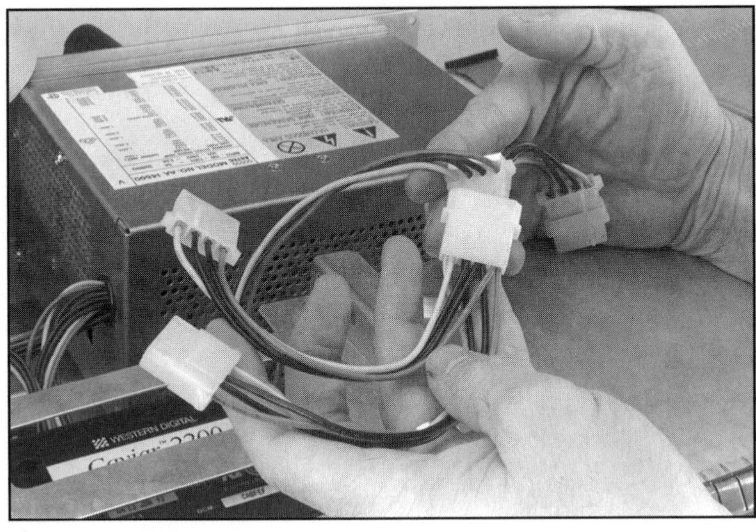

FIG. 11.3
A Y-connector can give you an extra power connector if you run out.

Choosing a Drive Bay

You also need to decide where your drive is going to go in the system. When replacing a drive outright, you can simply reuse the original drive bay. If you are adding a second hard disk, you need to locate an unused drive bay. Large desktop and tower chasses often have several drive bays available, as shown in Figure 11.4. You may have to hunt for an open bay in a mini-desktop enclosure.

Drive bays are typically referred to as *external* and *internal*. External drive bays are located behind those plastic plugs you see on so many plastic housings. Floppy disks, CD-ROM drives, and tape drives all demand these external drive bays. Internal drive bays are little more than metal brackets inside the chassis where you can bolt a drive securely. Because you do not need to insert or remove anything from a hard disk, you can use external or internal drive bays.

Another thing to consider when choosing a drive bay is to make sure that your power connector and signal cable are both long enough to reach the new hard disk, as shown in Figures 11.5 and 11.6.

NOTE For SCSI connections, you should not exceed 6 meters for total length of all cables (internal *and* external). This figure drops to 3 meters if you are using any Fast SCSI devices.

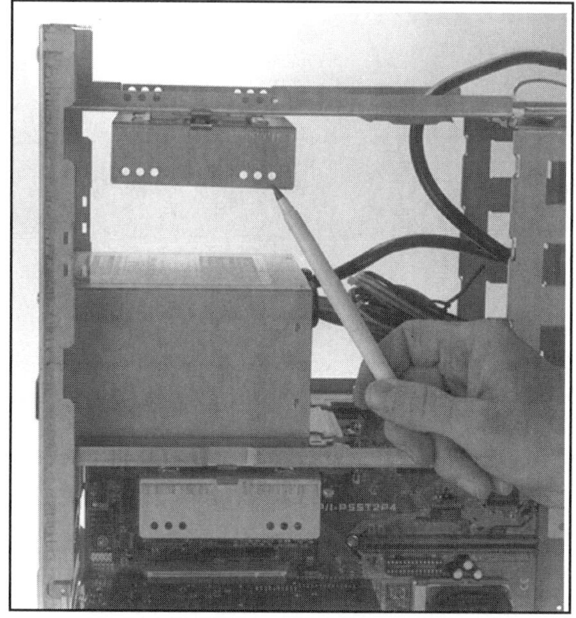

FIG. 11.4
This ATX case has removable internal drive bays for easy installation.

FIG. 11.5
Check the distance from the controller board to the hard drive to make sure your drive cable is long enough.

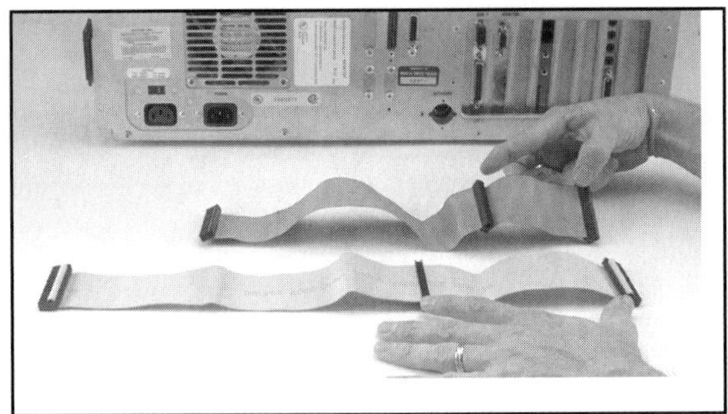

FIG. 11.6
You can always buy a longer cable if the one you have is too short.

Finally, consider whether the drive bay is 5 $\frac{1}{4}$ or 3 $\frac{1}{2}$ inches in size. Most hard drives are 3 $\frac{1}{2}$ inches in size, so if you want to use a 5 $\frac{1}{2}$-inch bay, you need to use mounting brackets, as shown in Figure 11.7. These mounting brackets and slides (see Figure 11.8) usually come with the drive but can be purchased separately from a local computer store if necessary.

FIG. 11.7
You can use a 3 $\frac{1}{2}$-inch drive in a 5 $\frac{1}{4}$-inch bay with mounting brackets.

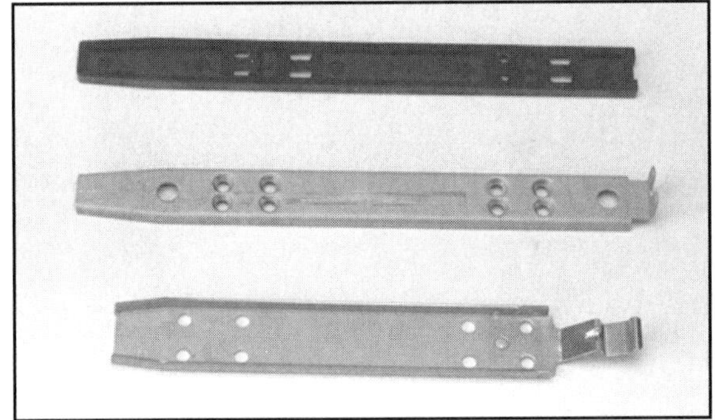

FIG. 11.8
Sometimes the slide rails are specific for the type of case.

Drive Configuration

Configuration of your new hard disk is paramount to its proper function. Examine your new drive and locate any jumpers (see Figures 11.9 and 11.10). For an IDE/EIDE drive, there are typically three ways to jumper the drive:

- As the only hard disk
- As the primary disk in a two-disk system
- As the secondary (slave) disk in a two-disk system

FIG. 11.9
An EIDE drive with the jumper set to Master.

FIG. 11.10
An EIDE drive with the jumper set to Slave.

If the hard disk is to be the *only* one in your system, the factory settings are usually correct. In this case, the jumper is not being used. You can skip to the next section.

When you use the new disk as a secondary drive—that is, the second drive on the same ribbon cable—make sure it is jumpered as the slave drive, and set the original disk so that it is the master drive (see Figure 11.11). This is the least intrusive method to adding a new disk to your system. You will still boot from the original drive with all files intact, but you just see an additional drive letter show up in your Windows 95 Explorer window (or File Manager if in Windows 3.x).

NOTE An EIDE controller can have two separate chains, each with its own master and slave drive for a total of four devices.

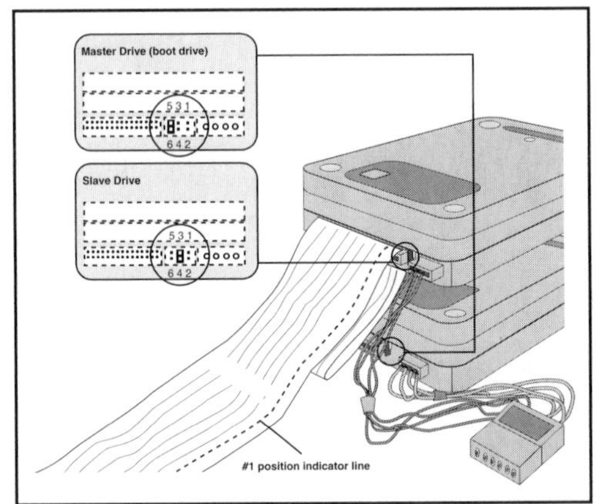

FIG. 11.11 *Note the location of the colored line on the ribbon (dotted in this example). It corresponds with the #1 pin on the drive.*

Making the new drive the master can get a bit messy. Because the drive is new, it will not have an operating system on it and will not boot. On an IDE/EIDE system, the master drive (the C: drive) has to be the boot drive. Therefore, you have to reinstall your OS on the new drive in order to use the system. All files should still be intact on the original drive; it will just be the next logical drive, usually D:. To get around this limitation, install the new drive as the slave. Boot the system, and duplicate the entire old disk to the new one. Shut off the system and switch master/slave status. Reboot the system to test. If all works well, you can reformat the old drive and you are ready to rock.

Is Your Controller IDE, or Is It EIDE?

It's OK to use the same controller with the new drive, but unless the controller is an EIDE controller, you will not be able to take advantage of all the performance enhancements of your new drive.

If your controller is embedded in the motherboard and you are not sure if it is IDE or EIDE, look for a Primary and a Secondary controller (refer to Figure 11.2). If you have these two controller, it is EIDE; only EIDE supports four devices (two on each connection). If you only have one controller (IDE), check your BIOS (Basic Input Output System) setup to see if you can disable the on-board hard drive controller. If so, you can buy an EIDE controller card and use it instead.

SCSI disks are a bit easier to configure because you need only select the proper device ID for the drive. By convention, the boot disk (the C: drive) in a SCSI system is set as ID0, and a second SCSI disk (the D: drive) can be set as ID1.

If your new SCSI disk falls at the end of a SCSI bus, you also need to install a set of SCSI terminating resistors on the drive. Fortunately, SCSI kits typically include terminating resistors, and provide specific instructions on how to install the terminators. Make sure to check the installation manual that came with your SCSI controller card. It's not always simple to terminate a SCSI chain; it depends on the type of controller (for example, some controllers support both internal and external SCSI chains, and both need termination).

NOTE Some newer devices have logical (auto or software) termination in addition to, or instead of, resistors.

NOTE IDE/EIDE and SCSI hard disks *can* coexist in the same system, but you cannot boot a PC from a SCSI disk if there is an IDE/EIDE disk in the system as well. IDE/EIDE disks automatically take precedence. If you need to boot from a SCSI disk, you have to remove any IDE/EIDE disks from the system first.

Installing a New Drive

Now that you've determined what type of drive configuration you have in the previous section, you can install the new drive. This section is divided into similarly appropriate parts, with steps common to all new installations here.

Before You Begin, You Need:

- ☑ A Phillips screwdriver
- ☑ An open drive bay (either 5¼- or 3½-inch)
- ☑ Slide rails

continues

continued

- ☑ 3 ½- to 5 ¼-inch mounting brackets (if you are putting the drive in a 5 ¼-inch bay)
- ☑ Mounting screws (come with the drive)
- ☑ Proper length ribbon cable

---

1. Shut down, turn off, and unplug the PC.
2. Open the system.
3. Discharge your static.

The following sections are specific to the type of drive configuration, and you should skip to the section that suits your needs.

Replacing an IDE Drive

This section describes the process of replacing a drive in a single drive system. For information on adding a new drive, skip to the next section.

TIP It is highly recommended that you replace your old IDE controller with a new EIDE controller. The additional cost is more than worth it in performance gains.

1. Locate the old drive, unplug the power connector (see Figure 11.12), and the 40-pin ribbon cable (see Figure 11.13).

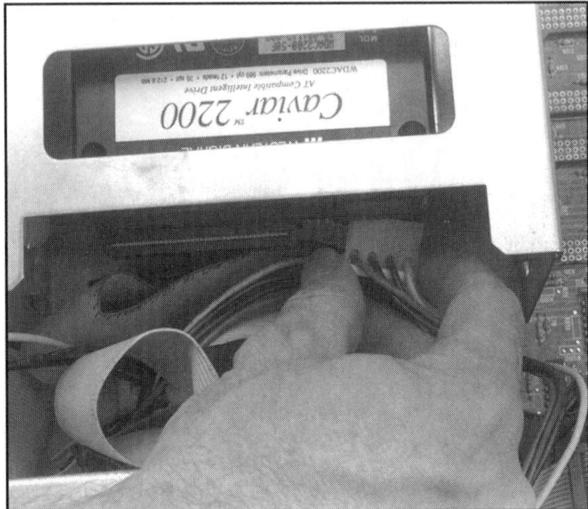

FIG. 11.12
Remove the 4-pin power connector.

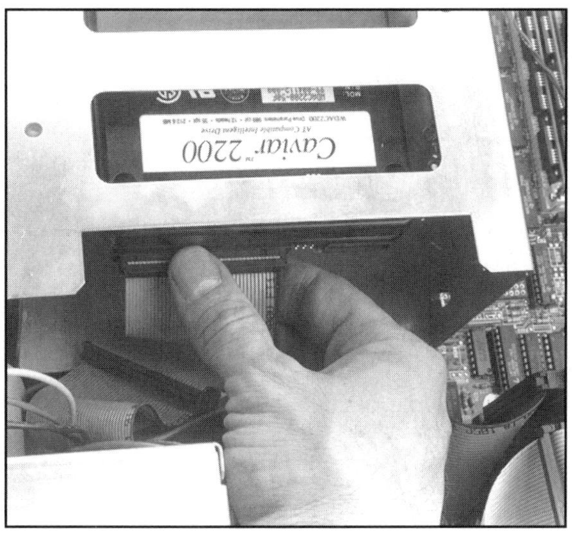

FIG. 11.13
Remove the 40-pin IDE ribbon cable.

2. Locate and remove the mounting screws. These are found either on the side of the drive bay or in front as shown in Figure 11.14.

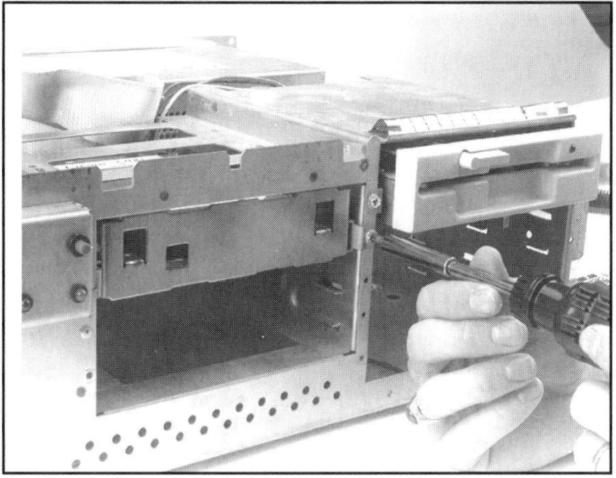

FIG. 11.14
Remove the drive mounting screws.

3. Carefully slide the drive out, making sure not to snag any other cables or wires in the process (see Figure 11.15).
4. Remove and save any mounting brackets, slide rails, and screws that may be attached. You can reuse them on the new drive. That's the surest way of getting a good fit.

FIG. 11.15
Remove the old drive.

5. Attach any mounting brackets and/or slide rails from the last step to the new drive.
6. Check the position of the key in your 40-pin ribbon cable, as in Figure 11.16. This key assures the correct alignment of the cable to the drive.

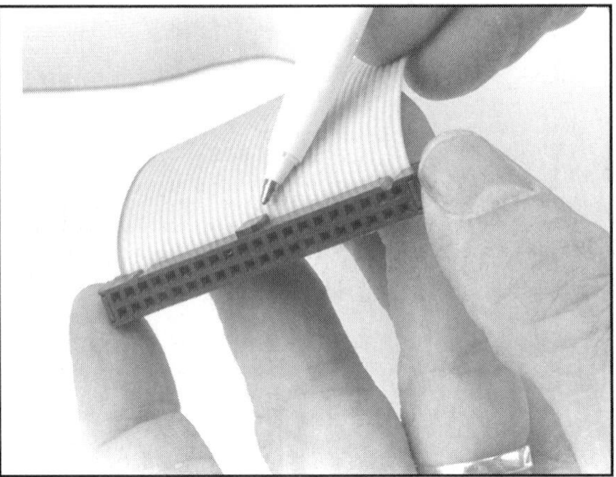

FIG. 11.16
The key in the connector corresponds to one on the drive to assure proper alignment.

TIP Don't panic if your ribbon cable does not have a key; not all do. There will be one colored wire at the side of the cable to indicate the #1 pin position, and the drive will also indicate this pin on its underside, as shown in Figure 11.17.

7. Slide the new drive in place of the old one, and replace all mounting screws, as shown in Figure 11.18.

FIG. 11.17
The bottom of the drive usually also indicates the #1 pin position. In this figure, a "1" is printed on the left side of the connector indicating the pin 1 position.

#1 pin position

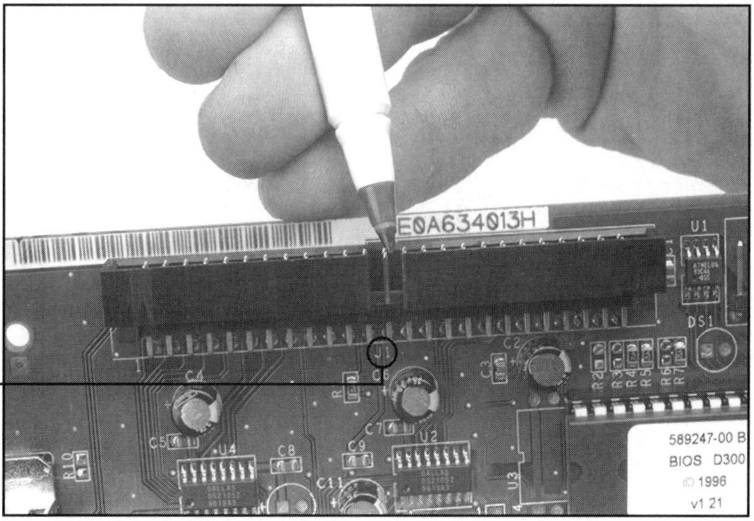

CAUTION When securing a hard disk, be extremely careful to avoid stripping or cross-threading a mounting hole. An unevenly mounted drive will vibrate excessively. This can lead to premature drive failure.

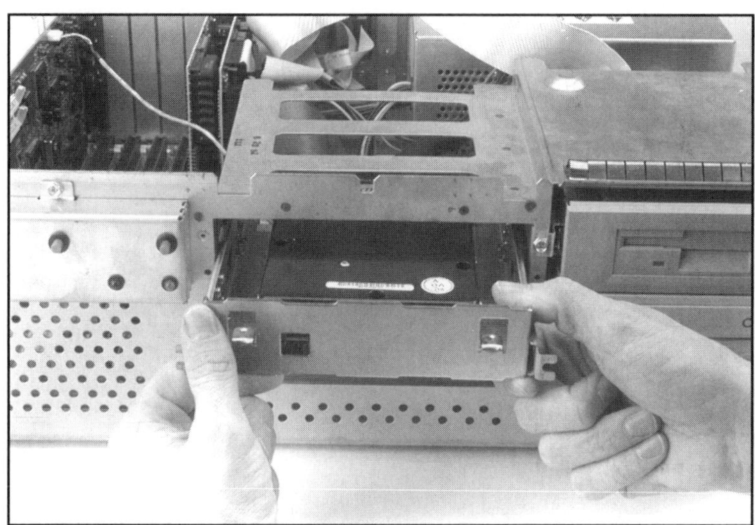

FIG. 11.18
Remount the new drive in the old drive bay.

8. Reattach the ribbon cable, noting the position of the key shown in Figure 11.19, or the #1 pin position.

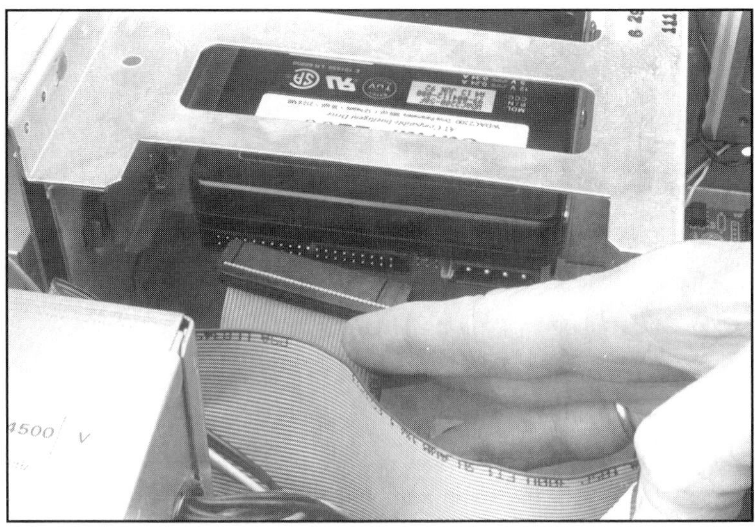

FIG. 11.19
Note the colored wire indicating the #1 pin position.

9. Reattach the 4-pin power connector (see Figure 11.20).

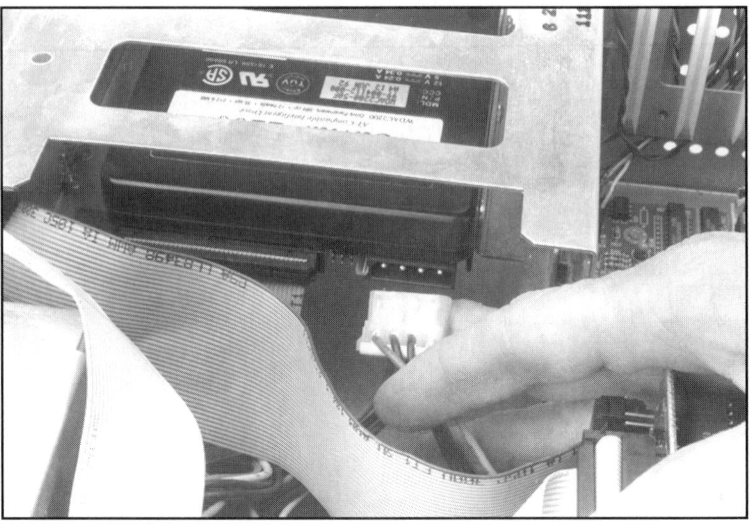

FIG. 11.20
Reinstall the power connector.

That's it! Sure not worth paying CompUSA $60 for, is it? Now you are ready to move to the next phase—preparing and formatting the drive.

Troubleshooting

My system doesn't even start when I turn the power on. What happened?
You may have inadvertently replaced the ribbon cable reversed (#40 wire to the #1 pin). Turn the power off and double-check that the #1 pin positions are lined up.

Adding a New EIDE Drive

This section describes the installation of an additional EIDE drive to a system with an IDE/EIDE drive already installed. This will be the most likely scenario because most people are unwilling—no matter how old and slow the old drive was—to simply discard it; it probably cost more than the new one! If this isn't you, you can skip to "Adding a New SCSI Drive" or back to "Replacing an IDE Drive."

Follow these steps to add a new EIDE drive:

1. Locate an open drive bay for your new drive, preferably one as close to the original drive as possible (see Figure 11.21). The reason for this is the limited distance between drive connectors on the ribbon cable (refer to Figure 11.5).

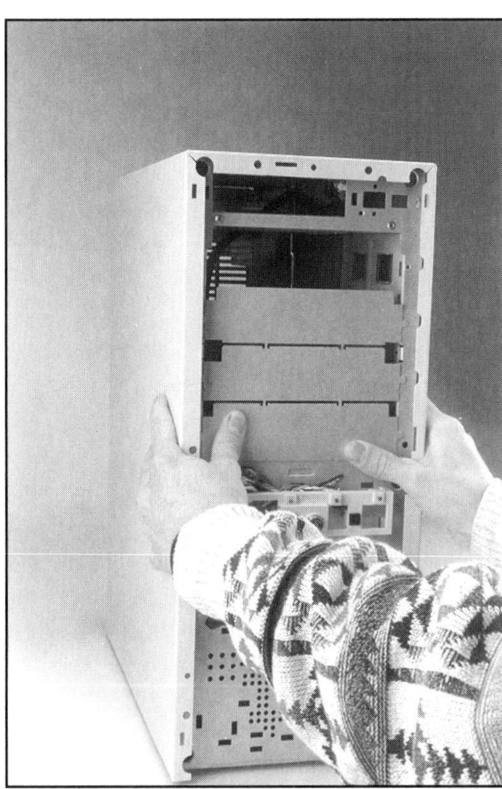

FIG. 11.21
Removing the facing of this mid-tower case shows five available external drive bays: one 3 1/2-inch and four 5 1/4-inch.

2. Attach any mounting brackets and/or slide rails, as required by your particular case design, to the new drive and slide it into place (see Figure 11.22). Note that some cases do not require any mounting brackets (3 $\frac{1}{2}$-inch bays) or slide rails.

FIG. 11.22
The new drive, with attached mounting brackets and slide rails (required by the 5 $\frac{1}{4}$-inch bay).

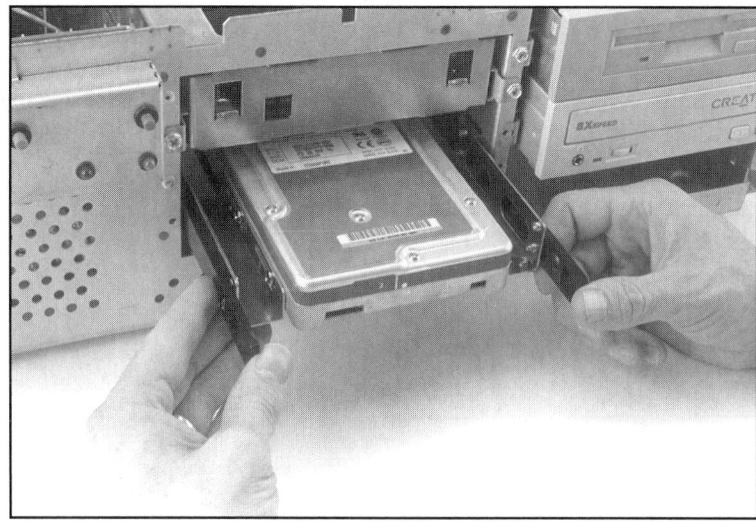

3. Check to see if you have an available 4-pin power connector; most systems will have at least one or two spares. If not, you can purchase a Y-connector (shown in Figure 11.23) that will split the power off one of the other power connectors.

FIG. 11.23
A Y-connector can give you an extra power connection if you find you've run out.

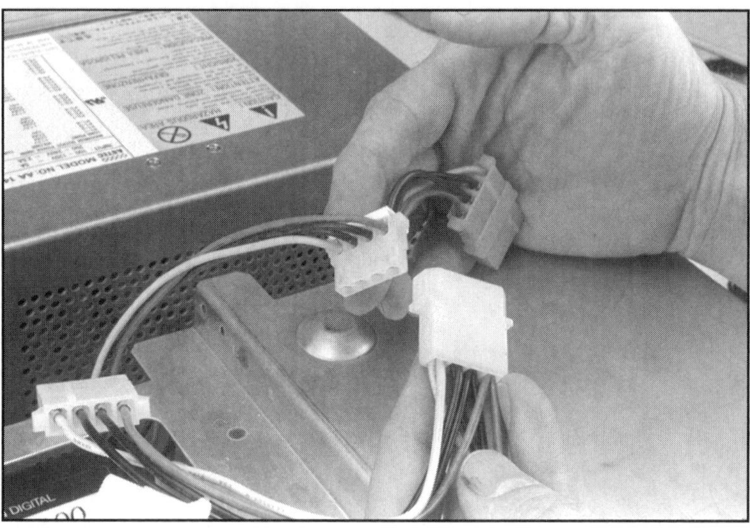

4. Attach the 4-pin power connector to the new drive (see Figure 11.24).

FIG. 11.24
Attach the power connector to the new drive.

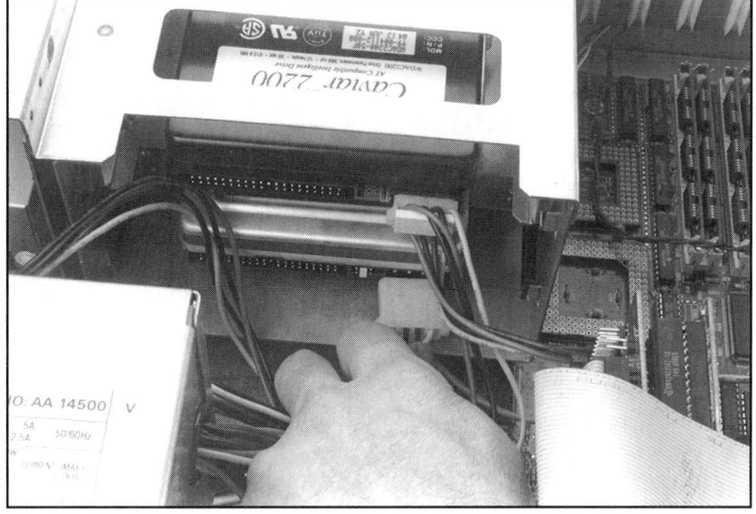

5. Attach an available drive connector from the 40-pin ribbon cable—note the key in the connector and the notch in the drive (refer to Figures 11.16 and 11.17)—to the new drive (see Figure 11.25).

FIG. 11.25
Attach the 40-pin ribbon cable to the new drive.

TIP It's worth mentioning that it doesn't matter which connector you use. The primary/master and secondary/slave relationships are determined by the jumpers on the disks themselves (refer to Figure 11.11), so feel free to reattach the cable in any manner necessary for optimum placement (see Figure 11.26).

FIG. 11.26
This motherboard has a built-in EIDE controller. Note the primary and secondary connections.

Secondary IDE

Primary IDE

NOTE If you have an EIDE controller and the secondary IDE connector is unused, you can attach an additional 40-pin ribbon cable to it to control your new drive (see Figure 11.27). In that case, the jumper settings on both the new drive and the old would be set to MASTER, because these controllers function as two separate controllers. The next device on either cable, whether hard disk or CD-ROM drive, would then be set to SLAVE.

FIG. 11.27
Note when connecting the IDE ribbon cable to the controller that the position of the #1 pin corresponds to the colored wire on the ribbon cable.

There you have it. A new drive is born. Now you are ready to move to the next phase, "Preparing and Formatting the Drive."

Adding a New SCSI Drive

In this section, you learn how to add a new SCSI hard drive to your system. If you don't have to complete this task, skip to the next phase "Preparing and Formatting the Drive," or refer to the earlier sections "Adding a New EIDE Drive" or "Replacing an IDE Drive."

About the Controller Card

The actual process of installing the card is no different than any other expansion card you might add (see Chapter 6, "Basic Device Configuration and Installation"). Very few new motherboards come with an embedded SCSI controller, as EIDE does, and neither do most home systems you might want to upgrade.

The first thing to note is that most SCSI controllers can have both an internal chain and an external chain, and both need to be terminated (see Figure 11.28).

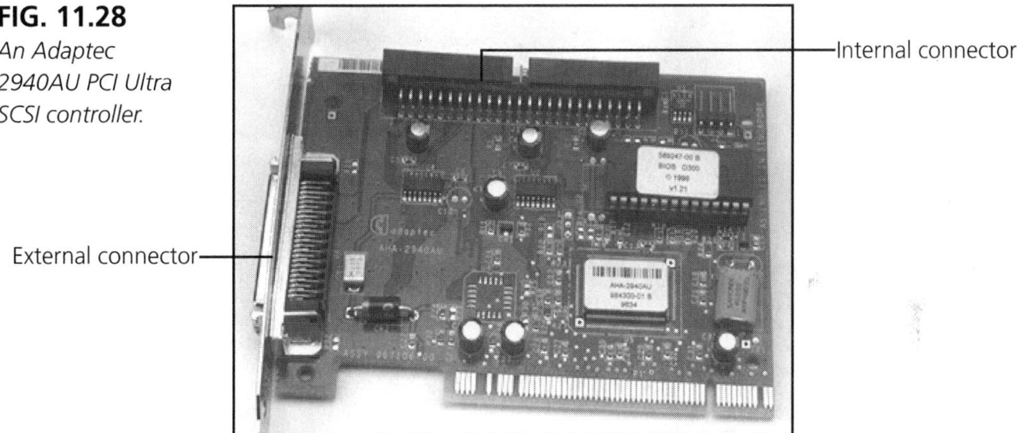

FIG. 11.28
An Adaptec 2940AU PCI Ultra SCSI controller.

Most internal connectors appear similar to the IDE counterpart except bigger—50 pins instead of 40 pins. The exception is an Ultra Wide SCSI connector (16-bit path rather than the standard 8-bit) which is actually visually smaller but uses 68 pins. External connections can be different, too. Some older controllers use a 50-pin connector that resembles a parallel port. Most newer controllers use a 50-pin mini-connector shown in Figure 11.29 or a 68-pin mini-connector for Ultra Wide. There are adapters available to change from one kind of connector to another, in the event a device you want to connect uses a different connection.

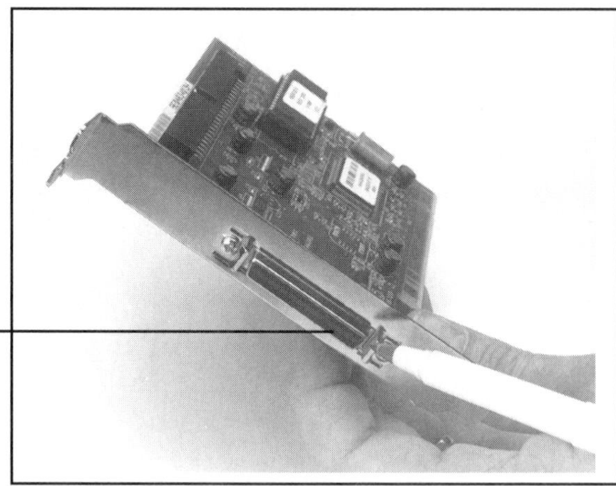

FIG. 11.29
You can use this connector to connect external SCSI devices like CD-ROM drives, scanners, printers, and so on.

Compatibility and Recommendations

As you are beginning to see, there is not quite the same standardization in the SCSI world as there is in the IDE. This is one reason SCSI has been relegated to the world of the "high-end" machine or computer geek. Only these people were willing to take the time to understand all the factors necessary for a properly functioning SCSI subsystem.

With this in mind, I recommend you purchase an Adaptec SCSI controller card, not because I get a commission on any sales derived from this book (I wish), but because it is the most standardized SCSI board out there. In fact, Adaptec has been pushing the standardization of SCSI for years. The ASPI (Advanced SCSI Programming Interface) was once Adaptec SCSI Programming Interface, before they turned it over to public domain. There are other SCSI boards out there with as good, if not better, price/performance ratio, but the headache you could get with incompatibilities and poorly written device drivers isn't worth the difference IMHO (In My Humble Opinion).

Also note in Figure 11.30 that the SCSI board has its own connection for the LED lights that flicker on the outside of your case to let you know there is some hard drive activity going on. It's not necessary to connect this, but some people like to use these lights for diagnostic reasons, or just because it looks cool.

Termination

Termination is one of the most important factors in setting up your SCSI subsystem. In a nutshell, the last device on a SCSI chain—internal *and* external—needs to have termination enabled. This can be accomplished in different ways, depending on the device, but this fact holds true of all SCSI chains.

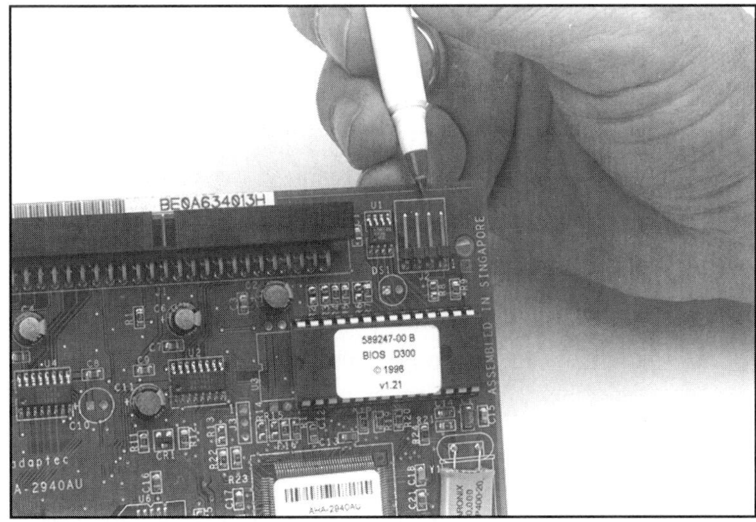

FIG. 11.30
Here's where you connect the external LED drive light indicator.

For example, if you have only two devices—a controller card (yes, it counts as a device) and an HD—they both need to be terminated. It's usually automatic for the controller; you do not need to do anything (not always the case if you are not using an Adaptec controller, though). The HD will have either terminating resistors that plug into the underside of the drive or have a jumper/dip switch to set, as in the case of the IBM Ultrastar ES 2.16G Ultra SCSI hard disk I used in this upgrade. Now add another device to this party, like an internal SCSI CD-ROM drive. If you were to install it *between* the HD and the controller, no termination is necessary. On the other hand, if you installed it after the HD, you would need to remove the termination from the HD and terminate the CD-ROM drive.

Got it? Think so, huh? Let's add an external scanner to this scenario. Both the scanner and the HD (or CD-ROM, in the last case) need to be terminated. Why? The controller card auto-terminates. In the case where the only devices were internal, the card was one terminator and the drive was the other. Both ends were terminated. When you added the external device, the controller card becomes non-terminated and the scanner becomes the other end of the chain. Now the scanner is one terminator and the internal drive is the other.

Simple, right? The bottom line is you need two terminating devices in any SCSI chain—one at both ends.

Setting SCSI IDs

Each device on a SCSI chain has its own unique ID called its *SCSI ID*. You choose this ID either through jumpers or switches, and they can be set to any number from 0 to 7. This has no relation to the device's physical orientation on the SCSI chain, nor does it affect termination in any way. There are some general rules though:

- The boot disk is usually set to ID 0.
- The host adapter is usually set to ID 7.

Some new SCSI devices are supporting *SCAM (SCSI Configured AutoMatically)*, where the host adapter assigns the unique IDs at bootup automatically. If your devices support this, be sure to enable this feature in the host adapter's BIOS, as described in the next section.

Configuring the Host Adapter

The SCSI controller card (also known as the *host adapter*) uses its own BIOS, similar to the motherboard BIOS, to configure the devices under its control. These settings are different for each host adapter, but in general there are a few important features you should learn about that are common to all:

- *Extended BIOS translation*. Enabling this feature allows MS-DOS 5.0 and above, including Windows 95, to support drives larger than 1G. This option is not necessary under OS/2 or Windows NT.
- *BIOS support for bootable CD-ROM*. Enabling this feature allows you to boot your system from special bootable CD-ROMs.
- *Plug and Play SCAM support*. SCAM automatically assigns a unique SCSI ID to any device attached to the SCSI chain that supports this feature.
- *Target Boot ID*. This is the SCSI ID of the disk you want to boot from. With SCSI, you can choose which disk you want to boot from, unlike with IDE.

Preparing and Formatting the Drive

Now that you've installed your new drive, made all the proper connections, and replaced the case cover, you need to let the computer know the new drive is there. This is done through the BIOS Setup program.

CMOS Considerations

The *CMOS (Complementary Metal-Oxide Semiconductor)* is the chip that holds the information your motherboard's BIOS has recorded on it. Some people use these terms interchangeably.

The BIOS reads the system information contained in the CMOS, and then checks out the system and configures it. Next, the BIOS looks for an operating system on the boot drive (drive 1 or C: drive), launches that OS, and then turns control over.

Once the BIOS setup is activated, most new BIOSes have the IDE HDD Auto Detection option. This is a great improvement over older BIOS programs that required you to know things like the cylinders, heads, sectors, and so on. You need to go through this process so your computer can register the new drive and make it "visible" to your OS.

In case you have one of these older BIOSes or the autodetect didn't correctly ID your drive, you need to enter this information manually. Your new drive will most likely have this configuration information printed on a label pasted to the top of the mounting chassis. You might also find the information on the manufacturer's WWW site. Here's a list of hard drive manufactures you can call:

Conner	408-456-3200
IBM	914-765-1900
Maxtor	408-432-1700
Western Digital	714-932-5000
Quantum	408-894-4000
Seagate	408-438-8222

Because every BIOS works a bit different, you need to read the BIOS Setup instructions that came with your computer, but some general instructions follow:

1. Go to User Defined Settings.
2. Enter the parameters from your drive. Usually, only the Cyls (cylinders), Heads, and S/T (number of sectors per track) are necessary; landing zone and capacity are usually not required.

The Meg field should then reflect the drives' unformatted capacity in megabytes.

NOTE Be sure to save your changes before exiting a CMOS Setup routine. If you forget to save, the new disk's parameters will be lost, and the drive will not be recognized.

Translating BIOS

It is important to note that not all older BIOSes will be able to recognize disk drives larger than 504M. Those that do are called *translating BIOSes*. Even if your BIOS correctly identifies the new drive's parameters, it doesn't mean the BIOS will translate those parameters. Here's how to check:

1. While at the BIOS Setup screen, look for a setting called LBA, Large Block Access, or Translation, and enable the option.
2. Check if the Autoconfigure Drive Type returns a heads value greater than 16; if so, you are probably OK.
3. Call your computer's vendor and/or manufacturer and ask. Here's a list of some major system manufacturers and their phone numbers:

AST	817-232-9824
Compaq	713-518-2000
Dell	512-728-3883
Gateway 2000	605-232-2191
HP	208-323-2551
IBM	404-238-1234
NEC	415-528-6000
Packard Bell	801-579-0161

What do you do if you don't have a translating BIOS? You can upgrade your BIOS (see Chapter 7, "Working with the BIOS," for help), or you can use software utilities like EZ-Drive that comes with all Western Digital hard drives over 528M (which is all of them these days), or Ontrack Disk Manager. The software works; I've used it. It does have some limitations, so read the instructions carefully and weigh these limitations against the cost of an upgraded BIOS.

Here is a list of phone numbers for common BIOSes you might use:

AMI	770-263-8181
Award	415-968-4433
Micro Firmware	405-321-8333
MR BIOS	508-686-6468
Phoenix	617-551-4000

Low-Level Format

Most drives come from the factory already in *low-level (physical) format.* This is where all the tracks and sectors of the disk are outlined and written. If your drive was low-level formatted (check the installation instructions), then you may want to skip to the section "Partitioning Your Drive." But if you are like me and want to make sure the job was done right, read on.

> **CAUTION** After a low-level format, you need to partition the drive into at least one active partition (done with the FDISK program), and then you can type the familiar **format c:/s** command (/s will make the drive bootable). As you might imagine, there will be nothing left of any data you might have had on the drive.

So why would you ever want to do this type of format?

- If your BIOS is having trouble recognizing the correct capacity of your hard disk. Some BIOSes do not like HDs that were low-level formatted with anything else than their own utilities. It's rare, but it happens.
- If you have many bad sectors. Occasionally, a low-level format will be able to recover some of them.

I always low-level format any SCSI drive I get because I've found that SCSI controllers are more picky about the drives they control than IDE controllers are, and I don't trust the manufacturer to do it right.

NOTE You may want to think twice about a low-level format of an IDE/EIDE drive if you are not having any problems (if it is new). You know what they say: "If it ain't broke, don't fix it."

The utilities that perform these low-level formats can be found in some BIOS Setup programs on your motherboard, in the case of IDE systems, or in the host adapter, in the case of SCSI systems.

Partitioning Your Drive

Any physical drive can have 1 to 24 *logical drives.* The easiest way to understand what a logical drive is is to think of the drive letters (C:, D:, E:, and so on) you see when you open the Windows Explorer (or File Manager). Each one can be a logical drive, but you still may only have one *physical* HD installed in your computer. You get these logical drives by partitioning the physical drive. Here are some primary reasons to do this:

1. There must be at least one master boot partition on the drive in order to high-level format the drive.
2. You may want to install more than one OS and keep them on separate logical drives.
3. You may want to install different file systems, like FAT on C: and NTFS on D:.
4. You may want to keep your applications separate from your OS. This will allow you to reformat one drive without losing the data stored on the other.
5. You may want to optimize your storage capacity. The FAT16 file system is limited as to how many clusters it can support. In order to support drives greater than 256M, it will use larger size clusters (*allocation units*) as shown in Table 11.1.

Table 11.1 Default Cluster Sizes

Hard Disk Partition Size	Cluster (Allocation Unit) Size	FAT Type
0 to less than 16M	8 sectors or 4,096 (4K) bytes	12-bit
16–128M	4 sectors or 2,048 (2K) bytes	16-bit
More than 128–256M	8 sectors or 4,096 (4K) bytes	16-bit
More than 256–512M	16 sectors or 8,192 (8K) bytes	16-bit
More than 512–1,024M	32 sectors or 16,384 (16K) bytes	16-bit
More than 1,024–2,048M	64 sectors or 32,768 (32K) bytes	16-bit

The problem with large clusters is that it is the smallest storage unit. So a small 1K file, when stored on a FAT system with 8K clusters, takes up 8K of disk space—a lot of waste. So if you want to maximize your storage capacity on a FAT file system, keep your logical drives to 255M or less.

TIP Modern file systems like FAT32 (in OEM release Windows 95) and NTFS (used in NT) are not as limited to the number of clusters, so they do not suffer from storage inefficiencies like FAT.

To partition the disk, you can use FDISK. FDISK comes with DOS and Windows 95 (in the WINDOWS\COMMAND folder). To use FDISK:

1. Place FDISK and FORMAT.COM (for the next phase) on a bootable floppy disk and reboot your system.
2. At the command prompt, type **FDISK**.
3. Select the physical drive ID.
4. Follow the on-screen option prompts.

CAUTION Step 3 is very important. By default, FDISK will operate on the boot or first drive. If you have data on that disk, a repartition of that disk will result in a complete loss of all that data!

Windows NT users do not need to use FDISK. Just insert your Setup Disk #1 and reboot. Setup is smart enough to know the disk is new and offers the proper partitioning information.

High-Level Formatting

Once the new drive has been low-level formatted and partitioned, it is ready for the more familiar **format c:** command.

If your new disk is not the boot disk, then you are ready to reboot your system. The new drive will show up in Explorer as the next logical drive. So if you had only one drive C:, then the new drive would be D:. You can then format the drive as you'd format any floppy disk, and you are set to start using your new drive.

If your new disk is the boot drive, you need to reinstall your OS. Follow the installation instructions that came with your operating system.

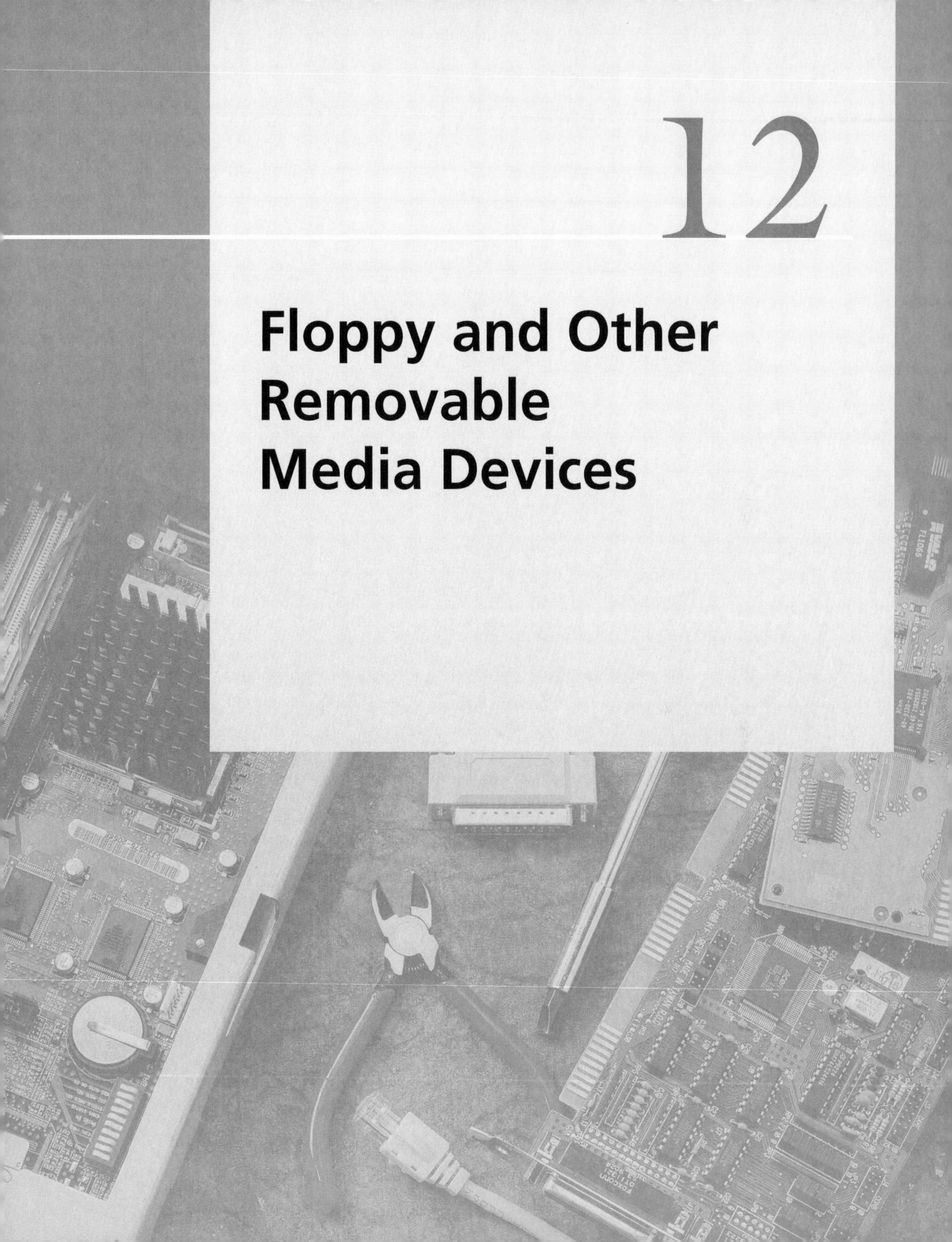

12

Floppy and Other Removable Media Devices

Floppy drives have been around since the IBM PC was introduced in 1981, and are still used today to transport data. Floppy drives have moving parts and use media from outside the computer, so they are more susceptible to breakage over time. If you own a computer long enough, you'll probably need to replace a broken floppy drive, add a new high capacity Zip drive, or upgrade an old 5¼-inch floppy at some point. The good news is that removable media drives are relatively easy to install.

By the end of this chapter, you will know how to:

- Identify different drive types
- Choose the correct drive type for your needs
- Install floppy drives
- Install Zip and Jaz drives
- Tell the BIOS what kind of removable media drives you have installed
- Choose between SCSI and Parallel drives

Before your install a new or replacement drive, you need to know what kind of drive you require. The next section gives you an overview of removable media types.

Drive Overview

All the drives discussed in this chapter have one common characteristic: *removable media*. This means that the drive reads and writes data on a spinning platter of magnetic media. The media in the drive spins at a constant speed and passes a *read/write head*. As the media surface moves past the head, it can *read* changes in the magnetic field on the media. These changes equate to *bits*—the ones and zeros that make up your Word documents, programs, and anything else you store on a floppy.

Unlike a CD-ROM, which can only read changes on the surface, all the drives in this chapter can also *write* changes to the magnetic field on the disk. When you've filled up a disk with data, you can *remove* it and put in another disk.

The Floppy Cable

All internal floppy drives connect to the computer's floppy drive controller via the *floppy cable* (see Figure 12.1). This cable is a 34-conductor flat ribbon cable. If you look carefully at the cable, you can see that a section on it is reversed between drives.

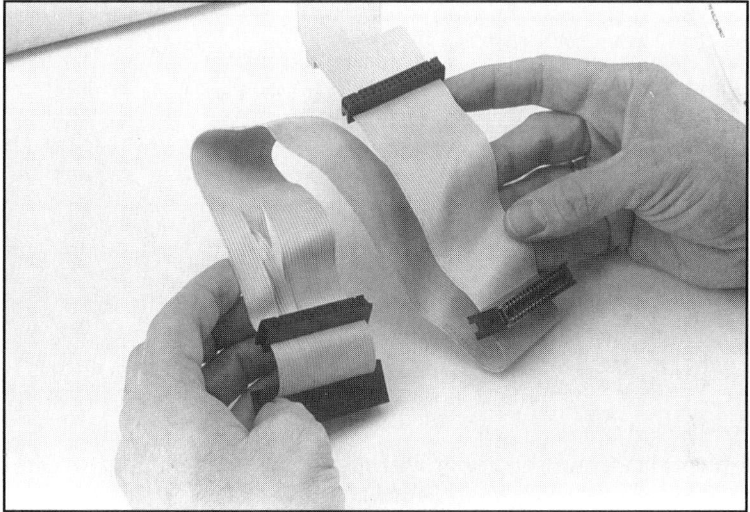

FIG. 12.1
A floppy cable with a "twist."

This is how the floppy controller can tell the difference between the A: drive and the B: drive: Following the cable from the adapter or motherboard to the end, a floppy drive connected before this twist is designated the second (B:) drive, and the drive connected after is designated as the first (A:) drive. As you learn in Chapter 13, "Tape Drives," floppy cable-attached tape drives often need to be attached specifically before or after this twist.

The Connectors

There are two different types of connectors on a floppy cable: an *edge connector* and a *pin connector* (see Figure 12.2). The floppy cable in Figure 12.2 has both types of connectors before and after the twist.

The edge connector is usually used to connect older devices like a 5 ¼-inch floppy drive. As you can see in Figure 12.2, the connector has a piece of plastic called a *gate* between pins 4 and 5. The edge to pin converter on the right has a notch in it so that you can't mistake putting the connector on backwards.

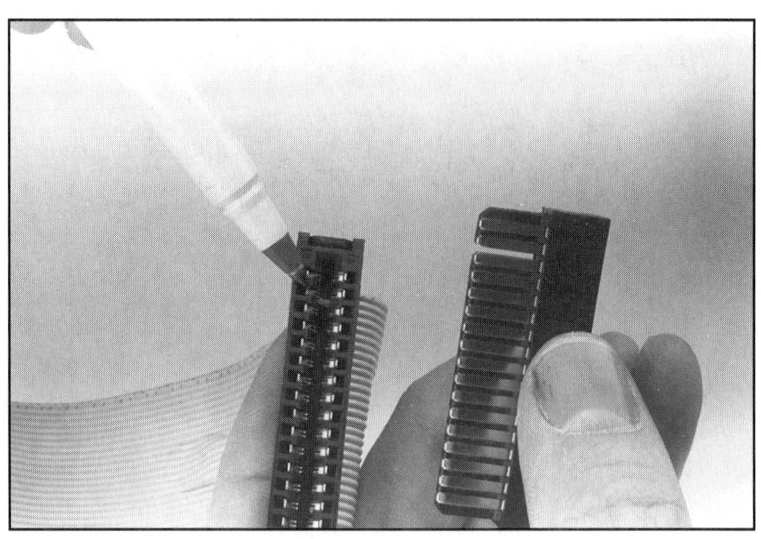

FIG. 12.2
An edge connector.

The other connector that you see is the pin connector (see Figure 12.3).

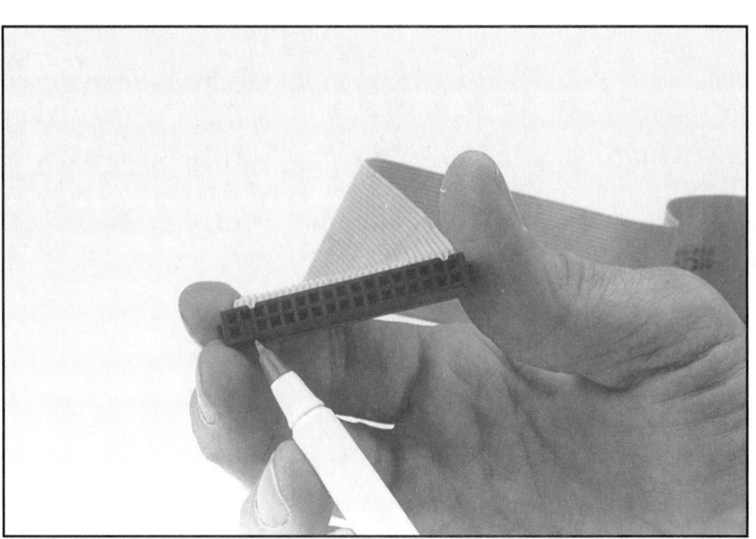

FIG. 12.3
A pin connector.

The pin connector has a similar device to keep you from putting the cable on backwards. As you can see in Figure 12.3, the connector has a blocked pinhole on pin 3. The floppy drives don't have a pin 3 so that you can't put this connector on backwards. While most floppy cables have the correct connectors, you may run across one that doesn't have pin 3 blocked. In this case, you can figure out which side of the cable pin 3 would be on by looking for pin 1. Pin 1 is covered in depth later in the section "Data Cable Compatibility," but you can find it by looking for the stripe on the data cable. Pin 3 will be two wires away from pin 1.

The 5 1/4-inch Drive

The floppy drive that came as original equipment on the IBM-PC in 1981, was a full height 5 ¼-inch drive that held a whopping 360K of data (see Figure 12.4). Later, a 1.2M version of this drive became the de facto standard.

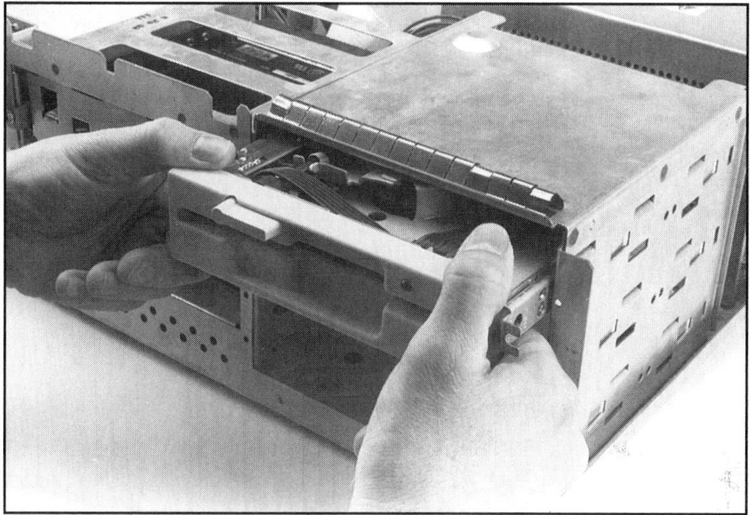

FIG. 12.4
A 5 1/4-inch disk drive.

TIP Depending on how old your computer is, you may have a 5 1/4-inch drive in it. If you do have a 5 1/4-inch drive, you probably aren't using it often. Computer and software manufacturers stopped using this media years ago. It may be a good idea to remove 5 1/4-inch drives to make space for CD-ROMs, a tape drive, or other removable media.

The actual disks for this drive need to be stored in a dust jacket to keep the magnetic media from being exposed. A notch on the right side of the disk indicates that this disk is writeable. If you want to write-protect the disk, place a sticker or tape over this notch. In addition, these floppy drives usually use an edge connector to connect to the data cable. The edge connector on this drive is an actual extension of the plastic that carries the drive electronics.

The 3 1/2-inch Disk Drive

The successor and still most commonly used floppy drive is the *3 1/2-inch disk drive* (see Figure 12.5). This disk has been introduced as an improvement to the 5 ¼-inch disk. Not only does it hold more, but it is also both sturdier and smaller.

FIG. 12.5
A 3 1/2-inch disk drive.

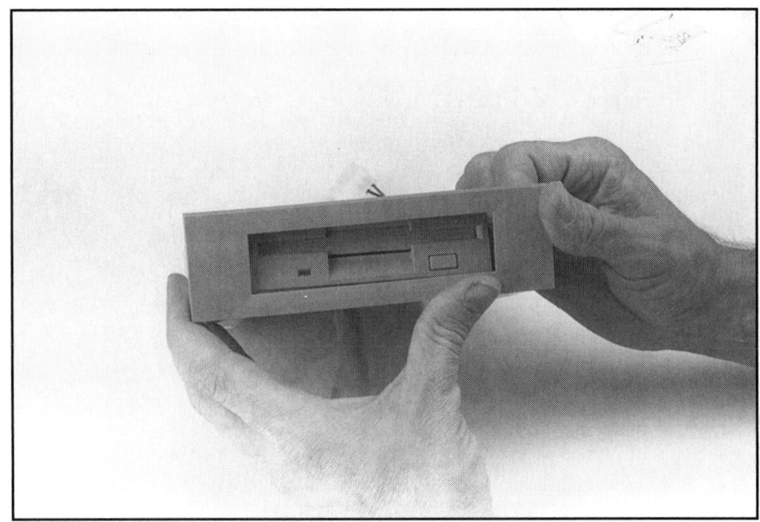

While it may seem strange to call a disk that is made of such a hard plastic case "floppy," the term actually refers to the media that plastic case protects. If you push the metal dust cover aside, you can tell that this media is practically the same as the 5 ¼-inch disk, but smaller. The drive first came in only 720K size, then 1.44M, and now 2.88M. The 2.88M floppy standard never really caught on, and it's quite hard to even find a 2.88M drive.

Choosing a Drive

Because floppy drives have moving parts and are open to invasion by dust, they have a tendency to fail more often than other components in your PC. Look for the following as indicators that your floppy drive is in need of repair or replacement:

- You format a disk on your computer, and another computer tells you that the disk isn't formatted.

- When copying a large file to the floppy, data errors occur.
- The drive makes strange noises or won't eject a disk easily.

If you have any of these problems, try some new disks. Quite often, the problem is just a disk gone bad. I usually throw out disks that give data errors right away. Even if a disk doctor program can make it usable, it will probably fail again. If the drive still doesn't work with new disks and a drive cleaner doesn't help, it may be time to replace the drive.

Once you have decided that you have to upgrade or fix your floppy drive, you'll need to choose a new drive. Before you go out and actually spend money, you need to first collect some information to make sure you buy the right drive and accessories.

Drive Bay Size

There are two different drive bay sizes for floppy drives: 3 ½-inch and 5 ¼-inch. Most computer cases have at least one 3 ½-inch drive bay and more than one 5 ¼-inch drive bays accessible from outside the case. If you want to install a 3 ½-inch drive and only have a 5 ¼-inch drive bay, you need to purchase a mounting bracket (see Figure 12.6) that screws onto the outside of the drive, and provides screw holes for the larger 5 ¼-inch drive bay.

FIG. 12.6
A 3 ½-inch drive mounting kit.

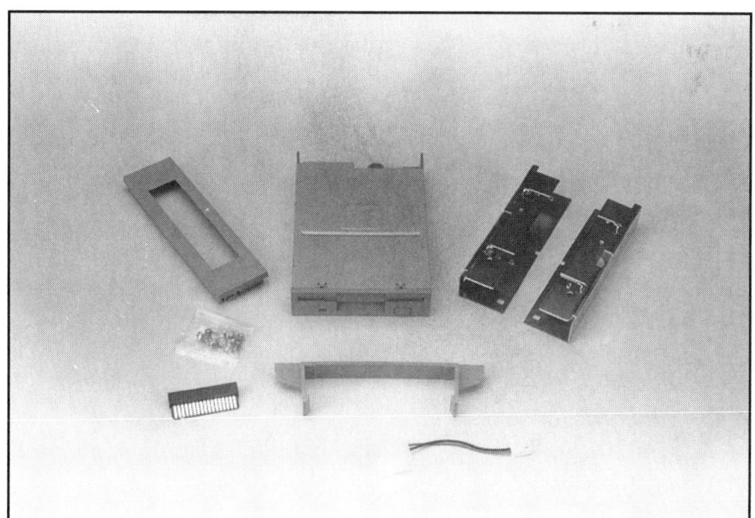

These mounting brackets may also provide converters for power plugs and data cables, if you need them.

Power Connector Compatibility

One of the two connections you will make to the floppy drive is the *power connector*. The good news about power cables is that they are notched so you can't plug one in backwards. The bad news is that there are two different connectors. Both connectors have four wires running into them; two are black, and the other two are (usually) red and yellow. There are two types of connectors: one is large and the other smaller. Your power supply will have many connectors coming out of it, most of which probably have the larger connectors. As a rule of thumb, most 3 ½-inch drives use the smaller connector.

Data Cable Compatibility

The data cable for floppy drives is a 34-conductor flat ribbon cable. This cable will have at least three connectors attached to it. One side of the cable will have a stripe on it. This stripe indicates that that wire terminates at what is called *pin 1*. This is important because you need to make sure the cable doesn't cross between the adapter and the drive. If you look closely near where the cable plugs into the floppy adapter (either your motherboard or an add-in card), you should see a small 1 or indicator which tells you which pin is the first pin. The cable in Figure 12.7 is an IDE cable (not a floppy cable), but illustrates both the stripe and the 1 on the motherboard.

Right now, it's important to identify the connector that you will be plugging into the drive. If you don't have an open connector, you may need to buy a new cable.

Purchasing the Drive

Replacement floppy drives are often available at electronic stores or through mail order. New floppy drives should cost about $50. If you need a mounting kit for a 3 ½-inch floppy (because you are putting it in a 5 ¼-inch bay), it should cost about $15.

FIG. 12.7
A data cable. Notice the 1 *on the motherboard and the stripe on the cable.*

Before you go and spend money, you should make sure you are purchasing a drive that will work in your computer. It pays off if you spend the time opening your computer and writing down what you've got. Here is a checklist of information you should have before purchasing a drive.

Before You Buy:

- ☑ Do you have a bay for the new drive?

  You need to open the case before you can really know the answer to this question. Just because you have a faceplate where it looks like a drive might fit doesn't mean there's space; the manufacturer may have hidden the hard drive behind that faceplate. A *faceplate* is a piece of plastic that covers an empty drive bay. If you don't check first, you may find a hard drive hidden behind the faceplate you plan on putting a new drive into. If you are adding a 3 1/2-inch drive and have a 3 1/2-inch bay, there is no problem. However, if you are putting a 3 1/2-inch drive into a 5 1/4-inch bay, you need to purchase and additional mounting bracket.

- ☑ Do you have a connector for the new drive?

  Take a look at the existing floppy cable. Does it have a connector for the drive you want to add? If not, you may have to buy a new cable.

☑ What kind of connector do you have?

Sometimes you'll find that you've only got an edge-card connector free on your cable. All 3 ½-inch drives have pin connectors, so an edge connector will not work. Some mounting kits will have pin connector to edge connector converters to solve this problem. The point is to make sure you have the appropriate connector type for the drive you plan to purchase.

☑ Do you have any power connectors free?

Check the power supply to make sure you have a free power connector for a new drive. Also make sure that the connector is the right size for your new drive. 3 ½-inch drives usually take smaller connectors than the power cable going to your hard drive. Again, buying a 3 ½-inch mounting kit may solve this problem, because many of these kits come with a power connector converter.

☑ Do know how to mount the new drive?

If you are adding a new drive, you need to be sure you know where and how it will mount to the case. Floppy drives need to be mounted very securely, because pushing the button to eject disks will quickly loosen a drive that isn't securely mounted.

Combo Floppy Drives

If you have a laptop computer and a free 5 ¼-inch drive bay, you might want to consider a combo PCMCIA (PC Card)/floppy drive. This drive provides slots to insert PC Cards, so you can use your modem, network card, or PC Card hard drive in both your laptop and stand-alone computer.

If you need both 5 ¼-inch and 3 ½-inch disk compatibility, you can purchase a combo drive that fits both drive types into one 5 ¼-inch drive bay. These drives let you select which drive is first in boot sequence (A:), and only need one connector.

Installing a Floppy Drive

The first step to installing a floppy drive is, of course, to open the case. Read through Chapter 5, "Taking Inventory," if you need help opening your computer.

Before Installing a Floppy Drive, You Need:

- ☑ About 30 minutes
- ☑ Screwdriver (usually Phillips, possibly flathead for older drive brackets)
- ☑ A floppy drive in static bag
- ☑ Brackets or sub-assembly (cage) if required by the case
- ☑ A place to put screws you remove

Removing the Old Drive

If you are removing a drive in this upgrade, first disconnect the power connector and the data connector.

> **CAUTION** As with all connections inside your computer, you may have to use some force to tighten/loosen the connection, but don't use too much. A good rule of thumb is to try not to use more force than that which would break a wooden popsicle stick. Also, never apply force to the wires, only to the connectors themselves. Power cables, for instance, can sometimes be sticky, and the impulse is to grab it by the wires and yank. Resist this impulse, because you can easily end up with a handful of useless wires.

Some cases will require you to unscrew and pull out the drive before you can access the power and data cable. If you can't reach the cables, skip to the next section and unscrew the drive. Pull it out until you can remove the connectors.

Screw Locations

Your floppy drive is attached to the case by one of three methods: rails, sub-assemblies, or screws.

Floppy drives originally used *rails* (see Figure 12.8) to slide into a case. The rails are attached to the outside of the drive itself, and allow you to slide the drive into the case. You secure the drive to the case either by screwing the front of the rail into the case or by snapping it into place (see Figure 12.9). The bottom of the three rails in Figure 12.8 has these snaps.

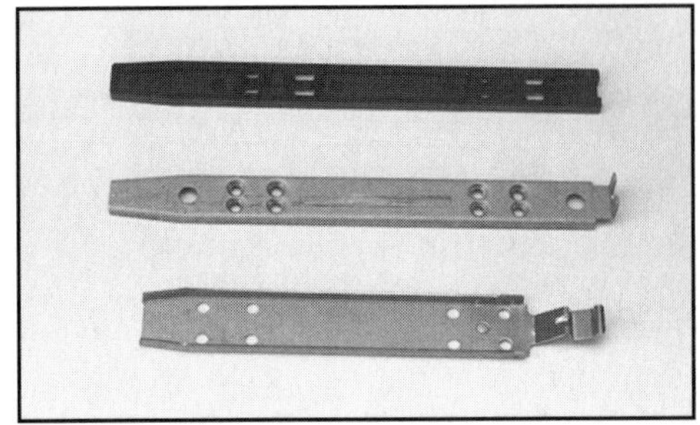

FIG. 12.8
Three different types of drive rails.

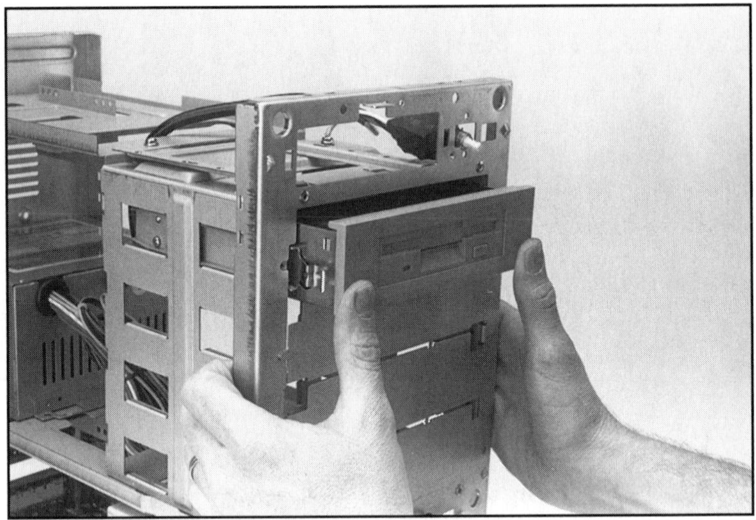

FIG. 12.9
Fastening a drive mounted with rails to the case.

Some cases have a separate "cage" or sub-assembly (see Figure 12.10) into which floppy drives fit or attach. You may need to detach this "cage" from the metal in the case in order to access the screws that hold down the floppy drive.

The third (and simplest) way floppy drives are fastened to cases is with four screws tightened directly into the side of the drive. Be very careful not to lose the screws when removing them, because they are smaller than the screws used in the rest of your computer. You need them later to fasten the new drive to the case.

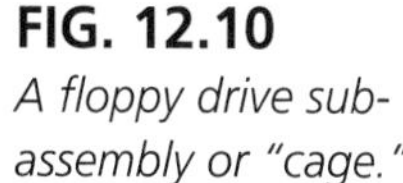

FIG. 12.10
A floppy drive sub-assembly or "cage."

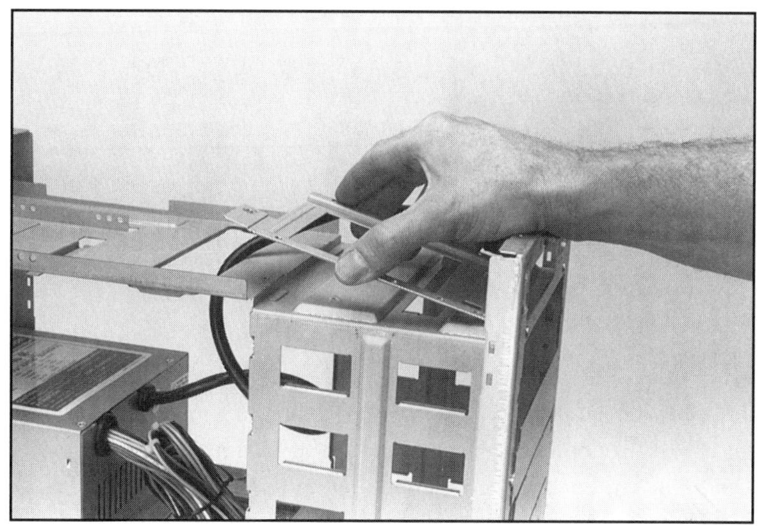

Installing the New Drive

When you're ready to install the new drive, remove it from its static bag and attach any rails or sub-assemblies your case requires. When all the pieces are together, you need to determine the best method to attach the power and data cables. Many cases allow you to access the back of the new drive after it has been installed. If you have room, slide the drive into the case and secure it with its screws, then attach the power and data cables.

On some cases, however, your hands won't have space to plug in the cables after the drive is screwed in. If your hands won't have space, pull the data and power cable in through the open slot, and attach them to the drive before you slide it into the case.

Regardless of how you are able to attach the data cable, remember to make sure that pin 1 (the side of the data cable with a red line) is attached to pin 1 of the floppy drive. After you have the drive physically installed, you can put the cover back on and reattach all the cables.

BIOS Configuration

Power on the system.

> **CAUTION** If your floppy drive lights stay on constantly as soon as you turn on the PC, it is an indication that one of the cables is connected backwards. Power down the system and look for a connector that isn't attached correctly.

If you have just replaced an old drive with a new one of the same type, no BIOS configuration should be required. However, if you have upgraded or changed the floppy configuration somehow, your BIOS will probably need to be notified. Some BIOSes autodetect the change in configuration when you turn the computer back on, while others may need to be manually set. Chapter 7, "Working with the BIOS," gives you instructions on how to edit the BIOS configuration, but these are the general steps you need to follow:

1. Press a key or key combination to get into the BIOS.
2. Change the drive type to match the new configuration.
3. Save the changes to the BIOS.
4. Reboot the computer.

The First Boot

After you have set up the BIOS, boot your computer from the hard drive to make sure it is working correctly. Put a disk in the drive, copy some files to it, and then open the files. If the drive you installed is the first logical drive (A:), reboot the system with a boot disk in it and make sure the computer will boot from that disk.

Your floppy drive upgrade is complete!

Installing a Zip/Jaz Drive

Iomega Zip drives have become very popular devices for storing and transporting data. This section covers how to install the external versions of these drives.

The Zip drive is essentially a 100M floppy disk drive in a cool blue case. It costs about $150, and the disks run about $10 apiece. The drive comes in two different versions: SCSI (pronounced "scuzzy") and Parallel.

You can think of the Iomega Jaz drive as the Zip's big brother—a removable 1G hard drive (see Figure 12.11).

FIG. 12.11
The external Jaz drive.

The drive spins a disk platter that is very similar to your internal hard drive's platter, and transfers data at hard drive speeds. Because of this speed and capacity, Jaz drives only come in a SCSI version. The external Jaz drive has SCSI-2 connectors on the back instead of the Zip drive's 25-Pin SCSI connector. SCSI connector types are covered in the next section.

In addition, the Jaz drive allows you to select the full range of SCSI IDs (0–7). The device that you put at SCSI ID 0 will be the boot device on a SCSI chain, so to get the Jaz drive to be your boot drive, put it at SCSI ID 0. Other than those two differences, you install the external Jaz drive the same way you would install an external SCSI Zip drive. You can follow the next section on installing the external SCSI Zip drive as a guide to installing an external Jaz drive.

Parallel versus SCSI

The two versions of the Zip drive are different only in the way you connect them to the computer. The *Parallel drive* attaches to your computer via the Parallel (Printer) port. You can then attach your printer to the Zip drive. If that sounds confusing, think of the parallel Zip drive as sitting between your PC and the printer. The advantage to the parallel drive is that almost every computer has a parallel port, so you can use your parallel Zip drive on almost any machine. The disadvantage is that it has a slower transfer rate than the SCSI version.

The SCSI version of the drive connects to your computer via a *SCSI adapter*, a card that probably doesn't come with your computer. Because the SCSI interface is faster, the SCSI version of the Zip drive can transfer data about six times faster than the parallel version. While the SCSI version of the Zip drive has a faster transfer rate, its "seek time" is the same as the parallel drive.

NOTE It is important to remember that transferring and finding data are two different things. The speed at which a drive can find a file on a disk is called the *seek time*, and the speed at which it can peel that file off the disk is the *transfer rate*.

Generally, you will want the SCSI version of the Zip drive only if you will be saving large (1M+) files and have a SCSI adapter. If you will be storing lots of smaller files on the disks, need to use the drive on many computers, or don't have (or want to purchase and install) a new SCSI adapter, the parallel version is a bit slower, but better, choice.

Installing an External Zip/Jaz Drive

The physical installation of the external Zip drive is straightforward. If you have a parallel Zip drive, remove the printer cable (if you have a printer) from the parallel port and plug in the Zip drive's cable. Next, plug the printer cable into the second port on the back of the Zip drive. Be sure the Zip drive is turned on before or at the same time the computer is, or it may not be recognized. After you run the install program from the Iomega disk, your Zip drive becomes the next logical drive letter (D:, E:, or F: depending on the next free drive letter).

If you have the SCSI version of the drive, your installation may be a bit more complex depending on what kind of SCSI connector you have on the back of you computer. The SCSI cable that comes with Zip drive has a SCSI-2 connector on the computer side.

Almost all SCSI connectors come in three different types:

- *The SCSI-2 Connector*. The SCSI-2 connector (see Figure 12.12) is the newest and most compact of the SCSI connectors. It is a high-density 50-pin female connector on the computer. The clips that secure the cable are a part of the cable, not the adapter or drive. If your PC has this type of connector, you are in good shape and can plug the Zip or Jaz drive's cable right into it.

FIG. 12.12
The SCSI-2 connector.

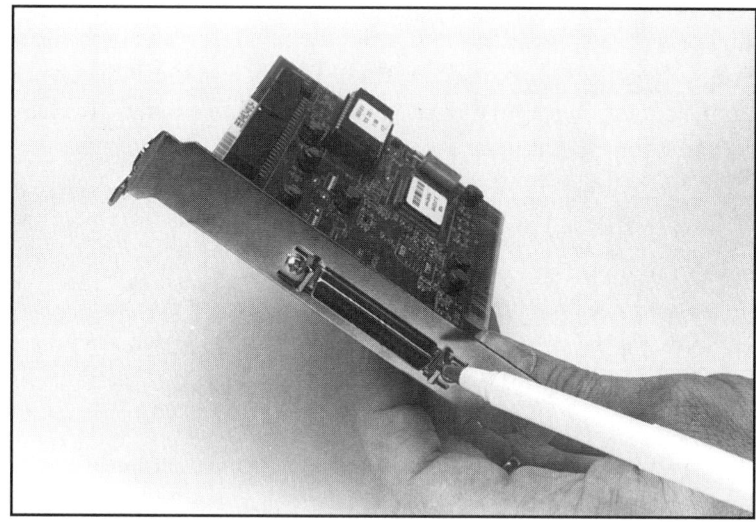

- *The SCSI-1 Connector.* You will know if you have a SCSI-1 connector because it will be the largest connector on the back of your computer. The connector has 50 pins total and is female at the back of the computer. It also has clips at its ends which hold the cable in place. If you have this type of connector, you need to purchase a different SCSI cable to attach the Zip drive.
- *The 25-pin Connector.* The 25-pin SCSI connector looks similar to a 25-pin RS-232 (COM) port, and is a female connector. This is the type of connector that is on the back of the SCSI Zip drive. If you have this type of connector on your computer, you need to purchase a different SCSI cable to attach the Zip drive.

Once you have the cables figured out, you need to connect the drive to the SCSI port on the back of the computer. Don't turn on your PC yet, because there are some additional things to check.

The SCSI Zip drive comes with two switches on the back, between the SCSI connectors. One switch is the selectable SCSI ID (ID 5 or 6). All devices connected to a SCSI adapter must have a unique SCSI ID. In most cases, there are no devices in your computer that will have a SCSI ID of 5 or 6, so either will be safe to choose. If, however, you have lots of SCSI devices (hard drives, tape drives, scanners, and so on), you need to make sure that none of them are at either ID 5 or 6, then choose that ID on the back of the Zip drive.

The other switch on the Zip drive is for SCSI Termination. *Termination* tells the SCSI adapter that this device is the last device in the SCSI chain. You usually won't need to move this switch from its default position unless your SCSI adapter isn't recognizing the Zip drive.

If you have an older SCSI card and a device with a SCSI ID between 0 and the Zip drive SCSI ID and no devices with a SCSI ID higher than your Zip drive, you may have to remove the termination on the last device before the Zip drive. For example, if you have a older computer with a SCSI controller and SCSI hard drive using SCSI ID 0, that drive may be the chain terminator, in which case the controller will not look higher than ID 0. Unless you remove the termination from that hard drive, the controller will never see your Zip drive at SCSI ID 5 or 6.

Before you turn on your PC, remember to first turn on the SCSI Zip drive. When the computer boots, the SCSI adapter identifies all the SCSI devices on the SCSI chain; if the Zip drive is turned off, it can't tell the adapter that it's available for use. After you have connected the Zip drive and configured the switches, you are ready to run the Iomega installation software and use the Zip or Jaz drive.

13

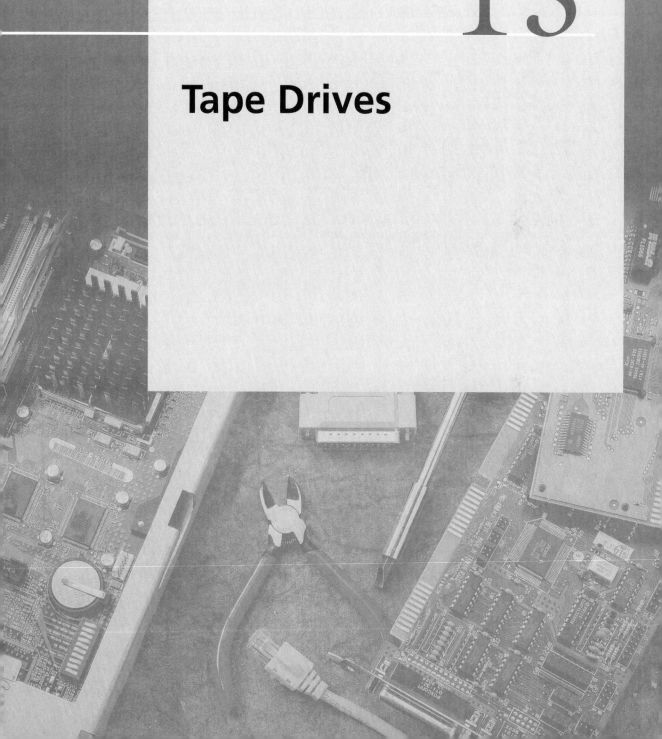

Tape Drives

Hard drives fail. Computers get stolen. People make mistakes. Regularly backing up your hard disk protects you from these calamities. But, a tape drive is like insurance. You need it only when you're in trouble. In the business world, a loss of data can be disastrous. Nearly half the businesses who lose their computer records go out of business within five years.

With that in mind, this is what you'll learn in this chapter:

- Why you need a tape backup drive
- Which tape sizes are available
- Which tape backup drive to get
- How to install various tape drives
- How to ensure a successful tape backup
- How to turn your tape drive into removable storage

Whether you want to protect someone's PC work or the files on an entire network, these next sections cover the various tape drives available to you and their installation procedures.

TIP I may use the term *backup* interchangeably with *tape* or *tape backup*. A backup is simply a copy of computer data on an external storage medium, such as a floppy disk or tape.

Tape Drive Basics

Backing up your computer is actually like making a *copy* of the information stored *inside* your computer. Your files are actually copied off the hard disk and onto one or more tape cartridges or disks. Those tapes or cartridges are then locked up or taken offsite for protection. Unlike using a floppy disk, the information on the backup tapes cannot be directly read by your computer.

NOTE Recent software called *direct tape access*, or *DTA*, allows a tape drive to be used for more than just backups. It allows the tape drive to double as a storage device, just like a an Iomega Zip or SyQuest EZ135 drive. Software from Imation (formerly 3M) and PGSoft, called *Tape-it,* makes this possible.

Why Back Up?

The value of a backup is often misunderstood. Your hard disk is equal to thousands of hours of labor. The value is not only in your data—the files you created, the letters you wrote, the addresses in your databases. Backups also save you the trouble of reinstalling programs and configuring them to your liking. For example, I have invested dozens of hours in customizing my Windows 95 and Windows 95 software programs. I've painstakingly removed unwanted files and have set my personal preferences, such as colors and fonts. If that work was lost, I would have to reinstall the software programs from the original program disks and customize the software... again. For these reasons, I recommend that you back up your programs as well as your data files.

A backup is useful for many purposes:

- *Emergencies.* With a backup, you can restore your work, or data, if your hard disk were to suddenly crash from mechanical failure, an electrical jolt, fire, water, or even dust. A properly backed-up hard disk can be restored within minutes.
- *Undeleting.* Backups are useful for restoring individual files or directories you or someone else might accidentally delete.
- *History.* A backup is also useful for accessing older versions of a file. The backup can contain earlier versions of important files that you may want to retrieve.
- *Archiving.* Backups are also useful for unburdening your hard disk of rarely used programs and old data. By archiving megabytes of information, your hard disk can focus on present work and not last year's budget or old correspondence. Archiving the information is safer than deleting files you may—gulp—need some day.
- *Sharing.* Backups are useful for transferring files from one computer to another. Whether moving the contents of your entire hard disk or just a few files, backup software provides an easy way to transfer files. You don't have to worry about how many files will fit on one disk or what to do with very large files.

The Backup Process

Backing up your computer involves copying files from your computer to another medium—a floppy disk or, more likely, a tape cartridge. Once done, the backup medium cannot be read directly by your computer; the files are often saved in a special format to conserve space and prevent errors.

If you want to back up more than 30M of data, I recommend a tape drive, because large floppy-disk backups can be slow, cumbersome, and require a dozen or more disks.

The backup process relies on the system of *attributes*. Each file on your computer has hidden marks to describe its status, as shown in Table 13.1. The archive *attribute*, or *flag*, is your computer's way of determining if a file needs to be backed up. Backup software uses the archive attribute to determine which files get backed up. If you view the attributes of your files in DOS or Windows, the presence of an "A" means the file has not been backed up.

CAUTION Some people consider floppy disks or even removable media such as Zip or SyQuest drives to be adequate for backup. These tape alternatives often are not because their media tends to get easily corrupted by age, magnetism, or contamination. Tape drives are like an old pair of shoes; they're comfortable, low-cost, and reliable.

Table 13.1 File Attributes

Letter	Meaning	Description
A	Archive	Needs to be backed up.
S	System	Important file required for the operating system.
H	Hidden	This file is hidden from view.
R	Read-only	This file cannot be deleted or saved to.

TIP To view the attributes of a file in Windows, open Windows Explorer (File Manager, if using Windows 3.x), highlight one file, and press Alt+Enter. The

Properties box displays check boxes for each attribute. If using DOS, type **ATTRIB** (and press Enter). The attributes for each file in the current directory are displayed.

By using these attributes, you will use a combination of two backup options:

- Full
- Partial (or *modified)*

The full backup backs up all files you select, whether the archive attribute is on or off. Usually, you would back up your entire hard disk, although you can perform a full backup of individual directories or folders. Once the files are safely backed up, the archive attributes of these files are turned off.

NOTE Every backup plan starts with making at least one full backup of the entire hard disk.

After a full backup, the partial backup is used to back up only those files that have been added or changed since the full backup. There are two types of partial backups:

- *Incremental.* The *incremental backup* backs up only those files that have changed or been added since the last full or partial backup. Just like its name, the incremental backup stores the changes to your data in increments. To restore your work, you must have the full backup set plus *all* the sets of incremental backups to restore your hard disk to the way it was up to the last incremental backup.
- *Differential.* The *differential backup* stores the files that have changed since the last full backup. However, the archive attribute is not turned off. If a differential backup is performed later, the same files are backed up plus any additional files that have been changed since then. With the differential option, the backup gets bigger and takes longer. The advantage is that the hard disk can be restored by having the full backup set and the single differential backup set.

The partial backup option you choose should reflect your personal style and the importance of your work. For example, if you want access to older versions of your files, you would prefer the incremental partial backup. Conversely, if you want the smallest backup and easiest restoration, you would prefer the differential backup.

Selecting a Backup Cycle

Because every backup routine starts with one full backup as its foundation, you need to determine the time between full backups. This is called the *backup cycle.* Two popular backup cycles are one week and one month. During this interval, you do partial backups, storing files that are new or have changed since the last full backup. Partial backups reduce the backup time, as well as wear and tear on your tape drive and tapes.

The backup cycle you select is determined by how many files and to what extent these files change. If you do not use your PC much and the files do not change much or are not that important, you could opt for a longer backup cycle. If your work is very important and difficult to reproduce, or you use your PC quite often, then select a shorter backup cycle.

Besides the full backup cycle, you also need to select how often you will do the partial backup. For example, your backup cycle may be one month and you may want to do a partial backup every week. If your files change often during that week or are very important, you may want to do a partial backup twice a week. You know your computer habits best, but consider these three points:

- If your number of backup tapes is limited, you need to estimate how many days they will last.
- If your number of backup tapes is unlimited, you have more flexibility in selecting a longer backup cycle.
- If you decide to save your backup tapes offsite for the ultimate in safety, keep your backup cycle fairly short, say one week.

> **CAUTION** One general rule of thumb is that the number of days between your partial backups should never encompass more work than you can afford to lose. For example, if you cannot afford to lose a single day's work, you should do a partial backup each day.

The Imation Data Storage Products Division recommends the "Grandfather, Father, Son" principle to backups. Covering 12 weeks, this concept allows you to restore your computer's hard disk to the way it was up to three months ago.

Simply put, this principle requires a weekly full backup of your computer for three consecutive weeks. Label each backup tape **Week 1**, **Week 2**, and **Week 3**. Throughout the week, do partial backups to store new or changed files. For example, you could have four tapes for each day of the week and use the weekly tapes on Fridays. On the fourth week, do another full backup but label it **Month 1**. Repeat these steps for the second month, but label the fourth week's backup set of the month **Month 2**. Repeat this for the third month and create **Month 3**.

TIP No matter how often you back up, label your backup media clearly. One way to avoid mix-ups is to use a different colored label or floppy disk for each day of the week: Monday backups on red, Tuesday on blue, and so on. Monthly backups could be kept on black labels or disks. If you back up weekly, you can also follow a color scheme. For example, use a different color disk for each week of the month, and a black disk for the end-of-the-month backup.

Besides selecting the length of your backup cycle, you also need to pick which kind of partial backup you will use between full backups: incremental or differential.

The incremental backup is ideal if you either work with different files or require older versions of the same files. If you frequently create several new files, like new correspondence, the incremental backup is also recommended. With this option, each partial backup is both fast and efficient because it is recording only the files that are changed or new since the previous incremental backup. If you need access to prior versions of the same file, the incremental backup lets you choose the file from any of the prior incremental backups.

If you ever need to use your backups, you must restore the full backup and then *all* incremental backups since then. If using disks as your backup medium, you may find yourself running out, because each incremental backup requires its own disk.

If you generally work with the same files each day, the differential backup is well suited as your partial backup. Also, the differential backup is ideal if you do not need to keep old versions of your files. With the differential backup, you use only two sets of backup media: the full backup set and the single differential backup set.

With the differential backup, the single partial backup records the changed or new files since the last full backup. For this reason, the differential backup grows larger and larger. Yet, if you tend to use the same files, the length of the backup may grow slowly. When you find the wait time or number of tapes too burdensome, you can do a full backup and repeat the cycle.

If you ever need to use your backup, you need to restore only these two sets: the full backup and the differential backup. This saves time and backup media (that is, fewer disks).

TIP You can combine the benefits of the differential and incremental backup by selecting the differential backup but putting it on different tapes. With this technique, you can have older versions of the same files, as well as keep restoration easy.

See Table 13.2 to learn how to select your type of partial backup.

Table 13.2 Selecting a Partial Backup Method

If You...	Then Use...
Create several new files (such as letters)	Incremental
Want fast partial backups	Incremental
Constantly update many different files	Incremental
Require access to older versions of files	Incremental
Have ample backup tapes	Incremental
Want fast restoration of your files	Differential
Often work on the same files each day	Differential
Do not need access to older file versions	Differential
Have few backup tapes	Differential

Protecting Your Tapes

The best backup plan can be thwarted by fire, flood, theft, and other calamities. To ensure the best data protection, you should always keep a backup set offsite, such as in a safe deposit box, a neighbor's house, or at work.

How do you maintain a backup copy offsite if you might need it at your computer? You simply maintain two backup sets and rotate between them each backup cycle. For example, if your backup cycle is one week, place the first week's backup set offsite. Then start the second week's backup set. The third week, you can either start a third backup set or reuse the first week's. In a worst-case scenario, the only work that would be lost if your onsite backup set were destroyed would be those few days since you stored the last backup offsite. Some backup software programs have full copy and incremental copy backup options so you can duplicate the current backup cycle's work and store it offsite. Also, when making partial backups, keep the tapes across the room away from your computer; thieves often steal the tapes that are conveniently nearby.

CAUTION Storing tapes in a fire-proof safe is not always safe. Although most safes protect papers from scorching in temperatures above 350°, backup tapes can be damaged by this heat. "Media-safe" safes are available, but cost three to four times as much as conventional fire safes.

Choosing a Tape Drive

Your choice of tape drives is limited by what tapes it can use. You have several different sizes of media from which to choose:

- Quarter-Inch Cartridge (QIC)
- Travan
- 4mm DAT
- 8mm
- Digital Linear Tape (DLT)
- Digital Data Storage (DDS)

Each of those formats (especially QIC) has splintered into numerous standards, which makes it even more difficult to find a tape drive that provides just the right mix of performance, price, and (where needed) backward compatibility.

The first step in picking a tape drive is determining the required capacity. One good rule of thumb is that you should be able to back up each drive onto one tape. You should consider your drive's entire capacity, rather than its current contents, because you will eventually fill it. By backing up your drive to one tape, you can keep better track of your backups.

NOTE You may choose a tape drive that holds less than your entire hard drive. However, your full backup may span more than one tape, and you will manually have to swap tapes when each one gets full.

Backing up your PC's contents is not a fast process. Speeds range from 9M per minute to 30M per minute. However, these numbers are affected by your CPU's horsepower and how much memory you have, as well as whether or not you're compressing your data. The higher the data rate, the faster your backup.

Backup speed is often not an issue with tape drives, although some drives are faster than others. Why not? Most tape backup software includes a scheduling feature that allows you to run the backup operation at night or other times when you aren't using the computer. Most backups require less than two hours.

NOTE If you do schedule late-night backups, you have to leave your PC on during the time the scheduled backup is to occur.

To get the most on the tape, the tape backup software, which either comes with your drive or is purchased separately, compresses the files as they are stored on tape. Tape drive vendors often quote tape capacity in terms of compressed rather than uncompressed, or *native*, capacity. For example, the Hewlett-Packard T1000 drive has a compressed capacity of up to 800M on one tape with an uncompressed capacity of 400M (see Figure 13.1).

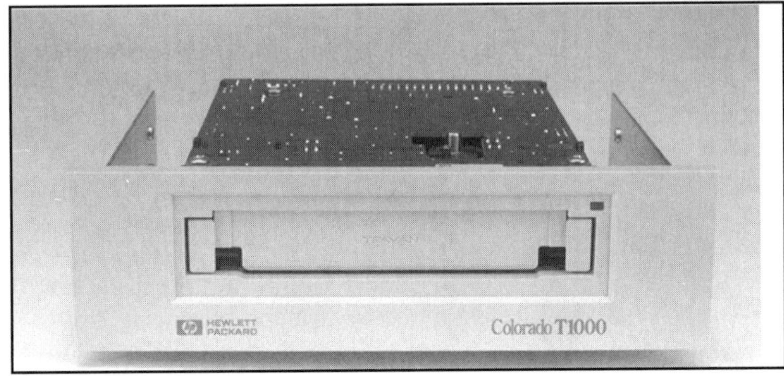

FIG. 13.1
The Colorado T1000 drive from Hewlett-Packard is a Travan drive that holds up to 800M on one tape when compression is turned on.

When vendors list compressed capacity figures for their drives, they assume a 2:1 compression, but real-world results don't always achieve this. For example, program files (those with .EXE or .COM extensions) don't compress as well as documents, database files, and other work-related files. My experience has been about 1.2:1 to 1.5:1.

NOTE Data compression onto a tape, unlike similar technology for hard drives, is a safe and proven process, especially if you turn on your tape software's Compare (Verify) feature to ensure that the information was saved to the tape.

The type of tape technology you pick determines which tape drive you will use. Your choices are simple and are explained in the following sections.

QIC

Of all the backup tapes available, quarter-inch cartridges (QIC) are the most economical. QIC tapes come in two sizes: the popular 3 ½-inch minicartridges (MC) and larger 5 ¼-inch data cartridges (DC).

The original QIC-40, which held 40M–60M, is obsolete. Today, the most common minicartridge is QIC-80, which holds up to 250M compressed. However, such capacity is outstripped by today's larger hard drives. To increase capacity, some manufacturers, such as Sony, changed the width of the tape from .25-inch to .315-inch. Such "QIC-Wide" drives can use both QIC-Wide and DC2000 tapes (see Table 13.3). More recent QIC drives are the QIC-3010, QIC-3020, and QIC-3080. Most QIC tape drives are either discontinued or heavily discounted.

Table 13.3 QIC Minicartridge Types (Capacities Shown Without Compression)

Format	DC-2000	QIC-Wide	Travan	QIC-EX (.315-in wide)
QIC-80	125M	200M	400M (TR-1)	500M
QIC-3010	340M	420M	800M (TR-2)	1.1G
QIC-3020	680M	850M	1.6G (TR-3)	2.2G
QIC-3040	840M	1G		2.5G
QIC-3050	1G	1.3G	2.3G	3.1G
QIC-3080	1.6G	2G		5G
QIC-3095		2G	4G (TR-4)	5G
QIC-3210		2.3G		5.1G
QIC-3230		8G	15G	20G

Options for Older Tape Drives

If you have an older QIC-80 drive or can't afford a new drive, consider a new high-capacity tape cartridge for existing QIC-80-style drives. The new cartridges that hold up to 800M—the QIC-XL from Gigatek and the QIC-EXtra from Verbatim—pack 1,000 feet of tape into the cartridge. Best of all, Travan drives can read both the Gigatek and Verbatim designs, so if you decide to upgrade to Travan sometime in the future, your backups will be useable.

To take advantage of this new tape cartridge, you need backup software that is XL- or EXtra-aware. Seagate (formerly Arcada) Backup for DOS and Windows version 4.3 or higher (including the 16-bit version 5.0 for Windows 95) and Seagate Backup for Windows 95 version 1.0 will automatically sense the longer tape length, allowing you to use the tape's full capacity when performing a backup. Software upgrades are available from either your drive's manufacturer or Verbatim.

Travan

Travan is one of the hottest tape technologies for desktop computers and is even now suitable for network file servers. Travan is simply a larger, modified QIC cartridge.

There are several generations of Travan tapes. First-generation TR-1 drives and cartridges hold up to 800M and can read QIC-Wide tapes. TR-2 drives and TR-3 drives and cartridges correspond to the QIC-3010 and QIC-3020 standards, respectively. Imation (formerly 3M) has continued to adapt Travan technology, and has introduced TR-4 minicartridges that hold up to 8G. TR-4 conforms to a recently established QIC-3095-MC format standard; TR-4 drives can read QIC-3020 tapes (see Table 13.4).

NOTE Imation is working on a 15G Travan cartridge to be released in 1997, as well as a Travan "jukebox" that autoloads Travan tapes.

Table 13.4 Travan Specifications and Compatibility

Format	TR-1	TR-2	TR-3	TR-4
Capacity				
Uncompressed	400M	800M	1.6G	4G
Compressed	800M	1.6G	3.2G	8G
Data Transfer Rate				
Minimum	62.5 Kbps	62.5 Kbps	125 Kbps	567 Kbps
Maximum	125 Kbps	125 Kbps	250 Kbps	567 Kbps
Drive Interface	Floppy	Floppy	Floppy	SCSI/EIDE
Compatibility	QIC-80 R/W	QIC-3010 R/W	QIC-3020/ 3010 R/W	QIC-3080/ 3095 R/W
R=Read, W=Write	QIC-40 R	QIC-80 R	QIC-80 R	QIC-3020 R

4mm DAT

Digital Audio Tape (DAT) is a recording technology that started in the music industry and has been adapted for data storage. Although smaller than QIC and Travan cartridges, DAT tapes hold quite a bit, from 2G–16G. The DAT tapes are about half to one-third the cost of QIC and Travan tapes, but the tape drives themselves cost twice to four times as much. DAT drives are known for their backup speed, and are often used for high-end individual computers or for backing up small workgroups of computers.

DAT devices use either of two formatting standards:

- *Digital Data Storage (DDS).* Most DAT drives use this format. DDS drives come in three styles: DDS-1 (2G uncompressed), DDS-2 (4G uncompressed), and DDS-3 (12G uncompressed).
- *Data/DAT.* Developed by Hitachi, this standard overwrites existing data files in place, reducing the inefficiencies of making multiple copies of the same file.

8mm

The 8mm cartridge owes its beginning to the conventional camcorder. Exabyte, which holds the patent for 8mm technology, adopted it for data storage. Single 8mm cartridges have a native capacity of up to 5G, with newer formulations pushing the capacity to 7G. The amount of data stored and the top transfer speed depend on the particular drive and the amount of compression used. Maximum transfer speed with full hardware-based data compression is about 21M/minute. 8mm tapes are often used to back up networks.

DLT

The ultimate in tape backup drives is digital linear tape (DLT). A new entry in the tape backup market, DLT is actually too fast for most computers because slowing the tape down below 40M per minute causes excessive wear. With a capacity of up to 20G (40G compressed) and a data-transfer rate of 1.5M/sec, DLT provides as much as four times the capacity and three times the speed of traditional tape products. Data reliability is also high. One-fourth of the data on DLT tapes is dedicated to error detection and correction. Also, the tapes are guaranteed for 500,000 passes, while the tape heads have a life of 10,000 hours. However, DLT tape drives cost at least $3,000.

Installing a Tape Drive

There are several ways to connect tape backup drives to a PC. The different methods include:

- Parallel (printer) port
- Floppy drive interface
- Enhanced IDE (EIDE) interface (also known as ATAPI)
- SCSI interface

The type of tape drive you select limits your choices of connections, as you learn in the following sections. For example, most low-end tape drives (such as QIC and TR-1, TR-2, and TR-3) use the floppy drive interface or parallel port. Higher-end drives (such as TR-4, DLT, or DAT) use either the Enhanced IDE (EIDE) or SCSI interface.

TIP Be practical. Tape drives come in many different flavors, so there's generally more than one approach to fit your situation. Think about the trade-offs in terms of capacity, usability, convenience, backup speed, and cost.

Parallel Port Tape Drives

Parallel port tape drives simply connect to your printer port. Parallel port tape drives are for those who want a simple, don't-wanna-open-my-computer tape drive. Parallel port drives are also for those who want a portable drive, often for backing up a laptop computer or several computers at one or more sites. Popular parallel port tape drives include Iomega Ditto or Hewlett-Packard's T-1000E.

Parallel port drives provide the slowest backup method of all drives. Speeds are often limited to about 5M per minute. In other words, backing up a 1G hard drive will take about three hours. If you turn on the Compare/Verify feature in your tape software, you can double that time.

NOTE The Iomega Ditto can hold as much as 2G of compressed data (1G uncompressed) with Iomega's proprietary tapes. However, it can only read the other popular formats such as Travan TR-1, TR-2, TR-3 and QIC-80, QIC-3010, and QIC-3020.

Installing the Parallel Port Tape Drive

Before You Install a Tape Drive, You Need:

- ☑ Parallel port, preferably bi-directional for faster backups. All PCs have at least one printer port. Ports are commonly referred to as LPT1. Additional ports are numbered LPT2 and LPT3. You won't have to worry about switching between the printer and tape drive. Parallel port tape drives often have a second connector to provide "pass-through" printing to your printer. In other words, you can have your tape drive and print through it, too.
- ☑ A 3 ½-inch floppy drive from which to install the tape backup software
- ☑ Small flat-bladed screwdriver to tighten cable connections
- ☑ Computer is turned off!

Installing a parallel port tape drive is as simple as plugging in a printer:

1. Verify that the computer is turned off.
2. Locate the parallel port connector on your computer. Parallel ports have receptacles for 25 pins. Your tape drive can share a parallel port with a printer.
3. If you have a printer cable attached to the computer's parallel port, disconnect it and plug it into the connector on the tape drive that says `To Printer`, if present. Hand tighten the screws.
4. Attach the data cable that came with your tape drive to the drive's other 25-pin connector.
5. Attach the tape drive data cable to your computer's parallel port and hand tighten its retaining screws.
6. Plug the tape drive's power cord into the drive and then into an electrical outlet.
7. Turn on your computer. Your PC should start as it normally does.

TROUBLESHOOTING

My PC doesn't act normally. If your PC doesn't start normally, check that the computer is plugged in, that each device is plugged in and turned on, and that all cables are plugged into the back of your computer. If you still have trouble, turn off your computer for 20 seconds before turning it back on.

Floppy Controller Tape Drives

Most low-end tape drives share the floppy drive cable for backing up your data. This would include QIC-80, TR-1, TR-2, and most TR-3 tape drives. Although popular, the floppy connection is much slower than the far better-performing SCSI and ATAPI (Enhanced IDE) interfaces.

Before You Install a Tape Drive, You Need:

- ☑ Phillips screwdriver or nut driver for removing case screws
- ☑ Available power connector to power the drive, or Y-splitter to share the power of another device

- ☑ Power-cable adapter (which may be included with the tape drive), in case your PC doesn't have the right size of power cable
- ☑ One available drive bay. Some tape drives can be installed in either a half-height (6×1 3/4 inches) or a 1-inch high bay (4×1 inches). Check your tape drive's documentation.
- ☑ A 3 1/2-inch floppy drive from which to install the tape backup software
- ☑ Any special mounting hardware required to place the drive in a 5 1/4-inch, half-height bay
- ☑ Small flat-bladed screwdriver to tighten cable connections
- ☑ Computer is turned off!

Installing a Floppy Controller Tape Drive

Installing a floppy-driven tape drive requires you to open the computer and "share" the floppy drive cable with the new tape drive. Just follow these steps:

1. Verify that the computer is turned off.
2. Unplug the computer and open it up. See Chapter 5 for details.
3. Determine whether you will be installing the tape drive in a half-height or 1-inch high drive bay. Many floppy-based tape drives will fit in the similar 1-inch opening as that used by the 3 1/2-inch floppy drive.
4. Remove the cover plate from the desired drive bay (see Figure 13.2).

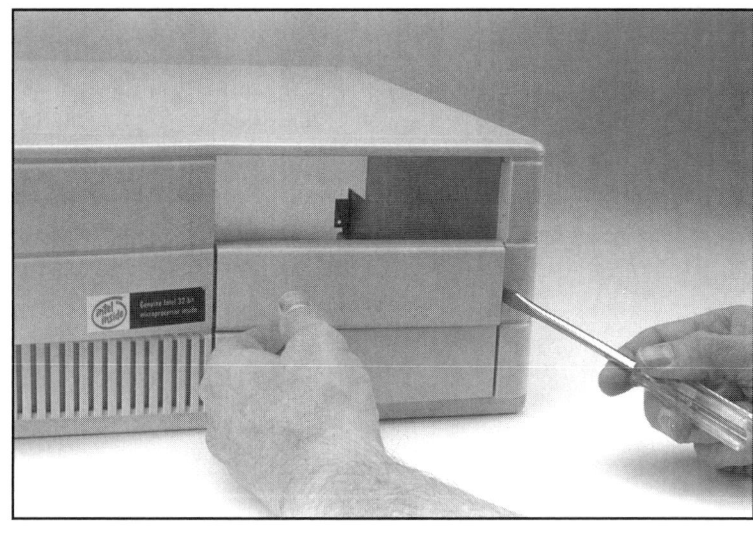

FIG. 13.2
Use the flat edge of the screwdriver to gently pry off the bay cover.

CAUTION Be careful when removing the drive bay cover. Because these are often made of plastic, they may be easily broken or chipped. Use a flat-edge screwdriver to gently pry off the cover. In some cases, these covers may be screwed in place.

CAUTION Before handling the tape drive or any other computer components, briefly touch your PC's metal case to drain yourself of static electricity. Avoid touching the printed circuit boards or the components on them.

5. If installing the tape drive in a 3 1/2-inch, 1-inch high drive bay, remove the mounting bracket from the tape drive, if necessary (see Figure 13.3). If installing the drive in a 5 1/4-inch, half-height drive bay, skip this step.

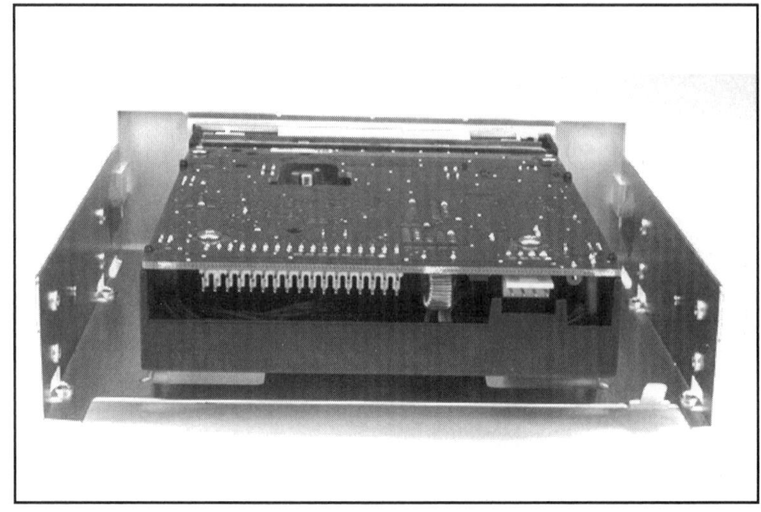

FIG. 13.3
Often, the tape drive comes in a 5 1/4-inch mounting bracket that can be removed if you want to put it in a 1×4-inch drive bay.

6. If installing the drive in a 5 1/4-inch, half-height drive bay, install any other mounting hardware, if required, for the tape drive to fit in the bay (see Figure 13.4).

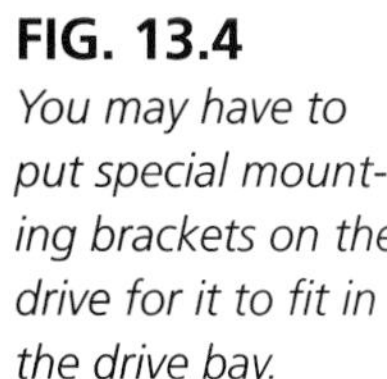

FIG. 13.4
You may have to put special mounting brackets on the drive for it to fit in the drive bay.

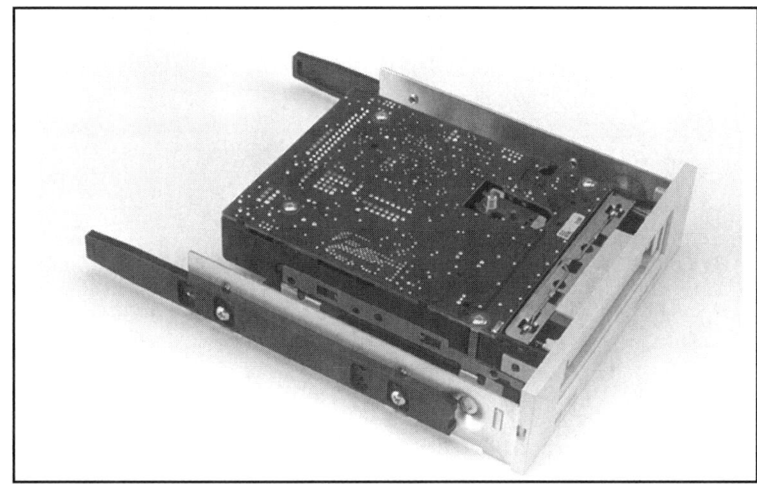

7. Locate your floppy controller connector, which may be either on the motherboard itself or attached to an adapter plugged into the motherboard. Note which end of the floppy controller has the colored stripe of the floppy drive cable attached to it.
8. Remove the existing floppy drive cable from the floppy connector.
9. Attach the cable that came with the tape drive to the back of the tape drive. This cable has a colored stripe (typically red) on the pin-one edge of the cable (see Figure 13.5). Mate this to the drive's "1" indicator, which is either printed on the circuit board or on the drive's housing. If unsure, check the drive's manual.

NOTE Having the cable on correctly so the colored edge is on the pin-one connection is crucial for the tape drive to work.

10. Thread the free end of the tape drive cable through the bay and slide the tape drive into the bay (see Figure 13.6).

FIG. 13.5
Ensure that the colored edge of the tape drive cable matches the pin-one side of the drive's connector.

FIG. 13.6
With the cables attached, slide the drive back into the bay.

11. Locate the computer's power supply. Find an unused power cable that fits the power connector on the tape drive. If the cable doesn't match your drive, you may need to use the power-cable adapter included with the drive, if included. If no free power cable is available, use a Y-power splitter to share the power from another device (see Figure 13.7). Attach this cable to the tape drive.

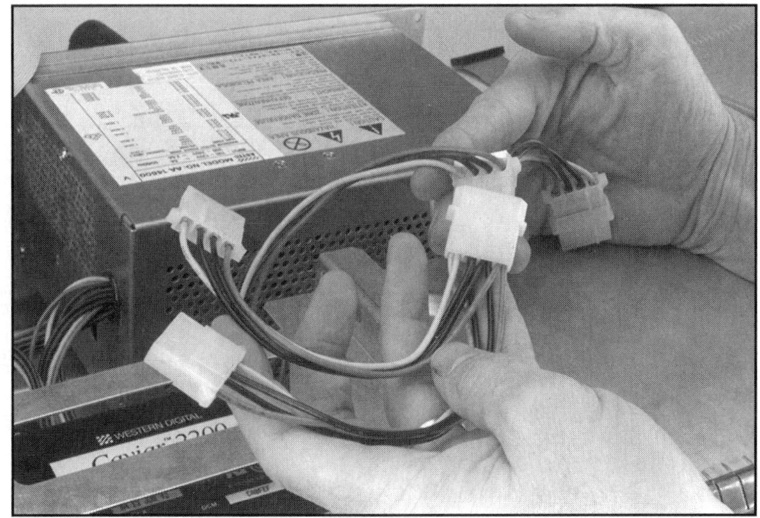

FIG. 13.7
If no power leads are available, you may have to use a Y-power splitter to share the power from another device.

12. Take the tape drive cable in one hand and the computer's floppy drive cable in the other. Match the cables' color stripes and plug the floppy drive cable into the middle connector of the tape drive cable. Be careful not to bend the connector's pins.
13. Attach the other end of the tape drive cable to the floppy connector. Place the cable's connector so the color stripe is on the same side of the floppy controller as noted in step 9.
14. Double-check that all pins of each connection are covered by the cable's connectors (see Figure 13.8). You want all pins to be snugly covered by the connectors.
15. After checking that the drive is flush with the front of the case (see Figure 13.9), insert and tighten the screws so the tape drive or mounting brackets are snug against the metal drive bay. This not only holds the drive in place but grounds it for proper electrical operation.

TIP Sometimes the mounting brackets may keep the drive from being fully inserted into the drive bay. If so, use side-cutters to trim the ends (see Figure 13.10).

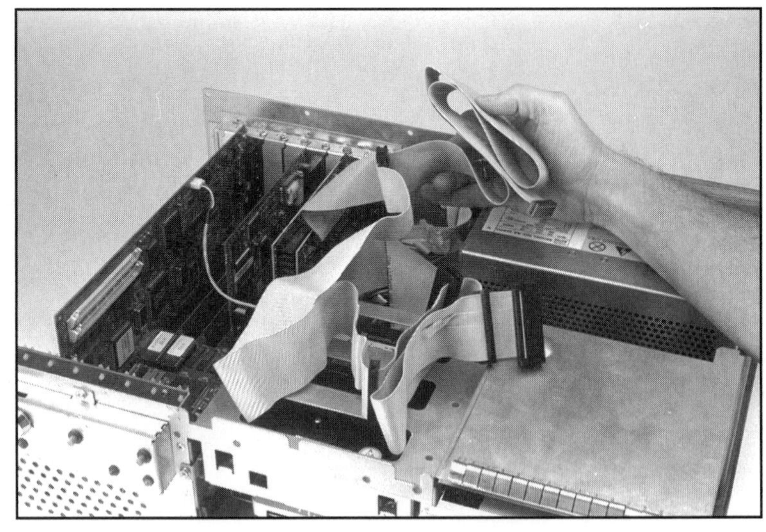

FIG. 13.8
Check that all connections are tight before closing the case.

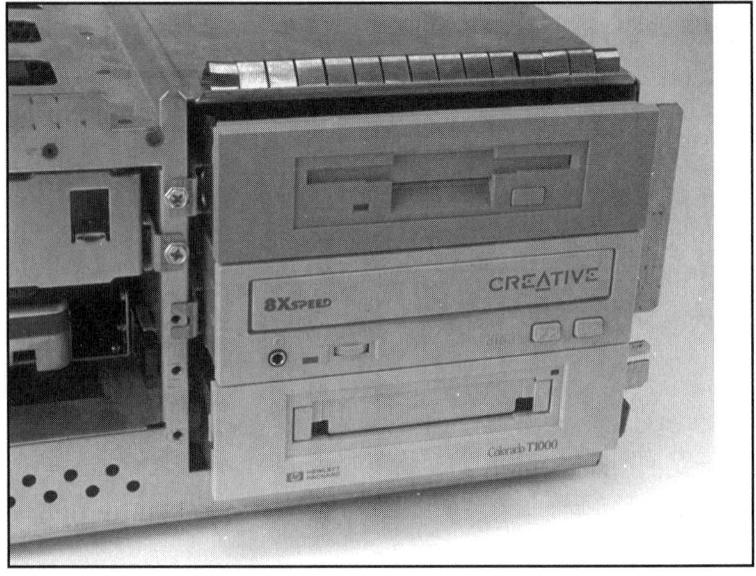

FIG. 13.9
Check that the new drive is flush with the front of the case and the other devices before screwing it into place.

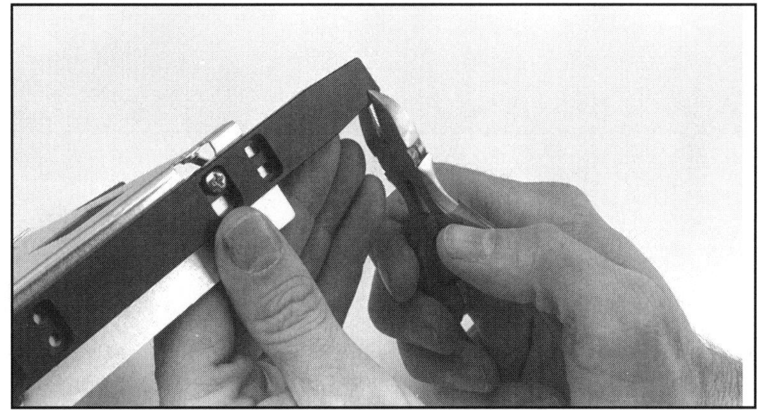

FIG. 13.10
If using mounting brackets that keep the drive from being fully inserted, you may need to trim them with side-cutters.

16. Put the cover back on your computer and secure it with any screws you removed earlier.
17. Plug in your computer, monitor, and any other devices, and turn them on.

TROUBLESHOOTING

My PC doesn't act normally. If your PC doesn't start normally, check that the computer is plugged in, that each device is plugged in and turned on, and that all cables are plugged into the back of your computer. If you still have trouble, turn off your computer for 20 seconds before turning it back on. Check that all expansion cards are firmly seated in their slots. If the lights of the floppy drives stay on or you receive a floppy-drive error, you may have plugged the cables in backwards. Open the computer and check that the colored stripes of all cables are on the same side and attached to the pin-one connectors.

IDE Tape Drives

Usually, tape drives that use the enhanced IDE (EIDE) interface often come with their own IDE controller cards. These controller cards often provide faster backup operation than using the typical IDE connector found on your motherboard or on an expansion card.

Before You Install an IDE Tape Drive, You Need:

- ☑ If using an IDE card that came with your tape drive, an available 16-bit ISA expansion slot
- ☑ If using an existing IDE connector in your PC, the slave (second) connector on your primary IDE cable or either connector on a secondary IDE connector

NOTE If you already have four IDE devices in your system (for example, three IDE hard drives and one CD-ROM drive), then you must consider an alternative tape drive, because enhanced IDE systems are limited to four IDE devices. One option similar to IDE in speed and price is a SCSI-based tape drive.

- ☑ Phillips screwdriver or nut driver for removing case screws
- ☑ Available power connector to power the drive, or Y-splitter to share the power of another device
- ☑ Power-cable adapter (which may be included with the tape drive), in case your PC doesn't have the right size of power cable
- ☑ One available drive bay. Some tape drives can be installed in either a half-height (6×1 3/4 inches) or a 1-inch high bay (4×1 inches). Check your tape drive's documentation.
- ☑ A 3 1/2-inch floppy drive from which to install the tape backup software
- ☑ Any special mounting hardware required to place the drive in a 5 1/4-inch, half-height bay
- ☑ Small flat-bladed screwdriver to tighten cable connections
- ☑ Computer is turned off!

Installing an IDE Tape Drive

Installing an IDE tape drive requires you to install inside your computer a tape drive and often a controller card for top performance. Some tape drives use a secondary IDE controller in your computer. Follow these steps:

1. Verify that the computer is turned off.
2. Unplug the computer and open it up. See Chapter 5 for details.
3. Determine whether you will be installing the tape drive in a half-height or 1-inch high drive bay. Many tape drives will fit in the similar 1-inch opening as that used by the 3 1/2-inch floppy drive.
4. Remove the cover plate from the desired drive bay.

CAUTION Be careful when removing the drive bay cover. Because these are often made of plastic, they may be easily broken or chipped. Use a flat-edge screwdriver to gently pry off the cover. In some cases, these covers may be screwed in place.

CAUTION Before handling the tape drive or any other computer components, briefly touch your PC's metal case to drain yourself of static electricity. Avoid touching the printed circuit boards or the components on them.

5. If installing the tape drive in a $3\frac{1}{2}$-inch, 1-inch high drive bay, remove the mounting bracket from the tape drive, if necessary. If installing the drive in a $5\frac{1}{4}$-inch, half-height drive bay, skip this step.
6. If installing the drive in a $5\frac{1}{4}$-inch, half-height drive bay, install any other mounting hardware, if required, for the tape drive to fit in the bay.
7. Locate a vacant ISA slot for the IDE controller that came with your tape drive. Remove its expansion slot cover.

NOTE With some IDE tape drives, you may have to use your PC's IDE connector, which may be either on the motherboard itself or attached to an adapter plugged into the motherboard (see Figure 13.11). The tape drive should use the secondary, not primary, IDE controller.

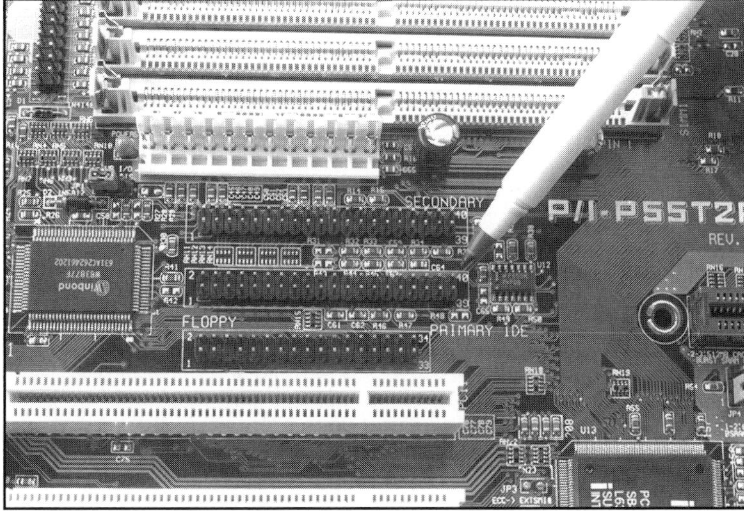

FIG. 13.11
Some IDE tape drives use the IDE connector on the motherboard.

8. Remove the controller card from its anti-static bag, and set any jumpers on the card, if required.
9. Holding the controller by its edges, insert it into the vacant expansion slot and secure it with the screw you removed in step 7.
10. Attach the cable that came with the tape drive to the controller card. This cable has a colored stripe (typically red) on the pin-one edge of the cable. Mate this to the controller's "1" indicator, which often is printed on the circuit board. Some cards and cables are keyed so they can only be installed correctly. If unsure, check the drive's manual.
11. Thread the free end of the tape drive cable through the bay and attach to the tape drive. Mate the colored pin-one edge of the cable to the drive's "1" indicator, which often is printed on the circuit board or on the drive's housing (see Figure 13.12). If unsure, check the drive's manual.

FIG. 13.12
Ensure the colored edge of the tape drive cable matches to the pin-one side of the drive's connector.

NOTE Having the cable on correctly so the colored edge is on the pin-one connection is crucial for the tape drive to work.

12. Set the tape drive to Master or Slave, according to the drive's manual.

TIP A drive is a master if it is connected to the end of the cable from either the drive's IDE controller card or the primary or secondary IDE controllers.

13. Locate the computer's power supply. Find an unused power cable that fits the power connector on the tape drive. If the cable doesn't match your drive, you may need to use the power-cable adapter included with the drive, if included. If no free power cable is available, use a Y-power splitter to share the power from another device. Attach this cable to the tape drive.
14. Slide the tape drive into the drive bay.
15. Double-check that all pins of each connection are covered by the cable's connectors. You want all pins to be snugly covered by the connectors.
16. After checking that the drive is flush with the front of the case, insert and tighten the screws so the tape drive or mounting brackets are snug against the metal drive bay. This not only holds the drive in place but grounds it for proper electrical operation.
17. Put the cover back on your computer and secure it with any screws you removed earlier.
18. Plug in your computer, monitor, and any other devices, and turn them on.
19. If using the IDE card that came with your tape drive, you must enter your computer's setup program (also called the BIOS or CMOS) and disable the secondary IDE controller, if possible. If using a secondary IDE controller already in your computer, you must enter your computer's setup and enable the secondary IDE controller if it isn't already.

TROUBLESHOOTING

My PC doesn't act normally. If your PC doesn't start normally, check that the computer is plugged in, that each device is plugged in and turned on, and that all cables are plugged into the back of your computer. If you still have trouble, turn off your computer for 20 seconds before turning it back on. Check that all expansion cards are firmly seated in their slots. If you receive a hard disk error, you may have plugged the cables in backwards. Open the computer and check that the colored stripes of all cables are on the same side and attached to the pin-one connectors.

If the tape drive is not found by the installation software, check that your tape drive is not conflicting with your sound card's IDE port, if present. Although most sound cards automatically disable the IDE port when not used to run a CD-ROM drive, some may need to have a jumper changed to disable the IDE port.

SCSI Tape Drives

Tape drives that use the SCSI (Small Computer Systems Interface) interface rely on an existing SCSI card in your system. A SCSI controller provides the fastest backup of all tape drives you've looked at, often reaching speeds of 30M per minute.

Before You Install a Tape Drive, You Need:

- ☑ An existing SCSI controller
- ☑ A list of the SCSI IDs of your existing SCSI devices, if any
- ☑ An available 50-pin connector on your internal SCSI cable
- ☑ Phillips screwdriver or nut driver for removing case screws
- ☑ Available power connector to power the drive, or Y-splitter to share the power of another device
- ☑ Power-cable adapter (which may be included with the tape drive), in case your PC doesn't have the right size of power cable
- ☑ One available drive bay. Some tape drives can be installed in either a half-height (6×1 3/4 inches) or a 1-inch high bay (4×1 inches). Check your tape drive's documentation
- ☑ A 3 1/2-inch floppy drive from which to install the tape backup software
- ☑ Any special mounting hardware required to place the drive in a 5 1/4-inch, half-height bay
- ☑ Small flat-bladed screwdriver to tighten cable connections
- ☑ Computer is turned off!

Installing an Internal SCSI Tape Drive

Installing an internal SCSI tape drive requires you to add the tape drive to the "chain" of SCSI devices you may already have in your computer. You must attach the tape drive to a free SCSI connector inside your computer, assign it a unique SCSI ID, and properly terminate the drive. Follow these steps:

1. Verify that the computer is turned off.
2. Unplug the computer and open it up. See Chapter 5 for details.

3. Determine whether you will be installing the tape drive in a half-height or 1-inch high drive bay. Many tape drives will fit in the similar 1-inch opening as that used by the 3 ½-inch floppy drive.
4. Remove the cover plate from the desired drive bay.

CAUTION Be careful when removing the drive bay cover. Because these are often made of plastic, they may be easily broken or chipped. Use a flat-edge screwdriver to gently pry off the cover. In some cases, these covers may be screwed in place.

CAUTION Before handling the tape drive or any other computer components, briefly touch your PC's metal case to drain yourself of static electricity. Avoid touching the printed circuit boards or the components on them.

5. If installing the tape drive in a 3 ½-inch, 1-inch high drive bay, remove the mounting bracket from the tape drive, if necessary. If installing the drive in a 5 ¼-inch, half-height drive bay, skip this step.
6. If installing the drive in a 5 ¼-inch, half-height drive bay, install any other mounting hardware, if required, for the tape drive to fit in the bay.
7. Set the drive's SCSI ID to an available ID. Often, this is done by setting jumpers on the drive (see Figure 13.13). If the default SCSI ID on your tape drive is already used in your system—such as by a SCSI hard drive, CD-ROM drive, or scanner—set the ID to one that is available. SCSI IDs range from 0 to 7. Most tape drives have their ID set to 2.

NOTE If adding an external SCSI tape drive, you must also give the drive a unique SCSI ID. Often this is done by a push-button selector or dial.

CAUTION If two or more devices have the same SCSI ID, they will not work properly.

8. Set termination, if required. The last device in a chain of SCSI devices must be terminated. Ideally, your tape drive should use the middle connector of an existing SCSI cable. If so, you do not need to terminate the drive. Ensure the jumpers are set to no termination. In some cases, termination is set by terminating resistor(s). If so, remove the terminating resistor(s).

If the tape drive will be at the end of the cable, then termination must be on. The drive may be terminated by either setting a switch or plugging in terminating resistor(s). The SCSI device that was previously at the end of the SCSI chain must then have its termination turned off.

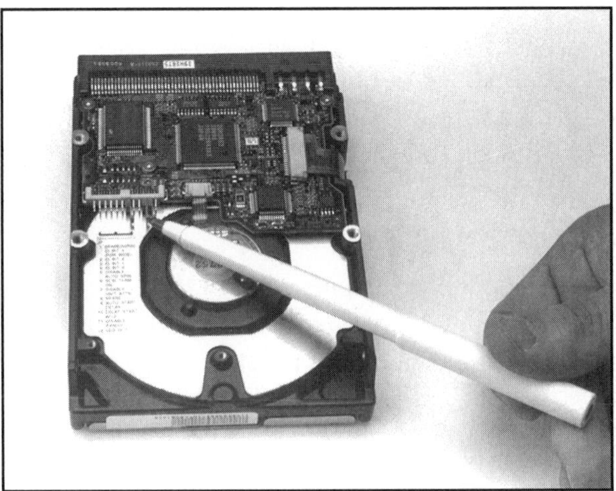

FIG. 13.13
SCSI devices, whether a hard drive (shown here) or a tape drive, have jumpers to set the SCSI ID as well as termination.

NOTE If adding an external SCSI tape drive, you must also terminate the drive, if it is the last device on the chain. You terminate the drive by installing a terminating plug on the SCSI out connector of the drive.

9. Thread the free end of the SCSI cable through the bay and attach to the tape drive. Mate the colored pin-one edge of the cable to the drive's "1" indicator, which often is printed on the circuit board or on the drive's housing. Some drives and cables are keyed so they can only be installed correctly. If unsure, check the drive's manual.

NOTE Having the cable on correctly so the colored edge is on the pin-one connection is crucial for the tape drive to work.

10. Slide the tape drive into the drive bay.
11. Locate the computer's power supply. Find an unused power cable that fits the power connector on the tape drive. If the cable doesn't match your drive, you may need to use the power-cable adapter included with the drive, if included. If no free power cable is available, use a Y-power splitter to share the power from another device. Attach this cable to the tape drive.

12. Double-check that all pins of each connection are covered by the cable's connectors. You want all pins to be snugly covered by the connectors.
13. After checking that the drive is flush with the front of the case, insert and tighten the screws so the tape drive or mounting brackets are snug against the metal drive bay. This not only holds the drive in place but grounds it for proper electrical operation.
14. Put the cover back on your computer and secure it with any screws you removed earlier.
15. Plug in your computer, monitor, and any other devices, and turn them on.

TROUBLESHOOTING

My new tape drive or other SCSI devices don't act normally. If the addition of the new SCSI device keeps your other devices from working, check that each device has a unique SCSI ID. Also, check that the devices on each end of the SCSI chain are terminated properly.

For example, if you have only internal SCSI devices, then only the SCSI card itself and the last device at the end of the internal cable should be terminated. If problems persist, then check that the colored edge of the SCSI cable is on the pin-one connector. Lastly, check that there is a minimum of 6 inches between each SCSI connector. If not, then you need a true SCSI cable. When there are fewer than 6 inches between connectors, signals can be scrambled with the addition of another SCSI device.

There also is a maximum length of both the internal and external cables connecting all of your SCSI devices, depending on your type of SCSI controller. The maximum length for Fast, Fast Wide, and Wide SCSI systems is 9.8 feet. If you have a SCSI-1 or SCSI-2 system, the maximum length is 19.7 feet. Check your SCSI controller's documentation to see which one you have and measure the total lengths of cables. An Ultra SCSI-3 system has a limit of 9.8 feet for up to four devices and 4.9 feet for five or more devices.

Software Installation

After installing your tape drive, you then need to install the tape backup software and drivers that came with it.

When using Windows 95, the attached tape drive often is detected by Windows 95. You are prompted for the drivers supplied with your tape drive. Consult your manual for installation instructions.

Often the backup software included with your drive may be insufficient for your needs. For example, some bundled backup software doesn't allow you to do a differential backup. If so, consider other backup software such as Seagate (formerly Arcada) Backup or Seagate (formerly Conner) Backup Exec.

Taking Care of Your Tapes

You can take an active role in ensuring your tape backups are successful and error-free.

If your tapes are exposed to heat or cold, give them time to adjust to the current environment. One rule of thumb is to place the tape cartridge in the backup environment one hour for each hour it spent outside the operating environment, up to eight hours. Also, do not expose the data cartridge to sudden temperature changes while it is in use. For example, don't let direct sunlight fall upon or heat vents blow on the tape during a backup.

Cleaning the heads of your tape drive is one way to ensure an accurate backup. The magnetic head is in contact with the tape when recording to, or reading from, the media. Any separation between the magnetic head and tape causes a decrease in signal strength, making it more difficult to interpret data and possibly causing errors.

To get the best performance from your tape drive, do routine head and motor puck cleaning. Cleaning these should be done after every eight hours of drive use. For example, if data is backed up daily, clean the drive once a week. Check with the drive manufacturer for recommended cleaning materials, although Imation (3M) provides a variety of drive-cleaning kits.

Another area that improves backup reliability is retensioning. *Retensioning* causes the tape to be wound tightly on its hub, eliminating the slack that causes the tape to skip over the drive's magnetic heads. Often, backup software has a retensioning command that rewinds the tape. Retensioning should be done each time a cartridge is loaded or whenever it has been exposed to extreme variances in temperature. A data cartridge should also be retensioned whenever it has been used continually over the same short length of tape.

Some other tips:

- Data cartridges should be retensioned prior to storage.
- Always remove data cartridges whenever the drive is turned off.
- When not in use, tapes should be stored in their protective covers.
- If possible, tapes should be stored in the same environment in which they'll be used.
- Do not store tapes in direct sunlight.

More Than Just a Tape Drive

In late 1996, Imation Corp. and PGSoft Inc. released a software product that allows desktop users to store and access data on tape cartridges as if they were a hard disk or floppy drive. This is called *direct tape access*, or *DTA*. By taking advantage of the tape's low cost-per-megabyte, Tape-it allows files to be opened or saved from any Windows 95 or Windows 3.1 application. This allows a tape drive to double as a storage device rather than just a backup device. With Tape-it, you can:

- Create a hard disk backup using a simple drag and drop.
- Open and save files to tape in any Windows/Windows 95 application.
- Save your favorite Internet download files or large multimedia files to a tape library.
- Move large numbers of files between computers at the office and at home.
- Exchange gigabytes of files with co-workers and customers.
- Browse and sort files on tape from within the Windows Explorer or the Windows File Manager.
- Organize information by customer or project, each with their own tape cartridge.
- Inexpensively increase the storage capacity of your computer by acquiring an inexpensive tape cartridge.

Both Pertec Memories Inc. (MyTape drives) and Seagate (TapeStore drives) are shipping their tape drives with Tape-it. A "light" version of Tape-it is available from Imation's Web site at:

http://burlapin.imation.com/dsp/travan/tape-it/

Although tape drives are slower than hard drives, Tape-it temporarily stores files in a "staging area" on the hard disk, and then transfers them to tape when it is convenient. Thus, you have the advantages of hard disk speed an unlimited low-cost tape storage in a single package.

With the correct tape drive and backup strategy, and utilities like Tape-it, you can protect yourself and your labor. Develop a thorough backup system that works for you…and use it religiously.

Multimedia Devices

14

Video

If the eyes are the windows to the soul, then your monitor is the window to your computer. Your monitor provides the link between you and your computer. You could get rid of your printer, disk drives, and expansion cards, but you couldn't sacrifice the monitor. Without a monitor, you would be operating blind. You couldn't see the results of your calculations or the mistyped words on the screen.

The first microcomputers were small boxes that lacked displays. Instead, you waited for the final output to a printer. When the monitor was added, the computer became more attractive to a wider audience. This trend continues today with graphical user interfaces such as Windows 95 and Windows NT.

The monitor doesn't work alone, however. The video card inside your computer determines the clarity, number of colors, size, and speed of the display.

With that in mind, this is what you'll experience through this chapter:

- The relationship between the monitor and video card
- The popular sizes and features of monitors
- How to understand the various resolutions and video standards
- How to choose the right features on a new video card
- How to install a new video card
- How to install more memory to an existing video card
- How to install a TV tuner card

Because the video card and monitor work hand in hand, you need to understand how the two interact, as you'll find out in this next section.

Video Overview

A computer monitor is very similar to a television set. Most monitors use a *cathode-ray tube* (*CRT*) to illuminate the screen. This is the same technology used in television sets. CRTs consist of a vacuum tube enclosed in glass. One end of the tube contains an electron gun. The other end contains a screen with a phosphorous coating.

NOTE Supposedly, CRT monitors will be replaced someday by thin, vibrant-looking *liquid-crystal displays (LCDs)*. These are the same displays found on active-matrix laptop computer screens.

When heated, the electron gun emits a stream of high-speed electrons that are attracted to the other end of the tube. On the way to the inside of the screen, a focus control and deflection coil steer the beam to a specific point on the phosphorous screen. When struck by the beam, the phosphor glows. This is the light that you see when watching TV or your word processor.

This electron beam moves very quickly. It sweeps the screen from left to right in lines from top to bottom, in a pattern called a *raster*. During its sweep, the beam strikes the phosphor wherever an image should appear on the screen. It also varies by intensity in order to produce different levels of brightness. Since the glow fades almost immediately, the electron beam must continue to sweep the screen in order to maintain an image, a practice called *redrawing* or *refreshing the screen*. Most displays have a *refresh rate* (also called a *vertical scan rate*) of about 70 hertz (Hz), meaning that the screen is refreshed 70 times a second. Low refresh rates cause the screen to flicker and contribute to eyestrain. The higher the refresh rate, the better for your eyes.

Monochrome, or one-color, monitors are very rare. Most people want to see various colors, which helps in making error messages and menu choices on the screen distinctive. Color monitors use more sophisticated technology than monochrome monitors, which accounts for their higher prices. A monochrome monitor may cost one-half the price of a color model. While a monochrome picture tube contains one electron gun, a color tube contains three guns arranged in a triangular shape. The color monitor contains phosphor *triads*, which consist of one red, one green, and one blue phosphor arranged in the same pattern as the electron guns. These three primary colors then are mixed to produce all other colors.

Monitors come in different sizes, from an inexpensive $100 12-inch monochrome monitor to a $10,000 42-inch color monitor. However, most popular sizes range from entry-level 14-inch monitors to large 21-inch monitors (see Figure 14.1).

Monitors, like television sets, are measured diagonally. However, these measurements are for the size of the tube, not the actual viewing area. For example, a 15-inch monitor may actually only show a diagonal image of 13.7 inches. This area varies slightly from monitor to monitor. As a result, comparing one company's 15-inch monitor to that of another may be unfair unless you actually measure the display area of each. Table 14.1 shows the approximate viewing area for the most common sizes.

FIG. 14.1
Monitors, like TVs, come in various sizes, from 12-inch to 42-inch models. Buy as large a model as you can afford and as your work area can hold.

Table 14.1 Possible Viewing Area of Various Monitors

Monitor Size	Possible Viewing Area
12-inch	10.5-inch
14-inch	13.1-inch
15-inch	13.7-inch
17-inch	15.8-inch
20-inch	19-inch
21-inch	19.8-inch

The larger the monitor, the more you'll pay. Often, the extra money is worth it. For example, jumping from a 14-inch monitor to a 15-inch monitor surprisingly provides 30 percent more viewing area. The larger monitors are handy for uses such as desktop publishing or live presentations. For example, a larger monitor allows you to design a letter-sized page at its actual size. This way, you can save yourself from printing several drafts before you get it right.

NOTE For Windows uses, I highly recommend a 15-inch monitor as the minimum you should consider. Also, the 15-inch monitor is the best bang-for-the-buck bargain in the industry.

Understanding Resolution

Resolution is the amount of detail the monitor can render. This quantity is expressed in the number of horizontal and vertical picture elements, or *pixels*, displayed on the screen. The greater the number of pixels, the more detailed the images. For example, higher resolutions such as 800×600 produce sharper images, but the images appear smaller and farther away. Also, the view of your desktop area expands and more information is visible. Conversely, as resolution decreases—640×480, for example—images appear larger and closer. However, the desktop area is smaller and less information is available.

The resolution required depends on your software program. DOS-based programs required little resolution, while Windows software requires a great deal. Surprisingly, the video card is the major player in what resolution a monitor will display, as you see later in the section "Matching Video Card and Monitor."

The *pixel* is the smallest unit that the monitor uses to produce an image. In a color monitor, the picture element is the trio of red, blue, and green phosphors.

The distance between these phosphor triads is called *dot pitch*. Dot pitch is measured in millimeters (mm). Monitors with a smaller dot pitch contain less distance between the phosphor triads. As a result, the picture elements lie closer together, producing a sharper picture. Conversely, less expensive screens that sport a larger dot pitch tend to produce "fuzzy" images. Most monitors have a dot pitch between .25 and .52mm. To avoid grainy images, look for a dot pitch of .28mm or smaller for 14- to 15-inch monitors, or .31mm or smaller for 17-inch and larger monitors. Avoid monitors with .39mm or larger dot pitches; the clarity is appalling.

Some monitors support *interlaced* resolution. In *noninterlaced* (conventional) mode, the electron beam sweeps the screen in lines from top to bottom, one line after the other, completing the screen in one pass. In interlaced mode, the electron beam also sweeps the screen from top to bottom but in two passes, sweeping the odd lines first and the even lines second. Each pass takes half the time of a full pass in non-interlaced mode. Therefore, both modes refresh the entire screen in the same amount of time. This technique redraws the screen faster and provides more stable images.

NOTE You already should be familiar with interlacing; broadcast television transmissions in the United States are interlaced.

The drawback is that interlacing depends on the ability of the eye to average two nearly identical lines separated by a gap into one solid line. Because unmatched lines produce flickering and shimmering images, interlacing is reserved for only high-resolution monitors mated to high-resolution video cards.

Video Card Standards

Like any computer device, a monitor requires a source of input. The signals that run your monitor come from the video card. While a few computers contain the video circuitry directly on the motherboard, most systems use a separate circuit board that fits into the expansion slot.

NOTE Video cards also are called *video adapters, graphics cards,* or *display adapters*. They're all the same thing.

Most video cards follow one of several industry standards. The first color video card was the *Color/Graphics Adapter* (*CGA*) from IBM. This card had a text resolution of 320×200 pixels, and could only display four colors from a palette of 16. The subsequent *Enhanced Graphics Adapter* (*EGA*), also from IBM, increased resolution to 640×350 pixels. Also, you could show 16 colors at one time from a palette of 64.

In 1987, the IBM Personal Systems/2 (PS/2) computers were introduced, sporting the video standard known as *Virtual Graphics Array*, or *VGA*. (Some people mistakenly call VGA "video graphics array.") As the most popular standard today, VGA adapters produce a maximum resolution of 640×480 pixels, and display up to 256 colors from a palette of 256,000. That's a lot of crayons.

To standardize video cards, several manufacturers formed the *Video Electronics Standards Association*, or *VESA*. VESA introduced the *Super VGA* (*SVGA*) video standard, which provides a starting resolution of 800×600 pixels and the same colors as VGA.

Which video standard do you select? The standard so far is VGA, with SVGA becoming predominant. (Many video cards support both.) Start by looking at the software you currently use or would like to run. Many games, for example, require VGA or VESA SVGA resolution.

SVGA is very popular for many reasons:

- If you want to be able to use multimedia (the melding of sound, sharp graphics, and information from a CD-ROM disk), you want to purchase a SVGA video card. This is the minimum requirement mandated by multimedia standards.
- SVGA is also convenient for Microsoft Windows, allowing you to see more icons and folders on the screen without having to scroll.
- SVGA is also better for your eyes, because it has a higher refresh rate than VGA—often 72Hz. By refreshing the screen more often, your eyes will not feel as fatigued.

How does the monitor adapt to each video card? Most monitors support at least one video standard, allowing them to operate with video cards and software compatible with that standard. For example, a monitor that supports VGA may operate with VGA video cards and VGA software. One drawback of this is that a monitor is limited to that display standard. A monitor that supports many different video standards is called a *multiple-frequency monitor*. Different vendors call their multiple-frequency monitors by different names, including *multisync*, *multi-frequency*, *multiscan*, and *auto synchronous*. Most monitors today support multiple frequencies.

Choosing a Video System

How do you know if you'd benefit from a faster video card? You're a victim of slow video if you're constantly waiting for the screen to redraw, or if there's an annoying delay between the time you request a window to open and the moment it actually does. Slow text scrolling, *artifacting* (when parts of the previous screen don't update as the display refreshes), jumpy video playback, and unreal-looking colors are also indications of poor video performance. If you would rather go to the dentist than run multimedia software on your PC, your system probably needs upgrading. The factors to consider are:

- Monitor size and resolution
- Number of colors
- Refresh rate
- Graphics and video acceleration

NOTE A new video card won't perform magic. If your system is anything less up-to-date than a Pentium, chances are a new video card won't do as much good as you'd like.

Monitor Size and Resolution

Monitor size and resolution depend on the applications you run on your computer. The standard resolutions are 640×480; 800×600; 1,024×768; 1,280×1,024 and 1,600×1,200. For example, 640×480 means that there are 640 columns and 480 rows of pixels on screen. The higher the resolution, the more pixels and the more viewing area.

However, you won't enjoy a high resolution on a small screen. Table 14.2 shows recommended maximum resolutions for popular screen sizes.

Table 14.2 Recommended Maximum Resolutions

Monitor Size	Recommended Resolution
14-inch	640×480
15-inch	640×480 or 800×600
17-inch	800×600 or 1,024×768
20-inch	1,024×768 or 1,280×1,024
21-inch	1,024×768 or 1,280×1,024

Some video cards generate all these resolutions, while many go only as high as 1,024×768. The monitor also must be capable of handling the highest resolution you want to use.

The shift from DOS to Windows through the first half of the 1990s has caused a significant increase in monitor size and resolutions. While 640×480 is fine for DOS character-based screens, a 17-inch monitor at 800×600 is much more enjoyable for Windows applications. Running Windows on a 20-inch or 21-inch monitor at 1,024×768 is better yet. However, you'll spend much more for any monitor larger than 15 inches.

Number of Colors

The standard number of colors displayed on a screen are 16; 256; 65,536 (64K); and 16,777,216 (16.8M). The number of colors is known as the *color depth*, or *bit depth* (see Table 14.3).

NOTE Sometimes a display adapter will offer an "in-between" 15-bit color depth, which is 32,768 colors.

Table 14.3 Color Depth Chart

Number of Colors	Color Depth	Known As
16	4-bit	Standard VGA
256	8-bit	Super VGA
32K	15-bit	High Color
64K	16-bit	High Color
16.8M	24-bit	True Color

To display multimedia applications, you need at least 64K colors, or 32K colors if your adapter supports it. The most realistic photographs and full-motion video are achieved with 16M colors, but 64K is often quite adequate. For standard business applications, such as word processing and spreadsheets, either 16 or 256 colors will suffice. Many online services and Internet sites require a minimum of 256 colors, while 64K is even better.

TIP If you do run your video card at 16M colors, don't be surprised if the display is slow, or some icons don't appear. For example, Microsoft Windows 3.x will not display some icons and warn of extremely low system memory if 16M colors is chosen.

What determines your maximum resolution and color depth is the amount of memory on the video card. Often, you can select how much memory you want on your video card, such as 512K, 1M, 2M, 4M, or more. The extra memory does not speed up your video card. Rather, it allows your monitor to display more colors and higher resolutions. For 256 colors drawn from a palette of 256,000, you need at least 512K of video memory. At 1,024×768 pixels, you need at least 1M. If you currently don't need this ability, bypass the extra memory. The next generation of video cards will probably provide other features you may need.

You easily can calculate the minimum amount of memory you will need on your video card:

> (Maximum Horizontal Resolution×Maximum Vertical Resolution×Color Depth in Bits)/8192 = Minimum Video Memory (in K)

For example, if you want SVGA resolution (800×600) with 65,536 (64K colors), you would multiply the horizontal resolution (800) by the vertical resolution (600) and the color depth (16). (Use Table 14.3 to get the color depth.) For example:

> (800×600×16)/8192=937.5K

In this case, you would require at least a 1M (1,024K) card.

The type of memory affects the overall speed of a video card, but again, more memory does not make the same video card faster. The types of memory available on memory cards are:

- *DRAM.* Most video adapters have used regular dynamic RAM (DRAM). Although inexpensive, this memory is rather slow. The slowness comes from the need to constantly refresh the visual data held in RAM. Also, like a revolving door, visual data in DRAM cannot be read at the same time it is being written to.
- *EDO RAM.* Extended Data Out (EDO) RAM is about 10 percent faster than DRAM because memory recharging can be done by separate circuits.
- *VRAM.* Video RAM (VRAM) is a popular type of memory available for some time now. More expensive than DRAM, VRAM has been the Cadillac of video memory for several years. VRAM is designed so that visual data can be put into memory while other images are being displayed.
- *WRAM.* Windows RAM (WRAM) is a modified VRAM from Samsung that offers a little better performance than VRAM at a lower cost.
- *MDRAM.* Multibank DRAM (MDRAM) is designed for graphics and video applications. MDRAMs have several small memory banks that draw the screen more efficiently than VRAM or WRAM.
- *SGRAM.* Synchronous Graphics RAM is a rarer high-end video card memory that is four times faster than DRAM.

Refresh Rate

The refresh rate, as mentioned earlier, is the number of times per second the image is painted onto the screen. Refresh is necessary, because the phosphors hold their glow for just a fraction of a second. The higher the refresh rate, the more rock solid the image will appear on screen. The higher the refresh rate, the better. Often a minimum of 70–72Hz is recommended to reduce eye fatigue. In general, higher resolutions require higher refresh rates to prevent noticeable screen flicker.

Graphics and Video Acceleration

Some video cards offer exceptional speed. They include a "thinking" video chip that frees your computer from having to draw the screen's images. Such video cards are called *video accelerators*. These special video cards are also called *Windows accelerator cards* because they can speed up all Microsoft Windows software. A video accelerator card can speed up a system by about 15 to 25 percent.

An accelerator card is built around a *video coprocessor*, a special computer chip that is mounted on the video card. This coprocessor may come from S3, Tseng Labs, or other companies. The coprocessor performs many of the video duties with little or no help from your computer's processor. With an accelerator card installed, your computer can concentrate on what it does best—handling data and responding to your needs. In other words, the accelerator card's video coprocessor offloads your computer from handling the pixels, lines, and other visual data. That reclaimed power is then focused on other tasks. Not only does the video coprocessor handle the work faster, but it also can address more memory at one time than conventional video cards.

To free your computer from these video duties, a video accelerator card requires a software driver that, once installed, tells Windows to let the video card handle the visual work. How much work is saved? Your computer can spend up to 40 percent of its time drawing your screen. In my own real-world experiences, my computer has been accelerated about 10 to 20 percent.

The video coprocessor can come in various speeds. Most today are powered by 64-bit processors, which determines the width of the data path. However, 128-bit graphics accelerators are on the rise. A 128-bit graphics card, such as the STB Lightspeed 128 or Number Nine's Imagine 128, can transfer huge amounts of display data between different parts of the card's circuitry. It can enhance a Pentium's

32-bit performance and get the information to the monitor fast so images can be displayed quickly and smoothly.

The latest trend in hardware-supported features is *video acceleration*, which puts several full-motion video functions into the chips. Features such as MPEG-1 support are desired if you plan to run a lot of multimedia movies.

Three-dimensional processing is another feature that is on the rise. Like video acceleration, it can be rolled into many of the new boards. A 3-D processor is responsible for applying the shading, or *skin*, onto the wireframe geometry that represents the 3-D image. 3-D improves the quality of displayed textures and depths, making them more realistic. 3-D features are recommended for games and business applications that support 3-D. For example, you can develop spreadsheets that give you a 3-D view of your data.

Some video cards have a *video feature connector (VFC)* (see Figure 14.2). This is an additional row of pins on the video card that connect to another internal expansion card. The VFC may also be called a *VESA advanced feature connector (VAFC)*. The video feature connector is desired if you think you might want to add an optional card, such as the higher-level MPEG-2 decoder or a TV tuner to watch television shows from your PC.

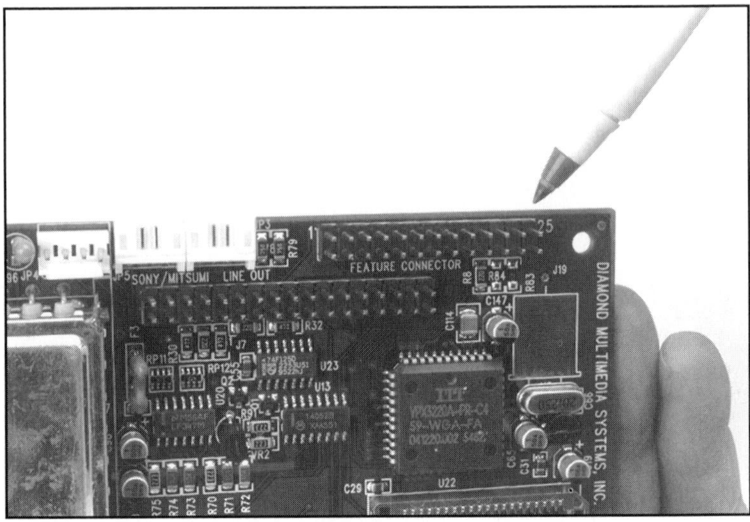

FIG. 14.2
The video feature connector, or VFC, provides a 26-pin connection to other cards inside your computer, such as TV tuners, MPEG decoders, and so on.

NOTE The MPEG-2 video-encoding scheme was initially created for digital satellite TV. Until last year, the most commonly targeted resolution of 720×480 at 30 framers per second (fps) was out of the realm of possibility for PCs. The new CD-ROM standard Digital Video Disc (DVD) was created to encompass MPEG-2.

Consider the Tradeoffs

The more colors, resolution, and refresh rate, the harder the display adapter has to work and the more expensive it is to purchase. Also, if you don't need the highest capacities of a card, don't purchase it, because another card can deliver what you need for less money. For example, if your monitor is smaller, you wouldn't want an adapter that displays 1,280×1,024; the text on the screen would be too small to read. Perhaps a video card that displays a maximum of 800×600 would be more appropriate…and affordable.

The higher the settings, the slower the adapter operates. Whenever there's a faster adapter that runs 16 million colors at yet a higher resolution, it's always a breakthrough.

Table 14.4 shows an example of video card specifications. The numbers are from Diamond Multimedia's 2001 Stealth 64 DRAM, which is an average display adapter that includes video acceleration.

Notice how the colors decrease as the resolution increases. Also, notice that it takes more memory (DRAM) on the display adapter to achieve higher resolutions and higher colors at the same time.

Table 14.4 Resolution versus Colors

Video Memory	Resolution	Maximum Colors	Maximum Refresh Rate
1M	640×480	64K	120Hz
2M	640×480	16M	100Hz
1M	800×600	64K	90Hz
2M	800×600	16M	100Hz
1M	1,024×768	256	100Hz

continues

Table 14.4 Continued

Video Memory	Resolution	Maximum Colors	Maximum Refresh Rate
2M	1,024×768	64K	100Hz
1M	1,152×864	256	70Hz
2M	1,152×864	64K	70Hz
1M	1,280×1,024	16	60Hz
2M	1,280×1,024	256	75Hz

Matching Video Card and Monitor

The trick is to pick a monitor that works with your selected video card. For example, you needn't purchase a monitor that handles all of the various resolutions. Rather, you want to purchase a monitor and video card that give you the most colors you require at the best refresh rate (more than 70Hz) and the optimum resolution. For example, a business computer used only for word processing can be suited with a 15-inch monitor and video card that displays 256 colors at up to 800×600 pixels with a refresh rate of 72Hz. There is no need for overkill features, such as 1,280×1,024 resolution or 16.8M colors.

CAUTION To save money, some buyers purchase a single-standard (fixed-frequency) monitor and a matching video card. For example, some computer superstores have sold VGA monitors as their "free" monitor bundled with a system. However, customers often find they need a new monitor and video card to get 800×600 resolution. For greatest flexibility, get a multisync monitor that accommodates a range of standards.

With multisync monitors, you must match the range of horizontal and vertical frequencies the monitor accepts with those generated by your video card. The wider the range of signals, the more expensive yet versatile the monitor. Your video card's vertical and horizontal frequencies must fall within the ranges supported by your monitor to work. The vertical frequency (or refresh/frame rate) determines how stable your image will be. The higher, the better. Typical vertical frequencies range from 50–150Hz. The horizontal frequency (or line rate) ranges between 31.5–91KHz.

To keep the horizontal frequency low, some video cards use interlacing signals, alternately displaying half of the lines of the total image. With some monitors, interlacing can produce a pronounced flicker. For this reason, your monitor should synchronize to twice the vertical frequency of the video card. If possible, avoid interlacing.

When shopping for a VGA monitor, make sure the monitor supports a horizontal frequency of at least 31.5KHz, the minimum a VGA card needs in order to paint a 640×480 screen. The VESA SVGA (800×600) standard requires a 72Hz vertical frequency and a horizontal frequency of at least 49KHz. The sharper 1,024×768 image requires a vertical frequency of 60Hz and a horizontal frequency of 58KHz. If the vertical frequency is upped to 72Hz, the horizontal frequency must be 58KHz.

Also, consider the size of your desk before you think about monitors 16 inches or larger. A 16-inch monitor is typically at least a foot and a half deep, and a 20-inch monitor takes up 2 square feet. (Typical 14-inch monitors are 16 to 18 inches deep.)

Picture-tube quality is another consideration. Many monitors are curved because it's easier to send electron beams across them. Flat-screen monitors, which are a bit more expensive, look better to most people. As a general rule, the less curvature a monitor has, the less glare it reflects.

You also should check the dot pitch of the monitor. The lower the number, the better. You can save money by picking a smaller monitor and one with a higher dot pitch. The tradeoff, of course, is clarity but often tolerable. Selecting a monitor with .31mm dot pitch over one with .28mm dot pitch may save you up to $200.

Get a monitor with horizontal and vertical positioning and image controls that can be easily reached. High-end monitors have digital (push-button), not analog controls (dials), which last longer. Look for more than basic contrast and brightness controls; many monitors let you adjust the width and height of your screen images. A tilt-swivel stand should be included with your monitor, allowing you to move the monitor to the angle best for your use.

TIP If ordering by mail, watch out for excessive shipping costs. Better yet, try to find a vendor that includes prepaid shipping for such a large purchase. When your new monitor finally arrives, check for external damage to the box.

Tire-Kicking a Monitor

A monitor is such an important part of your computer that knowing its technical specifications doesn't go far enough. Knowing that the monitor has a .28mm dot pitch doesn't necessarily tell you that it is ideal for you. It's best to "kick the tires" of your new monitor at a showroom or, with a liberal return policy, in the privacy of your office.

To test your monitor:

1. Load a black-on-white word processor or graphics program, such as Microsoft Windows' Paintbrush. Stare at one side of the monitor and take in the screen without focusing on it. Then chomp your teeth while looking directly at the screen. Does the screen flicker or pulsate? If it does, you'll find that even a couple of hours of work at this monitor will tire your eyes and give you a headache.
2. Draw a circle with the graphics program. If the result is an oval, not a circle, this monitor won't serve you well with graphics or design software.
3. Type some words in 8- or 10-point type (1 point =1/72-inch). If they are fuzzy or if the black characters are fringed with color, select another monitor.
4. Are the brightness, contrast, power, and other controls at the front of the monitor? Controls at the front or more easily accessible than those on the back or side.
5. Turn the brightness up and down while examining the corner of the screen's image. If the image blooms or swells, it's likely to lose focus at high brightness levels.
6. Load Windows to check for uniform focus. Are the corner icons as sharp as the rest of the screen? Are the lines in the title bar curved or wavy? Monitors are usually sharply focused at the center, but seriously blurred corners indicate a poor design. Bowed lines may be the result of a poor graphics card, so don't dismiss a monitor that shows them without double-checking with another card.
7. Is the screen prone to glare? A showroom's subdued lighting can make glare hard to detect, so instead look for curved tubes that catch light from many directions. A flatter or flat-screen monitor reduces glare.

Some SVGA cards also support higher resolutions, such as 1,024×768; 1,280×1,024; and even 1,680×1,280. Such a high resolution requires a 17-inch or larger monitor to comfortably read the text. Also, such high resolution slows down your monitor, because the video card must draw all those pixels. On typical 15-inch monitors, such resolutions cram too much detail into too small an area.

The type of bus slot into which you want to put the video card also is very important (see Figure 14.3). The bus connection provides the data entry point to the graphics board. Your purchase is restricted to the type of bus supplied on your PC's motherboard. While many graphics boards come in ISA, VL-Bus, and PCI bus formats, all the newer, faster products come only in PCI, the bus format found with virtually all Pentium computers. With PCI, graphics controllers can use such features as bus mastering, which boosts speed, and Plug and Play support, which eases installation.

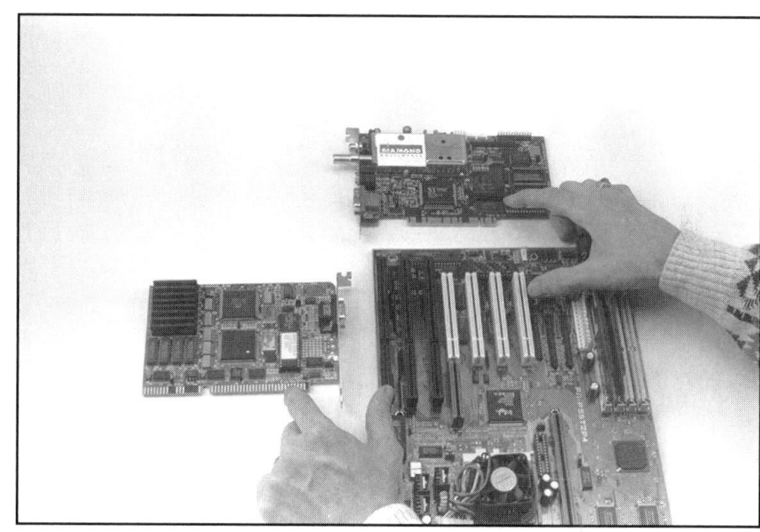

FIG. 14.3
The video card you use must match your available expansion slots. Preferably, use a PCI video card if your motherboard has such slots.

NOTE For assistance in determining your available bus slots, see Chapter 5.

Installing a Video Card

Installing a new video card can spring some traps. If, for some reason, the new video card doesn't work correctly, you won't be able to see anything on the screen, so you won't know why the card is misbehaving. And if you have any software that depends on the video card you are removing, it may not run correctly on the new card.

Before You Install a New Video Card, You Need:

- ☑ Phillips screwdriver or nut driver for removing case screws
- ☑ Available expansion slot that uses the same connector your new video card has (most likely you are replacing an existing video card)
- ☑ Original operating system installation disks, such as Windows 95 or Windows for Workgroups 3.11, containing generic VGA video card drivers
- ☑ A 3 1/2-inch floppy drive from which to install the video card software. A CD-ROM drive may be required because video drivers recently come on CD-ROM, not floppy disks.
- ☑ Small flat-bladed screwdriver to tighten cable connections
- ☑ Computer is turned off!

To install the video card:

1. Disable or remove any software that relies on your current video card. Your computer's startup files may rely on your video card. When you replace your card with another, the software may be surprised by the different video card and possibly not even work. For example, your current video card may be using Windows drivers. To minimize problems, return Windows to work in plain VGA mode, bypassing the special drivers that came with your existing card.

   If using Windows 3.x, run the Windows Setup program found in the Main group. Choose Options, Change System Settings. From the Display drop-down menu, choose VGA. Select OK to confirm your choice. You may be asked to insert one or more of your original Windows 3.x installation disks. When finished, you are asked to restart Windows for the VGA setting to take effect.

   If using Windows 95/NT 4.0, choose Start, Settings, Control Panel. Next, double-click Display. Select Change Display Type. For the Adapter Type, select Change. Select Show All Devices. Select Standard Display Types from the top of the list and the matching Standard Display Adapter (VGA). Choose OK to save your changes and then Close. You are prompted to restart your computer for the VGA setting to take effect.
2. Turn off your computer and remove its case. See Chapter 5 for details.
3. Unplug the monitor from the existing video card.

4. Remove or disable the current video card.

   If your computer has a video card built into its motherboard rather than on an expansion card, you must disable it. Most computers with a built-in video card allow you to turn off this internal circuitry by either changing a jumper or a DIP (dual inline package) switch. In most cases, an on-off switch labeled `VGA` must be turned off. A few manufacturers do not allow you to disable the onboard video card. Check your owner's manual for directions.

   If your video card is an expansion card, remove the screw holding it in place and lift the card straight up. Grab the card by its metal bracket or edges, not by its components.

CAUTION Before removing the video card, briefly touch your PC's metal case to drain yourself of static electricity. Avoid touching the printed circuit boards or the components on them. Instead, grab the card by its edges or frame.

5. Configure your new video card.

   Before inserting the new video card, you may need to configure it using the card's switches or jumpers. In most cases, the factory default settings should work fine. For example, some cards allow you to disable the software interrupt used to avoid conflicts with a network card. Others require you to set the scan rate of the card so it is compatible with your monitor. The documentation should tell you the purpose of each and suggest the situations in which a setting is useful. Even if you decide to use the default or factory settings, look at the board carefully to make sure it is set to the defaults.

NOTE Most video cards today have few if any jumpers. The advent of Plug and Play makes installation easier than ever.

6. Select a slot for your new video card.

   Select an expansion slot that perfectly fits the edge connector on your new video card. For example, use a PCI expansion slot for a PCI-based video card, or a VLB slot for a VLB type of video card. If you removed an existing video card, you may be able to use the same slot. If your video card was built into your computer's motherboard, select an empty expansion slot and remove its slot cover.

7. Install the new video card (see Figure 14.4).

   Insert the video card into the expansion slot. Firmly press the copper-edged connector of the card into the expansion slot until it snaps into place. There should be a snug fit between the edge connector of your card and the expansion slot. If the connection in the slot is too loose or too tight, try installing the card into another slot where a better fit might be achieved.

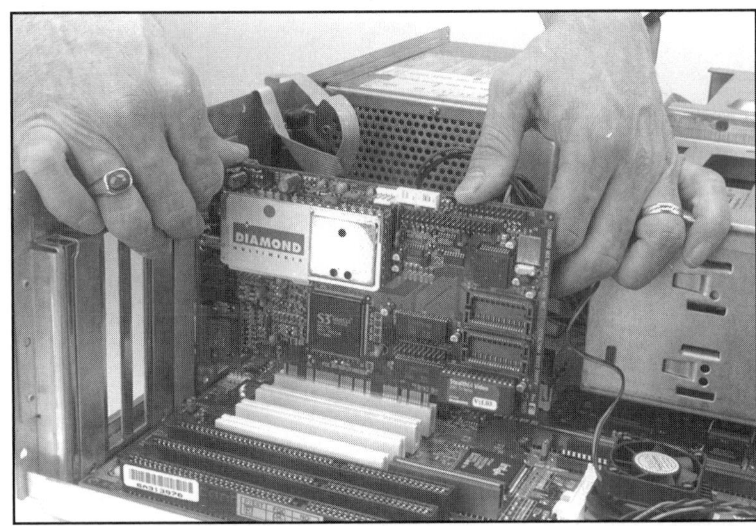

FIG. 14.4
Insert the video card firmly into its slot. The copper-edged connectors should be virtually hidden in the slot.

8. Visually inspect the expansion card to ensure it is fully inserted into the slot. The edge connector's copper fingers should be fully and evenly inserted.
9. Use the screw removed from the slot to fix the card in place.
10. Plug in your computer, monitor, and keyboard. Before assembling the rest of your computer, you should test the new video card. Plug in your computer and monitor. Connect your keyboard to your computer.

    Don't forget to plug the monitor cable from your monitor to the new video card. First, turn on your monitor and then your computer. After you turn on your computer, the new video card's copyright notice should appear on the screen almost immediately. If so, you know it is working correctly.

    If you noticed anything wrong as your computer warmed up, immediately turn it off, remove the card, and reinsert it. Test again. If it still doesn't work, study it to see if you have set a switch on the card incorrectly, if applicable.

11. Replace your computer's case and prepare your computer for operation.

12. Set up your software to work with the new video card.

    Some operating systems have built-in support for a higher-resolution video card. For example, Windows 3.x and Windows 95/NT have drivers for most video cards, although your video card may have a newer, more powerful version.

    If using Windows 95, turn on your computer and start Windows 95. When Windows 95 detects the new video card and asks which drivers to use, choose Driver from Disk Provided by Hardware Manufacturer, and click OK. Insert the manufacturer's CD-ROM or floppy disk containing the Windows 95 driver.

TIP If necessary, select Browse to browse the CD or floppy to find the directory containing the drivers.

    Select the software driver for your graphics accelerator card, and choose OK. At the Install from Disk screen, choose OK. When prompted, restart your computer to adopt the new settings.

    If installing drivers for Windows 3.x, start Windows 3.x and insert the manufacturer's CD-ROM or floppy disk containing the Windows 3.x driver. From the Program Manager's File menu, select Run. Choose the Browse button and browse the drive where the CD-ROM or disk is located. If your software is on CD-ROM, you may have to choose a Windows 3.1 directory. Often, the installation software is called SETUP.EXE or INSTALL.EXE. Find this installation file and choose OK to select it. Next, choose OK to run it. Follow the instructions on the screen. When asked to restart your computer, choose Yes.

    Once the software driver is installed for its intended program, your video card performs to its full powers. For example, you may be able to see more on your screen. Characters on the screen are easier to read because more pixels are being used to form the letters, and graphical images are smoother and more representative of how they will look when printed.

13. Fine-tune your screen, if needed. Some cards let you customize the configuration—the horizontal and vertical scanning frequencies to use for a given graphics mode—either interactively or by entering timing values or specifications found in your monitor's manual. Usually, a graphics card's

Setup utility lets you pick from a list of supported monitors. If yours is missing from the menu, try other similar models to find the best match.

TIP When running Windows, don't use a higher resolution or more color depth than necessary. Maxing out at 1,280×1,024 instead of 1,024×768 resolution is a headache with a 17-inch or smaller monitor. Also, limit your colors. A 16.8 million-color palette is generally useful only for photographic image editing, while motion video looks fine at 65,536 colors. The exponentially greater content of high-color images can slow down performance considerably.

NOTE Some video cards include software utilities that ease switching resolutions and colors. For example, Diamond Multimedia video cards have the InControl Tools utility. Number Nine video cards use HawkEye. These utilities often need to be installed separately. If you intend to stay with one resolution or color depth most of the time, I recommend you not install these programs, because they require system resources and memory by constantly "lurking" in the background.

TROUBLESHOOTING

My screen is smaller or off-center. Because the new video card may have a different resolution than your previous card, you may need to use your monitor's horizontal and vertical controls to center the image on your screen. You may also have controls to widen or lengthen the screen image.

My screen size fluctuates. If you must fiddle with the image-position and size controls on your monitor every time you switch between DOS and Windows, the problem may lie with your graphics card and not the display. Image size and position are affected by the signal timing that the graphics adapter uses, so you may need to adjust the card's configuration using the utility software that came with it.

My computer sometimes locks up or the display looks garbled. Display problems that can't be isolated may be the simple result of an outdated software driver. Check the driver version by accessing Windows 95's Control Panel or Microsoft's MSD.EXE Diagnostic utility. Most graphics card companies provide Web sites and bulletin board systems from which to download the latest drivers, and Microsoft's site includes a collection of current drivers.

Upgrading Video RAM

Many video cards today come with 1M or 2M of memory, with sockets for additional memory. Often, more memory is required if you want to run at 24-bit color (16.8 million colors) or if you plan to move to a higher resolution.

One way to save money is to buy a video card today with less than the maximum memory and add more later when prices drop or you can better afford it.

Installing additional memory is a simple operation. You simply plug memory chips into empty sockets on the video card.

Before You Add Additional Memory, You Need:

- ☑ Phillips screwdriver or nut driver for removing case screws
- ☑ Video card that has empty sockets for adding additional memory
- ☑ Upgrade memory chips that meet the manufacturer's specifications. For example, Diamond Stealth 64 cards often take two 256K×16 chips. To find the chips required by your card, consult your manual or the video card's manufacturer.
- ☑ Computer is turned off!

---

1. Turn off your computer and remove its case. See Chapter 5 for details.
2. Unplug the monitor from the existing video card.
3. Remove the video card. Remove the screw holding it in place and lift the card straight up. Grab the card by its metal bracket or edges, not by its components.

> **CAUTION** Before removing the video card, briefly touch your PC's metal case to drain yourself of static electricity. Avoid touching the printed circuit boards or the components on them. Instead, grab the card by its edges or frame.

4. Install the additional memory (see Figure 14.5). Video cards often have two or four sockets for additional memory. The new memory chips must be installed in a certain direction to work properly. The memory chips you insert often have a notch or circle on one end of the chip to show polarity. Match this to the notch, beveled edge, or circle on the video card's printed circuit board next to the memory socket. In other words, look for a marking on one of the two long sides of the socket that is distinctive. Press each memory chip firmly into each socket.

FIG. 14.5
Insert the additional video memory. In this case, a SIP (single-inline pin) memory chip is being inserted.

5. Re-install the new video card (see Figure 14.6).

   Insert the video card into the expansion slot. Firmly press the copper-edged connector of the card into the expansion slot until it snaps into place. There should be a snug fit between the edge connector of your card and the expansion slot.

FIG. 14.6
Press firmly to insert the video card in its slot.

6. Visually inspect the expansion card to ensure that it is fully inserted into the slot. The edge connector's copper fingers should be fully and evenly inserted.

7. Use the screw removed from the slot to fix the card in place.
8. Plug in your computer, monitor, and keyboard and test the upgraded video card.

   Before assembling the rest of your computer, you should test the upgraded video card. Plug in your computer and monitor. Connect your keyboard to your computer. Don't forget to plug the monitor cable from your monitor to the new video card.
9. Turn on your computer and test the video card. First, turn on your monitor and then your computer. After you turn on your computer, the new video card's copyright notice should appear on the screen almost immediately. The new amount of video memory should be indicated at this startup screen. If so, you know it is working correctly.

   If you noticed anything wrong as your computer warmed up, immediately turn it off, remove the card, and reinsert it. Test again. If it still doesn't work, study it to see if you have set a switch on the card incorrectly, if applicable.
10. Replace your computer's case and prepare your computer for normal use.

Adding a TV Card

Want to watch TV periodically from your PC? New television-tuner cards can be connected to a cable or antenna, allowing you to watch television on your monitor. The TV image can be run full-screen or reside in a small window on your Windows desktop. From a more practical standpoint, these TV-tuner add-in cards allow you to capture frames from live video sources. Some models can also record full-motion video.

Most TV tuners are simply expansion cards that connect to your existing video card's 26-pin video feature connector (VFC) to display TV images on your screen. Others simply commandeer the card's VGA port, guaranteeing compatibility with virtually any system.

Other video cards, such as the Stealth64 Video 2201TV, include the TV tuner and audio features on the basic card (see Figure 14.7). Otherwise, the Diamond Stealth64 Video 2201TV is nearly identical to the Stealth64 Video 2201XL.

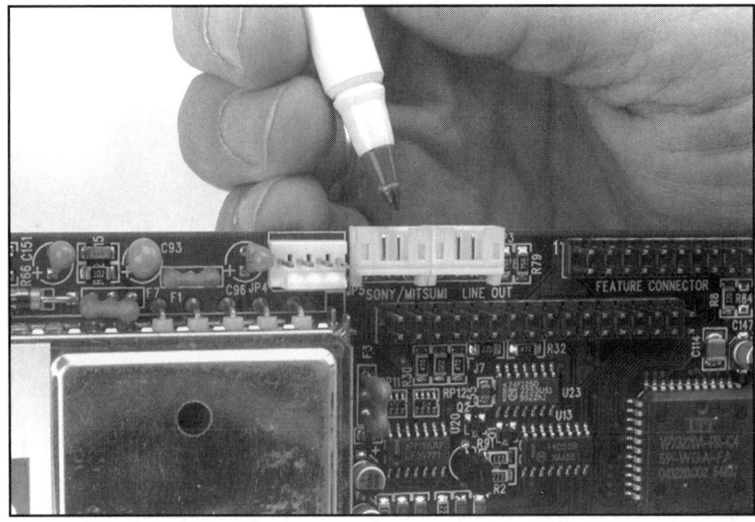

FIG. 14.7
The Diamond Stealth64 Video 2201XL includes a TV tuner, as well as audio features.

Once operating, the software controls are quite flexible: You can switch to a full-screen display without borders. You also can fine-tune stations and adjust color, hue, saturation, and contrast of the broadcast images.

Installing a TV Tuner

Installing a TV tuner requires lots of cables and connections, but overall is a simple operation.

Before You Add a TV Tuner, You Need:

- ☑ Phillips screwdriver or nut driver for removing case screws
- ☑ Video card that has a video feature connector (VFC)
- ☑ TV tuner card that connects to the VFC
- ☑ If possible, a list of interrupts (IRQs) and addresses used by your other expansion cards (such as network cards, video cards, and so on) in your computer

- ☑ Sound card with a line-in connector and speakers, to play TV sound or external amplified speakers
- ☑ A 3 ½-inch floppy drive from which to install the TV-tuner card software
- ☑ Windows 3.x or Windows 95
- ☑ Computer is turned off!

---

1. Turn off your computer and remove its case. See Chapter 5 for details.
2. Remove the TV tuner card from its anti-static bag.

CAUTION Before removing the TV tuner from its anti-static bag, briefly touch your PC's metal case to drain yourself of static electricity. Avoid touching the printed circuit boards or the components on them. Instead, grab the card by its edges or frame.

3. Set the I/O address and interrupt settings. TV tuners require a unique I/O address and interrupt (IRQ) to work properly in your computer. You often set jumpers to select an available IRQ (see Figure 14.8). For more information on interrupts and addresses, see Chapter 6.

FIG. 14.8
You may have to change jumpers on the TV tuner to change the address and interrupt (IRQ) to avoid conflicts with other cards.

CAUTION Some TV cards use address 300h (hex) as their default I/O port address. This may conflict with network cards, which often use the same address. You have to change the address of either the TV tuner card or the network card.

4. Select an empty expansion slot and remove the screw holding its slot cover.
5. Insert the TV tuner card into the slot.

   Firmly press the copper-edged connector of the card into the expansion slot until it snaps into place. There should be a snug fit between the edge connector of your card and the expansion slot.
6. Visually inspect the TV tuner to ensure it is fully inserted into the slot. The edge connector's copper fingers should be fully and evenly inserted.
7. Use the screw removed from the slot to fix the card in place.
8. Connect the 26-pin flat cable between the feature connector on the TV tuner card and the video feature connector on the video card (see Figure 14.9). When plugging the cable, make sure that pin 1 on both ends of the cable is connected to pin 1 of the TV and VGA card's connectors. Pin 1 is indicated by the colored edge on the cable.

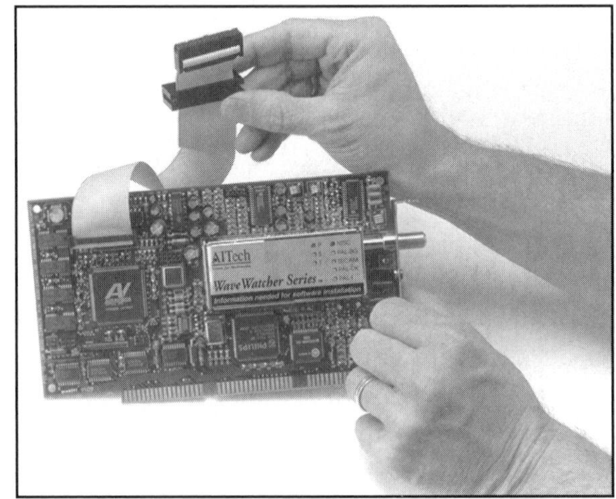

FIG. 14.9
To display TV signals, the cable from the TV tuner card attaches to the VFC connector on your video card.

9. Replace your computer's case and prepare your computer for operation.
10. Connect the TV or coaxial cable. Screw the threaded connector that comes with the TV tuner card to your TV or cable antenna. Next, plug the connector into the antenna jack of the TV tuner card.

NOTE Firmly plug in the cable to ensure good TV/cable reception.

11. If you have no sound card or want to play TV sound through a separate pair of amplified speakers, connect the speakers to the speaker port of the TV card. If using separate speakers, skip the next step.
12. If you want to use your existing sound card and speakers to play TV sound, connect the audio cable between the speaker port on the TV card to the sound card's LINE IN port.
13. Plug your pair of speakers to the sound card's SPEAKER OUT (if the speakers are unamplified/unpowered) or LINE OUT (if amplified) connector.
14. If desired, connect any composite video source to the TV card, such as a VCR or camcorder. A video input cable is often supplied with the TV tuner to allow you to watch and capture videos from an external video device. Connect this cable from the video input port to the VCR or camcorder.
15. Connect the TV tuner to your video card. Most TV tuners come with a VGA loopback plug. This connects the TV tuner to the video card (see Figure 14.10).

FIG. 14.10
A VGA loopback plug connects the TV tuner to the existing video card so TV and video signals can be combined.

16. Connect your monitor to the TV tuner's VGA connector. Note that the monitor is now hooked up to the TV tuner, not the video card.
17. Turn on your computer and test the TV card. First, turn on your monitor, and then your computer. After you turn on your computer, the video card's copyright notice should appear on the screen almost immediately. If so, you know it is working correctly.

Troubleshooting

My screen is blank. Check that the monitor cables are plugged into the TV tuner card. Also, check that the VGA loopback cable is connected between the TV tuner and video card. If that fails, you may have to open the computer and reinsert the TV tuner card for a good connection. Test again. If it still doesn't work, consider changing the interrupt or I/O address.

18. Install the TV tuner software. Start Windows 3.x or Windows 95.

If installing software for Windows 3.x, start Windows 3.x and insert the manufacturer's floppy disk containing the Windows 3.x driver. From the Program Manager's File menu, select Run. Choose the Browse button and browse the drive where the disk is located. Often, the installation software is called SETUP.EXE or INSTALL.EXE. Find this installation file and choose OK to select it. Next, choose OK to run it. Follow the instructions on the screen. When asked to restart your computer, choose Yes.

If installing software for Windows 95, start Windows 95 and insert the manufacturer's floppy disk containing the Windows 95 driver. From the Start menu, select Run. Choose the Browse button, and browse the drive where the disk is located. Often, the installation software is called SETUP.EXE or INSTALL.EXE. Find this installation file and choose Open to select it. Next, choose OK to run it. Follow the instructions on the screen. When asked to restart your computer, choose Yes.

19. Change the resolution of your Windows screen to VGA resolution. To first use a TV tuner, it's best to start in VGA, 16-color mode.

If using Windows 3.x, run the Windows Setup program found in the Main group. Choose Options, Change System Settings. From the Display drop-down menu, choose VGA. Select OK to confirm your choice. You may be asked to insert one or more of your original Windows 3.x installation disks. When finished, you are asked to restart Windows for the VGA setting to take effect.

If using Windows 95/NT 4.0, choose Start, Settings, Control Panel. Next, double-click Display. Select Change Display Type. For the Adapter Type, select Change. Select Show All Devices. Select Standard Display Types from the top of the list and the matching Standard Display Adapter (VGA). Choose OK to save your changes and then Close. You are prompted to restart your computer for the VGA setting to take effect.

20. Test and configure the TV card in VGA mode. When first running the TV tuner software, you may have to scan all channels so that the tuner can remember only clear channels.
21. Using step 19, reconfigure your display to its original setting.
22. Adjust TV display settings to work best with your display. You may have to adjust your TV tuner to give you the best color available. Options include filters, brightness, hue, saturation, contrast, centering, and others. When finished, you may be asked to save these settings.

TIP The options for a TV tuner card are much more elaborate than a normal TV set. Read your owner's manual to understand each control before you change it.

TROUBLESHOOTING

My screen is too dark. Change the brightness and contrast in your TV tuner software.

The display goes outside the edges of the TV/video screen. Find options for alignment to crop or align the image.

There are colored shadows at the edges of the screen. Find the display alignment options and change the horizontal or vertical alignment. If this fails, your software may have a VGA DAC Skew option to clear this problem.

The picture is distorted. If using a VGA monitor that is set at 1,024×768 resolution and interlacing is being used, the live TV/video will be distorted. In this case, choose the interlace setting in your tuner software. If your monitor is non-interlaced, then this choice must be off.

The display is abnormal. If your video card supports 64K colors, you may have options to display at this color mode.

The picture is jittery. If the pixels in the image jitter, find the skew options and adjust until the jitter disappears.

Reducing Glare

After a few hours of work at your computer, your eyes may become aching and tired. Most likely, the glare from your computer's monitor is the culprit. *Glare* is light that is bounced off your screen directly into your eyes. Because most monitors are slightly curved, they channel the light from the sides at you.

continues

continued

You can easily tell if you have a glare problem. First, turn off your monitor. If parts of your screen have an especially bright spot, such as a window reflection or other light source, you may have a problem. Glare easily can be reduced. The best solution is to buy a monitor with a flat screen and either etched or coated glass designed to reduce glare. If you cannot afford a new monitor, here are some affordable ways to reduce glare:

- Change the light that is bounced off your screen. Point your screen away from any bright light sources, such as windows and lamps. Also, avoid facing a window directly. Looking at a monitor with a bright window in front of you is especially straining. It's best to have windows to the left or right of your screen. Also rearrange the other lights in your room. Window blinds can control outside light. Meanwhile, try to reduce the amount of surrounding light in your room without relying on a single reading lamp. A single lamp causes uneven lighting, which also causes eye fatigue. Your goal is to have indirect, uniform lighting.
- Change the position of your monitor. Tilt your screen down slightly, about 10 to 15 degrees below eye level. While an upward-tilting screen is ideal to look at for bifocal and contact-lens wearers, it reflects more light than one perpendicular to your desk. Also, you should sit more than 18 inches from your monitor. When setting the monitor's brightness, start out at a low level to avoid headaches and eye fatigue. How low? Load a program that has a light background and set the brightness accordingly. You'll not only avoid eye problems but also lengthen the life of your monitor.
- Use software to change your screen. It is best to have dark characters on a light screen, rather than light characters on a dark background. Microsoft Windows and other programs enable you to change your colors.
- A filter of tinted glass or plastic can improve your monitor's contrast by darkening the screen uniformly. These are called *glare filters* or *anti-glare screens*. These filters are available for as little as $50. Because of the filter, you may need to increase the monitor's contrast and brightness—in that order—so the screen seems as bright as usual. You can get an inexpensive black mesh screen, but it may cause more trouble than it solves. These screens reduce glare by absorbing any light that isn't traveling perpendicular to the screen. Unfortunately, mesh screens absorb light that comes in at sharp angles from the side, producing glare. Also, the coarser meshes may interfere with the screen's images. For portable glare reduction, consider wearing Polaroid™ sunglasses.

15

Sound

Personal computers have been seen as physical devices requiring physical means of input and output. You have to type in much of your information, and what you get back is visual—either on screen or on a printout.

When your use is more directed at entertainment than productivity, the experience is limited. So, what happens when you add sound to the experience? It becomes more real and easier to understand.

In this chapter, you look at possible uses for sound systems, what the equipment can produce, and how to put it all together:

- Sound overview—what sound can accomplish for you
- Choosing sound equipment
- Installing a sound card
- Connecting add-on peripherals to the sound card
- Configuring a sound card

Sound Overview

Equipping a computer for sound has reached a stage where the quality created by computer-based sound systems equals that of professional needs. Not only can you create your own music CDs, but the systems can be used for speech recognition and synthesis. You can "tell" your computer what to do, and you can ask it to "read" back some information to you.

The first place you are going to hear about the special effects delivered by sound systems is in the entertainment field. Space games, sports, action games, Carmen Sandiego adventures, and even Scrabble have a new level of participation with the addition of sound effects.

Another use in the entertainment area is with a CD player for playing music in your workspace. You can use many computer CD-ROM devices with most sound cards, or you can plug your portable CD player into your sound card.

Education benefits from the realism of speech and sound effects that are added to reference material. The electronics and software in the sound cards are equal to that of many stereo systems in homes.

As you surf the Web, you will see RealAudio™ icons. If you have a sound card, you can receive information and instructions orally. When designing your own Web page, include your own recorded links.

Sound systems also provide a means for people with visual challenges to expand the use of their computers. With the right software, you can run your computer programs with voice commands or review entered material using a speech synthesis program.

The software has been available to read back most text for a long time. Foreign language programs can be created that teach accurate pronunciation through phonetics.

Choosing Sound Equipment

When adding a sound system to your personal computer, you need to decide what equipment you want in addition to the sound card. If you have recently shopped for a stereo system, you will be well prepared. The decisions are the same: What speakers, microphone, or MIDI equipment do you need?

Sound Card

Are you a high-quality devotee of the audio world? If so, you will be looking for a sound card like the Creative Labs Sound Blaster AWE32 PnP. This card supports 16-channel, 32-voice, and 128 instruments and 10 drums sound reproduction; CD-ROM interface; and upgradable memory for additional downloadable sound samples.

As you increase the functions and capabilities of your sound system, keep in mind the memory requirements. The higher-quality and higher-priced boards have *SIMM* (*Single Inline Memory Modules*) adapters for easy upgrade by the owners.

By adding the same memory modules used on your motherboard, you can download additional samples of sounds to use in your production studio.

ON THE WEB

A primary provider of downloadable sound fonts is E-mu Systems, located on the World Wide Web at:

http://www.emv.com/sndbanks.htm

An additional feature to check out is the possibility of daughterboards for additional features. Several Creative Labs sound and modem boards accept a Wave Blaster® II daughterboard to add wave-table editing capabilities.

Some of the advanced sound system boards and software make specific requirements of your computer. Some can use 8-bit slots, some use 16-bit slots, and some require a PCI slot. The "hot" cards require a 486 or better system. No longer can a 386 be considered an upgradable model.

Speakers

Unless you have speakers built into a monitor, you need to consider the power requirements of the speakers in your equation for a sound system. Speakers designed for computers can be used without any power, but the output is not as audible and the quality suffers.

Most speakers can be powered with either batteries or an external power supply. When you use the external supply, you need another plug on your powerbar(s). It is great when you can use standard batteries, preferably AA for small speakers and D cells for larger speakers.

Make sure that you do not use speakers with a higher watt rating than the sound card can handle. You can probably patch your sound system into your stereo system if you need more volume.

Headphones

It is not necessary to invade your office space with music or other sound effects from your new sound system. You can use headphones with most, and many sound cards come with headphones and a microphone. Check the ohm and watt requirements, and make sure that you have a cord with enough length. Nothing is more disconcerting than being yanked back in your chair if you forget about the cord.

Microphone

Microphones allow for a range in ease of use and quality. Most sound cards are bundled with a microphone; otherwise, you can use most standard microphones with the right plug (see Figure 15.1). You can also use telephone type headsets with some models of sound cards.

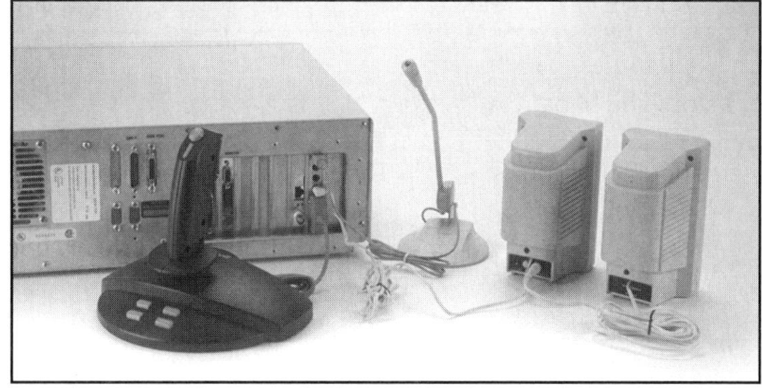

FIG. 15.1
This system uses a microphone on a pedestal for hands-free ease.

In a conference room setting, a multi-directional microphone could be used with the sound system. These microphones are designed to pick up voices anywhere in a room with the same volume and clarity.

Keyboard and Other MIDI

Musicians have been jumping on the PC bandwagon with the introduction of sound systems and interfaces. You can connect instruments (such as your electronic keyboard) when they are equipped with a MIDI (Musical Instrument Digital Interface) interface.

A portable computer has become as important as any other instrument in a musician's band. Band members store their music on disk, mix the cuts from a recording session, add effects, and change the qualities of prerecorded sounds.

CDs

If you want to add a CD-ROM player at the same time, you may find it easiest to get a sound card with a CD-ROM adapter. Is your machine new enough that the existing hard drive controller can handle a CD-ROM device? If you have a hard drive with a capacity greater than 500M, your controller can probably support a CD-ROM. Otherwise, you need to invest in an Enhanced IDE (EIDE) controller. The EIDE controllers are necessary for large capacity hard drives and IDE CD-ROM drives.

CAUTION If you are buying a used sound card, check the specification for the CD-ROM. Older cards used SCSI and proprietary interfaces.

Having the CD-ROM controller on the sound card does not mean that you are going to have to use fewer interrupts. An IRQ needs to be set for each type of device on your sound card. Most current CD-ROM interfaces incorporated in sound cards support both a proprietary and a standard interface.

NOTE I've installed several of these, and it is always a royal pain to use the sound card's IDE controller. Whenever possible, I use the integrated controller for the CD-ROM. The SCSI controllers on these cards are generally inferior, also.

Other Devices to Connect to the Sound Card

The type of things that you can connect to your sound system is usually very extensive. Your stereo system can be plugged into the Line In and Line Out connectors for playback or recording. Bring your portable CD player to play music through your CD-challenged personal computer.

NOTE Use an adapter cord, rather than an adapter plug, to make the transition between the two sizes of plugs. Because of the limited space on the back of the card, large plugs with adapters can quickly crowd out other plugs. Adapters and cords are readily available at most electronics stores.

Don't forget that if you do not already have a game port, you can also plug a joystick into the MIDI port of the sound card.

The Creative Labs Sound Blaster AWE32 even comes with WebPhone™ Lite. WebPhone Lite is a software package that lets you make phone calls to similarly equipped people over the Internet. The only additional requirements are a modem or direct connection to the Internet and a telephone.

Placement

It is probably not a surprise to you, but sound cards use up more desk space than any other peripheral. Speakers and microphones with cords between all of them can cause a big traffic jam on your desktop. Add to that a portable CD player for music, and you have created a jungle.

An interesting solution to the clutter issue is the incorporation of speakers and a microphone in your monitor case. If you are at a point where you are upgrading your monitor or looking at a whole new system, consider this design feature.

You can find additional ways to address the challenge of the tangle at many electronics stores. Just as there are cordless mouse devices and many peripherals such as printers with infrared connectors, there are probably ways to go cordless in the audio arena.

Installing a Sound Card

Now that you have your new sound card, let's install it in your computer so you can start getting that great sound.

Before Buying or Installing a Sound Card, You Should Know:

- ☑ What sound quality do you need?
- ☑ Do you have a CD-ROM?
- ☑ Do you need a CD-ROM interface?
- ☑ Do you need a SCSI or Enhanced IDE interface for the CD-ROM?
- ☑ Does the CD-ROM player require CD caddies?
- ☑ Do you want to hook up MIDI equipment to your computer?
- ☑ Do you have enough "machine" for the sound card?
- ☑ How much space will these take up on your desk?
- ☑ Do you have all the necessary cables?
- ☑ How many IRQs will the sound card use?
- ☑ Will a sound card conflict with another device in your computer?
- ☑ Do you already have a joystick/game port?
- ☑ If you are upgrading the sound system memory, does it use 30-pin or 72-pin SIMMs?

What to Check First

Before you pick up a screwdriver, you need to check your existing equipment for its configuration first. Use the MSD.EXE or MSINFO.EXE, a couple of Microsoft diagnostics programs provided with DOS and Windows 95, respectively, to check your equipment for hardware interrupt (IRQ) settings and memory address exclusions. If you are using Windows 95, MSINFO.EXE is installed in the folder labeled \WINDOWS\MSAPPS\MSINFO.

The following is a list of the typical Interrupt Request (IRQ) settings:

Interrupt Request	Used By
IRQ 0	Internal Timer*
IRQ 1	Keyboard*
IRQ 2	Video adapter or network interface card
IRQ 3	COM2: and COM4:
IRQ 4	COM1: and COM3:
IRQ 5	LPT2:
IRQ 6	Floppy drive*
IRQ 7	LPT1:
IRQ 8	Real-time clock*
IRQ 9	Video or network adapter
IRQ 10	Unassigned
IRQ 11	Unassigned
IRQ 12	Unassigned
IRQ 13	Numeric coprocessor
IRQ 14	Hard drive controller
IRQ 15	Unassigned

**IRQ cannot be reassigned*

These settings are required to determine what settings to use to identify your sound card to the computer system. Interrupts 2, 3, 4, and 7 are used by system devices such as the parallel and serial ports, and network interface cards. Each hardware feature on your sound card may require an additional IRQ and memory address. Sound cards commonly use interrupts 10 and 11.

Setting Jumpers and Making Other Internal Connections

If your sound card uses jumpers, you must first locate any jumpers on the sound card and identify what they control. Otherwise, the settings are made with the setup software included with the card.

There may be jumpers that set the MIDI port to use with a joystick, or jumpers that set the IRQ for the controller for your CD-ROM. Jumpers may change the CD-ROM interface from a standard to a proprietary configuration or enable a type of sound-editing standard.

Locate the jumpers for the IRQ setting. When a bridge is made with a jumper between two adjacent posts, the jumper is said to be ON (see Figure 15.2). When the jumper is removed, it is OFF.

FIG. 15.2
Setting IRQ jumpers on a sound card is similar to any expansion card.

When you want to use IRQ 10 for the sound card, place a jumper across the IRQ 10 posts and make sure that the other IRQ jumpers (for this feature) are removed.

Except when you are using the MIDI port for a joystick, the IRQ jumpers are the only other jumpers you will probably need to set. Because each brand and model of sound card can have different features and settings, it is important to refer to the manual provided with the sound card. Many manufacturers provide documentation on their Web or BBS sites if you do not have the manual.

CD-ROM Drives

The only other internal connections you need to make are those needed for a CD-ROM player. CD-ROM players support both a drive interface cable and sound interface cords.

The drive interface cable is a wide-ribbon cable. The width depends upon the type of interface you are using. Check the cable and connectors to make sure that the number one pins line up. Figure 15.3 shows the connectors on a typical CD-ROM drive.

Check the manual for your sound card to determine if there are any conflicts with specific CD-ROM players. Some of the conflicts may be handled with an additional jumper or connector on the sound card.

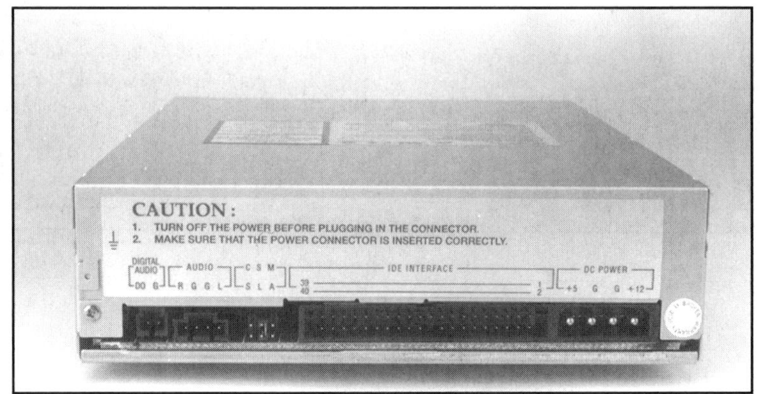

FIG. 15.3
Digital Audio, Audio, configuration jumpers, IDE Interface, and power connections on a CD-ROM player.

Installing the Sound Card in the Computer Case

The first thing to look for in the computer case is the right type of slot for your sound card. If your card is a 16-bit, use a standard 16-bit slot. If you have a PCI card, locate an open PCI slot.

NOTE While your sound card may be used with an 8-bit slot, installing it in a 16-bit slot gives you a greater selection of hardware settings. If you encounter hardware conflicts while using an 8-bit slot, change to a 16-bit slot and rerun your configuration software.

Maneuver the card so that the mounting bracket drops into the alignment slot in the back of the expansion slot. Press firmly on the upper edge of the card, possibly rocking the card from back to front, to seat it in the edge connector on the motherboard (see Figure 15.4).

FIG. 15.4
Firmly rock the card into the interface slots on the motherboard.

When the mounting bracket is completely seated, screw in the retaining screw to secure the card.

After getting the card secured in the case, run the CD-ROM cable and cords from the sound card to the CD-ROM (see Figure 15.5). Check the alignment of the cable and cords before inserting them into their appropriate connections on the CD-ROM drive.

FIG. 15.5
The image on the top shows the audio channel cable coming from the sound card to the CD-ROM shown on the bottom.

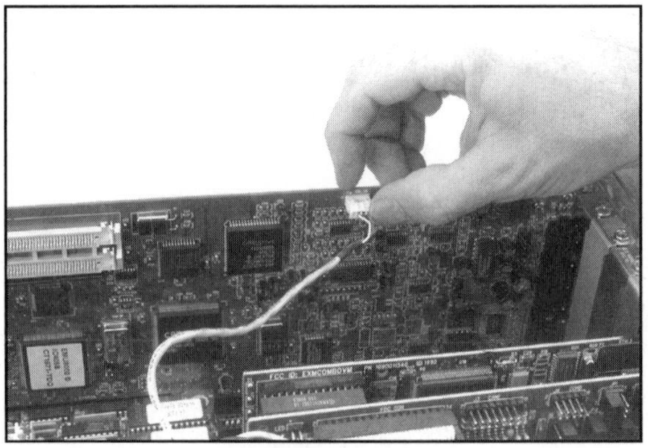

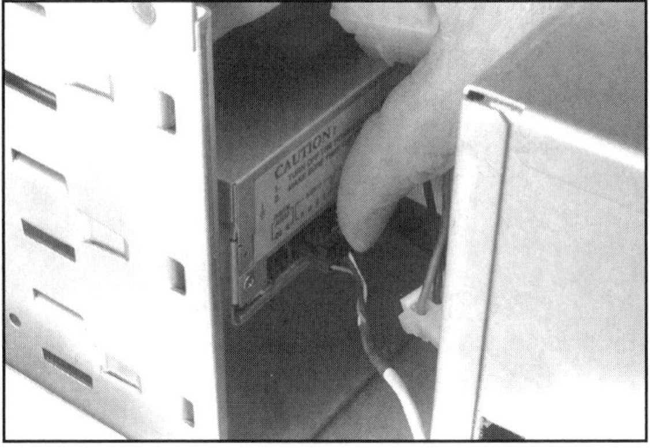

NOTE Test the new equipment before closing your computer case, especially if this is the first time you have added a peripheral. Unless you have very little workspace to use temporarily, leave the case open until you are sure of the new configuration.

Memory Upgrades

The new sound cards designed for professional-quality sound include the ability to add more sound samples. More instrument and other sound samples can be used to re-create sounds by upgrading and adding more memory to the sound card. Just as with video cards, additional memory can be added, but it is necessary to configure the operating system to avoid potential memory-addressing conflicts.

Locate the SIMM sockets on the sound card and check the orientation of the memory module to the socket. This is accomplished by identifying the registration notch on the bottom edge of the SIMM (see Figure 15.6).

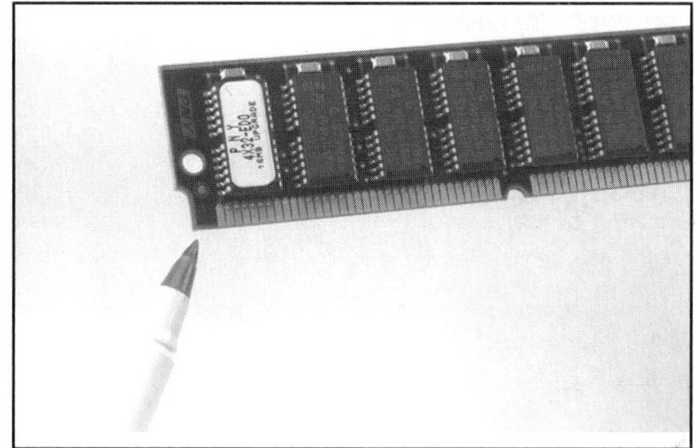

FIG. 15.6
Locate the registration notch on the SIMM before inserting the SIMM socket.

Insert the SIMM into the socket at an angle until the SIMM is completely seated (see Figure 15.7). After seating the module, push it to the back or front of the socket to set the retaining clips. The amount of maximum addressable memory may not match the total amount you install. In the case of the Creative Labs Sound Blaster AWE32 PnP, only 28M are read when two 16M SIMMs are installed.

FIG. 15.7
Insert the SIMM into the memory expansion socket.

Connecting Devices to the Card

Adding speakers, a microphone, or other devices to your sound system is just as simple as hooking them up to your stereo system. Figure 15.8 shows a PC set up for games with speakers, microphone, and a joystick.

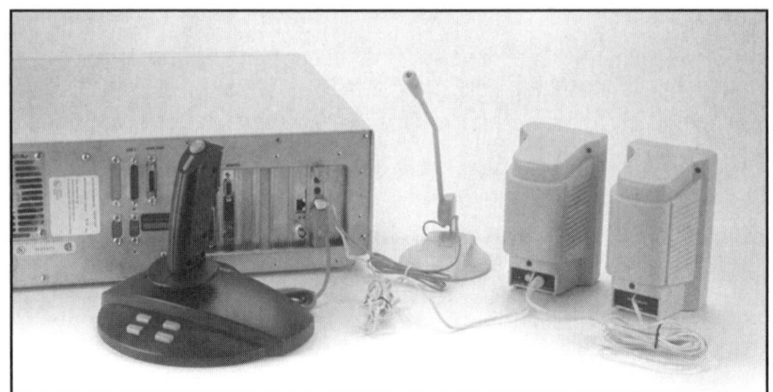

FIG. 15.8
A fully configured sound system with joystick on the MIDI port.

Speakers and Other Output Devices

There are two connectors on most sound expansion cards for output. One is usually dedicated to speakers, and the other is a line output to Line In connectors on amplified devices.

Both connectors require a stereo mini-jack on the speakers and other connections for stereo output. When you are running the sound output onto your stereo, use a cable from the Line Out jack to the Line In jack or plugs on the stereo amplifier.

Headphones

If you are working in a shared environment or have other concerns, you can use headphones instead of speakers. You can plug in your Walkman headset to listen to your favorite CDs at your desk or continue to play Sky Warrior IV after your family has gone to bed.

Plug the headphones into the Speaker jack on the back of your sound card. The Volume control included with your sound card can be used to control the volume out of the Speaker jack.

If you plug your headphones into the jack on a CD-ROM player, only the volume control on the player can be used to control the output.

Microphone and Other Inputs

There are two connectors on most sound expansion cards for input. One is dedicated to a microphone, and the other is a line input to Line Out connectors on amplified devices.

The Microphone jack uses a monaural mini-jack on the microphone. To connect the sound output from another device to the Microphone jack, use a stereo-to-mono cable from the Microphone jack to the Line Out plugs on the other unit.

The Line In jack accepts a stereo mini-jack for two-channel input. When you are running the sound output from your stereo, for example, use a stereo-to-stereo cable from the Line In jack to the Line Out plugs on the stereo amplifier.

Line Out plugs on stereos are typically RCA plugs, so when you look for the connecting cable, make sure it is a monaural mini-jack-to-stereo RCA plug. Most configurations of these audio cables can be found at many electronics stores.

Keyboard and Other MIDI

MIDI devices are popular in the home as well as the recording studio. You can add an electronic keyboard, organs, synthesizer, or other MIDI-equipped devices, further enhancing the audio qualities. MIDI-capable sound systems come with a MIDI interface box. The box is connected with a single DB15 plug to the MIDI connector on the sound card.

The MIDI interface boxes typically have separate plugs and jacks for a variety of MIDI input and output.

Other Sound Tips

The sound card systems provide a means to add and edit a multitude of different sound effects to anything you do with a computer. You can hook up your portable CD player or your television sound if you want to capture a specific sound bite or quote.

TIP If you have a Macintosh with sound effects that you want to use on your Windows machine, plug into the Line In and Out jacks and play-and-record the sound effects.

When you are creating an ultra-efficient office, you could use a wireless microphone and earphone headset for freedom of movement. Because some sound systems are incorporated with a voice messaging and auto-dialing system, the hands-free feature expands the high-tech environment.

Configuring a Sound Card

It is important to restate here that the most important preinstallation task to do is get the current IRQ and memory addresses. After determining by these are using a system utility such as Microsoft's MSD.EXE or MSINFO.EXE, you either set the IRQ setting using jumpers or use a system utility to configure the IRQ through software.

After installing the sound card in your computer, it is necessary to configure software to work with the card. This process differs according to what version of Windows you are using. The software settings for the sound system software are consistent regardless of the Windows version.

Windows 95

If you have a Plug and Play-compatible sound card, Windows 95 automatically opens the Add New Hardware Wizard to install the new device. Otherwise, open the Control Panel on the Windows 95 desktop and click the Add New Hardware icon to open the wizard.

The wizard prompts you to allow it to automatically search your computer for the new card. It is faster to do a Manual selection of the sound card than using the Automatic Search. In the second window of the Add New Hardware Wizard, click the No option button and the Next button to select the sound card manually.

In the next window, select Sound, Video and Game Controllers from the Hardware Types list box. Select the manufacturer from the Manufacturers list box to see a list of the included Models list. From the Models list box, select your sound system and click the Next button.

The next window in the wizard may display the settings it wants to use, based on the devices and settings it has already found and used. This list shows the Direct Memory Access (DMA) address, Input/Output (I/O) memory address (the memory range that may need to be excluded in the CONFIG.SYS), and the Interrupt Request (IRQ) that the system wants to use for the card. If the IRQ does not match the IRQ jumper setting on the card, cancel the installation and recheck the jumper.

After Windows 95 has finished installing any required files, you have to restart the computer for the new sound system to come to life. You can finish installing the sound software by following the software instructions, but a fast way to test a sound system is to play a CD in the player.

If you have set the IRQ jumper to the same settings that the Add New Hardware Wizard selects and are still having problems, run the System program from the Control Panel.

Click the Device Manager tab and look for Sound, Video and Game Controllers. Click the plus icon to the left, highlight the sound device, and click Properties. In the Properties dialog box, click the Resources tab to view the hardware settings.

The primary area for potential conflict is the IRQ setting. If you find that you are experiencing problems, check the IRQ setting for network cards, modems, and other serial devices for a duplicate IRQ assignment.

Windows 3.x and Windows for Workgroups

In the Windows 3.x world, the required system configuration is performed in the CONFIG.SYS and AUTOEXEC.BAT files. The configuration is then loaded after DOS loads. The setup software included with many sound cards will modify the files for you.

Your CONFIG.SYS file may include the following statements to configure a Creative Labs SoundBlaster:

```
DEVICE=[Path]\CTCM.EXE
DEVICE=C:\SBCD\DOSDRV\SBIDE.SYS /D:MSCD001 /V /P:1E8,11
```

The AUTOEXEC.BAT file may include the following lines:

```
SET CTCM=[Path]
[Path]\CTCU /s /W=[Windows Directory Path]
```

CD-ROM and CD-R Drives

CD-ROM technology is advancing at a steady clip. What was yesterday's state-of-the-art 3x CD-ROM is now a museum piece. The nice thing about the advancing technology is that it is getting easier to add or replace these older models. A small consolation, I know, when you probably paid $400 plus for that 3x museum piece, but a benefit just the same. If this is your first CD-ROM, that should make you feel better about dropping a whole $130 for that 12x CD-ROM. CD-Rs (CD-Recordables) are covered here, too; they are installed and used in the same way a standard CD-ROM is, with the added ability to record data onto special recordable CD media.

In this chapter, you learn how to

- Compare and contrast features of CD-ROM and CD-R drives to get the most value per buck before you purchase
- Determine the right CD-ROM/CD-R for your system
- Demonstrate a typical installation of the drive
- Build a CD duplicating system

Overview of CD-ROM and CD-R Drives

CD-ROMs have become a standard component of modern day PCs for one reason—their ability to distribute massive amounts of data in a compact and inexpensive way. I remember getting my first copy of OS/2. It came in a box with a small manual and 21 floppy disks. I thought, "This is crazy. It's going to take me all day to get this loaded." Actually, it took me three days, but that was an OS/2 thing.

In that same vein, CD-Rs are becoming popular for their ability to store large amounts of data. You can even back up your hard disk on one CD-R, and at about $10 a pop for the media, that's a lot cheaper than tape media of equal capacity. CD-R drives have also dropped in price to the point of becoming affordable to the mainstream consumer. The drawback is that it's not reusable.

CD-RWs (CD-Rewritables), however, are reusable. This latest technology will allow you to read, write, and *rewrite* CDs. The down side is CD-RW won't be 100 percent backward compatible. CD-RW drives will read CD-ROMs, but existing CD-ROM drives won't read CD-RW disks. CD-R drives won't be able to read or write CD-RW discs, either.

Drive Specifications

CD-ROMs and CD-Rs share the same read mechanisms (see Figure 16.1), so many of the comparison specifications are similar as well.

FIG. 16.1
The major components of a typical CD-ROM.

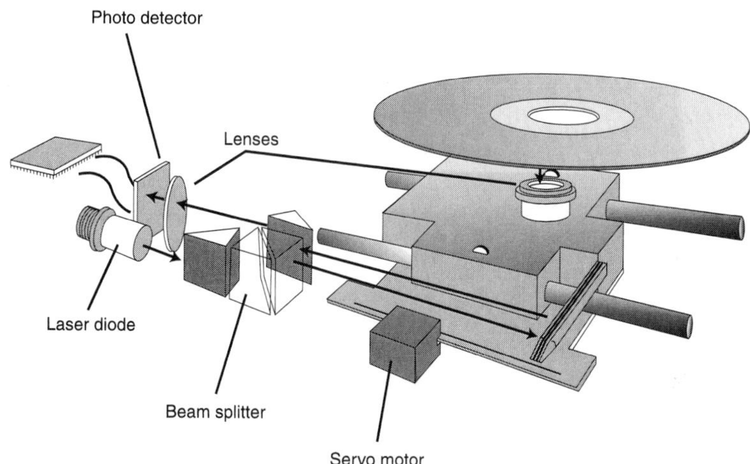

Similar to hard drives, CD-ROM drives have a set of specifications that help you decide which drive is best for your system. These specifications, in order of importance, are:

- *Transfer rate.* This tells you how much data the drive can transfer at a sustained rate from the CD to the CPU, measured in kilobytes per second. A 1x drive will sustain a transfer rate of 150K/s. This is the base number; all higher rates are a multiple of this number. For example, a 2x drive has a transfer rate of 300K/s or 2 times 150. The higher, the better.
- *Average seek time (also known as access time).* The access time is the amount of time that lapses between a request for information and its delivery. The lower the value, the better. The time is recorded in milliseconds. A good access time is 150ms, but the lower the value, the better.
- *Buffer or cache.* Onboard cache acts as a buffer for data being transferred from the drive. Typical is 256K, but again, the larger the better.
- *Interface type.* IDE (Integrated Drive Electronics) or SCSI (Small Computer System Interface) are the two most common drive interfaces. For the least amount of hassle and the greatest amount of savings, stick with the interface type you already have, that is, unless you plan to record CDs. All CD-Rs are

SCSI. This has to do with the way a CD-R is recorded. Once the recording process is started, it cannot be stopped. If it is, the CD will be ruined. The IDE interface was not designed to provide this kind of sustained throughput; the SCSI interface can.

- *Loading mechanism.* The way you load the CD in the CD-ROM comes in two flavors—tray and caddy. The *tray* method (see Figure 16.2) is the same you see in audio CD players. It's a slide-out drawer that you just drop your CD in and close. The *caddy* is a special container you place the CD in before you slide it in the drive. The tray method is the most convenient way, because you eliminate the step of placing the CD in the caddy, then the caddy in the CD drive. However, I do not know of any CD-R drives that use a tray system; they all use the caddy method. The caddy allows more accurate laser positioning, which is paramount when recording a CD.
- *Internal or external.* All IDE type CD-ROMs are internal because the IDE interface does not support external devices. SCSI-based CD-ROMs can be either *internal* (housed inside the computer case) or *external* (separate stand-alone units with their own power supply). It is best to use an internal model if your system has the space for it, especially if you will be doing CD recording. Internal models are less expensive, and the case acts as a shield for the cabling to electromagnetic (EM) and radio frequency (RF) interference that can cause unpredictable results.

FIG. 16.2
This IDE 8x CD-ROM drive from Creative Labs uses a tray type loading mechanism.

General Recommendations

If your system currently has an IDE/EIDE controller, an open connection point on the ribbon cable (IDE supports 2, EIDE 4), and you need a CD-ROM drive and not a CD-R, go with the fastest (highest transfer rate) IDE compatible CD-ROM drive you can afford. You get the most "bang for your buck" from IDE. The transfer rates are up to 16x now.

If you have no available IDE connections, have a SCSI-based system, or plan on using a CD-R, your best choice is a SCSI-based CD-ROM—the fastest you can afford. On an IDE system, this gives you at least six more devices you can support (SCSI systems support up to seven devices on one card). On a SCSI system, this is the cheaper way to go because you can use the controller card you already have. And for a system you plan to have a CD-R drive on, it's your only choice.

Planning the Installation

Once you have decided on the type of drive to buy (and you've picked out a controller), it's time to plan your installation process. CD drive installations are usually straightforward, but proper planning is the key to avoiding problems.

Power Considerations

Power is the first consideration. A typical CD drive requires about 10 watts of power for proper operation. This may not sound like much, but you must be sure that your power supply is able to provide that much power; otherwise, your supply may become overloaded. Overloaded supplies often cause unpredictable PC operation, or prevent the PC from booting at all. In extreme cases, a severely overloaded power supply can even break down. Here are some rules to help avoid power problems:

- If your system has not been upgraded before, it can usually stand an extra drive without any problem.
- If your system has been significantly upgraded already, pay attention to the system's operation after you add a new drive. If the system behaves erratically, you may need a higher voltage power supply.

TIP Refer to Chapter 26's section on "Checking the Power Supply" for more help.

You also need to have a 4-pin power connector available for the new drive. If you're replacing an existing CD drive, you can reuse the power connector on the replacement drive. When adding a new drive, be sure there is an extra power connector available from the power supply.

If you don't have a power connector available, you can purchase a *Y-connector* that splits an existing connector into two separate connectors, as shown in Figure 16.3.

You simply remove a power connector from a drive, install the Y-connector, plug one arm of the Y-connector back into the original drive, and you've got a spare connector for that new drive.

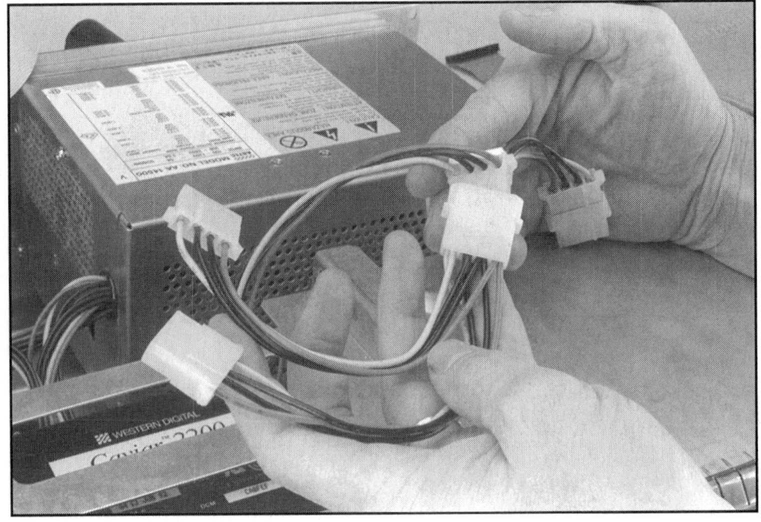

FIG. 16.3
A Y-connector can give you an extra power connector if you run out.

Choosing a Drive Bay

You also need to decide where your drive is going to go in the system; only a 5 ¼-inch drive will do. When replacing a drive, you can reuse the original drive bay. If you are adding a CD drive for the first time, you need to locate an unused drive bay (see Figure 16.4). Large desktop and tower chassis often have several drive bays available, but you may have to hunt a bit for an open bay in a mini-desktop enclosure.

Drive bays are typically referred to as *external* and *internal*. External drive bays are located behind those plastic plugs you see on so many plastic housings. Floppy disks, CD-ROM drives, and tape drives all demand these external drive bays. Internal drive bays are basically metal brackets inside the chassis to which you can bolt a drive securely. Because you need access to the drive to insert or remove the CD media, you can only use external drive bays.

As mentioned earlier in the section "Drive Specifications," an external SCSI CD drive is exempt from this process for obvious reasons.

Another point to consider when choosing a drive bay is to make sure that your power connector and signal cable are both long enough to reach the new hard disk (see Figures 16.5 and 16.6).

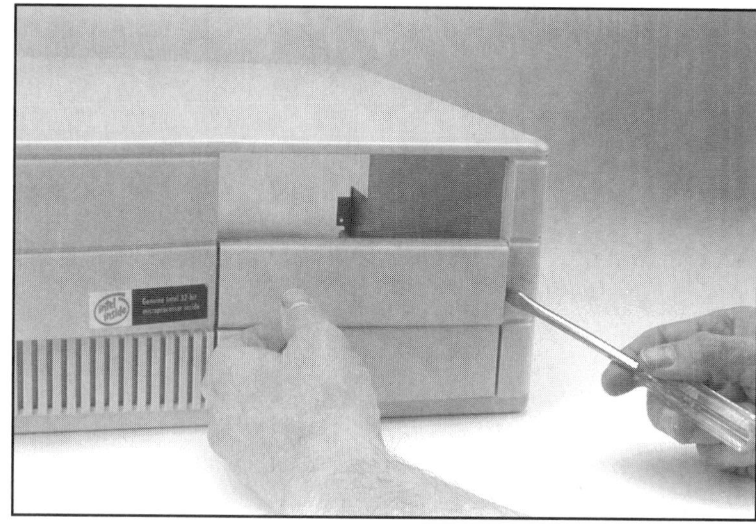

FIG. 16.4
Remove the plastic plug over an available 5 $\frac{1}{4}$-inch external drive bay.

FIG. 16.5
Check the distance from the controller board and the CD drive.

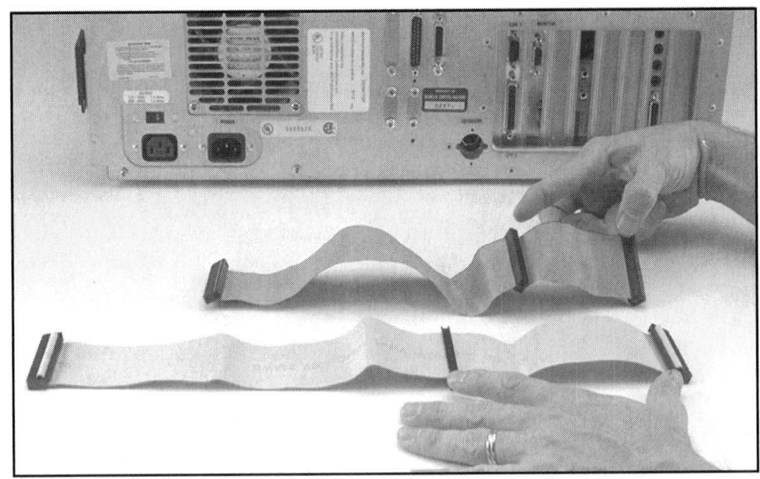

FIG. 16.6
You can always buy a longer cable if the one you have is too small.

Finally, you need to determine whether or not your particular case design requires the use of slide rails. Slide rails usually come with the computer case, if the manufacturer uses a specific design, and attach to the drive to allow for easier/quicker access to the drive, as shown in Figure 16.7. CD drives usually come with a generic type of slide rail.

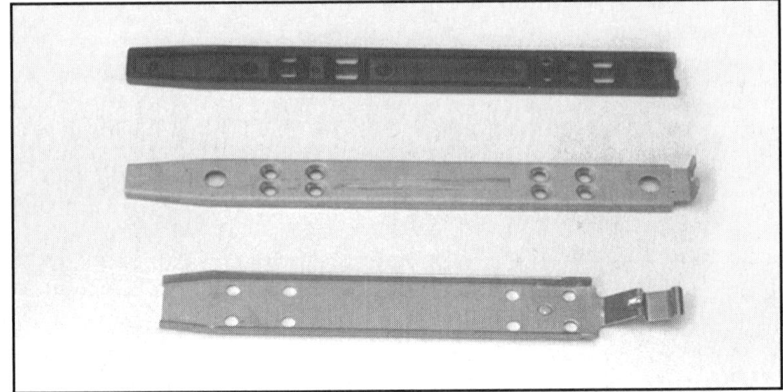

FIG. 16.7
Sometimes the slide rails are specific for the type of case.

Drive Configuration

Configuration of your new CD disk is paramount to its proper function. Examine your new drive (see Figure 16.8) and locate any jumpers. For an IDE drive, here are the typical ways to jumper the drive:

- As the primary (master) drive on the secondary IDE connection
- As the secondary (slave) drive to a current hard disk drive

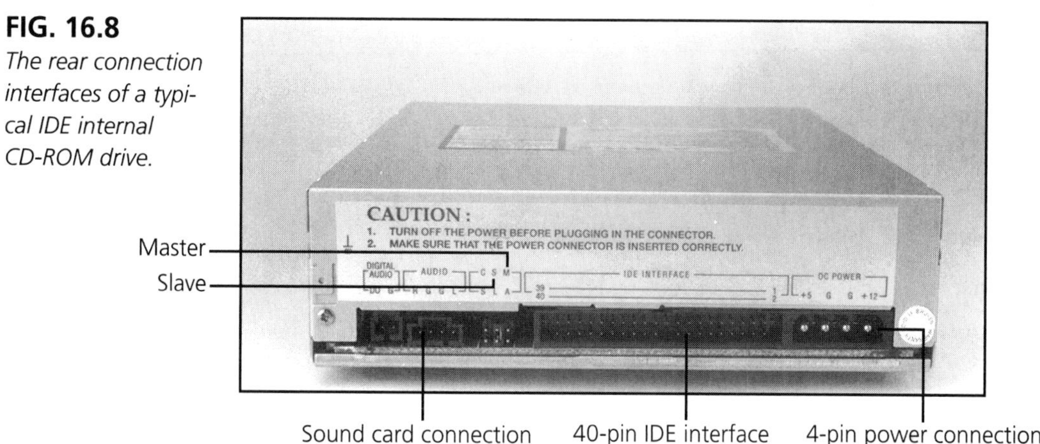

FIG. 16.8 *The rear connection interfaces of a typical IDE internal CD-ROM drive.*

If the CD drive is to be the only drive on your secondary EIDE interface, the factory settings are usually correct. In this case, the jumper is not being used. You can skip to the next section.

NOTE Some motherboards have embedded EIDE controllers, as in Figure 16.9. This means that it will support two IDE chains, both with a master and a slave drive for a total of four devices.

FIG. 16.9 *This motherboard has an embedded EIDE interface with a primary and secondary IDE connection.*

When you use the CD-ROM as a secondary drive—that is, the second drive on the same ribbon cable—make sure it is configured as the slave drive, and set the hard disk so that it is the master drive. In most cases, the CD-ROM shows up as the next logical drive, or D: drive.

SCSI drives are a bit easier to configure because you only select the proper device ID for the drive. By convention, the boot disk (the C: drive) in a SCSI system is set as ID0, and the host adapter has the ID of 7. You are free to choose any other available ID. If your new SCSI drive falls at the end of a SCSI bus, you need to terminate the drive (covered later in this chapter in the section "Termination").

NOTE IDE/EIDE disks and SCSI CD drives can coexist in the same system. The CD drive needs its own controller or host adapter. Some sound cards have a SCSI interface built in.

Installing a CD-ROM or CD-R Drive

The installation of a CD-ROM and a CD-R is identical. The only difference is that IDE type CD-ROMs only come in the internal flavor, while CD-Rs use the SCSI interface, and therefore can come in both internal and external flavors. The common installation instructions are as follows, and any specific information to the type of interface you choose can be found in its own section.

Before You Begin, You Need:

- ☑ A Phillips screwdriver
- ☑ The CD drive
- ☑ IDE or SCSI ribbon cable
- ☑ Audio cable to connect the CD drive to your sound card
- ☑ Mounting screws and slide rails (the latter is case-dependent)
- ☑ An open 5 $^1/_4$-inch external drive bay

Adding an Internal IDE CD-ROM Drive

This section describes the installation of an internal IDE CD-ROM drive to a system with an IDE/EIDE hard disk drive already installed. If this isn't for you, you can skip to "Adding a New SCSI Drive."

TIP If your system uses an older IDE controller, that's OK. Even the newest and fastest CD-ROMs can't take advantage of the Enhanced IDE features.

NOTE Adding a controller card is the same as adding any other card. Refer to Chapter 6, "Basic Device Configuration and Installation," for help.

To add an internal IDE CD-ROM drive, follow these steps:

1. Locate an open drive bay for your new drive, preferably one as close to your hard drive as possible. The reason for this is that the distance between drive connectors on the ribbon cable is usually short.
2. Attach any slide rails, as required by your particular case design, to the new drive. Note that some cases do not require slide rails.
3. Check to see if you have an available 4-pin power connector. Most systems have at least one or two spares. If not, you can purchase a Y-connector (shown in Figure 16.10) that splits the power off one of the other power connectors.

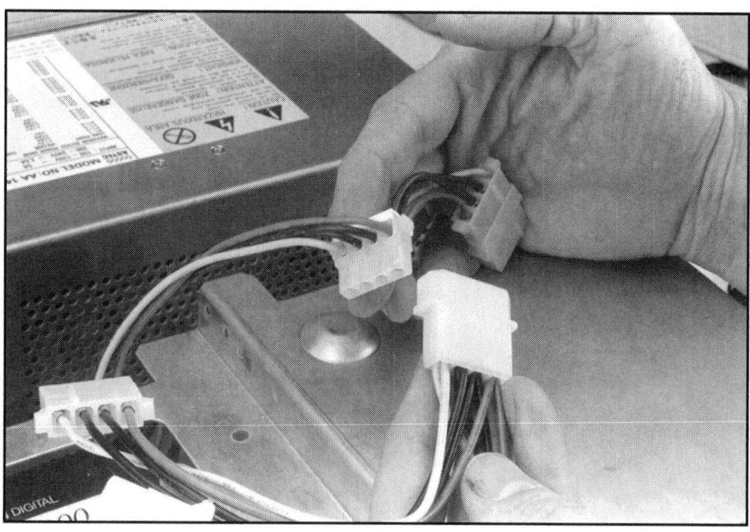

FIG. 16.10
A Y-connector can give you an extra power connection, if you find you've run out.

4. Attach the 4-pin power connector before you insert the drive (see Figure 16.11). This is usually easier than trying to do it after the drive is in place, but that depends on the type of case you have.

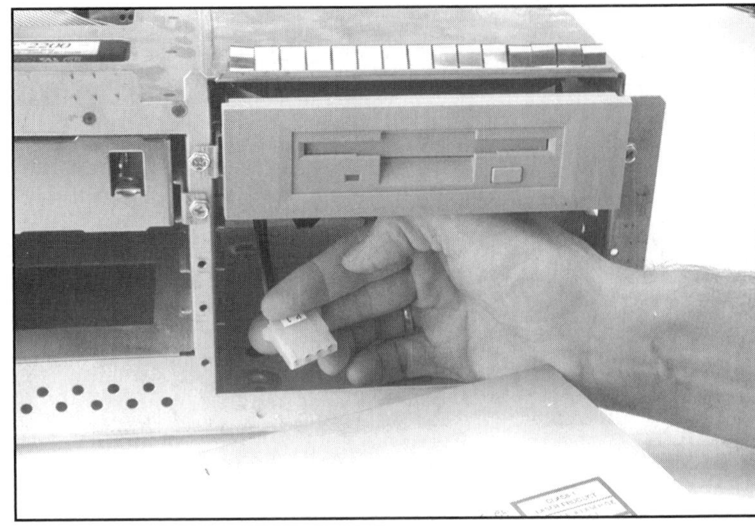

FIG. 16.11
Attach the power connector to the new drive.

5. Slide the new drive into the 5 $^{1}/_{4}$-inch expansion bay see (see Figure 16.12), and attach the supplied mounting screws.

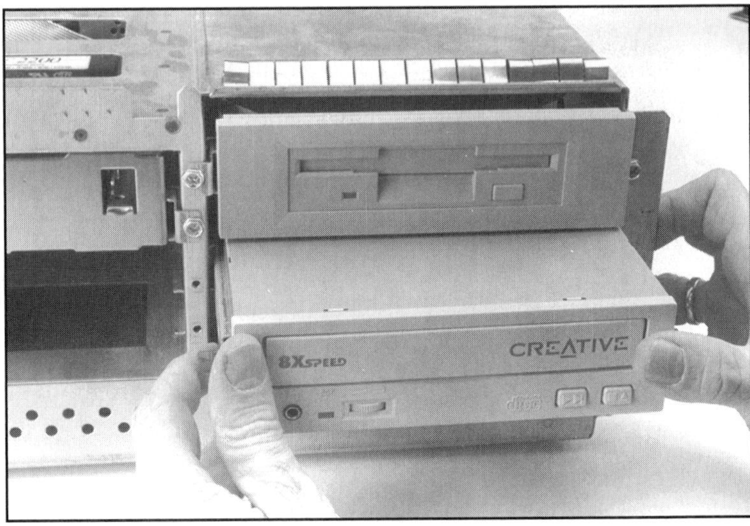

FIG. 16.12
Add the new internal CD-ROM to an external 5 $^{1}/_{4}$-inch bay.

6. If possible, attach an available drive connector from the 40-pin ribbon cable already in your system, noting the key in the connector (see Figure 16.13).

TIP It's worth mentioning that it doesn't matter which connector you use. The primary/master and secondary/slave relationship is determined by the jumpers on the drives themselves (see Chapter 11), so feel free to reattach the cable in any manner necessary for optimum placement.

FIG. 16.13
Note that the #1 pin position is indicated on the ribbon cable, usually with a color.

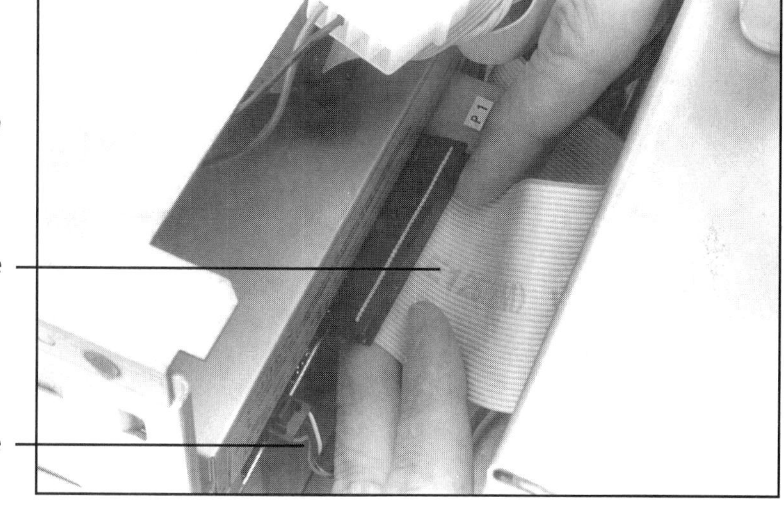

NOTE If you have an EIDE controller and the secondary IDE connector is unused (refer to Figure 16.9), you can attach an additional 40-pin ribbon cable to it to control your new drive. In that case, the jumper settings on both the new drive and the old would be set to MASTER, because these controllers function as two separate controllers. The next device on either cable, whether hard disk or CD-ROM drive, would then be set to SLAVE.

7. Connect the audio cable supplied with your CD drive to your sound card. This is how you will be able to hear your music CDs from you CD-ROM. See Chapter 15 for more on connecting your sound card.
8. Replace the computer case cover.

And there you have it. A new drive is born.

Adding a New SCSI Drive

This section discusses the addition of a new SCSI CD-ROM drive to you system. If your drive interface is IDE, skip back to "Adding an Internal IDE CD-ROM Drive."

External SCSI CD-ROM/CD-R Drives

Because the SCSI interface supports external devices, you have two flavors of SCSI CD drives—internal and external. Adding an external SCSI device is about as easy as adding an external modem—plug it in, flip a few switches, and you are ready to go.

Of course, you need to have the SCSI controller card installed and configured properly (if not, see the later section "About the Controller Card"). Assuming this is true, you simply locate the external SCSI connection port on the back of your computer, connect the drive cable, plug in the power supply, configure the drives' SCSI ID and termination (see the later sections "Termination" and "Setting SCSI IDs"), and turn on the computer. The SCSI card should recognize the drive and make it available to Windows 95 or NT. If you are still using Windows 3.x, you need to install some real-mode device drivers in your CONFIG.SYS and AUTOEXEC.BAT files. A software setup program is provided by the controller's manufacturer for this purpose. Check your documentation.

Internal SCSI CD-ROM/CD-R Drives

Adding an internal SCSI CD drive to your system is the same as adding the IDE CD drive. The drive is configured a bit differently, though, so you should read the next section before you refer to the previous section "Adding an Internal IDE CD-ROM Drive."

About the Controller Card

This section briefly discusses the SCSI controller card (sometimes called the *host adapter*), even though the actual process of installing the card is no different than any other expansion card you might add (see Chapter 6, "Basic Device Configuration and Installation"). This is because very few new motherboards come with an embedded SCSI controller, as EIDE does, and neither do most home systems you might want to upgrade.

The first thing to note is that most SCSI controllers can have both an internal chain and an external chain (see Figure 16.14), and both need to be terminated. Most internal connectors appear similar to the IDE counterpart except bigger—50 pins instead of 40. The exception is an Ultra Wide SCSI connector (16-bit path rather than the standard 8-bit), which is actually visually smaller but uses 68 pins.

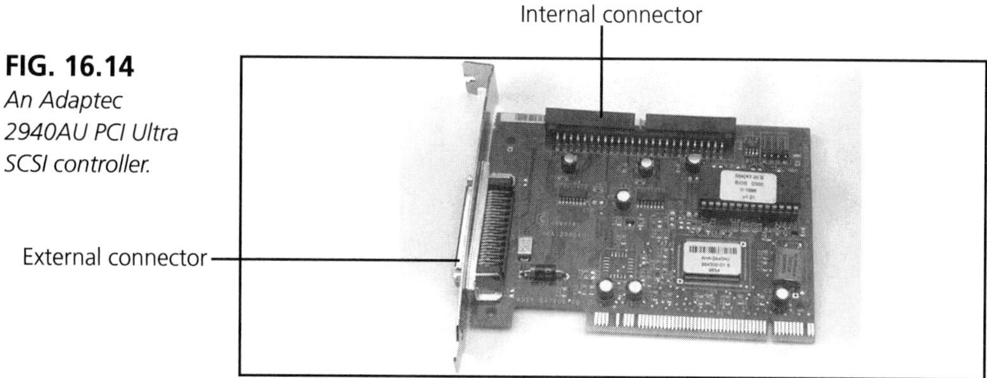

FIG. 16.14
An Adaptec 2940AU PCI Ultra SCSI controller.

External connections can be different, too. Some older controllers use a 50-pin connector that resembles a parallel port. Most newer controllers use a 50-pin mini-connector shown in Figure 16.15 or a 68-pin mini-connector for Ultra Wide. There are adapters available to change from one kind of connector to another, in the event that a device you want to connect to uses a different connection.

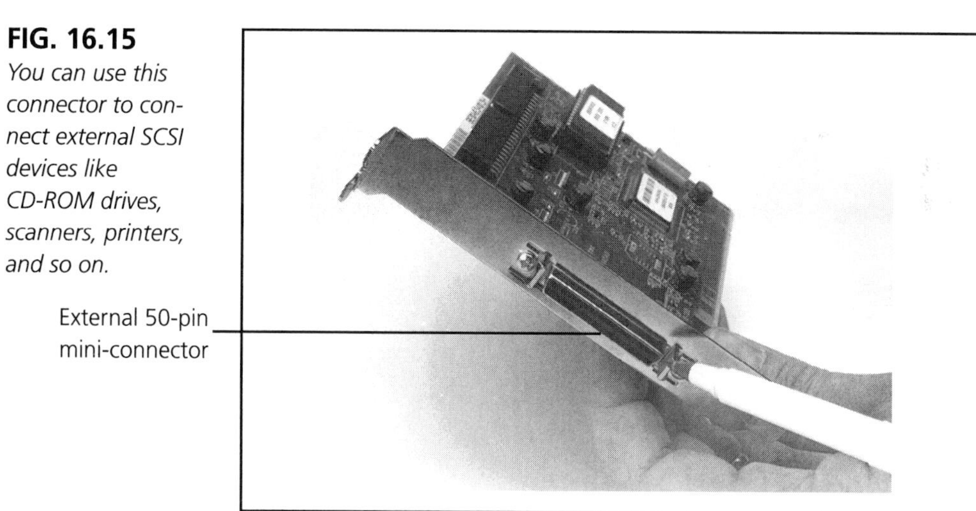

FIG. 16.15
You can use this connector to connect external SCSI devices like CD-ROM drives, scanners, printers, and so on.

Compatibility and Recommendations

As you are beginning to see, there is not quite the same standardization in the SCSI world as there is in the IDE. This is one reason why SCSI has been primarily used in "high-end" computers or by computer "geeks." Only these people were willing to take the time to understand all the factors necessary for a properly functioning SCSI subsystem. With this in mind, I recommend you purchase an Adaptec SCSI controller card.

I make this recommendation not because I get a commission on any sales derived from this book (I wish), but because it is the most standardized SCSI board out there. In fact, Adaptec has been pushing the standardization of SCSI for years. The ASPI (Advanced SCSI Programming Interface) was once Adaptec SCSI Programming Interface before they turned it over to the public. There are other SCSI boards out there with as good, if not better, price/performance ratio, but the headache you could get with incompatibilities and poorly written device drivers isn't worth the difference.

Termination

Termination is one of the most important factors in setting up you SCSI subsystem. In a nutshell, the last device on a SCSI chain—internal and external—needs to have termination enabled. This can be accomplished in different ways, depending on the device.

For example, if you have only two devices—a controller card (yes, it counts as a device) and a hard drive—they both need to be terminated. It is automatic for the controller; you do not need to do anything (not always the case if you are not using an Adaptec controller). The hard drive will have either terminating resistors that plug into the underside of the drive or have a jumper to set, as in the case of the IBM Ultastar ES 2.16G Ultra SCSI hard disk I used in this upgrade. Now add another device to this party, like an internal SCSI CD-ROM drive. If you were to install it between the hard drive and the controller, no termination is necessary. On the other hand, if you installed it after the hard drive, you would need to remove the termination from the HD and terminate the CD-ROM drive.

Think so, huh? Let's add an external scanner to this scenario. Both the scanner and the hard drive (or CD-ROM, in the last case) need to be terminated because the controller card auto-terminates. In the case where the only devices were internal, the card was one terminator, and the drive was the other. Both ends were terminated. When you added the external device, the controller card became non-terminated and the scanner became the other end of the chain. Now the scanner is one terminator and the internal drive is the other. Simple, right? The bottom line is that you need two terminating devices in any SCSI chain, one at each end.

Setting SCSI IDs

Each device on a SCSI chain has its own unique ID called its *SCSI ID*. You choose this ID either through jumpers or switches, and they can be set to any number from 0 to 7. This has no relation to the device's physical orientation on the SCSI chain, nor does it effect termination in any way. There are some general rules, though:

- The boot disk is usually set to ID 0.
- The host adapter is usually set to ID 7.

Some new SCSI devices are supporting *SCAM (SCSI Configured AutoMatically)*, where the host adapter assigns the unique IDs at bootup automatically. If your devices support this, be sure to enable this feature in the host adapter's BIOS, as described in the controller's manual.

IDE CMOS Considerations

The *CMOS (Complementary Metal-Oxide Semiconductor)* is the chip that holds the information that your motherboard's BIOS (basic input/output system) has recorded on it. Some people use these terms interchangeably.

The BIOS reads the system information contained in the CMOS, then checks out the system and configures it. Next, the BIOS looks for an operating system on the boot drive (drive 1 or C: drive) and launches that OS, then turns control over. For more on BIOS setup, refer to Chapter 7, "Working with the BIOS."

Once the BIOS setup is activated, most new BIOSes have the IDE HDD Auto Detection option. Your BIOS should give you some prompt as how to activate the detection process. Usually, it is simply a matter of moving the cursor to the indicated field and pressing Enter (F1 usually pulls up a Help menu in most BIOS programs). You need to go through this process so your computer can register the new drive and make it "visible" to your OS.

In case you have an older BIOS or the autodetect didn't correctly ID your drive as an IDE CD-ROM, you need to configure software drivers in order to allow DOS or Windows 3.x to recognize the CD-ROM drive. Setup software is provided with your drive for this task. Windows 95 and Windows NT can usually autodetect the drive, so no hassles there.

It's worthwhile to mention that Windows 95 and NT usually don't recognize a CD-R without specific drivers from the manufacturer. This is not that big of a deal because the software used to write CDs will. You only need the OS to be aware of the CD-R if you also want to use it as a standard CD-ROM.

> **CAUTION** Be sure to save your changes before exiting a CMOS Setup routine. If you forget to save, the CD-ROM parameters will be lost, and the drive will not be recognized.

Building a CD Duplicator

Because most software companies allow you to make one copy of licensed software for archive purposes, what better/safer media than a CD? They are tamperproof, impervious to magnetic fields, random access, and, best of all, cheap. Also, if you are going to invest in a recordable CD drive, you will most likely be creating your own content, and may have a need to copy that content in a convenient way.

Building a CD duplicator is really nothing more that putting a SCSI CD-ROM in the same machine as your CD-R. Software is usually provided with the CD-R that copies the contents of the CD in the CD-ROM to the CD-R media. The reason you need a SCSI CD-ROM for the job is tied into the CD recording process. Basically, when you start a write to a CD-R, the process must continue uninterrupted until the completion of the entire session. This is not possible with the IDE/EIDE interfaces.

Recommendations and Tips for Perfect Writes

Having ruined more than my fare share of CD-R media, I have a few things to say so you will not have to share in my pain:

- Try to use internal rather that external drives if you can. The external SCSI chain is fairly susceptible to RF and EM radiation, which will exhibit itself as random, brain-scrambling write errors. The computer case will shield you from this. If you must go external, pay extra to get shielded cables—they're worth it.

- Buy an Adaptec SCSI controller card if possible. This is the most common SCSI controller on the market, and everyone supports it. I have a wall of trashed CD-R media due to a cheap controller that returns *buffer under run* (the RAM buffer runs out of data during a write) errors.
- Make sure you have your termination properly set. Sometimes SCSI devices operate without correct termination, just not very well or consistently.
- Try not to use the machine while in the recording process. Theoretically, the SCSI sub-system runs independently of other processes in the computer, that is, unless the other process hangs your whole computer.

PART V

Communications, Internet, and Networking

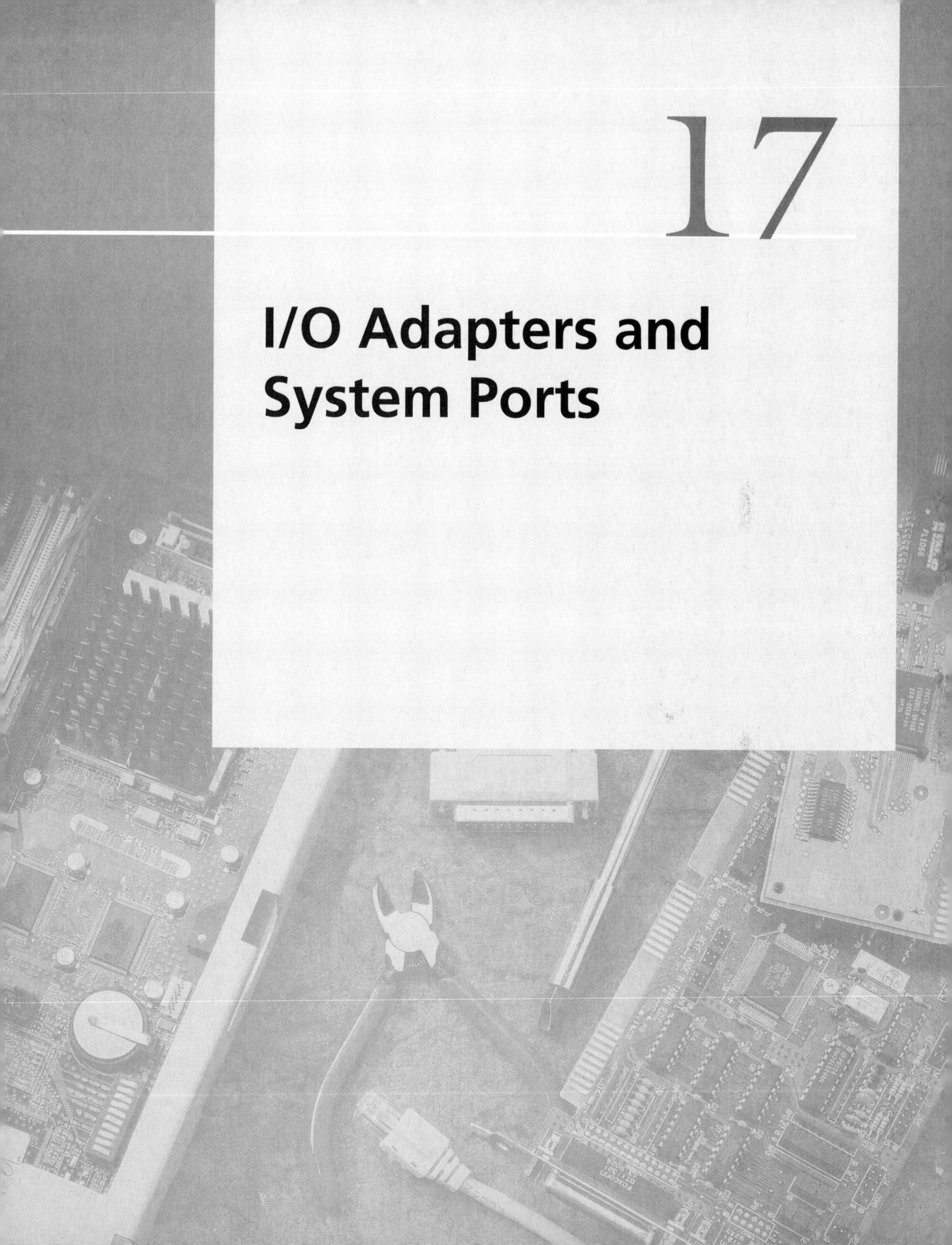

17

I/O Adapters and System Ports

Most users need only one physical parallel port for a printer and two serial ports: one for a mouse and another for a modem. In some situations, though, it's good to have more ports. For example, you might have two printers and therefore need two parallel ports. Or, maybe you're using a mouse, a modem, and another serial device, so you need three serial ports. You can easily add more ports to your system. And, there is one upgrade you should consider adding to your system even if you have plenty of ports. This chapter covers all these topics, including the following:

- Understanding parallel and serial ports
- Choosing a multiport adapter
- Upgrading 16450 UARTs to 16550 UARTs for better performance
- Installing a multiport (I/O) adapter
- Adding ports under your operating system

First, you should understand some background about parallel and serial ports.

Device and Port Overview

Your computer probably contains at least one *parallel port* and two *serial ports*. If yours is a relatively new system, the ports are probably built right onto the motherboard (see Figure 17.1) and ribbon cables run from these motherboard connections to port connectors on the back of the case.

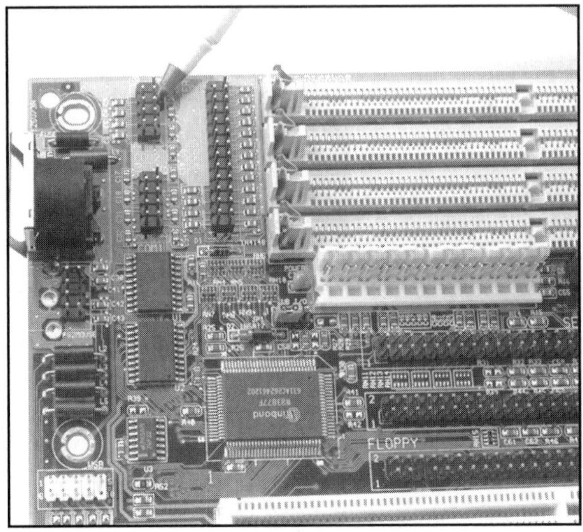

FIG. 17.1
This is a serial port connection on a motherboard. Below it is a second serial port and to the right, a parallel port.

If yours is an older system or contains more than one parallel port or two serial ports, at least some of the ports are probably located on an adapter installed in one of the bus slots. I/O adapters, which sometimes are called *multiport adapters*, contain parallel and serial ports. Usually, these adapters contain one or two parallel ports and two serial ports, and often include at least one game port (for a joystick).

Except in the case of an internal modem, which is configured as one of the computer's serial ports, devices that connect to serial and parallel ports do so from the back of the computer. When the ports are built onto the motherboard, a ribbon cable connects from the port connection on the motherboard to a connector on a bracket in front of an empty bus slot (on the right in Figure 17.2) or through a cutout in the chassis (on the left in Figure 17.2). An example of a parallel port cable and connector is shown in Figure 17.3.

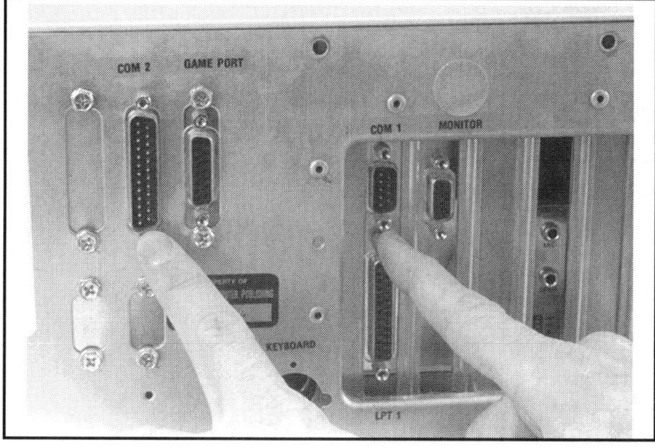

FIG. 17.2
The parallel and serial ports are accessible from the rear of the computer, either through a bus bracket slot or a special cutout in the chassis.

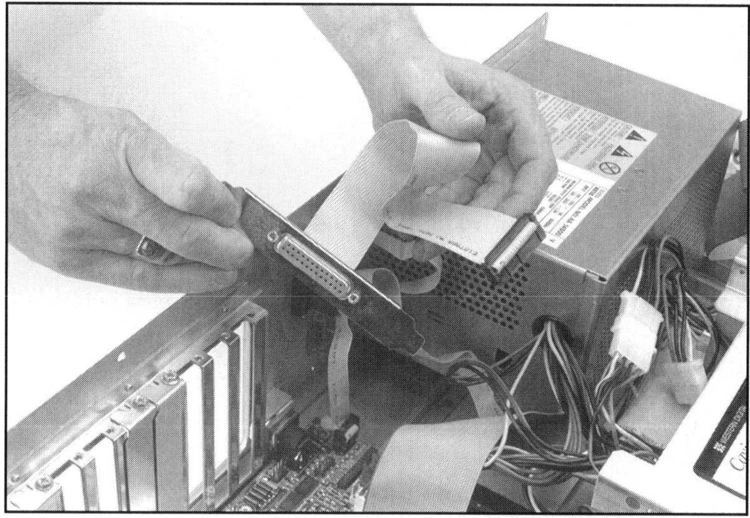

FIG. 17.3
This parallel port connector mounts in an empty bus bracket slot and connects to the motherboard or an I/O card by a ribbon cable.

TIP If you take a close look at a port bracket assembly, notice that the port connector itself is held on the bracket by two threaded studs. The studs not only hold the connector on the bracket, but also accept retaining screws for the cable being connected to the port. You can remove the studs to get the connector off of the bracket for mounting in the back of the chassis. This is a good solution when you don't have a bracket slot available for the bracket assembly. It's also a good solution when the ribbon cable is too short to make it from the I/O connectors on the motherboard to the bracket slot.

If you decide to remove the connector from the bracket, just use the same studs to mount the connector to the back of the computer's chassis.

Understanding Parallel (LPT) Ports

You'll often see or hear parallel ports referred to as *LPT ports*. LPT is taken from *Line PrinTer*, and refers to the fact that the parallel port is most commonly used to connect printers to the computer. However, parallel ports have been used in recent years to connect other types of devices to the computer. Some special SCSI (Small Computer System Interface) adapters can be used to connect SCSI devices such as CD-ROM drives to the parallel port—a great solution for adding SCSI devices to a notebook computer. Also, you'll find certain other types of mass-storage devices that connect through the PC's parallel port.

Parallel ports get their name from the fact that data travels through the parallel port in parallel, one byte at a time. The port includes eight data lines, and each bit of the byte travels through a different line more or less at the same time as all the other bits in the byte. The parallel ports in the PC are labeled LPT1, LPT2, and so on.

NOTE A *bit* is the smallest unit of computer data. A *byte* comprises 8 bits. It takes 1 byte to represent a character, such as the letter R or the number 7. A parallel port can therefore send one full character at a time. Fortunately, it does so very quickly.

In addition to the standard parallel ports used in PCs since the first IBM PC crawled out of the computer-evolution soup, you'll find ECP and EPP ports in most of today's computers. *ECP* stands for *Enhanced Capabilities Port*, and *EPP* stands for *Enhanced Parallel Port*.

NOTE The original parallel port was unidirectional. That is, data flowed out to the peripheral and not back the other way. The bi-directional parallel port was introduced in 1987 and provided a means for peripheral devices to communicate back to the PC. A printer, for example, could send information back to the PC concerning its state (paper jam, out of paper, and so on).

The EPP, which was introduced in 1991, is occasionally referred to as a *Fast Mode parallel port*. EPP increases by a factor of 10 the speed of the port over a standard bi-directional parallel port. EPP was designed primarily with LAN adapters, disk drives, tape drives, and CD-ROM drives in mind.

The ECP, which was introduced in 1992, offers similar performance advantages over a standard bi-directional port. ECP is primarily intended to service high-speed printers, however. Unlike EPP, ECP requires a DMA channel.

NOTE Regardless of the type of parallel port, the port uses a 25-pin female connector, as shown in Figure 17.3.

Most systems manufactured since about 1992 support each of the three parallel port modes: standard (bi-directional), EPP, and ECP. You'll get the best performance with EPP and ECP, so that's how you should configure your parallel ports. Note that port configuration is handled through the BIOS Setup program, and is covered later in the section "Installing an I/O Adapter."

TIP You can use a special parallel cable to connect two computers together to share files, creating a poor man's network. DOS includes a program called Interlink that lets you accomplish this link. You can use Direct Cable Connection in Windows 95 to accomplish the same thing.

Be aware, though, that Direct Cable Connection in the original Windows 95 release can cause a memory hole to form that will cause your system to run out of RAM. Before using Direct Cable Connection, you should download and install the Windows 95 service pack from Microsoft's Web site.

For a complete discussion of using Direct Cable Connection in Windows 95, refer to the *Windows 95 Communications Handbook* from Que.

Update for home users:
http://www.microsoft.com/windows95

Understanding Serial (COM) Ports and UARTs

Serial ports get their name from the fact that data is sent through the port in serial fashion, one bit at a time. This is because the port has only one data line for each direction. Serial ports also are referred to as *COM ports* because they provide a means of communication between external devices and the PC. The most common devices that connect to serial ports are modems, mice, and serial printing devices, including printers and plotters.

The connectors for a serial port come in two configurations: 9-pin and 25-pin. If you look at Figure 17.2, you see a 9-pin connector on the right and a 25-pin connector on the left. You can use *port adapters* to connect different types of devices to the ports. Figure 17.4 shows an adapter for connecting a PS/2 connector to a 9-pin serial port. Figure 17.5 shows an adapter for connecting a 25-pin device to a 9-pin port. Other adapters are available for other situations, such as connecting a 9-pin device to a 25-pin port.

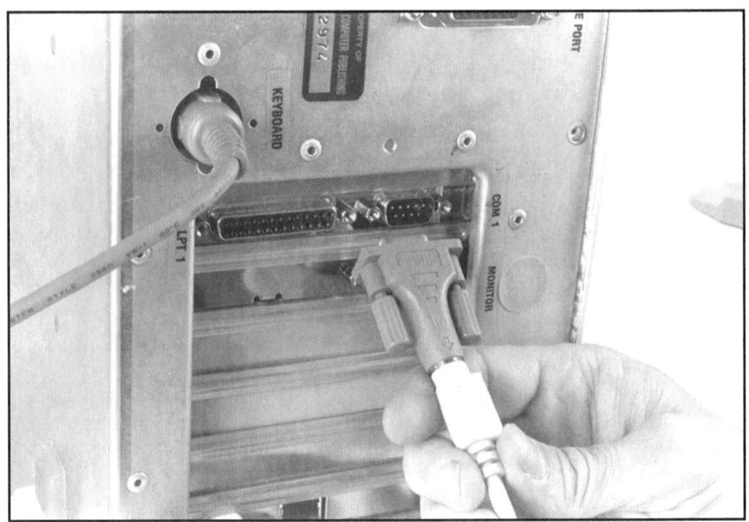

FIG. 17.4
This adapter connects a PS/2-style mouse to a 9-pin serial port.

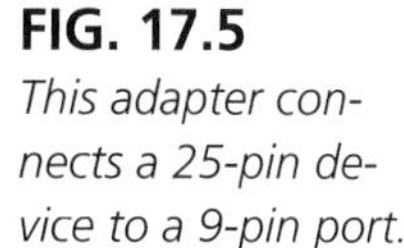

FIG. 17.5
This adapter connects a 25-pin device to a 9-pin port.

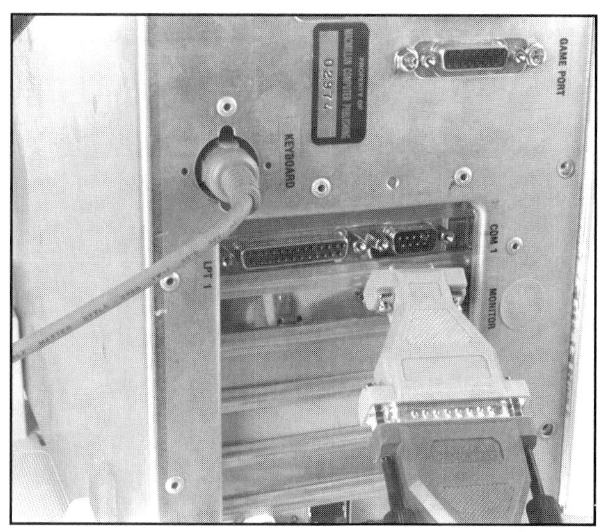

Although the serial port handles one bit at a time, the computer works with bytes. You cannot cram a byte through a serial port any more than you can drive eight cars side-by-side across a one-lane bridge. Some mechanism is needed to break each byte into individual bits that can be sent through the serial port. That's the role the UART plays.

UART stands for *Universal Asynchronous Receiver Transmitter*. The UART is a chip on the I/O card (or built into the super I/O chip on the motherboard). The UART converts bytes into serial bits that can be transmitted through the serial port. The UART also translates incoming bits back into bytes so they can be processed by the PC. The UART also controls the flow of data through the port. Figure 17.6 shows a UART chip on an I/O adapter.

FIG. 17.6
The UARTs serve to translate bits into bytes and vice versa. They also control the flow of data through the serial port.

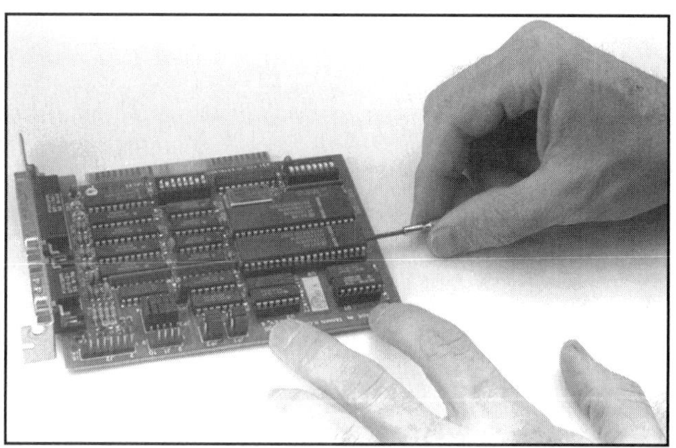

There are three types of UARTs used on I/O adapters, each designated by a different number: 8250, 16450, and 16550 (the number references a generic part number and has no real significance in itself). The 8250 UART was used in the original IBM PC. If you have an old system, it might contain 8250 UARTs.

The 16450 UART came next and provided better performance than the 8250, making it more suitable for high-speed communications. The 16550 improves on the 16450's design by adding a 16-byte FIFO (*First In First Out*) buffer for temporary storage of data as it moves in and out of the port. The buffer eliminates ***data overrun***, which occurs when the port receives information faster than it can process it. The buffer lets the port continue to receive data while it continues to process.

TIP The original 16550 UART suffers from a few bugs, but these bugs were corrected in the 16550A UART. When you read 16550 in the rest of this chapter, you can assume that it means 16550A. If you decide to upgrade the 16450 UARTs in your system to 16550s, make sure you get 16550 chips with at least the letter A after the numbers (such as 16550AFN).

The surest way to tell if your I/O adapter contains 16550 UARTs is to look for the part number on the UART itself. If the serial ports are built onto the motherboard, however, you won't be able to tell by looking. You can use the DOS-based MSD utility to check the COM ports. Here's how:

1. Boot the system to a DOS prompt.
2. Change to the DOS directory (**CD \DOS**).
3. Enter **MSD** to start the MSD utility.
4. Press C to open the COM port window.
5. Note the type of UART reported at the bottom of the display.

Although you can run MSD within Windows 3.x and Windows 95, it might not report the correct type of UART. So, you should run MSD outside of Windows.

To check for 16550 UART support under Windows 95, use this procedure:

1. Start Windows 95 and open the Control Panel.
2. Double-click the System icon.
3. Click the Device Manager tab to display the Device Manager property sheet (see Figure 17.7).

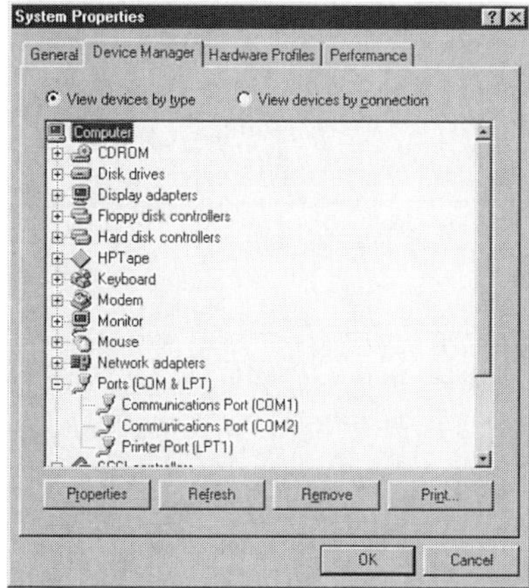

FIG. 17.7
Use the Device Manager property sheet to view the settings for the COM ports, as well as other devices.

4. Expand the Ports branch.
5. Double-click a serial port, or select a port and click Properties to display the property sheet for the port.
6. Click the Port Settings tab to display the Port Settings page (see Figure 17.8).

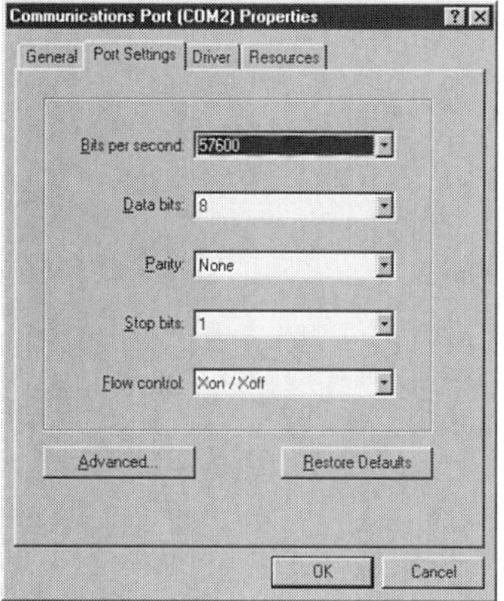

FIG. 17.8
Use the Port Settings page to set the serial port's properties.

7. Click the Advanced button to display the Advanced Port Settings dialog box (see Figure 17.9).

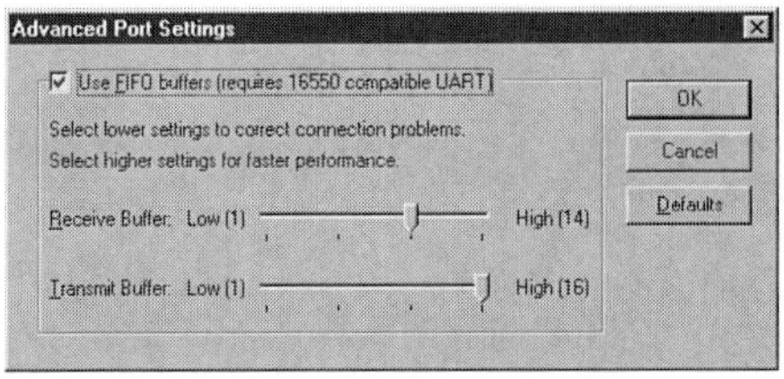

FIG. 17.9
Use the Advanced Port Settings dialog box to determine if your system contains 16550 UART support.

8. If the Use FIFO Buffers check box is available (not dimmed), your system contains 16550 UARTs or the equivalent circuitry in the I/O chip.

You can check for the presence of 16550 UARTs on a Windows NT system through the Ports object in Control Panel:

1. Open the Control Panel and double-click the Ports icon.
2. In the Ports dialog box, select the port you want to check and click the Settings button.
3. In the Settings dialog box for the port, click the Advanced button to display the Advanced Settings dialog box (see Figure 17.10).

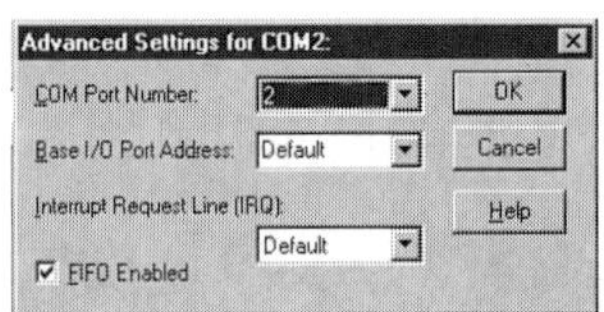

FIG. 17.10
Check the Advanced Settings dialog box in Windows NT 4.0 for 16550 support.

4. Availability of the FIFO Enabled check box indicates support for 16550 UARTs.

Later in the section "Upgrading UARTs," you find a procedure to explain how to replace the socketed UART chips on an I/O adapter.

Choosing Multiport (I/O) Adapters

Why add a multiport adapter to your PC? There are two reasons:

- Add 16550 UART support
- Increase the number of ports

If you need another LPT port, for example, you can add a relatively inexpensive adapter to the system to gain not only the LPT port, but also a couple of new COM ports.

TIP If you don't plan to use both LPT ports at the same time, another solution is to get a parallel port switch box to which you can connect more than one printer. The switch box connects to the LPT port, and the printers connect to the switch. You then select on the switch the printer you want to use.

Check for these features when you're shopping for an I/O card:

- *Number of ports.* Most adapters contain at least one LPT port and two COM ports. You also can find adapters that have three LPT ports and four COM ports if you need that many.
- *ECP/EPP support.* Make sure the parallel ports support ECP and EPP modes.
- *Game port.* Most I/O adapters contain a game port.
- *16550 or 16C650 UART support.* Look for an adapter that contains either 16550 UARTs or 16C650 UARTs. The 16C650 contains a 32-byte buffer compared to the 16550's 16-byte buffer.
- *IDE controller.* Most IDE controllers also contain parallel and serial ports. If you also need a new IDE controller, get one with ports.
- *Ports can be disabled.* Keep in mind that your system motherboard or another adapter in the system probably contains parallel and serial ports. Most I/O boards enable you to disable ports so they don't conflict. Or, you can disable the ports on the motherboard or other adapter, if necessary.

TIP A 16-bit I/O adapter will give you more choices for IRQ settings than an 8-bit card. This can help avoid IRQ conflicts by making more interrupts available for the ports.

Installing an I/O Adapter

Installing an I/O adapter is a lot like installing any other adapter. One step you have to perform that isn't required by some other types of adapters is setting the IRQ and base address for the ports. You also might need to disable ports if the system already contains some.

The following procedure will help you install a multiport adapter in your system. The later section "Configuring Serial Ports" helps you configure the ports to work properly under your computer's operating system.

Before Installing an I/O (Multiport) Adapter, You Need:

- ☑ Phillips screwdriver for the cover and bracket screws
- ☑ I/O adapter
- ☑ Motherboard manual if disabling or configuring ports on the motherboard
- ☑ Adapter manual if disabling or configuring ports on a secondary adapter (such as an IDE controller)
- ☑ Manual for the new I/O adapter

1. Determine how many ports you have in the system now, and decide if you need to disable any existing ports or disable any ports on the new adapter.
2. Use the system logs, MSD, or Device Manager to determine the IRQ and base address settings for the existing ports.
3. Shut down, turn off, and unplug the PC.
4. Remove the PC's cover.
5. Use the I/O adapter manual as a guide to configure the IRQ and base addresses of the ports on the adapter card so they don't conflict with any other devices or ports in the computer. Typically, configuration is accomplished through DIP switches or jumpers on the adapter card.

TIP If you're not sure what IRQ and base addresses are, read Chapter 6, "Basic Device Configuration and Installation."

6. Install the adapter in the PC (see Figure 17.11).

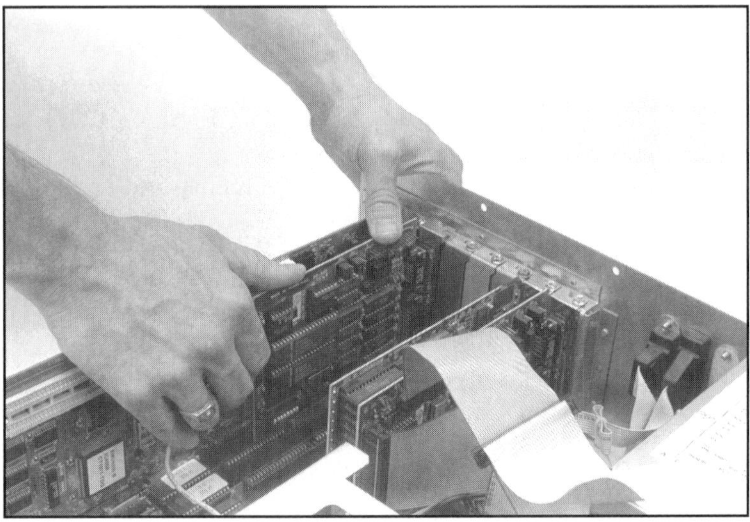

FIG. 17.11
After you configure the IRQ and base address settings, install the card in the PC.

TIP You might find it easier to connect the ribbon cables for the I/O connectors to the adapter before installing the adapter.

7. If you need to reconfigure or disable ports on the motherboard or on another adapter, do so now using the manual for the motherboard or adapter.
8. Check the location of pin 1 on each of the connectors on the adapter (see Figure 17.12).

FIG. 17.12
Pin 1 on each of the adapter's connectors is probably marked by a number 1 on the board itself.

9. Install the I/O connectors either in an appropriate mounting hole in the chassis (see Figure 17.13) or in a bus bracket slot (see Figure 17.14). If you decide to use the mounting hole in the chassis, you need to remove the connector from its bracket.
10. Connect the serial and parallel port cables to the appropriate connectors on the adapter (see Figure 17.15), making sure to align the colored stripe on the ribbon cable with pin 1 on the connector.
11. Replace the PC's cover and plug in the computer.
12. Start the system and run the BIOS Setup program. Configure the LPT ports, if desired, for ECP/EPP.

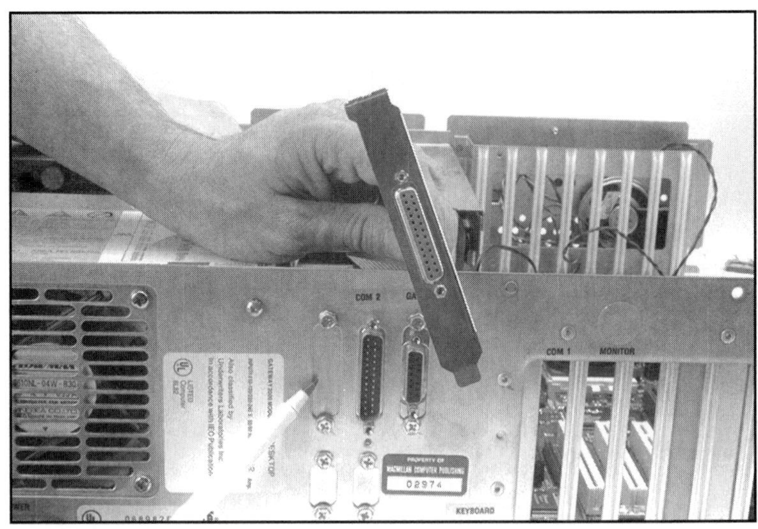

FIG. 17.13
You can mount the connectors in the mounting holes in the back of the computer's chassis.

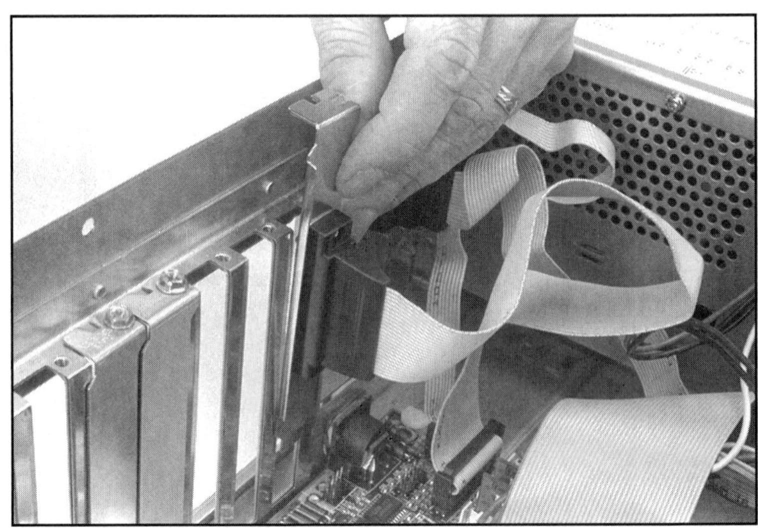

FIG. 17.14
If you have available bracket slots, you can use the bracket adapters to install the connectors.

FIG. 17.15
Connect the ribbon cables to the adapter, making sure to line up pin 1 on the connector with the colored stripe on the ribbon cable.

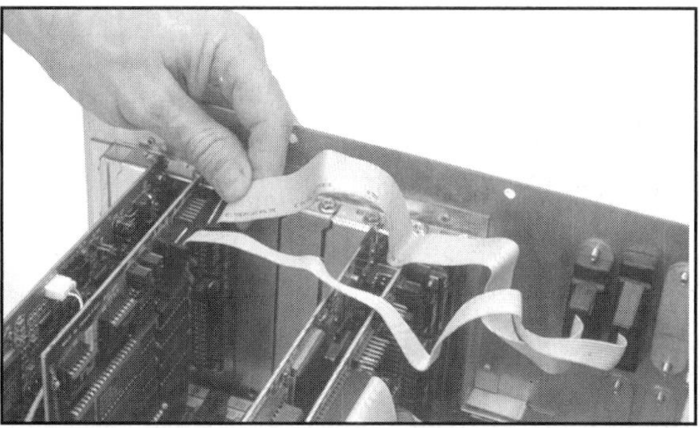

Troubleshooting

By far, the most common source of trouble with serial and parallel ports is using the same IRQ and base address settings for two or more ports on a system that doesn't support IRQ sharing. If you have problems with the serial or parallel ports, try these suggestions:

- *Verify port resource settings.* Go through the port configuration steps to make sure you have unique IRQ and base address settings for the ports. You'll find an explanation of how to check those settings in the following section, "Configuring Serial Ports." The settings must be unique if you plan to use the ports at the same time.
- *Verify physical port settings.* If the port settings in the operating system are correct, make sure the adapter card is physically configured to match those settings.
- *Make sure an internal modem or motherboard ports are not conflicting.* If the system contains ports on the motherboard or an internal modem, make sure these ports don't conflict with the ones you just installed. For example, you might have the internal modem configured as COM2 and forgot to disable COM2 on the new I/O adapter (or configure it as COM4).
- *Check cable connections.* Make sure you connected the ribbon cables to the I/O adapter, and that the external connections to the ports are secure.
- *Check the requirements of the peripheral device.* The device you've connected to the port might require specific settings. Check the device's manual, then set the port settings accordingly.

- *Check cables.* If the previous steps failed to turn up the culprit, you might have a bad cable. If you have a spare cable, try it.

Configuring Serial Ports

If you set the IRQ and base addresses properly, your system should automatically recognize the new serial ports. However, you might need to configure the ports within the operating system. For example, you might want to enable the FIFO buffers for the 16550 UART. This section explains how to configure serial ports under Windows 3.x, Windows 95, and Windows NT.

General Configuration Topics

Serial ports are somewhat more complex than parallel ports in the number of settings you can change within the operating system. Chapter 6 described IRQ and base address settings. The following list briefly describes the other settings that apply to serial ports:

- *Bits per second (bps).* The number of bits the serial port transfers each second. In general, a communications program overrides this setting with its own. If you're not sure what to use, specify 9600 for this setting.
- *Data bits.* The number of data bits in a data word. You can choose a value from 4 through 8. Most systems use either 7 or 8 data bits. As with bits per second, a communications program typically overrides this setting. If you're not sure what to use, specify 8 data bits for this setting.
- *Parity.* The type of parity checking, if any, the port uses. The choices are None, Space, Even, Odd, and Mark. A communications program overrides this setting with its own. If you're not sure what to use, specify Even.
- *Stop bits.* The number of bits used to indicate the end of a data word. You can choose 1, 1.5, or 2. If you're not sure what to use, choose 1.
- *Flow control.* The method the port uses to control the flow of data through the port. A communications program typically overrides this setting with its own. You can choose Xon/Xoff, Hardware, or None. If you're not sure what to use, choose Xon/Xoff.
- *FIFO settings.* These settings control the 16550 UART's FIFO buffer. You can enable/disable the port and set the *trigger level* for the send and receive

buffers. The trigger level indicates the number of bytes in the buffer that will trigger an interrupt and allow the port to be serviced by the CPU. The default values provide good performance in almost all cases.

NOTE Because the default values for all these settings work well in most cases, this book doesn't cover them in detail. If you want or need more explanation about port values, refer to the *Windows 95 Communications Handbook* and *Windows NT Communications Handbook*, both from Que. The primary focus of this part of the chapter is to tell you where to find these settings under various operating systems in case a specific application you have requires you to change them.

Configuring Serial Ports Under Windows 3.x

You configure the serial port settings using the Ports icon in the Control Panel. Use this procedure to specify serial port settings:

1. Open the Control Panel and double-click the Ports icon.
2. In the Ports dialog box, click the port whose settings you want to specify, then click Settings to display the Settings dialog box (see Figure 17.16).

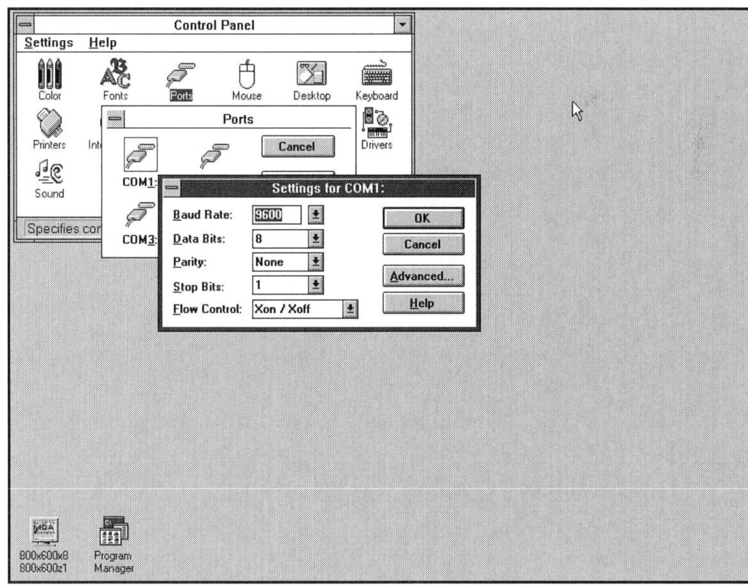

FIG. 17.16 *Control basic serial port settings through the Settings dialog box for the port.*

3. Choose in the Settings dialog box the appropriate settings for the port.
4. Choose the Advanced button if you want to set the IRQ and base address for the port. The Advanced Settings dialog box appears (see Figure 17.17).

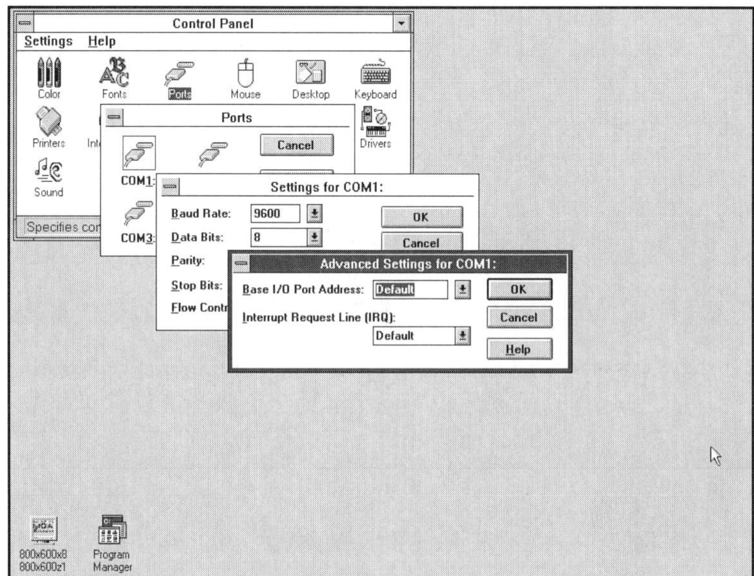

FIG. 17.17 *Use the Advanced Settings dialog box to specify the IRQ and base address for a port.*

5. Choose OK in each of the three dialog boxes to close them.

To enable the 16550 FIFO buffers for a port, you need to add a setting to the SYSTEM.INI file. Edit SYSTEM.INI using Notepad or SysEdit and add the setting **COM*n*FIFO=True** to the [386Enh] section, where *n* is the number of the port. To enable the FIFO buffer for COM2, for example, add the setting **COM2FIFO=True**. You have to restart the system for the change to take effect.

Configuring Serial Ports Under Windows 95

Windows 95's Plug-and-Play support should enable Windows 95 to automatically detect and configure the settings for the new serial ports. If you decide to change the IRQ or base address settings or want to change the basic or advanced settings for a port, use this procedure:

1. Open the Control Panel and double-click the System icon to display the System property sheet.
2. Click the Device Manager tab to display the Device Manager.
3. Expand the Ports branch to list the installed ports.
4. Double-click the port you want to change, or select the port and choose Properties.
5. Click the Port Settings tab to display the Port Settings property sheet (see Figure 17.18). Specify settings according to your needs.

FIG. 17.18
Use the Port Settings property sheet in Windows 95 to control basic serial port settings.

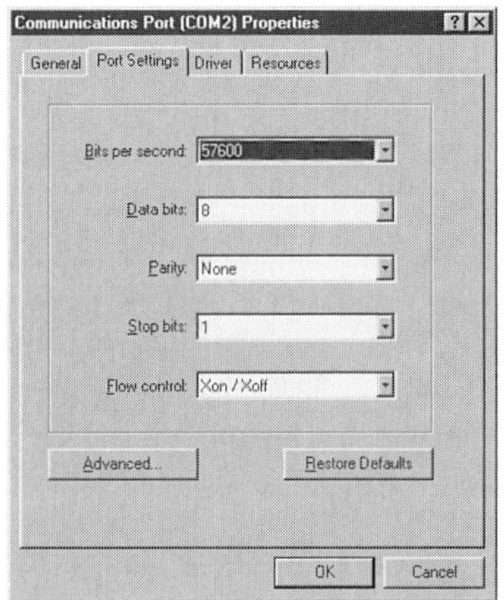

6. If you want to set the FIFO trigger values or enable/disable the FIFO buffer for the port, click the Advanced button.
7. In the Advanced Port Settings dialog box (see Figure 17.19), enable the FIFO port by placing a check in the Use FIFO Buffers check box.

FIG. 17.19
Use the Advanced Port Settings dialog box to control FIFO support and trigger values.

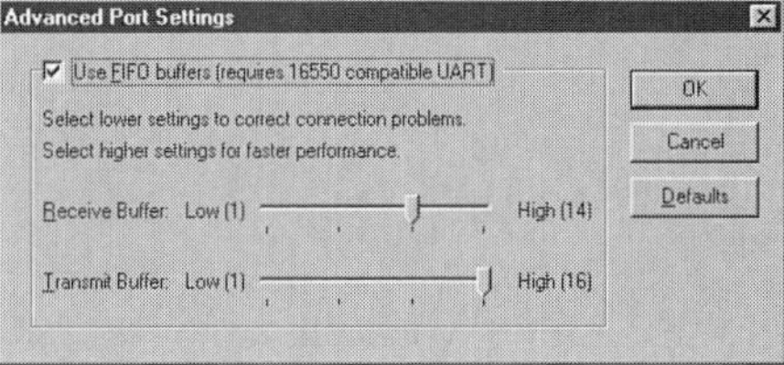

8. In general, you should use the default trigger values for best results. If you need to change them, however, simply slide the Receive Buffer or Transmit Buffer control to the desired setting. Then, choose OK. Choose OK again to close the property sheet.

Configuring Serial Ports Under Windows NT

You use the same procedure under Windows NT 3.x and 4.0 to configure serial port settings. The following procedure shows you how:

1. Open the Control Panel and double-click the Ports icon.
2. In the Ports dialog box, select the port whose settings you want to change, then click Settings.
3. In the Settings dialog box (see Figure 17.20), choose the settings you need.

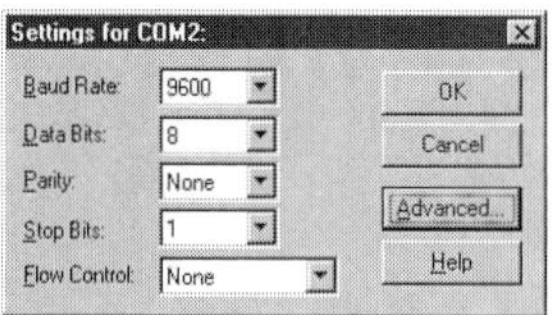

FIG. 17.20
Use the Settings dialog box to control serial port settings in Windows NT.

4. If you need to change the IRQ, base address, or enable/disable FIFO support, click the Advanced button.
5. In the Advanced Settings dialog box (see Figure 17.21), specify the settings you need, then choose OK.

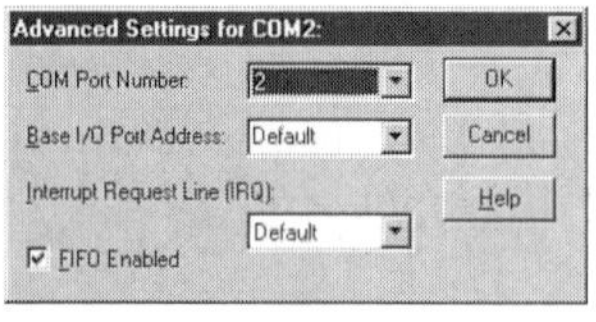

FIG. 17.21
Use the Advanced Settings dialog box to control base address, IRQ, and FIFO support.

6. Choose OK to close the Settings dialog box.

Upgrading UARTs

You might think that replacing the UART chips on an I/O adapter is a tough, tricky job. Actually, it's very easy, and you don't need any special tools. Before you buy the UARTs, however, make sure the I/O adapter uses socketed UARTs, rather than soldered UARTs. If the UARTs are soldered to the board, your best bet is to buy a new I/O adapter.

TIP If you can't find UARTs locally, you should be able to buy them from just about any computer mail-order supplier. Or, call JDR Microdevices at 408-494-1400.

To Replace UARTs on an I/O Adapter, You Need:

- ☑ I/O adapter with socketed, not soldered, 16450 UARTs
- ☑ New 16550AFN UARTs to replace the old ones
- ☑ Phillips screwdriver for case and adapter screws
- ☑ Small, flat-bladed screwdriver or chip extractor tool to remove UARTs
- ☑ Anti-static protection

1. Shut down, turn off, and unplug the PC.
2. Open the PC and locate the I/O adapter.
3. Discharge your static, then disconnect the ribbon cables from the I/O adapter and remove the adapter.
4. Note the location of the semicircular notch on top of the UART. This notch indicates pin 1.
5. Using a chip extractor or a small, flat-bladed screwdriver, remove the old UARTs from their sockets (see Figure 17.22).

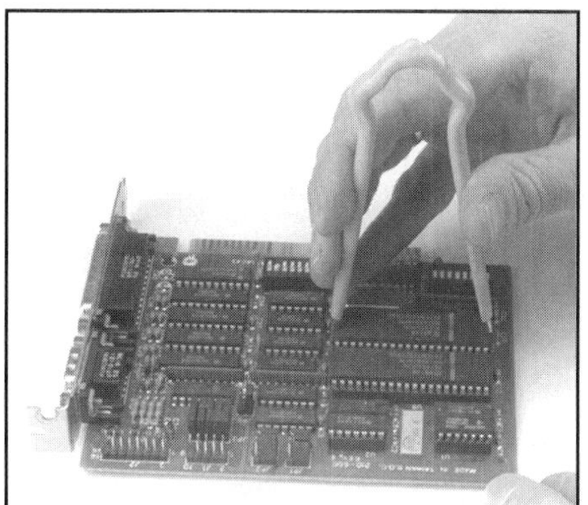

FIG. 17.22
You can use a chip extractor to remove the UARTs, but a small, flat-bladed screwdriver or spare bus slot bracket cover will do for prying the chip out of its socket.

6. Taking care to align the pin 1 notch on the UART with the correct end of the socket (see Figure 17.23), place the UART gently in the socket, making sure to align all the pins (see Figure 17.24).

FIG. 17.23
The notch on top of the UART indicates the location of pin 1 and helps you orient the chip correctly in the socket.

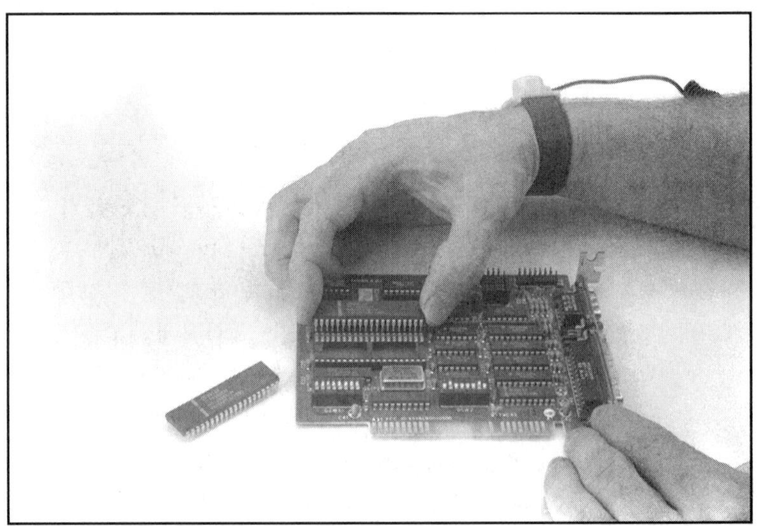

FIG. 17.24
Lay one row of pins over their holes in the socket, then rotate the chip down to insert the other row.

7. After you verify that the pins are all aligned properly, press on the chip to seat it fully in the socket (see Figure 17.25).

FIG. 17.25
Push the UART firmly into the socket to seat it.

8. Reinstall the I/O adapter in the case, and reconnect any ribbon cables you disconnected in step 3.
9. Reassemble the PC, then boot the operating system.
10. Use the appropriate method to enable FIFO support for the ports. See the section "Configuring Serial Ports" earlier in this chapter for instructions on how to do that.

18

Modems

Modems have always been the PC accessory that turned the island of a stand-alone home computer into a world of information. Slow 300bps modems were used to connect to mainframes. Later as we moved up to the "high speed" of 2.4Kbps, the modem was used often to connect to bulletin board systems (BBSes). Now most people use a 28.8Kbps or 33.6Kbps modem to access the Internet. And manufacturers are promising 56Kbps modems soon.

By the end of this chapter, you will know:

- How to choose a modem that's right for your needs
- How modems talk to each other and your PC
- How to configure internal and external modems
- How to install internal and external modems
- What to do to achieve peak modem performance

Overview of Modems

The basic function that a modem performs is turning digital bits into an analog signal and back—a process called *modulation*. The word *modem* is actually shorthand for *Modulator/Demodulator*. If you're not sure what an analog signal is, well, it's sound. When you dial into another computer or the Internet, your modem places a phone call by "picking up" the phone line and using the same touch tones your home phone generates. When the other end answers, the two modems "negotiate" how they will talk to each other. This process is not unlike two people trying to find a common language and dialect.

After the modems have decided on a common signaling rate, compression, error correction, and other language options, the "Carrier Detect" light turns on, and your modem is "talking" to the modem at the other end. If you have the speaker turned on, you can hear this entire setup process. If you've ever picked up an extension that a modem is using, you have heard (and maybe interrupted) the conversation.

Choosing a Modem

When you shop for a modem, it may seem that the modem manufacturers are deliberately trying to confuse you with the width of their product line. There are so many standards and features available that just deciphering the box can be a challenge.

Most of those standards and options are discussed later in this section, but you need to make the most important decision first: whether you want the modem inside or outside your PC.

Internal versus External Modems

External modems:

- Have indicator lights. While this may not seem important, it really is a nice feature. You can get a lot of information about what the modem is doing by which lights are flashing.
- Are easier to install than internal modems. Internal modems can be difficult to set up (unless you use Windows 95 and buy a Plug and Play modem), but an external modem (once your have the right equipment) can be Plug and Play.
- Require a free serial (COM) port on your computer. Just as important is that this free serial port is a equipped with a high speed (16550 or 16650 AFN) UART. Take a look at Chapter 17, "I/O Adapters and System Ports," for a discussion of what UARTs are and how to find out what kind you have.
- Cost a little more than internal modems. The extras that go into an external modem cost money.
- Require the purchase of a separate cable. You need to find the right kind of cable for your computer.
- Are easily moved to another computer.

Internal modems:

- Take up less space and wiring than an external modem. The less cables there are outside of your computer, the better.
- Can be difficult to install. Don't worry—this chapter will help you do it, but it may be a bit confusing.
- Come with a high-speed serial (COM) port. You don't need to worry about a free port, or the port type—it's built into the card.
- Don't have any indicator lights. While most communications programs (and Windows 95 Dial-Up Networking) provide on-screen send and receive lights, they aren't real time and don't convey as much information as a full set of lights.
- Are cheaper than external modems.

After you have decided which type of modem is best for your needs, speed is the next biggest decision.

Modem Speeds

Different modems "talk" over the phone line at different speeds. Because many manufacturers build modems, they all use standards which define a common language. These standards are usually proposed by a working group of manufacturers and then ratified into an official "standard" by the *ITU-T* (*International Telecommunications Union Telecommunication Standardization Sector*). Here are the common standards for connection speed:

Standard	Speed
V.34	28.8, 33.6Kbps
V.32bis	14.4Kbps
V.32	9.6Kbps
V.22bis	2.4Kbps

These modulation rates are the speeds that a modem will talk to another modem. *Kbps* means how many kilobytes a modem can transfer every second. The higher the number, the faster the modem can transfer data. The V.32bis modulation speed and slower speeds almost always connect at their highest speed, but V.34 modems almost never connect at top speed. Modem manufacturers are promising new modems that connect at 56Kbps under pristine line conditions, and some modems being sold now offer an upgrade to this new 56Kbps speed when its standard is finalized. Because the speed of your modem is directly related to how long you are on the phone line, you should always buy the fastest modem you can afford.

Error Correction

Modems also come with error correction. When a modem is transmitting information with error correction, it can signal to the other modem when it encounters an error. While this may seem like common sense, error correction at the modem level takes the burden of checking every incoming bit for correctness off the PC's CPU and onto the modem's hardware. This speeds up your overall operations. The most common error correction protocol in use today is called *V.42*, and you should make sure that your modem supports it.

Data Compression

Most modems offer data compression. It will be useful to take a closer look at PC and modem communications before we discuss data compression.

If you place a call to your Internet service provider (ISP) with your computer, it is easy to think of this as all one connection. In reality, there are actually three connections. First, there is a connection between your PC and your modem (called the *DTE*), then a connection from your modem to the ISP's modem (the *DCE*), and finally a connection from that modem to the ISP's computer (another *DTE*). Now for the confusing part—each of these three connections can be happening at different speeds. For example, your PC can be talking to your modem at 57.6Kbps, your modem talking to ISP's modem at 28.8Kbps, and the ISP's modem talking to the computer it's connected to at 38.4Kbps. The reason for this speed difference will become clearer when we talk about data compression later.

When modems talk to one another with data compression, they can compress and decompress data on-the-fly. Practically, if you are receiving data from your ISP, the ISP's modem is compressing data and your modem is decompressing it. This is why the computers talk to the modems at a higher speed than the modems talk to each other; data compression allows the computers to send more data (over the DTEs) than the rate of their connection (the DCE).

If your modem is connected to your ISP at 28.8Kbps, it gets data from the ISP's modem at 28.8Kbps, but because decompressed data is bigger than compressed data, it may have actually shipped more than 28.8K worth of data in a second. This is why the DTE (modem-to-computer) speeds are always higher than the DCE (modem-to-modem) speeds. As you can see, this process of data compression can radically speed up your data transmission. The trick with data compression is that it doesn't work when the data you are sending or receiving is already compressed—data like .ZIP, .GIF, or .JPG files. Data compression will have no effect on these files. Enough data on the World Wide Web is compressible that data compression can speed up your Web browsing. The most common standard for data compression is called *V.42bis*, and you should make sure that the modem you are buying supports this standard.

Fax

Almost all modems sold today include fax functionality and basic software. Additional programs like WinFax Pro and Windows 95's Microsoft Fax allow you to send and receive facsimiles. You should make sure that the modem you are buying has send-and-receive fax capabilities.

Plug and Play

Some internal modems can be a pain to install because of all the settings you need to configure. New modems advertised as Plug and Play (PnP) modems make the installation a lot easier by automating those configuration settings. You can read Chapter 6, "Basic Device Configuration and Installation," for detailed information on how PnP works. PnP modems configure themselves with a COM port setting automatically, so you can skip the later section "Configuring an Internal Modem," entirely.

Additional Features and Functionality

Lately, modem manufacturers are pouring more features into their products in an effort to differentiate their modem from the competition. As a result, you can buy a cheap modem that will do everything but make coffee for you. This section offers a brief overview of some of these new features.

Simultaneous Voice and Data

Modems that offer *Digital Simultaneous Voice and Data (DSVD)* or *Voiceview* allow you to talk to the other party over the same phone connection—as long as the modem you are calling supports the same feature. Remember that this feature will only allow you to talk the people your modem is connected to; you can't "still use your phone" to call other people. This feature can be useful if you make data calls to a person who you want to talk to and only have one phone line.

Full-Duplex Speakerphone

This feature gives you the functionality of a regular office speakerphone, only with better sound quality. Most speakerphones operate at *half-duplex*—only one party can speak or be heard at a time. The advanced circuitry in the modem allows for *full-duplex* speakerphone functionality where both parties can talk and be heard at the same time. Some modems come with software that allows you to keep a phonebook or dial numbers from your contact manager.

Answering Machine/Voice Mailboxes

Some modems answer the phone for you and take messages. Many models offer advanced functionality that is far beyond that of a regular answering machine, including multiple voice mailboxes. Your computer could answer the phone with "Press 1 to leave a message for Chris, 2 to leave a message for Linda, 3 to have Chris paged, or 4 to leave a fax." The only disadvantage is that you have to leave your computer on any time you want it to answer the phone, probably 24 hours a day.

Caller ID

For a monthly fee, the phone company sends the phone number of the calling party to your modem along with the first ring. This service is called *Caller ID*, and a modem that supports it will usually include software that pops up a window with the calling number on the screen. Some contact manager applications also support these modems, so they pop up a window with the contact's name and personal information if it has the number on record. You can also purchase a separate display unit from the phone company that displays the calling party's number.

Distinctive Ringing

Another service the phone company can provide is *Distinctive Ringing*. Instead of the expense of an additional phone line, the phone company can assign a second or third number to your existing line. You can tell which number the person called because each has a different ring pattern. The idea is that you can answer the phone appropriately for a business call at home without the expense and hassle of a separate phone line.

Modem manufacturers have provided their modems with the ability to determine distinctive ring patterns. With this feature, you could have a voice number, a fax number, and a data number that would all ring on the phone line the modem is plugged into. If configured in this manner, the modem could answer calls to the data line with a BBS, fax calls with a fax program, and let the voice calls ring through to an answering machine. The downside again is that for most applications, you have to leave your computer on 24 hours a day.

Feature Overview

After reading through all these features, it may be helpful to know that most (probably 80 percent or more) of the modems for sale today offer the same basic features:

V.34 speed, V.42 error correction, V.42bis data compression, and fax. If you have decided on an internal modem, spend the extra time to find one that is PnP; it will be quite a bit easier to install. As a consumer, you can buy knowing that most modems are compatible with one another. The only thing to watch out for are *Winmodems*—modems that are only usable within windows because of the special drivers they come with. They may be a bit cheaper, but offer proprietary solutions, and should be avoided. If all you plan to do is dial into your ISP and maybe send some faxes, all you need is a basic internal PnP modem. If you need some of the fancier features discussed earlier in this section, you have some more involved shopping and comparisons ahead of you.

One requirement all modems share is an *analog phone line*. You can use a phone line already installed in your house as your data line, or have the phone company add a new line. If you are installing a modem for use at work, beware that just because you have a phone on your desk doesn't mean that you have an analog phone line. Many office phone systems operate as digital systems, and modems aren't compatible with these line types. Check with the phone system administrator before you plug into the office phone line. Once you know where you'll plug in the modem, make sure you meet the other items on the following checklist for your modem type.

Configuring a Non-Plug and Play Internal Modem

Welcome to the wonderful and exciting world of jumper setting. If you are installing a modem that isn't PnP, you will have to make manual configuration changes via jumpers to set the COM port. *Jumpers* (see Figure 18.1) are tiny plastic connectors that slide over different sets of pins on the internal modem. When you put the jumper on a set of pins, the jumper *shorts* (provides an electrical path) between the pins and causes a configuration setting to change.

The location and configuration of the jumpers on internal modems differ by manufacturer, and should be well documented in the manuals that come with the modem. If you don't have any jumpers on your modem, you probably have purchased a PnP model and can skip ahead to the next section.

FIG. 18.1
Typical internal modem jumpers.

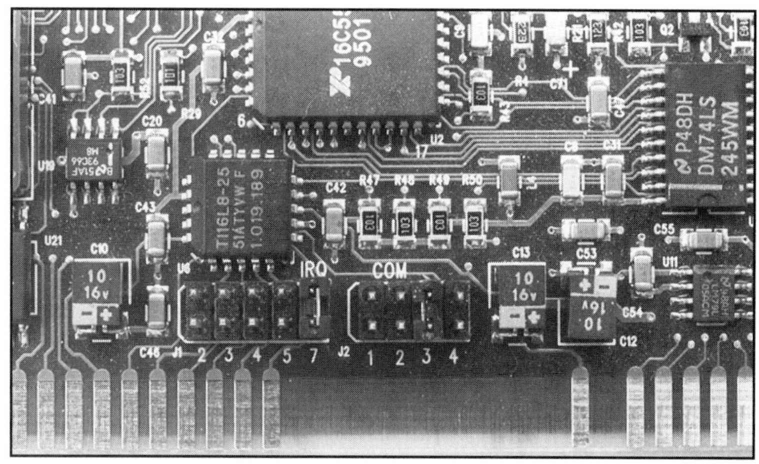

Choosing Which COM Port to Use

The PC talks to your modem through a COM port. This communication requires two parts: an IRQ and an IO address. The *IRQ* is where the modem can "interrupt" the CPU to tell it that it has new data, and the *IO address* is the location that the PC uses to pass data to the modem. The default settings for COM ports in a PC are:

Port	IO Address	IRQ
COM 1	3F8-3FF	4
COM 2	2F8-2FF	3
COM 3	3E8-3EF	4
COM 4	2E8-2EF	3

This is the way IBM chose to implement serial ports back when it designed the IBM PC, and the standard still exists today. One problem about the way the COM ports are arranged is that they share IRQs. Specifically, COM 1 and COM 3 share IRQ 4, and COM 2 and COM 4 share IRQ 3. The only implication of this sharing is that you don't want to put your internal modem on an IRQ that is being used often.

Essentially, if you have a mouse (or any other often-used peripheral) on COM 1 and you put your modem on COM 3, you will have problems because the mouse and the modem will both be fighting for IRQ 4. Assuming your PC has two COM ports (COM 1 and COM 2), the following applies: If you have a frequently used serial device (such as a mouse) on COM 1, put the modem on COM 4. If the mouse is on COM 2, put the modem on COM 3. If, however, your PC has only one COM port (COM 1), it is safe to put your new modem at COM 2.

Figure 18.2 shows a modem being configured via the jumper settings. Once you have configured the modem correctly, you can install it in your PC.

FIG. 18.2
Configuring an internal modem.

Installing an Internal Modem

The hard part of internal (non-PnP) modem installation is the correct configuration of the COM port. Physical installation of an internal modem is the same as any other card, so you can follow the guidelines in Chapter 6, "Basic Device Configuration and Installation."

After you have installed the modem, proceed to the upcoming section "Installing Modem Drivers and Software."

To Install an Internal Modem, You Should Have:

- ☑ An available ISA slot

  Because modems transfer data at relatively slow rates (compared to a hard drive, for instance), the internal modems don't need a bus any wider than a 16-bit ISA slot.

Refer to Chapters 5 and 6 if you don't know how to identify an ISA connector. If you have a PCI motherboard, make sure that the slot you are planning to put the modem in is an ISA slot. For more information on buses and slots, see Chapter 5, "Taking Inventory."

- ☑ A place to put the COM port

  Most computers come with two serial ports (COM1 and COM2), and can handle up to four without special hardware. Installing an internal modem adds a new serial port (usually COM3 or COM4) to your PC. You should know what COM ports your PC has so that you can configure the modem to use the correct spot.

- ☑ What is attached to your existing COM ports

  You should know what devices use your existing COM ports before installing a new modem. The reason for this becomes clear in the next section, but for now, write down a list of which devices are using each port.

Installing an External Modem

After you have the correct cable, installing the modem is pretty straightforward. Connect the modem to the COM port on the back of your PC with the cable (see Figure 18.3).

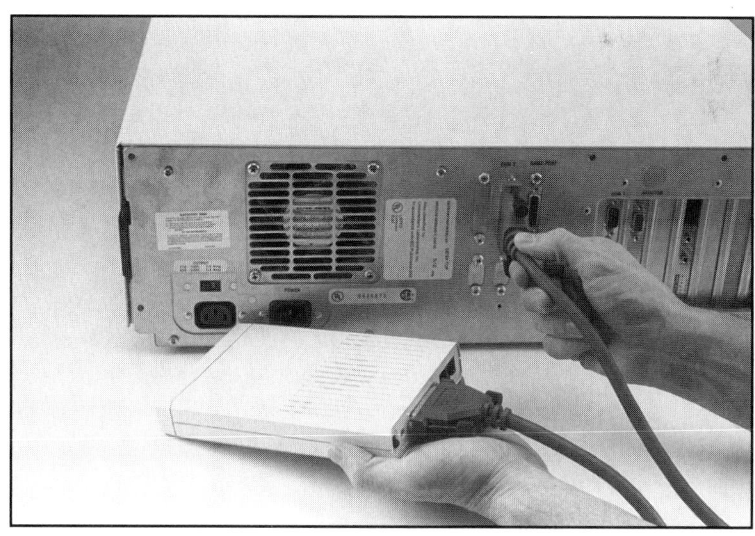

FIG. 18.3
An external modem connected to a PC.

You also need to plug the external modem into a power plug and then plug the phone line into the modem. There are usually two jacks on the back of an external modem: One is to a connected modem to the phone line, and the other is for an extension phone. This extension phone can be used to place calls anytime the modem isn't online.

Once you turn on the modem, at least one of the indicator lights turns on. Here's a quick overview of some common external modem indicators:

- *CD (Carrier Detect)*. The CD light is the most important indicator on your modem. When this light is on, the modem is connected to another modem. If a connection is dropped, you see this light turn off even before your computer tells you that it "lost carrier."
- *SD/RD (Send Data/Receive Data)*. These lights should be self-explanatory. These two lights indicate that the modem is sending or receiving data from the modem it is connected to. If you are performing a file transfer and one of the lights is on almost all the time, you are getting a good transfer rate. If the light is off for a good period of time or is only on intermittently during a file transfer, you are having a less than optimal transmission.
- *AA (Auto Answer)*. If the modem is configured (by your communications software) to answer the phone anytime it rings, this light is on. Note that if this light is not on, the modem can still answer the phone; a communications program can look for a "RING" signal from the modem and tell it to pick up the call.
- *ARQ (Error Correction)*. When the modem is connected with error correction, this light is on. If the modem senses an error, this light flashes while the modem retransmits the affected data.
- *TR (Data Terminal Ready)*. This light is on when the modem sees a connection to your PC.
- *CS (Clear to Send)*. If you have a "full-flow" cable, your computer can tell the modem if it is able to accept incoming data. This indicator tells you that the modem has received this indicator from the computer. Under normal conditions, this light should always be on. If the computer becomes extremely busy, or if you aren't using a high-speed (16550 AFN) UART, the computer may tell the modem to stop sending information until it can catch up.

Before Installing an External Modem, You Need:

☑ A free high-speed serial (COM) port

An external modem attaches to the computer via a COM port on your computer. For just about any modem you can buy today, a high-speed UART (a 16550 AFN or 16650) is required. This chapter won't go into detail about the serial ports themselves, but Chapter 17, "I/O Adapters and System Ports," covers them in detail. You need to know how many pins your COM port has (9- or 25-pin) before you can buy the next item, the cable. Figure 18.4 shows the type and labeling of the ports you are looking for.

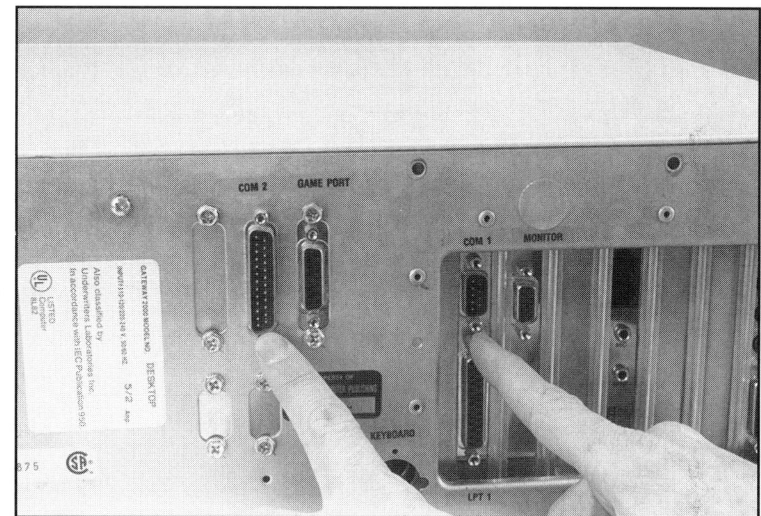

FIG. 18.4
Finding serial (COM) ports.

☑ A "Full-Flow" serial cable

You need to purchase a cable to connect the modem to the PC that fits the ports you are using. Most external modems have a 25-pin COM port, so that side of the cable should be easy. The size of the other side depends on how many pins the COM port on your computer has. You need to take a look at the port you plan on plugging the modem into to see if it has 9 or 25 pins, then buy an appropriate cable. Also, you should make sure the cable you buy is *Full-Flow*—meaning that all pins are connected. Some cheaper cables will be missing the connections that are required for hardware flow control.

Installing the Modem Drivers and Software

Once you have installed the modem, turn on the PC. If you are using Windows 95, the operating system detects that a new modem has been added to the system, and tries to install drivers if it can identify the modem correctly. If it can't find drivers for the modem, it asks for you to provide a disk from the manufacturer. Once you have gotten the drivers installed, you are ready to use communications software to connect to another computer or the Internet. Windows 95 comes with a terminal program called HyperTerminal that allows you to dial into BBSes. You can also use Windows 95 to connect to the Internet; see Chapter 20, "Making Internet Connections," to learn more about how to configure the connection.

If you are using Windows 3.1, you need to load software like Trumpet WinSock to connect to the Internet. Your ISP will often have software available to connect to the Internet. If you want to call online services like bulletin board systems (BBSes), you can try the Windows Terminal program. A more full-featured communications package like Procomm for Windows will probably be more suitable for using BBS systems.

If you are using America Online (AOL), CompuServe (CIS), or Prodigy, you need to load the software they provide to access their services. Each of their programs allow you to select your new modem as a communications device.

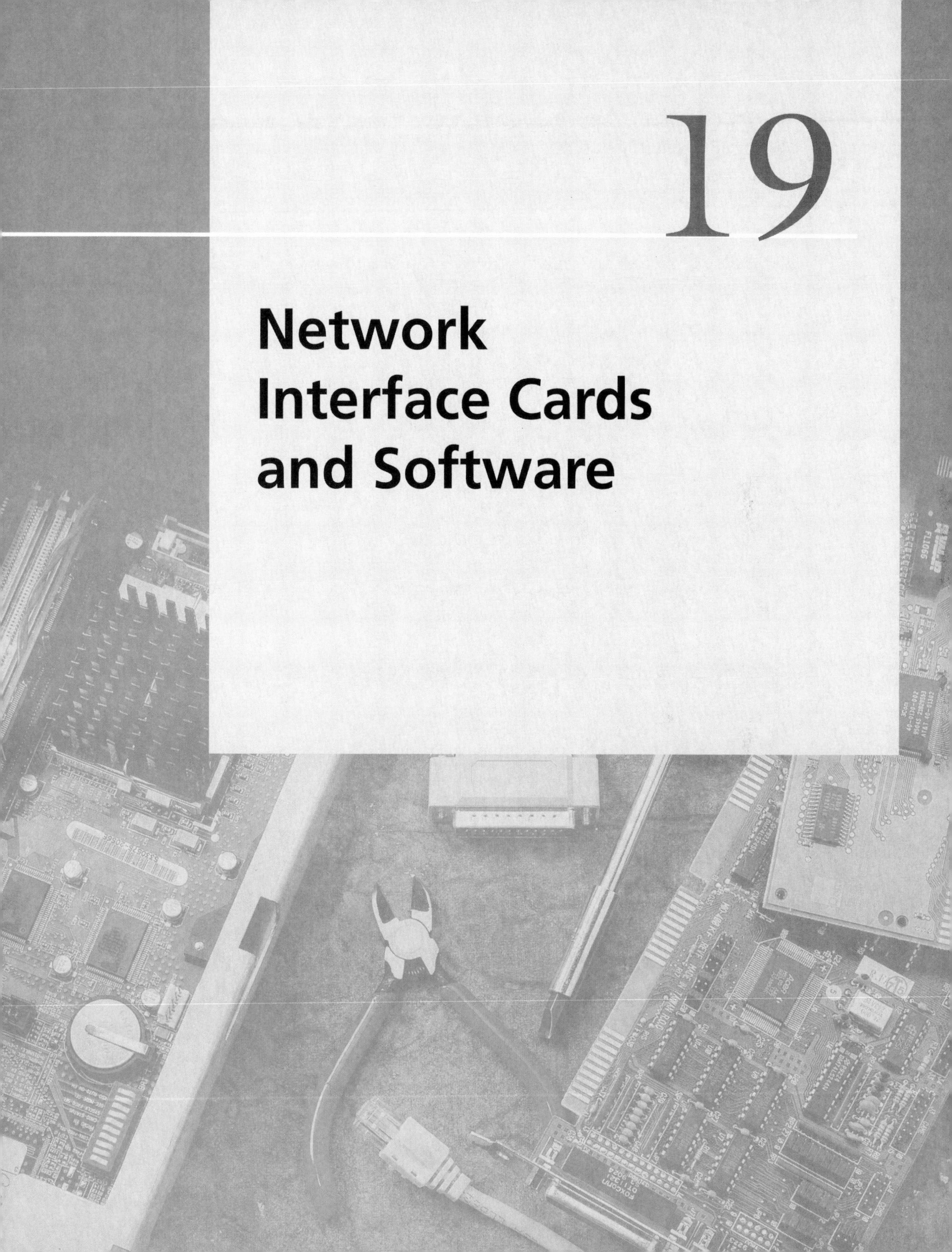

19

Network Interface Cards and Software

If your family of computers has grown to more than one, sharing the data and printers between these computers would be a good step. This decision is the first step in creating your own network. In a network, all computers can have access to the files on the other computers and can share other devices such as printers and CD-ROM drives.

This chapter concentrates on the following topics for setting up a network in your home or small office:

- Understanding network concepts
- Overview of network hardware
- Installing and configuring a network interface card
- Installing network drivers and protocols

This chapter looks at setting up simple networks for Windows 95 and Windows for Workgroups using The Microsoft Network software included with the Windows software. After completing these steps, you will have a network up and running, share your data with the other systems, and share access to printers.

NOTE Unless otherwise stated, assume that you are working in Windows 95.

Understanding Network Concepts

Networks are designed as a means to eliminate the use of *sneaker nets.* In the early 1980s, sneaker nets were the outcome of having to copy files onto floppy disks and taking the disks to another computer to use the files.

However, a network can also extend the use of your office resources. Economics do not always allow each computer in a home to have a letter-quality printer, such as a laserjet. Networked computers can send output across the network to any desired printer.

In addition, networking software provides different levels of security, allaying concerns about access to sensitive data on specific systems or to specific users. Access can be limited to disk, directories or folders, files, by user group, by user, and so forth. The home office or small business can extend the capabilities of a group of computers with the right use of networking.

Several types of network hardware are commonly in use in business and home settings. The most common are Ethernet and Token Ring in large settings, and Ethernet for the small or home business.

The primary difference between Ethernet and Token Ring is how the data is passed between workstations (that is, your individual computer) and what type of cabling is used. If you are using an Ethernet setup, you use either 10Base-T or coaxial cabling in a star or straight backbone layout, respectively.

A *Token Ring layout* uses a complete ring of wiring. Token Ring networks are usually seen in companies with an investment in IBM mainframe or other IBM-dedicated systems. Because of the unsuitability of Token Ring for home and small business use, this chapter does not cover Token Ring networks.

Overview of Network Hardware

When you are writing your checklist of hardware to purchase for your network, remember that like anything in computers, there is always a cable that the sales person forgot. In this section, I discuss the required equipment to create a network for a home office.

The Required Equipment Includes:

- ☑ Network interface cards (NIC)
- ☑ A hub if you are using 10Base-T NICs
- ☑ T-connectors and terminators if you are installing Thinnet NICs
- ☑ Unshielded twisted-pair (UTP) or Thinnet coaxial cable for a 10Base-T or Ethernet network, respectively

While you are looking at a range of networking solutions, the concentration will be on an Ethernet-based network.

Network Interface Cards

A *network interface card (NIC)* is the add-in card that you put in a slot in your desktop system, in a PC Card (PCMCIA) socket in your laptop, or possibly attach through a parallel port. The NIC takes the data to be sent, breaks it into packets, transmits it to the destination system, and puts the packets back into the original file or data structure. Along the way, the *firmware* (instructions in the cards) performs error-checking to detect data loss during the transmission to guarantee the arrival of the right information.

The type of NIC that you purchase depends upon two main factors:

- What kind of network you want to build
- What type of cabling you want to use

As already mentioned, there are two main types of networks—Ethernet and Token Ring—with Ethernet the more common and easier to build. Token Ring uses only one type of cabling, but Ethernet has a variety of cabling options.

Most common in Ethernet networks are *10Base-T* and *coaxial*, also known as *10Base-2*. A 10Base-T wiring system uses telephone-type wires and connectors, and requires a hub to connect all of the PCs together. *Thinnet*, also referred to as *Thin Ethernet*, is a cable similar to your TV cable running directly from PC to PC.

Hubs

In a network layout using 10Base-T wiring, all of the systems are connected with a device called a *hub*. The hub handles the "traffic" across the network, passing the packets of data from PC to PC. You can use some hubs to make a transition from a 10Base-T network to a 10Base-2 (coaxial cable), minimizing the impact of changing from one wiring to another.

Cabling

The type of Ethernet cabling you use determines how you lay out the cable. With *coaxial cable* (this cable looks like your TV cable), the cable is laid out as a continuous cable, also known as a *backbone*. T-connectors are installed for each workstation, and the two ends of the cable have terminators installed.

An Ethernet network based on 10Base-T cabling is laid out like a star. The individual runs of the twisted-pair wire from the hub to the individual PCs make the layout look like a star or starfish.

Other Network Interface Hardware

There are two other pieces of hardware that you may need for a network. A *transceiver* may be used on Ethernet adapters equipped with a DB15 AUI connector. *AUI transceivers* can be purchased for use with UTP or coaxial cabling. These are typically used, if your adapter has one, when you move your system to a new network that is based on a different system.

Internal NICs can come with any combination of connectors. You can get a card with just an RJ45 or just a BNC, maybe an RJ45 and AUI or BNC and AUI, or possibly all three. The more flexibility you look for, the greater the initial cost.

If you purchased a PCMCIA network interface, you need to be sure that it has a dongle for the right type of cable system. Some PC cards provide you with two different cables—10Base-T and Thinnet. Because laptops are very portable machines, you may find yourself needing both types of dongles. Leave one in the office, and use the second at home.

Installing a Network Interface Card (Putting NIC in PC)

It is important to refer to the section in this chapter which pertains to your type of NIC: internal, PCMCIA (also called PC Card), or external. The internal NICs may require that you set jumpers on the cards before installing them in systems, but PCMCIA interfaces and external NICs use software configuration to set the interrupts.

Before Installing Your NIC, You Need to Know:

- ☑ What IRQs are already in use on your system?
- ☑ What IRQs and memory addresses will the NICs use?
- ☑ Do you have all the necessary cables?
- ☑ Do you need or have T-connectors and terminators, transceivers, or a hub?

What to Check First

There are two items that you need to check before you pick up a screwdriver:

- Your existing equipment for its hardware setup
- What type of cabling you are using (to determine what type of NIC to buy)

Use the MSD.EXE or MSINFO.EXE, a couple of Microsoft diagnostics programs provided with Windows, to check your equipment for hardware interrupt (IRQ) settings and memory address exclusions.

Setting Jumpers on Internal NICs

After getting a list of the IRQs already in use, check the manual for your NIC to see what IRQs it can be set to use. Then compare the in-use IRQ list to the following list to identify an IRQ that you can use. The following table provides a list of the typical IRQ settings:

Interrupt Request	Used By
IRQ 0	Internal Timer*
IRQ 1	Keyboard*
IRQ 2	Video adapter or network interface card
IRQ 3	COM2: and COM4:
IRQ 4	COM1: and COM3:
IRQ 5	LPT2:
IRQ 6	Floppy drive*
IRQ 7	LPT1:
IRQ 8	Real-time clock*
IRQ 9	Video or network adapter
IRQ 10	Unassigned
IRQ 11	Unassigned
IRQ 12	Unassigned

Interrupt Request	Used By
IRQ 13	Numeric coprocessor
IRQ 14	Hard drive controller
IRQ 15	Unassigned

**IRQ cannot be reassigned*

Interrupts 2, 3, 4, and 7 are used by system devices such as the parallel and serial ports, and NICs. The NIC requires only one IRQ and memory address.

You must first locate any jumpers on the NIC and identify what they control. There may be jumpers that set the network card to boot to the network from an optional ROM chip set. Jumpers may be used to change the NIC setup from a hardware configuration to a software-configurable mode.

Locate the jumpers for the IRQ setting. When a bridge is made with a jumper between two adjacent posts, the jumper is said to be ON. When the jumper is removed, it is OFF.

When you want to use IRQ 11 for the NIC, place a jumper across the IRQ 11 posts and make sure that the other IRQ jumpers (for this feature) are removed.

Unless you are using a ROM chip to boot, these are the only jumpers that you will probably need to set.

Installing an Internal NIC in Your PC

Once you have set any jumpers, you can put the card in your computer. When you are installing an internal NIC, the first thing to look for in the computer case is the right type of slot for your NIC.

If your card is 16-bit, use a standard 16-bit slot. If you have a PCI card, locate an open PCI slot. Network cards are available for installing in 8-bit ISA, 16-bit ISA (see Figure 19.1), 32-bit EISA, 32-bit MCA (Microchannel), and 32-bit PCI slots.

NOTE While your NIC card may be used with an 8-bit slot, installing it in a 16-bit slot gives you a greater selection of hardware settings. If you encounter hardware conflicts while using an 8-bit slot, change to a 16-bit slot and rerun your configuration software.

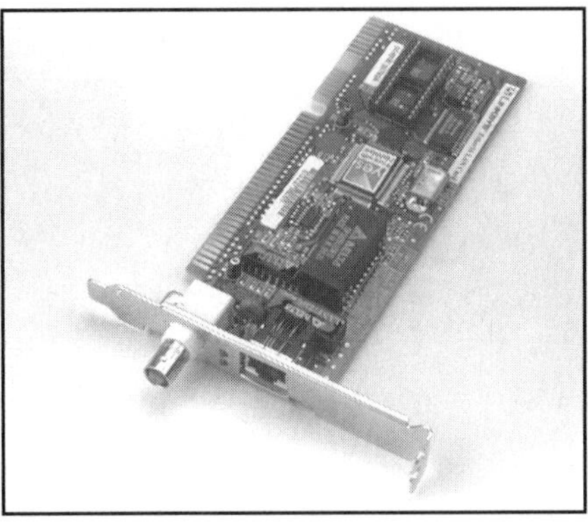

FIG. 19.1
An Ethernet network interface card (NIC) with a 10Base-T RJ45 connector above a 10Base-2 BNC connector.

Maneuver the card so that the mounting bracket drops into the alignment slot in the back of the expansion slot. Press firmly on the upper edge of the card, possibly rocking the card from back to front, to seat it in the edge connector on the motherboard (see Figure 19.2).

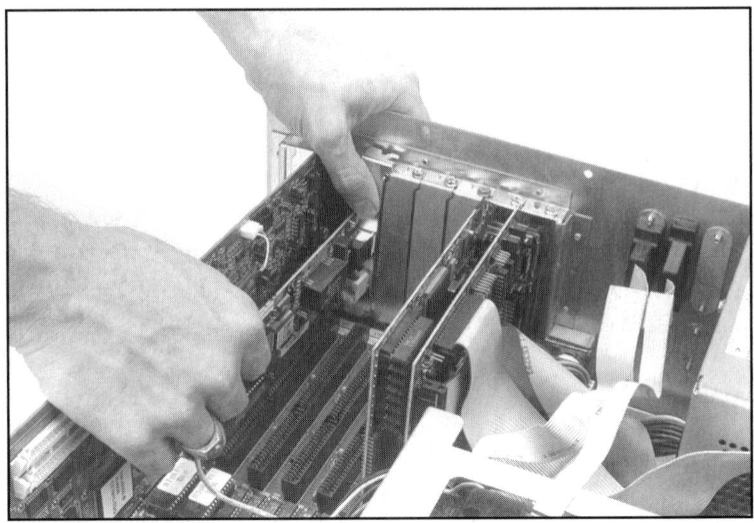

FIG. 19.2
Insert the network adapter into an expansion slot with firm, even pressure.

When the mounting bracket is completely seated, screw in the retaining screw to secure the card.

NOTE Test the new equipment before closing your computer case, especially if this is the first time you have added a peripheral. Unless you have very little work space to use temporarily, leave the case open until you are sure of the new configuration.

Installing a PCMCIA or External Interface

There are two other types of network interfaces—*PCMCIA cards* and *external adapters*. The PCMCIA adapters (also referred to as *PC Cards*) are designed primarily for use with laptops or other systems equipped with a PCMCIA Type II slot.

PCMCIA adapters use either a pop-out jack or a dongle to connect to the network. A *dongle* is a cable that dangles from your PC Card and makes a connection with another device. The dongles usually come with a jack for either 10Base-T or Thinnet wiring.

An external adapter typically is a small box attached to a parallel port on your computer system. They can be used with desktop computers or laptops and other portables. External network interface adapters usually require an external power supply (using up yet another outlet on your powerbar). You can purchase external adapters for either type of cabling system.

Connecting to the Network Cabling

An Ethernet-based layout requires that you run a single, continuous backbone of Thin or Thick Ethernet cable. Each end of the backbone has a terminator attached and workstations are attached along the backbone with T-connectors.

The horizontal, straight-through leg at the top of the T-connector is put in the length of the cable to attach the computers (see Figure 19.3). The vertical leg of the T is connected to or disconnected from the BNC connector of the network interface. All interfaces designed for Thinnet have a BNC, twist-on connector.

> **CAUTION** If you are removing a computer from a Thinnet-cabled network, disconnect the short, vertical leg of the T-connector from the network card on the computer. Do not disconnect either of the legs of the straight-through section of the T-connector.

It is necessary to put a terminator on each end of the backbone on the straight-through legs of the last T-connectors (see Figure 19.4). The T can be attached to an adapter or laid out for future expansion.

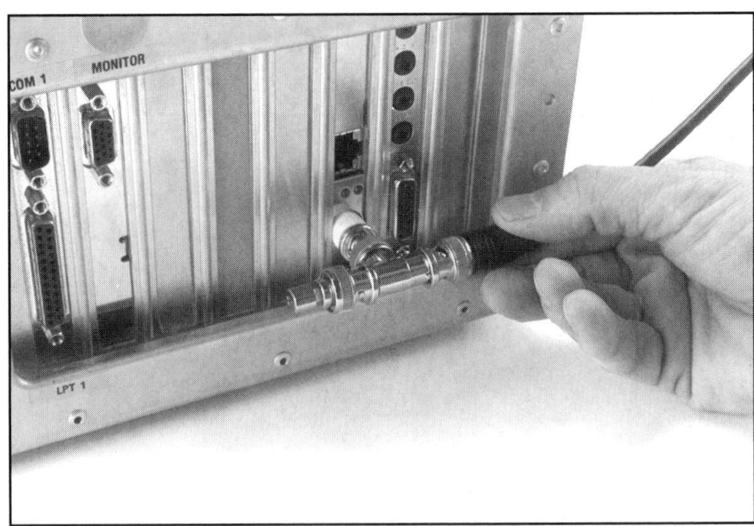

FIG. 19.3
Attach the coaxial cable to the second leg of the straight-through section of the T-connector.

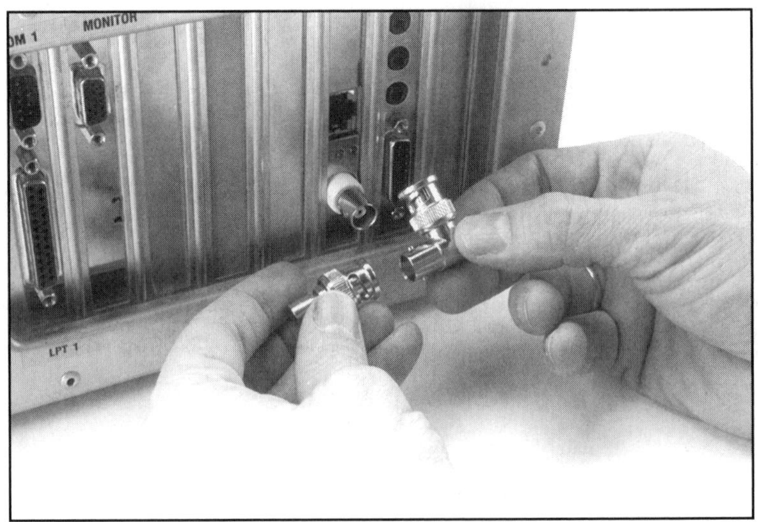

FIG. 19.4
Place the terminator on one end of the straight-through leg of the T-connector.

The downside of a Thinnet, 10Base-2, layout is that network will crash if you break the backbone. That is why it is necessary to disconnect the single, short leg of the T-connector from the adapter, not either of the straight-through connectors making the top of the T (see Figure 19.5). Also, the entire cable backbone has to go to the BNC connector of your NIC. You cannot use any extension cables between the short leg of the T-connector and BNC connector.

The up side to a network based on Thinnet is that all you need for your network are NIC adapters and a cable. You could set up a two-machine network with a hardware cost less than $100.

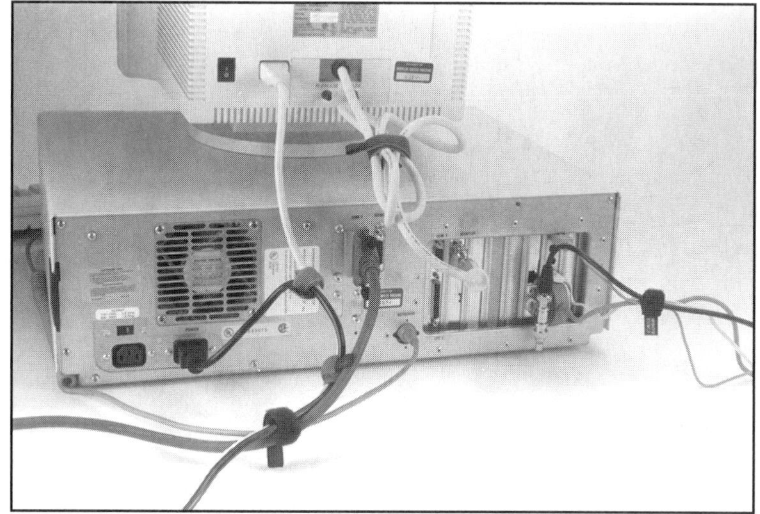

FIG. 19.5
A Thinnet, or 10Base-2, network with a terminator on the end of the cable run.

A *10Base-T network* is based on a star topology—a hub in the center with network cables running out to each workstation. The cable used in a 10Base-T layout is called *Unshielded Twisted-Pair (UTP)*. The connectors are standard telephone RJ45 jacks (see Figure 19.6). Even though the jacks handle eight wires and most cables are four pairs, only two of the pairs of wires in UTP are used. The pairs of wires in the sheath are twisted throughout their run as part of their electrical design to provide shielding.

A down side of a 10Base-T network is that you must also have a hub that is the backbone for its segment and handles the passing of the data between the workstations. Hubs come with any number of ports and can be expanded to handle more workstations and other networked devices by adding more hubs to the "chain."

The up side is that it is easier to add and remove computers from the network without crashing the network. You just unplug the cable from the computer or the hub. Also, you get a very "clean" connection. All you need from the hub to the computer is a single cord.

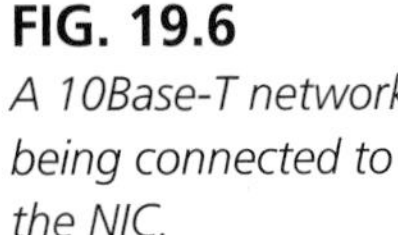

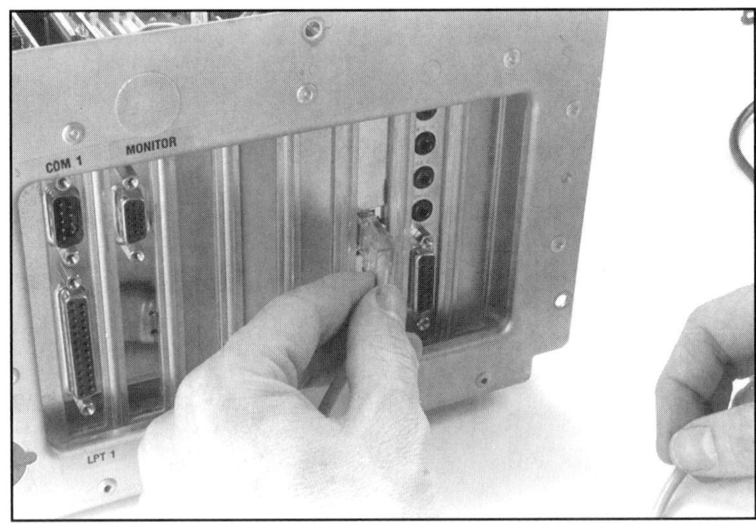

FIG. 19.6
A 10Base-T network being connected to the NIC.

The tools and materials, cable, and connectors, are readily available at electronics stores, and the cables are not difficult to put together. However, unless you are going to run the cable in a conduit, premade cables of all lengths are common through catalogs and at the same electronics stores and are easier to use—no assembly required.

Hubs and Bridges

Hubs are used to control the interchange of network data, creating a concentration, junction, or hub. Hubs are the most commonly purchased devices aside from the cabling and NICs in networks.

A *bridge* is a device between two independent networks that connects the two together while restricting the exchange of data. The bridge adds another layer of security in network environments as well as providing a means to connect networks. These are not very common in small applications.

It is important to match the speed of the hub to that of the network interfaces in use. Two speeds are in common use in 1997: 10mps and 100mps. 10mps interface equipment transmits at a maximum of 10M/sec, and 100mps devices can transmit at 10 times that speed.

If you have a 10mps hub and want to use 100mps cards, you may not benefit from the increased throughput speed of the 100mps cards. You will benefit as much as possible if you have a 100mps hub with any combination of 100mps and 10mps interfaces. Systems talking to other similarly equipped systems will communicate at the fastest speed; therefore, a system with all 100mps interfaces will work the fastest.

Hubs can be specifically for one type of cabling, such as all 10Base-T, or can connect two different cables sets, usually a 10Base-T hub with a coax connector for tying two cable systems together in an Ethernet configuration.

Configuring a Network Interface Card

Once you have installed the network card in the computer, you still have to complete the configuration of the card and the software. If you did not have any jumpers or switches to set on the NIC or set jumper to software-configurable, you need to complete the next step for configuring the network card through software.

The software configuration program that you use depends upon the operating system that you have. Windows 95 finds and automatically sets most modern NICs. Otherwise, you need to run the manufacturer's configuration program.

Windows 95 Configuration

If the network interface you have installed is Plug and Play (PnP) compatible, Windows 95 automatically detects and sets up your card. It detects the card, and checks the settings on any existing devices; the New Hardware Found Wizard sets the IRQ, memory, and I/O address on the card.

The wizard then installs the necessary software to support the NIC, modifies the CONFIG.SYS file and any necessary .INI files, and prompts you to restart your computer.

If your card is not PnP but is software-configurable, use the Add New Hardware Wizard in the Control Panel folder to configure and install the network drivers. The Add New Hardware Wizard is used to set up the network drivers for a non-PnP NIC with manually set jumpers, but the interrupts and other jumper settings cannot be changed through software.

After running the wizard, if the network card does not work, go to the Control Panel and click the System icon. Click the Device Manager tab in the System Properties dialog box. When you click the plus icon to the left of Network Adapters, a list of installed adapters is displayed.

NOTE If your network card is not displayed in the Network Adapter list, close the dialog box and shut down Windows. When you have turned off your computer, check your earlier list of IRQs and change to an alternate. Then restart your computer and Windows.

Highlight the name of your network card in the list and click the Properties button. In the adapter Properties dialog box, click the Resources tab.

To change one of the settings, highlight to setting and click the Change Setting button. In the Edit dialog box, change the setting by clicking the Value spinner arrows. You can see if there are any devices that conflict with your setting while you increment the setting. If there is a conflict, the conflicting device is named in the Conflict Information box at the bottom of the dialog box.

If any changes need to be made to the CONFIG.SYS file and any .INI files, they are made by the wizard.

Windows 95, used with PnP-compatible devices, is one of the easiest ways to fly. The old days of setting jumpers and switches, then configuring the CONFIG.SYS, and finally determining what network support software to install, are over.

Configuring DOS/Windows 3.x

If you are using the Windows or Windows for Workgroups 3.x, it is necessary to run the manufacturer's configuration software to set the IRQ, memory address, and I/O address on a software-configurable adapter. Some of the programs also edit the CONFIG.SYS file for you, but you still need to run the network configuration for the version of Windows you are using.

In the configuration program, you need to set the IRQ, memory address, and *I/O address*, a set of addresses for the hardware to communicate and manage itself. Some of the advanced programs tell you if there is a potential address conflict, but most do not give any warning. Typically, set the IRQ to 10 or 11. The memory address and I/O address can be reset if there is a conflict with other devices, but the IRQ settings are usually the source of any conflict.

If your software does not make the necessary change to the CONFIG.SYS file, you need to use your editor to make the change to the text file. The most common modification is to the EMM386 statement, excluding the memory range of the network card memory. This is the information returned in the memory address section of your configuration. The change might read like this:

```
DEVICE=C:\WIN95\EMM386.EXE NOEMS X=D000-D100 X=D400-D900
```

After running the configuration software from DOS, start Windows. In Windows, you need to go to the Main group and select Windows Setup. Choose Options, Change System Settings to open the Change System Settings dialog box. Open the Network drop-down list box and select Microsoft Network (or 100% Compatible).

Windows prompts you to insert Disk 1, copying the Microsoft Network drivers to your hard drive, and then suggests that you restart Windows for the drivers to be loaded. Then, proceed with the steps in the "Installing Network Drivers and Protocols" section for configuring your network and adapter.

Installing Network Drivers and Protocols

The final step in this process is to set up the network and adapter to work together. As you read earlier, PnP cards installed with Windows 95 install all of the basic stuff for you. However, you may still need to add a different protocol to those supported by your network software.

Network drivers are the program extensions which tell Windows (or your network program if you are not in a Windows environment) how to "talk" to the network adapter. Network protocols are standard data-handling methods specified by the network companies.

Setting Up System Software Drivers

When you configure the network software, you are telling it what kind of interface card you are using on the current workstation. The driver that is loaded instructs the network software in how the interface communicates with the computer's bus.

Windows 95 automatically senses the NIC and loads the interface drivers. Because the interface cards do not all work the same, it is also necessary for Windows to load the appropriate protocol files for the adapter. If Windows does not have the drivers and other support files in its shipped database, the drivers are available from the vendor. If you do not have the shipped disk of software, you can order them from the vendor or download them from forums on most online service providers.

If the card is not PnP, you must run the network setup program. In Windows 95:

1. Open the Control Panel.
2. Select the Add New Hardware Wizard to set up the card.
3. Select Networks from the Control Panel to install the network software after setting up the NIC in the Add New Hardware Wizard.
4. Check the Configuration list to ensure that the NIC drivers are loaded and the desired protocols are installed (see Figure 19.7). IPX/SPX and TCP/IP are the most commonly used protocols.

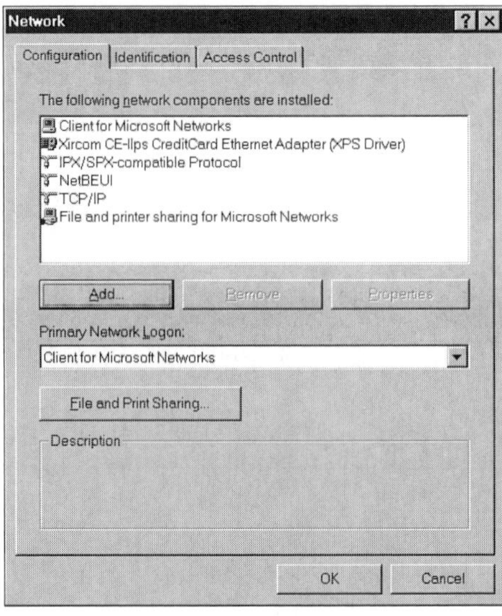

FIG. 19.7
Windows 95 Network Control Panel is opened to Configuration to show installed network adapter and protocols.

5. Click the Add button in the Network dialog box if either protocol is not installed. The Select Network Component Type dialog box is opened.
6. Click the Add button with Protocol highlighted to open the Select Network Protocol dialog box.

7. Select the software manufacturer whose protocol driver you want to load from the Manufacturers list. Then select the protocol from the Protocol list and click the OK button.
8. Windows returns you to the Network dialog box. If you click the OK button, the protocol drivers will be installed. Click the Cancel button to throw away any undesired changes.

Windows for Workgroups uses different steps for setting up the network and network adapters:

1. Start Windows for Workgroups and open the Main group. From the Main group, double-click the Windows Setup icon.
2. Choose Option, Change Network Settings on the Windows Setup menu bar. The Network Setup dialog box is displayed with three groups with buttons: Networks, Sharing, and Drivers.
3. It is necessary to specify the type of network software you are setting up your workstation to use. Click the Networks button to open the Networks dialog box. If you want to add Microsoft Windows Network with or without another network defined, click the Install Microsoft Windows Network radio button and click the OK button.
4. Click the Drivers button to open the Network Drivers dialog box when you are returned to the Setup window. This box is used to select an adapter and then the protocols to install. Click the Add Adapter button to open the Add Network Adapter dialog box.
5. Windows provides a Detect Wizard that you can use at this point to find your network card. Click the Detect button to start this wizard and click Yes to start the automatic detection of your NIC. When the NIC has been found, you are notified with a Windows Setup dialog box. Click the Yes button to accept the NIC and install the driver.

   When you have selected your card and closed the window, you are prompted to pick the IRQ setting. This is the setting you picked when you ran the NIC configuration program or set jumpers.
6. In the NIC setup dialog box which is now displayed, set the Interrupt Value in the Value drop-down list box and click OK. You are returned to the Network Drivers dialog box where the NIC is displayed with the default protocol drivers—Novell NE2000 with Microsoft NetBEUI and IPX/SPX Compatible Transport with NetBIOS, for example.

7. Click the Add Protocol button and select any additional protocols you want to install, such as TCP/IP. After selecting the desired protocol, click OK to return to the Network Drivers dialog box.
8. Click Close to accept all the changes or additions and return to the Network Setup dialog box.
9. Click the Sharing button to open the Sharing dialog box where you set the options to share files and printers with other people on your network.
10. Place a check mark in the I Want to Be Able to Give Others Access to My Files check box to enable file sharing. Place a check mark in the I Want to Be Able to Allow Others to Print to My Printer(s) check box to enable printer sharing. Click OK to return to the Network Setup dialog box.
11. Click OK to close the Network Setup dialog box and complete the network setup in the Microsoft Windows Network Names dialog box.
12. Type a single word name in the User Name text field, accept Workgroup or enter a new name in the Workgroup combo box, and type a name to identify your computer (this will appear in network dialog boxes to identify you) in the Computer Name text field. Click OK to complete the setup.
13. You are prompted to put Windows Setup disks in your computer as the files are copied to your system.
14. Restart your system and Windows for Workgroups when prompted.

When you return to Windows, you see a new group in the Program Manager—Networks. You make further changes to the Network and customize Mail, Remote Access, Chat, and other network functions from the Network group. A Network control is added to the Windows Control Panel.

NOTE It is necessary to set Sharing in the Network dialog box to Share Files or Printers. You limit access to files through the File Manager and sharing of printer through the Print Manager.

Selecting Network Protocol

Network protocols are different layers of programs which each handle data in their specific modes. The primary two protocols used with Ethernet networks are IPX and TCP/IP.

Internetwork Packet eXchange (IPX) protocol is the most common protocol used with Microsoft and Novell networks. *IPX/SPX (Sequenced Packet eXchange)* is installed by default by both network setup programs.

Transmission Control Protocol/Internet Protocol (TCP/IP) is a packet routing protocol to route data across multiple servers, such as the Internet. If you intend to go on the Internet, install TCP/IP.

NOTE If you are going to create a guest-to-host network using Microsoft's Direct Cable Connection Wizard, you must have TCP/IP protocol loaded. Open the Control Panel and use the Network control to install TCP/IP if it is not configured.

TCP/IP is a multilayered protocol stack with the ability to connect a long list of different operating systems. This makes it a perfect choice for the Internet.

Sharing Files and Printers

Installing the cards, cables, and other parts and configuring the software is one of the last steps in the process of networking your computers for file and printer sharing. You must also define on each computer what areas or specific files are intended to be shared with others. At the same time, you specify whether to let other users use printers on other workstations.

The definition of sharing is done in two steps:

1. Click the Sharing button (in Windows for Workgroups) or the File and Print Sharing button (in Windows 95) in the Network Setup dialog box. In the Sharing dialog boxes, click the Files check box to enable File Sharing and the Print check box to enable Printer Sharing (see Figure 19.8). Now close all of the dialog boxes and restart your system and Windows.
2. Open the File Manager, highlight a directory or file, and choose Disk, Share As.
3. In the Share Directory/File dialog box, enter a name to appear in the other users' network directories and set the Access Type to Read-Only, Full, or Depends on Password to limit the type of access. Enter any desired password (for access over the network) in the Read-Only Password text field or the Full Access Password field, according to the Access Type.
4. File or directory sharing is turned off in the File Manager by highlighting the file or directory and by choosing Disk, Stop Sharing.

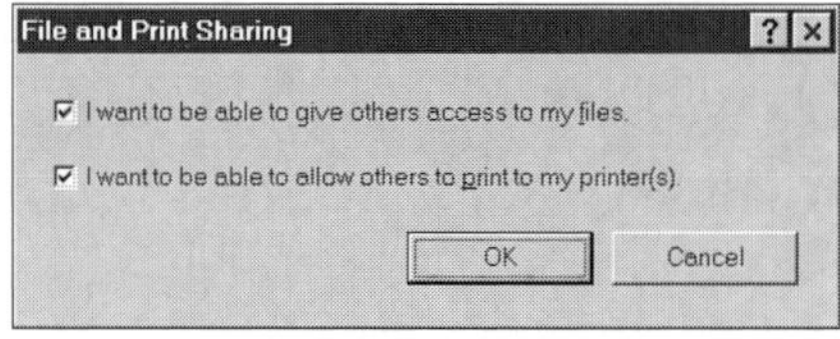

FIG. 19.8
Windows 95 File and Print Sharing dialog box opened in the Network control panel with file and printer sharing enabled.

5. Open the Print Manager to set sharing for printers. Highlight the desired printer on your system, and choose Printer, Share Printer As.
6. In the Share Printer dialog box, select the printer to be shared in the Printer drop-down list box. Enter a name to identify the printer in the other users' Print Managers in the Share As text field. You enter any desired password (for access over the network) in the Password text field.
7. Printer sharing is turned off in the Print Manager by highlighting the printer, selecting Printer and then selecting Stop Sharing Printer. Click OK in the Stop Sharing Printer dialog box to disable the ability of others to access the specified printer over your network.

To finish setting up file/folder and printer sharing in Windows 95:

1. Open the Windows Explorer, highlight a folder or file, and choose File, Sharing.
2. In the File/Folder Properties dialog box, click the Shared As option button. Type a name to appear in the other users' network directories in the Share Name text field and set the Access Type to Read-Only, Full, or Depends on Password to limit the type of access (see Figure 19.9). Enter any desired password (for access over the network) in the Read-Only Password text field or the Full Access Password field, according to the Access Type.
3. File or directory sharing is turned off in the Explorer by highlighting the file or folder and choosing File, Sharing, Not Shared.
4. Open the Printer control in the Control Panel to set sharing for printers. Highlight the desired printer on your system, and choose File, Sharing.
5. In the Printer Properties dialog box, click the Sharing tab to bring it to the front. Enter a name to identify the printer in the other users' Print Managers in the Share Name text field. You enter any desired password (for access over the network) in the Password text field.

6. Printer sharing is turned off in the Printer control by highlighting the printer and choosing File, Sharing, Not Shared. The printer does not appear in the Print Manager list of other users.

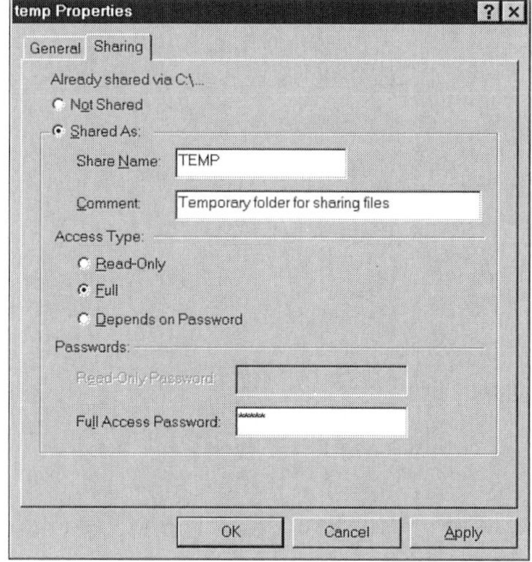

FIG. 19.9 *The Windows 95 Properties dialog box is opened with the Shared As option enabled for the folder named Temp.*

Networking also lets you share other types of devices. CD-ROM players can be shared between systems by setting file sharing for the drive in the File Manager, just as you share a directory.

Finally, You Are Networking

Now that you have completed the physical installation of the network hardware and configured all of the software, be sure to restart your computer and Windows to load the drivers.

You should now be able to turn on all of your networked computers and share files and printers between any of the workstations.

NOTE You can also mix non-Windows computers such as Macintosh systems with the right software. Novell NetWare supports using computers running DOS, Windows, Macintosh, and OS/2 operating systems. With this type of flexibility, you can support the needs of your home-based business and those of your school-age family across a variety hardware.

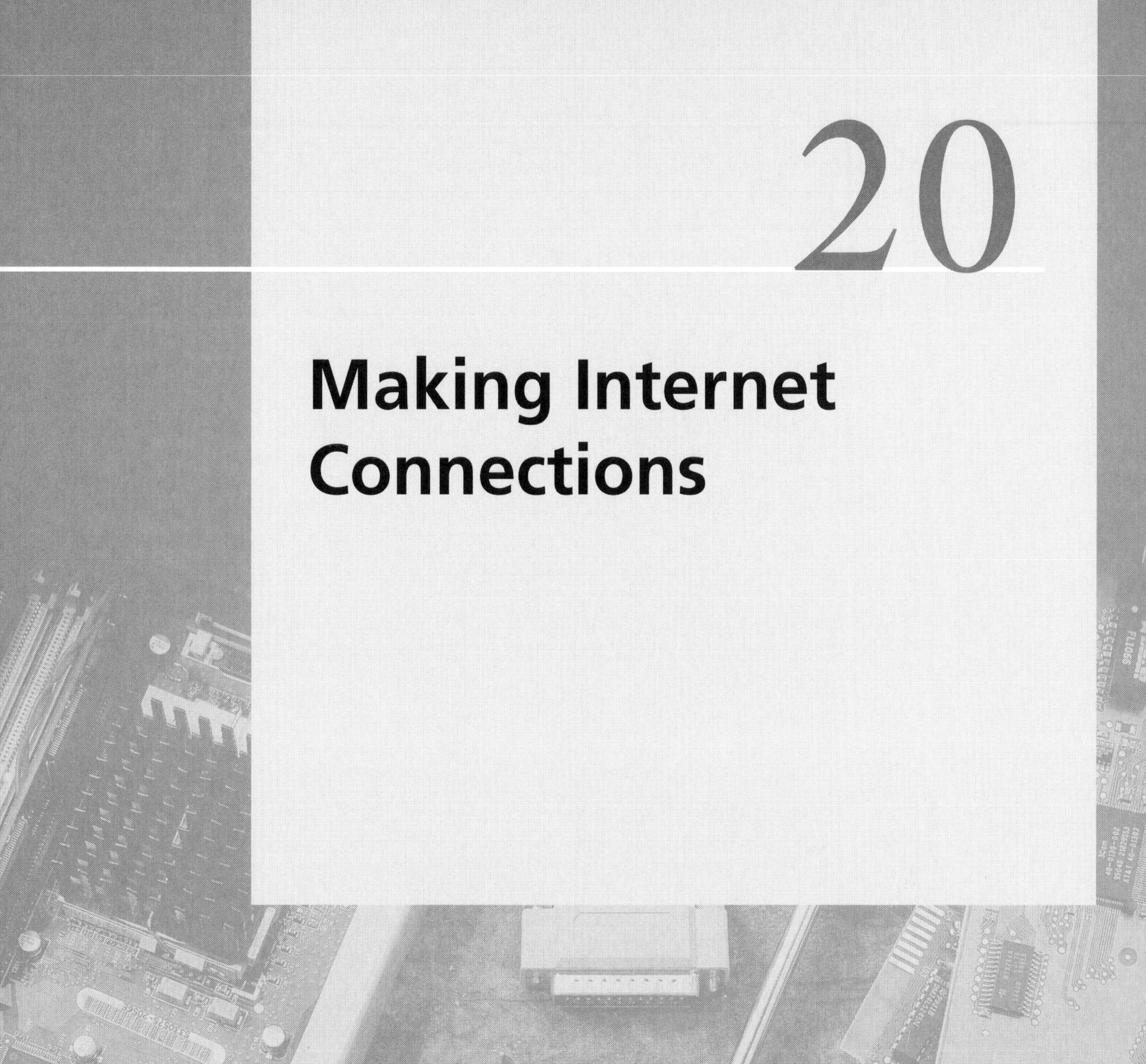

20

Making Internet Connections

Now that you have your PC upgraded with all the newest hardware and software, and you finally have your machine back into one piece again, you probably want to try it out. What better way to test your new silicone-based supermachine than by spending a few hours cruising the Internet and seeing what lies out there on the so-called Information Superhighway. In this chapter, you learn what is required to get your machine connected to the Internet.

After reading this chapter, you will:

- Have an overview and understanding of the Internet
- Know what resources you need to make your Internet connection
- Know how to install software that will allow you to connect to the Internet
- Know how to establish a dial-up connection to the Internet
- Know how to connect to the Internet through a local area network (LAN)
- Know how to use certain utilities to troubleshoot your Internet connections

First, you should know how the Internet came into being and then take a brief look into this global network.

Internet Overview

The foundation of what today is called the Internet was established in the late 1960s by the United States government. Starting with *ARPAnet (Advanced Research Projects Agency Network)*, the government began researching ways to exchange information among various government sites located in the United States. The research and implementation of ARPAnet led to the early beginnings of the Internet. This network allowed government officials at various sites to exchange files, documents, and messages with one another, even though they were physically separated by many miles.

The early pioneers of ARPAnet wanted to create a network that was robust, reliable, and did not have a single point of failure. A *single point of failure* would be a network designed with one device that was the *master node*, or controlling device, for the network. This leads to problems in that when your master node goes down, you lose your entire network. These early pioneers of ARPAnet acknowledged this single point of failure concept and, in turn, created a network that had no central controlling device; rather, it was made up of individual devices, or *nodes*, that all worked together and participated on the network. Although these first networks consisted of few machines, it laid the foundation for things to come.

It was apparent that this early network design would not be able to withstand large amounts of data traffic. It was these limitations that led researchers to invent a new protocol that would allow for open, fast, and efficient communications between all the devices attached to this now growing network. This creation was *Transmission Control Protocol/Internet Protocol (TCP/IP)* and it was this protocol that became not only the standard communication protocol for the Internet, but is slowly becoming the standard communication protocol for all computer-based network transmissions. In 1983, ARPAnet began to use TCP/IP as its network communications protocol, and so, by some historical accounts, on January 1, 1983, the Internet as we know it was born.

Most people weren't using the Internet in 1983. Although the groundwork for the Internet may have been in place that year, it wasn't until the late 1980s and early 1990s that the Internet as it is used and thought of today was really pushed into the public eye. It was in 1992 that Tom Brenners-Lee, a physicist for CERN (European Laboratory for Particle Physics), invented *HTML (HyperText Markup Language)* which was used for what Brenners-Lee called the *WWW (World Wide Web)*.

In 1993, a group of developers from the NCSA (National Center for Supercomputing Applications), led by Marc Andressen, created *Mosaic*, which was the first graphical-based WWW browser. With Mosaic, the Internet was opened up to allow the exchange of richly formatted text pages, graphics, high-quality images, and multimedia.

The development of HTML and the Mosaic browser led to the explosion of Internet usage and of the WWW in particular. But the WWW is not the only aspect of the Internet that has grown since 1983. E-mail still remains the number one used application on the Internet. Other usage of the Internet includes:

- FTP (File Transfer Protocol)
- UseNet (Internet newsgroups)
- Archie
- Gopher
- Telnet
- IRC (Internet Relay Chat)

It is all these applications together that have led to the growth of the Internet. Today, there are more than 30 million users who are using the Internet. This is a 6,000 percent increase over the number of users who were using the Internet in 1983.

Now that you have had a brief introduction to the Internet, it's time to start getting your computer online. Before you begin, you should make a list of resources that you are going to need to establish your Internet connection.

TCP/IP Software Packages

When establishing a connection to the Internet, you need TCP/IP software. As mentioned earlier, TCP/IP is how your machine communicates with other machines on the Internet. These software packages are sometimes referred to as an *IP stack*. You can purchase TCP/IP products at any software store, and many companies offer bundled packages for connecting to the Internet, which include not only your TCP/IP software, but other Internet applications to get you started. You should check out your local software store for some of the packages that are available.

If you are connecting to the Internet through a local or national *ISP (Internet service provider)*, your ISP may have given you TCP/IP software to help you establish your Internet connection. Most ISPs include this software in their monthly charge or you are charged a one-time setup fee. If you have friends who are already online, you could ask them to download software from the Internet, and once you have established your connection, you can then register these products.

You should decide on the package that you feel comfortable with, because you will be spending the time to install and configure the software.

TIP If you are using an ISP for your Internet access, it is a good idea to find out what package your ISP recommends. If you choose a package that is recommended by your ISP, the ISP's technical support team is probably familiar with the product. If you encounter any problems during your installation, you can rely on your ISP to provide you with support in installing and configuring your software.

NOTE Microsoft has included a utility called *Dial-Up Networking* in its recent operating systems. Dial-Up Networking can be used the same way as most TCP/IP software packages when establishing connections to the Internet. Most major TCP/IP software vendors have versions of their software that run on both Windows 95 and NT, so if you are familiar with certain TCP/IP communications programs, you can probably use them under the new Microsoft operating systems. To find out more information on Dial-Up Networking, refer to Chapter 21, "Using Dial-Up Networking."

Internet Utilities

You also need some basic Internet software to establish your Internet connection. You can find many applications on the Internet, but because you have yet established your connection, you need some utilities to get you going.

As mentioned in the previous section, most ISPs provide you with software products that allow you to connect to the Internet. Also, new operating systems such as Windows 95 and Windows NT come with some of these utilities built into the operating system themselves. At minimum, you will want to have Web browsing software (such as Netscape, Microsoft Internet Explorer, or Mosaic) and a mail package (such as Eudora, Pegasus, or Microsoft Outlook). In addition, you might want to get a newsreader, Telnet application, FTP applications, and some type of testing utility such as ping or traceroute, which is covered later in this chapter. Most TCP/IP packages include some if not all of these utilities.

TIP One thing to keep in mind, though, is that once you establish your Internet connection and you find that you are missing a certain Internet utility, you will more than likely be able to find it on the Internet.

If you are feeling a little lost in trying to decide what packages and applications you need to establish your Internet connections, don't worry—you learn where to obtain these utilities in the next few sections.

Provider Information

With the growing trend in the number of ISPs providing low-cost Internet access, many users are attaching to the Internet through these provider's networks. In establishing a connection to your provider, you need some basic information. Most ISPs have documentation that they provide to their users which contains information you need in establishing your Internet connection. Information that you need from your ISP includes:

- The phone numbers for your specific modem (14.4Kbps, 28.8Kbps, and so on)
- Does the ISP provide SLIP or PPP connectivity?
- Does the ISP use dynamic or static IP number assignments?
- The IP numbers for DNS servers
- Any special settings for your provider's network (MTU, PAP, CHAP, and so on)

Information from Your Network Administrator on How Your LAN Connects to the Internet

If you are trying to establish a connection to the Internet from your office LAN, you need information on the procedure your company uses to establish its connections to the Internet. Most companies have standard documentation on how to establish this connection, or a help desk which can help answer your questions. Most corporations today use some type of Internet firewall or proxy server in providing users access to the Internet. A *firewall* or *proxy server* protects your company's LAN by securing and monitoring all Internet-based transactions. Some of these systems require user authentication, and hence a user ID and password to access them.

Companies and most universities have an *open network*, which means that every device or node on the network is in essence a node on the Internet. In these types of network setups, you don't need to access the Internet through a proxy server. These setups provide ease of use to the end user, but provide a less secure network environment. Your network administrator can give you the information that you need to establish your Internet connection.

Now you should have everything you need to establish your Internet connection. You are ready to install your TCP/IP software, which is the first step in getting you connected to the Net.

Installing TCP/IP Software

To Install TCP/IP Software, You Need:

- ☑ Your TCP/IP software
- ☑ Internet applications (Web browser, mail package, Telnet utility)
- ☑ Information from your ISP
- ☑ Information from your network administrator on how your company establishes connections to the Internet

Now you are ready to install your TCP/IP software:

1. You need either the disks from the software vendor or the executable file that installs the software for you.
2. Once you have your files available, place the install disks into your A: drive (or equivalent drive letter) and start the setup process.
3. If you are installing your software from a single executable, start that executable from the appropriate drive. For example, you would type either of the following:

   a:\inet.exe

   c:\temp\inet.exe

4. Once you have begun the setup process, files are copied to your hard drive. During the installation process, you may be prompted to provide certain information.

TIP Some of the message boxes that display during the installation may be confusing, so you should understand them all before continuing. Also, be sure to have the information that your ISP has provided you or the information from your network administrator.

As mentioned in step 4 of the preceding section, you may encounter various message boxes in the installation of your IP software. One such message box can be seen in Figure 20.1. This is the dreaded Winsock message, and if you have had any type of Internet software on your machine before, there is a good chance that you may run across this message when installing your TCP/IP software.

The Winsock.dll and What It Does

First off, you are probably asking yourself, "What is a Winsock and how did it get on my machine?" The Winsock.dll (Dynamic Link Library) could be the most vital component in establishing Internet connectivity. The Winsock.dll acts as a holding tank or *library* (hence the name) of information about your machine and your connection to the Internet. Every time you establish a connection to the Internet, your Winsock.dll is initialized with your current session's parameters. The type of information that can be held in the Winsock is your IP number, your domain name (suba.com), your request information (HTTP, FTP, Telnet), and much more information.

continues

continued

Once you make contact with another machine on the Internet, your Winsock will pass that machine your information to establish a communication session between your machine and the remote machine.

If you have ever installed any type of Internet software, from bundled Internet packages to CompuServe, there is a good chance that one of these applications installed a Winsock.dll onto your machine. A good way to find out if you have a Winsock installed on your machine is to search your C:\Windows folder and any subfolders for Winsock.dll.

Once you have located any older Winsocks, you may want to back them up into another directory or rename the older Winsock. Most TCP/IP software packages ask you if you would like to back up older Winsocks on your machine, much like the message box in Figure 20.1.

By backing up and replacing your older Winsock, you can eliminate any confusion when you attempt to install your new TCP/IP software. Once you have your Winsock renamed or moved, you can proceed with the installation of your TCP/IP software.

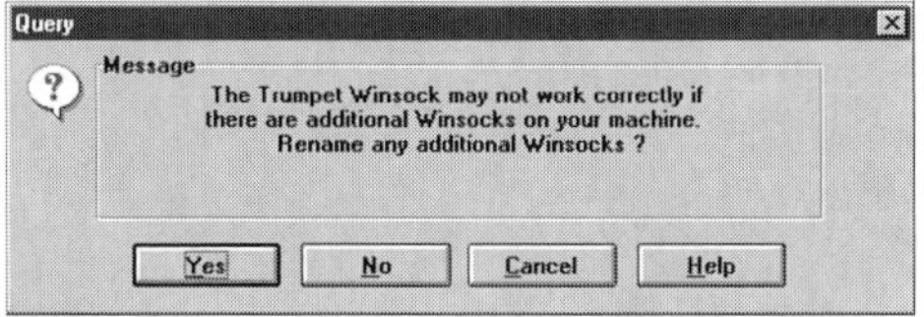

FIG. 20.1
A common Winsock message box.

NOTE With various applications available to connect to the Internet, it is becoming common to have multiple Winsocks installed on your machine. Although all providers are working on standardizing their applications to work with various Winsocks, there are still applications out there that require certain Winsocks to have their applications function properly. If you find that some of your older applications don't function properly after installing your new TCP/IP software, this may be the problem. You need to ask your application vendor what Winsocks they currently support.

Environment Settings

During installation, your TCP/IP software may need to make changes to your environment settings. This usually entails adding the software directory into your PATH statement. Figure 20.2 shows a common message box prompting you to make changes to your environment settings. Be sure to make backup copies of your

AUTOEXEC.BAT and CONFIG.SYS before you install your TCP/IP software. If prompted to change your AUTOEXEC.BAT and CONFIG.SYS, allow your software to make the changes and be sure to reboot your machine after the installation is complete.

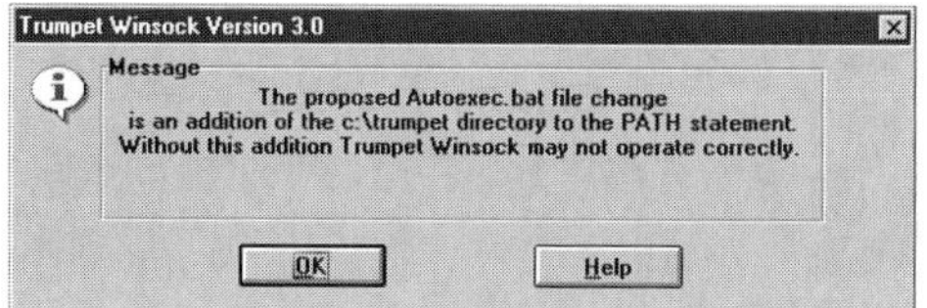

FIG. 20.2
This common dialog box prompts you to make changes to your environment settings.

You are also asked other information during the setup process. Figure 20.3 shows some of the typical information that you would be asked to supply. Take a look at this information, and then find out what role each of these pieces plays in establishing your Internet connection.

Trumpet Winsock Setup
IP address
DNS server(s) 198.87.202.35,198.87.202.10
Domain suffix suba.com
Driver
SLIP
PPP
Packet driver Vector 00
Netmask 0.0.0.0
Gateway 0.0.0.0
Dialler settings...
MTU 576 TCP MSS 512
TCP RWIN 2048 TCP RTO MAX 60
Demand load timeout 5 seconds
Ok Cancel Help

FIG. 20.3
A typical TCP/IP installation screen.

IP Address

All TCP/IP software packages ask you for your IP address. This may be a little outdated with the current trend in how IP addresses are assigned. Today, most ISPs assign IP numbers *dynamically*—meaning that users who log onto the network will have an IP number assigned to them when they log in. This is a convenient way to assign IP numbers and alleviates countless headaches that statically assigned IP addresses brought with them. You may still run across a service provider that statically assigns IP addresses, so this is where you would put in that IP address. You will only enter in an IP address if you are given an address from your LAN administrator or ISP. This is the difference between static IP addresses and dynamic: The static IP address is going to stay the same, and the dynamic is constantly changing. For most Internet users, you do not have to worry about assigning an IP address.

DNS

Domain Name Service (DNS) is another critical component in establishing any type of Internet connectivity. DNS is the mechanism that allows domain names (such as iquest.com) to be translated into their corresponding IP numbers. This means that when users type **http://www.microsoft.com**, they can get to the Microsoft home page. In reality, though, they are going to **207.68.137.53**. The DNS scheme works in a top-down hierarchy. Figure 20.4 shows an example of how host names are resolved using DNS.

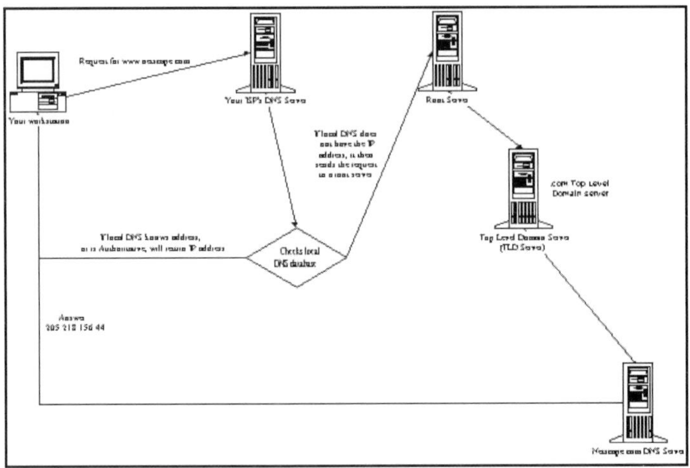

FIG. 20.4
An example of how host names are resolved using DNS.

There are currently 10 major TLDs (Top Level Domains) in the world. Refer to Table 20.1 for a listing of these 10 major TLDs. These numbers represent the number of domains on the Internet, not the number of machines. For example, **microsoft.com** is just one domain in the .com TLD. But, Microsoft has hundreds of machines that are part of the Internet, such as **ftp.microsoft.com www.microsoft.com**, **news.microsoft.com**, and so on.

Table 20.1 Ten of the Internet's Largest TLDs

Domain on the Internet	Approximate Number of Machines	Domain Name
.com	290,000	Commercial
.uk	24,000	United Kingdom
.org	22,500	Organizations
.net	16,000	Networks

Domain on the Internet	Approximate Number of Machines	Domain Name
.de	15,000	Germany
.jp	12,500	Japan
.edu	11,500	Educational
.au	10,000	Australia
.ca	10,000	Canada
.us	9,500	United States

(source: Net Wizards' July 1996 Domain Survey, ***http://www.nw.com****)*

A majority of the DNS entries on the Internet are maintained by a division of Network Solutions, Inc., called *InterNIC*. InterNIC maintains a majority of all registered domains on the Internet.

What does this mean to the Internet user? For one, it allows for ease of use in connecting to your favorite Web sites. Imagine if to surf the Net, you had to have a listing of every IP number for every Web site that you wanted to visit. It wouldn't be much fun, and, needless to say, a very big waste of time. Also, with DNS's entries, companies can use an already well-known market name to attract users to their Web sites.

The most important point to remember in setting up DNS entries for your connection to the Internet is that you use the correct DNS server. Once again, this information would be supplied to you by your ISP or your network administrator.

NOTE There is a current frenzy in the way DNS entries operate and how TLDs are maintained or established. Alternatives exist to InterNIC, one of the largest being AlterNIC, which allows for various TLDs in the DNS structure. There are also proposals out to change the current DNS structure on the Internet.

To learn more about these changes and how DNS operates, visit **http://www.alternic.net/draft_postel.html**, **http://www.alternic.net/rfcs/1500/rfc1591.txt.html**, and **http://www.alternic.net**.

Domain Suffix

The *domain suffix* is the domain to which you will be connecting. Simply put, if you use Netwalk as your provider, then your domain suffix is

netwalk.com

Some TCP/IP packages also ask for a *host name*, which would be a name for your machine. This in turn makes your machine

yourmachine.providers.domain

Going back to the Netwalk example, if your machine was named Arkanoid, then you would be

arkanoid.netwalk.com

Some TCP/IP packages make this domain suffix a required parameter, while other packages have this being an optional parameter.

SLIP and PPP

Two protocols allow for communication between your modem and your ISP's modem or equivalent device—SLIP and PPP.

SLIP (Serial Line Internet Protocol) is the older method for providing dial-up access to the Internet. It served as a way for users to dial into a host device, often called a *terminal server*, and allowed this terminal server and the user's modem to communicate with one another. SLIP is the older of the two communication protocols, but there are still some ISPs around that provide SLIP service.

PPP (Point-to-Point Protocol) is a newer communication protocol. Although which protocol provides faster communication has been researched and studied, there is still much dispute if any difference really exists. PPP provides better error-checking, and hence, many people feel it is a more stable communication platform than SLIP. PPP also handles dynamic assignment of IP information much better than its SLIP predecessor.

Although most ISPs are using the new PPP protocol in providing Internet connections to their users, there still may be a few SLIP shops around. The easiest way to find out is to refer to your provider's documentation. It is very likely that it states clearly which method it uses.

Packet Driver

A *packet driver* acts almost as a middle man between your network card and your TCP/IP software. Your packet driver takes information from your TCP/IP software, communicates it to your network card, and then takes information from your network card and passes it along to your TCP/IP software. The packet driver allows you to communicate with the Internet while you are attached to a LAN. There is some information that you need to supply to your TCP/IP software in order for it to work correctly with your packet driver. Some of this information is covered in the next few sections.

The only time you would be concerned with a packet driver is if you where installing your TCP/IP software on a machine connected to your LAN. You can refer to the later "Connecting to the Internet Through a LAN" section of this chapter for more information. When installing software on a machine connected to a LAN, you should contact your network administrator and ask if there are any specifics that you should be aware of before continuing.

Vector

The *vector* is simply the software interrupt of your packet driver. This interrupt allows your packet driver to communicate with your operating system. Although different TCP/IP software packages refer to this by different names, they all will have this interrupt in their respective packages somewhere. Contact your network administrator for help in determining which interrupt you should use for your perspective packet driver.

Netmask

A *netmask* can be used to locate *segments*, or parts, of the same network. Netmasks are usually directly related to your IP address. For example, if your IP address is 199.50.201.2 (this is commonly referred to as a *Class C IP address*), then your netmask would be 255.255.255.0.

> **CAUTION** Netmask and IP subnetting can be a very confusing and very difficult topic to understand, so you want to be sure to refer to your documentation when entering your netmask value. If you put in the wrong value for your netmask, you can cause your TCP/IP software to function improperly.

Gateway

When you see *gateway* or *default gateway* in your TCP/IP settings, this refers to a device that contains information on how your data will be delivered on the Internet. This is commonly referred to as a *router*, or any machine that is routing enabled.

Basically, what your gateway does is take the request for the network that you want to reach and find the appropriate route for your request.

Explaining routing and its associated concepts is far outside of what I want to accomplish in this book, but it is significant to bring up here in that you must have the appropriate gateway setup for your Internet connection if you want to be successful in establishing your link to the Internet. Most ISPs are using *dynamic IP allocation*, which not only gives you an IP address when you request connection, but also knows the location of your gateway. This is convenient in that you don't have to remember your gateway IP number, and if it changes, it does not affect you Internet connection. For those connections that still require you to statically assign your gateway address, this should be documented in your ISP's information or the information that your network administrator has given you.

Other Information

You may be asked for some other information in setting up your TCP/IP software (refer to Figure 20.3).

MTU (Maximum Transmission Unit) is the maximum amount of data that can be transmitted in any one frame of data. Any time you as a user request or send any information on a computer network, you are not sending or receiving one large packet of data. On the contrary, you are actually sending hundreds of small frames of data to your remote device. The MTU setting allows you to set how much data can be sent in each of those data frames.

TCP RWIN (TCP Receiving Window) is a setting that tells your TCP/IP software how much data a remote machine can receive while you are communicating with it. If this setting is low, it results in slow communication between your machine and the remote machine.

TCP MSS (TCP Maximum Segment Size) is a setting that specifies the largest amount of data that your Winsock would receive in one session. This is accomplished by two machines: your machine and a remote machine agreeing on the segment size at the beginning of the communication process.

TCP RTO MAX (TCP Retransmission Time-out Maximum) sets the maximum amount of time between TCP retransmission of data packets.

Demand load time-out is how long your Winsock stays loaded after all Winsock applications have closed. These applications would include your Web browser, e-mail program, Telnet package, or FTP or other Internet utility.

Different TCP/IP software packages contain different information, but if you refer to the software's online help program or the software manuals, they should tell you the properties and provide a description of all the software configuration options.

In most cases, this information can remain at the software's default settings; it is only if your ISP or Internet connection requires special settings in regard to these attributes that you would need to change them. This is on a provider-by-provider basis, so once again, you would have to refer to your documentation to see if any of these settings needed to be changed.

AOL, CompuServe, MSN

AOL (America Online), *CompuServe*, and *MSN (The Microsoft Network)* are the largest of the online service providers in the country. These service providers provide a wide range of services to their members. These major online services now offer full Internet connectivity to their members, to go along with the already existing services. Some of these include chat rooms, interest groups, bulletin board areas, software download sites, game areas, and many other services.

These online providers offer their own software, usually free for installation by their customers. They usually offer a free number of hours for your first month's membership. They also offer various pricing packages that you can choose from that best suit your needs. These providers' software offer you a very easy, step-by-step configuration process that sets you up on their system and gets you acquainted with their various services. For more information on these providers, visit their respective Web sites at:

- **http://www.aol.com**
- **http://www.compuserve.com**
- **http://www.msn.com**

Establishing Dial-Up Connection to the Internet

Now that you have your TCP/IP software configured, you are ready to dial into your ISP. You need the phone number(s) that you can access for your appropriate modem speed. Once again, your ISP should provide you with these numbers.

Modem Properties

You want to put the properties of your modem into the appropriate area. Assume that you have already installed your modem, so all that you need to enter is the COM Port settings and the speed of your modem. Figure 20.5 shows how you would set your modem properties in your TCP/IP software.

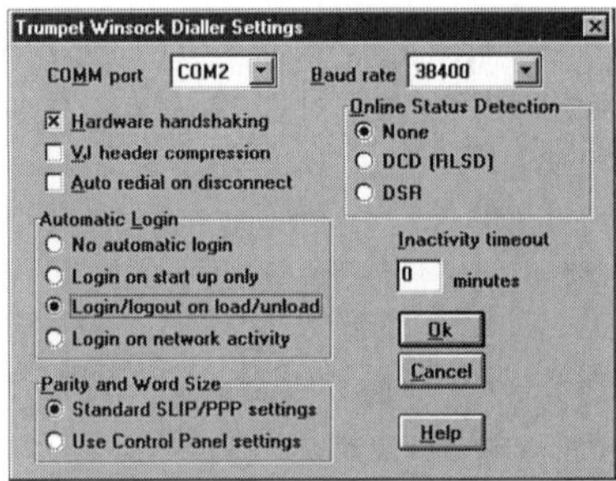

FIG. 20.5
Set up modem properties and automatic dialing.

Most TCP/IP software packages also enable you to automatically log into your ISP. This allows for a very easy way to establish your Internet connection whenever you need it.

Manual Dial

You should try to dial into your provider manually to make sure you do not have any configuration problems. Refer to Figure 20.6 to find how to start the manual dialing process.

Once you have chosen manual dial, the whitespace of the screen should become available for you to enter information into. In the whitespace, you want to run a quick check of your modem. Type the following:

```
AT
```

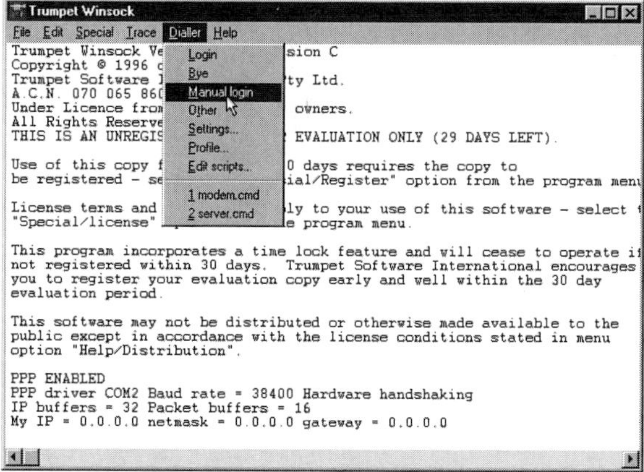

FIG. 20.6
Start the manual dialing process.

You should receive an OK message. This is telling you that your modem is responding correctly. If you do not receive an OK message, you should check your modem parameters to see if they are correct, that your modem is turned on if external, and that your modem is configured properly. Once your modem checks out OK, type:

atdt *your provider's phone number*

Once you have logged into your provider, you will usually switch into PPP mode, which can usually be accomplished by some type of keystroke command. In this example, you switch into PPP mode by pressing the Esc key. Figure 20.7 shows what your screen should look like after manually dialing into your provider.

NOTE As you can see in Figure 20.7, some ISPs ask for information other than user ID and password. This is not a problem when doing a manual dial, but it adds complexity when setting your TCP/IP software to dial your provider automatically. You need to find out how you log into your ISP and what prompts are asked. You can find this out by using any standard terminal package and dialing your provider's number. An even easier way is just asking your provider the logon sequence or by referring to your documentation.

Now you should be dialed into your ISP. To test this connection, see the later "Troubleshooting Your Internet Connection" section of this chapter.

Once you have seen that you have no problems with your TCP/IP configuration, you can set up your software to automatically connect to the Internet.

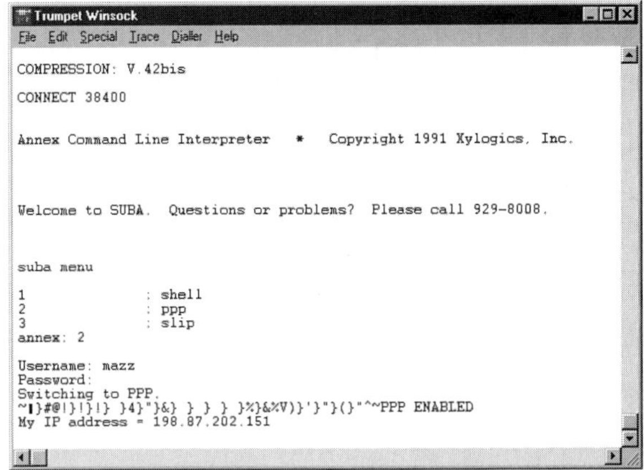

FIG. 20.7
The screen as it appears after the manual dial is completed.

Automatic Dialing

You need to set up your TCP/IP software to automatically dial whenever TCP/IP connectivity is requested. The benefit of this is that whenever you click your e-mail icon or Web browser, your TCP/IP software automatically dials into your provider and establishes a connection. If you refer to Figure 20.5, you can see how you can tell your TCP/IP software to establish an Internet connection automatically. Each TCP/IP package varies on how it states the automatic connection method, but almost all packages have this option available.

Also, you need to provide your user name and password to establish your Internet connection (see Figure 20.8).

FIG. 20.8
Provide your user name and password to your TCP/IP software.

Once you have entered your appropriate information, you should choose Dialer, Login from Your TCP/IP Software. This should attach you to your provider. Once you have dialed into your provider, you now want to see if you can automatically dial into your provider when you open any application that needs to use your TCP/IP software. (You can set this up by choosing the Login/Logout on Load/Unload option as seen in Figure 20.5.) Locate your Web browser and open it. Your TCP/IP software should start up and dial into your service provider. You now have your automatic connection to the Internet established.

TIP When you open an Internet application such as Netscape and you receive an error message stating that your machine was unable to locate your TCP/IP software, you may want to check your AUTOEXEC.BAT file. Your TCP/IP software directory should be included in your path settings. Also, be sure that you have rebooted your machine since installing your TCP/IP software.

As mentioned in the previous "Manual Dial" section, some ISPs ask for more information than the standard user name and password. If this is the case for your ISP, you may have to customize your dialing properties. Most of today's TCP/IP software packages use some type of dialing scripts when establishing these automatic connections. You can refer to your software's documentation on how to customize any scripts to meet the needs of your ISP. You should also contact your ISP; many of them will have copies of these scripts customized for their environment that they give to their users.

Connecting to the Internet Through a LAN

If you are connecting to the Internet through a LAN, you need to understand what type of LAN environment you have in regards to Internet connectivity. There are two types of LAN environments: open and closed. The *open environment* is the easiest way to connect to the Internet, while the *closed environment* is a much more secure LAN environment. To find out what type of LAN you have or to learn more about how your LAN accesses the Internet, ask your network administrator to explain what type of environment you have. At minimum, you need some type of documentation that has the specifics of your LAN in regards to Internet connectivity.

Open LAN Environment

An *open LAN environment* is one that is directly connected to the Internet. More specifically, in an open LAN environment, every machine on your LAN is also a machine on the Internet. Most open LANs are found in educational and research facilities. Establishing a connection to the Internet in an open environment is fairly straightforward and simple. You need some type of Internet software (browser, FTP, Telnet). Also, you need to make sure that you have at least one DNS entry.

Now, before you go looking into the guts of your computer and changing anything, be sure you know what you're looking for. In most open LAN environments, network administrators and managers spend countless hours setting up each machine's TCP/IP software and configuring it to their LANs' requirements, so be careful when looking at your TCP/IP software configuration.

One of the simplest ways to test if your machine can connect to the Internet is by trying to run an Internet application:

1. Locate your Web browser on your machine, and then open it.
2. Once open, try and connect to the Internet. You can do this by typing any location in the URL bar of your browser. Refer to Figure 20.9 to locate the URL entry bar.

FIG. 20.9
The location of the URL bar for Microsoft Internet Explorer.

3. Type in any known destination on the Internet, such as **http:// www. microsoft.com** or **http://www.yahoo.com**.

If your browser returns a Web page, then you are connected to the Internet. If the browser returns some type of error message, first try another URL, and if the error continues, your machine may not be configured correctly to access the Internet. As mentioned earlier, you should contact your network administrator before trying to make any changes to your machine's TCP/IP configuration. It may take some time to hunt someone down who can help you, but in the long run, this may end up saving you many hours of lost time while you wait for you machine to be re-configured.

As mentioned in the previous section, making a connection to the Internet in an open LAN environment is not that difficult to do. In today's LAN environments, most company LANs don't supply open connectivity to the Internet; on the contrary, most of today's LANs are part of a closed environment.

Closed LANs

The most common type of LAN in regards to Internet connectivity is the *closed* or *protected LAN*. When a LAN is said to be closed, it is not that the LAN does not have access to the Internet. A closed LAN is a LAN that is somehow protected from the Internet by some sort of security mechanism.

The most common type of security for these types of LANs is referred to as a *firewall* or *proxy server*. A firewall is a way of protecting your LAN from users on the public Internet. In the previous section on open LANs, it was stated that every machine on the LAN was part of the Internet. In a closed environment, only the firewall and machines that it distinguishes are part of the Internet. This allows for your LAN to be secure from the perennial hackers found on the Internet. In today's corporate world, data is valued as one of the most important items a company possesses, so this type of security is a must if your company is going to provide Internet access to its LAN users.

In regards to connecting to the Internet in a closed environment, it is a little more troublesome than that of an open LAN, but if you have the right information, you shouldn't have any problems. Your machine needs to be configured with the appropriate TCP/IP or equivalent software. As mentioned in the previous section, talk to your network administrator before trying to configure or make any changes to your TCP/IP software.

Once you have your software configured, you need to obtain the IP number or host name of your firewall. You also need any port settings that are specific to your firewall setup. Your documentation that you received from your network administrator should contain this information. In most popular Internet software packages, there are configuration options that allow you to enter in your firewall information. In Figure 20.10, you can see how to set up Microsoft Internet Explorer to connect to the Internet via a firewall.

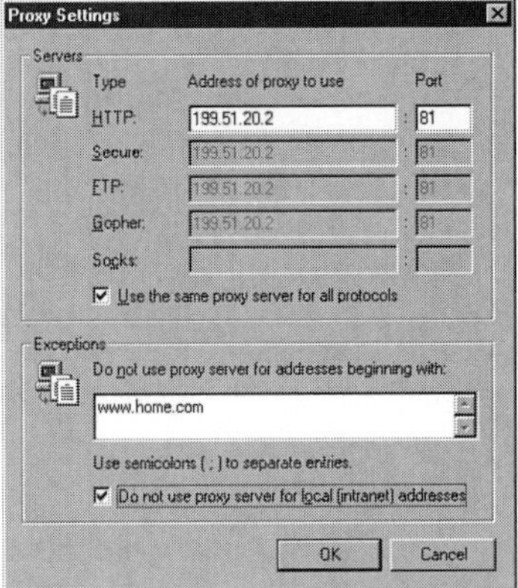

FIG. 20.10 *Internet Explorer proxy settings.*

Depending on how your company has designed and implemented your firewall, you may have to provide information in order to be authenticated by the firewall. This is usually performed in the form of a user ID and password. Other companies do not require authentication to get through their firewalls; they just check to see if the user who is requesting access to the Internet actually resides on one of the company's legal networks. Some companies implement another type of firewall security called *packet filtering*, which allows only certain machines to access the Internet. No matter what type of firewall your company uses, if you have the correct information, you should be able to access the Internet in no time.

NOTE Just like anything in technology, not all firewalls are created equal. Because of this, you may see some limitations when connecting to the Internet via a firewall. Some of these are limitations of the firewall itself, while others are imposed by companies that want to add extra security to their networks. Some firewall setups will not allow Real-Audio, Java applets, ActiveX Controls, and other new Internet technologies to be passed through them.

Troubleshooting Your Internet Connection

This section will help you become familiar with certain utilities and concepts when troubleshooting your Internet connection. As is always the case with any computer-related component, there is always a time when a component is not functioning as it is supposed to. That is why you need some tools and techniques that can help you troubleshoot your Internet connection.

ping

ping is probably the most common utility used in troubleshooting any IP connectivity problem on the Internet. ping is a quick tool that can tell you whether or not you can reach another device. ping sends out echo packets, trying to bounce them off remote machines. If the remote machine receives this packet, it sends the response back to the machine originating the ping request. When you receive this response, that means that the remote device is reachable by your machine.

Suppose you have just set up your dial-up connection and you want a quick way to see if it works. Go to your ping utility, and try to ping **www.microsoft.com**. Figure 20.11 shows a successful ping test. Notice that it states the number of requests sent, the number received, and packet loss percentage. This means that you can reach this remote machine on the Internet.

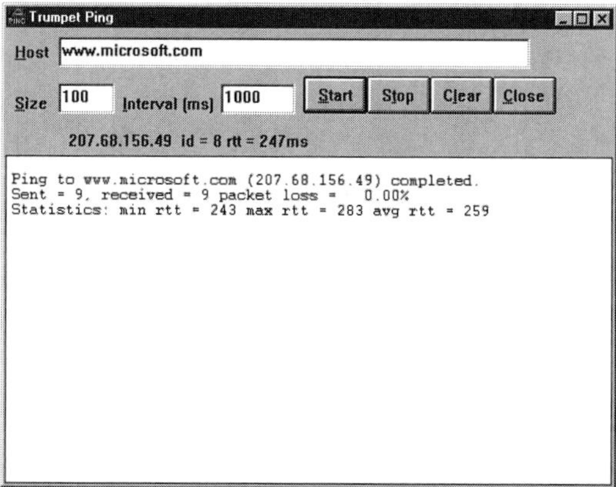

FIG. 20.11
A successful ping test.

Now see Figure 20.12. This shows an unsuccessful ping command. Notice the number of requests sent, that 0 were received by the remote machine, and that packet loss was 100 percent. This means that you cannot reach the remote machine on the Internet. You should try and ping another remote machine, and if you are still unsuccessful, you may need to check your configuration parameters again.

Using ping can provide you a quick and reliable way to troubleshoot your Internet connections.

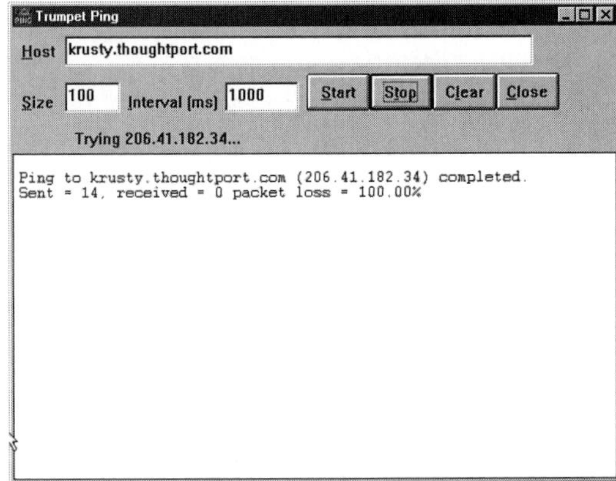

FIG. 20.12
An unsuccessful ping test.

Telnet

Although many people use Telnet to carry on sessions or log into remote machines on the Internet, Telnet can be a very useful troubleshooting tool. When you open your Telnet application, you are asked for a remote machine to connect to. By entering in a machine name, such as **vulcan.ohiou.edu**, you are requesting to log onto that remote machine. Your machine in turn requests the IP address of **vulcan.ohiou.edu** from your DNS server. Once your machine gets the IP address, it then connects you to the remote machine. If any of these pieces are not responding, such as if your DNS is down or you have lost your IP number, you get a message similar to that in Figure 20.13. Telnet can provide you one more way of testing to see if your Internet connection is established and working properly. Using Telnet as a troubleshooting utility can give you a quick, accurate test of whether you can reach remote sites on the Internet.

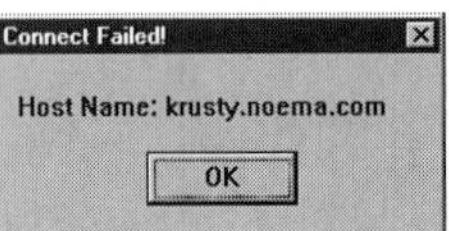

FIG. 20.13
A Telnet connection failed message.

Traceroute

This utility provides you with more information than the ping utility does. Traceroute is true to its name, in that it traces the route that you take to a remote machine and returns to you all devices along the way. Because traceroute reports all devices that lie along your route, it takes longer to execute than ping.

Traceroute basically reports every router or routing-enabled device that lies in the path from your machine to a remote machine. Traceroute can provide you with information such as what is the last device your transmission can reach, what devices lie on your transmission route, and how many devices away on the Internet the remote machine is. Although traceroute is used mostly by those individuals who set up the routing of data packets on the Internet, it can be used by the end user who may have a problem or who may be just curious. Traceroute can provide you with a map of devices that you communicate with while talking with remote machines on the Internet. Figure 20.14 shows the results from a traceroute.

> **CAUTION** It is not recommended to run traceroute on high production devices, such as backbone routers or production servers, or during peak traffic times. Because traceroute reports every device in your path to a remote machine, you may take processing power which could be used for your normal data traffic.

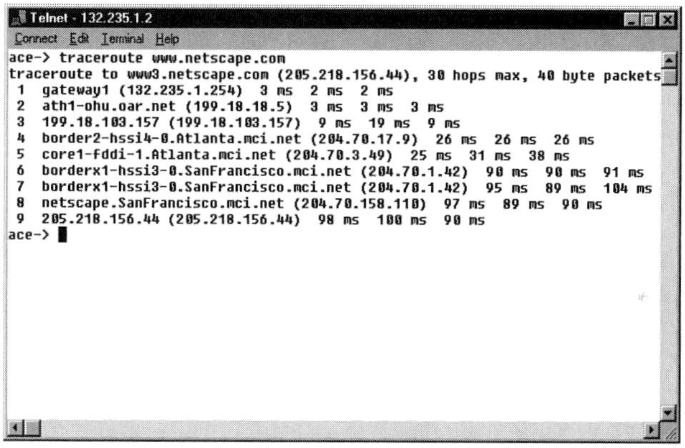

```
Telnet - 132.235.1.2
Connect Edit Terminal Help
ace-> traceroute www.netscape.com
traceroute to www3.netscape.com (205.218.156.44), 30 hops max, 40 byte packets
 1  gateway1 (132.235.1.254)  3 ms  2 ms  2 ms
 2  ath1-ohu.oar.net (199.18.18.5)  3 ms  3 ms  3 ms
 3  199.18.103.157 (199.18.103.157)  9 ms  19 ms  9 ms
 4  border2-hssi4-0.Atlanta.mci.net (204.70.17.9)  26 ms  26 ms  26 ms
 5  core1-fddi-1.Atlanta.mci.net (204.70.3.49)  25 ms  31 ms  38 ms
 6  borderx1-hssi3-0.SanFrancisco.mci.net (204.70.1.42)  90 ms  90 ms  91 ms
 7  borderx1-hssi3-0.SanFrancisco.mci.net (204.70.1.42)  95 ms  89 ms  104 ms
 8  netscape.SanFrancisco.mci.net (204.70.158.110)  97 ms  89 ms  90 ms
 9  205.218.156.44 (205.218.156.44)  98 ms  100 ms  90 ms
ace->
```

FIG. 20.14
Results of a traceroute to Netscape's Web site.

Other Internet Troubleshooting Techniques

Suppose, for example, that you are receiving an error from your Internet application saying that the host is unreachable. This could be a number of things:

- What is probably the case is that the remote machine you are trying to attach to is not available, either because it is offline, not currently configured for the network, or is physically shut off.
- Your DNS may not be responding.

To troubleshoot this, dial into your provider and then try to carry on a Telnet session with your host machine (**www.myprovider.com**). If your Telnet software returns a `Connection failed` message, as shown in Figure 20.13, then it is a pretty safe assumption to say that your DNS is not responding. One way around this is to ask your provider if it has a secondary, and even a third, DNS server. Then get the IP numbers of these DNS servers and place them in the DNS entries of your TCP/IP software. This way, three DNSes must be down before you are left off the Net.

Another trick that may be useful is to Telnet to your service provider or any machine on the public Internet, and run the host executable. The syntax and results for this command can be seen in Figure 20.15.

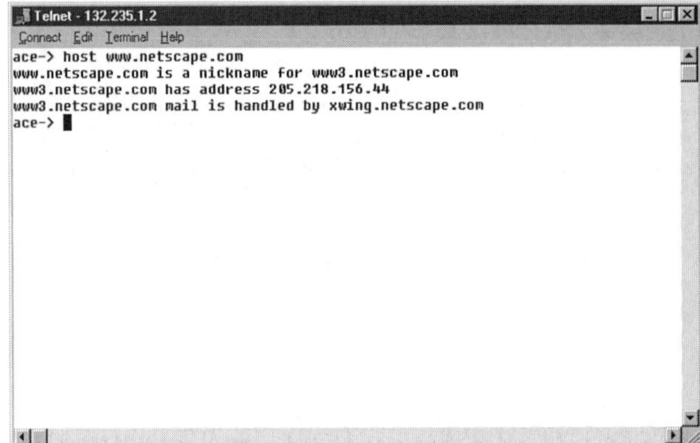

FIG. 20.15
Syntax and results from running the host application to Netscape's Web site.

You can see that you receive some very good information. Now, if you wanted to attach to Netscape's home page and your DNS was down, you could still reach it by typing **http://205.218.156.44**.

21

Using Dial-Up Networking

One feature in Windows 95 and Windows NT 4.0 that you might find useful after an upgrade is Dial-Up Networking. You can use Dial-Up Networking to connect through your modem to a remote local area network (LAN), Internet service provider, another Windows 95/NT user's PC, and other remote systems. If you've just added a new modem to the system or have set up your own network, you can use Dial-Up Networking to connect to the Internet, connect from home to your network, and more. Dial-Up Networking also works in conjunction with Exchange's Remote Mail to enable you to send and receive e-mail through remote mail servers. Dial-Up Networking is an important part of the operating system because it supports so many other features and programs in Windows 95 and Windows NT.

In this chapter, you explore Dial-Up Networking and learn about the following topics:

- Understanding Dial-Up Networking
- Installing and configuring Dial-Up Networking
- Using a Dial-Up Networking session
- Using remote LAN resources
- Using SLIP and CSLIP connections
- Creating Dial-Up scripts
- Setting up a Dial-Up Networking server

Before you begin setting up Dial-Up Networking, you should have a basic understanding of how Dial-Up Networking works. The following section provides an overview.

NOTE This chapter focuses on using Dial-Up Networking to connect to the Internet and to another computer. For that reason, connections to NetWare networks and a few other topics involving Dial-Up Networking aren't covered. For complete coverage of Dial-Up Networking and other communications topics, turn to *Windows 95 Communications Handbook* and *Windows NT Communications Handbook*, both from Que. This chapter focuses primarily on Windows 95, but also includes information about Dial-Up Networking in Windows NT.

Understanding Dial-Up Networking

In a Dial-Up Networking session, one computer acts as a *server* and another acts as a *client*. If you're connecting to a remote LAN, for example, the computer that you dial into is the server, and your PC is the client. So the server provides access to the client (see Figure 21.1).

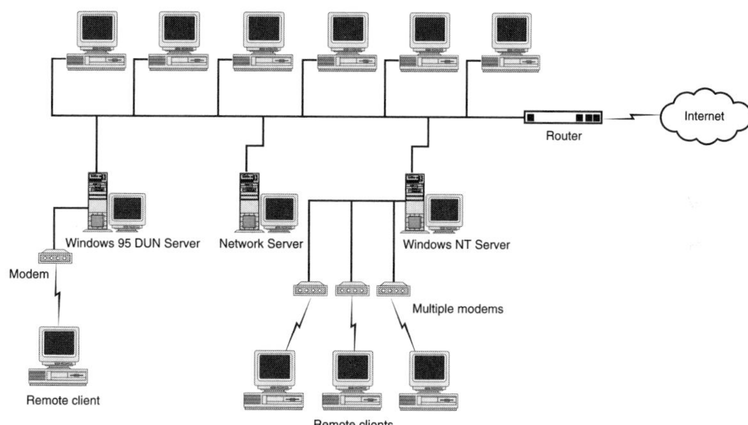

FIG. 21.1
Dial-Up Networking clients can connect to individual machines or networks.

Windows 95 and Windows NT include the software you need to turn your PC into a Dial-Up Networking client. You can connect to a variety of remote servers, including NetWare and Windows NT servers, Point-to-Point Protocol (PPP) servers (many Internet service providers use PPP), and other types of dial-up servers. In addition, the Microsoft Plus! add-on for Windows 95 includes software that turns your PC into a Dial-Up Networking server, enabling other users to dial into your PC. Windows NT has this feature built in.

TIP Dial-Up Networking is a great way to connect your PC to a friend's PC to share files over a modem. One of you must be running the Dial-Up Networking Server software.

As you can see in Figure 21.1, a Windows 95 computer can act as a Dial-Up Networking server for one computer at a time, provided you install the Dial-Up Networking server software on the Windows 95 server. Windows NT, NetWare, and other remote access servers can support multiple modems and multiple dial-in users at one time.

TIP Most Internet service providers use PPP as their connection protocol. A few UNIX-based systems require a *SLIP (Serial Line Interface Protocol)* connection. The Windows 95 and Windows NT Dial-Up Networking clients support SLIP, but this book doesn't cover SLIP because it applies to relatively few people. Also, you'll find the capability to create dial-up scripts useful when working with SLIP. These two topics are covered thoroughly in the *Windows 95 Communications Handbook* and the *Windows NT Communications Handbook*, both from Que.

What can you do once you're connected to the remote system? To a degree, that depends on the server. If you're connecting to a remote LAN, you can access the shared resources on the LAN just as if you were sitting at a computer connected directly to the LAN. You can use files, send and receive mail, and print, although the speed at which you can perform these tasks naturally is slower because you're working through a modem connection. You can't run a program from the server, for example. For that, you need to use a remote control program (which are not covered in this book).

If you're connecting to a Windows 95 computer running the Dial-Up Networking Server software, you can access that computer's resources, as well as the resources on the network to which the server is connected. A Windows 95 Dial-Up Networking server doesn't support the same number of protocols as other types of remote access servers, however. This is explained next.

The Windows 95 Client

The Dial-Up Networking software in Windows 95 includes a *Dial-Up Adapter*, which essentially is a driver that makes your modem work like a network card. When you install Dial-Up Networking, Windows 95 installs the Dial-Up Adapter software automatically.

With the Windows 95 Dial-Up Networking client, you can connect to remote access servers that support these protocols:

- *Point-to-Point Protocol (PPP)*. PPP is supported by an increasing number of remote access servers, including many Internet service providers, Windows 95, and Windows NT 3.5x.
- *Novell NetWare Connect*. NRN is NetWare's proprietary remote access protocol that enables clients to connect to NetWare-based LANs.
- *Windows NT 3.1 and Windows for Workgroups 3.11 RAS*. These two operating platforms use asynchronous NetBEUI protocol, and a Windows 95 client can connect to remote access servers running either Windows NT 3.1 or Windows for Workgroups 3.11.
- *Serial Line Interface Protocol (SLIP)*. The SLIP protocol originated in UNIX. Through its support for SLIP, the Windows 95 Dial-Up Networking client enables you to connect to a UNIX server. The SLIP software for the Windows 95 client is included on the Windows 95 CD.

NOTE The Windows 95 Dial-Up Networking server software doesn't support SLIP. It supports only NetBEUI and PPP protocols. Therefore, a Windows 95 Dial-Up Networking server can't act as a gateway to the Internet because the server software doesn't support TCP/IP.

The Windows NT Client

The Dial-Up Networking client in Windows NT supports these connection protocols:

- *Point-to-Point Protocol (PPP)*. See the explanation of PPP in the previous section.
- *Serial Line Interface Protocol (SLIP)*. See the explanation of SLIP in the previous section.
- *Point-to-Point Tunneling Protocol (PPTP)*. This protocol allows secure connections across the Internet. If your computer is connected to the Internet, you can use PPTP to connect to a remote LAN.

Requirements for Dial-Up Networking

To use Dial-Up Networking, you need the following:

- A modem compatible with Windows 95/Windows NT
- Roughly 3M of available hard disk space to store the Dial-Up Networking software (about 2M with Windows NT)
- One of the file and printer sharing services (included with Windows 95/ Windows NT) if you want to use the remote server's or LAN's resources

As explained previously, only the Dial-Up Networking client software is included with Windows 95. You also need the Microsoft Plus! for Windows 95 add-on to use the Dial-Up Networking server software. Both client and server software is included with Windows NT.

Installing and Configuring Dial-Up Networking

Adding and configuring Dial-Up Networking on your system requires two steps:

- Install the Dial-Up Networking software
- Bind a protocol to the Dial-Up Adapter

The next section explains how to add the Dial-Up Networking software to your system.

NOTE The following sections assume you're setting up Dial-Up Networking to connect to an Internet service provider. If you're connecting to another Windows 95 or Windows NT computer or network, add the NetBEUI protocol.

Installing Dial-Up Networking in Windows 95

Setup gives you the option of installing Dial-Up Networking when you install Windows 95. If you didn't install Dial-Up Networking when you installed

Windows 95, you can add the software through the Control Panel. Use the following steps to add Dial-Up Networking to your PC:

1. Open the Control Panel and double-click the Add/Remove Programs icon.
2. Click the Windows Setup tab to display the Windows Setup property page.
3. Click the Communications item in the list of installed components; then choose the Details button.
4. In the Communications dialog box, place a check beside the Dial-Up Networking item; then choose OK.
5. On the Add/Remove Programs Properties sheet, choose OK. Windows 95 then adds the Dial-Up Networking software to your PC, prompting you for the Windows 95 disks or CD if necessary. Follow the prompts to complete the installation process.

Adding Protocols

The next step in configuring Dial-Up Networking for Windows 95 is to bind one or more network protocols to the Dial-Up Adapter. *Binding* a protocol associates it with the adapter and causes the adapter to use the protocol when communicating with the server.

To add a protocol to the Dial-Up Adapter, follow these steps:

1. Open the Control Panel and double-click the Network icon to display the Network property sheet (see Figure 21.2).

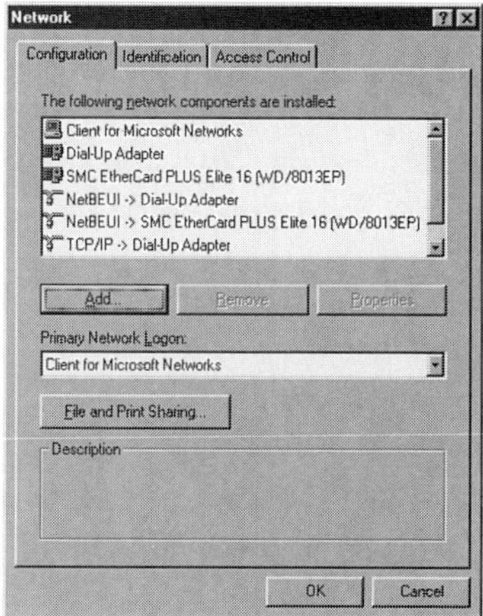

FIG. 21.2
Use the Configuration page to add a protocol to the Dial-Up Adapter.

2. Scroll through the list of installed services to determine if the protocol you need to use with the Dial-Up Adapter is already installed. If so, it should already be associated with the Dial-Up Adapter, and you can skip to step 6.
3. If the TCP/IP protocol is not yet installed, click the Add button.
4. From the Select Network Component dialog box, choose Protocol; then choose Add.
5. In the Select Network Protocol dialog box, choose Microsoft and TCP/IP, then choose OK.
6. When the Configuration page reappears, select the Dial-Up Adapter, choose Properties, and click the Bindings tab to display the Bindings page (see Figure 21.3).

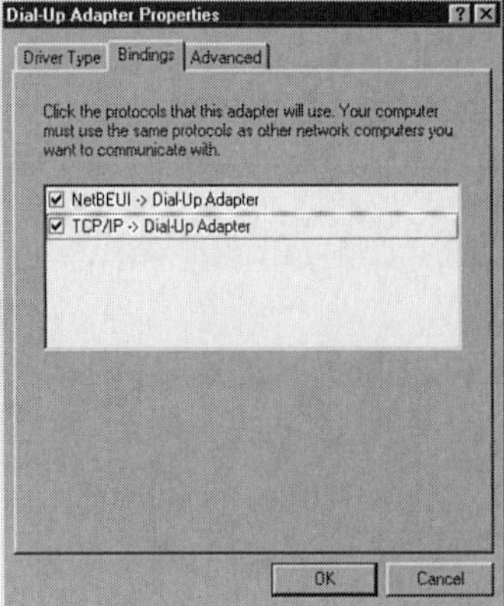

FIG. 21.3
Use the Bindings page to specify which protocols the Dial-Up Adapter will use.

7. Place a check beside each of the protocols you want the Dial-Up Adapter to use; then choose OK.
8. If you need to configure the TCP/IP protocol, refer to Chapter 20 to learn what settings you need to provide. When you finish configuring the protocol(s), choose OK. Windows 95 prompts you to reboot the system.

TIP The Dial-Up Adapter requires a protected mode NDIS driver in order to work. While the Dial-Up Adapter property sheet is open, click the Driver Type tab and verify that the Enhanced Mode option button is selected.

After the PC reboots, you're ready to start using Dial-Up Networking. Windows 95 creates a new folder named Dial-Up Networking in the My Computer folder. Windows 95 stores your Dial-Up Networking connections in this folder. Your next step, therefore, is to create Dial-Up Networking connections for the servers you want to access.

Do I Really Need a Client?

You don't need to use a network client with Dial-Up Networking, but you do need to use at least one network protocol. If you want to access shared resources on the remote computer or its LAN, you do need to use a network protocol. Use the Client for Microsoft Networks if you're connecting to a Windows 95, Windows NT, or Windows for Workgroups server.

If you're just connecting to the Internet, then you don't need—and should not use—a client. If you bind a client to the TCP/IP connection and file sharing is enabled for that client, you make it possible for other people on the Internet to browse your computer. That's a big, potential security and privacy risk. Without a client, you're safe.

You install a client in much the same way as you install a network protocol. Use the steps listed previously in this section for installing a protocol, but in step 4, choose Client rather than Protocol. Follow the prompts to select and install the client you need.

Installing Dial-Up Networking in Windows NT

You can install Dial-Up Networking when you install Windows NT. Or, you can add it later. Use these steps to add Dial-Up Networking in Windows NT:

1. If you haven't already done so, click the Modems icon in the Control Panel to install the modem you'll be using for the Dial-Up Networking connection.
2. Open the Control Panel.
3. Choose the Network icon, then select the Services tab to display the Service property sheet.
4. If Remote Access Service is not already listed in the Network Services list, click the Add button.

5. Select the Remote Access Service item from the Select Network Services dialog box and click OK.
6. When prompted to do so, enter the path to the appropriate directory (Alpha, I386, and so on) on the Windows NT CD. Then, choose OK.
7. After the files have been copied, an Add Port dialog box appears. Select the modem port you want Dial-Up Networking to use, then click OK.
8. RAS Setup next asks you if you want it to automatically detect the modem. Choose OK if you want it to (recommended), or Cancel if you want to choose the modem manually.
9. Next, RAS setup displays the Configure Port Usage dialog box (see Figure 21.4). You can configure RAS to dial out only, receive calls only, or both dial out and receive calls. Choose the option that you want and click OK.

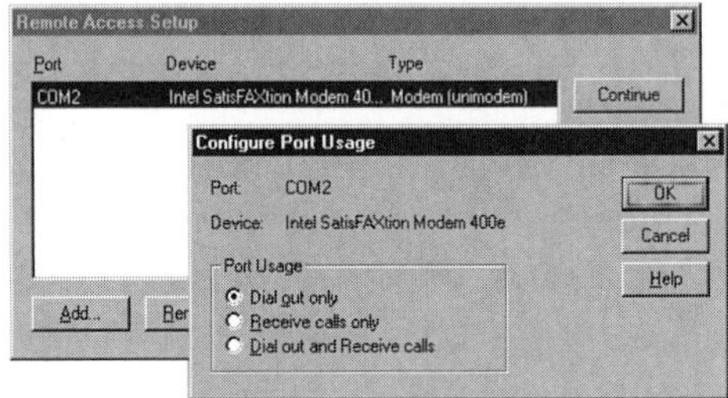

FIG. 21.4
You can configure Dial-Up Networking to dial out, receive calls, or both.

10. RAS setup configures the software, then returns to the Network Settings property sheet. Choose OK to close the property sheet.
11. You are prompted to restart your computer. You must do so before using Dial-Up Networking.

Using a Dial-Up Networking Session

When you choose a resource or feature available only by a Dial-Up Networking connection, Windows automatically connects for you. You also can start a Dial-Up Networking session yourself. The next section explains how.

Creating a Dial-Up Networking Connection—Windows 95

To open the Dial-Up Networking folder, double-click My Computer; then double-click the Dial-Up Networking folder icon. Or choose Start, Programs, Accessories, and Dial-Up Networking. At first, the Dial-Up Networking contains only one icon—the Make New Connection icon. Selecting the Make New Connection icon starts a wizard that helps you set up a Dial-Up Networking session. As you create various Dial-Up Networking connections, their icons appear in the Dial-Up Networking folder.

Use the following steps to run the Make New Connection Wizard and create your first Dial-Up Networking session:

1. If you haven't set up your modem yet, do so now. See Chapter 18 for an explanation of how to install a modem.
2. Double-click My Computer; then double-click the Dial-Up Networking folder icon to open the Dial-Up Networking folder.
3. Double-click the Make New Connection icon. The dialog box shown in Figure 21.5 appears.

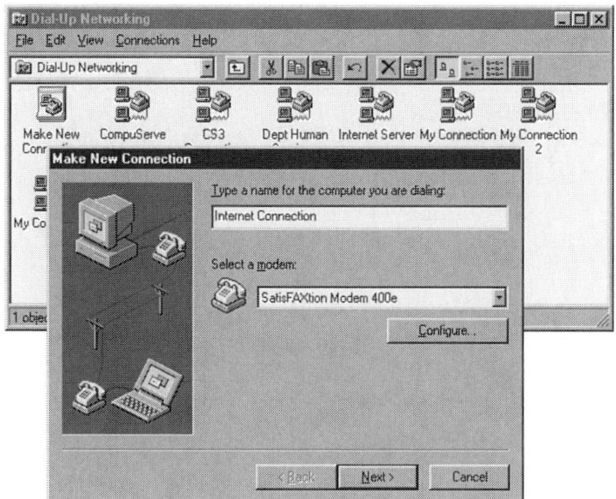

FIG. 21.5
The Make New Connection Wizard automates the process of creating a Dial-Up Networking session.

4. Type a name for the computer you're dialing in the text box provided. This is the name that appears under the session icon as its description. The name also appears in the list of available servers whenever Windows 95 prompts you to select a Dial-Up Networking connection for Remote Mail or other features or programs that use Dial-Up Networking.
5. From the Select a Modem drop-down list, choose the modem you want to use for the Dial-Up Networking connection.
6. If you need to set options for the modem, choose the Configure button to open the property sheet for the modem and set its properties.
7. After you have configured the modem, return to the Make New Connection Wizard and click Next.
8. The wizard prompts you to provide the area code, phone number, and country code of the server you are dialing. Specify these items of information; then choose Next and Finish. Windows 95 adds the icon for the session to the Dial-Up Networking folder.

Creating a Dial-Up Networking Connection—Windows NT 4.0

Creating a Dial-Up Networking connection is easy in Windows NT. Here are the steps to follow:

1. Double-click the My Computer icon on the desktop.
2. Double-click the Dial-Up Networking icon in My Computer.
3. In the Dial-Up Networking dialog box (see Figure 21.6), click the New button.
4. Enter a name for the connection, as well as the phone number, then choose OK.
5. Click the More button, then click Edit Entry and Modem Properties.
6. Set the options in the resulting property sheet according to the settings required by the server you're calling.
7. Choose OK to close the property sheet when you're satisfied with the settings.

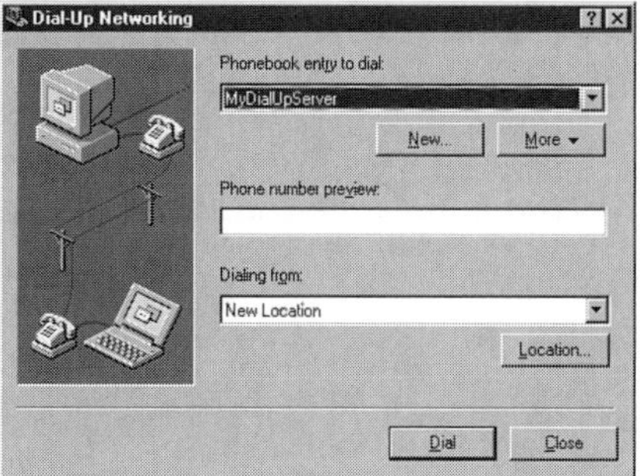

FIG. 21.6
Use the Dial-Up Networking dialog box to select and create connections.

Connecting to a Remote Server—Windows 95

Connecting to a remote server in Windows 95 is easy. Just open the Dial-Up Networking folder and double-click the icon of the session you want to use. Dial-Up Networking displays a Connect To dialog box similar to the one shown in Figure 21.7.

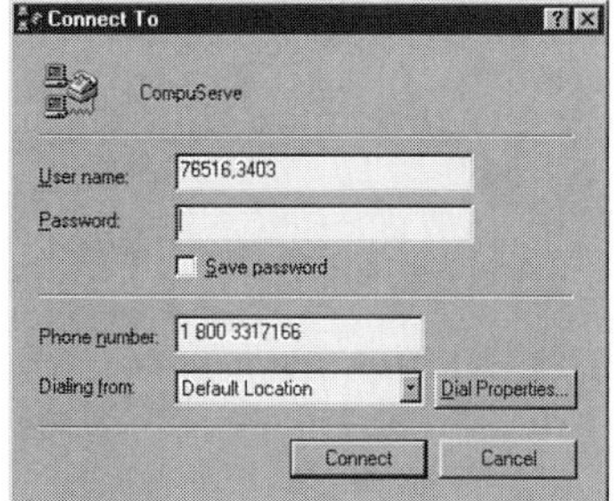

FIG. 21.7
The Connect To dialog box lets you set options before connecting.

In the User Name text box, enter the user name under which you want to log onto the remote server. In the Password text box, enter the password for your logon account. If you want Dial-Up Networking to save the password so that you don't have to type it next time, enable the Save Password check box. Dial-Up Networking stores the password in your password cache file.

If you want to change settings such as the phone number, dialing properties, or dialing location, use the controls in the Connect To dialog box to set them. Then click the Connect button. Dial-Up Networking dials the server and attempts to connect. After the connection is established, you can begin using the remote server's resources, such as browsing the Internet.

Connecting to a Remote Server—Windows NT

Connecting with Dial-Up Networking under Windows NT is even easier than with Windows 95. Open My Computer and double-click the Dial-Up Networking icon. In the Dial-Up Networking dialog box that appears, select the phonebook entry you want to use, then click Dial.

Setting a Session's Properties—Windows 95

The Make New Connection Wizard doesn't give you much control over a Dial-Up Networking session's properties, but you can change the properties after you create the session. To do so, open the Dial-Up Networking folder and right-click the session's icon; then choose Properties from the context menu. Windows 95 displays a property sheet for the connection similar to the one shown in Figure 21.8.

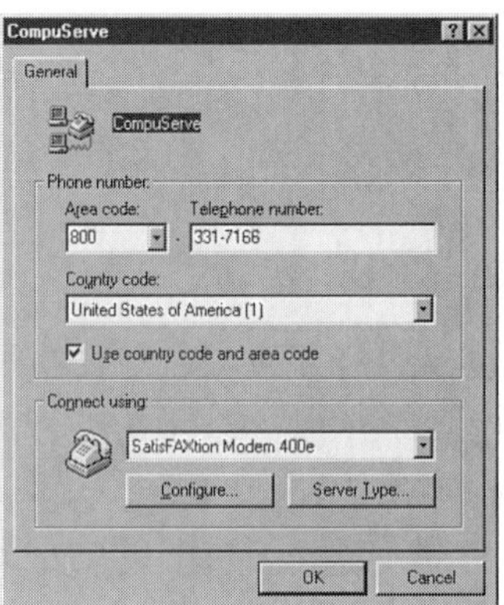

FIG. 21.8
Use the session's property sheet to control its settings.

As you can see in Figure 21.8, you can change the area code, phone number, and modem for the session. You also can click the Configure button to configure the modem for the session. Enabling the Use Country Code and Area Code check box causes Dial-Up Networking to include the country and area codes in the dialing string. Clear the check box if the number is a local one.

Next, specify which protocol you want the session to use by clicking the Server Type button. Windows 95 displays the Server Types dialog box shown in Figure 21.9.

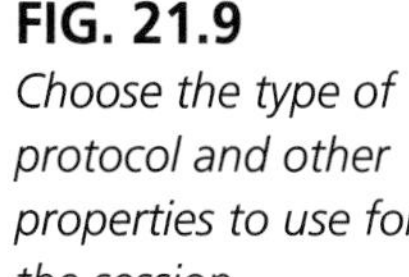

FIG. 21.9
Choose the type of protocol and other properties to use for the session.

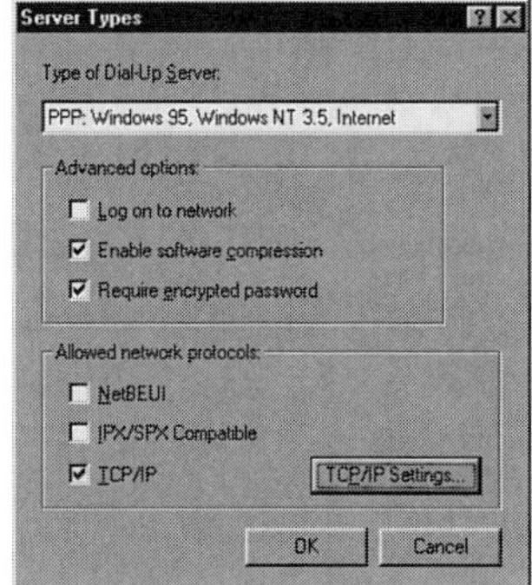

The following list explains options you can set in the Server Types dialog box:

- *Type of Dial-Up Server.* From this drop-down list, select the type of server to which you're connecting. Choose PPP for a Windows NT 3.5x or Windows 95 remote access server, or for a PPP-based Internet service provider. Choose Windows for Workgroups and Windows NT 3.1 to use asynchronous NetBEUI.
- *Log on to the Network.* Enable this check box if you want Dial-Up Networking to attempt to log onto the remote server using the user name and password you supplied in the Connect To dialog box.
- *Enable Software Compression.* Enable this check box if you want Dial-Up Networking to compress data as it is sent to speed performance. The server must also support software compression.
- *Require Encrypted Password.* Enable this check box to ensure maximum security for your password. With this check box enabled, Dial-Up Networking encrypts your password before sending it to the server. If the server doesn't support encrypted passwords, the password is sent unencrypted.
- *NetBEUI, IPX/SPX Compatible, TCP/IP.* Choose one or more of these check boxes to select the network protocol you want to use for the connection. The server must support the protocol(s) you select. For an Internet service provider, all you need is TCP/IP.
- *TCP/IP Settings.* Click this button if you want to specify settings for the TCP/IP protocol different from the default settings stored in the Control Panel. Dial-Up Networking displays the dialog box shown in Figure 21.10.

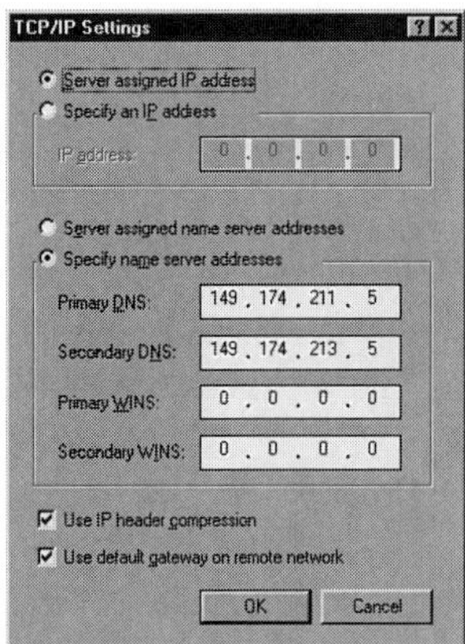

FIG. 21.10
Use the TCP/IP Settings dialog box to specify TCP/IP settings different from your Windows 95 default settings.

TIP Each Dial-Up Networking session can use a different set of TCP/IP settings. For example, one server might require an explicit IP address, and another server might assign one to you when you log on. You can configure each session appropriately through the TCP/IP Settings dialog box.

Use the TCP/IP Settings dialog box to set the following properties:

- *Server Assigned IP Address.* Choose this option button if the server assigns an IP address to you when you log on.
- *Specify an IP Address.* Choose this option button to specify an explicit IP address. Enter the IP address in the IP Address box.
- *Server Assigned Name Server Addresses.* Choose this option button if you want the server to assign DNS and WINS server IP address to you when you log on.
- *Specify Name Server Addresses.* Choose this option button to specify explicit IP addresses of your primary and secondary DNS and WINS servers. Enter the appropriate server IP addresses in the boxes provided.
- *Use IP Header Compression.* If the remote server supports IP header compression, enable this check box to improve performance. If the server doesn't support IP header compression, clear this check box.
- *Use Default Gateway on Remote Network.* Enable this check box if you want the Dial-Up Networking to automatically route all your TCP/IP traffic to the remote network's default router.

After you specify the settings you want to use, choose OK to close the TCP/IP Settings dialog box. Then choose OK to close the Server Types dialog box. Choose OK a third time to close the property sheet for the connection.

NOTE Another connection protocol you can use is SLIP. SLIP is often required to connect to some UNIX-based servers, although most Internet service providers support the PPP protocol. For more information about SLIP, refer to the *Windows 95 Communications Handbook* and *Windows NT Communications Handbook*, both from Que.

Setting a Session's Properties—Windows NT

After you create a Dial-Up Networking connection in Windows NT, you can modify almost all of its properties to suit your preferences and the requirements of the remote server or network. To change a connection's properties, first open the Dial-Up Networking client by double-clicking the Dial-Up Networking icon in My Computer. When the Dial-Up Networking dialog box appears, choose from the Phonebook Entry to Dial drop-down list the connection you want to edit. Then, click More and choose Edit Entry and Modem Properties to display the Edit Phonebook Entry property sheet (see Figure 21.11).

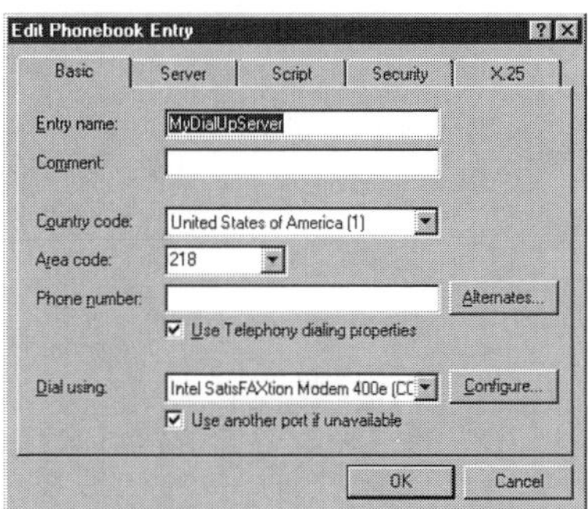

FIG. 21.11 *Use the Edit Phonebook Entry property sheet to modify the settings for a connection you've already created.*

The pages on the Edit Phonebook Entry property sheet are:

- *Basic.* This page lets you set the name of the connection, phone number, and a couple of other basic settings.
- *Server.* Use this page to specify the type of connection protocol to use, as well as the network protocol to use (PPP and TCP/IP for Internet).

- *Script.* Use this page to select a script to run after dialing. A script can help automate the connection process. Some Internet providers require that you enter information when you connect, and you can use a script to enter that information for you.
- *Security.* This page lets you specify the type of security used by the Dial-Up Networking client.
- *X.25.* This page applies only to those users who connect through an X.25 network. You probably do not.

Setting Up a Dial-Up Networking Server

Windows 95 includes all the client software you need to dial into a remote access server with Dial-Up Networking. You also can set up your Windows 95 workstation as a Dial-Up Networking server, but you need the Microsoft Plus! for Windows 95 add-on to do it. Plus! includes Dial-Up Networking server software that lets other users dial into your PC to access your PC's resources, and to access the resources of your LAN if the PC is connected to a LAN.

NOTE This section explains how to use the Dial-Up Networking Server software included with Plus! for Windows 95. Server capability is built into Windows NT's Dial-Up Networking software. Just enable dial-in when you install Dial-Up Networking (explained in the earlier section "Installing Dial-Up Networking in Windows NT").

The Windows 95 Dial-Up Networking server software supports NetBEUI and IPX/SPX protocols, enabling clients that use those protocols to dial in and use resources. The Windows 95 Dial-Up Networking server doesn't support TCP/IP or NetWare's NRN protocols, however, which means you can't connect with a NetWare dial-up client or use the Windows 95 server as a TCP/IP gateway. The Windows 95 server supports PPP and asynchronous NetBEUI (used by Windows NT 3.1 and Windows for Workgroups 3.11); but it doesn't support SLIP, CSLIP, or NetWare's NRN protocols.

The Windows 95 Dial-Up Networking server supports two types of security: *share-level* and *user-level.* With share-level security, shared resources are protected using passwords. Any user that has the correct password can access the shared resource.

All Windows 95 workstations use share-level security to protect resources they are sharing.

User-level security provides greater security by requiring access to be handled through a Windows NT or NetWare security provider. When a user tries to access a resource, the request is directed to the security server. The server checks its security database to determine if the user is authorized to use the resource. If so, the security server grants access to the resource. Access is denied if the user doesn't have the necessary access privilege. Using user-level security requires that your Windows 95 Dial-Up Networking server be connected to a LAN that contains a Windows NT or NetWare server that can act as a security server.

Installing the Dial-Up Networking Server

To install the Windows 95 Dial-Up Networking server software, run the Setup program for your Microsoft Plus! product. In Setup, choose the Custom option to enable you to select which items to install. Select the Dial-Up Networking Server from the Options list; then follow the remaining instructions in Setup to complete the installation process.

Configuring the Dial-Up Networking Server

After you install the Dial-Up Networking server, you might not know it's there. The only real indication is a new item in your Dial-Up Networking folder's menu. Open the Dial-Up Networking folder; choose Connections, then Dial-Up Server. Dial-Up Networking displays a Dial-Up Server property page similar to the one shown in Figure 21.12.

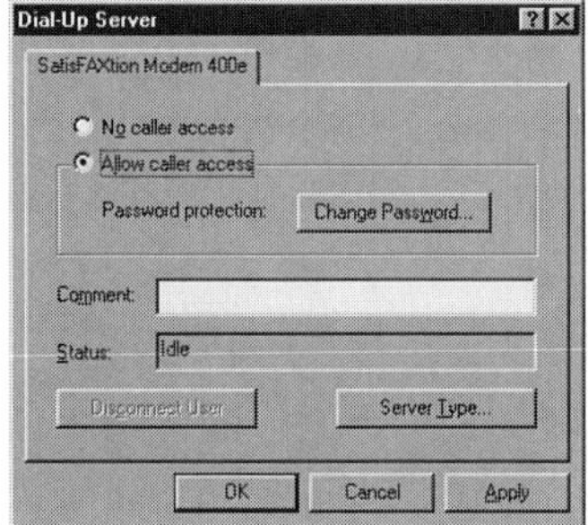

FIG. 21.12
Use the Dial-Up Server dialog box to enable callers to dial into your PC.

To allow others to dial into your PC, choose the Allow Caller Access option button. If you're using share-level security, you can assign a password for call-in access. Anyone calling in must provide the correct password to be connected. To assign the password, click the Change Password button to open a simple dialog box in which you specify the password for your PC.

If you're using user-level security, the Dial-Up Server dialog box is slightly different. With user-level security, you must click the Add button and add each user who you want to have access. The list of available user names comes from the security server on the LAN. After you add names, they show up in the User Name list on the Dial-Up Server dialog box.

NOTE User-level security applies not only to dial-in users, but also to users on your local network who want to access resources on your PC. Share-level security is the default. To turn on user-level security, open the Control Panel, double-click the Network icon, and then click the Access Control tab of the Network property sheet. Select the User-Level Access Control option button; then choose OK. Windows 95 restarts your PC to apply the change.

After you configure the security options, you need to specify the type of connection protocol your Windows 95 Dial-Up Networking server will use. On the Dial-Up Server dialog box, click the Server Type button to display the Server Types dialog box shown in Figure 21.13.

FIG. 21.13
You must specify the type of connection protocol to use.

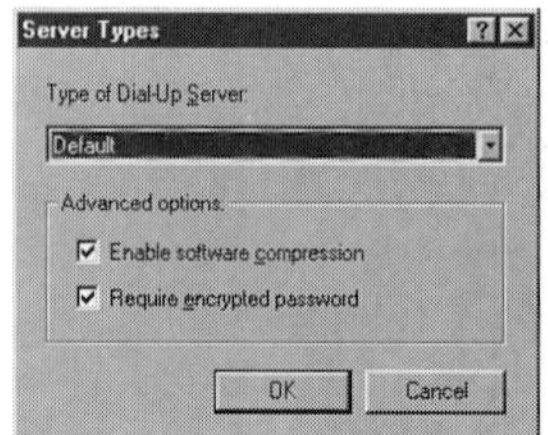

If you select the Default server type, your Dial-Up Networking server attempts to use PPP to connect callers, and if the PPP connection fails, attempts asynchronous NetBEUI. If the NetBEUI connection fails, the call terminates. If you want to limit calls specifically to either PPP or NetBEUI, select the desired protocol from the drop-down list.

Two other options on the Server Types dialog box let you control the connection:

- *Enable Software Compression*. Enable this check box if you want the server to use software compression to improve data transfer speed. The remote user must also be using software compression. If not, the server connects without compression.
- *Require Encrypted Password*. Enable this check box to require the caller's client to transmit the logon password in encrypted format. If you clear this check box, the password is sent unencrypted.

Choose OK to return to the Dial-Up Server dialog box; then click OK to begin monitoring the port for incoming calls.

Terminating a User

Occasionally, you might need to terminate a user's connection to your Dial-Up Networking server. The user might have forgotten to log off and terminate the connection, for example, which is tying up the line and preventing other callers from connecting. Or, you might need to disconnect a user for security reasons.

To disconnect a user, open the Dial-Up Networking folder and choose Connections, Dial-Up Server to open the Dial-Up Server dialog box. Click the Disconnect User button. Dial-Up Networking prompts you to verify that you want to disconnect the current caller.

Voice and Fax Messaging

Going online means many things today. You can transfer data to another computer, browse the World Wide Web, send a fax, and now have your computer answer the telephone and take your messages. All it takes is a modem with the right features and a telephone line.

Communications-impaired users would need a printer and a fax machine to send a fax. To take and pass on messages, such users would need an answering machine or a secretary. A properly equipped computer can minimize these tasks by requiring just a couple of keystrokes to accomplish the same things.

In this chapter, I cover these topics:

- Installing a modem
- What your system settings are and how to find them
- Checking the features to look for
- An overview of Voice Messaging
- Faxing from your PC

Installing the Modem

This section looks at the installation of different modems. Regardless of which features you decide to get, the installation of the modems is the same.

Before You Install a Modem, You Need:

- ☑ A Phillips screwdriver (internal modem)
- ☑ A cable between the modem and computer (external modem)
- ☑ A phone cord (all flavors)
- ☑ The current system settings

General Installation Information

Whether you have purchased an external, internal, or PC Card modem with any of these features, you still have to connect the modem to your computer.

If you have a Plug-and-Play compatible modem, it is easy to set this up with your computer. There are no switches or jumpers to set because you configure the modem using software.

Windows 95 and NT 4.0 automatically sense that you have added a Plug and Play device and prompt you through the Setup Wizard. The Setup Wizard even suggests settings to use based upon the equipment you already have.

When you have a modem that has jumpers or switches that have to be set, you need to determine what IRQs and addresses are used by other devices already installed in your system. If you are using a computer with Windows 3.x or Windows for Workgroups, go to a DOS prompt and run MSD.EXE. MSD, the Microsoft Diagnostics program included with DOS, determines how your computer hardware is set up.

MSD prints out a report of the information it gathers, so it is not necessary to take notes yet. Print out a report for LPT Ports, COM Ports, and IRQ Status.

Considering the used ports and interrupts (IRQ), you then enter nonconflicting settings in the appropriate software configuration. If you have switches on the modem, set these to match the software settings.

The most common setting to determine on a modem and in the software configuration is the COM port—the serial communications device and setting. Most often, computers will have two serial ports: COM 1 and COM 2.

If you have two connectors on your computer and get an internal modem, you have to disable one of the internal COM ports. Usually there is either a switch in the internal card or motherboard to designate, enable, and disable the COM ports.

At the same time, check whether you are using a serial mouse on one of the ports. Obviously, you will not want to disable that port. It is possible to have up to four COM ports—COM 1, COM 2, COM 3, and COM 4. The four ports share only two IRQ addresses. COM 1 and COM 3 use the same IRQ, and COM 2 and COM 4 share the other IRQ.

Because of this sharing of IRQs, it is important to try to set up your serial devices to minimize concurrent use of the shared IRQs. If you have a mouse on COM 1 and a printer on COM 2, consider assigning the modem to COM 4. It is a relatively common practice to wait until you are offline before printing, so this setting avoids possible interrupt conflict. If you share the IRQ between a mouse and a modem and are using Windows software, you can potentially have problems—losing your mouse, modem, or both—until you restart your system.

The same decisions hold true if you are setting switches or jumpers on a modem (see Figure 22.1). Set the COM port to avoid conflict with other serial devices, and select memory addresses that do not overlap memory addresses being used by other cards or equipment—internal or external.

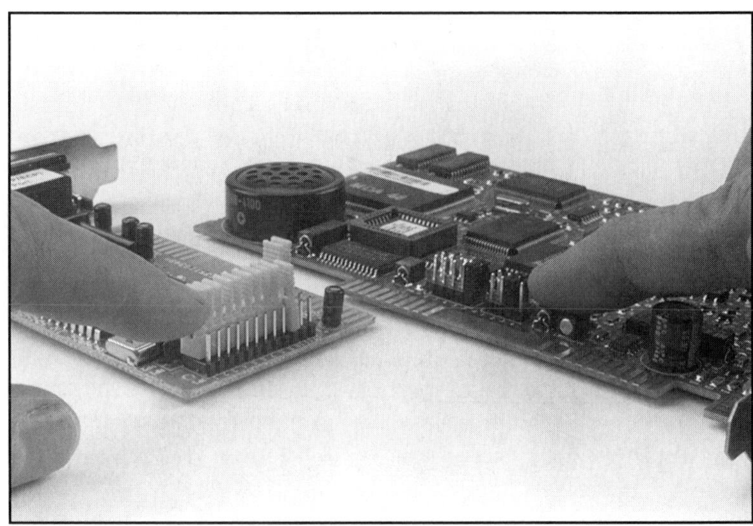

FIG. 22.1
The jumpers on modems can be located anywhere on the circuit board.

If you have a modem with voice messaging, you need to check the manual to see if you can use your telephone to record and review messages, or if you need speakers and a microphone. If you want to use speakers and a microphone, you need to locate the appropriate jacks on the modem.

Speakers, and even microphones, can be located in many places. Some designs stand alone and some attach to monitors, removing them from precious desk space. Some monitors come with speakers and microphones built into the monitor case.

Installing an Internal Modem

Internal modems have become one of the simplest devices to add to your personal computer (see Figure 22.2). Most modem cards are switchless, using software to set up the modem hardware configuration. If there are DIP switches, you have to check your existing hardware for COM port, interrupt, and memory address settings already in use.

FIG. 22.2
Installing an internal modem requires a vacant slot in your computer system.

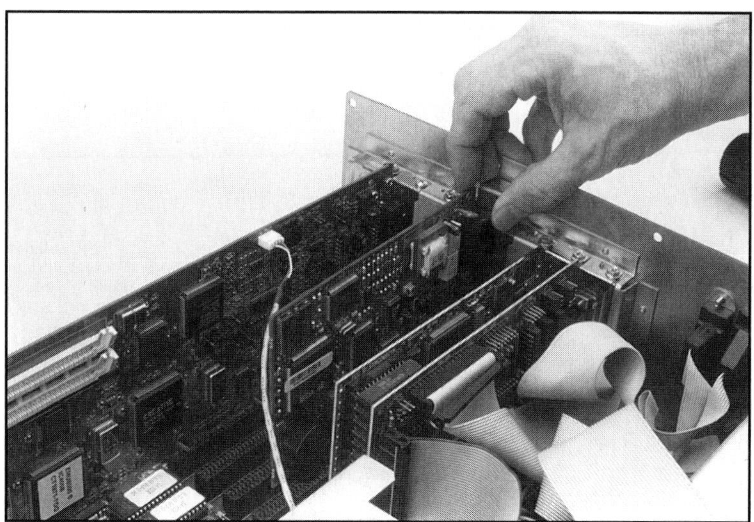

NOTE If the modem has two phone jacks, it is important to check the manual to determine which one is dedicated to the incoming phone line. If you hear a click when connecting to a service or performing any other phone operation—but are not able to dial—reverse the phone jack used to connect to the wall jack.

Usually, the only cords you need for an internal modem are the cords to the phone jack and your telephone, and any cords necessary for sound equipment for a voice messaging system.

Installing an External Modem

An *external modem* has the operational advantage of external lights that you can watch to see what is happening. This is a leftover feature from the days when computers had banks of lights which the operators had to interpret. Also, it is easier to move an external modem if you want.

The downside is that external modems do not get their power from the computer. A separate power supply is necessary, usually raising the price. Also, the external modem takes up additional desk space, and it requires that you have another outlet on your powerbar.

Connect external modems to the computer using a serial cable and a phone cord to the wall jack (see Figure 22.3). You can use a straight-through cable with as few as four wires. Most external modems have a DB25 connector. PCs, laptops, or whatever type of system you have may have DB25 or DB9 connectors.

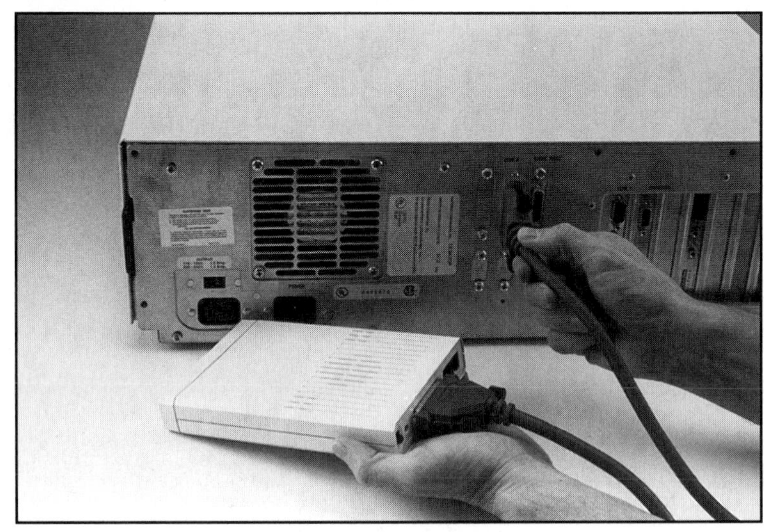

FIG. 22.3
Installing an external modem requires a cable to connect the modem to your computer system.

These designations—DB25 and DB9—describe the pin types and number of pins in a connector. A DB25 connector is a 25-pin connector. In Figure 22.3, you can see a desktop PC with both DB25 and DB9 serial connectors. Usually when both types of connectors are on a PC, the DB9 is preset as COM 1 and the DB25 is COM 2 (see Figure 22.4).

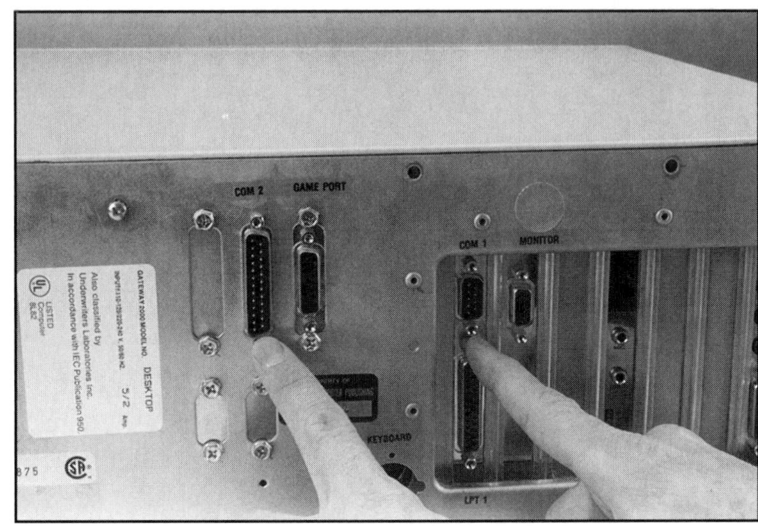

FIG. 22.4
In this computer system, COM 1 has a DB9 connector and COM 2 uses a DB25 connector.

If you are connecting to a DB25 on your computer, a DB25M to DB25F cable is all you need (see Figure 22.5). When you are using a DB9 on the PC, look either for a DB25M to DB9F cable or a similar adapter for a DB25M to DB25F cable.

FIG. 22.5
Use an adapter to connect a cable with a DB25 connector to COM 1 port with a DB9.

Getting on the Road with PC Card Modems

Another type of internal modem is the *PC Card modem*, formerly referred to as *PCMCIA*. A PC Card is the size of a small stack of business cards, and slips into a slot on the side of laptops. Just as with internal devices, PC Card devices connect directly to the bus on the motherboard and provide fast access between the CPU and the modem.

PC Card adapters are available for desktop and tower type computers. However, because of the extra cost of the PC Cards themselves, you commonly purchase one for use with laptops and other portable devices with limited internal space. The PC Card slots are defined as Type II and Type III slots.

NOTE The cords you use to connect PC Card modems to the phone lines are called *dongles* because they dangle from the side of our laptops. Dongles break in accordance with how much you use the PC Card modem. It is important to know where to get a replacement or to have a replacement on hand if you use it often or are traveling.

After inserting your PC Card modem into a PC slot, the only other hardware setup is connecting to the phone lines. Plug the dongle into the modem and the phone cord into the dongle jack. If you have a PC Card modem with the patented XJack connector, you can plug the standard phone cord directly into the PC Card through the XJack.

Connecting to the Telephone Lines

The phone lines that you connect to are the simplest part of the equipment needs for faxing and voice messaging, and the most important. You can use any standard phone line in your home or in the office. It may even be possible to use your cellular phone to make the connection to the phone company's trunk system.

If you are working in an office with a PBX system, it may be necessary for you to have a dedicated line that does not go through the PBX system.

If you are using a phone service that has call waiting from the local phone company, this feature needs to be disabled when you are using the phone line for faxing or voice messaging. This is as simple to do as calling the phone company for the codes to disable the feature, and entering the codes in the modem setup.

For example, Pacific Bell says to press ***70** before dialing your number. Call waiting will be turned off for the duration of this one phone call, restarting automatically when the call is discontinued.

TIP If you are including the code in the phone number dialed by your software, make sure that there are several commas before the code and the phone number. The commas pause the dialing of the subsequent number for several seconds. The pause is used to wait for a second dial tone after the call waiting feature is disabled. Do not hang up after entering ***70** (or other code), because hanging up restores the feature.

NOTE If you find that you are losing fax transmissions partway through and are dropped from your online service without reason, get your phone company to check your lines. Especially in the winter, the lines become fouled with condensation, causing communications problems.

Using Voice-Over Data

A separate category of modems is the *Digital Simultaneous Voice and Data (DSVD)* modems that can mix spoken communications with concurrent transmission of digital data over one telephone line. By using a DSVD modem with another user with a DSVD modem, you can talk to each other while transferring files, playing a game, or running a program. This is a valuable capability for a computer support person when showing a client how to do something on his or her computer while using a remote control program.

Sharing a Line for Voice, Data, and Fax

The world of online communication is not without its downsides. One of these drawbacks is the possible need for another phone line to dedicate to your online needs. However, it is possible to get along with just one phone line in your home, and there are solutions for those times when you seem to need more than one line.

Most fax modems and voice messaging capable modems can discriminate the type of calls coming in and start the appropriate software. If a fax is being sent to you, the multi-featured communications program automatically switches to the fax mode when it "hears" the fax signal being transmitted by the incoming call.

When you do not answer a call manually and no fax signal is detected, the program switches to the phone answering mode, and answers the call with your default message. If you have created *mailboxes*, authorized callers can then access their mailboxes, picking up their messages or leaving new messages.

NOTE The mailboxes, or message boxes, created and used with voice messaging software are simply separate areas used to organize the messages. They are referred to as *mailboxes* because an analogy to a post office is accurate—a place for handling incoming and outgoing communications or messages.

Contacting Your Telephone Service

As part of the installation of your modem, you may need to contact your telephone company. You may want information about ISDN service, how to disable your call waiting feature, or the condition of your phone lines. Because you are going to be using the telephone for any of the features you have decided upon, the telephone has become even more indispensable to you.

The main question for you to ask before you purchase an ISDN modem is whether you want to gain speed when you are online by using an ISDN phone line. If the telephone company does not provide this service in your area, do not spend the money on an ISDN modem.

After determining whether to use ISDN, you need to determine what phone-service features you have that could cause problems for your digital communications. The feature that does cause problems is call waiting. When call waiting beeps you to indicate another phone call, the beep can disconnect your modem or possibly distort any transmitted data. Table 22.1 lists the customer service numbers to dial to contact the major telephone service providers in the continental United States and Canada.

Table 22.1 Contact Information for Various Telephone Companies

Phone Company	Telephone Number
Ameritech	(800) 832-6328 or (800) TEAM-DATA
Bell Atlantic	(800) 570-4736 or (800) 570-ISDN
Bell South	(800) 428-4736
Cincinnati Bell	(513) 566-3282 or (513) 566-DATA
GTE	(800) 448-3795 or (800) 483-4926
NYNEX	(800) 438-4736 or (800) GET-ISDN
Pacific Bell	(800) 995-0346
Rochester Telephone	(716) 777-1200
Southwestern Bell	(314) 235-9553
SNET	(800) 430-4736 or (800) 430-ISDN
Stentor (Canada)	(604) 663-5734
U.S. West	(800) 898-9675

Decisions to Make Before Upgrading Your Modem

An important hardware question to ask at the computer store is whether a modem has a Flash ROM and is upgradable by the user. Many add-in devices like modems are being designed with rewritable memory chips that contain the operating instruction for the device. With devices with Flash ROM, a manufacturer can notify you of an upgrade that you can download, and you can perform the upgrade yourself without opening the PC case or having to touch a screwdriver.

Shopping for a New Modem

- ☑ Do you want voice messaging as well as fax?
- ☑ How fast is the fax capability of the modem?
- ☑ Are you ready to get an ISDN-capable modem?
- ☑ Is the modem Plug-and-Play compatible?
- ☑ Do you have to set switches or jumpers on the modem?
- ☑ Are there any cables or other devices needed?
- ☑ Do you need to add speakers or a microphone to your system?
- ☑ Does the modem have Flash ROM for easy upgrading?

An Overview of Voice Messaging

Voice messaging—or, as you may call it in your office, *voice mail*—has become affordable for the home and small business to match the capabilities of the large company telephone systems.

In the "Configuring for Voice Messaging" section of this chapter, you learn how your computer can:

- Be an answering machine
- Handle incoming phone calls
- Set up multiple message boxes
- Customize outgoing messages
- Create a Fax on Demand system

One thing to remember about using your computer system for faxes or voice messaging is that you must leave your computer on. Don't worry that someone else will be able to get on your computer and create havoc. That can only happen if you connect directly to another computer or system, such as to a network or the Internet.

Configuring for Voice Messaging

Unless you have just upgraded to a completely new computer system, the Voice Messaging software will have to be configured to meet your needs. The following sections look at basic setup, customizing outgoing messages, creating message boxes, and creating a Fax on Demand system.

Using Your Computer as an Answering Machine

The simplest way to use your voice-messaging feature is as an answering machine. To put your personal voice-messaging system online, you just have to find the controls for the messaging software and find the Play feature. You can then listen to the messages and review your outgoing greeting through the speakers or headphones connected to your system, or through the handset of your telephone.

Many voice-messaging programs come with a prerecorded outgoing message. You may want to change this to your personal greeting. Click the appropriate Record button or menu option and record your new message. You can probably use a microphone connected to the modem or just pick up the handset of your telephone and record the message.

Handling Incoming Phone Calls

Receiving an incoming phone message is as simple as leaving your computer on with the voice messaging software set to receive calls. When you open the voice messaging software, a message box tells you when you have messages. Just click the Play button to listen to any messages.

A great feature of computer-based voice messaging is what you can do with the messages. If you want, you can save the message for later review, forward it to another person for action, save it in a personal message box, or delete the message from the computer.

When you receive a fax, the voice messaging system determines that it is a fax and then starts the fax program. When your software has an integrated notification feature, you receive a notification for incoming faxes as well.

You can retrieve your waiting messages from the system even when you are on the road. Just call your system, press the appropriate keys on the telephone keypad to access the system, review the message, and determine what action you want for each message.

Setting Up Multiple Message Boxes

A major advantage of your computer-based voice messaging system over a traditional answering machine is the capability to create separate message—or mail—boxes. You can create an area for each member of your family or staff as if each of you had your own extension.

When you create the message boxes, each person can have his or her own password assigned to each assigned box for privacy. You still can have access to these boxes while on the road.

Customizing Outgoing Messages

Just as you can have individual message boxes, you can customize your outgoing message for each box, or just for specific callers, using entered codes from the telephone. The custom messages can provide any type of information, and even direct the caller to do other operations on the messaging system for additional features.

Some of the voice messaging programs also allow you to change your messages remotely by pressing the appropriate keys on the phone to start the record-and-review process.

Fax on Demand

Fax on Demand is a feature of modems with the messaging features. Fax on Demand can handle sets of faxes for retrieval by creating message boxes for the faxes. Faxes to be accessed are placed in different message boxes for organization and security purposes.

You can direct a user to a specific message box that has the instructions for downloading the faxes. Then, by pressing the specified keys on the phone keypad, the users can have the faxes forwarded to another fax machine or fax-equipped computer.

Remote Notification

A small feature to consider when you are comparing different voice messaging software is *remote notification*. Some programs notify your pager or online service when you receive an incoming message or fax.

You could take this feature another step by enabling the remote notification just for specific message boxes, selectively paging you with the notification.

Faxing from Your PC

A fax, or facsimile of an original, has become the business instrument of the 1990s, providing a copy of a document as it originally looked. The only task you cannot do with just a fax modem and your computer is to include your handwritten notes, unless you have a scanner. You can handle any kind of incoming fax and can increase the creative uses for your computer.

Fax systems transmit a document for review by someone at a remote location. The fax modem reduces the amount of paper you use because you can review the received document on-screen. Also, because you transmit original material directly from your computer, it is not necessary to print something out first and then throw it away after transmission. So, your computer is "green" in more ways than just being a power conserving model.

Setting Up Software

There are two primary sources for fax software:

- Third-party publishers
- The OEM software for Windows 95 and NT 4.0

This section uses Windows 95 Mail and Fax setup as an example of the information you need, and where to enter it.

The following steps show you how to configure Windows 95 for fax capabilities:

1. Press Alt+S to open the Start menu from the Windows 95 desktop. Choose Settings, Control Panel.
2. In the Control Panel, select and open the Modem control. If you have not installed your modem, it does not appear in the list. Select Add, and follow the steps in the New Modem Wizard to configure Windows 95 for your modem.
3. Close the Modem Control Panel when you see the modem in the Modem control. Double-click the Mail and Fax icon to open the MS Exchange Properties Settings control.
4. Highlight Microsoft Fax in the list and click the Properties button. The Microsoft Fax Properties dialog box opens.
5. Click the User tab and enter your name, phone number, and other personal or business information that you want to have appear on the cover page of each fax.
6. Select the Modem tab and make sure that your modem is in the list. If you are on a network, check the Let Other People on the Network Use My Modem for Sending Faxes check box to share your modem.
7. Click the Dialing tab to set your location for the software. As you travel through different telephone area codes and time zones, you can use the Dialing preferences to automatically determine when to send a fax. It also decides whether to dial an area code with an outgoing fax.
8. Select the Message tab. You can decide whether to use a cover page or not, what cover page to use, when to send faxes, and other settings related to the sending of faxes.
9. Click OK to return to the MS Exchange Properties Settings dialog box. From here, you can also create a phone book for people you call often. Click OK in the MS Exchange Properties Settings dialog box to close the box and apply the new settings.

The Modem sheet is used to verify the Answer mode setting in the Properties section. Click the Properties button in the Modem tab and check your setting in the Answer Mode group. If you have this set to answer, indicate the number of rings in the Answer After box that you want.

Use the Answer After setting to give yourself a chance to answer the phone before the fax program picks up the call. If you are using a third-party fax/voice-messaging program, check what the program reaction is if you want to answer the call yourself.

Selecting Fax as Printer

Sending a document as a fax is as simple as printing a file. Open the document or file in the program you created it in and choose File, Print. In the Print dialog box, make sure that you have the Fax driver selected as your printer. If the current printer is not the Fax driver, click the Printer button and select the Fax driver.

As with any printout, select the range of pages to print and click the OK button. The Compose New Fax Wizard walks you through the steps of selecting the recipients and cover page, entering a subject and message, and finally dialing and sending the fax.

Your fax is delivered, looking exactly as you intended including any graphics or anything else you have placed in the document. You could have even had your signature scanned at a shop and inserted it into your document.

TIP You may encounter a situation where the fax crashes after one page. If you have been faxing a document—a resume, for example—to different companies and then encounter this situation, check the speed that your fax modem is connecting to the destination machine. If the connection is at 14.4Kbps, set your modem to connect at 9.6Kbps. Some fax machines cannot receive at 14.4Kbps, even though they may connect at that speed.

NOTE Remember to change your Windows Printer setting back to your printer. Unfortunately, Windows sets the printer changes to its Default output device rather than letting you make the device change temporarily.

Formatting Considerations

Because faxes usually included information at the top or bottom of the final page, it can squash the information on the "printed" page slightly or reduce the page symmetrically.

When you change from a printer to the Fax driver, you will see that some margins, tabs, page count, and other page features may have changed. Review your documents before you actually send them.

TIP Have you ever been away from your home or office and needed a printout of something? Hotels, motels, trailer parks, and even gas stations and truck stops have fax machines set up for incoming and outgoing communications. With permission, you can just plug your laptop modem into a telephone, dial the motel's fax number, and go pick up the fax.

Faxing with a Data Modem

It is not even necessary to have fax capability in your modem if you are using an online service. Most online services let you address your messages to their fax server where they can transmit the fax to the number you give them.

On the Road

For the really active business person, consider getting a modem adapter for your cellular phone and a cell phone-compatible modem for your laptop. Cell phone-compatible modems have additional error-checking for signal handling.

Not only can you use the laptop in its communications-on-the-road mode for faxing, but you can also go on to your online service and continue using those services. Get your stock quotes as easily as in your office. Watch out for your phone charges. Cellular services charge by the minute and "surfin'" can run up the per-minute charges regardless of the type of online service you have.

NOTE Check which type of service you have from your cellular provider—analog or digital. Analog is the desired service for making cellular connections to the online world at the time of this writing.

Receiving a Fax

Receiving a fax is almost as simple as sending one. Just as importantly, you do not have to print it out to review. Just open your fax manager software and select the new facsimile, or reopen a saved one.

If you have set the Answer mode for the modem properties to Do Not Answer, follow these steps for configuring MS Exchange in Windows 95 to receive a fax:

1. Press Alt+S to open the Start menu from the Windows 95 desktop. Choose Settings, Control Panel.
2. Close the Modem Control Panel when you see the modem in the Modem control. Click the Mail and Fax icon to open the MS Exchange Properties Settings control.
3. Highlight Microsoft Fax in the list and click the Properties button. The Microsoft Fax Properties dialog box opens.
4. Select the Modem tab and click Properties to open the Fax Modem Properties dialog box.
5. Set the Answer After option in the Answer mode group by pressing Alt+A to select the Answer After radio button. Then press Tab to set the number of times the telephone rings before the program answers. Press Enter to close the dialog box.
6. Click OK in the Microsoft Fax Properties dialog box. Then click OK in the MS Exchange Properties Settings dialog box to close and apply the new settings.

When you receive a fax, the software saves it to your hard drive with a temporary name. You can then view the fax on your screen or make a printout. The fax can also be forwarded to another machine or saved for later review.

A fax is actually received as graphic images and is saved as graphic files. If you have the necessary software and want to convert the text back into data, you can run most faxes through an *OCR (Optical Character Recognition)* program that attempts to read the text. However, OCR only has about an 80 to 90 percent accuracy rate. It may be necessary to review the data to correct any errors afterward, so it may not pay off in the long run.

Now that you have looked at all of the possibilities that buying a modem loaded with fax and voice messaging features can add to your office, get out there and put that modem in your computer.

PART VI

Maintenance and Disaster Recovery

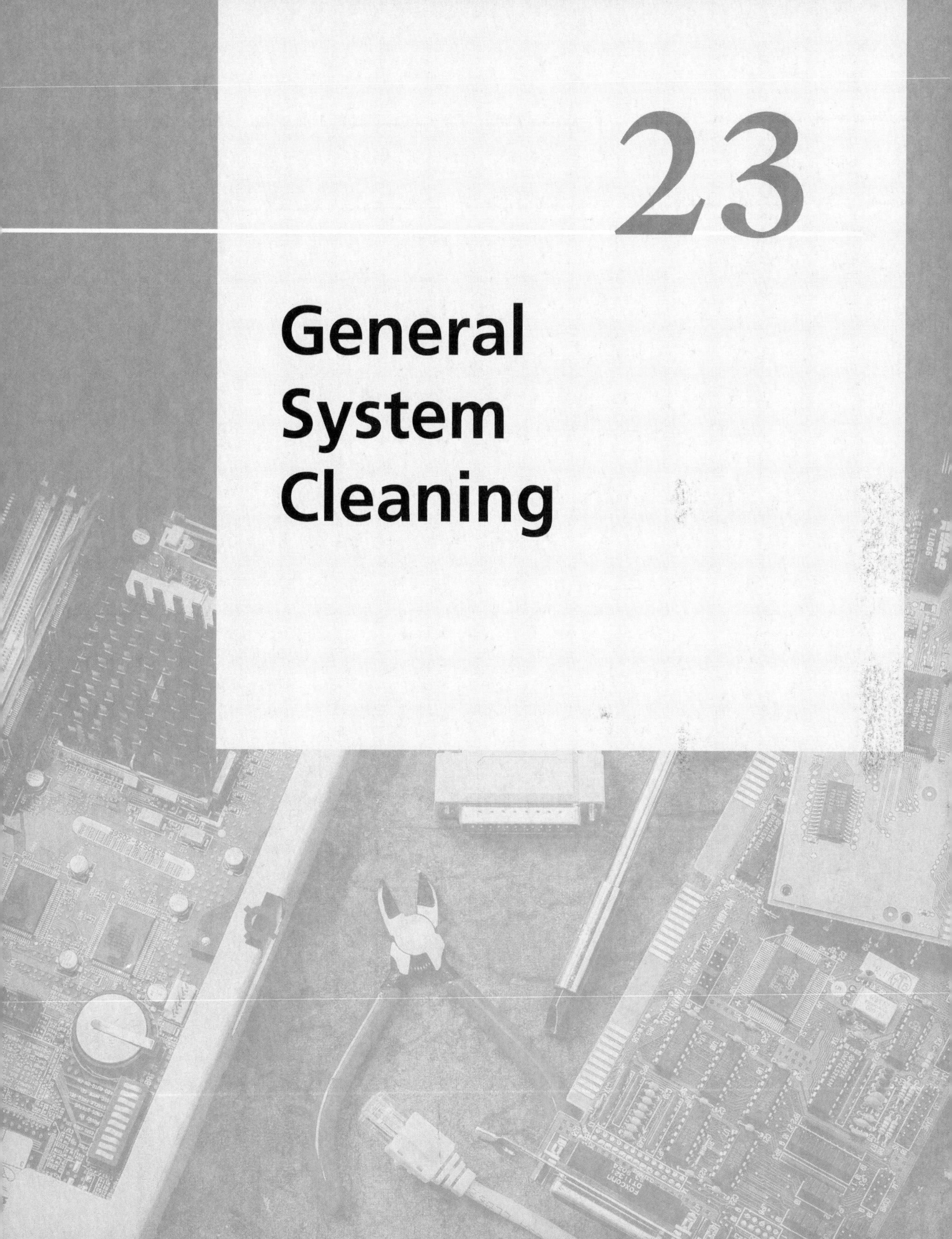

23

General System Cleaning

This book is about upgrading, so why cover maintenance topics like cleaning? As long as you have the system open to perform an upgrade, you might as well take the time to clean it up a bit. Plus, a little maintenance now and then will help you put off an upgrade a little longer and prolong the life of your computer.

This chapter explains some simple ways to keep your system working well, including the following:

- Cleaning the keyboard
- Cleaning the system unit
- Cleaning disk drives and drive heads
- Cleaning the monitor
- Cleaning mice and other input devices

System Unit

Many upgrades involve opening the system to install or remove adapters or other devices. You'll probably find that your computer is a magnet for dust and that you have an entire warren of dust bunnies living inside your computer. Although the dust won't cause any problems electrically, it does cut down the efficiency of the cooling fans and can act as an insulating blanket to keep heat from radiating away from components. So, you should clean out the system unit each time you open it to perform an upgrade, and every two or three months, depending on how dusty your office environment is.

> **CAUTION** Make sure you shut down, turn off, and unplug the PC before you open it and start cleaning inside it.

The best tools for this job are a clean, stiff-bristle paintbrush and a vacuum cleaner (see Figure 28.1). Use the brush to knock the dust loose so the vacuum can remove it. Although you should vacuum any dust you find in the system (within reason, of course), pay particular attention to these areas:

- *The power supply.* Never open the power supply to try to clean inside it! You should vacuum the dust from the holes in the side of the power supply, though. This helps the power supply run cooler and enables it to pull more air from the case. Also, working from the back of the power supply, vacuum the dust from the fan blades. You might want to temporarily remove the metal wire guard covering the fan (if it is removable) so you can get to the fan blades, but be sure to replace the guard when you're finished.
- *The CPU fan.* This area can build up almost as much dust as the power supply. Because the CPU generates so much heat, it's important to keep the fan clean to retain its cooling efficiency.
- *Secondary fan.* Some computers have a secondary cooling fan at the front of the case. If so, clean the dust from the blades.
- *Empty bus slots.* Keeping the dust out of these slots ensures that you'll have a good connection if you later install an adapter in the slot.
- *Floppy disk drives.* The floppy drives—particularly the top one—tend to collect dust. You probably won't be able to get to them very easily, but remove as much dust as you can from them.

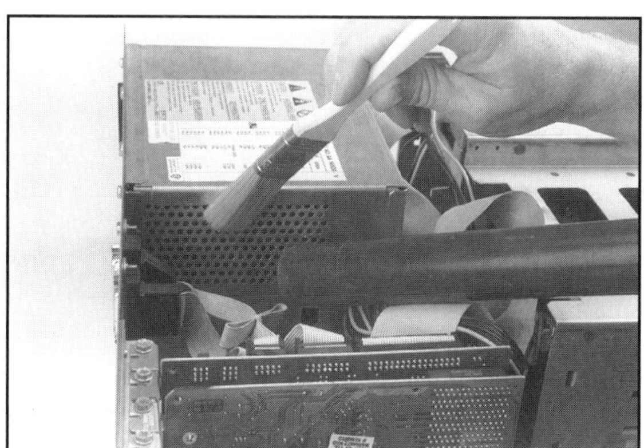

FIG. 23.1
Cleaning out the system increases cooling efficiency and potentially prolongs the life of the computer.

CAUTION You should resist the temptation to reverse the vacuum or use compressed air to blow the dust out of the computer. First, all you're doing is blowing the dust back into the room so it can get sucked back into the computer! More important, however, is the fact that the dust has a tendency to work its way into the floppy drives, bus slots, and other hard-to-reach places. Also, take care with the brush and vacuum nozzle not to bang or damage anything.

After you've cleaned up the inside of the computer and put it back together, give some thought to tidying up all those cords sticking out the back. You'll find different types of wire ties at your local computer or electronics store. One type I particularly like is a Velcro strap that you wrap around cables to keep them neat (see Figure 23.2).

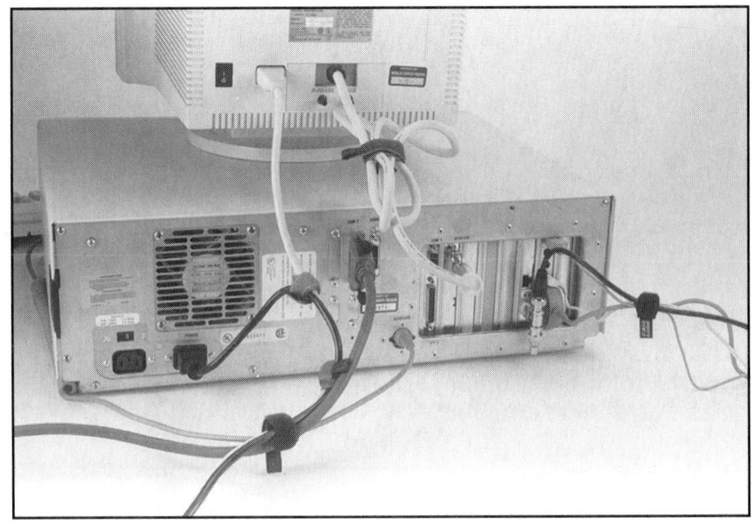

FIG. 23.2
Take some time to tidy up all those cords hanging out the back of your computer.

TIP You can find small, hand-held, battery-powered vacuums with tiny collector bags attached to them sold in some computer and electronics stores. Don't bother buying one. They suck…or rather, they don't suck.

Keyboard

You would probably be amazed and a little horrified at all the crud that collects in your keyboard. Skin cells, hair, dust, and all sorts of other junk have a tendency to call your keyboard "home." The first line of defense is a can of compressed gas (see Figure 23.3), which you can find at computer and electronics stores. The can includes a tiny straw that fits in the can's nozzle to let you direct the gas into tight spots, like between the keys.

FIG. 23.3
Use compressed gas to clean the crud out of your keyboard.

Yes, I know that you're just blowing that junk all over the desk so it can get into everything else, and eventually back into the keyboard. So, you should shut down and turn off the computer, then disconnect the keyboard, and take it outside to blow the crud out of it. Or, use the vacuum to collect the junk as you blow it out with the compressed gas.

Although you normally don't need to disassemble the keyboard to clean the dust and debris from it, you might need to disassemble the keyboard to clean up something you've spilled in it. Water won't do much damage if you don't spill a lot. If it's just a few drops, forget it—just let it evaporate on its own. If you spill cola or something else with sugar in it, you really should open the keyboard and give it a thorough cleaning. The following procedure will help you do that.

Before Cleaning Inside the Keyboard, You Need:

- ☑ A Phillips screwdriver to disassemble the keyboard
- ☑ Compressed gas and/or brush and vaccum
- ☑ Rubbing alcohol and lint-free cloth

1. Shut down and turn off the computer.
2. Disconnect the keyboard from the computer and lay it upside-down on a flat, clean work surface.

TIP If you plan on disassembling the keyboard and removing the keys to clean under them, this is a good time to make a photocopy of the keys. You can use the photocopy later to make sure you get all the keys back in the right locations. Just lay the keyboard keys down on the copier and press the Copy button. You won't get a perfect copy, but it should be acceptable.

3. Remove the screws that hold together the keyboard case (see Figure 23.4).

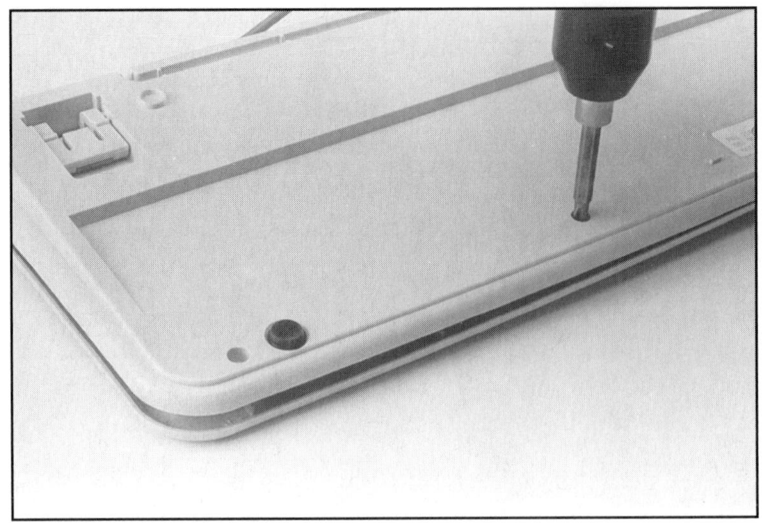

FIG. 23.4
Use a Phillips screwdriver to remove the screws that hold together the keyboard.

4. Holding the case together, turn the keyboard over, then remove the top cover. Use the compressed gas and/or brush and vacuum to clean out the keys (see Figure 23.5).

FIG. 23.5
With the cover off, you'll be able to get more of the crud out from under the keys.

NOTE If you're just cleaning dust and miscellaneous crud out of the keyboard, stop here and reassemble the keyboard. The remaining steps are for cleaning up spills.

5. Taking care not to dislodge any keys, remove the key assembly from the case.
6. If the keyboard has a circuit card attached to the key assembly (see Figure 23.6), remove it and set it aside (noting, if necessary, how to reconnect it to the key assembly).

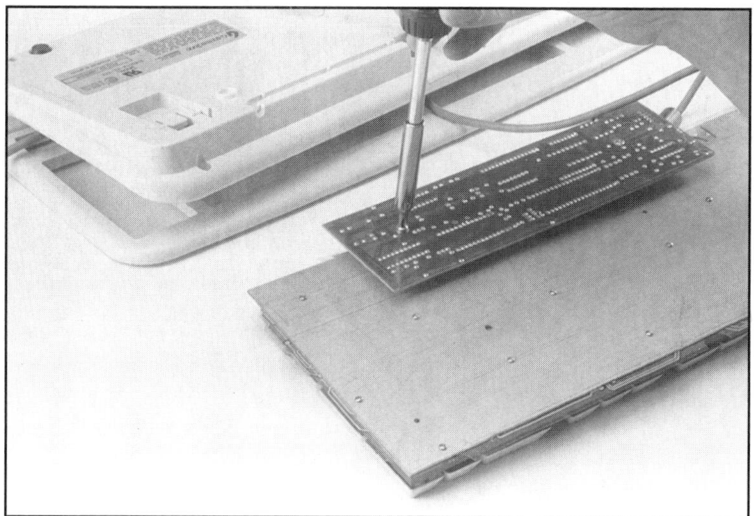

FIG. 23.6
Some, but not all, keyboards have a circuit card attached to the key assembly.

7. Remove the four million little screws that hold the back metal plate to the key assembly (perhaps I exaggerate the number). Put the screws in a cup or other container so you won't lose them. See Figure 23.7.

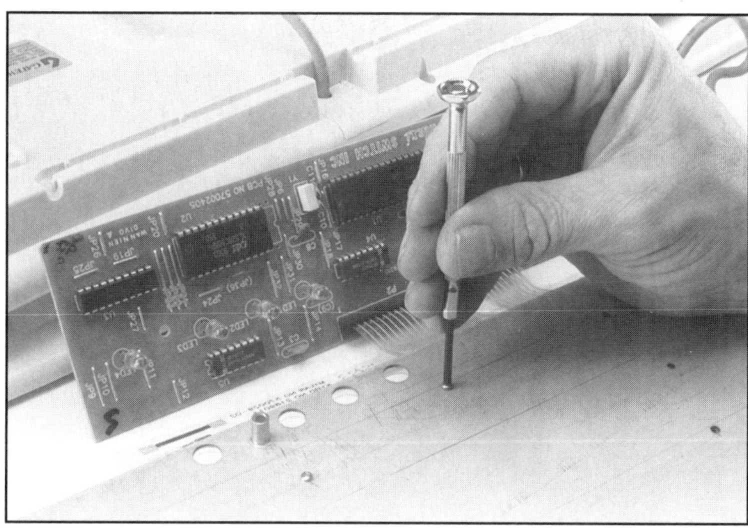

FIG. 23.7
The back plate is held on with numerous little screws.

8. Carefully lift off the metal plate. What you find underneath depends on the design of the keyboard, but Figure 23.8 is fairly typical of what you'll see—some type of printed circuit card. Carefully lift up and clean the contacts on the card with the alcohol and cloth.

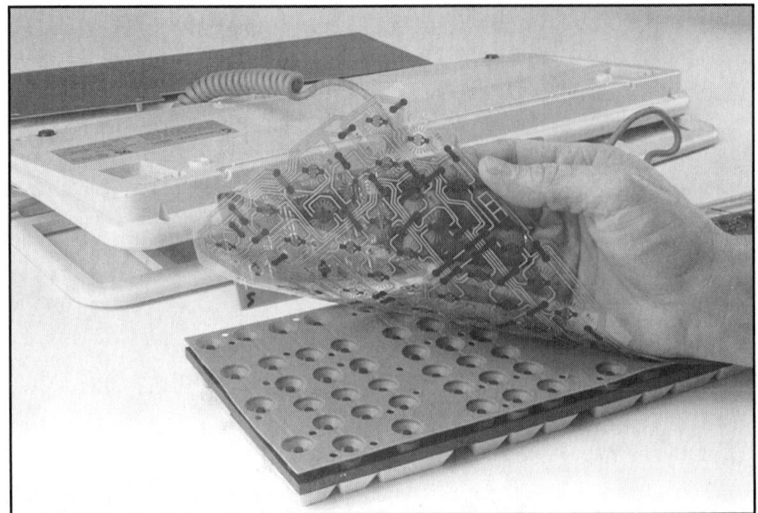

FIG. 23.8
When you push a key, you close contacts on the printed circuit card, which generates a signal indicating that a specific key was pressed.

9. Probably, there will be some type of rubber pad between the printed circuit and the backs of the keys (see Figure 23.9). Carefully lift this up and clean any spill residue from the pad as well as the backs of the keys.

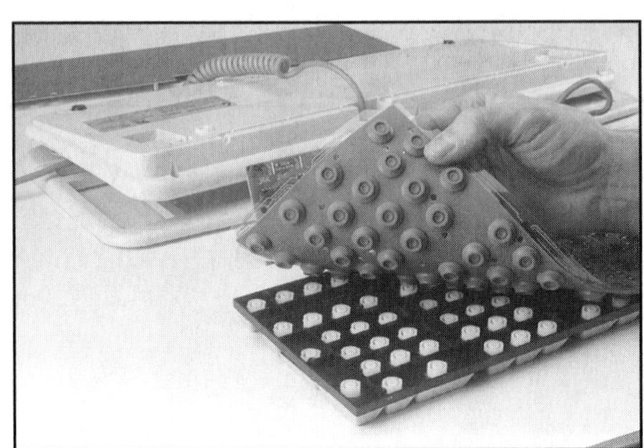

FIG. 23.9
Individual cups or a rubber pad serve as springs to make the keys move back up after you press them.

10. Reassemble the pads, printed circuit, circuit card, and metal plate, then turn the assembly right-side up again.
11. It would be a good idea to remove the keys and clean under them, as well. They should pop off. Just don't remove more than a few at a time, because you'll have a real nightmare trying to figure out which keys go where. Clean under them with the alcohol and cloth.

> **CAUTION** Some of the keys have retaining wires under them (see Figures 23.10 and 23.11). It's best if you don't remove these, because it can be difficult to get the wires back in the right spots. If you do have to remove them, you might find it easier to attach the wire to the keys first, then attach the wire and key to the keyboard. Reassemble these keys before putting the cover back on the keyboard to make it easier to access the wires and connectors.

FIG. 23.10
Some keys have wires that clip to the key and the keyboard.

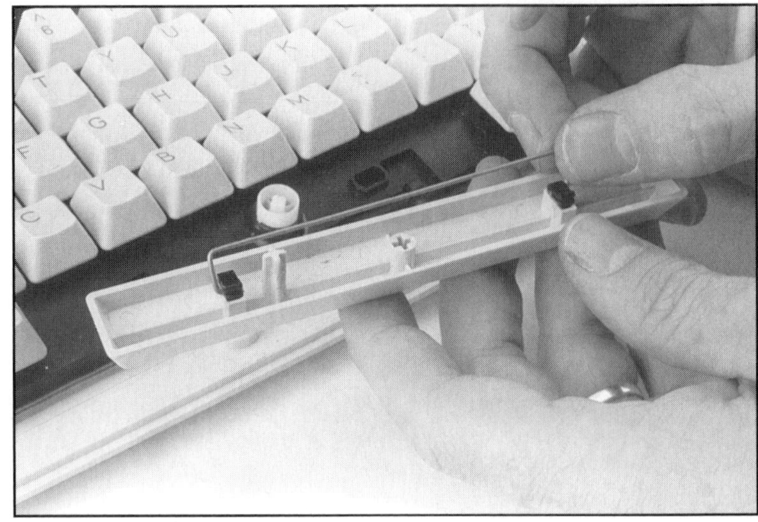

FIG. 23.11
Sometimes it's easier to connect the wire to the key, then mount the whole assembly to the keyboard.

Disk Drives

Another task you might want to perform every few months is to clean the computer's floppy disk drives. Unlike the heads on a hard disk, which ride above the disk on a cushion of air, the heads of a floppy disk drive rest right on the floppy disk media's surface. So, the head has a tendency to pick up crud from the disk over a period of time. If the heads get too dirty, the drive won't be able to read or write to the disk.

Cleaning a floppy drive doesn't require disassembling anything. Instead, it requires a special cleaning disk that you can buy from most computer stores. The cleaning disk looks like a regular disk, except the part inside the jacket is made of a soft, porous fabric instead of the plastic/magnetic substrate used in a regular disk. The cleaning kit includes a liquid that you apply to the fabric disc. You then insert the disk and try to read from it. For example, you might open a DOS box and enter **DIR A:**, or double-click drive A in My Computer (Windows 95 and Windows NT 4.0), or on the drive A button in File Manager (Windows 3.x and Windows NT 3.x).

Generally, you shouldn't need to clean out a CD-ROM drive, because these drives use a laser to read the disc. There is no contact between the laser and the disc, so unless the drive gets full of dust, the laser continues to read the discs without any problem. If you do have some problems reading CDs and the problem occurs with different CDs, try blowing out the drive with a can of compressed gas. If that doesn't help, you might have a problem with the CD itself. You can buy cleaning kits for CDs, which typically consist of a package of circular lint-free wipes. They seem to work well enough, but so does the sleeve of a clean sweatshirt.

There is typically nothing to do to clean a hard disk. In fact, if you open a hard disk, you'd immediately render it unusable. The smallest particle of smoke or dust can crash a hard disk head.

Monitor

Don't even think about opening your monitor to clean inside it. The monitor contains high-capacity capacitors that can deliver a nasty, deadly shock even after the monitor is turned off and unplugged. There won't be much to clean inside the monitor, anyway.

Instead, concentrate on cleaning the outside of the monitor and the screen. I generally use a good glass cleaning solution to clean not only the glass but the case. Use a lint-free cloth, and spray the cleaner on the cloth, not on the glass. This keeps cleaner from running down between the case and the glass.

Mice and Trackballs

It's a good idea to occasionally clean inside your trackball or mouse. The design of both types of pointing devices is very similar, with two primary types in each: optical and mechanical.

Mechanical devices have a featureless ball that moves small rollers as you move the trackball or mouse. Figure 23.12 shows the ball removed from a trackball. Figure 23.13 shows the rollers underneath. The movement of the rollers is translated into an electrical signal that is passed to the PC.

Over time, crud builds up on the rollers and eventually causes problems with the ball's movement. You can use a cotton swab or cloth dipped in alcohol to clean the rollers. Or, just scrape off the stuff with your thumbnail. Make sure you dump the crud out of the assembly before you put the ball back in place.

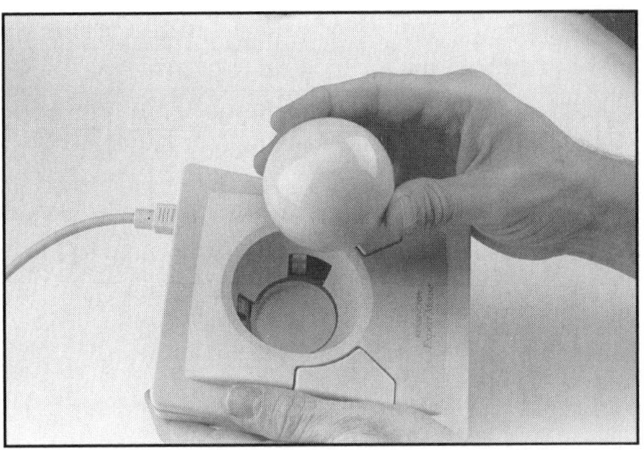

FIG. 23.12
Typically, the ball in a trackball simply lifts out of the unit.

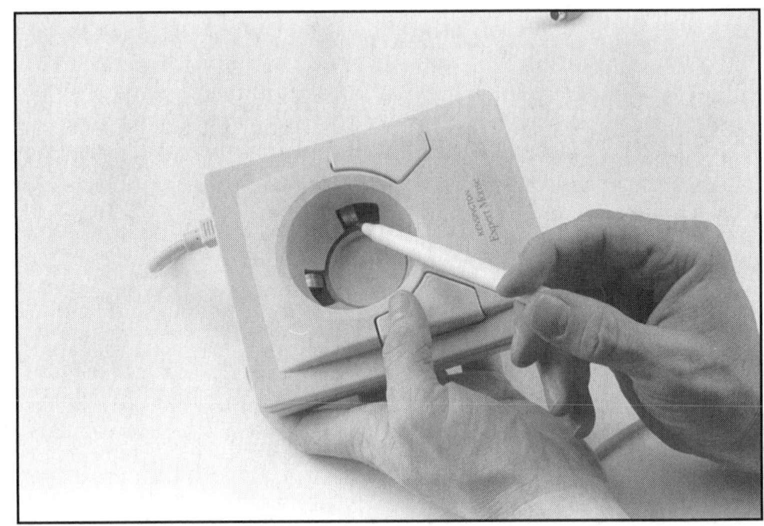

FIG. 23.13
The ball moves rollers as it rotates, and that movement is converted to an electrical signal.

Mice, as well as some trackballs, have a retaining ring that holds the ball in place (see Figure 23.14). To remove the ball, you must twist the ring counterclockwise and lift off the ring. You will then be able to remove the ball.

Some devices, including the trackball shown in Figure 23.14, are *optical devices.* Rather than relying on the motion of the rollers to translate movement to the PC, these devices use an optical sensor to detect when the ball moves and translate the movement to the PC. In these devices, the ball is covered with tiny dots that enable the sensor to determine when and how the ball is moving. In addition to cleaning the ball occasionally, you should also remove the ball and make sure the clear cover over the sensor (if there is one) is free of dust (see Figure 23.15). Use a cotton swab dipped in alcohol to clean it.

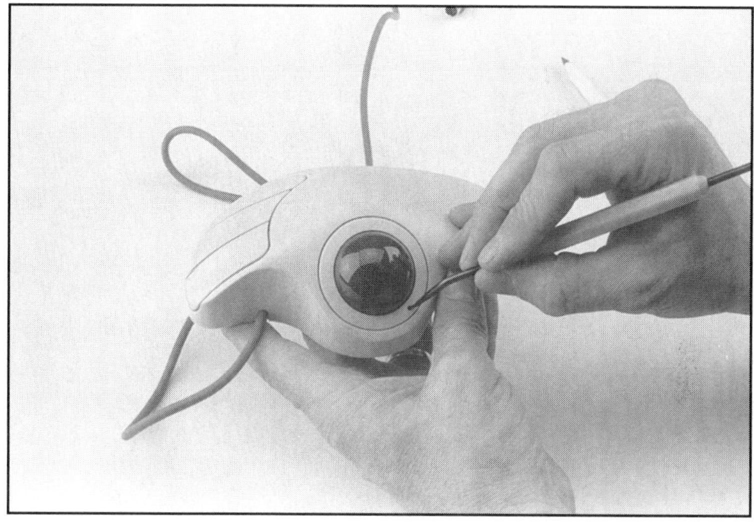

FIG. 23.14
Mice and some trackballs have a retaining ring to hold the ball in place.

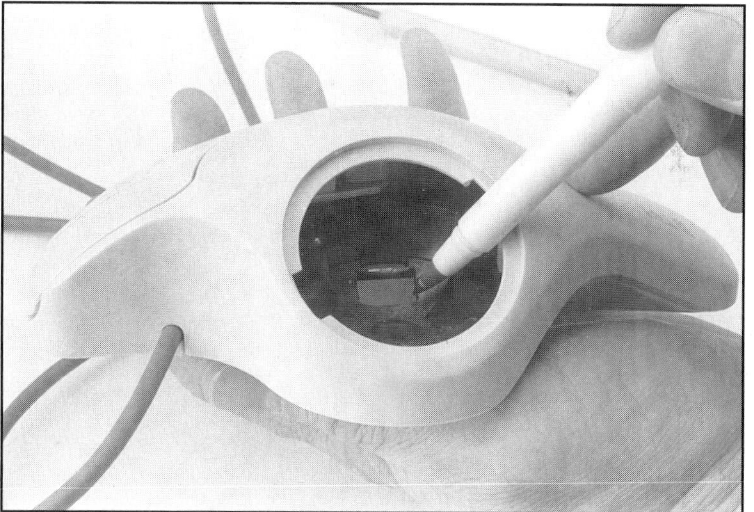

FIG. 23.15
Keep the optical sensor cover clean and free of dust.

24

Basic Troubleshooting

Usually, you'll be able to complete an upgrade without any problems. After the new gadget is in and any necessary software installed, the device will work fine. Now and then, however, something will go wrong and you'll have to start troubleshooting the problem. This chapter gives you some suggestions on how to begin a thorough, logical process to track down the problem. The chapter covers these topics:

- Using system logs and backups
- Using single-step boot to track down a driver problem
- Using a clean boot and minimal configuration to minimize drivers and memory use
- Booting in safe mode in Windows 95
- Using a boot or recovery disk

TIP If your computer was working for a while and suddenly started experiencing problems, and you don't think you've changed anything, make sure drive C hasn't become full. That can lead to all sorts of problems that often seem unrelated to available disk space.

Most of the techniques in this chapter apply to DOS/Windows 3.x and Windows 95. Windows NT doesn't offer much in the way of control over how you boot the system. Some of the procedures will, however, work for Windows NT. I've noted those accordingly.

Using Logs

If you installed something new in your computer and it doesn't work, or the computer itself doesn't seem to work, you might need to uninstall the new gadget and start from scratch. In most cases, though, you should be able to locate the problem and fix it fairly easily. First, you should check the system logs.

I hope you've been faithful about keeping a system log, adding notes and comments each time you make a change to the system or add a new device. If the PC worked for a while and suddenly is having problems, it's more than likely you changed a setting (or installed some software that changed a setting), and that change is causing the problem. It might be the last thing you added or changed, but not necessarily. Some problems won't crop up right away.

Have you recently performed any of the following tasks?

- Installed some new hardware in the PC
- Changed a setting, however minor, in AUTOEXEC.BAT, CONFIG.SYS, SYSTEM.INI, WIN.INI, or the Registry
- Installed some new software
- Let someone else work with your system
- Run SysEdit or RegEdit

Any of these actions can alter your PC's configuration files, and even a seemingly minor change can throw a wrench into the works if it's not correct. Pull out your system logs and see what changes you've made recently. If you've changed some hardware settings, try changing them back to see if the problem goes away. If you've recently installed some software, you might need to uninstall it and test for the problem again. Before you do that, however, read through the rest of the chapter and perform the procedures that apply to your situation and system. You might be able to clear up the problem without doing anything as drastic as uninstalling hardware or software.

Using a Single-Step Boot

Changes to the CONFIG.SYS and AUTOEXEC.BAT files can cause all sorts of problems. If your system is having problems booting, check to see if you have performed any of these tasks lately:

- Modified CONFIG.SYS or AUTOEXEC.BAT yourself
- Installed new software
- Installed new hardware that included installing software

If you answer "Yes" to any of the above, there is a good possibility that something in the installation process has modified CONFIG.SYS or AUTOEXEC.BAT. An easy way to troubleshoot this type of problem is to *single-step* through the boot process. This means that you execute the statements in CONFIG.SYS and AUTOEXEC.BAT at boot one at a time, pausing after each. If a driver or program in one of these files is causing a problem, you'll be able to figure out which one it is. When the system hangs, the statement that was executing is probably the one causing the problem.

TIP To single-step through CONFIG.SYS, you have to be using DOS version 6.0 or higher (or Windows 95, which essentially is DOS 7.0). Previous versions of DOS don't support single-step boot. Also, Windows 95 offers additional single-step control over boot processing in addition to CONFIG.SYS and AUTOEXEC.BAT (covered a little later in the section "Single-Step Boot—Windows 95").

When you find out which step is causing the problem, you can remark that step from the file, eliminate it, or modify it to overcome the problem. To turn a statement into a *remark* in CONFIG.SYS, place a semicolon or the keyword **REM** at the beginning of the line. To turn a statement into a remark in AUTOEXEC.BAT, place the keyword **REM** at the beginning of the line.

NOTE Bear in mind that turning a statement into a remark effectively bypasses that statement in the boot process. If the statement loads a device driver, that driver will no longer load. This might cure your problem (assuming the device driver is the problem), but it also might mean that the device controlled by the driver won't work. At least you'll be able to identify and begin troubleshooting the problem. If you turn a statement into a remark, reboot the system, and the problem goes away, the line you just changed was causing the problem.

If the problem goes away when you single-step through the configuration files, but reappears when you let the system boot normally, the order in which the lines in the configuration file are being processed is probably causing the problem. Make sure that any lines that load or configure memory managers come first in the configuration files. Then, you can try shuffling lines around in the files to try to overcome the problem.

Single-Step Boot—DOS 6.x

Follow these steps to single-step through the boot process on a computer running DOS 6.x:

1. If Windows is running, exit Windows. Then press Ctrl+Alt+Delete, or press the Reset button on your PC (or just turn off, then turn on the PC).
2. When you see the message `Starting MS-DOS` appear on the display, press F8.
3. If you use a multi-boot configuration menu, the menu is displayed. Choose the option under which you've been having the problem.

4. The system displays each line in CONFIG.SYS, prompting you to either execute it (press Y) or bypass it (press N).
5. If the system hangs trying to process a line, return to step 1, but this time, bypass the line that caused the system to hang.
6. After all entries in CONFIG.SYS are either processed or bypassed, execute the steps in AUTOEXEC.BAT to look for problems there.

NOTE DOS version 6.0 lets you single-step through CONFIG.SYS, but process AUTOEXEC.BAT in its entirety without stepping through it. DOS 6.2x, however, single-steps through AUTOEXEC.BAT. To pause execution so you can read the screen, press Ctrl+S or Shift+Pause. Press the spacebar to continue.

If the problem is generated by HIMEM.SYS or EMM386.EXE, there could be a problem with the computer's memory or the PC's extended CMOS setup. If you've just installed some new memory, go back and check the installation. Check out Chapter 10, "Adding Memory," for specific troubleshooting tips.

NOTE If you've recently installed software, the setup program you used might have added optional switches to the EMM386 statement, and these switches could be causing the problem.

If the problem occurs when loading a device driver, the problem might be cause by a command-line switch included in the statement. *Command-line switches* are additional information included with the device driver statement that control the way the driver is loaded. Check the manual for the device using the driver to see if the switches are correct. If the switches are correct, the problem could be caused by a hardware resource conflict (two devices using the same IRQ, for example).

NOTE You won't be able to run Windows 3.x if HIMEM.SYS does not load successfully from CONFIG.SYS. This means you can't bypass HIMEM.SYS and still run Windows 3.x.

If you're running DOS 6.0 and can't single-step through AUTOEXEC.BAT, use this procedure to accomplish the same end:

1. Print a copy of AUTOEXEC.BAT for reference. To do so, bypass CONFIG.SYS and AUTOEXEC.BAT, then type the command **TYPE**

AUTOEXEC.BAT > PRN at the DOS prompt. Or, you can print the file from Edit or Notepad.

2. Reboot the system and perform a single-step boot. When asked whether or not to process AUTOEXEC.BAT, press N.
3. One at a time, enter the commands from AUTOEXEC.BAT. Watch the display as you press Enter for each command, looking for potential error messages. Before processing a line, make sure you've entered it properly.

If a problem occurs after you enter a command, you've located the source of the problem. If no errors occur, the problem probably lies elsewhere.

Single-Step Boot—Windows 95

Follow these steps to single-step through the boot process on a computer running Windows 95:

1. If your system displays a boot menu at startup, choose option 5, then skip to step 3.
2. If your system doesn't display a boot menu at startup, press Shift+F8 when you see the message `Starting Windows 95`.

NOTE Pressing F8 when you see the message `Starting Windows 95` causes the boot menu to appear. You then can choose option 5 to single-step through the boot.

3. Confirm or bypass each step by pressing either Y or N, respectively.

Notice as you single-step through the Windows 95 boot process that you have the option not only of single-stepping through CONFIG.SYS and AUTOEXEC.BAT, but also of controlling whether or not the DoubleSpace/DriveSpace driver loads, the Registry is processed, a boot log file is created, the GUI is started, and all drivers are loaded.

NOTE Some of the options in the single-step boot process in Windows 95 depend on how your system is configured. If you don't have any DoubleSpace or DriveSpace drives, for example, you won't see a message about loading the associated driver.

Using a Clean Boot

A single-step boot, which was explained in the previous section, lets you step through the boot process one step at a time. In some cases, you might want to bypass your system's configuration files altogether. This is called *performing a clean boot*. With a clean boot, you bypass all the device drivers and programs loaded by CONFIG.SYS and AUTOEXEC.BAT. This eliminates possible conflicts with drivers or other programs loaded by CONFIG.SYS and AUTOEXEC.BAT. Any devices that require drivers loaded by CONFIG.SYS or AUTOEXEC.BAT won't function, but at least you'll be able to boot the system and begin editing the CONFIG.SYS and AUTOEXEC.BAT files to overcome the problem.

Using a Clean Boot Under DOS/Windows 3.x

Follow these steps to perform a clean boot on DOS/Windows 3.x systems:

1. Press Ctrl+Alt+Delete or the reset switch to reboot the computer.
2. When the message `Starting MS-DOS` appears on the display, press the F5 function key. (This only works for DOS 6.x and higher.)
3. When the DOS prompt appears, try executing the program that has been causing the problem.

NOTE You won't be able to run Windows after performing a clean boot because Windows requires HIMEM.SYS. Performing a clean boot bypasses HIMEM.SYS, which is loaded through CONFIG.SYS. Try using a minimal configuration instead (see the section "Using a Minimal Configuration" later in this chapter).

Also, most device drivers can't be loaded from the command line, but instead must be loaded through CONFIG.SYS. Typically, any device driver that has a SYS file extension must be loaded by CONFIG.SYS. Device drivers with an EXE file extension typically can be loaded from the command line.

The result of a clean boot is that there won't be any device drivers or other programs running or resident in memory. The primary reason for performing a clean boot is to enable the system to boot when it otherwise would not, and allow you to begin editing CONFIG.SYS and AUTOEXEC.BAT (or replace them with backup copies of the previous versions of the files).

Here are a few things to keep in mind about a clean boot:

- PATH. Because the AUTOEXEC.BAT file wasn't process, the system PATH environment variable will not have been set. If you try to start a program by typing its name at the command prompt and you receive the message `Bad command or file name`, the program or command is probably located in a different directory from the current one. Use the CD command to change to the directory where the command or program is stored. Or, look at the AUTOEXEC.BAT file and enter on the command line the PATH statement contained in AUTOEXEC.BAT.

TIP To set the PATH environment variable from the command line, enter the command PATH=***drives and directories***, where *drives and directories* are the drives and directories you want on the path, separated by semicolons. Example: **PATH=C:\;C:\DOS;C:\WINDOWS**.

- *Memory managers.* Neither the HIMEM.SYS or EMM386.EXE memory managers will be running (or a third-party memory manager, if you're using one). Applications that require a memory manager, such as Windows 3.x, won't run. If you need the memory manager for troubleshooting, try using a minimal configuration instead of a clean boot.
- *Device drivers.* None of the device drivers normally loaded by CONFIG.SYS or AUTOEXEC.BAT will be present in memory. This means that any device requiring such a driver won't work. For example, you might not be able to use the mouse or CD-ROM drive until you load the necessary device drivers. Use a single-step boot to process only the essential device drivers needed for troubleshooting.
- *The UMA.* With no memory manager to manage the Upper Memory Area (UMA), all of the DOS operating system is loaded into conventional memory below 640K. The *UMA* is the area of conventional memory between 640K and 1M. If you load device drivers from the DOS command prompt, those drivers go into conventional memory below 640K, rather than into the UMA.

Using a Clean Boot Under Windows 95

In most cases, a Windows 95 computer doesn't even need a CONFIG.SYS or AUTOEXEC.BAT file. This is because Windows 95 provides support for most devices, and those that it doesn't are usually supported by vendor-supplied device drivers that load within Windows 95, not from CONFIG.SYS or AUTOEXEC.BAT. Usually, the only reason to use a CONFIG.SYS or AUTOEXEC.BAT file with Windows 95 is to load a real-mode device driver when there is no Windows 95 driver for the device. Or, you might want to set environment variables (such as the PATH) through AUTOEXEC.BAT.

You have a few ways to perform a clean boot under Windows 95. First, you can simply rename CONFIG.SYS and AUTOEXEC.BAT to something else, like **Config.old** and **Autoexec.old**. Or, use these steps:

1. Reboot the system with Ctrl+Alt+Delete or press the Reset button.
2. If your system is configured to show the boot menu, choose option 7, Safe Mode Command Prompt Only to bypass the startup files and boot to a command prompt. Or, choose option 3, Safe Mode, to bypass the startup files and load the GUI.
3. If your system is not configured to show the boot menu, press F8 when you see the message `Starting Windows 95`. The boot menu appears, and allows you to select either option 3 or 7, as needed.

NOTE See the later section "Using Safe Mode and Overcoming Hardware Conflicts" for a more complete description of safe mode and its effects on the boot process.

Using a Minimal Configuration

On DOS/Windows 3.x systems, it's sometimes useful to process only some of the device drivers and other statements in CONFIG.SYS and AUTOEXEC.BAT. For example, you might need to load HIMEM.SYS and a mouse driver, but nothing else, to boot the system and troubleshoot a problem. Or, you might need to load just HIMEM.SYS and a CD-ROM driver so you can read from the CD-ROM drive in Windows.

A *minimal configuration* means that the system is booted using only the minimum device drivers needed to get the system up and running, but still be able to access critical devices like the mouse and CD-ROM drive.

You need to edit CONFIG.SYS and AUTOEXEC.BAT to create a minimal configuration for boot. Boot the system to DOS, bypassing CONFIG.SYS and AUTOEXEC.BAT if necessary, to get the system up. Then, edit CONFIG.SYS and

AUTOEXEC.BAT, turning into comments those lines that aren't absolutely necessary to get the system up and running for troubleshooting. For CONFIG.SYS, place a semicolon at the beginning of each line you want to bypass (or use the **REM** keyword at the beginning of the line). For AUTOEXEC.BAT, place the **REM** keyword at the beginning of each line you want to turn into a comment. When you've finished editing the files, reboot the system and let DOS process CONFIG.SYS and AUTOEXEC.BAT.

Following is a suggested minimal CONFIG.SYS file to use for troubleshooting:

```
; Minimal CONFIG.SYS file
DEVICE=C:\DOS\HIMEM.SYS
FILES=20
BUFFERS=10
SHELL=C:\DOS\COMMAND.COM /P
```

Here is a minimal AUTOEXEC.BAT file to use for troubleshooting:

```
REM Minimal AUTOEXEC.BAT file
PROMPT $P$G
PATH=C:\DOS;C:\WINDOWS;C:\
REM  Change the previous line according to your
REM  system's configuration, but only include the
REM  DOS, Windows, and root directory on the path
```

Using Safe Mode and Overcoming Hardware Conflicts

Windows 95 provides a special operating mode called *safe mode* that is very useful for troubleshooting and overcoming driver- and hardware-specific problems. Safe mode is a lot like a minimal configuration in DOS because it causes Windows 95 to load only those device drivers and operating system components that are absolutely necessary to boot the system. In addition, safe mode uses a VGA display driver, which helps you overcome problems with a non-functioning or incorrectly configured video driver. Safe mode also bypasses CONFIG.SYS and AUTOEXEC.BAT.

If you're having trouble booting Windows 95, try using safe mode. After Windows 95 starts, you'll be able to open the Control Panel to change driver resource settings, disable devices, remove drivers, or install different drivers to troubleshoot and hopefully overcome the system's problems.

You can choose from three different safe modes when you boot:

- *Safe Mode.* Boots a minimal Windows 95 operating system, excluding the majority of device drivers except those necessary to boot the system (such as disk drivers). Safe mode uses a VGA display driver to overcome potential conflicts with the currently installed display driver.
- *Safe Mode with Network Support.* Identical to safe mode, but Windows 95 also loads real-mode support for your network interface card and network. This option lets you bypass unnecessary device drivers but still have network access.
- *Safe Mode Command Prompt Only.* Bypasses all your Windows 95 configuration files and boots the system to a command prompt. In effect, it is a clean boot to DOS 7. This option doesn't boot the GUI or any of your system's device drivers. If you need CD-ROM access, for example, you won't have it under safe mode. You can, however, execute DOS commands and programs.

If you are having problems with the display driver, boot the system in Safe mode. Then, open the Control Panel and change the settings on the display driver and boot the system again to test it.

If you're having a problem with a specific device, try one of the following solutions presented in the following sections.

Change the Device's Resource Settings

The problem might be caused by a *resource conflict,* which is two or more devices trying to use the same IRQ, DMA, or base memory address settings. Here's the process for changing the resources used by a device:

1. Boot the system in Safe mode.
2. Open the Control Panel and double-click the System icon.
3. Click the Device Manager tab to display the Device Manager property page (see Figure 24.1).
4. Locate the device that is causing the problem. The device list should already be open and displaying the device if Windows 95 detected a problem with it. You'll find an exclamation mark beside the device name, indicating that there is a problem with it.

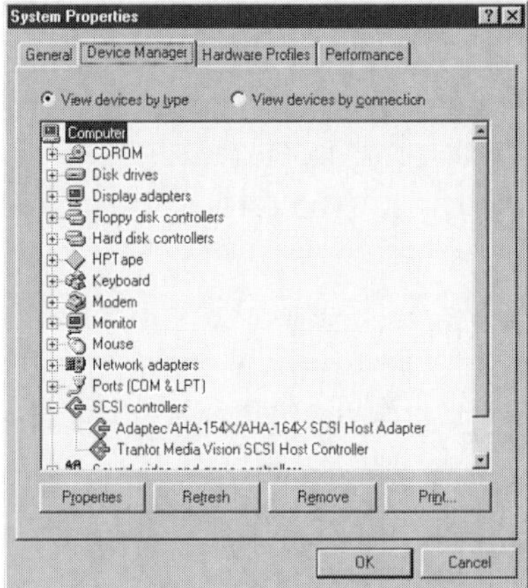

FIG. 24.1
Use the Device Manager to control the resources assigned to a device.

5. Select the device and click Properties to display the property sheet for the device (see Figure 24.2).

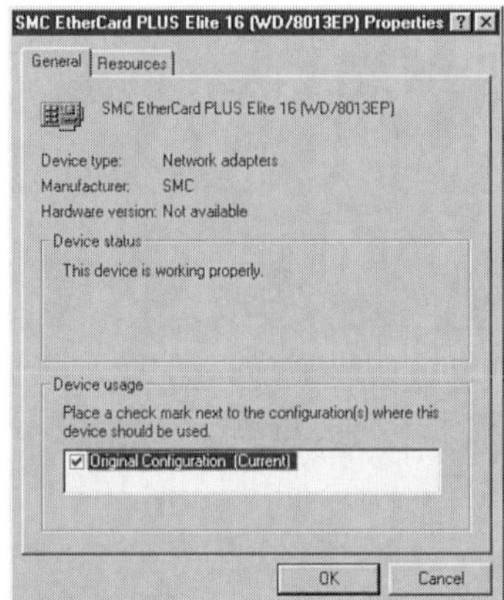

FIG. 24.2
This is a typical property sheet for a device.

6. Click the Resources tab to display the device's Resources page (see Figure 24.3).
7. Clear the Use Automatic Settings check box if it is selected.
8. Using the device manual and your system logs as a guide, change the resources assigned to the device so they don't conflict with any other device.
9. Close the Resource property sheet for the device, then close the Device Manager.
10. Reboot the system to test the new configuration.

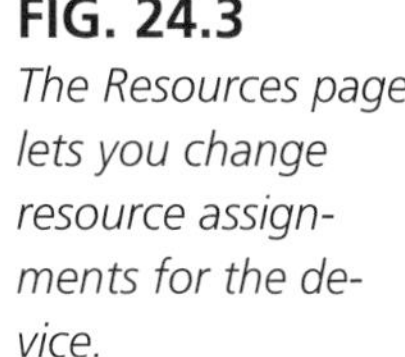

FIG. 24.3
The Resources page lets you change resource assignments for the device.

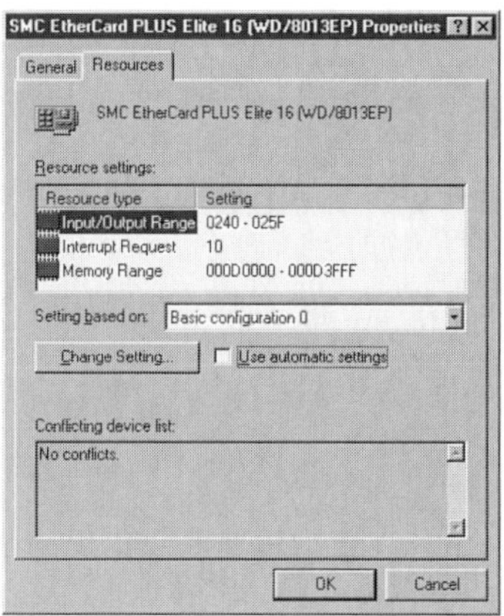

Disable the Device

Another option you have for overcoming a problem with a device is to disable the device. If you're not using the device now and simply want to get the system back up, disabling the device is a quick way to do so. You can troubleshoot the problem with the device later when you have the time and the inclination.

Your capability to disable a device relies on Windows 95's support for hardware profiles. A *hardware profile* is a named hardware configuration. Windows 95 keeps track of which devices should be included with a specific profile, and loads the device drivers only for those devices in the profile. This lets you switch at boot between different hardware configurations.

By default, Windows 95 creates one hardware profile called *Original Configuration*. All of your devices are enabled by default for this profile. To temporarily disable a device, all you have to do is turn it off for that profile. Use these steps to do so:

1. Boot the system in safe mode.
2. Open the Control Panel and double-click the System icon.
3. Click the Device Manager tab to display the Device Manager.
4. Locate in the device list the device you want to disable.
5. Select the device to be disabled and click Properties.
6. In the General property page for the device, clear the Original Configuration check box (see Figure 24.4).
7. Close the property sheet and the Control Panel, then shut down and restart the system.

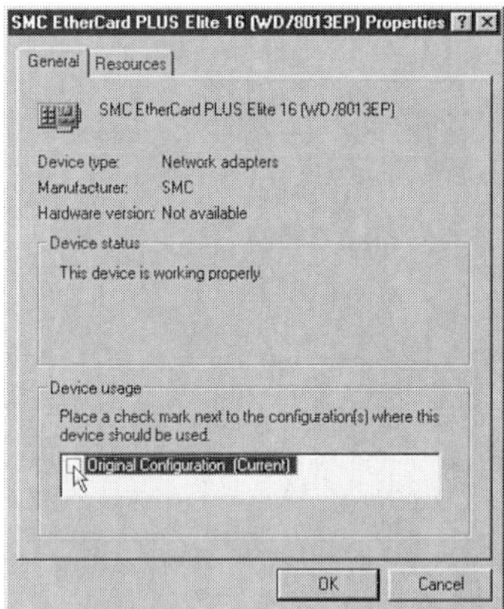

FIG. 24.4
Clear the Original Configuration check box to temporarily disable a device.

TIP When you want to troubleshoot the device, re-enable it by placing a check in the Original Configuration check box. For more information on using hardware profiles, consult *Windows 95 Installation and Configuration Handbook* from Que.

Reinstall the Device Driver

In some cases, reinstalling a device driver can overcome a problem and get the device working again. The first step is to remove the existing driver for the device. Then, you can reinstall the driver and test the system to see if you've overcome the problem. You can use the following steps to remove and reinstall a device driver under Windows 95:

1. Boot the system in safe mode.
2. Open the Control Panel and double-click the System icon.
3. Click the Device Manager tab to display the Device Manager.
4. Locate in the hardware list the device whose driver you want to remove.
5. Select the device from the list, then click Remove. Windows 95 prompts you to verify that you really want to remove the device driver. Choose OK to remove the device, or choose Cancel to abort the process.
6. If you want to let Windows 95 detect the device and install support for it through Plug and Play, shut down and restart the system in normal mode. Windows 95 should detect the device and attempt to install support for it. If Windows 95 doesn't detect the device, open the Control Panel and choose the Add New Hardware Wizard.

7. If the device came with its own setup program, run that program to install support for the device.

TIP If you're reinstalling a video driver, first select the standard VGA driver and reboot the system. Then, run the video driver's setup program or reinstall the video driver automatically through Plug and Play.

Using a Boot/Recovery Disk

Sometimes you'll find it impossible to boot the system from the hard disk because it has suffered some catastrophic failure. Or, maybe you're installing a new hard disk and forgot to format the drive as a system disk. Without the system files on the hard disk, the system won't boot.

In the case of DOS/Windows 3.x and Windows 95, you can use a boot disk to start the system. Booting from a floppy disk boots the system to a command prompt and you can begin using FDISK, FORMAT, or other utilities to format and troubleshoot the disk. In the case of Windows NT, the Recovery Disk helps you boot the system and begin rebuilding the file system or repairing the operating system.

There isn't much to explain about using a boot/recovery disk. The only prerequisite is that you have one. Chapter 2, "Building a Software Safety Kit," explains how to create a boot/recovery disk under DOS, Windows 95, and Windows NT. I hope you took the time to create the disk. If not, you'll probably have to find someone who has one or can make one for you. See "Creating Boot/Recovery Disks" in Chapter 20.

When you have the boot/recovery disk, just insert the disk in drive A and restart the system.

NOTE Your system's BIOS might have an option that causes the system to bypass an attempt to boot from the floppy drive. Usually this option is available in the advanced CMOS setup page for the BIOS. If your system doesn't attempt to boot from the floppy, run the CMOS setup program and enable the option to boot from the floppy drive. Refer to Chapter 7, "Working with the BIOS," for help with CMOS settings.

Using Switches to Start Windows

Windows 3.x and Windows 95 both support a selection of command-line switches that start Windows in specific modes or with certain options to facilitate troubleshooting. Using the switches can help you track down and overcome potential problems. To use the switches, you just include them on the command line you use to start Windows. The following sections explain the options available under both Windows 3.x and Windows 95, as well as how to use them to start Windows.

TIP If you forget the command-line switches, you can use with the WIN command; just enter **WIN /?** at the command prompt. You are treated to a list of the available options and their use.

Using Windows 3.x Command-Line Switches

You use the WIN command to start Windows 3.x from the DOS command prompt. Normally, you simply enter **WIN**, which starts Windows with its default options. However, you can use a selection of command-line switches with the WIN command to control how Windows starts and operates. The format for the WIN command is as follows:

```
WIN [/3] [/S] [/B] [/D:[F][S][V][X]]
```

The following list explains each of the switches:

- `/3`. Starts Windows in 386 enhanced mode.
- `/S`. Starts Windows in standard mode.
- `/B`. Creates a file called BOOTLOG.TXT that records system messages generated during system startup.
- `/D`. Use with the following options for troubleshooting when Windows won't start correctly:

  :F. Turns off 32-bit disk access, and is equivalent to the SYSTEM.INI file setting `32BitDiskAccess=FALSE`. Try this switch if you're having trouble with corrupted data on the hard disk or can't access the drive.

  :S. Specifies that Windows should not use ROM address space between F000:0000 and 1M for a breakpoint. It's equivalent to the SYSTEM.INI file setting `SystemROMBreakPoint=FALSE`. In general, you shouldn't have to use this switch.

:V. Specifies that the ROM routine will handle interrupts from the hard disk controller instead of Windows. It's equivalent to the SYSTEM.INI file setting `VirtualHDIRQ=FALSE`. Use this option when you're having trouble accessing the hard disk.

:X. Excludes all of the adapter area (UMA) from the range of memory that Windows scans to find unused space. It's equivalent to the SYSTEM.INI file setting `EMMExclude=A000-FFFF`. Use this option if you think a memory conflict might be causing your problem.

To use any of these switches, comment out the WIN statement if it exists in your computer's AUTOEXEC.BAT file. Then, boot the system to a command prompt. Enter the **WIN** command, along with any switches, to boot the system for troubleshooting. The following example creates a boot log and excludes all of the UMA memory:

```
WIN /B /D:X
```

Using Windows 95 Command-Line Switches

Like Windows 3.x before it, Windows 95 supports command-line switches that control the way the operating system starts and runs. The format for the WIN command is as follows:

```
WIN [/D:[F][M][S][V][X]]
```

Use the `/D switch` with the following options to troubleshoot Windows 95 startup:

- *:F.* Turns off 32-bit disk access and is equivalent to the SYSTEM.INI file setting `32BitDiskAccess=FALSE`. Use this option when you're having trouble with corrupted data or accessing the disk.
- *:M.* Starts Windows 95 in safe mode.
- *:N.* Starts Windows 95 in safe mode with networking support.
- *:S.* Specifies that Windows 95 should not use ROM address space between F000:0000 and 1M for a breakpoint. It is equivalent to the SYSTEM.INI file setting `SystemROMBreakPoint=FALSE`. Generally, you shouldn't have to use this option.
- *:V.* Specifies that the ROM routine will handle interrupts from the hard disk controller. It is equivalent to the SYSTEM.INI file setting `VirtualHDIRQ=FALSE`. Use this option when you have problems accessing the disk drive.

- *:X*. Excludes all of the adapter (UMA) area from the range of memory that Windows scans to find unused space. It is equivalent to the SYSTEM.INI file setting `EMMExclude=A000-FFFF`. Use it when you suspect a memory conflict is causing problems.

The primary difference between Windows 3.x and Windows 95 as far as startup is concerned is that Windows 95 automatically attempts to boot the GUI and full operating system. A Windows 3.x system only starts Windows automatically if the WIN command is added to the AUTOEXEC.BAT file.

Because Windows 95 boots automatically, you have to use an extra step or two to be able to specify startup switches. If your system is configured to display a boot menu, choose the Command Prompt Only option. Then, enter the **WIN** command with the desired switches to start Windows 95. If your system doesn't show a boot menu, press F8 when you see the message `Starting Windows 95`. This displays the boot menu and lets you choose the option to start a command prompt only. Then, enter the desired WIN command.

Working with Backups

Before you make any change to the system, you should back up the system's configuration files. In fact, you should back them up on a regular basis—once a day isn't unreasonable if you use your system a lot. Otherwise, just make sure to back up the files before adding any new software or hardware. Take a look at Chapter 2, "Building a Software Safety Kit," for a discussion of which files to back up for your operating system See "Backing Up System Files," in Chapter 20.

In many cases, you can overcome a problem by restoring your previous configuration files. This might mean you lose the function of whatever you've just added, but at least your system should work.

For example, say you just installed a new gadget and the system suddenly stopped working. You've removed the offending gadget, but the system still doesn't work. More than likely, the installation procedure for the device modified your computer's configuration files and something in that modification is causing the problem. Restoring your original files should at least get the system up again so you can begin tracking down the cause of the problem.

TIP Before you start restoring your system's configuration files, you should back up the current ones. If restoring the previous set doesn't fix the problem, you should restore the current set to make sure you don't lose any functionality that has been added through them.

Restoring a Configuration—DOS/Windows 3.x

Before you try restoring a set of previous configuration files, try the steps outlined in the previous sections of this chapter. If all else fails, you can try restoring the files. Here's the process to use to restore your backup configuration files:

1. Copy the current CONFIG.SYS and AUTOEXEC.BAT files to a directory on your hard disk. If you don't have a good place to put them, use the command **MD C:\BACKUP** to create a directory called BACKUP. Then, use the COPY command or File Manager to copy the files to the directory.
2. Copy the previous backup copies of CONFIG.SYS and AUTOEXEC.BAT to the root directory of drive C, then reboot the system to test it.

TIP When DOS or Windows makes changes to your system's configuration files, it retains the old copies and renames them to something like CONFIG.003 and AUTOEXEC.003. Look in the root directory of drive C for multiple copies of CONFIG.* and AUTOEXEC.*. The files with the highest numbered extension are probably be the latest ones. You might try using those instead of what you have backed up (or if you have no backups).

Comparing Current and Backup Files for Differences

You can manually go through your current and backup configuration files to check for differences, but there is an easier way: use the FC command. *FC* stands for *File Compare*, and the FC command does just that—it compares two files for differences between them and displays the results. FC offers a quick way to find the differences between two files.

To use the FC command, boot the system to a command prompt (or open a DOS session in Windows). At the command prompt, enter the following command, where *file1* is the name of the current configuration file and *file2* is the name of the backup configuration file:

```
FC file1 file2
```

FC generates a report that shows the lines in both files that are different. This helps you spot lines that have been changed or added by an installation program or other process. Following are the syntaxes of the FC command, followed by an explanation of its command-line switches:

```
FC [/A] [/C] [/L] [/LBn] [/N] [/T] [/W] [/nnnn] [drive1:][path1]filename1
[drive2:][path2]filename2
FC /B [drive1:][path1]filename1 [drive2:][path2]filename2
```

- `/A`. Causes FC to display only first and last lines for each set of differences.
- `/B`. Performs a binary comparison.
- `/C`. Disregards the case of letters.
- `/L`. Compares files as ASCII text.
- `/LB`*n*. Sets the maximum consecutive mismatches to the number of lines specified by *n*.
- `/N`. Displays the line numbers on an ASCII comparison.
- `/T`. Prevents tabs from being expanded to spaces.
- `/W`. Compresses white space (tabs and spaces) for comparison.
- /*nnnn*. Specifies the number of consecutive lines (*nnnn*) that must match after a mismatch.

TIP You can redirect the output of the FC command to a text file instead of the screen, then print or view the text file with any text editor. To redirect the output to a file, just add the right chevron and a file name to the end of the command line, such as **FC FILE1 FILE2 > TEXTFILE**.

Restoring Original Configuration Files

If you think that one or more changes to your configuration files is causing a problem with your system booting or running properly, you can try restoring your backup configuration files to see if the problem goes away. Before you restore the backup files, though, you should make a copy of the current configuration files. If restoring the backup copies doesn't work, you should copy the latest configuration files back into place. That way, any changes that were made to the latest set of files are restored, possibly restoring features or support for hardware that isn't present in the backup copies. See "Backing Up System Files" in Chapter 20.

25

The Computer Won't Start

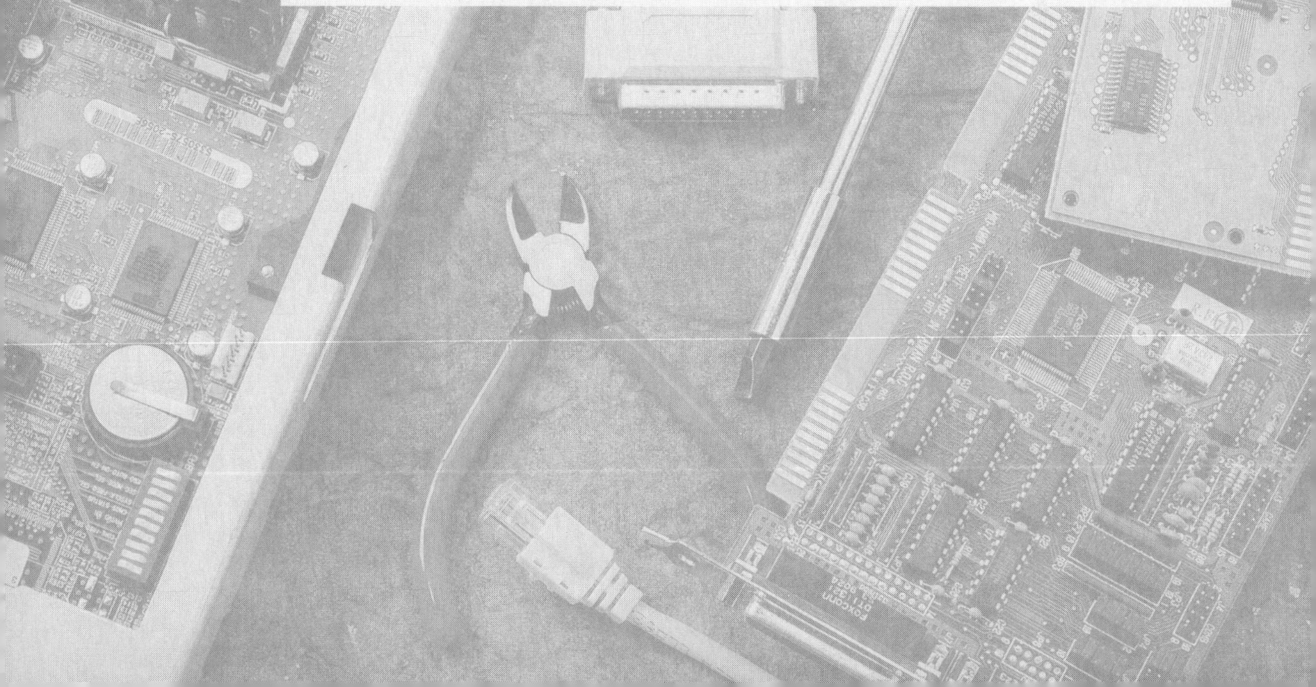

I really hope you're not reading this chapter, because if you are, it means you've performed some upgrade and now your system won't work. Or, maybe the system has been working for awhile but suddenly went *kaput!* and stopped working. Hopefully, the problem is relatively minor or something you've simply overlooked. This chapter helps you track down and fix the problem. The chapter covers these topics:

- Checking the computer for signs of life
- Checking the power supply and cables
- Checking motherboard connections
- Overcoming problems with the boot process

You're probably reading this chapter for one of two reasons: Either the computer is completely lifeless, or it tries to boot and isn't successful. These are two very different problems in terms of troubleshooting, so I've covered them separately. The first section covers situations in which the computer won't try to boot at all. The later section "Problems with the Boot Process" covers situations in which the computer at least attempts to boot.

The Computer Is Lifeless

You've pushed or flipped the power switch on your computer to the On position and nothing happens. The computer sits silent, daring you to make it work. The problem could be a loose connection, bad cable, bad power supply, or some other failure of the system. Or, you might be experiencing a problem completely unrelated to the computer. Maybe you've popped a circuit breaker. In any case, the first thing to do is look for signs of life.

Checking for Noises and Signs of Life

When you turn on your computer, it should make some noise. For example, you should be able to hear the power supply fan turning. Aside from the disk drives, the power supply fan usually is the noisiest part of the computer. If the power supply fan is turning, you at least have an indication that the power supply is getting electricity. What the power supply is doing with that electricity remains to be seen (it still might not be working properly), but at least you'll know that the electrical outlet and power cord are doing their jobs.

I know you'll find some of the following steps very obvious, but I've included them just to make sure you don't overlook something:

1. Make sure the power cord is plugged into the wall *and* to the back of the PC. Jiggle the connections to make sure they're tight.
2. Turn on the PC and listen for any kind of noise that will indicate signs of life from the computer.
3. Put your hand behind the computer in front of the power supply fan. Is the fan pushing any air?
4. If you don't feel any air, maneuver the computer around so you can look at the power supply fan. Is it turning?

If the power supply fan is turning, there's a good chance that the power supply is good. The problem might lie with a bad connection to the motherboard. Read the sections "Checking Motherboard Connections" and "Checking the Power Supply" for additional items to check.

If the power supply fan isn't turning, you probably have one of the following three problems:

- *The outlet is dead.* This might seem like an obvious problem, but you might not have thought to check it. Just because it was working 10 minutes ago doesn't mean it is working now.
- *The PC's power cord is loose or bad.* If you've checked that the power cord is securely plugged into the back of the PC and the wall outlet, and the computer still shows no signs of life, the power cord itself might be bad.
- *The power supply is toast.* If neither of the previous two items generated any luck with the computer, you might have a bad power supply. If you have a multimeter (volt-ohm meter), you can check the power supply for output.

The following section offers some tips that help you troubleshoot these possible problems.

Checking the Cables and Power Source

The first things to check are sometimes the most obvious, and because they're so obvious, you might overlook them (I assume you've already verified that the computer is plugged in). Try these steps if your computer is showing no signs of life.

To check the power source:

1. Check the outlet. Plug in a lamp or something else into the outlet to see if it is working. I use a small tester that plugs into the outlet and has three lights on the end of it (see Figure 25.1). A good outlet gives you two yellow lights. You'll find this type of tester at your local discount retailer or hardware store. Of course, a lamp, clock, or anything else electrical works almost as well. The nice thing about the tester is that it will identify problems with the circuit, such as open ground, hot and neutral reversed, and so on.

FIG. 25.1
A typical AC circuit tester can test the correctness of the circuit and not just whether it is providing power.

2. If the socket isn't working, or the tester indicates a problem with it, check the circuit breaker.
3. If the circuit breaker is tripped, find out why it is tripped. Do you have too many things going on that one circuit?

TIP Although computers don't draw a lot of current, other devices in your building or home do. If you are working out of a home office, for example, make sure you don't have the computer on the same circuit as a refrigerator, freezer, air conditioner, or resistance-heating appliance (like an electric heater or oven).

If you've determined that you're getting power from the wall socket, the problem might be in the computer's cable. Here are some steps to help you check the power cord:

1. If you have a spare power cord, try it. For example, temporarily use the cord from your monitor or printer to see if you can get the computer to hum. If the computer starts with the new cord, jog down to the nearest place that sells computers and buy a new cord. You've probably located the problem.
2. If you can't find a spare cord or don't want to buy one at the moment, use a multimeter to test the cord. Unplug the cord from the computer, then plug it into the wall outlet. Set the multimeter to test AC voltage. Taking care not to touch the metal parts of the multimeter's probes, insert the probes into the two holes in the end of the cord (the part that connects to the computer's power supply). Be careful so you don't get zapped. You should get a reading somewhere around 120 volts (see Figure 25.2). If you get a reading of zero, or less than 110 volts, you have a bad cord.

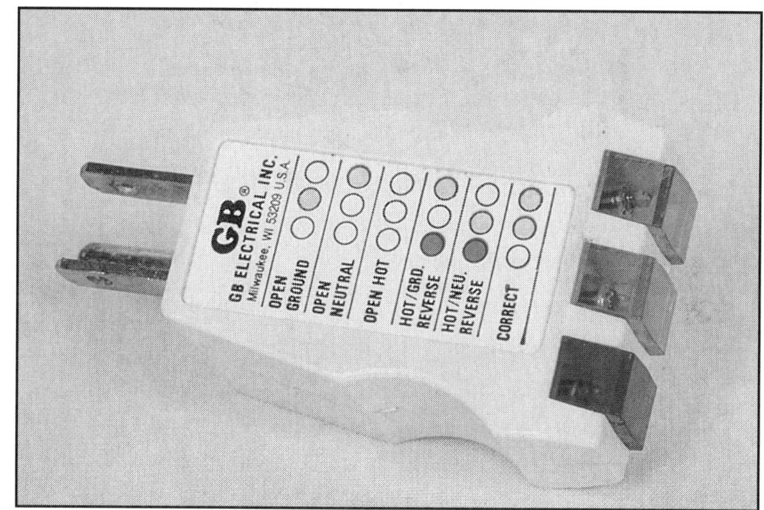

FIG. 25.2
You can test a power cord with a multimeter. You should get a reading close to 120 volts.

3. If you can't check the cord for voltage for some reason, or you don't like the idea of sticking the probes into a live cord, you can check the cord for continuity. In other words, you're checking to make sure the wire inside the cord isn't broken. Set the multitester to measure ohms (resistance).

Unplug the cord from the wall outlet. Touch one probe to one prong of the plug, and the insert the other probe in the other end of the plug (see Figure 25.3). The reading should drop to zero. If you don't get a reading of zero, check the other hole to make sure you don't have the wrong one. Also, test the ground plug (it's the round one). You should get a reading of zero not only for both the hot and neutral wires, but also for the ground.

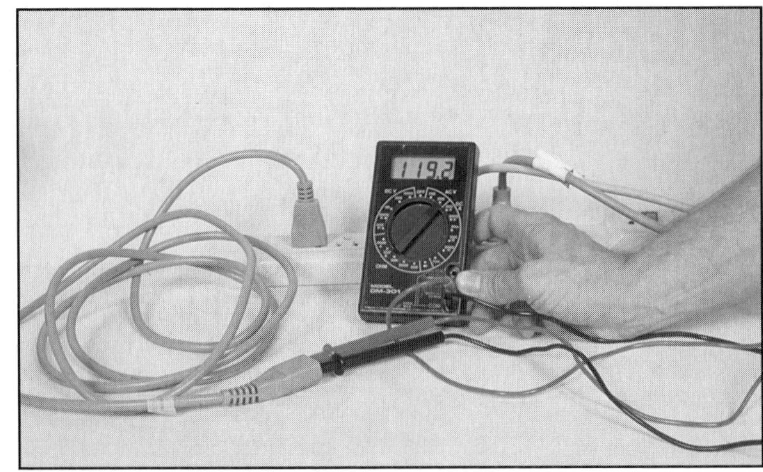

FIG. 25.3
You can use a multitester to check a cord for continuity with the cord unplugged from the wall.

If neither of these steps identifies or fixes the problem, you might have a bad power supply. Before you start blaming the power supply, though, you should check the motherboard power connections.

Checking Motherboard Connections

Even if you haven't replaced the motherboard, it's still possible that you accidentally (or purposely) disconnected the power supply connections to the motherboard. If the outlet and the power cord seem to be good, follow these steps to check the connections to the motherboard:

1. Unplug the computer from the wall outlet.
2. Open the PC and locate the power supply. It's the large silver box at the right rear (desktop) or top (tower) of the case. It has lots of wires coming out of it.
3. Locate the two wiring assemblies that connect from the power supply to the motherboard (see Figure 25.4).

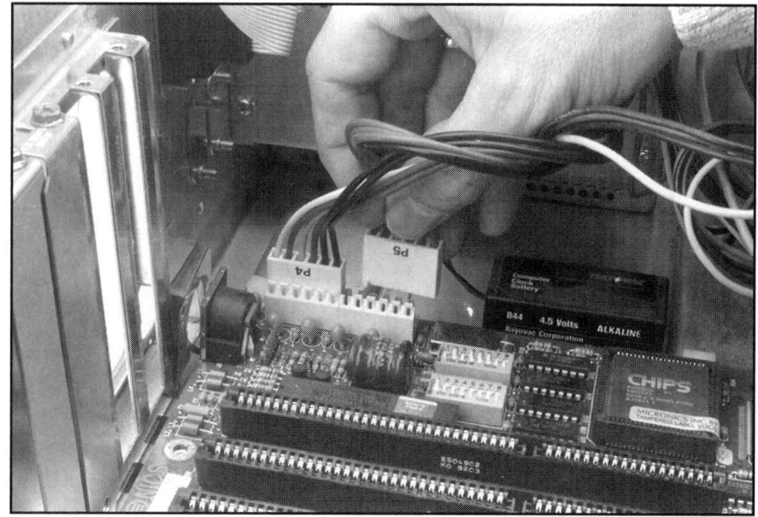

FIG. 25.4
Unless yours is an ATX case, you'll have to power connections from the power supply to the motherboard. ATX designs have one long connector instead of two.

4. The power connections to the motherboard are usually labeled P4 and P5 or P8 and P9. The black wires should be toward the center of the two connectors. Make sure the connections are secure and in the right location (check the motherboard manual to be sure).

Checking the Power Supply

If the power supply connections to the motherboard are correct and secure, the problem might be in the power supply. If you have a multimeter, you can test the power supply to see if it is putting out the correct voltage (if any) to the motherboard.

CAUTION This is the only procedure in the book in which I have you work inside the computer with the computer plugged in and turned on. Be *very careful* working inside the PC in this procedure, and make sure you don't drop anything inside while it is on.

Also, **do not remove the power supply from the case or disconnect it from the motherboard!** I've read and heard that some power supplies can explode if they are not connected to a load when they are turned on. Honestly, I don't know if that's true or not, but I don't want you to find out.

1. Turn off the PC, but leave it connected to the wall outlet.
2. Open the system unit.
3. Set the multimeter to read DC voltage in the next range higher than 12 volts (such as 20 volts, for example).
4. Locate an unused peripheral power supply connector or disconnect the power supply connection from a hard disk or floppy disk to use for the test.
5. Turn on the PC.
6. Insert the black probe into the power connector on one of the black wires (it doesn't matter which one).
7. Touch the red probe to the yellow wire on the connector. You should get a reading of +12 volts.
8. Touch the red probe to the red wire on the power connector. You should get a reading of +5 volts.
9. If you didn't get any readings in steps 7 and 8, you don't have to go any further with the test. Replace the power supply.
10. Insert the black probe into P4/P8 at one of the black wires.
11. Insert the red probe into the P4/P8 connector to the motherboard at a red wire. You should get a reading of +5 volts (see Figure 25.5).

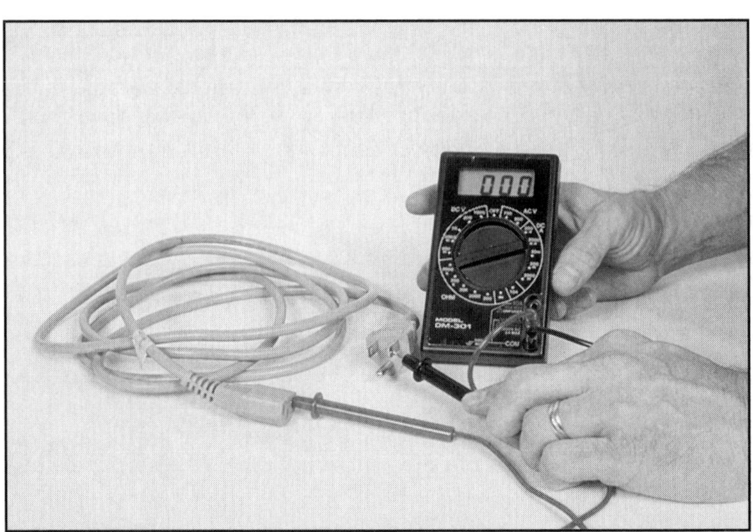

FIG. 25.5
Use a multimeter to test the power going to the motherboard connections.

12. Insert the red probe into P4/P8 at the yellow wire. You should get a reading of +12 volts.
13. Check the blue wire. You should get a reading of -12 volts.
14. Move the black probe to one of the black wires on P5/P9. Use the red probe to test the white wire. You should get a reading of -5 volts.
15. Check each of the red wires on P5/P9. You should get a reading of +5 volts on each one.

You won't get exactly 5 or 12 volts on these connections, but you should be close (like 5.03, for example). If the power supply reading is a couple of volts off, or there is no reading, you have a bad power supply.

Replacing the Power Supply

It's a simple matter to replace the power supply. All it takes is a screwdriver and about 20 minutes.

Before Replacing the Power Supply, You Need:

- ☑ A Phillips screwdriver for the case screws and power supply screws
- ☑ A new power supply of sufficient wattage for your system (typically, 200 watts or better)

---

1. Turn off and unplug the PC.
2. Remove the PC's cover.
3. Disconnect all of the power connections to the peripherals (disk drives, CPU fan, and so on).
4. Disconnect the power connections to the motherboard.
5. Locate and remove the screws holding the power supply to the chassis (see Figures 25.6 and 25.7).

FIG. 25.6
There probably will be four screws holding the power supply to the chassis.

FIG. 25.7
Here are the screws that hold the power supply in place in an ATX tower design.

6. Remove the power supply (see Figure 25.8).
7. Place the new power supply in the chassis and screw it into place.
8. Connect the power connections to the motherboard.
9. Connect all the peripherals.
10. Check all connections, then replace the PC's cover.
11. Test the system.

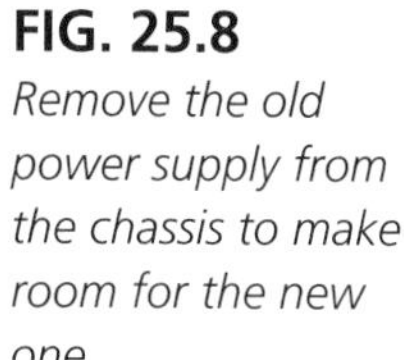

FIG. 25.8
Remove the old power supply from the chassis to make room for the new one.

Problems with the Boot Process

If the computer makes humming and whirring sounds when you turn it on, the power supply and connections are probably good. But, the system still might not boot. This section covers some possible problems and their solutions.

Dreaded Black Screen

If your PC hums and whirs but you don't see anything at all on the screen, the problem might be as simple as a loose cable. Use these steps to check for problems (some might seem overly obvious, but check them anyway):

1. Make sure the power cord is plugged into the wall and monitor, and the monitor is turned on.
2. Make sure the contrast and brightness knobs are not turned all the way down.
3. Make sure the video cable is securely attached to the video card and to the monitor (some monitors have removable cables).
4. If your PC uses a special-purpose video adapter (such as TV or video capture) in addition to the video card, it probably uses a pass-through connector that connects the two video cards. Check the connections between the cards to make sure they are correct and secure.

If the problem was a monitor that wasn't plugged in, I suggest you get a power cord for the monitor that you can plug into the power supply (see Figure 25.9). Then, you can leave the monitor turned on all the time, and it will power up when you turn on the computer. Using this type of cord doesn't put any additional load on the power supply, so it won't have a negative effect on your system.

FIG. 25.9
You can get a power cord for the monitor that connects to the computer's power supply, making the monitor come on when you turn on the computer.

If your brightness or contrast knobs were turned all the way down, don't feel bad. I've done the same thing.

Disk Boot Errors

Some of the problems described in this section can only be overcome by reformatting the hard disk. I hope you already have backups of your important files if that becomes necessary. If you're having a problem reading the disk, it's too late to make backups.

General failure error reading drive C:

This error usually is caused by the BIOS' inability to read the boot sector on the hard disk. A virus could have infected and trashed the boot sector, the boot sector could have been damaged through wear and tear, or the computer suffered a nasty kick or jolt.

If the problem is being caused by a bad master boot record and there is no physical damage to the disk, you might be able to re-create the boot record. The FDISK program, which you normally use to create and prepare disk partitions, also lets you re-create the master boot record:

> **CAUTION** The FDISK command can wipe out everything on the hard disk. No kidding—everything on the drive can be irretrievably lost in about a second. However, the command explained in the next procedure won't do anything to your disk other than re-create the master boot record. If you issue the FDISK command without any command-line switches, you see an FDISK menu that, among other things, lets you delete partitions. If you see any menus after issuing the FDISK command, press the Esc key immediately to get out of the program.

1. Find your emergency boot/repair disk, insert the disk into drive A, and reboot the PC.
2. When the command prompt appears, locate the FDISK.EXE program on the floppy disk.
3. At the command prompt, type **FDISK /MBR** and press Enter. Don't omit the /MBR switch, or you'll find yourself in the FDISK program, ready to delete a partition. When you issue the FDISK /MBR command, it will seem like nothing happens. You are returned almost immediately to a command prompt. But, FDISK has re-created the boot record (if it could).
4. Remove the floppy disk and reboot the system to see if the system can boot from the hard disk.

Bad or missing command interpreter

This error is caused by DOS not being able to locate the COMMAND.COM file. It might be due to a corrupted COMMAND.COM file, but sometimes it's caused by DOS not being able to find COMMAND.COM. Check out these possibilities:

- You booted the system from a floppy disk, but now have a different floppy disk in drive A:. Place the correct disk in drive A: and reboot.
- You have inadvertently copied a different version of COMMAND.COM into the root directory of the boot drive of the hard disk. Boot from the emergency boot disk, and copy the COMMAND.COM file from it to the root directory of the hard disk.

- You logged onto the network with a network copy of COMMAND.COM and are now logged off the network. Reboot and log back on. Check with your network administrator to find a fix for the problem.
- You might have a corrupted copy of COMMAND.COM. Reboot from the emergency boot disk and copy COMMAND.COM from the floppy to the root directory of drive C:.
- Maybe you erased COMMAND.COM from the root directory of drive C:. Restore it from the emergency boot disk.
- You might be booting from a bootable floppy disk that for some reason doesn't contain a copy of COMMAND.COM. Copy COMMAND.COM onto the disk.

Non-system disk or disk error

You might have a non-bootable floppy disk in drive A. If there is a disk in drive A:, remove it and attempt to reboot the system. If you receive this error message and there is no disk in drive A:, you have a problem with the hard disk. It might be that IO.SYS or MSDOS.SYS are missing from the disk. Try this procedure:

1. Boot the system using your emergency boot floppy disk and make active drive A: (type **A:** and press Enter).
2. At the command prompt, type **SYS C:** and press Enter. This command copies the system files IO.SYS, MSDOS.SYS, and COMMAND.COM to the hard disk, making it bootable.
3. Remove the disk from drive A: and reboot the system for testing.

File allocation table bad

This error is typically caused by a trashed file allocation table (FAT). Unfortunately, there is no way to recover the FAT without a utility program such as Norton Utilities. If you have such a utility, however, you might be able to recover the FAT and boot the system. Before doing anything else, however, you might want to call the technical support department (Symantec for Norton Utilities, for example), explain the problem, and ask about the best way to proceed with the repair. The technicians might be able to help you overcome the problem more quickly and without unforeseen problems.

Configuration too large for memory

If you see this message, you're probably using EMM386 to manage upper memory and there is an error in the line in CONFIG.SYS that loads EMM386. Single-step through the boot process, bypassing the line that loads EMM386. Then, edit CONFIG.SYS to correct the problem with that line.

CMOS Errors

The error message you receive at boot (if any) could be caused by a CMOS configuration problem. The following identifies possible CMOS errors and solutions. Note that some of these errors do not prevent the system from booting.

CMOS display type mismatch

This error appears if you've set the CMOS video setting different from the type of video adapter installed in the system. Run CMOS setup and reset the video adapter setting.

CMOS memory size mismatch

This error is common after you've installed additional memory, because the amount of memory in the system no longer matches the stored CMOS memory setting. Run the CMOS Setup program and specify the correct amount of RAM.

CMOS battery state low

This error indicates that the CMOS battery backup is running low on juice. If the computer uses an auxiliary battery pack or a button-type replaceable battery, you can replace the battery pack or battery with a new one. If the motherboard uses an on-board device such as a capacitor for CMOS backup power, you have to contact the system vendor or motherboard manufacturer to find out how to proceed.

TIP Without its CMOS settings, the computer might not be able to boot, because it forgets what type of hard disk is installed. If you can't replace the battery right away, leave the system running until you can. That way, you won't lose the CMOS settings and won't have boot problems. Before you shut down the computer to replace the battery, make sure you make a hard copy of the CMOS settings.

CMOS checksum failure

This error is generally caused by corrupted data in CMOS, and could be caused by bad battery backup or a loose connection. Check the CMOS backup power, and if that doesn't fix the problem, check with the system vendor or motherboard manufacturer. You might have to replace the CMOS or motherboard.

CMOS system options not set

Some or all of the CMOS settings have become corrupted or lost. Run the CMOS Setup program and restore all the settings. This problem can be caused by a bad CMOS backup battery.

CMOS time & date not set

Like some of the previous problems, this one was probably caused by a bad CMOS battery backup. Run the CMOS Setup program and reset the date and time. Then, check the battery backup.

System lock up when writing to floppy drive—OverDrive systems

If you are using an OverDrive CPU and the system locks up when you try to write to the floppy disk, your system probably requires an interposer between the OverDrive CPU and the CPU socket. Check with the technical support staff for your computer manufacturer on how to proceed.

Appendixes

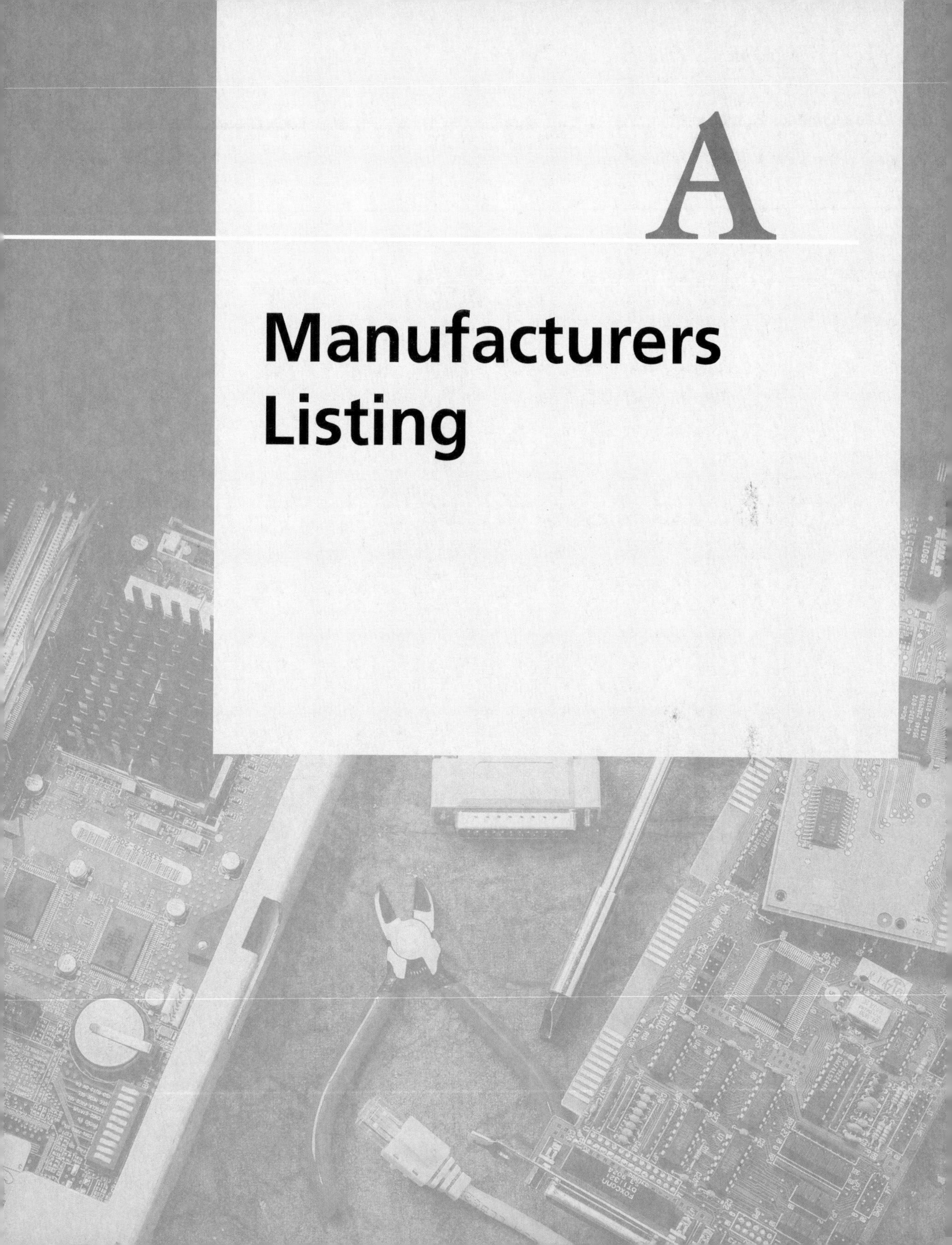

A

Manufacturers Listing

This appendix includes a comprehensive list of the major hardware and software manufacturers. The first half of this appendix lists the names of the manufacturers under each major product category. The second half lists each manufacturer alphabetically with extensive information, including:

- Name and address
- Toll-free and main phone numbers
- Web site
- Fax number
- Direct sales phone number
- Tech support phone number
- Tech support BBS number

Product Categories

The following are categories of both hardware and software products, listed alphabetically. Companies that make such products are listed under the appropriate categories. Once you find a company in which you are interested, use the second half of this appendix for information on how to contact them.

BIOS Upgrades

American Megatrends, Inc.

Award Software International, Inc. (subsidiary of GCH Systems, Inc.)

Phoenix Technologies Ltd.

CD-ROM and CD-R Drives

Aztech Labs, Inc. (subsidiary of Aztech Systems, Ltd.)

Chinon America, Inc. (Information Equipment Division)

CMS Enhancements (subsidiary of AmeriQuest)

Creative Labs, Inc. (subsidiary of Creative Technology, Ltd.)

Hewlett-Packard Co.

IBM Storage Systems (division of IBM)

MicroSolutions, Inc.

Mitsumi Electronics Corp., Inc. (division of Mitsumi Electric Co., Ltd.)

Nakamichi America Corp.

NEC Technologies, Inc.

Panasonic Communications & Systems Co. (Office Automation Group)

Philips Electronics, Inc. (Professional Solutions Division)

Pinnacle Micro, Inc.

Pioneer New Media Technologies, Inc. (Optical Memory Systems Division)

Plextor (subsidiary of Shinano Kenshi Co., Ltd.)

Procom Technology, Inc.

SONY Electronics, Inc.

TEAC America, Inc. (Data Storage Products Division)

Toshiba America Information Systems, Inc. (TAIS) (subsidiary of Toshiba Corp.)

Turtle Beach Systems (subsidiary of Integrated Circuit Systems, Inc.)

UMAX Technologies, Inc. (subsidiary of UMAX Data Systems, Inc.)

Wearnes Peripherals Corp. (division of Wearnes Peripherals International)

CPUs

Advanced Micro Devices, Inc.

Cyrix Systems Direct (division of Cyrix Corp.)

Intel Corp.

Desktop PCs

Acer America Corp. (subsidiary of The Acer Group)

ALR (Advanced Logic Research, Inc.)

Apple Computer, Inc.

APS Technologies

AST Research, Inc.

Austin Direct (an IPC Co.)

Blackship Computer Systems, Inc.

Compaq Computer Corp.

Comtrade Computer, Inc.

Cyrix Systems Direct (division of Cyrix Corp.)

Dell Computer Corp.

Digital Equipment Corp. (DEC)

Everex Systems, Inc. (subsidiary of Formosa Plastics Group)

Gateway 2000, Inc.

Hewlett-Packard Co.

IBM (International Business Machines)

Micron Electronics, Inc.

MidWest Micro

Packard Bell NEC, Inc. (CA)

Quantex Microsystems, Inc.

SONY Electronics, Inc.

Toshiba America Information Systems, Inc. (TAIS) (subsidiary of Toshiba Corp.)

Tri-Star Computer Corp.

USA Flex, Inc.

Vektron International, Inc.

Floppy Drives

Chinon America, Inc. (Information Equipment Division)

Mitsumi Electronics Corp., Inc. (division of Mitsumi Electric Co., Ltd.)

TEAC America, Inc. (Data Storage Products Division)

Hard Drives

Digital Equipment Corp. (DEC)

Fujitsu Computer Products of America, Inc. (subsidiary of Fujitsu America, Inc.)

Hitachi America, Ltd. (Computer Division)

IBM Storage Systems (division of IBM)

Maxtor Corp. (subsidiary of Hyundai Electronics America)

Micropolis Pte, Ltd. (subsidiary of Singapore Technologies)

Quantum Corp.

Samsung Electronics America, Inc. (Information Systems Division)

Seagate Technology, Inc.

Toshiba America Information Systems, Inc. (TAIS) (subsidiary of Toshiba Corp.)

Western Digital Corp.

I/O Cards

Adaptec, Inc.

Boca Research, Inc.

BusLogic, Inc. (subsidiary of Mylex Corp.)

DTC (Data Technology Corp.)

Promise Technology, Inc.

QLogic Corp.

SIIG, Inc.

Western Digital Corp.

Memory

Kingston Technology Corp.

PNY Electronics Inc.

Modems

Best Data Products, Inc.

Boca Research, Inc.

Cardinal Technologies, Inc.

Creative Labs, Inc. (subsidiary of Creative Technology, Ltd.)

Diamond Multimedia Systems, Inc.

DTC (Data Technology Corp.)

Hayes Microcomputer Products, Inc.

MaxTech Corp.

Microcom, Inc.

Motorola UDS (unit of Motorola Information Systems Group)

Multi-Tech Systems, Inc.

Practical Peripherals (product division of Hayes Microcomputer Products, Inc.)

Reveal Computer Products, Inc.

SIIG, Inc.

U.S. Robotics Access Corp. (subsidiary of U.S. Robotics Corp.)

Xircom, Inc.

Zoltrix, Inc.

Zoom Telephonics, Inc.

ZyXEL (a Zero One NetWorking Co.)

Monitors

ADI Systems, Inc. (subsidiary of ADI Corp.)

Amdek

AOC International (U.S.A.), Ltd.

CTX International, Inc.

Eizo Nanao Technology, Inc. (subsidiary of NANAO Corp.)

Hyundai Electronics America (subsidiary of Hyundai Electronics Industries Co., Ltd.)

IBM (International Business Machines)

MAG Innovision Co., Inc.

MaxTech Corp.

NEC Technologies, Inc.

Nokia Display Products, Inc. (division of Nokia Consumer Electronics)

Panasonic Communications & Systems Co. (Office Automation Group)

Sampo Technology, Inc. (Industrial Products Division)

Samsung Electronics America, Inc. (Information Systems Division)

Samtron Displays, Inc. (division of Samsung Electronics Co., Ltd.)

SMILE International, Inc. (subsidiary of Kuo Feng Corp.)

SONY Electronics, Inc.

Tatung Co. of America, Inc. (subsidiary of Tatung Co.)

ViewSonic Corp. (division of Keypoint Technology Corp.)

Wyse Technology, Inc.

Motherboards

ASUS Computer International, Inc. (subsidiary of ASUSTek Computer, Inc.)

DTK Computer, Inc. (division of Datatech Enterprises Co., Ltd.)

Shuttle Technology, Inc.

Vektron International, Inc.

Network Interface Cards and Hubs

Accton Technology Corp.

Adaptec, Inc.

Allied Telesyn International Corp.

Asante Technologies, Inc.

Boca Research, Inc.

CNet Technology, Inc.

D-Link Systems, Inc.

Farallon Communications

Intel Corp.

Kingston Technology Corp.

Linksys (division of The Linksys Group, Inc.)

MaxTech Corp.

Newbridge Networks, Inc.

SIIG, Inc.

Xircom, Inc.

Notebooks

Acer America Corp. (subsidiary of The Acer Group)

Apple Computer, Inc.

AST Research Inc.

Austin Direct (an IPC Co.)

Compaq Computer Corp.

Comtrade Computer, Inc.

Dolch Computer Systems, Inc. (division of Dolch American Instruments, Inc.)

Dell Computer Corp.

Digital Equipment Corp. (DEC)

Everex Systems, Inc. (subsidiary of Formosa Plastics Group)

Gateway 2000, Inc.

Hewlett-Packard Co.

IBM (International Business Machines)

MaxTech Corp.

Micron Electronics, Inc.

MidWest Micro

Packard Bell NEC, Inc. (CA)

Quantex Microsystems, Inc.

Sager Midern Computer, Inc.

Samsung Electronics America, Inc. (Information Systems Division)

Sharp Electronics Corp. (Information Systems Group)

Toshiba America Information Systems, Inc. (TAIS) (subsidiary of Toshiba Corp.)

Vektron International, Inc.

WinBook Computer Corp. (subsidiary of Micro Electronics, Inc.)

Printers

Brother International Corp. (Business Machine Group)

Canon Computer Systems, Inc. (subsidiary of Canon, Inc.)

Citizen America Corp. (subsidiary of Citizen Watch Co., Ltd.)

Epson America, Inc. (subsidiary of Seiko Epson Corp.)

Hewlett-Packard Co.

Lexmark International, Inc.

NEC Technologies, Inc.

Okidata Corp. (division of Oki America, Inc.)

Panasonic Communications & Systems Co. (Office Automation Group)

QMS, Inc.

Star Micronics America, Inc. (subsidiary of Star Micronics Co., Ltd.)

Tektronix, Inc. (Color Printing and Imaging Division)

Removable Media

CMS Enhancements (subsidiary of AmeriQuest)

Epson America, Inc. (subsidiary of Seiko Epson Corp.)

Iomega Corp.

MicroSolutions, Inc.

New Media Corp.

SyQuest Technology, Inc.

Scanners

Caere Corp.

Fujitsu Computer Products of America, Inc. (subsidiary of Fujitsu America, Inc.)

Hewlett-Packard Co.

Howtek, Inc.

Logitech, Inc. (division of Logitech International)

Microtek Lab, Inc. (subsidiary of Microtek International, Inc.)

Mustek, Inc.

UMAX Technologies, Inc. (subsidiary of UMAX Data Systems, Inc.)

Visioneer, Inc.

Software

Adobe Systems, Inc.

Borland International, Inc.

Broderbund Software, Inc.

Corel Corp.

Davidson & Associates, Inc.

Disney Interactive, Inc.

Intuit, Inc. (Personal Finance Division)

Lotus Development Corp. (Word Processing Division)

Microsoft Corp.

Novell, Inc.

Parsons Technology, Inc. (subsidiary of Intuit, Inc.)

Peachtree Software, Inc. (subsidiary of Automatic Data Processing, Inc.)

Quark, Inc.

Sierra On-Line, Inc.

Symantec Corp.

Symantec Corp. (Delrina Group)

Sound Cards

Advanced Gravis Computer Technology, Ltd.

Aztech Labs, Inc. (subsidiary of Aztech Systems, Ltd.)

Creative Labs, Inc. (subsidiary of Creative Technology, Ltd.)

DSP Solutions, Inc.

ENSONIQ Corp.

Genoa Systems Corp.

MediaMagic (division of IPC Technologies, Inc.)

Orchid Technology, Inc. (subsidiary of Micronics Computers, Inc.)

Reveal Computer Products, Inc.

Turtle Beach Systems (subsidiary of Integrated Circuit Systems, Inc.)

Standby Power Supplies and Surge Protectors

American Power Conversion Corp.

Best Power (unit of General Signal)

Curtis Manufacturing Co., Inc.

Kensington Microware, Ltd. (subsidiary of ACCO World Corp.)

Newpoint Corp. (subsidiary of Proxima Corp.)

SL WABER, Inc. (subsidiary of SL Industries, Inc.)

TrippLite

ViewSonic Corp. (division of Keypoint Technology Corp.)

Tape Drives

CMS Enhancements (subsidiary of AmeriQuest)

CORE International, Inc. (an AIWA Co.)

Datasonix Corp.

Exabyte Corp.

Hewlett-Packard Co. (Colorado Memory Systems Division)

Hitachi Data Systems Corp.

IBM Storage Systems (division of IBM)

Iomega Corp.

MicroNet Technology, Inc.

MicroSolutions, Inc.

Procom Technology, Inc.

Reveal Computer Products, Inc.

Seagate Technology, Inc.

SONY Electronics, Inc.

Tandberg Data, Inc. (subsidiary of Tandberg Data ASA)

TEAC America, Inc. (Data Storage Products Division)

Video Cards

AITech International

ATI Technologies, Inc.

Boca Research, Inc.

Cardinal Technologies, Inc.

Creative Labs, Inc. (subsidiary of Creative Technology, Ltd.)

DFI, Inc.

Diamond Multimedia Systems, Inc.

Genoa Systems Corp.

Hercules Computer Technology, Inc.

Matrox Graphics, Inc.

Number Nine Visual Technology Corp.

Orchid Technology, Inc. (subsidiary of Micronics Computers, Inc.)

Reveal Computer Products, Inc.

SIIG, Inc.

STB Systems, Inc.

Truevision, Inc.

UMAX Technologies, Inc. (subsidiary of UMAX Data Systems, Inc.)

Alphabetical Listing

Acer America Corp. (subsidiary of The Acer Group)
2641 Orchard Pkwy.
San Jose, CA 95134
800-733-2237; 408-432-6200
http://www.acer.com/aac/
Direct sales: 800-239-2237 (Acer Direct)
Fax: 408-922-2953
Tech support: 800-637-7000
Tech support BBS: 408-428-0140

Accton Technology Corp.
1962 Zanker Rd.
San Jose, CA 95112
800-926-9288; 408-452-8900
http://www.accton.com
Direct sales: 408-452-8080
Fax: 408-452-8988
Tech support: Use toll-free number
Tech support BBS: 408-452-8828

Adaptec, Inc.
691 S. Milpitas Blvd.
Milpitas, CA 95035
800-934-2766; 408-945-8600
http://www.adaptec.com
Direct sales: 800-442-SCSI
Fax: 408-262-2533
Tech support: 800-959-SCSI
Tech support BBS: 408-945-7727

ADI Systems, Inc. (subsidiary of ADI Corp.)
2115 Ringwood Ave.
San Jose, CA 95131
800-228-0530; 408-944-0100
http://www.adi-online.com
Fax: 408-944-0300
Tech support: Use main number

Adobe Systems, Inc.
1585 Charleston Rd., P.O. Box 7900
Mountain View, CA 94039-7900
800-833-6687; 415-961-4400
http://www.adobe.com
Direct sales: 800-642-3623
Fax: 415-961-3769
Tech support: 415-961-4992
Tech support BBS: 408-562-6839

Advanced Gravis Computer Technology, Ltd.
3750 N. Fraser Way, Ste. 101
Burnaby, BC, CD V5J 5E9
800-663-8558; 604-431-5020
http://www.gravis.com
Fax: 604-431-5155
Tech support: 604-431-1807
Tech support BBS: 604-431-5927

Advanced Micro Devices Inc. (AMD)
1 AMD Place
Sunnyvale, CA 94088-3453
http://www.amd.com.
800-222-9323; 408-749-5703
Fax: 408-749-4753

AITech International
47971 Fremont Blvd.
Fremont, CA 94538
800-882-8184; 510-226-8960
http://www.aitech.com
Fax: 510-226-8996
Tech support: 510-226-9246
Tech support BBS: 510-226-8267

Allied Telesyn International Corp.
950 Kifer Rd.
Sunnyvale, CA 94086
800-424-4284; 408-730-0950
http://www.alliedtelesyn.com
Fax: 408-736-0100
Tech support: 206-488-5888
Tech support BBS: 206-820-2594

ALR (Advanced Logic Research, Inc.)
9401 Jeronimo Rd.
Irvine, CA 92718
800-444-4257; 714-581-6770
http://www.alr.com
Fax: 714-581-9240
Tech support: 714-458-0863
Tech support BBS: 714-458-6834

Amdek
9020-II Capital of Texas Hwy., N, Ste. 400
Austin, TX 78759
800-722-6335
Fax: 800-742-6335
Tech support: 800-800-9973

American Megatrends, Inc.
6145-F Northbelt Pkwy.
Norcross, GA 30071
800-828-9264; 770-246-8600
http://www.megatrends.com
Fax: 770-246-9381
Tech support: 770-246-8645
Tech support BBS: 770-246-8780

American Power Conversion Corp.
132 Fairgrounds Rd.
West Kingston, RI 02892-9906
800-800-4272; 401-789-5735
http://www.apcc.com
Fax: 401-789-3180
Tech support: Use toll-free number

AOC International (U.S.A.), Ltd.
311 Sinclair Frontage Rd.
Milpitas, CA 95035
800-775-1262; 408-956-1070
http://www.aocltd.com
Direct sales: 800-228-7744
Fax: 408-956-1516
Tech support: 800-343-5777

Apple Computer, Inc.
1 Infinite Loop
Cupertino, CA 95014
800-776-2333; 408-996-1010
http://www.apple.com
Direct sales: 800-538-9696 (Hardware); 800-325-2747 (Software/Claris Corp.)
Fax: 408-996-0275
Tech support: 800-767-2775
Tech support BBS: 800-877-8221

APS Technologies
6131 Deramus Ave., P.O. Box 4987
Kansas City, MO 64120-0087
800-235-3707; 816-483-1600
http://www.apstech.com
Direct sales: 800-235-3708
Fax: 816-483-3077
Tech support: 800-344-7550
Tech support BBS: 816-483-4541

Asante Technologies, Inc.
821 Fox Lane
San Jose, CA 95131-1601
800-662-9686; 408-435-8388
http://www.asante.com
Direct sales: 800-566-6680
Fax: 408-432-1117
Tech support: 800-622-7464
Tech support BBS: 408-432-1416

AST Research Inc.
16215 Alton Pkwy., P.O. Box 57005
Irvine, CA 92718
800-876-4AST; 714-727-4141
http://www.ast.com
Fax: 714-727-9355
Tech support: Use toll-free number
Tech support BBS: 714-727-4132

ASUS Computer International, Inc. (subsidiary of ASUSTek Computer, Inc.)
721 Charcot Ave.
San Jose, CA 95131
408-474-0567
Fax: 408-474-0568
Tech support: Use main number
Tech support BBS: 408-956-9084

ATI Technologies, Inc.
33 Commerce Valley Dr., E
Thornhill, ON, CD L3T 7N6
905-882-2600
http://www.atitech.ca
Fax: 905-882-2620
Tech support: 905-882-2626
Tech support BBS: 905-764-9404

Austin Direct (an IPC Co.)
2121 Energy Dr.
Austin, TX 78758
800-483-9938; 512-339-3500
http://www.austindirect.com
Direct sales: 800-952-9816
Fax: 512-454-1357
Tech support: 800-752-4171
Tech support BBS: 512-339-3582

Award Software International, Inc. (subsidiary of GCH Systems, Inc.)
777 E. Middlefield Rd.
Mountain View, CA 94043-4023
415-968-4433
http://www.award.com
Fax: 415-968-0274
Tech support BBS: 415-968-0249

Aztech Labs, Inc. (subsidiary
of Aztech Systems, Ltd.)
47811 Warm Springs Blvd.
Fremont, CA 94539-7400
800-886-8859; 510-623-8988
http://www.aztechca.com
Fax: 510-623-8989
Tech support: 510-623-9037
Tech support BBS: 510-623-8933

Best Data Products, Inc.
21800 Nordhoff St.
Chatsworth, CA 91311
800-632-BEST; 818-773-9600
http://www.bestdata.com
Fax: 818-773-9619
Tech support: Use main number
Tech support BBS: 818-773-3943

Best Power (unit of General Signal)
P.O. Box 280
Necedah, WI 54646
800-356-5794; 608-565-7200
http://www.bestpower.com
Fax: 608-565-2221
Tech support: 800-356-5737
Tech support BBS: 608-565-7424

Blackship Computer Systems, Inc.
2031 O'Toole Ave.
San Jose, CA 95131
800-531-7447; 408-432-7500
http://www.blackship-computers.com
Fax: 408-432-1443
Tech support: Use toll-free number

Boca Research, Inc.
1377 Clint Moore Rd.
Boca Raton, FL 33487-2722
407-997-6227
http://www.bocaresearch.com
Fax: 407-997-0918
Tech support: 407-241-8088
Tech support BBS: 407-241-1601

Borland International, Inc.
100 Borland Way
Scotts Valley, CA 95066-3249
800-233-2444; 408-431-1000
http://www.borland.com
Direct sales: 800-331-0877;
800-245-7367 (Interbase)
Fax: 408-431-4122
Tech support: 408-461-9155
Tech support BBS: 408-431-5096

Broderbund Software, Inc.
500 Redwood Blvd., P.O. Box 6125
Novato, CA 94948-6121
800-521-6263; 415-382-4400
http://www.broderbund.com
Fax: 415-382-4419
Tech support: 415-382-4700
Tech support BBS: 415-883-5889

Brother International Corp.
(Business Machine Group)
200 Cottontail Lane
Somerset, NJ 08875-6714
908-356-8880
http://www.brother.com
Fax: 908-356-4085
Tech support: 800-276-7746
(computer printers); 800-284-4329
(fax machines)

BusLogic, Inc. (subsidiary
of Mylex Corp.)
4151 Burton Dr.
Santa Clara, CA 95054-1564
800-707-7274; 408-492-9090
http://www.buslogic.com

Fax: 408-492-1542
Tech support: 408-654-0760
Tech support BBS: 408-492-1984

Caere Corp.
100 Cooper Court
Los Gatos, CA 95030
800-535-SCAN; 408-395-7000
http://www.caere.com
Fax: 408-354-2743
Tech support: 800-462-2373
Tech support BBS: 408-395-1631

Canon Computer Systems, Inc.
(subsidiary of Canon, Inc.)
2995 Redhill Ave.
Costa Mesa, CA 92626
800-848-4123; 800-387-1241 (CD);
714-438-3000
http://www.ccsi.canon.com
Fax: 714-438-3099
Tech support: 800-423-2366
Tech support BBS: 714-438-3325

Cardinal Technologies, Inc.
1827 Freedom Rd.
Lancaster, PA 17601
800-775-0899; 717-293-3000
http://www.cardtech.com
Direct sales: 717-293-3049
Fax: 717-293-3055
Tech support: 717-293-3124
Tech support BBS: 717-293-3074

Chinon America, Inc.
(Information Equipment Division)
615 Hawaii Ave.
Torrance, CA 90503-9747
800-441-0222; 310-533-0274
http://www.chinon.com
Fax: 310-533-1727
Tech support: Use main number

Citizen America Corp. (subsidiary
of Citizen Watch Co., Ltd.)
P.O. Box 4003, 2450 Broadway,
Ste. 600
Santa Monica, CA 90411-4003
800-477-4683; 310-453-0614
http://www.citizen-america.com
Fax: 310-453-2814
Tech support: 310-453-0614, ext. 266
Tech support BBS: 310-453-7564

CMS Enhancements (subsidiary
of AmeriQuest)
1051 S. East St.
Anaheim, CA 92805
800-327-5773; 714-517-0915
Fax: 714-956-8156
Tech support: 800-555-1671
Tech support BBS: 714-437-9794

CNet Technology, Inc.
2199 Zanker Rd.
San Jose, CA 95131
800-486-2638; 408-954-8000
http://www.cnet.com.tw
Direct sales: 408-954-8888
Fax: 408-954-8866
Tech support: 408-954-8800
Tech support BBS: 408-954-1787

Compaq Computer Corp.
20555 State Hwy. 249
Houston, TX 77070-2698
800-345-1518; 713-514-0484
http://www.compaq.com
Direct sales: 800-888-5925 (Compaq
DirectPlus)
Fax: 713-514-4583
Tech support: 800-OKCOMPAQ
Tech support BBS: 713-378-1418

Comtrade Computer, Inc.
1215 Bixby Dr.
City of Industry, CA 91745
800-969-2123; 818-961-6688
http://www.comtrade-pc.com
Direct sales: 800-868-5588
Fax: 818-369-1479
Tech support: 800-899-4508
Tech support BBS: 818-961-6098

CORE International, Inc. (an AIWA Co.)
6500 E. Rogers Circle
Boca Raton, FL 33487-2655
800-688-9910; 407-997-6044
http://www.aiwa.com
Direct sales: 800-920-CORE
Fax: 407-997-6009
Tech support: 408-997-6033
Tech support BBS: 407-241-2929

Corel Corp.
1600 Carling Ave., The Corel Bldg.
Ottawa, ON, CD K1Z 8R7
800-772-6735; 613-728-8200
http://www.corel.com
Direct sales: 800-950-5378, ext. 196
Fax: 613-728-9790
Tech support: 613-728-6173
Tech support BBS: 613-728-4752

Creative Labs, Inc. (subsidiary of Creative Technology, Ltd.)
1901 McCarthy Blvd.
Milpitas, CA 95035
800-998-1000; 408-428-6600
http://www.creaf.com
Direct sales: 800-998-5227
Fax: 408-428-2394
Tech support: 405-742-6622
Tech support BBS: 405-742-6660

CTX International, Inc.
748 Epperson Dr.
City of Industry, CA 91748
818-839-0500
http://www.ctxintl.com
Direct sales: 800-289-9157
Fax: 818-810-6703
Tech support: 800-888-2012
Tech support BBS: 909-594-8973

Curtis Manufacturing Co., Inc.
225 Secaucus Rd.
Secaucus, NJ 07096
800-955-9514; 201-422-0240
Fax: 201-422-0254
Tech support: Use toll-free number

Cyrix Systems Direct (division of Cyrix Corp.)
P.O. Box 853923
Richardson, TX 75085-3923
800-340-7501
http://www.cyrix.com
Direct sales: 800-340-7544
Fax: 800-340-7463

D-Link Systems, Inc.
5 Musick
Irvine, CA 92618
800-326-1688; 714-455-1688
http://www.dlink.com
Fax: 714-455-2521
Tech support: Use main number
Tech support BBS: 714-455-1779

Datasonix Corp.
5700 Flatiron Pkwy.
Boulder, CO 80301
800-328-2779; 303-545-9500
http://www.datasonix.com/datasonix

Fax: 303-545-9249
Tech support: Use toll-free number
Tech support BBS: 303-473-0305

Davidson & Associates, Inc.
19840 Pioneer Ave.
Torrance, CA 90503
800-545-7677; 310-793-0600
http://www.davd.com
Fax: 310-793-0601
Tech support: 800-556-5571
Tech support BBS: 310-793-9966

Dell Computer Corp.
2214 W. Braker Ln., Ste. D
Austin, TX 78758
800-289-3355; 512-338-4400
http://www.dell.com
Direct sales: 800-289-1180
Fax: 512-728-3653
Tech support: 800-624-9896
Tech support BBS: 512-728-8528

DFI, Inc.
135 Main Ave.
Sacramento, CA 95838-2041
916-568-1234
http://www.dfiusa.com
Direct sales: 800-808-4334
Fax: 916-568-1233
Tech support: Use main number

Diamond Multimedia Systems, Inc.
2880 Junction Ave.
San Jose, CA 95134-1922
800-4-MULTIMEDIA; 408-325-7000
http://www.diamondmm.com
Fax: 408-325-7070
Tech support: 408-325-7100
Tech support BBS: 408-325-7175

Digital Equipment Corp. (DEC)
146 Main St.
Maynard, MA 01754-2571
800-344-4825; 508-493-5111
http://www.pc.digital.com
Direct sales: 800-642-4532
(Digital PC/PCs Compleat)
Fax: 508-493-8780
Tech support: 800-354-9000
Tech support BBS: 508-496-8800

Disney Interactive, Inc.
500 S. Buena Vista St.
Burbank, CA 91521-8114
818-553-4345
Direct sales: 800-900-9234;
800-899-0431 (CD)
Fax: 818-502-0827
Tech support: 800-228-0988

DSP Solutions, Inc.
1157 San Antonio Rd.
Mountain View, CA 94043
800-560-1817; 415-919-4000
http://www.dsps.com
Fax: 415-919-4040
Tech support: 415-919-4100
Tech support BBS: 415-919-4199

DTC Data Technology Corp.
1515 Centre Pointe Dr.
Milpitas, CA 95035
408-942-4000
http://www.datatechnology.com
Fax: 408-942-4027
Tech support: Use main number
Tech support BBS: 408-942-4010

DTK Computer, Inc. (division of Datatech Enterprises Co., Ltd.)
770 Epperson Dr.
Los Angeles, CA 91748
800-289-2385; 818-810-8880
http://www.dtkcomputer.com
Direct sales: 818-810-0098
Fax: 818-810-0090
Tech support: Use main number
Tech support BBS: 818-854-0797

Eizo Nanao Technology, Inc.
(subsidiary of NANAO Corp.)
23535 Telo Ave.
Torrance, CA 90505
800-800-5202; 310-325-5202
http://www.traveller.com/nanao
Fax: 310-530-1679
Tech support: Use main number

ENSONIQ Corp.
P.O. Box 3035, 115 Great Valley Pkwy.
Malvern, PA 19355-0735
800-942-0096; 610-647-3930
http://www.ensoniq.com
Fax: 610-647-8908
Tech support: Use main number

Epson America, Inc.
(subsidiary of Seiko Epson Corp.)
20770 Madrona Ave., P.O. Box 2842
Torrance, CA 90509-2842
800-289-3776; 310-782-0770
http://www.epson.com
Direct sales: 800-374-7300 (EPSON Direct)
Fax: 310-782-5220
Tech support: 800-922-8911
Tech support BBS: 310-782-4531

Everex Systems, Inc.
(subsidiary of Formosa Plastics Group)
5020 Brandin Court
Fremont, CA 94538
800-821-0806; 510-498-1111
http://www.everex.com
Fax: 510-683-2186
Tech support: 800-262-3312
Tech support BBS: 510-226-9694

Exabyte Corp.
1685 38th St.
Boulder, CO 80301
800-EXABYTE; 303-442-4333
http://www.exabyte.com
Fax: 303-417-5500
Tech support: 800-445-7736
Tech support BBS: 303-447-7100

Farallon Communications
2470 Mariner Square Loop
Alameda, CA 94501-1010
510-814-5100
http://www.farallon.com
Fax: 510-814-5023
Tech support: 510-814-5000
Tech support BBS: 510-865-1321

Fujitsu Computer Products of America, Inc.
(subsidiary of Fujitsu America, Inc.)
2904 Orchard Pkwy.
San Jose, CA 95134
800-626-4686; 408-432-6333

http://www.fcpa.com
Fax: 408-894-1716
Tech support: Use toll-free number
Tech support BBS: 408-944-9899

Gateway 2000, Inc.
610 Gateway Dr., P.O. Box 2000
North Sioux City, SD 57049-2000
800-846-2000; 605-232-2000
http://www.gw2k.com
Fax: 605-232-2023
Tech support: 800-846-2301
Tech support BBS: 605-232-2109

Genoa Systems Corp.
6850 Santa Teresa Blvd.
San Jose, CA 95119
408-362-2900
http://www.genoasys.com
Fax: 408-362-2998
Tech support: 408-362-2990

Hayes Microcomputer Products, Inc.
P.O. Box 105203
Atlanta, GA 30348-5203
770-840-9200
http://www.hayes.com
Fax: 770-441-1213
Tech support: 770-441-1617
Tech support BBS: 770-446-6336

Hercules Computer Technology, Inc.
3839 Spinnaker Court
Fremont, CA 94538
800-532-0600; 510-623-6030
http://www.hercules.com
Fax: 510-623-1112
Tech support: 800-323-0601
Tech support BBS: 510-623-7449

Hewlett-Packard Co.
3000 Hanover St.
Palo Alto, CA 94304
800-752-0900; 800-387-3867 (CD); 415-857-1501
http://www.hp.com
Direct sales: 800-637-7740 (HP Direct)
Tech support: 800-858-8867
Tech support BBS: 415-852-0256

Hewlett-Packard Co.
(Colorado Memory Systems Division)
800 S. Taft Ave.
Loveland, CO 80537-9929
970-669-8000
Fax: 970-667-0997
Tech support: 970-635-1500
Tech support BBS: 970-635-0650

Hitachi America, Ltd. (Computer Division)
2000 Sierra Point Pkwy., Hitachi Plaza
Brisbane, CA 94005-1835
800-HITACHI; 415-589-8300
http://www.hitachi.com
Fax: 415-244-7647
Tech support: Use main number

Hitachi Data Systems Corp.
P.O. Box 54996, 750 E. Central Expwy.
Santa Clara, CA 95056-0996
800-227-1930; 800-982-5815 (CA); 408-970-1000
http://www.hdshq.com
Fax: 408-727-8036
Tech support: 619-537-3000

Howtek, Inc.
21 Park Ave.
Hudson, NH 03051
800-444-6983; 603-882-5200
http://www.howtek.com
Fax: 603-880-3843
Tech support: Use main number

Hyundai Electronics America
(subsidiary of Hyundai Electronics Industries Co., Ltd.)
510 Cottonwood Dr.
Milpitas, CA 95035
800-568-0060; 408-232-8000
http://www.hea.com
Direct sales: 408-232-8650
Fax: 408-232-8146
Tech support: Use toll-free number

IBM (International Business Machines)
Old Orchard Rd.
Armonk, NY 10504
800-426-3333; 914-765-1900
http://www.ibm.com
Direct sales: 800-426-7255 (IBM PC Direct)
Tech support: 800-237-5511
Tech support BBS: 919-517-0001; 800-847-7211 (OS/2)

IBM Storage Systems (division of IBM)
5600 Cottle Rd.
San Jose, CA 95193
800-426-7299; 408-256-1600
http://www.ibm.com
Fax: 408-256-5082

Intel Corp.
2200 Mission College Blvd.
Santa Clara, CA 95051
800-548-4725; 408-765-8080
http://www.intel.com
Fax: 408-765-1821
Tech support: 800-628-8686

Intuit, Inc. (Personal Finance Division)
P.O. Box 3014
Menlo Park, CA 94026-3014
800-624-8742; 415-322-0573
http://www.intuit.com
Direct sales: 800-781-5999
Fax: 415-322-1597
Tech support: 505-896-7266

Iomega Corp.
1821 W. Iomega Way
Roy, UT 84067
800-697-8833; 801-778-1000
http://www.iomega.com
Fax: 801-778-3748
Tech support: 801-629-7629
Tech support BBS: 800-456-5522

Kensington Microware, Ltd.
(subsidiary of ACCO World Corp.)
2855 Campus Dr.
San Mateo, CA 94403
800-535-4242; 415-572-2700
http://www.kensington.com
Fax: 415-572-9675
Tech support: Use main number

Kingston Technology Corp.
17600 Newhope St.
Fountain Valley, CA 92708
800-435-2620; 714-435-2600
http://www.kingston.com
Direct sales: 800-337-8410
Fax: 714-435-2699
Tech support: 800-435-0640
Tech support BBS: 714-435-2636

Lexmark International, Inc.
740 New Circle Rd., NW
Lexington, KY 40511-1876
800-358-5835; 606-232-2000
http://www.lexmark.com
Direct sales: 800-438-2468
Fax: 606-232-2403
Tech support: 606-232-3000
Tech support BBS: 606-232-5238

Linksys (division of The Linksys Group, Inc.)
17401 Armstrong Ave.
Irvine, CA 92614
800-LINKSYS; 714-261-1288
http://www.linksys.com
Fax: 714-261-8868
Tech support: Use main number
Tech support BBS: 714-261-2888

Logitech, Inc.
(division of Logitech International)
6505 Kaiser Dr.
Fremont, CA 94555
800-231-7717; 510-795-8500
http://www.logitech.com
Fax: 510-792-8901
Tech support: 510-795-8100
Tech support BBS: 510-795-0408

Lotus Development Corp.
(Word Processing Division)
1000 Abernathy Rd., NE, Ste. 1700
Atlanta, GA 30328
800-343-5414; 770-391-0011
http://www.lotus.com
Fax: 770-698-7654
Tech support: 770-399-5505
Tech support BBS: 770-395-7707

MAG Innovision Co., Inc.
2801 S. Yale St.
Santa Ana, CA 92704
800-827-3998; 714-751-2008
http://www.maginnovision.com
Fax: 714-751-5522
Tech support: Use toll-free number

Matrox Graphics, Inc.
1055 St. Regis Blvd.
Dorval, QC, CD H9P 2T4
800-361-1408; 514-685-0270
http://www.matrox.com/mga
Direct sales: 514-969-6320
Fax: 514-969-6363
Tech support: Use main number
Tech support BBS: 514-685-6008

MaxTech Corp.
13915 Cerritos Corp. Dr.
Cerritos, CA 90703
800-936-7629; 310-921-1698
http://www.maxcorp.com
Direct sales: 800-289-4821
Fax: 310-802-9605
Tech support: Use main number
Tech support BBS: 310-921-4438

Maxtor Corp. (subsidiary of Hyundai Electronics America)
211 River Oaks Pkwy.
San Jose, CA 95134-1913
800-2-MAXTOR; 408-432-1700
http://www.maxtor.com
Fax: 408-432-4510
Tech support: Use toll-free number
Tech support BBS: 303-678-2222

MediaMagic (division of IPC Technologies, Inc.)
10300 Metric Blvd.
Austin, TX 78758-9846
800-624-8654; 512-339-3500
Direct sales: 800-752-1577
Fax: 512-339-3522
Tech support: 800-246-7073
Tech support BBS: 512-339-3582

Microcom, Inc.
500 River Ridge Dr.
Norwood, MA 02062-5028
800-822-8224; 617-551-1000
http://www.microcom.com
Fax: 617-551-1968
Tech support: Use main number
Tech support BBS: 617-255-1125 (modems); 617-762-5134 (carbon copy)

Micron Electronics, Inc.
900 E. Karcher Rd.
Nampa, ID 83687-3045
800-347-3490; 208-893-3434
http://www.mei.micron.com
Direct sales: 800-388-6334
Fax: 208-893-3424
Tech support: Use toll-free number
Tech support BBS: 208-465-7755

MicroNet Technology, Inc.
80 Technology
Irvine, CA 92718
800-800-3475; 714-453-6000
http://www.micronet.com
Direct sales: 714-453-6100
Fax: 714-453-6101
Tech support: 714-453-6060

Micropolis Pte Ltd. (subsidiary of Singapore Technologies)
21211 Nordhoff St.
Chatsworth, CA 91311
800-395-3748; 818-709-3300
http://www.microp.com
Fax: 818-718-5312
Tech support: 818-709-3325
Tech support BBS: 818-709-3310

Microsoft Corp.
One Microsoft Way
Redmond, WA 98052-6399
800-426-9400; 206-882-8080
http://www.microsoft.com
Direct sales: 800-MSPRESS
Fax: 206-93-MSFax
Tech support: 206-454-2030; 206-637-7098 (Windows)
Tech support BBS: 206-936-6735

MicroSolutions, Inc.
132 W. Lincoln Hwy.
DeKalb, IL 60115
800-890-7227; 815-756-3411
http://www.micro-solutions.com
Direct sales: 800-890-7227, ext. 200
Fax: 815-756-2928
Tech support: 815-754-4500
Tech support BBS: 815-756-9100

Microtek Lab, Inc. (subsidiary of Microtek International, Inc.)
3715 Doolittle Dr.
Redondo Beach, CA 90278-1226
310-297-5000
http://www.mteklab.com
Direct sales: 800-654-4160
Fax: 310-297-5050
Tech support: 310-297-5100
Tech support BBS: 310-297-5102

MidWest Micro
6910 U.S. Rt. 36, E
Fletcher, OH 45326
800-445-2015; 513-368-2309
http://www.mwmicro.com
Direct sales: 800-682-7260
Fax: 800-562-6622
Tech support: 800-262-6622
Tech support BBS: 513-368-3741

Mitsumi Electronics Corp., Inc.
(division of Mitsumi Electric Co., Ltd.)
6210 N. Beltline Rd., Ste. 170
Irving, TX 75063
800-MITSUMI; 214-550-7300
http://www.mitsumi.com
Fax: 214-550-7424
Tech support: 415-691-4465
Tech support BBS: 415-691-4469

Motorola UDS (unit of
Motorola Information Systems Group)
5000 Bradford Dr.
Huntsville, AL 35805-1993
800-365-6394; 205-430-8000
http://www.mot.com/MIMS/ISG/
Direct sales: 205-430-8449
Fax: 205-430-8926
Tech support: 205-430-8047
Tech support BBS: 508-261-1058

Multi-Tech Systems, Inc.
2205 Woodale Dr.
Mounds View, MN 55112-9907
800-328-9717; 612-785-3500
http://www.multitech.com
Fax: 612-785-9874
Tech support: 800-972-2439
Tech support BBS: 800-392-2432

Mustek, Inc.
1702 McGaw Ave.
Irvine, CA 92714
800-4-MUSTEK; 714-250-8855
http://www.mustek.com
Fax: 714-250-3372
Tech support: 714-250-4880
Tech support BBS: 714-250-4263

Nakamichi America Corp.
955 Francisco St.
Torrance, CA 90502
800-421-2313; 310-538-8150
http://www.nakamichi-corp.com
Fax: 310-324-7614

NEC Technologies, Inc.
1250 N. Arlington Hgts. Rd., Ste. 500
Itasca, IL 60143
800-NEC-INFO; 630-775-7900
Direct sales: 800-284-4484
Fax: 508-635-4666
Tech support: 800-632-4662

New Media Corp.
One Technology Park, Bldg. A
Irvine, CA 92718-2339
800-453-0550; 714-453-0100
http://www.newmediacorp.com
Fax: 714-453-0114
Tech support: Use main number
Tech support BBS: 714-453-0214

Newbridge Networks, Inc.
593 Herndon Pkwy.
Herndon, VA 22070-5241
800-343-3600; 703-834-3600
http://www.newbridge.com
Fax: 703-471-7080
Tech support: 703-834-5300

Newpoint Corp. (subsidiary
of Proxima Corp.)
6370 Nancy Ridge Dr.
San Diego, CA 92121-3297
800-321-5987; 619-677-5700
Fax: 619-558-1408

Nokia Display Products, Inc.
(division of Nokia Consumer Electronics)
1505 Bridgeway Blvd., Ste. 128
Sausalito, CA 94965
800-BY-NOKIA; 415-331-0322
http://www.intltech.com/nokia
Fax: 415-331-6211
Tech support: Use toll-free number
Tech support BBS: 800-483-7952

Novell, Inc.
1555 N. Technology Way
Orem, UT 84757
800-453-1267; 801-222-6000
http://www.novell.com
Fax: 800-NOVLFax
Tech support: 800-858-4000

Number Nine Visual Technology Corp.
18 Hartwell Ave.
Lexington, MA 02173-3103
800-GET-NINE; 617-674-0009
http://www.nine.com
Fax: 617-674-2919
Tech support: 617-674-8595
Tech support BBS: 617-862-7502

Okidata Corp. (division
of Oki America, Inc.)
532 Fellowship Rd.
Mt. Laurel, NJ 08054
800-OKI-TEAM; 609-235-2600
http://www.okidata.com
Fax: 609-778-4184
Tech support: 609-273-0300
Tech support BBS: 609-234-5344

Orchid Technology, Inc. (subsidiary
of Micronics Computers, Inc.)
45365 Northport Loop West
Fremont, CA 94538
800-767-2443; 510-683-0300
http://www.orchid.com
Fax: 510-490-9312
Tech support: 510-683-0323

Packard Bell NEC, Inc. (CA)
31717 La Tienda Dr.
Westlake Village, CA 91362
800-733-5858; 818-865-1555
http://www.packardbell.com
Tech support: 800-733-4411
Tech support BBS: 905-542-7359

Panasonic Communications & Systems
Co. (Office Automation Group)
2 Panasonic Way
Secaucus, NJ 07094-9844
800-742-8086; 201-348-7000
http://www.panasonic.com
Fax: 201-392-4441
Tech support: 800-222-0584
Tech support BBS: 201-863-7845

Parsons Technology, Inc.
(subsidiary of Intuit, Inc.)
One Parsons Dr., P.O. Box 100
Hiawatha, IA 52233-0100
800-679-0670; 319-395-9626
http://www.parsonstech.com
Direct sales: 800-223-6925
Fax: 319-395-0102
Tech support: 319-395-7314

Peachtree Software, Inc. (subsidiary of Automatic Data Processing, Inc.)
1505-C Pavilion Place
Norcross, GA 30093
800-228-0068; 770-564-5800
http://www.peach.com
Direct sales: 800-247-3224
Fax: 770-564-6000
Tech support: 770-279-2099

Philips Electronics, Inc.
(Professional Solutions Division)
2099 Gateway Place
San Jose, CA 95110
800-235-7373; 408-453-5129
http://www.pps.philips.com
Fax: 408-453-0680
Tech support: 408-467-3628
Tech support BBS: 408-453-5837

Phoenix Technologies Ltd.
2770 De La Cruz Blvd.
Santa Clara, CA 95050
800-677-7305; 408-654-9000
http://www.ptltd.com
Fax: 408-452-1985
Tech support: 800-767-5465

Pinnacle Micro, Inc.
19 Technology Dr.
Irvine, CA 92718
800-553-7070; 714-789-3000
http://www.pinnaclemicro.com
Fax: 714-789-3150
Tech support: Use toll-free number
Tech support BBS: 714-789-3048

Pioneer New Media Technologies, Inc.
(Optical Memory Systems Division)
2265 East 220th St.
Long Beach, CA 90810
800-444-6784; 310-952-2111
http://www.pioneerusa.com
Fax: 310-952-2100
Tech support: 408-496-9140
Tech support BBS: 310-835-7980

Plextor (subsidiary of Shinano Kenshi Co., Ltd.)
4255 Burton Dr.
Santa Clara, CA 95054
800-886-3935; 408-980-1838
http://www.plextor.com
Fax: 408-986-1010
Tech support: Use toll-free number
Tech support BBS: 408-986-1569

PNY Electronics Inc.
200 Anderson Avenue
Moonachie, NJ 07074
201-438-6300
http://www.pny.com
Fax: 201-438-9097
Tech support: 800-234-4597

Practical Peripherals (product division of Hayes Microcomputer Products, Inc.)
5854 Peachtree Corners, E.
Norcross, GA 30348-5203
770-840-9966
http://www.practinet.com
Fax: 770-734-4601
Tech support: Use main number
Tech support BBS: 770-734-4600

Procom Technology, Inc.
2181 Dupont Dr.
Irvine, CA 92715
800-800-8600; 714-852-1000
http://www.procom.com
Fax: 714-852-1221
Tech support: Use toll-free number

Promise Technology, Inc.
1460 Koll Circle, Ste. A
San Jose, CA 95112
800-888-0245; 408-452-0948
http://www.promise.com
Fax: 408-452-1534
Tech support: 408-452-1180
Tech support BBS: 408-452-1267

QLogic Corp.
3545 Harbor Blvd., P.O. Box 5001
Costa Mesa, CA 92626
800-662-4471; 714-438-2200
http://www.qlc.com
Direct sales: 800-867-7274
Fax: 714-668-5008
Tech support: 714-668-5037
Tech support BBS: 714-708-3170

QMS, Inc.
One Magnum Pass, P.O. Box 81250
Mobile, AL 36689-1250
800-622-5546; 334-633-4300
http://www.qms.com
Direct sales: 800-523-2696
Fax: 334-633-0013
Tech support: 334-633-4500
Tech support BBS: 334-633-3632

Quantex Microsystems, Inc.
400B Pierce St.
Somerset, NJ 08873
800-836-0566; 908-563-4166
http://www.quantex.com
Fax: 908-563-0407
Tech support: 800-864-8650

Quantum Corp.
500 McCarthy Blvd.
Milpitas, CA 95035
800-624-5545; 408-894-4000
http://www.quantum.com
Fax: 408-894-3218
Tech support: 800-826-8022

Quark, Inc.
1800 Grant St.
Denver, CO 80203
800-788-7835; 303-894-8888
http://www.quark.com
Fax: 303-894-3399
Tech support: Use main number

Reveal Computer Products, Inc.
6045 Variel Ave.
Woodland Hills, CA 91367
800-326-2222; 818-704-6300
http://www.reveal.com
Direct sales: 800-REVEAL-1
Fax: 818-340-9957
Tech support: Use main number

Sager Midern Computer, Inc.
18005 Cortney Court
City of Industry, CA 91748
800-669-1624; 818-964-8682
http://www.sager-midern.com
Fax: 818-964-2381
Tech support: Use toll-free number

Sampo Technology, Inc.
(Industrial Products Division)
5550 Peachtree Industrial Blvd.
Norcross, GA 30071
770-449-6220
Fax: 770-447-1109
Tech support: Use main number

Samsung Electronics America, Inc.
(Information Systems Division)
105 Challenger Rd.
Ridgefield Park, NJ 07660-0511
800-726-7864; 201-229-4000
http://www.samsung.com

Direct sales: 800-656-2785
Fax: 201-229-4110
Tech support: Use toll-free number
Tech support BBS: 201-691-6238

Samtron Displays, Inc.
(division of Samsung Electronics Co., Ltd.)
18600 Broadwick St.
Rancho Dominguez, CA 90220
800-SAMTRON; 310-537-7000
Fax: 310-537-1033
Tech support: Use toll-free number

Seagate Technology, Inc.
920 Disc Dr.
Scotts Valley, CA 95066-4544
800-SEAGATE; 408-438-6550
http://www.seagate.com
Direct sales: 408-438-8111
Fax: 408-438-7852
Tech support: 408-438-8222
Tech support BBS: 408-438-8771

Sharp Electronics Corp.
(Information Systems Group)
P.O. Box 650, Sharp Plaza
Mahwah, NJ 07430-2135
800-BE-SHARP; 201-529-8200
http://www.sharp-usa.com
Direct sales: 800-993-9737
Fax: 201-529-8413
Tech support: 800-732-8221

Shuttle Technology, Inc.
43218 Christy St.
Fremont, CA 94538
510-656-0180
Fax: 510-656-0390
Tech support: Use main number
Tech support BBS: 510-656-0282

Sierra On-Line, Inc.
3380 146th Place, SE, Ste. 300
Bellevue, WA 98007
800-649-4904; 206-649-9800
http://www.sierra.com
Direct sales: 800-757-7707
Fax: 206-641-7617
Tech support: 206-644-7697
Tech support BBS: 209-683-4463

SIIG, Inc.
6078 Stewart Ave.
Fremont, CA 94538-3152
510-657-8688
Fax: 510-657-5962
Tech support: Use main number
Tech support BBS: 510-353-7532

SL WABER, INC.
(subsidiary of SL Industries, Inc.)
520 Fellowship Rd., Ste. C-306
Mt. Laurel, NJ 08054
800-634-1485; 609-866-8888
Fax: 609-866-1945
Tech support: 800-257-8384

SMILE International, Inc.
(subsidiary of Kuo Feng Corp.)
1575 Sunflower Ave.
Costa Mesa, CA 92626
800-U-SMILE-2; 714-546-0336
Fax: 714-546-0315
Tech support: Use main number

SONY Electronics, Inc.
3300 Zanker Rd.
San Jose, CA 95134-1901
800-352-7669; 408-432-1600
http://www.sony.com
Fax: 408-943-0740
Tech support: 800-326-9551
Tech support BBS: 408-955-5107

Star Micronics America, Inc.
(subsidiary of Star Micronics Co., Ltd.)
70-D Ethel Rd., W
Piscataway, NJ 08854
800-506-7827; 908-572-9512
http://www.starmicronics.com
Direct sales: 800-782-7636
Fax: 908-572-5095
Tech support: 908-572-3300
Tech support BBS: 908-572-5010

STB Systems, Inc.
1651 N. Glenville Dr., Ste. 210
P.O. Box 850957
Richardson, TX 75085-0957
888-234-8750; 214-234-8750
http://www.stb.com
Fax: 214-234-1306
Tech support: 800-234-4334
Tech support BBS: 214-437-9615

Symantec Corp.
10201 Torre Ave.
Cupertino, CA 95014-2132
800-441-7234; 408-253-9600
http://www.symantec.com
Direct sales: 800-453-1193
Fax: 408-253-3968
Tech support: 415-892-1424
Tech support BBS: 541-484-6669

Symantec Corp. (Delrina Group)
895 Don Mills Rd., 500-2 Park Centre
Toronto, ON, CD M3C 1W3
800-441-7234; 416-441-3676
http://www.delrina.com
Direct sales: 800-879-5075
Fax: 416-441-0333
Tech support: 416-441-3086

SyQuest Technology, Inc.
47071 Bayside Pkwy.
Fremont, CA 94538
800-245-CART; 510-226-4000
http://www.syquest.com
Direct sales: 510-226-4150
Fax: 510-226-4100
Tech support: 800-249-2440
Tech support BBS: 510-656-0473

Tandberg Data, Inc. (subsidiary
of Tandberg Data ASA)
2685-A Park Center Dr.
Simi Valley, CA 93065-6211
800-826-3237; 805-579-1000
http://www.tandberg.com
Fax: 805-579-2555
Tech support: Use main number

Tatung Co. of America, Inc.
(subsidiary of Tatung Co.)
2850 El Presidio St.
Long Beach, CA 90810
800-827-2850; 310-637-2105
http://www.tatung.com.tw
Fax: 310-637-8484
Tech support: Use main number
Tech support BBS: 310-635-9090

TEAC America, Inc.
(Data Storage Products Division)
7733 Telegraph Rd.
Montebello, CA 90640
800-888-4XCD; 213-726-0303
Fax: 213-727-7652
Tech support: Use main number
Tech support BBS: 213-727-7660

Tektronix, Inc. (Color Printing
and Imaging Division)
26600 Southwest Pkwy., P.O. Box 1000
Wilsonville, OR 97070-1000
800-835-6100; 503-682-7370
http://www.tek.com
Fax: 503-682-2980
Tech support: Use toll-free number
Tech support BBS: 503-685-4504

Toshiba America Information Systems,
Inc. (TAIS) (subsidiary of Toshiba Corp.)
9740 Irvine Blvd., P.O. Box 19724
Irvine, CA 92713-9724
800-334-3445; 714-583-3000
http://www.toshiba.com
Direct sales: 800-959-4100
Fax: 714-583-3645
Tech support: 800-999-4273
Tech support BBS: 714-837-4408

Tri-Star Computer Corp.
2424 West 14th St.
Tempe, AZ 85281-6900
800-844-2993; 602-731-4926
http://www.tri-cad.com
Direct sales: 800-800-1714
Fax: 602-731-4979
Tech support: Use toll-free number
Tech support BBS: 602-731-9383

TrippLite
500 N. Orleans St.
Chicago, IL 60610
312-755-5400
http://www.tripplite.com
Fax: 312-644-6505
Tech support: 312-755-5401

Truevision, Inc.
2500 Walsh Ave.
Santa Clara, CA 95051
800-522-TRUE; 408-562-4200
http://www.truevision.com
Fax: 408-562-4066
Tech support: Use toll-free number
Tech support BBS: 317-577-8777

Turtle Beach Systems (subsidiary of
Integrated Circuit Systems, Inc.)
5690 Stewart Ave.
Fremont, CA 94538
800-884-0190; 510-624-6200
http://www.tbeach.com
Fax: 510-624-6291
Tech support: 510-624-6265
Tech support BBS: 510-624-6279

UMAX Technologies, Inc. (subsidiary
of UMAX Data Systems, Inc.)
3353 Gateway Blvd.
Fremont, CA 94538
800-468-8629; 510-651-8834
http://www.umax.com
Tech support: 510-651-4000
Tech support BBS: 510-651-2550

U.S. Robotics Access Corp. (subsidiary
of U.S. Robotics Corp.)
8100 N. McCormick Blvd.
Skokie, IL 60076-2999
800-DIAL-USR; 847-982-5010
http://www.usr.com
Direct sales: 847-982-5001
Fax: 847-933-5800
Tech support: 847-982-5151
Tech support BBS: 847-982-5092

USA Flex, Inc.
444 Scott Dr.
Bloomingdale, IL 60108
800-777-2450; 630-582-6206
http://www.usaflex.com
Direct sales: 630-582-6202
Fax: 630-351-7204
Tech support: 800-955-1488
Tech support BBS: 630-351-6048

Vektron International, Inc.
2100 N. Hwy. 360, Ste. 1904
Grand Prairie, TX 75050
800-725-0047; 214-606-0280
http://www.vektron.com
Direct sales: 800-725-0038
Fax: 214-606-1278
Tech support: 800-725-0026
Tech support BBS: 214-606-0444

ViewSonic Corp. (division of Keypoint Technology Corp.)
20480 E. Business Pkwy.
Walnut, CA 91789
800-888-8583; 909-444-8800
http://www.viewsonic.com
Direct sales: 909-869-7976
Fax: 909-468-3756
Tech support: 800-888-8383
Tech support BBS: 909-468-1241

Visioneer, Inc.
2860 W. Bayshore Rd.
Palo Alto, CA 94303
800-787-7007; 415-812-6400
http://www.visioneer.com
Fax: 415-493-0399
Tech support: Use main number

Wearnes Peripherals Corp. (division of Wearnes Peripherals International)
2210 O'Toole Ave.
San Jose, CA 95131
408-432-1888
Fax: 408-432-1884

Western Digital Corp.
8105 Irvine Center Dr.
Irvine, CA 92718
800-275-4932; 714-932-5000
http://www.wdc.com
Fax: 714-932-6498
Tech support: 714-932-4900
Tech support BBS: 714-753-1234

WinBook Computer Corp. (subsidiary of Micro Electronics, Inc.)
1160 Steelwood Rd.
Columbus, OH 43212
800-293-1644; 614-481-7460
Direct sales: 800-293-1641
Fax: 800-448-0308
Tech support: 614-481-7465
Tech support BBS: 614-481-0726

Wyse Technology, Inc.
3471 N. First St.
San Jose, CA 95134-1803
800-438-9973; 408-473-1200
http://www.wyse.com
Fax: 408-473-1222
Tech support: 800-800-9973
Tech support BBS: 408-922-4400

Xircom, Inc.
2300 Corporate Center Dr.
Thousand Oaks, CA 91320-1420
800-438-4526; 805-376-9300

http://www.xircom.com
Direct sales: 800-376-9300
Fax: 805-376-9311
Tech support: 805-376-9200
Tech support BBS: 805-376-9020

Zoltrix, Inc.
47273 Fremont Blvd.
Fremont, CA 94538
510-657-1188
http://www.zoltrix.com
Fax: 510-657-1280
Tech support: 510-657-5737
Tech support BBS: 510-657-7413

Zoom Telephonics, Inc.
207 South St.
Boston, MA 02111
800-631-3116; 617-423-1072
http://www.zoomtel.com
Direct sales: 800-666-6191
Fax: 617-423-3923
Tech support: 617-423-1076
Tech support BBS: 617-423-3733

ZyXEL (a Zero One NetWorking Co.)
4920 E. LaPalma Ave.
Anaheim, CA 92807
800-255-4101; 714-693-0808
http://www.zyxel.com
Fax: 714-693-8811
Tech support: Use main number
Tech support BBS: 714-693-0762

B

Online Resources

This appendix provides a list of resources on commercial online services and the Internet. This list helps you find information related to computer upgrades and repairs.

General PC Resources

There are several places to get help with general PC issues, such as product reviews, industry news, and even basic PC operation.

Internet Sites

http://www5.zdnet.com/products/

has hundreds of product reviews (categorized) and a search engine. Plus, you'll find original daily content.

http://web1.zdnet.com/zdbop/

Ziff-Davis' industry-standard testing programs are available for download (well, most of them).

http://www.smalloffice.com/expert/archive/tearchive.html

contains an archive of articles/reviews from Home Office Computing and Small Business Computing magazines.

http://www.techweb.com/

leads you to technology super site from CMP Media, Inc., that contains news, reviews, comparisons, videos, and lots of other resources for computer users, including a search engine for the site.

http://www.cnet.com/

offers news, reviews, software, how-tos, and other interesting items related to PCs.

http://www.sresearch.com/

contains many articles about data storage, backups, and network products.

http://204.96.68.153/ (http://www.bugnet.com)

is home of BugNet Online, The Global Resource for PC Bugs, Glitches, Incompatibilities...and their Fixes.

http://www.dfw.net/~sdw/index.html

is a gargantuan site devoted to system optimization information. It not only covers hardware and software, but includes a search engine and lots of links.

http://www.xmission.com/~trevin/help/trevhelp.html

is dedicated to helping ordinary users with basic PC issues.

http://www.prodworks.com/universl.htm

is a Universal Accessibility resource for users with special needs.

http://www.microsoft.com/athome/yourpc/special/neworup.htm

Deciding whether to buy new or upgrade? Find an interesting article about when and how to upgrade a hard drive. This site is created by Microsoft.

http://www.compusa.com/ask_pc.html

contains CompUSA's P.C. Modem Q&A with an archive. This site also links to the vendors who sell products at CompUSA.

http://www.dataquest.com

Want to discover computer trends before they happen? Dataquest Interactive provides market research from Dataquest, Inc. You can see industry news, opinions, analysis, forecasts, and statistics.

http://aloha.com/~gemdrtgi/pages.html

contains a page of links to helpful Web sites with hardware, software, and configuration information.

http://t2.technion.ac.il/~s3180792/bookmark.html

contains a very large list of links to various hardware and software resources.

http://www.verinet.com/pc/
is called "Build your own PC" with step-by-step instructions and links to other resources.

http://www.css.msu.edu/pc-guide.html
provides a guide to buying and upgrading a home computer; it's written to be part of a college course.

America Online

Keyword: **CC** (or **COMPANY CONNECTION**)

The Company Connection acts as a gateway to the support staffs of many manufacturers. To begin your search, you simply select the product category.

Keyword: **MAGAZINE RACK**

Read articles from more than two dozen computer magazines, including *PC World*, *WINDOWS Magazine*, *PC Computing*, and others.

Keyword: **PC MULTIMEDIA**

The Multimedia Forum combines several existing areas into a coalition of computer resources. This forum encompasses music, games, graphics, animation, and other areas. There are both software and video clips to download.

Keyword: **NEW PRODUCTS**

This area provides the full text press releases for new PC and Macintosh products. You can scroll through 300 articles in each newsgroup or use the search capabilities to scan all news from the past 12 months for specific information.

Keyword: **PDA**

The Personal Digital Assistants (PDA) forum covers every aspect of PDA and palmtop computing. It contains information, discussion, and software for all handheld devices including the Newton PDAs, Hewlett-Packard palmtop computers, and others.

Keyword: **ZDNET**

This area from computer magazine publisher Ziff-Davis has product reviews, software downloads, troubleshooting guides, and more.

Keyword: **FC**

The Family Computing forum focuses on computing products, software, and hints to help the home computer user.

Keyword: **FORUMS**

Select from one of more than 15 computer-related forums, including Windows 95, OS/2, and others.

CompuServe

GO SUPPORT

This forum allows you to search by category, company, or keyword for help in almost any hardware or software area.

GO ZDNET

This area from computer magazine publisher Ziff-Davis has product reviews, software downloads, troubleshooting guides, and more.

Hardware

The following are sources of information on various hardware, from modems to motherboards.

Internet Sites

As you probably already know, the Internet can provide you with a vast, unending amount of resources, right at your fingertips. The following sections are organized as follows: general, mass storage, memory, modems, motherboards, network adapters and networks, processors, sound cards, and video cards.

General

http://theref.c3d.rl.af.mil/

TheRef™ Hardware Specs at Your Fingertips provides information about interfaces, controllers, hard drives, and more.

http://www.cam.org/~agena/computer.html

The Computer Hardware Performance Site provides many pages, covering video accelerators, benchmarks, motherboards, CPUs, and Windows 95.

http://www.venus.it/homes/spumador/driver.htm

contains very complete list of links to hardware vendors.

http://www.randomc.com/~dperr/pc_hdwe.htm

is a PC hardware information and links page with lots of both!

http://www.blackdown.org/~qtech/hw.html

The Hardware Book shows you an electronic reference guide to connectors, cables, adapters, and more.

http://www.atipa.com/InfoSheets/

provides information about and how-tos for various hardware installations.

http://pclt.cis.yale.edu/pclt/pchw/platypus.htm

offers you an introduction to PC hardware.

http://dragon.herts.ac.uk/data/company.html

provides a list of links to access online data sheets from various semiconductor manufacturers.

Mass Storage

http://www.seagate.com/support/disc/papers/papers.html

contains a collection of technical papers about mass storage devices and platforms.

http://www.maxtor.com/tn-9607-005.html

presents you with a technical paper on formatting Maxtor HDDs with a capacity greater than 2.048G.

http://www.maxtor.com/ide_cmos.html

shows you a chart of CMOS parameters for Maxtor IDE drives.

http://thef-nym.sci.kun.nl/cgi-pieterh/atazip/atafq.html

provides you with an Enhanced IDE/Fast-ATA resource with frequently asked questions, background info, and links.

http://www.powerquest.com/partitionmagic/whypartition.html

gives you three reasons why you should partition your hard disk.

http://www.iomega.com/product/whatineed/index.html

This Iomega quiz helps you determine the type of storage you need, including tape backup and removable storage alternatives.

http://www.imation.com

Imation Online from Imation, Inc., a 3M Co. spin-off, features information on its data storage and document systems products. Areas to visit include Virus Education, Compatibility Guides, and CD-ROM Services.

Memory

http://www.kingston.com/king/mg0.htm

The Ultimate Memory Page contains complete information on memory.

Modems

http://dragon.herts.ac.uk/data/datasheets/

provides questions and technical information about PC ports.

http://www.nb.rockwell.com/mcd/56kmodem/56k_wp.html

contains a technical paper about Rockwell's 56K modem technology.

http://x2.usr.com

offers information about U.S. Robotics X2 technology.

http://www.diamondmm.com/product-support/white-paper-index.html

provides discussions of current and new communications subjects.

http://www.rosenet.net/~costmo/

The "Everything You Ever Wanted To Know About Modems...But Were Afraid To Ask" site includes massive lists of links to related resources.

http://www.igc.org/support4/modems.html

The Institute for Global Communications (IGC) Modems and Data Communications page contains lots of information and links.

http://www.mountain.net/MNW/mos.html

contains communications and operating system-related topics.

http://www.practinet.com/ppi-tips.htm

presents you with articles about file transfer protocols and other telecommunications issues, including optional telephone features.

Motherboards

http://www.ping.be/bios/

is devoted to flash BIOS information and updates.

http://web2.iadfw.net/ksm/software.htm

contains Intel Triton drivers and information about bus mastering.

http://www.os2zone.aus.net/demo/art/marius/mboards.html

provides a discussion and comparison of various motherboards and related components.

http://www.lemig.umontreal.ca/bios/bios_sg.htm

contains the BIOS Survival Guide.

http://www.mrbios.com

contains BIOS and Triton questions and suggestions.

Network Adapters and Networks

http://plainfield.bypass.com/~gzaret/hiband.html#Cable Modems

This is the High Bandwidth Web page; its name says it all.

http://www.shiva.com/remote/prodinfo/index.html

shows you articles about remote access and security issues.

http://www.gdc.com/ATMRoom.html

provides technical information about asynchronous transfer mode (ATM).

http://www.fore.com/html/atm-edu/index.html

provides complete information about ATM.

http://www.ascend.com/techdocs/techindex.html

contains a technical library of telecommunications terms and subjects.

http://t2.technion.ac.il/~s3180792/bookmark.html

contains several links to various network resources.

http://www-leland.stanford.edu/~llurch/win95netbugs/faq.html

holds an archive of Windows 95 networking questions and suggestions.

http://www.sresearch.com

The Strategic Research Corp. site offers The Network Buyer's Guide, which contains a collection of data on enterprise networking and storage products. Among the many resources are product listings, white papers, and links to evaluation software tools online.

http://alumni.caltech.edu/~dank/isdn/

offers an ISDN resource and much more.

Processors

http://www.x86.org/

The Intel Secrets page shows you what Intel doesn't want you to know!

http://sysdoc.pair.com/

explains the important hardware aspects of a modern Pentium/Pentium Pro machine.

Sound Cards

http://www.creaf.com/zonemenu.html

Enter the Creative Zone from Creative Labs Inc. In its Tech Lab, you'll find product data sheets, technical tips, access to drivers and patches, and information for developers.

Video Cards

http://www.diamondmm.com/product-support/white-paper-index.html

offers information on current and new video technology subjects.

http://www.nine.com/tech/whitepages/

contains articles about video-related subjects.

America Online

Keyword: **HARDWARE** (or **PC HARDWARE**)

The PC Hardware Forum provides a place to discuss hardware-related topics in the various message areas and weekly conferences, as well as files to help test, analyze, and configure your computer hardware to keep it running at its best.

Keyword: **CC HARD**

The Company Connection for hardware acts as a gateway to the support areas of various hardware manufacturers, including Acer, Diamond Multimedia, Gateway 2000, and others.

CompuServe

GO NOVFF

This forum provides a comprehensive keyword searchable database of file descriptions from Novell-related forums. It helps you find any of thousands of files for Novell networks. This forum is downloadable if you have WinCIM or DOSCIM.

GO NAP-1

contains Novell's Application Technical Information Database (AppTID), which houses all of Novell's technical information documents, files, patches, and fixes. For example, you may be instructed to get a specific file, patch, or fix from AppTID.

GO TID-1

contains Novell's technical solutions database, which houses all of Novell's technical information documents, files, patches, and fixes.

Software

The following are sources for information and files for general software issues.

Internet Sites

http://www.microsoft.com/msdownload/

is a one-stop shop for all free MS downloadable software, from betas to development tools to product add-ons to trial versions, and more.

http://www.hotfiles.com/

is ZDNet's categorized downloadable software library of shareware, and includes the year's top 100 shareware files. This site includes a wonderful search engine.

http://www.stroud.com

contains Stroud's Consummate Winsock Applications, the best one-stop-shop for free Windows software, with reviews and a search function.

http://www.spa.org

The Software Publishers Association (SPA) provides a trove of information, links, and resources, including the searchable Software Industry Directory. Visitors can learn about SPA special-interest groups, publications, activities, and upcoming conferences.

http://www.winsite.com/

is the Planet's Largest Software Archive for Windows with search capabilities.

http://www.jumbo.com/

offers a humongous collection of shareware and freeware with a search function.

http://www.tucows.com/

contains The Ultimate Collection Of Winsock Software.

http://www.shareware.com/

is another giant collection of shareware with a search capability.

http://www.software.ibm.com/download/

contains IBM's software download site for all of its products, including OS/2 and Lotus.

http://www.halcyon.com/cerelli/

is devoted to Windows 95 installation, configuration, and maintenance.

http://www.windowatch.com/

is an online magazine for Windows 95/NT users.

http://www.conitech.com/windows/

gives you news, information, and drivers for Windows 95, NT, and CE.

http://www.creativelement.com/win95ann/

is a site called "Windows 95 Annoyances" and is dedicated to fixing, tweaking, and coping.

http://www.gate.net/~jsharit/windows_95/win95tips_and_tweaks.html

This Windows 95 tips site is complete with background music.

http://www.windows-nt.com/

is a site for Windows NT users with tips and online help desk.

http://members.gnn.com/jstein/wintips.htm

offers Windows 3.x tips and optimization suggestions.

http://www.inquiry.com

contains searchable product databases, reviews from industry publications, and discussion forums. Visit the Tech Tips section for advice and resources on a variety of programming languages.

http://www.intergate.net/OS2/

offers OS/2 "must-have" utilities and FTP links.

http://www.ugu.com

contains the UNIX Guru's Universe for system administrators.

America Online

Keyword: **SOFTWARE**

From the PC Software Center, you can look for certain files or help in certain areas. This one-stop center allows you access to software help and file searching.

Keyword: **FILESEARCH**

This keyword takes you to America Online's software search engine. You can limit your search to any combination of 11 software categories, or search the entire database for a specific software program. You also have the power to find new software uploaded in the past month or even week.

Keyword: **SOFTWARE HELP**

This area features a software "survival kit" as well as live help, message forums, and visual aids in mastering common PC or America Online functions.

CompuServe

GO ASP

Sponsored by the Association of Shareware Professionals (ASP), the ASP Forum allows you to download and register your shareware.

GO WINSUPPORT

provides one-stop support for Windows 95, including a link to Microsoft Corp., driver updates, shareware downloading, and more.

GO FILEFINDER

contains a comprehensive keyword searchable database of file descriptions from all CompuServe forums, and is downloadable if you have WinCIM or DOSCIM. It's a great one-stop source for freeware, shareware, or drivers in many areas.

You also can more quickly get to any of its sub-areas, such as:

GO ARF-1	Free and shareware adult images and utilities.
GO GAMESFF	Free and shareware games.
GO GRAPHFF	Free and shareware graphics files and utilities.
GO INETFF	Free and shareware Internet sites, utilities, and more.
GO PCFF	Free and shareware general-purpose DOS files.

GO WINFF

offers a comprehensive keyword-searchable database of file descriptions from Windows-related forums. This forum helps you find any of thousands of files for Microsoft Windows and Windows 95, and is downloadable if you have WinCIM or DOSCIM.

GO MSFF

is a comprehensive keyword-searchable database of file descriptions from Microsoft forums. It's downloadable if you have WinCIM or DOSCIM.

Safety and Security

Concerned about viruses and protecting your computer from other calamities? Use the following sources to keep your computer tuned up.

Internet Sites

http://www.mcafee.com/

provides complete information and history of viruses.

http://www.symantec.com/avcenter/reference/corpst.html

contains a complete article on viruses and anti-viruses, and why to use them.

http://www.ncsa.com/library/

offers a library of information relating to all security issues published by the National Computer Security Association (NCSA).

http://www.apcc.com/english/power/index.htm

tells you all about power: events, risks, and how to protect your investments.

http://www.powerexpress.com/battbible.html

provides important battery information for laptops and other portable devices.

http://www.apcc.com

APC On-line from American Power Conversion Corp. spotlights its uninterruptible power supply and network software products. The All About Power section includes an interactive worksheet to calculate the total dollar value of data lost due to power outages.

America Online

Keyword: **VIRUS**

This Virus InfoCenter provides comprehensive information and software about computer viruses. You can also leave messages in a forum dedicated to viruses.

Internet Access

There are also Internet sites for Internet answers, including Internet dialers, top Web sites, and more.

Internet Sites

http://www.winsock.com/wsdir/

The Stardust WinSock Software Directory is a source for Internet and TCP/IP software for Microsoft Windows with complete descriptions.

http://www.pbs.org/internet

Want to see the impact of the Internet? This online version of the public television series "Life on the Internet" provides a good example of the Web's multimedia capabilities. Topics covered include Internet commerce, software encryption, the history of the Internet, and electronic cash.

http://www.100hot.com

The most popular Web sites are listed here, based on a combination of surveys, logs, and traffic samples. Web 21 uses this data to compile its Top 100 list.

CompuServe

GO INETFF

This forum contains a comprehensive keyword searchable database of file descriptions from Internet-related forums. It includes the best Internet sites, utilities, and more. This forum is downloadable if you have WinCIM or DOSCIM.

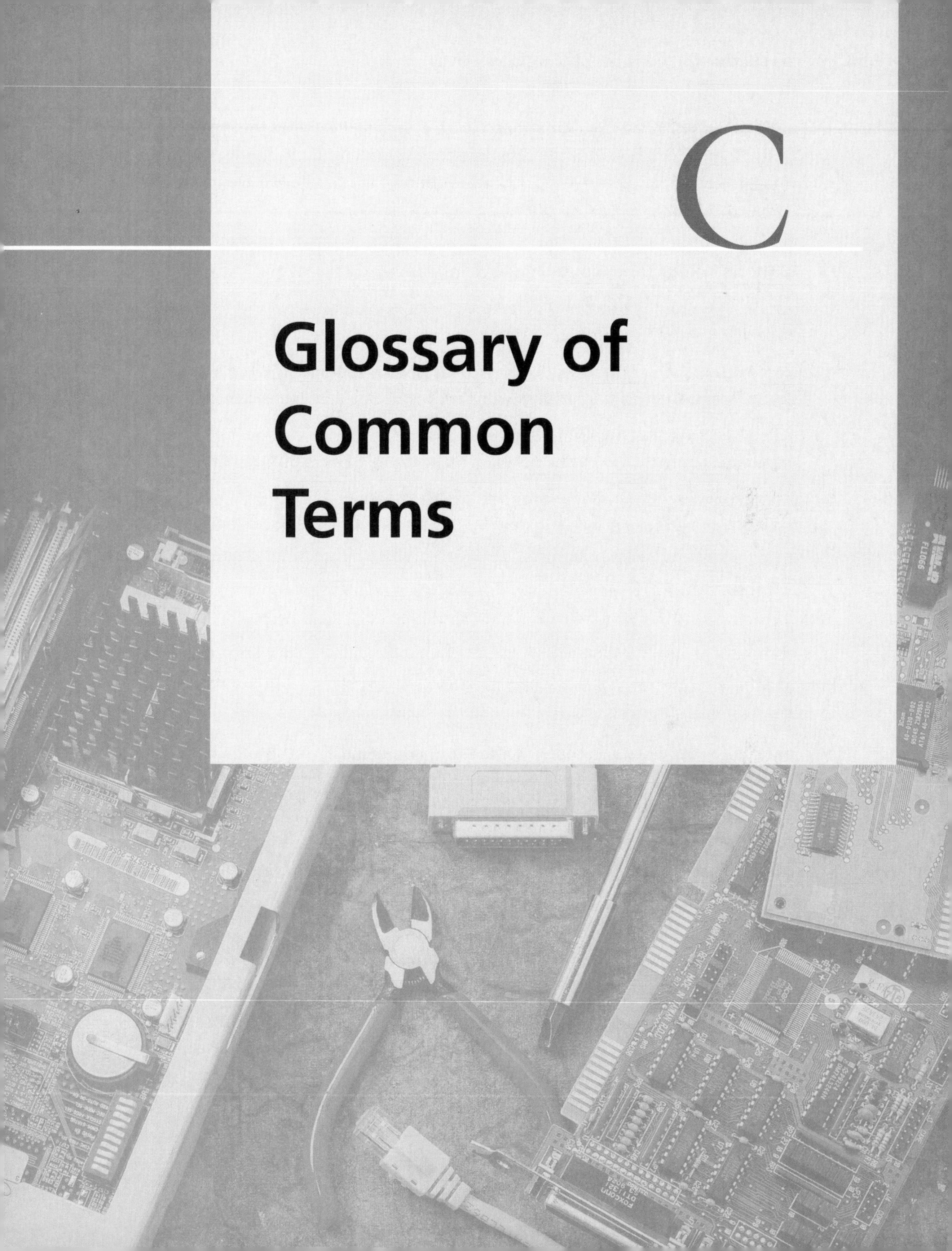

C

Glossary of Common Terms

access time The average time it takes a device (usually a disk drive) to find a random piece of data on a disk. Access time is measured in milliseconds (the lower the number, the faster the drive). Good access times for a hard drive are between 10 ms and 15 ms. See also *transfer rate*.

AMPS Advanced Mobile Phone Service. AT&T's Bell Laboratories' term to describe its cellular technology. Digital cellular is called D-AMPS.

Analog Signals Voice tones and data carried as continuous, varying waveforms over phone lines (as opposed to digital signals).

application Also known as *program*; a set of instructions that enable a computer to perform a specific task, such as word processing or data management.

ASCII file A file containing characters that any program on any computer can use. Sometimes called a *text file* or an *ASCII text file*. (ASCII is pronounced "ASK-key.")

Auto Answer A modem with the ability to answer incoming telephone calls without the use of a telephone set.

Auto Dial The ability of a modem to dial telephone numbers without the use of a telephone set.

AUTOEXEC.BAT A file that DOS reads whenever you boot or reboot your computer. This file contains a series of commands that DOS automatically executes.

AWE Advanced WavEffects synthesis. A Creative Labs trademarked name for digital effects editing software.

batch file Any file that contains a series of commands. You run the batch file just as you would run a program file (by entering its name at the DOS prompt). The most famous batch file is AUTOEXEC.BAT.

baud A unit for measuring the speed of data transmission, which is usually used to describe the speed at which a modem transfers data, such as 2,400 baud. A more accurate measure of transmission speed is bps (bits per second).

BIOS Basic Input-Output System. Pronounced "BUY-ose," the start-up instructions for a computer. The BIOS tells the computer how to control traffic between the various elements that make up the computer, including disk drives, the printer, ports, and the monitor.

bit The basic unit of data in a computer. A computer's alphabet consists of two characters: 1 and 0. 1 stands for on, and 0 stands for off. Bits are combined in sets of eight to form "real" characters, such as A, B, C, and D. See also *byte*.

bits per second (bps) A unit for measuring the speed of data transmission. Remember that it takes 8 bits to make a byte (the equivalent of a single character). Modems have common bps ratings of 14,400 and 28,800.

boot To start a computer with the operating system software (usually DOS) in place.

bps See *bits per second.*

bulletin board system (BBS) Not to be confused with the British Broadcasting System, a BBS is a program that enables a computer to automatically answer the phone when other computers call. A BBS allows the calling computer to copy files to it (*upload* files) and copy files from it (*download* files). Although you can purchase a BBS program to set up your own BBS, most users work with BBSes set up by computer companies and professional associations.

bus A superhighway that carries information electronically from one part of the computer to another. There are three such highways:

- A *data bus* carries data back and forth between memory and the microprocessor.
- An *address bus* carries information about the locations (addresses) of specific information.
- A *control bus* carries control signals to make sure the data traffic flows smoothly, without confusion.

byte A group of eight bits that usually represents a character or a digit. For example, the byte 01000001 represents the letter A.

cache Pronounced "cash," this is a part of memory that makes your computer run faster by holding the most recently accessed data from a disk. The next time the computer needs the data, the computer gets it from memory rather than from the disk, which would be slower. Sometimes called a *RAM cache.*

capacity A measure of how much data a disk can store. For example, you can format a 3.5-inch, high-density floppy disk to store 1.44M; 1.44M is the disk's *capacity.*

CD-ROM Compact-Disc Read-Only Memory. A storage technology that uses the same kind of discs you play in an audio CD player for mass storage of computer data. A single disc can store more than 600M of information. Pronounced "see-dee-RAHM."

cell The box formed by the intersection of a row (1,2,3,...) and column (A,B,C,...) in a spreadsheet. Each cell has an *address* (such as B12) that defines its column and row. A cell may contain text, a numeric value, or a formula.

chat To "talk" to another person by typing at your computer. What you type appears on the other person's screen, and what the other person types appears on your screen. You can chat on the Internet or on an online service, such as Prodigy or America Online.

click To move the mouse pointer over an object or icon and press and release the mouse button once without moving the mouse.

client Of two computers, the computer that's being served. On the Internet or on a network, your computer is the client, and the computer you're connected to is the *server.*

Clipboard A temporary storage area that holds text and graphics. The cut and copy commands put text or graphics on the Clipboard, replacing the Clipboard's previous contents. The Paste command copies Clipboard data to a document.

CMOS Complementary Metal-Oxide Semiconductor. Pronounced "SEA-moss," CMOS is an electronic device (usually battery operated) that stores information about your computer.

COM port Short for COMmunications port. A receptacle, usually at the back of the computer, into which you can plug a serial device such as a modem, mouse, or serial printer. If your computer has more than one COM port, the ports are numbered COM1, COM2, and so on.

command An order that tells the computer what to do. In command-driven programs, you have to press a specific key or type the command to execute it. With menu-driven programs, you select the command from a menu.

computer Any machine that accepts input (from a user), processes the input, and produces output in some form.

CPU Central Processing Unit. See also *microprocessor.*

crash Failure of a system or program. Usually, you realize that your system has crashed when you can't move the mouse pointer or type anything. The term *crash* is also used to refer to a disk crash (or head crash). A disk crash occurs when the read/write head in the disk drive falls on the disk. This would be like dropping a phonograph needle on a record. A disk crash can destroy any data stored where the read/write head falls on the disk.

cursor A horizontal line that appears below characters. A cursor acts like the tip of your pencil; anything you type appears at the cursor.

cyberspace The universe created by the connection of thousands of computers. Computer users can use modems to enter cyberspace and converse with other users.

database A type of computer program used for storing, organizing, and retrieving information. Popular database programs include Access, Approach, and Paradox.

density A measure of the amount of data that can be stored per square inch of storage area on a disk.

dialog box An on-screen box that allows you to enter your preferences or supply additional information. You use the dialog box to carry on a "conversation" with the program.

Direct Memory Address (DMA) The line used by the expansion card to send data directly to memory without using the central processor (CPU).

directory A division of a disk or CD, which contains a group of related files. Think of your disk as a filing cabinet and think of each directory as a drawer in the cabinet. By keeping files in separate directories, it is easier to locate and work with related files.

disk A round, flat, magnetic storage medium. A disk works like a cassette tape, storing files permanently, so you can play them back later. See also *floppy disk* and *hard disk*.

disk drive A device that writes data to a magnetic disk and reads data from the disk. Think of a disk drive as being like a cassette recorder/player. Just as the cassette player can record sounds on a magnetic cassette tape and play back those sounds, a disk drive can record data on a magnetic disk and play back that data.

DOS Disk Operating System (rhymes with "boss"). An essential program that provides the necessary instructions for the computer's parts (keyboard, disk drive, central processing unit, display screen, printer, and so on) to function as a unit.

DOS prompt An on-screen prompt that indicates DOS is ready to accept a command. It looks something like C> or C:\.

download To copy files from another computer to your computer usually through a modem. See also *upload*.

DSVD Digital Simultaneous Voice and Data. A protocol developed by U.S. Robotics, Intel, Creative Labs, and Hayes and Rockwell International to let users share data and talk to each other over a single phone line.

Error Correction Typically refers to the programming used to verify that all the data is being received successfully.

ETC Enhanced Throughput Cellular; an AT&T Paradyne wireless cellular protocol enhancement, developed to allow modems equipped with ETC to transmit data at 14.4 bps.

Fax on Demand A feature that allows callers to request faxes to be sent to their fax machines or fax-equipped computer.

e-mail Short for *electronic mail*, e-mail is a system that enables people to send and receive messages from computer to computer. E-mail is usually available on networks and online information services.

EMS (Expanded Memory Specification) See *expanded memory.*

environment A setting in which you perform tasks on your computer. Microsoft Windows, for example, displays a graphical environment that lets you enter commands by selecting pictures rather than by typing commands. This makes it much easier to use your computer (assuming you know what the pictures stand for).

executable file A program file that can run the program. Executable files end in BAT, COM, or EXE.

expanded memory Additional memory that a computer uses by swapping data into and out of a reserved portion of a computer's standard memory area. With expanded memory, additional memory is added to the computer in the form of memory chips or a memory board. To access this additional memory, an expanded memory manager reserves 64 of the standard 640K as a swap area. The 64K represent 4 *pages*, each page consisting of 16K. Pages of data are swapped into and out of this 64K region from expanded memory at a high speed. Old DOS programs commonly used expanded memory, but Windows and its programs prefer extended memory. See also *extended memory.*

expansion slot An opening on the motherboard (inside the system unit) that allows you to add devices to the system unit. Expansion slots allow you to add an internal modem, sound card, video accelerator, or other enhancements.

extended memory Any memory above the standard 640K that performs the same way as the standard memory. Extended memory is directly available to the processor in your computer, unlike expanded memory, in which data must be swapped into and out of the standard memory. Most additional memory in new computers is extended. See also *expanded memory.*

extension The portion of a file's name that comes after the period. Every file name consists of two parts: the base name (before the period) and an extension (after the period). The file name can be up to eight characters in DOS and Windows 3.x (up to 255 characters in Windows 95). The extension (which is optional) can be up to three characters.

field A blank in a database record into which you can enter a piece of information (for example, a telephone number, ZIP code, or a person's last name).

file A collection of information stored as a single unit on a floppy or hard disk. Files always have file names to identify them.

file allocation table (FAT) A map on every disk that tells the operating system where the files on the disk are stored. It's sort of like a seating chart for files.

file format The patterns and standards that a program uses to store data on a disk.

File Transfer Protocol (FTP) A set of rules that governs the exchange of files between two computers on the Internet. To copy a file from the Internet, you need a special program that can handle FTP file transfers.

fixed disk drive A disk drive that has non-removable media, as opposed to floppy drives, which have removable media.

Flash ROM Read Only Memory commonly used in add-in devices for storing the device configurations and command programs. Flash ROM can be updated by the user.

floppy disk Flexible, Mylar-encased, removable magnetic media. Floppy disks are used in your computer's floppy disk drive (located on the front of the computer).

folder Windows 95's name for a directory, a division of a hard disk or CD that stores a group of related files. See also *directory*.

font Any set of characters of the same *typeface* (design) and *type size* (measured in points). For example, Times Roman 12-point is a font: Times Roman is the typeface, and 12-point is the size. (There are 72 points in an inch.)

format (disk) To prepare a disk for storing data. Formatting creates a map on the disk that tells the operating system how the disk is structured. The operating system uses this map to keep track of where files are stored.

format (document) To establish the physical layout of a document, including page size, margins, running heads, line spacing, text alignment, graphics placement, and so on.

FTP See *File Transfer Protocol.*

function keys The 10 or 12 F keys on the left side of the keyboard, or 12 F keys at the top of the keyboard (on some keyboards there are both). F keys are numbered F1, F2, F3, and so on, and you can use them to enter specified commands in a program.

gigabyte (G) A thousand megabytes. See also *megabyte (M).*

Gopher An area of the Internet that allows you to navigate the Internet using menus. You use a menu to tell the Gopher what you want. The Gopher will then "go for" the item you requested.

graphical user interface (GUI) Pronounced "GOO-ey," a type of program interface that uses graphical elements, such as icons, to represent commands, files, and (in some cases) other programs. The most famous GUI is Microsoft Windows.

hard disk Usually synonymous with fixed disk drive, the primary storage method of your computer.

hard drive See *hard disk.*

Hayes-compatible Used to describe a modem that uses the Hayes command set for communicating with other modems over the phone lines. Hayes-compatible modems usually are preferred over other modems because most modems and telecommunications software is designed to be Hayes-compatible.

HTML Short for HyperText Markup Language, the code used to create documents for the World Wide Web. These codes tell the Web browser how to display the text (titles, headings, lists, and so on), insert anchors that link this document to other documents, and control character formatting (by making it bold or italic).

icon A graphic image on-screen that represents another object, such as a file on a disk.

initialize To reset a computer or program to some starting values. When used to describe floppy or hard disks, the term means the same as *format.*

Input/Output Address (I/O) The line used by the expansion card to send data to the central processor (CPU).

interactive A user-controlled program, document, or game. Interactive programs commonly display on-screen *prompts* asking the user for input so they can decide how to carry out a particular task. These programs are popular in education, allowing children to follow their natural curiosity to solve problems and gather information.

interface A link between two objects, such as a computer and a modem. The link between a computer and a person is called a *user interface*, and refers to the way a person communicates with the computer.

Internet A group of computers all over the world that are connected to each other. Using your computer and a modem, you can connect to these other computers and tap their resources. You can view pictures, listen to sounds, watch video clips, play games, chat with other people, and even shop.

Interrupt ReQuest (IRQ) The line used by the expansion card to make a "request" of the central processor (CPU).

ISDN Integrated Services Digital Network. High-speed digital phone lines that allow simultaneous transmission of data, high-quality sound, video, and voice.

ITU-TSS International Telecommunications Union-Telecommunications Standards Section; the body responsible for establishing telecommunications standards.

keyboard The main input device for most computers. You use the keyboard to type and to enter commands.

kilobyte (K) A unit for measuring an amount of data. A kilobyte is equivalent to 1,024 bytes (each byte is a character).

load To read data or program instructions from disk and place them in the computer's memory, where the computer can use the data or instructions. You usually load a program before you use it or load a file before you edit it.

macro A recorded set of instructions for a frequently used or complex task. In most programs, you create a macro by telling the program to record your actions. You then name the macro or assign it to a keystroke combination. You can replay the macro at any time by selecting its name or by pressing the keystroke combination you assigned to it.

megabyte (M) A standard unit used to measure the storage capacity of a disk and the amount of computer memory. A megabyte is 1,048,576 bytes. This is roughly equivalent to 500 pages of double-spaced text.

memory An electronic storage area inside the computer, used to temporarily store data or program instructions when the computer is using them. The computer's memory is erased when the power to the computer is turned off. Also referred to as RAM.

menu A list of commands or instructions displayed on-screen. Menus organize commands and make a program easier to use.

microprocessor Sometimes called the *central processing unit* (CPU) or *processor*, this chip is the computer's brain; it processes all the instructions for the computer.

MIDI Musical Instrument Digital Interface. A standard for connecting electric devices together for sharing audio data.

MNP Microcom Networking Protocol. Asynchronous error control protocol using CRC (cyclic redundancy check) error detection and retransmission of damaged frames.

MNP-4 Error correction protocol used with existing data compression standards such as V.42 bis or MNP-5 to improve data throughput.

MNP-10 EC Microcom Networking Protocol Class 10 Enhanced Cellular standard for modem designed for use with cellular telephones.

modem An acronym for MOdulator/DEModulator. A modem is a piece of hardware that enables a computer to send and receive data through an ordinary telephone line.

modem pool Group of modems used to facilitate modem usage in network and other telecommunications settings, such as cellular phone service providers.

monitor A television-like screen on which the computer displays information.

mouse A hand-held device that you move across the desktop to move an arrow, called a mouse pointer, across the screen. Used instead of the keyboard to select and move items (such as text or graphics), execute commands, and perform other tasks.

MS-DOS (Microsoft Disk Operating System) See *DOS*.

multitasking The process of performing two computer tasks at the same time. For example, you might be printing a document from your word processor while checking your e-mail in Prodigy. One of the primary advantages of Windows is that it allows you to multitask.

newsgroup An Internet bulletin board for users who share common interests. There are thousands of newsgroups ranging from body art to pets. Newsgroups let you post messages and read messages from other users.

Nonvolatile Memory (NVRAM) Random Access Memory that has backup power and does not lose its data when the power is turned off.

online Connected, turned on, and ready to accept information. Used most often in reference to a printer or modem.

Packet-Switching The transfer of data divided into data packets, each with its own identification and destination address, between computer systems.

pane A portion of a window. Most programs display panes, so you can view two different parts of a document at the same time.

parallel port A connector used to plug a device, usually a printer, into the computer. Transferring data through a parallel port is much faster than transferring data through a serial port, but parallel cables can only carry data reliably for 15 or 20 feet.

partition The seperation between two logical drives. One physical hard disk drive can be divided (or partitioned) into one or more logical drives (don't be fooled; it's still one disk drive).

path The route that the computer travels from the root directory to any subdirectories when locating a file.

PC Card Credit-card-sized devices, including modems, network connection cards and memory cards, that comply with the PCMCIA (Personal Computer Memory Card International Association) standards.

peripheral A device that's attached to the computer but is not essential for the basic operation of the computer. The system unit is the central part of the computer. Any devices attached to the system unit are considered *peripheral*, including a printer, modem, or joystick. Some manufacturers consider the monitor and keyboard to be peripheral, too.

pixel A dot of light that appears on the computer screen. A collection of pixels forms characters and images on the screen. Think of a pixel as a single peg in a Lite Brite toy.

Plug and Play Certification by Microsoft that a device installed in a computer system is sensed and installation of supporting software is initiated automatically.

ports The receptacles at the back of the computer. They get their name from the ports where ships pick up and deliver cargo. In this case, the ports allow information to enter and leave the system unit.

post To tack up a message in a bulletin board or newsgroup for all to see.

POST Power-On Self Test. A series of internal checks the computer performs on itself whenever it is first turned on. If the test reveals that any component is not working properly, the computer displays an error message on-screen giving a general indication of which component is causing problems.

PPP Point-to-Point Protocol. When you choose an Internet service provider, you get the right connection: SLIP or PPP.

program A group of instructions that tells the computer what to do. Typical programs are word processors, spreadsheets, databases, and games.

prompt A computer's way of asking for more information. The computer basically looks at you and says, "Tell me something." In other words, the computer is *prompting* you or *prodding* you for information or for a command.

protocol A group of communications settings that control the transfer of data between two computers.

PSTN Public Switched Telephone Network. The worldwide voice telephone network.

pull-down menu A menu that appears at the top of the screen, listing various options. The menu is not visible until you select it from the menu bar. The menu then drops down, covering a small part of the screen.

random-access memory (RAM) The location where your computer stores data and programs temporarily. RAM is measured in kilobytes and megabytes. In general, the more RAM a computer has, the more powerful the programs it can run. Also called *memory*.

record Used by databases to denote a unit of related information contained in one or more fields, such as an individual's name, address, and phone number.

ROM-BIOS See *BIOS*.

sampling rate The range of instrument sampling, ranging from 5KHz, that determines the output quality. 5KHz would be in relation to music from a radio as 44KHz is to CD quality.

scanner A device that converts images, such as photographs or printed text, into an electronic format that a computer can use. Many stores use a special type of scanner to read bar code labels into the cash register.

scroll To move text up and down or right and left on a computer screen.

server Of two computers, the computer that's serving the other computer. On the Internet or on a network, your computer is the *client*, and the computer you're connected to is the *server*.

service provider A company that you pay in order to connect to their computer and get on the Internet.

shareware Computer programs you can use for free, and then pay for if you decide to continue using them. Many programmers start marketing their programs as shareware, relying on the honesty and goodwill of computer users for their income. That's why most of these programmers have day jobs.

shell A program that enables you to enter commands to the operating system by choosing them from a menu. Shell programs make it easier to use the operating system.

SIMM Single Inline Memory Module. A slim board with memory chips mounted on the board that is inserted in a SIMM socket for device memory.

SLIP Serial Line Internet Protocol. A type of Internet connection that allows you to connect directly to the Internet without having to run programs off your Internet service provider's computer. See also *PPP*.

software Any instructions that tell your computer (the hardware) what to do. There are two types of software: operating system software and application software. *Operating system software* (such as DOS) gets your computer up and running. *Application software* enables you to do something useful, such as type a letter or chase lemmings.

spreadsheet A program used for keeping schedules and calculating numeric results. Common spreadsheets include Lotus 1-2-3, Microsoft Excel, and Quattro Pro.

status bar The area at the bottom of a program window that shows you what's going on as you work. A status bar may show the page and line number where the insertion point is positioned, and indicate whether you are typing in Overstrike or Insert mode.

style A collection of specifications for formatting text. A style may include information for the font, size, style, margins, and spacing. Applying a style to text automatically formats the text according to the style's specifications.

switch A value you can add to a command to control the manner in which the command is carried out. For example, in DOS, you can use the /v switch with the COPY command to have DOS verify that the copied files are exact duplicates of the originals.

TCP/IP Transmission Control Protocol/Internet Protocol. A set of rules that governs the transfer of data over the Internet. In order to do anything on the Internet, you need a TCP/IP program. This program connects your computer to your service provider's computer, which is part of the Internet. You can then run other programs that let you do fun stuff, like browse the World Wide Web.

telnet The process of connecting to a server and using it to run programs, just as if you were sitting at its keyboard (or sitting at the keyboard of a terminal that's connected to the server). Think of it as using the computerized card catalog at the local library.

throughput The actual speed of transmission of uncluttered data.

trackball A device, often used with laptop computers, that works like an upside-down mouse. It requires less desk space for use than a mouse, because instead of moving it around the desk to move the pointer on-screen, you roll it in place to move the pointer. Some arcade video games use devices similar to trackballs.

transfer rate A measure of how much information a device (usually a disk drive) can transfer from the disk to your computer's memory in a second. A good transfer rate is in the range of 500 to 600K/s. The higher the number, the faster the drive. See also *access time.*

Trojan horse See *virus.*

uninterruptible power supply (UPS) A battery-powered device that protects against power spikes and power outages. If the power goes out, the UPS continues supplying power to the computer so you can continue working or safely turn off your computer without losing data.

upload To send data to another computer, usually through a modem and a telephone line or through a network connection.

URL Uniform Resource Locator. An address for an Internet site. The Web uses URLs to specify the addresses of the various servers on the Internet and the documents on each server. For example, the URL for the Whitehouse server is **http://www.whitehouse.gov**. The **http** stands for HyperText Transport Protocol, which means this is a Web document. **www** stands for World Wide Web. **whitehouse** stands for the White House. And **gov** stands for Government.

V.17 ITU-T standard for fax transmission at 14,400 bps.

V.32 ITU-T standard for data transmission at 9600 bps.

V.32 bis ITU-T standard for data transmission at 14,400 bps. Higher data transmission speeds are achieved when V.42 and V.42 bis data compression is used.

V.34 ITU-T standard for data transmission at 28,000 and 33,600 bps.

V.42 ITU-TSS standard for modem error checking using LAP-M protocol. MNP-2, -3, and -4 are alternative protocols included for backward compatibility.

V.42 bis ITU-TSS standard for data compression to increase throughput speed.

virtual memory Disk storage that is treated as RAM (memory). Both Windows 3.1 and Windows 95 can use disk space as virtual memory.

virus A program that attaches itself to other files on a floppy or hard disk, duplicates itself without the user's knowledge, and may cause the computer to do strange and sometimes destructive things. The virus attacks the computer by erasing files from the hard disk or by formatting the disk.

voice A sample of types of instruments in different uses to use as templates for generated sound effects and music. The pitch, speed, and volume of voices can be modified for clarity.

voice mail Telephone message storage and retrieval, including the ability to set up specific welcoming messages and private "mailboxes" for multiple users.

Web browser A program that lets you navigate the World Wide Web (the most popular feature of the Internet). The World Wide Web consists of documents (pages) that may contain text, graphics, sound clips, video clips, and other items. A Web browser pulls the pages into your computer (using a modem or network connection) and displays them on your screen. See also *World Wide Web.*

wild card Any character that takes the place of another character or a group of characters. Think of a wild-card character as a wild card in a game of poker. If the Joker is wild, you can use it in place of any card in the entire deck of cards. In DOS, you can use two wild card characters: a question mark (?) and an asterisk (*). The question mark stands for a single character. The asterisk stands for a group of characters.

windows A way of displaying information in different parts of the screen. Often used as a nickname for Microsoft Windows.

word processor A program that lets you enter, edit, format, and print text.

word wrap A feature that automatically moves a word to the next line if the word won't fit at the end of the current line.

World Wide Web A part of the Internet that consists of multimedia documents that are interconnected by links. To move from one document to another, you click a link, which may appear as highlighted text or as a small picture or icon. The Web contains text, sound and video clips, pictures, catalogues, and much, much more. See also *Web browser.*

write-protect To prevent a computer from adding or modifying data stored on a disk.

Index

Symbols

A

B

C

D

E

F

G

J-K

L

M

N

O

P

Q

R

T

U

V

W

X-Y-Z

Technical Support:

If you need assistance with the information in this book or with a CD/Disk accompanying the book, please access the Knowledge Base on our Web site at **http://www.superlibrary.com/general/support**. Our most Frequently Asked Questions are answered there. If you do not find the answer to your questions on our Web site, you may contact Macmillan Technical Support **(317) 581-3833** or e-mail us at **support@mcp.com**.

Complete and Return this Card for a *FREE* Computer Book Catalog

Thank you for purchasing this book! You have purchased a superior computer book written expressly for your needs. To continue to provide the kind of up-to-date, pertinent coverage you've come to expect from us, we need to hear from you. Please take a minute to complete and return this self-addressed, postage-paid form. In return, we'll send you a free catalog of all our computer books on topics ranging from word processing to programming and the internet.

Mr. ☐ Mrs. ☐ Ms. ☐ Dr. ☐

Name (first) ____ (M.I.) ____ (last) ____

Address ____

City ____ State ____ Zip ____

Phone ____ Fax ____

Company Name ____

E-mail address ____

1. Please check at least (3) influencing factors for purchasing this book.

- Front or back cover information on book ☐
- Special approach to the content ☐
- Completeness of content ☐
- Author's reputation ☐
- Publisher's reputation ☐
- Book cover design or layout ☐
- Index or table of contents of book ☐
- Price of book ☐
- Special effects, graphics, illustrations ☐
- Other (Please specify): ____ ☐

2. How did you first learn about this book?

- Saw in Macmillan Computer Publishing catalog ☐
- Recommended by store personnel ☐
- Saw the book on bookshelf at store ☐
- Recommended by a friend ☐
- Received advertisement in the mail ☐
- Saw an advertisement in: ____ ☐
- Read book review in: ____ ☐
- Other (Please specify): ____ ☐

3. How many computer books have you purchased in the last six months?

- This book only ☐
- 2 books ☐
- 3 to 5 books ☐
- More than 5 ☐

4. Where did you purchase this book?

- Bookstore ☐
- Computer Store ☐
- Consumer Electronics Store ☐
- Department Store ☐
- Office Club ☐
- Warehouse Club ☐
- Mail Order ☐
- Direct from Publisher ☐
- Internet site ☐
- Other (Please specify): ____ ☐

5. How long have you been using a computer?

- ☐ Less than 6 months
- ☐ 6 months to a year
- ☐ 1 to 3 years
- ☐ More than 3 years

6. What is your level of experience with personal computers and with the subject of this book?

	With PCs	With subject of book
New	☐	☐
Casual	☐	☐
Accomplished	☐	☐
Expert	☐	☐

Source Code ISBN: 0-7897-0986-4

7. Which of the following best describes your job title?

Administrative Assistant ☐
Coordinator ☐
Manager/Supervisor ☐
Director ☐
Vice President ☐
President/CEO/COO ☐
Lawyer/Doctor/Medical Professional ☐
Teacher/Educator/Trainer ☐
Engineer/Technician ☐
Consultant ☐
Not employed/Student/Retired ☐
Other (Please specify): ________________ ☐

8. Which of the following best describes the area of the company your job title falls under?

Accounting ☐
Engineering ☐
Manufacturing ☐
Operations ☐
Marketing ☐
Sales ☐
Other (Please specify): ________________ ☐

9. What is your age?

Under 20 ☐
21-29 ☐
30-39 ☐
40-49 ☐
50-59 ☐
60-over ☐

10. Are you:

Male ☐
Female ☐

11. Which computer publications do you read regularly? (Please list)

____

Comments: ________________

Fold here and scotch-tape to mail.

NO POSTAGE NECESSARY IF MAILED IN THE UNITED STATES

BUSINESS REPLY MAIL

FIRST-CLASS MAIL PERMIT NO. 9918 INDIANAPOLIS IN

POSTAGE WILL BE PAID BY THE ADDRESSEE

ATTN MARKETING
MACMILLAN COMPUTER PUBLISHING
MACMILLAN PUBLISHING USA
201 W 103RD ST
INDIANAPOLIS IN 46290-9042

Check out Que® Books on the World Wide Web

http://www.quecorp.com

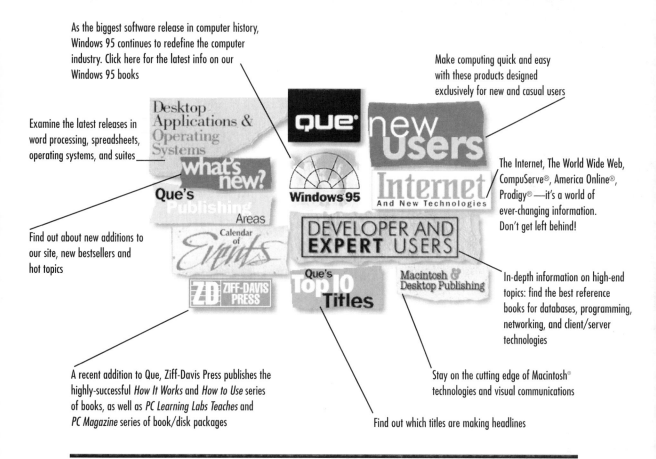

As the biggest software release in computer history, Windows 95 continues to redefine the computer industry. Click here for the latest info on our Windows 95 books

Make computing quick and easy with these products designed exclusively for new and casual users

Examine the latest releases in word processing, spreadsheets, operating systems, and suites

The Internet, The World Wide Web, CompuServe®, America Online®, Prodigy®—it's a world of ever-changing information. Don't get left behind!

Find out about new additions to our site, new bestsellers and hot topics

In-depth information on high-end topics: find the best reference books for databases, programming, networking, and client/server technologies

A recent addition to Que, Ziff-Davis Press publishes the highly-successful *How It Works* and *How to Use* series of books, as well as *PC Learning Labs Teaches* and *PC Magazine* series of book/disk packages

Stay on the cutting edge of Macintosh® technologies and visual communications

Find out which titles are making headlines

With 6 separate publishing groups, Que develops products for many specific market segments and areas of computer technology. Explore our Web Site and you'll find information on best-selling titles, newly published titles, upcoming products, authors, and much more.

- Stay informed on the latest industry trends and products available
- Visit our online bookstore for the latest information and editions
- Download software from Que's library of the best shareware and freeware